Biographia Evangelica: or, an historical account of the lives and deaths of the most eminent and evangelical authors or preachers, ... By the Rev. Erasmus Middleton, ... Volume 1 of 4

Erasmus Middleton

Eighteenth Century
Collections Online
Print Editions

Gale ECCO Print Editions

Relive history with *Eighteenth Century Collections Online*, now available in print for the independent historian and collector. This series includes the most significant English-language and foreign-language works printed in Great Britain during the eighteenth century, and is organized in seven different subject areas including literature and language; medicine, science, and technology; and religion and philosophy. The collection also includes thousands of important works from the Americas.

The eighteenth century has been called "The Age of Enlightenment." It was a period of rapid advance in print culture and publishing, in world exploration, and in the rapid growth of science and technology – all of which had a profound impact on the political and cultural landscape. At the end of the century the American Revolution, French Revolution and Industrial Revolution, perhaps three of the most significant events in modern history, set in motion developments that eventually dominated world political, economic, and social life.

In a groundbreaking effort, Gale initiated a revolution of its own: digitization of epic proportions to preserve these invaluable works in the largest online archive of its kind. Contributions from major world libraries constitute over 175,000 original printed works. Scanned images of the actual pages, rather than transcriptions, recreate the works *as they first appeared.*

Now for the first time, these high-quality digital scans of original works are available via print-on-demand, making them readily accessible to libraries, students, independent scholars, and readers of all ages.

For our initial release we have created seven robust collections to form one the world's most comprehensive catalogs of 18th century works.

Initial Gale ECCO Print Editions collections include:

History and Geography
Rich in titles on English life and social history, this collection spans the world as it was known to eighteenth-century historians and explorers. Titles include a wealth of travel accounts and diaries, histories of nations from throughout the world, and maps and charts of a world that was still being discovered. Students of the War of American Independence will find fascinating accounts from the British side of conflict.

Social Science

Delve into what it was like to live during the eighteenth century by reading the first-hand accounts of everyday people, including city dwellers and farmers, businessmen and bankers, artisans and merchants, artists and their patrons, politicians and their constituents. Original texts make the American, French, and Industrial revolutions vividly contemporary.

Medicine, Science and Technology

Medical theory and practice of the 1700s developed rapidly, as is evidenced by the extensive collection, which includes descriptions of diseases, their conditions, and treatments. Books on science and technology, agriculture, military technology, natural philosophy, even cookbooks, are all contained here.

Literature and Language

Western literary study flows out of eighteenth-century works by Alexander Pope, Daniel Defoe, Henry Fielding, Frances Burney, Denis Diderot, Johann Gottfried Herder, Johann Wolfgang von Goethe, and others. Experience the birth of the modern novel, or compare the development of language using dictionaries and grammar discourses.

Religion and Philosophy

The Age of Enlightenment profoundly enriched religious and philosophical understanding and continues to influence present-day thinking. Works collected here include masterpieces by David Hume, Immanuel Kant, and Jean-Jacques Rousseau, as well as religious sermons and moral debates on the issues of the day, such as the slave trade. The Age of Reason saw conflict between Protestantism and Catholicism transformed into one between faith and logic -- a debate that continues in the twenty-first century.

Law and Reference

This collection reveals the history of English common law and Empire law in a vastly changing world of British expansion. Dominating the legal field is the *Commentaries of the Law of England* by Sir William Blackstone, which first appeared in 1765. Reference works such as almanacs and catalogues continue to educate us by revealing the day-to-day workings of society.

Fine Arts

The eighteenth-century fascination with Greek and Roman antiquity followed the systematic excavation of the ruins at Pompeii and Herculaneum in southern Italy; and after 1750 a neoclassical style dominated all artistic fields. The titles here trace developments in mostly English-language works on painting, sculpture, architecture, music, theater, and other disciplines. Instructional works on musical instruments, catalogs of art objects, comic operas, and more are also included.

The BiblioLife Network

This project was made possible in part by the BiblioLife Network (BLN), a project aimed at addressing some of the huge challenges facing book preservationists around the world. The BLN includes libraries, library networks, archives, subject matter experts, online communities and library service providers. We believe every book ever published should be available as a high-quality print reproduction; printed on-demand anywhere in the world. This insures the ongoing accessibility of the content and helps generate sustainable revenue for the libraries and organizations that work to preserve these important materials.

The following book is in the "public domain" and represents an authentic reproduction of the text as printed by the original publisher. While we have attempted to accurately maintain the integrity of the original work, there are sometimes problems with the original work or the micro-film from which the books were digitized. This can result in minor errors in reproduction. Possible imperfections include missing and blurred pages, poor pictures, markings and other reproduction issues beyond our control. Because this work is culturally important, we have made it available as part of our commitment to protecting, preserving, and promoting the world's literature.

GUIDE TO FOLD-OUTS MAPS and OVERSIZED IMAGES

The book you are reading was digitized from microfilm captured over the past thirty to forty years. Years after the creation of the original microfilm, the book was converted to digital files and made available in an online database.

In an online database, page images do not need to conform to the size restrictions found in a printed book. When converting these images back into a printed bound book, the page sizes are standardized in ways that maintain the detail of the original. For large images, such as fold-out maps, the original page image is split into two or more pages

Guidelines used to determine how to split the page image follows:

• Some images are split vertically; large images require vertical and horizontal splits.
• For horizontal splits, the content is split left to right.
• For vertical splits, the content is split from top to bottom.
• For both vertical and horizontal splits, the image is processed from top left to bottom right.

Biographia Evangelica:

OR, AN

HISTORICAL ACCOUNT

OF THE

LIVES AND DEATHS

Of the moſt eminent and evangelical

AUTHORS OR PREACHERS,

BOTH BRITISH AND FOREIGN,

IN THE SEVERAL

DENOMINATIONS OF PROTESTANTS,

From the Beginning of the Reformation, to the preſent Time

WHEREIN

Are collected, from authentic Hiſtorians, their moſt remarkable ACTIONS,
SUFFERINGS, and WRITINGS, exhibiting the Unity of their FAITH
and EXPERIENCE in their ſeveral *Ages, Countries* and *Profeſſions,* and
illuſtrating the Power of DIVINE GRACE in their *Faith, Living* and *Dying.*

By the Rev ERASMUS MIDDLETON,

Lecturer of *St Bennet's,* Grace church Street, and of *St Helen's,* Biſhopſgate Street

The FAITHFUL are— *bleſſed in Chriſt,* Eph 1 4.—*called, Grace,* Gal 1 15 —
juſtified freely by Grace, Rom 111 24.—*produced,* Col 111 1. —*Lives
by Faith,* Gal 111 11 —*obtain a good Report through Faith,* Heb x 30 —*are
bleſſed in the Lord,* Rev xiv 13 —*ſhall appear with him in Glory,* Col 111 4

VOL. I

LONDON

Printed by J W PASHAM, for the AUTHOR,

And ſold by ALEX HOGG, No 16 Pater noſter Row, G KEITH,
Grace church ſtreet, and J MATHEWS, No 8 in the Strand,
M DCC LXXIX,

PREFACE.

AT a Time, when Infidelity and Irreligion abound on the one Hand, and Popery and other heretical Tenets are making large Strides upon the Reformed Religion on the other, it hath been thought neceſſary, by many ſerious Perſons, of all the Proteſtant Denominations among us, to oppoſe a Torrent of Wickedneſs and Deluſion, which threatens to bear down all before it The Judgements of GOD, which ſeem to hang over us as a Nation, and the dreadful Scourge of War, with which we are already viſited, may juſtly be imputed to the prevailing Iniquity of the Times, the Diſſoluteneſs of our public Principles and Manners, and the open Diſregard for the LORD OF HOSTS, which ſo many among us, in Practice if not in Words, have dared to avow We have reaſon to tremble as a Nation, under the awful Viſitations of the ALMIGHTY, and to fear, that, unleſs a Reformation of our general Conduct take place, and a greater Regard be paid to the Intereſts of Religion and Truth, we ſhall be afflicted with yet heavier Diſpenſations, and that what we ſee already, is only *the Beginning of Sorrows.*

With this View it hath been ſuggeſted, that (as nothing makes ſtronger Impreſſions upon the Mind than *Example*) a Review of the Lives and Principles of the moſt eminent Perſons in the Proteſtant Churches, from the Beginning of the Reformation to the preſent Day, might be a providential Means of aſſiſting, at leaſt, in giving a Check to

this

this general Inundation of Infidelity and falfe Opinions. The attentive Perufal and Confideration of what thofe great and good Men maintained, fuffered for, or died in Poffeffion of, may, in the Hand of G O D, be inftrumental in leading others to follow their Example, or at leaft deter many from reviling and contemning thofe peculiar Principles of the Proteftant Doctrine, which their Indolence or their Ignorance have not fuffered them to underftand It may fafely be faid, that nothing has contributed fo much to the Reception of impious or fuperftitious Tenets among us, as the fpiritual Darknefs of our *prefent enlightened Age*, which indeed has made great Improvements in the Knowledge of every Thing *but* one—and that is, *the One Thing Needful*. Our Youth are trained up, according to the Fafhion, in the Ignorance and Contempt of every Thing facred, and no Man is allowed either Senfe or Difcretion, unlefs he is quite at Eafe with refpect to Religion, and indifferent to the great Concerns of Eternity. In fhort, to be polite, in the common Acceptation, is to be profane, and to gain a Character of Underftanding and Honor, a Man muft affect to defpife the confcientious Purity of the Gofpel, and openly difregard the AUTHOR of all Wifdom What can be hoped for from Maxims like thefe, but what we have already found, viz. *Irreligion* on the one Side, and *fpiritual Error* on the other? And thefe, we may expect, will draw upon us (as they did upon the Churches of *Afia*) the dreadful Scourges of G O D, by *outward* Calamities, and in the Progrefs of *inward* Blindnefs or Abandonment.

 Every Man, therefore, who has any Concern for the Glory of G O D, the Purity of the Gofpel, and the beft Interefts of Pofterity, will readily (we fhould hope) give his earneft Encouragement to a Work, which feems calculated for thefe important Purpofes, as well as his own Edification. It is a FAMILY-BOOK, and may be put

into

into the Hands of Youth, both for their Information as a History, and for their Profit as an Instructor. Mr Fox's *Acts and Monuments* were ordered by Authority to be placed in every Church, that the People of the several Parishes in the Kingdom, might be led, to a thorough Detestation of the poisonous Principles and bloody Practices of the *Papists* 'Tis to be regretted, that this Order, like many others, is grown obsolete Perhaps, in no Case, is the Disuse of wholesome Injunctions more to be lamented, than in the unbridled Liberty, which is taken in the Education of our Youth. People, of the worst Principles, may, without Examination, inculcate them freely upon the rising Generation And thus, insidiously, Popery, Infidelity, and Immorality, are scattered all over the Land However, it cannot be unseasonable for Parents, in particular, to lay a Work of this Kind before their Children, when the Tenets of *Rome*, dangerous to all civil and religious Liberty, seem to be gaining Ground among us. Those, indeed, are the most *ignorant* of the Community, who are infected or most likely to be infected by that corrupt Leaven, for, it may be truly said, no Man was ever seduced into its erroneous Principles, either by the Conviction of his *Reason* or his *Senses*, and much less by the Sanctions of *Scripture*. And we must do the Papists the Justice to say, that they do not attempt this Sort of Conviction Their Arguments and Inducements are laid in the Fears of the *Simple*, who know neither the true Doctrines of Christianity nor themselves, and in their own self-sufficient, or rather all-sufficient, *Authority*, which, if it was properly explained, would sooner excite the Contempt and Abhorrence, than the Approbation of any reasonable Being.

As to the Work itself, we have freely made use of the several Authors who penned the Lives of these illustrious Men, omitting what was either too prolix for our Plan,

or

or what, upon Comparifon with other Accounts, did not appear fufficiently founded, and adding many Circumftances, which had efcaped them or have fince been collected by others. By this Method, we may, without Vanity, hope, that thefe Relations are in general more complete than thofe which have been hitherto offered to the Public In the feveral Accounts of thefe evangelical Men, the great Object of our Plan has been the general Edification, as well as Information, and, for this End, the Reader will find many ferious Reflections interfperfed throughout the Work How far we have fucceeded, muft be fubmitted to the Judgement of the Reader, whom, if a fincere Chriftian, we fhall truft to pleafe, and, if otherwife, we ought not to be anxious about it.

We will only detain the Reader to affure him, that no bigotted Partiality to Sects or Denominations, whether eftablifhed or tolerated, will be found in this Collection, but our whole Attention has been paid to truly great and gracious Characters of all thofe Perfuafions, which hold the diftinguifhing Principles of the Gofpel, and are united in the main Endeavor to promote our common Chriftianity.

The Copper-plates are the Performance of an ingenious young Artift, and fufficiently befpeak his Merit. The Encouragers of this Undertaking will perceive, that this Part of the Work has been performed in a Manner much fuperior to what is generally given, and, we doubt not, it will be fully agreeable to their Expectation.

May the GOD of all Grace be pleafed to blefs our Attempt, to the Inftruction of *the Ignorant and them that are out of the Way*, to the Edification of humble Profeffors of the Gofpel, and to the Satisfaction of all thofe, whatever be their outward Denomination, who *love our* LORD JESUS CHRIST *in Sincerity.*

INDEX.

INDEX.

INDEX.

Biog.

LETTERS

OF

RECOMMENDATION

Received from the following DIVINES.

DEAR SIR,

I Have perufed the firft Volume of your BIOGRAPHIA EVANGELICA with great Pleafure, and admire both the Plan and Execution thereof. May the great Head of the Church blefs this Undertaking, fo highly feafonable at this critical Period, when the glorious Doctrines of the Reformation (in Defence whereof many of thofe illuftrious Worthies laid down their Lives) are too generally denied on the one Hand, and the Errors of Popery are evidently gaining Ground on the other! This Publication therefore, I doubt not, will be bleffed to the Glory of our GOD and SAVIOUR, and to the Eftablifhment of His People in the fundamental Truths of the Gofpel and I truft you will meet with the utmoft Encouragement from Believers of every Denomination For my own Part, I fhall be happy to recommend it as far as my little Influence may be fuppofed to extend Your enriching this valuable Work with fo many excellent Plates renders it one of the cheapeft Publications I have feen, and muft be a great Recommendation of it to the Public Praying therefore for a Blefling on this and every Labour of Love for the REDEEMER's Sake, I remain, with great Efteem and Regard,

Dear Sir,

Dec. 2, 1779 At the Countefs of   Your affectionate Friend,
HUNTINGDON's Houfe,   J. WILLS.
Spa-Fields, London.

REV. SIR,

AS you have been fo obliging as to folicit me to give my Opinion of a Work which you are now publifhing, I am happy to affure you that it gives me great Pleafure to find that a Thing of this Nature is undertaken. The Plan, you have adopted, has often paffed through my own Mind, and I have myfelf purpofed to *attempt*, what I hope you will be encouraged to *finifh*

You may be apprehenfive, and a little fearful perhaps, that the BIOGRAPHIA EVANGELICA will not meet with general Acceptance. you will at leaft have the Honour of having defigned a Work which, if I miftake not, is *original* in its Way, and which, if properly regarded, is calculated to be of *extenfive* and *lafting Benefit* to Mankind

Hiftory is certainly *the Key of Knowledge* and biographical Hiftory has this peculiar Advantage, that it contains the Knowledge of *Men* and *Things* at the fame Time. and evangelical Biography has

this

this still greater Advantage, that it unites the *utile dulce,* and conveys not only the most entertaining, but the most important Science, I mean, the *Wisdom that maketh wise to Salvation* without which all other Wisdom is at the best comparative Folly

You have my hearty Wish, that your valuable Publication may meet with the Success it deserves, and that it may be instrumental in opposing the fatal Increase of Popery in this Kingdom, and in promoting that Zeal for our Religion, which has always distinguished the most eminent Protestants of every Denomination

I am, Rev Sir,

Your's most respectfully,

Lower Grosvenor-Place.   C DE COETLOGON.

DEAR SIR,

THE REFORMATION of this Kingdom, from the Superstition, Idolatry and Cruelty of the Church of Rome, is such a national Blessing, as should excite our constant Praises to that GOD by whom we possess it The Memory, also, of those illustrious Men, who were the Instruments of bringing about and maintaining it, should not be forgotten by us The BIOGRAPHIA EVANGELICA seems calculated to answer these valuable Ends The Prints, likewise, are so well executed, that they much enhance the Value of the Work. That it may be much and profitably read is the sincere Desire of,

SIR,

Watling Street,   Your's, &c.

Nov 26th, 17/9.   HEN. FOSTER.

TO THE REV. ERASMUS MIDDLETON.

DEAR SIR,

I Have perused, with great Pleasure and Profit, your very excellent BIOGRAPHIA EVANGELICA The Plan adopted, I most highly approve of, but especially the just, impartial, and faithful Account you have given us of those great and glorious Luminaries of the Church, the blessed REFORMERS, whose precious Names and Characters must ever be dear and valuable to all who love our LORD JESUS CHRIST, for the noble Testimony they bore, living and dying, to the Truth of the ever blessed and eternal Word of GOD —In a day like this, when the precious and invaluable Word of GOD is so slighted and despised, it is most heartily to be wished, that your very excellent Publication might be attentively read, by every Lover of Truth, as a Work, highly calculated, to instruct, settle, and establish, every unprejudiced and impartial Reader —That you may meet with every Encouragement in so laudable an Undertaking, and behold with Pleasure, Gratitude, and Joy, many happy and blessed Effects resulting from it, is the earnest Prayer of,

Your very affectionate Friend,

Northampton Chapel,   WM. TAYLOR.

Dec. 2d, 1779.

Letters of Recommendation, &c.

NEITHER the *Author* or *Engraver* need the Recommendation of their Admirer,

British Museum, A GIFFORD
Nov 6th, 1779

REV. SIR,

I Have read the first Volume of the BIOGRAPHIA EVANGELICA, and sincerely wish it may meet with Success, as it is a Work which seems calculated to afford a considerable Degree of profitable Entertainment

Hackney, JOHN CONDER.
Sept 26th, 1779

REV AND DEAR SIR,

I Have looked into your valuable Work, intitled BIOGRAPHIA EVANGELICA, I highly esteem it, as it contains what may indeed be called a PRESENT TRUTH, as it exhibits what the Grace of GOD can do, and has actually done for the Souls of Men, who have felt its Power on their Hearts

The extensive Nature of your Plan also exhibits to our View, that the Grace and Favour of GOD is not confined to the party Names and Distinctions that have divided Christians from one another in these latter Days, but extends to all of every Denomination who love the LORD JESUS, who believe in his Name, and walk according to his Gospel, and this may, and should, encourage all of the same Stamp to be Followers of them who through Faith and Patience do now inherit the Promises.

That part of your Work particularly that holds forth to our View, the Sufferings and Patience of the eminent Ministers and Christians who suffered from and under the Synagogue of Satan at Rome, deserves particular Regard, at a Time when the Wound the Beast received at the REFORMATION seems to be, as it were, healing among us May the LORD in Mercy deliver us from ever falling under that heavy Yoke any more If you think this honest and well meant Testimony can be of any Service to your Work, you are at Liberty to make what Use of it you please, and I am,

Your affectionate Brother, in the Work and Bonds of the Gospel,

Braintree, in Essex, THOMAS DAVIDSON.
Dec 2, 1779

THE Lives of illustrious Men have been read with Greediness, and Attention in all Ages, whether in the Pagan, the Jewish, or the Christian World The Lives of the famous Greeks and Romans, written by the judicious and excellent Plutarch, is a Work of such Importance and Use, that we may truly affirm with a learned Man, "If it were proposed to destroy all the literary Works of the Pagan World, except one, Plutarch's Lives should be preferred as the most pleasing, instructive and useful"

Now

Letters of Recommendation, &c.

Now if we set such a Value on the Lives of the Pagan Philosophers, Statesmen and Warriors, how much more should we prize the History of the great Generals and Commanders in the Christian Church those greatest Heroes that have lived since the Reformation from Popery. and whose Lives, Labours, and Characters, are here faithfully recorded and if we pursue Plutarch's Manner of running a Parallel between the Character of one great Man and another, and compare the Christian with the Pagan Heroes, we shall find the Advantages most abundantly on the Christian Side. Where can we find in the Heathen World, any Characters that can equal Wickliffe, Tindale, Luther, and Calvin, with a long Series more here enumerated.

In the brightest Pagans you see Traces of Genius, Policy, Fortitude, Justice, and the Love of their Country but all flowing from the Principles of Nature, and actuated by a violent Ambition or Love of Fame, but in the Christian Heroes exhibited in this Work, you see heavenly Wisdom, ardent Love of God, Faith in the Blood of CHRIST, Zeal for the Divine Glory, invincible Fortitude to dare even the most dreadful Forms of Death, strong Compassion for immortal Souls; yea, and what is still higher, a Love of their bitterest Enemies, and fervent Prayers for them in the Agonies of Death Who would not esteem and venerate such exalted Characters? Who would not read with Avidity and Delight the Lives, the Virtues, and the glorious Martyrdom of many of these great Men?

How seasonable and useful at this singular Point of Time is such a Work! I do therefore most cordially express my Approbation of the Design and Execution of it, and heartily recommend it to my Friends and fellow Protestants of all Denominations

Northampton,   JOHN RYLAND.
Nov. 21st, 1779.

To the PRINTER.

SIR,

HAVING long wished to see the Lives of all eminently holy Men from the Dawn of the Reformation to the present Time, collected in one Book, I was happy to find my Wish about to be accomplished in the Publication of the *Biographia Evangelica* Such a Work is peculiarly seasonable at this alarming Crisis, and will (through the Blessing of God) prove an effectual Antidote against Popery, as well as the Means of reviving that Spirit for the Things of CHRIST, which, alas! is now so languid among Christians of all Denominations. It is my sincere Desire the Work may be generally read, and my earnest Prayer that it may fully answer the End of the pious Author.   I am,

SIR,

Great Portland Street,   Your most obedient Servant,
Nov 24, 1779.   JOHN TROTTER.

From an Original Picture in the Collection of the Duke of Norfolk

Biographia Evangelica.

JOHN WICKLIFFE,

THE FIRST REFORMER.

WHEN we look back upon the days of barbarism, and the grofs ignorance of the true light of the gofpel, which prevailed in the Chriftian world, for fo many ages together, before the Reformation, when we reflect upon the ftupid ceremonies and abominable fuperftitions and cheats, practifed by the monks and others, and then furvey the hand of GOD, working, in a moft extraordinary manner, through all this mafs of corruption and folly, and bringing about, by degrees, the clear fhining of the everlafting gofpel We muft ftand aftonifhed at the whole, and, from the wonderful contraft of the times, may fay, *This hath GOD wrought, it is the Lord's doing, and it is marvellous in our eyes*

GOD vouchfafed to honor *England* with the firft dawning of the Reformation And an *Englifhman* was the firft champion of that caufe, which afterwards received the name of PROTESTANTISM This remarkable inftrument of the divine blefling was JOHN WICKLIFF, or JOHN de WICKLIFFF, taking his firname from a village once called *Wickliffe*, near *Richmond*, in *Yorkfhire*, where he was born in the year 1324. It has been obferved, that no fuch place exifts at prefent under that name, but it is well known, that great numbers of our villages, and even towns and hundreds, have received different denominations from change of poffeflors in the courfe of ages *Wickliffe* was fent early to *Oxford*, and was firft admitted commoner of *Queen's College*, and afterwards of *Merton*, where he became fellow.

B

Merton

Merton Coll ge was then the beſt ſeminary for great and learned men in the whole univerſity, and the following eminent perſons belonged to it, about this time. 1 *Walter Burley*, called the Plain Doctor, who was preceptor to king *Edward* III. 2 *William Occam*, called the Singular Doctor 3 *Thomas Bradward ι e*, the Profound Doctor, who was called to court by archbiſhop *Stratford*, and ſucceeded him in the ſee of *Canterbury* 4. *Simon Mepham*, archbiſhop of *Canterbury*, in 1330 5 *Simon Iſlip*, who was alſo promoted to the ſame ſee, in 1349, was lord privy ſeal, and ſecretary to the king 6 *William Rede*, an excellent mathematician, and biſhop of *Chicheſter* in 1369 7 *Geoffry Chaucer*, the Father of *Engliſh* Poetry *Wickliffe* was afterwards called *Doctor Evangelicus*, or the Goſpel Doctor, and he certainly deſerved the title, as the ſtudy of the holy ſcriptures was his principal delight He was indeed (to uſe the words of biſhop *Newton*) ‘ deſervedly famous, the honour of his “ own, and the admiration of all ſucceeding times.’

Wickliffe was ſoon diſtinguiſhed, among theſe illuſtrious contemporaries, for the cloſeneſs of his application to ſtudy, and the vivacity of his genius He became celebrated in philoſophy and divinity, being ſo remarkable for an elegancy of wit, and ſtrength in diſputations, that he was eſteemed more than human by the common ſort of divines. He adorned the learning of the ſchools, by acquiring a deep knowledge of the civil and canon law, as alſo of the municipal laws of his own country, which have been always too much neglected till our own times, when we find the Vinerian profeſſorſhip of the laws of *England* eſtabliſhed in the univerſity of *Oxford* *Wickliffe* not only ſtudied and commented upon the ſacred writings, but he tranſlated them into his native language, and wrote homilies on ſeveral parts of them. He alſo diligently ſtudied the writings of St. *Auſtin*, St *Jerom*, St *Ambroſe*, and St *Gregory*, the four fathers of the Latin church But he was thirty-ſix years of age before he had a proper opportunity of exerting his excellent talents, ſo as to attract the obſervation of the univerſity, and even of the whole kingdom ; for it was in the year 1360 when he became the advocate for the univerſity againſt the encroachments made by the mendicant friars, who had been very troubleſome from their firſt eſtabliſhment in *Oxford*, in 1230, and occaſioned great inquietude to the chancellor and ſcholars,

lars, by infringing their statutes and privileges, and setting up an exempt jurisdiction

Popery was established in *England* by *Austin* the monk, and continued to be the only religion till the Reformation   The church of *Rome* had infected all *Christendom* with its errors and corruptions, and the whole church was degenerated from its primitive purity by the artifices of the monks, who had polluted the clear stream of religion with the rank weeds of superstition

The clergy had engrossed the greatest part both of the riches and power of *Christendom* But the corruptions of their worship and doctrine were easily detected, nor had they any varnish to color them by, except the authority and traditions of the church   When some studious men began to read the antient fathers, and councils, they found a vast difference between the first five ages of the Christian church, in which piety and learning prevailed, and the last ten ages, in which ignorance had buried all their former learning   Only a little misguided devotion was retained for six of those ages, and, in the last four, the restless ambition and usurpation of the popes were supported by the seeming holiness of the begging friars, and the false counterfeits of learning, consisting only of a vile metaphysical jargon, or vain school-divinity, which prevailed among the canonists, school-men, and casuists

It may be noted, that soon after and about the year 1300, flourished several able and pious men, who boldly withstood the errors of the church of *Rome*, and the insolence of its popes   Of these, perhaps, none was more remarkable than *Marsilius* of *Padua*, who wrote his *Defensor Pacis* for the emperor *Lewis*, of *Bavaria*, against pope *John* XXII, and who is execrated by name in the bull of pope *Gregory* against *Wickliffe*   He vehemently opposed the enormities of the court of *Rome*, and maintained, that believers are freely justified by grace alone, and that works are not the efficient causes of our salvation, though justification and salvation are ever attended with them.   He and others paved the way for our great countryman, who soon afterwards appeared and distinguished himself above them.

Wickliffe was indeed the morning-star of the Reformation, though he appeared like a meteor to the monks, when he opposed them in support of the university   The number of students there had been thirty thousand, but, in 1357, they were so far decreased that the whole was not above six thousand. This was entirely owing to the

bad

bad practices of the preaching friars, who took all opportunities to entice the students, from the colleges, into
their convents, which made people afraid of sending
their children to the univerfity The friars difregarded
the determination of the parliament in 1366, whereby it
was enacted, that they fhould receive no fcholar under
the age of eighteen, and that the king fhould have power
to redrefs all controverfies between them and the univerfity *Wickliffe* foon diftinguifhed himfelf by his bold
and zealous oppofition againft the ufurpations and errors
of the friars, who juftified their begging trade, by afferting, that the poverty of *Chrift*, and his apoftles, made
them poffefs all things in common, and beg for a livelihood This opinion was firft oppofed by *Richard Kil-
myngton*, dean of St *Paul's*, who was feconded by *Richard
Fitz-Ralph*, archbifhop of *Armagh*, after which, *Wickliffe*,
Thorefby, *Bolton*, *Hereford*, *Bryts*, and *Norris*, openly oppofed this doctrine at *Oxford*, where they made the friars
blufh for their audacity.

Wickliffe wrote with an elegance uncommon in that
age, efpecially in the *Englifh* language, of which he
may be confidered as one of the firft refiners, and his
writings afford many curious fpecimens of the old *Englifh*
orthography In one of his tracts, intitled " Of Clerks
" Poffeffioners," he expofes the friars for drawing the youth
of the univerfity into their convents, and fays, " Freres
" drawen children fro *Chrift's* religion into their private
" order by hypocrific, lefings, and fteling For they
" tellen that their order is more holy than any other,
" that they fhullen have higher degree in the blifs of
" heaven than other men that been not therein, and
" feyn, that men of their order fhullen never come to
" hell, but fhullen dome other men with *Chrift* at
" domefday."

Wickliffe wrote and publifhed feveral tracts againft the
beggary of the friars, particularly " Of the Poverty of
" Chrift, againft able Beggary," and " Of Idlenefs in
" Beggary " He afferts, that " Chrift bad his apoftles
" and difciples that they fhould not bere a fatchell, ne
" fcrip, but look what man is able to hear the gofpel,
" and eat and drink therein, and pafs not thence, and
" not pafs fro houfe to houfe —Sith there were poor
" men enough to taken mens alms before that freres
" camen in, and the earth is now more barren than it was,
" other freres, or poor men, moten wanten of this alms
" but

" but freres, by fubtle hypocrifie, gotten to themfelves,
" and letten the poor men to have theſe almes."

He diſputed with a frier, on able begary, before the
duke of *Gloucefter*, to whom he fent an account of both their
arguments, and addreffed his highnefs in thefe words,
" To you lord, that herde the diſputaſion, be geve the
" tyle to rubbe away the ruft in either partye."

Theſe controverfies gave *Wickliff* fuch great reputation
in the univerfity, that, in 1361, he was advanced to be
mafter of *Baliol College*, and four years after he was made
warden of *Canterbury-hall*, founded by *Simon de Iflip*,
archbifhop of *Canterbury*, in 1361, and now fwallowed up
in *Chrift-church.* The royal licence granted to the archbifhop, for founding the college, is dated the twentieth of
October 1361, and only mentions ' a certain number of
' fcholars,' religious and fecular. There were to be a
warden and eleven fcholars, who were to ftudy logic, the
civil and canon law, for whofe maintenance the archbifhop fettled on them the rectory of *Pageham* in *Suffex*,
and the manor of *Wodeford* in *Northamptonfhire.* He purchafed fome old houfes in the parifh of St. *Mary's* in
Oxford, and fitted them up for the reception of his fcholars, whom he placed there himfelf, and appointed *Henry
de Wodehall*, or *Woodhall*, to be the warden. This man
was a monk of *Chrift-church, Canterbury*, and doctor of
divinity. But he was at fuch variance with the fecular
fcholars, that the archbifhop, in 1365, turned him, and
three monks, out of his new-founded *Hall*, in whofe room
he appointed *Wickliff* to be warden, and three other fe-
culars to be fcholars. It was afterwards pretended, that
the warden, and three of the fcholars, were to be monks
of *Chrift-church, Canterbury*, and the other eight, fecular
priefts, though this limitation could not be proved from
the writings relating to the foundation.

The letters of inftitution, whereby the archbifhop appointed *Wickliff* to this wardenfhip, were dated the fourteenth of *December*, 1365, in which he is ftyled ' a perfon
' in whofe fidelity, circumfpection, and induftry, his
' grace very much confided, and one on whom he had
' fixed his eyes for that place, on account of the ho-
' nefty of his life, his laudable converfation, and know-
' ledge of letters.'

Wickliff behaved with univerfal approbation, till the
death of the archbifhop, who had a great efteem for
him. His grace died the twenty-fifth of *April*, 1366,
and was fucceeded in the archiepifcopal dignity by *Simon*

Langham,

Langham, bishop of *Ely,* who had been a monk, and was inclined to favor the religious against the seculars. The monks of *Canterbury* applied to *Langham* to eject *Wickliffe* from his wardenship, and the other seculars from their fellowships   They alledged, that the warden was to be a monk, nominated by the prior and chapter of *Canterbury,* and appointed by the archbishop   But that *Wickliffe* craftily obtained the wardenship   Archbishop *Langham* ejected *Wickliffe* from the wardenship, and the three other seculars, in 1367, in consequence of which, he also issued out his mandate, requiring *Wickliffe* and all the scholars to yield obedience to *Wodehall* as their warden   This was refused by them, as being contrary to the oath they had taken to the founder, but the archbishop sequestered the revenue, and took away the books and other things, which the founder by his last will had left to the *Hall.*

Wickliffe, and the three expelled fellows, appealed to the pope, to which appeal the archbishop made a reply, and the pope commissioned cardinal *Andruynus* to examine and determine the affair, who, in 1370, ordained, by a definitive sentence, which was confirmed by the pope, that only the monks of *Christ-church, Canterbury,* ought to remain in the college called *Canterbury-hall,* and that the seculars should be all expelled; that *Wodehall* and the other monks, who were deprived, should be restored, and that perpetual silence should be imposed on *Wickliffe* and his associates.   *Wickliffe,* and three poor clerks, could not oppose such a powerful combination, and the decree was strictly put in execution, pursuant to the papal bull, dated at *Viterbium,* the twenty-eighth of *May,* 1370, directed to *Simon de Sudbury,* bishop of *London,* and others, who were to restore *Wodehall* and the monks, and to compel all those who contradicted them by ecclesiastical censures, without permitting any appeal.

In this arbitrary manner *Wickliffe* was dispossessed of the wardenship of *Canterbury-hall,* which had been conferred on him by the founder, whose munificent intentions were frustrated by the papal sentence, which was directly contrary to the form of the licence of *Mortmain* that empowered the founder to endow his seminary for a certain number of scholars, religious and secular, who now, by this papal sentence, were to be all religious. It was, therefore, a question in law, whether the *Hall* and endowment were not forfeited to the crown? But the monks, in 1372, procured the royal pardon, and confirmation

firmation of the papal sentence, on paying 200 marks, which was equivalent to 800 pounds of our money

While the dispute was carried on about the right to *Canterbury-hall*, king *Edward* had notice from pope *Urban*, that he intended to cite him to his court at *Avignon*, to answer for his default in not performing the homage which king *John* acknowledged to the see of *Rome*, and for refusing to pay the tribute of 700 marks a year, which that prince granted to the pope. The king laid this before his parliament, in 1366, who were determined to assist him with all their power against such arbitrary attempts from the pope. The firmness of the parliament caused the pope to stop short, and prevented his successors from ever after troubling the kings of *England* on that account. However, one of the monks ventured to defend the claim made by the pope, to which *Wickliffe* replied, and proved, that the resignation of the crown, and promise of a tribute made by king *John*, ought not to prejudice the kingdom, or oblige the present king, as it was done without consent of parliament. No wonder, then, that *Wickliffe* should incur the resentment of the pope, who was impatient of contradiction, and could not bear any opposition to his pretensions. But *Wickliffe* thereby made himself known to the court, and particularly to the duke of *Lancaster*, who took him under his patronage. At this time *Wickliffe* stiled himself *peculiaris regis clericus*, or the king's own clerk or chaplain. But he professed himself an obedient son of the *Roman* church, to avoid the personal injury intended him by his adversaries

However, this deprivation was no injury to the reputation which *Wickliffe* had acquired. Every body saw it was a party business, and that it was not so much against his person that the monks had a prejudice, as against all the seculars that were members of the college. Shortly after, *Wickliffe* was presented, by the favor of the duke of *Lancaster*, to the living of *Lutterworth*, in the diocese of *Lincoln*, and then it was that he published, in his writings and sermons, certain opinions which appeared to be novel, because contrary to the received doctrine of those days. As he did not declare his sentiments till after he had lost his rectorship, his enemies have taken occasion, from thence, to accuse him of acting out of a spirit of revenge, by reason of the injury that had been done him. ' I shall not, says *Rapin*, undertake to clear him from this ' charge. As there is none but God alone that sees into ' the hearts of men, it is rashness to accuse or excuse ' them,

' them, with regard to the ſacred motives of their actions.
' I ſhall only take notice, that *Wickliffe's* bittereſt enemies
' have never taxed him with any immoralities.'

Wickliffe was turned out of his rectorſhip by the court
of *Rome*, and a man muſt be poſſeſſed of a very diſin-
tereſted way of thinking, not to reſent ſuch uſage, eſpecially as *Wickliffe* was irreproachable in his morals. The
ſpirit of the times was no little encouragement to his reſentment. 'I muſt however,' ſays Mr *Guthrie*, ' do
' *Wickliffe* the juſtice, which has *not been done him before*,
' of obſerving, that he ſeems to have maintained his re-
' forming opinions even before he was turned out of his
' rectorſhip.' This is to his honor, and removes one
of the ſtrongeſt objections againſt the motives of *Wickliffe's* Reformation, as we have it from an author unfavorable to his memory.   This opinion is alſo farther
confirmed by the ingenious Mr *Gilpin*.

But *Wickliffe* began more early to attempt the Reformation of thoſe diſorders and corruptions which he ſaw in
men of his own profeſſion, and particularly the exactions
and uſurpations of the pope. This is evident from his
tract, " Of the laſt Age of the Church," which he publiſhed in the year 1356, fourteen years before he loſt the
rectorſhip.

Wickliffe, in 1372, took his degree as doctor of divinity,
which he publickly profeſſed, and read lectures in it with
very great applauſe, for he had ſuch authority in the
ſchools, that his opinion was received as an oracle, inſtead of being diſregarded after his ejectment. In theſe
lectures, he more ſtrongly expoſed the follies and ſuper-
ſtitions of the friars. He charged them with holding fifty
hereſies and errors. He ſhewed their corruptions, and detected their practices. This was ſtriking at the root of
all the abuſes which had crept into the church, at a time,
when the greater and more neceſſary articles of faith, and
all genuine and rational knowledge of religion, had generally given place to fabulous legends, and romantic ſtories,
fables which, in this reſpect, only differed from thoſe of
the antient heathen poets, that they were more incredible,
and leſs elegant.

The pope diſregarded the ſtatute of proviſors, by ſtill
continuing to diſpoſe of eccleſiaſtical benefices and dignities as he thought fit. Theſe were enjoyed by *Italians*,
Frenchmen, and other aliens, who had the revenues of
them remitted abroad. The parliament frequently complained to the king and the pope of this intolerable griev-
ance,

ance, by reprefenting its fatal inconveniences to the church, and pernicious confequences to the kingdom

This oppreffion was fo infupportable, in 1373, that the king fent the bifhop of *Bangor*, and three other ambaffadors, to the pope, to require of him that he would not interfere with the refervation of benefices But this embaffy was ineffectual, for though the pope entered into a concordate about that matter, it was only a temporal conceffion, and the parliament renewed their requeft, that remedy fhould be provided againft the provifions of the pope, whereby he reaped the firft fruits of ecclefiaftical dignities. It has always been the policy of the court of *Rome* to play faft and loofe with temporal princes in its tranfactions with them, waiting diligently for advantageous feafons, and preffing them clofely whenever they occurred But, when it met with dangerous oppofitions, it dextroufly waved the conteft without renouncing its claims, and temporized, and foothed, and flattered, and lay by, for a more convenient opportunity

The king, in 1374, iffued out a commiffion for taking an exact furvey of all the ecclefiaftical dignities and benefices, throughout his dominions, which were in the hands of aliens The number and value of them aftonifhed the king, who then appointed feven ambaffadors to treat with the pope upon the bufinefs of the former embaffy Doctor *Wickliffe* was the fecond perfon mentioned in this commiffion, and the ambaffadors were met at *Bruges* by the pope's nuncio, two bifhops, and a provoft, to treat concerning the liberties of the church of *England* The treaty continued two years, when it was concluded, that the pope fhould defift from making ufe of refervations of benefices But all treaties with that corrupt court were of no fignification, and the parliament, the very next year, complained the treaty was infracted, A long bill was brought into parliament againft the papal ufurpations, as the caufe of all the plagues, injuries, famine, and poverty of the realm They remonftrated that the tax paid to the pope amounted to five times as much as the tax paid to the king, and that God had given his fheep to the pope to be paftured, not fleeced Doctor *Wickliffe* was now made more fenfible of the pride, avarice, ambition, and tyranny of the pope, whom he boldly expofed in his public lectures, and private converfation He called him " Antichrift, " the proud worldly prieft of *Rome*, and the moft curfed " of clippers and purfe-kervers " He alfo very freely reproved the corruptions which prevailed among the pre-

C lates

lates and inferior clergy, obferving, " that the abomi-
" nation of defolation had its beginning from a perverfe
" clergy, as comfort arofe from a converted clergy " Of
prelates, he fays, " Oh Lord, what token of mekenefs,
" and forfaking of worldly riches is this? A prelate, as
" an abbot or priour that is dead to the world, and pride
" and vanity thereof, to ride with fourfcore horfe, with
" harnefs of filver and gold and to fpend with earls and
" barons, and their poor tenants, both thoufand marcs
" and pounds, to meyntene a falfe plea of the world, and
" forbare men of their right " But *Wickliffe* fufficiently
experienced the hatred and perfecution of thofe, whom he
endeavored to reform. The monks complained to the pope
that *Wickliffe* oppofed the papal powers, and defended
the royal fupremacy, on which account, in 1376, they
drew up nineteen articles againft him, extracted from his
public lectures and fermons Thefe articles were fent to
the pope, and were principally as follow

" That there is one only univerfal church, which is the
" univerfity" [or entire number] " of the predeftinate.
" *Paul* was never a member of the devil, although" [be-
fore his converfion] " he did certain acts like unto the
" acts of the church malignant The reprobate are not
" parts of the" [invifible] " church, for that no part
" of the fame finally falleth from her becaufe the charity"
[or grace] " of predeftination, which bindeth the church
" together, never faileth "

" The reprobate, although he be fometime in grace,
" according to prefent juftice" [i e by a prefent appearance of outward righteoufnefs,] " yet is he never a part
" of the holy church" [in reality] " and the predefti-
" nate is ever a member of the church, although fometime
" he fall from grace *adventitia*, but not from the grace of
" predeftination ever taking the church for the convo-
" cation of the predeftinate, whether they be in grace or
" not, according to prefent juftice " i e whether they
be converted already, or yet remain to be fo, the predeftinate, or elect, conftitute, as fuch, that invifible church,
which God the Father hath chofen, and God the Son
redeemed.

" The grace of predeftination is the band, wherewith
" the body of the church, and every member of the fame,
" is indiffolubly joined to Chrift their head "

" That the eucharift, after confecration, was not the
" real body of Chrift, but only an emblem or fign of it.
" That the church of *Rome* was no more the head of the
                                        " univerfal

" univerfal church than any other church, and that St
" Peter had no greater authority given him than the reft
" of the apoftles   That the pope had no more jurifdic-
" tion in the exercife of the keys, than any other prieft
" That if the church mifbehaved, it was not only lawful,
" but meritorious, to difpoffefs her of her temporalities.
" That when a prince, or temporal lord, was convinced
" that the church made an ill ufe of her endowments, he
" was bound, under pain of damnation, to take them
" away   That the gofpel was fufficient to direct a Chrif-
" tian in the conduct of his life.   That neither the pope,
" nor any other prelate, ought to have prifons for the
" punifhing offenders againft the difcipline of the church,
" but that every perfon ought to be left at his liberty in
" the conduct of his life."

This was oppofing the rights, which the popes had long
afferted, of a fuperiority over temporal princes, and of
depriving them of their kingdoms, whenever they thought
proper.   It was juftifying the regal, in oppofition to the
papal, pretenfions of an ecclefiaftical liberty, or an exemption of the perfons of the clergy, and the goods of the
church, from the civil powers   It was denying the power
that the pope maintained of remitting, or retaining, the
fins of individuals abfolutely   It was fhewing the abufe of
ecclefiaftical cenfures, and rejecting the opinion of papal
indulgences

Such are the tenets with which this famous reformer is
charged   And it is rather wonderful that he fhould have
the courage to proceed fo far, than extraordinary, that he
did not go farther, confidering the prejudices of education,
which the wifeft and beft of men, without a particular
effort of divine grace, feldom or never fubdue

The followers of *Wickliffe* went greater lengths than he
intended   But all the opinions which they have fathered
upon the Wickliffites are not to be regarded, any more
than the cenfures, which were afterwards thrown upon
Luther for the fubfequent heterodoxies of the Lutherans,
the Anabaptifts, and other fects in *Germany*, which he
oppofed himfelf while living, and to which his writings
are a ftanding contradiction

Wickliffe had opened the eyes of the people, and they
began to think, the moment they could fee, to which they
were the more incited by the example fet them by the duke
of *Lancafter*, and the lord *Henry Percy*, earl-marfhal, who
took *Wickliffe* under their patronage and protection. This
alarmed the court of *Rome*, and pope *Gregory* XI fent

forth feveral bulls againft *Wickliffe*, all dated the twenty-
fecond of *May*, 1377 One was directed to *Simon Sudbury*,
archbifhop of *Canterbury*, and *William Courtney*, bifhop of
London, whom he delegated to examine into the matter of
the complaint   Another was difpatched to the king himfelf And a third to the univerfity of *Oxford* In the firft
bull, to the two prelates, he tells them, ' he was informed
' that *Wickliffe* had rafhly proceeded to that deteftable
' degree of madnefs, as not to be afraid to affert, and
' publicly preach, fuch propofitions, as were erroneous
' and falfe, contrary to the faith, and threatening to fub-
' vert and weaken the eftate of the whole church.' He
therefore required them to caufe *Wickliffe* to be apprehended and imprifoned by his authority, and to get his
confeffion concerning his propofitions and conclufions (of
which they deemed *nineteen* to be heretical) which they
were to tranfmit to *Rome*, as alfo whatever he fhould fay,
or write, by way of introduction or proof But, if *Wickliffe*
could not be apprehended, they were directed to publifh a
citation for his perfonal appearance before the pope within
three months. The pope requefted the king to grant his
patronage and affiftance to the bifhops in the profecution
of *Wickliffe*, who had promulgated ' opinions full of errors
' and containing manifeft herefy, fome of which appeared
' to be the fame with thofe of *Marfilius* of *Padua*, and
' *John de Gandun*, condemned by pope John XXII ' In
the bull to the univerfity, he fays, the heretical pravity
of *Wickliffe* tended ' to fubvert the ftate of the whole
' church, and even the civil government ' And he orders
them to deliver *Wickliffe* up in fafe cuftody to the delegates.

King *Edward* III died the twenty-firft of June 1377,
before the bulls arrived in England. The univerfity
treated their bull with contempt, or with very little devotion, They favored and protected *Wickliffe*, who was
powerfully fupported by the duke of *Lancafter*, and the
earl-marfhal Thefe noblemen openly declared, they
would not fuffer him to be imprifoned And, indeed, there
was yet no act of parliament, which empowered the bifhops
to imprifon heretics without the royal confent But the
delegated prelates, on the nineteenth of *February* 1378,
iffued out their mandate to the chancellor of the univerfity
of *Oxford*, commanding him to cite *Wickliffe* to appear
before them in the church of St *Paul*, *London*, in thirty
days.

Before that day came, the firft parliament of king *Richard*
II. met at *Weftminfter*, where it was debated, ' whether
' they

' they might lawfully refuse to fend the treafure out of the
' kingdom, after the pope required it on pain of cenfures,
' and by virtue of the obedience due to him?' The refolution of this doubt was referred, by the king and parliament, to doctor *Wickliffe*, who anfwered it was lawful,
and undertook to prove it fo, by the principles of the law
of *Chrift*

Wickliffe appeared to the fummons of the delegates at
St *Paul's*, where a vaft concourfe of people affembled to
hear the examination The doctor was attended by the
duke of *Lancafter*, and the lord-marfhal *Percy*, who had
conceived fuch a very high opinion of his learning and
integrity, that they affured him he had nothing to fear,
and that he might make his defence with courage againft
the bifhops, who were but mere ignorants in refpect to
him When *Wickliffe* came near the place of the affembly,
there was fo great a croud of people attending, that it was
with difficulty he and his two patrons got admittance into
the church This manner of their appearance, by introducing *Wickliffe* as to a triumph, rather than a trial,
touched the bifhop of *London*, who told the earl-marfhal,
' if he had known what mafteries they would have kept
' in the church, he would have ftopped them from coming
' there '

The archbifhop, and the bifhop of *London*, held their
court in the chapel, where feveral other prelates, and fome
noblemen, attended to hear the trial *Wickliffe* ftood before the commiffioners, according to cuftom, to hear what
was laid to his charge But the earl-marfhal bid him fit
down, ' as he had many things to anfwer, and had need of
' a foft feat to reft him upon, during fo tedious an attend-
' ance.' The bifhop of *London* objected to this, which was
anfwered by the duke of *Lancafter*, in fuch warm terms,
that he told the bifhop, ' he would bring down the pride
' of all the prelacy in the kingdom ' The bifhop made a
fpirited reply And the duke faid foftly, to one who fat
by him, that, ' rather than take fuch language from the
' bifhop, he would drag him out of the church by the hair
' of his head.' This was over-heard by fome of the bye-
ftanders, and the affembly was inftantly in a violent commotion The Londoners declared they would oppofe any
infults upon their bifhop The noblemen treated the citizens with difdain, they carried off *Wickliffe* in fafety, and
the court broke up without entering into an examination
of the bufinefs But the Londoners plundered the duke of
Lancafter's palace in the *Savoy*, and the duke turned the

mayor and aldermen out of the magistracy, for not restraining the sedition Wickliffe had the happiness to find his doctrine embraced by men of letters, and persons of quality Some would make us believe, that people were frightened into a feigned approbation of his doctrine But it may be said, with much greater probability, that fear deterred many from being his followers The truth is, a man ran no risk in continuing to adhere to the old tenets, whereas it might be dangerous to embrace the new ones

The duke of *Lancaster* was made president of the council, and the bishops were afraid to offend the avowed protector of *Wickliffe*. However, the two prelates summoned the doctor a second time before them, at *Lambeth*. He appeared, when the Londoners forced themselves into the chapel, to encourage the doctor, and intimidate the delegates. *Wickliffe* seemed willing to give the prelates some sort of satisfaction, and delivered them a paper, wherein he explained the several conclusions with which he was charged. In all appearance, the delegates would not have been contented with so general an explanation, if the king's mother had not obliged them to desist, by sending Sir *Lewis Clifford* to forbid their proceeding to any definitive sentence against *Wickliffe* The delegates were confounded with this message, and, as their own historian says, ' at the wind of a reed shaken, their speech became ' as soft as oil, to the public loss of their own dignity, ' and the damage of the whole church ' They dropped the thoughts of all censures against *Wickliffe*, and dismissed him, after enjoining him silence, to which injunction he paid no regard, and maintained his opinions in the utmost latitude. This steadiness ill agrees with the explanation of his opinions, which it is pretended he made before the bishops, and is represented as full of equivocations and evasions The disguising his sentiments is little conformable to his natural temper, which was far enough from being fearful Though a modern writer takes upon him to say, ' that *Wickliffe* appears to have been a ' man of slender resolution ' He also calls *Wickliffe*'s explanations aukward apologies But he should have remembered they are only such as are given us by *Walsingham*, whom he calls a prejudiced writer

The duke of *Lancaster* flattered himself with the hopes of being sole regent during the minority of the king his nephew, who was crowned on the thirteenth of July 1377, but the parliament joined some bishops and noblemen with him in the regency. This was a damp upon the Wickliffites,

liffites, or Lollards, who were become so numerous, that two men could not be found together, and one not a Lollard But pope *Gregory* XI died the twenty-seventh of *March* 1378, which was a great advantage to *Wickliffe*, for, by his death, an end was put to the commission of the delegates Here the historian seems to be mistaken, when he says, the demise of the pope occasioned grief to the faithful. Because *Wickliffe* did not make his appearance before the delegates of *Lambeth*, till almost three months after the death of *Gregory* A schism ensued, by a double election of two popes, which was a real advantage to the Wickliffites, since *Urban* VI was not acknowledged by the kingdom to be lawful pope till the end of the next year. On this occasion, *Wickliffe* wrote a tract " Of the Schism " of the *Roman* Pontiffs " And soon after published his book " Of the Truth of the Scripture " In the latter he contended for the necessity of translating the scriptures into the *English* language, and affirmed, that the will of God was evidently revealed in two Testaments, that the law of Christ was sufficient to rule the church, and that any disputation, not originally produced from thence, must be accounted profane

The fatigues which *Wickliffe* underwent, by attending the delegates, threw him into a dangerous fit of illness, on his return to *Oxford* The mendicant friars took this advantage, and sent a deputation to him, to inform him of the great injuries he had done them, by his sermons and writings. The deputies told him, he was at the point of death, and exhorted him to revoke whatever he had advanced to their prejudice *Wickliffe* immediately recovered his spirits, raised himself on his pillow, and replied " I " shall not die, but live to declare the evil deeds of the " friars " The unexpected force of his expression, together with the sternness of his manner, drove away the friars in confusion

The parliament, which assembled in 1380, was famous for a statute made against the blood-suckers that had long devoured the land, viz the foreign ecclesiastics, who, by this statute, were rendered incapable of holding any benefices in *England* At the same time, the parliament petitioned the king to expel all foreign monks, for fear they should instil notions into the people of *England*, repugnant to the good of the state While *Wickliffe*, in his lectures, sermons, and writings, embraced every opportunity of exposing the Romish court, and detecting the vices of the clergy both religious and secular

The

The feſtivals of *Wickliffe*, which are extant, and his
ſermons on the *Commune Sanctorum*, gave great offence to
the monks, who kindled a ſeditious ſpirit among the people on account of the poll-tax, which ſoon broke out into
thoſe inſurrections headed by *Wat Tyler*, *Ball*, and *Littſtar*
Theſe rebels beheaded *Simon Sudbury*, archbiſhop of *Canterbury*, the lord high-treaſurer, and put many others to
death   Their deſign was to murder the king, root out the
nobility, and deſtroy all the clergy except the mendicant
friars. Some hiſtorians accuſe the Wickliffites with cauſ-
ing this rebellion, but without any foundation   It is certain, that religion had no hand in theſe commotions, ſince
the duke of *Lancaſter*, the avowed protector of *Wickliffe*,
was the principal object of the rebels fury   Beſides, *Wickliffe* then reſided on his living of *Lutterworth*, and was
never charged with any thing on that account   Nor can
we hardly find an inſtance of inſurrections, cauſed by a
religious zeal, appeaſed in ſo ſhort a time as this was,
which continued only about a month, from the beginning
to the end

The holy ſcriptures had never been tranſlated into *Engliſh*, except by *Richard Fitz-Ralph*, archbiſhop of *Armagh*,
and *John de Treviſe*, a *Corniſh-man*, who both lived in the
reign of *Edward* III   That taſk was now undertaken
by *Wickliffe*, and other learned aſſociates, which made it
neceſſary for *Wickliffe* to apologize for their undertaking,
by ſhewing that *Bede* tranſlated the bible, and king *Alfred*
the pſalms, into the *Saxon* tongue   It had long given *Wickliffe* great offence (ſays Mr. *Gilpin*), and indeed he always
conſidered it as one of the capital errors of popery, that
the bible ſhould be locked up from the people   He reſolved, therefore, to free it from bondage. The bible,
he affirmed, contained the whole of God's will, which,
he ſaid, was ſufficient to guide his church. Theſe, and
other arguments, paved the way for the publication of
this great work, and ſatisfied the minds of all ſober men

This work it may eaſily be imagined raiſed the clamors
of the clergy   *Knighton*, a canon of *Leiceſter*, and contemporary with *Wickliffe*, affords a ſample of the language of
his brethren   ' *Chriſt* entruſted his goſpel (ſays he) to the
' clergy, and doctors of the church, to miniſter it to the
' laity and weaker ſort, according to their exigencies and
' ſeveral occaſions   But this maſter *John Wickliffe*, by
' tranſlating it, has made it vulgar, and laid it more open
' to the laity, and even to women who can read, than it
' uſed to be to the moſt learned of the clergy and thoſe of
                                                    ' the

' the beſt underſtanding And thus the goſpel-jewel, the
' evangelical pearl, is thrown 'bout, and *trodden under*
' *foot of ſwine*' However, ſome great and learned men
were of opinion, there was an older tranſlation, which muſt
have been *that* above mentioned Though it has been
aſſerted, ' the firſt tranſlation that was ever made of the
' *whole* bible into the *Engliſh* language, is ſpoke after the
' conqueſt, was made by doctor *Wickliffe*' He and his
aſſiſtants were very careful in making their tranſlation, by
correcting the *Latin* text, collecting the gloſſes, and con-
ſulting the antient divines, after which they ſet about the
tranſlation, not literally, but as clearly as they could to
expreſs the ſenſe and meaning of the text according to the
Hebrew, as well as the *Latin* bibles In this he had much
aſſiſtance from the commentators, and particularly from
the annotations of *Nicholas Lyra* They diſtinguiſhed
which books had the authority of holy writ, and which
were apocryphal, They juſtified their tranſlations, and
affirmed, " that he that kepeth mekeneſs and charitie, hath
" the trewe underſtandynge and perfection of holi write "

The zeal of the biſhops to ſuppreſs *Wickliffe's* bible
only made it, as is generally the caſe, the more ſought
after They, who were able, among the reformers, pur-
chaſed copies, and they, who were not able, procured it
leaſt tranſcripts of particular goſpels, or epiſtles, as their
inclinations led In after times, when Lollardy increaſed,
and the flames were kindled, it was a common practice,
to faſten about the neck of the condemned heretic, ſuch
of theſe ſcraps of ſcripture as were found in his poſſeſſion,
which generally ſhared his fate,

Wickliffe proceeded in detecting the errors and abuſes
that had crept into the church, and oppoſed the popiſh
doctrine of tranſubſtantiation, which was aſſerted by *Rad-
bertus* about the year 820 It is confeſſed by the papiſts,
that this man was the firſt who wrote ſeriouſly and copi-
ouſly on this ſubject, ' the truth or reality of the body
' and blood of the euchariſt ' This was contrary to the
catholic doctrine that had exiſted near a thouſand years
after *Chriſt*, and particularly in the church of *England*
according to the *Saxon* homilies *Wickliffe* attacked this
error in his divinity lectures, in 1381, and maintained the
true and antient notion of the Lord's ſupper On this
account he publiſhed ſixteen concluſions, the firſt of which
is, that " the conſecrated hoſt, ſeen upon the altar, is not
" *Chriſt*, or any part of him, but an effectual ſign of him "
He offered to enter into a public diſputation with any man

D upon

upon thefe conclusions, which was prohibited by the religious, who were doctors in divinity, and *Wickliffe* then published his opinion concerning the eucharist

In his tract *de Blasphemia*, he observed, that the true doctrine of the facrament of the eucharist was retained in the church a thoufand years, even till the loofing of Satan but this oppofition to the doctrine of tranfubftantiation foon brought *Wickliffe* into more difficulties, for he was attempting to eradicate a notion, that exalted the myftical and hierarchical powers of the clergy *William de Barton* chancellor of the univerfity, and eleven doctors, of whom eight were of the religious, condemned *Wickliffe's* conclufions as erroneous affertions *Wickliffe* told the chancellor, that neither he, nor any of his affiftants, were able to confute his opinion, and he appealed from their condemnation to the king

William Courtney, bifhop of *London*, fucceeded archbifhop *Sudbury* in the fee of *Canterbury*, and was entirely devoted to the intereft of his patron the pope. This prelate had before fhewn himfelf a violent oppofer of *Wickliffe*, and now proceeded againft him and his followers, But as foon as the parliament met, in 1382, *Wickliffe* prefented his appeal to the king, and both houfes, *Walfingham* reprefents this, as done with a defign to draw the nobility into erroneous opinions, and that it was difapproved by the duke of *Lancafter*, who ordered *Wickliffe* to fpeak no more of that matter Others fay, that the duke advifed the doctor, not to appeal to the king, but fubmit to the judgement of his ordinary, upon which, the monks affert, he retracted his doctrine at *Oxford*, in the prefence of the archbifhop of *Canterbury*, fix bifhops, and many doctors, furrounded with a great concourfe of people It is true, he openly read a confeffion in Latin, which was fo far from being a retractation, that it feems rather a vindication of his opinion of the facrament, for it declares his refolution to defend it with his blood, and cenfures the contrary as herefy He at large explains his meaning, how he underftood the body of *Chrift* to be in the eucharift, or facrament of the altar, and exprefsly fays, " this vener-" able facrament is naturally bread and wine, but is " facramentally the body and blood of *Chrift*."

The new archbifhop prevailed upon the king to empower the bifhops to imprifon heretics, without afking the royal permiffion But the houfe of commons complained to the king, that this was a breach of the peoples privileges, and very deftructive to liberty, fince the clergy thereby became the absolute masters of the honour and fortune of private persons The king revoked the grant, but the revocation is not to be found on the parliament rolls, where it was expunged by the artifices of the clergy, whose chief view was to punish the Wickliffites

The king, in 1382, married *Anne* of *Luxemburg*, sister of the emperor *Wenceslaus*, and this princess became a great patroness of the Wickliffites to the time of her death, which happened in 1394 But archbishop *Courtney* prosecuted *Wickliffe*, and appointed a court of select bishops, doctors and batchelors, which assembled in the monastery of the preaching friars, *London* This court declared fourteen conclusions of *Wickliffe*, and others, heretical and erroneous

It is said, *Wickliffe* was cited to appear at this court, but was prevented by his friends, who advised him, that a plot was laid by the prelates to seize him on the road However, his cause was undertaken by the chancellor of *Oxford*, the two proctors, and the greatest part of the senate, who, in a letter, sealed with the university seal, sent to the court, gave him a great commendation for his learning, piety, and orthodox faith Doctor *Nicholas Hereford*, Doctor *Philip Rapyngdon*, and *John Ayshton*, M A were the principal followers of *Wickliffe*, and appeared at this court, where they defended his doctrine, as also in the convocation Doctor *Hereford* afterwards took a journey to *Rome*, and offered, in the confistory before the pope, to defend the conclusions lately condemned by the archbishop, who committed him to prison on his return to *England* It has also been said, that the duke of *Lancaster* deserted the Wickliffites, and that all of them, except *Wickliffe*, submitted to the established church Archbishop *Courtney* exerted all his own authority, and all his interest at court, to punish the Wickliffites, and suppress their doctrine. He ordered the condemnation of the heretical articles to be published in the university But *Wickliffe* increased in reputation, and his doctrine gained ground in the affections of the people, while he was obliged to quit his professorship, and retire to *Lutterworth*, where he still vindicated his doctrine, and justified his followers

Doctor *Wickliffe* was seized with the palsy, in 1382, soon after he left *Oxford*, and the pope then cited him to appear at Rome. *Wickliffe* returned a letter of excuse to this citation, wherein he tells the pope, that " *Christ* " taught him more obedience to God than to man " His enemies were sensible that his distemper would soon put

a period

a period to his life, and therefore they permitted him to
spend the remainder of his days in tranquillity, after he had
been many years exposed to continual danger   He was
seized with another violent fit of the palsy, on Innocents'
day 1384, as he was in his church of *Lutterworth*, when
he fell down, never recovered his speech, and soon expired, in the sixtieth year of his age

The Christian world has not had a greater man in these
last ages than doctor *Wickliffe* He had well studied all
the parts of theological learning, and he was endowed,
by the grace of God, with an uncommon gravity and
sanctity of manners, from whence arose that vehement
desire of restoring the primitive purity of the church in
that ignorant and degenerate age   His most inveterate
adversaries never presumed to call in question his excellent
piety, and unblemished life   But many of them have sufficiently acknowledged his great learning, and uncommon
abilities.   Indeed, in those writings of his which are yet
remaining, doctor *Wickliffe* has shewn an extraordinary
knowledge of the scriptures, he discovers a sound judgement, argues closely and sharply, breathes a spirit of true
piety, and preserves a modesty becoming his character.
Nothing is to be found in him either puerile or trifling, a
fault very common to the writers of that age, but every
thing he says is grave, judicious, and exact   He wanted
nothing to render his learning consummate, but his living
in a happier age.

The great *Bradwardin* was, in some sense, *Wickliffe*'s
spiritual father, for it was the perusal of *Bradwardin*'s
writings, which, next to the holy scriptures, opened that
proto-reformer's eyes to discover the genuine doctrine of
faith and justification   *Bradwardin* taught him the nature
of a true and justifying faith, in opposition to merit-
mongers and pardoners, purgatory and pilgrimages

The censure which *Melancton* passed on *Wickliffe* was
made great use of by the papists   And some protestant
writers have charged him with maintaining several erroneous opinions, but what *Collier* says of him is beneath
contempt.   *Guthrie* affects to condemn him for being a
predestinarian, but he acknowledges, however, that ' his
' notions about the fopperies of religion, images, pilgrim-
' ages, legends, and the like, are many of them sensible,
' and most of them allowable   That his opinions with
' regard to the sacraments of the church, as then believed
' in *England*, are free, and such as have been adopted by
' many strict foreign churches   That, however immo-
                                                ' derate

‘ derate he was in his principles, he appears to have been
‘ a wise and moderate man in his practice, witness his
‘ dying in peace upon his own living, amidst an universal
‘ combustion which his tenets had raised And that he
‘ must be allowed to have left behind him the dawn of that
‘ Reformation which was afterwards completed ’

Mr *Guthrie*, observed that *Wickliffe* ‘ seems to have
‘ been a strong predestinarian ’ It will presently appear
(says a later writer) that he more than seemed to have been
such, and that *Luther* and *Calvin* themselves were not
stronger predestinarians than *Wickliffe* I shall open the
evidence with two propositions, extracted from his own
writings

1 " The prayer of the *reprobate* prevaileth for no man "

2 " All things that happen, do come *absolutely* of ne-
" cessity "

The manner in which this great harbinger of the Reformation defended the latter proposition, plainly shews
him to have been (notwithstanding *Guthrie*'s insinuation
to the contrary) a deep and skilfull disputant " Our
" Lord," says he, " affirmed that such or such an event
" should come to pass. It's accomplishment, therefore,
" was unavoidable. The antecedent is infallible By
" parity of argument, the consequent is so too For the
" consequent is not in the power of a created being, for-
" asmuch as *Christ* affirmed so many things" [before they
were brought to pass] " Neither did [pre] affirm any
" thing accidentally Seeing, then, that his affirmation
" was, not accidental, but necessary, it follows, that
" the event affirmed by him, must be necessary likewise
" This argument," adds *Wickliffe*, " receives additional
" strength, by observing, that, in what way soever God
" may declare his will, by his after-discoveries of it in
" time, still, his determination, concerning the event, took
" place before the world was made *Ergo*, the event will
" surely follow The necessity, therefore, of the ante-
" cedent, holds no less irrefragably for the necessity of
" the consequent. And who can either promote or hin-
" der the inference, namely, That this was decreed of
" God before the formation of the world " I will not
undertake (says Mr *Toplady*) to justify the whole of this
paragraph. I can only meet the excellent man half-way
I agree with him, as to the *necessity of events* But I cannot, as he evidently did, suppose God himself to be *a
necessary agent*, in the utmost sense of the term That
God *acts* in the most exact conformity to his own *decrees*,

is a truth which scripture asserts again and again But that God was *absolutely* FREE *in decreeing*, is no less asserted by the inspired writers, who, with one voice, declare the Father's predestination, and subsequent disposal, of all things, to be entirely founded, not on any antecedent necessity, but on the single, sovereign pleasure of his own *will*.

The quotation however, proves, that *Wickliffe* was an absolute necessitarian And he improves, with great solidity and acuteness, the topic of *prophecy* into (what it most certainly is) a very strong argument for *predestination*. As the *prophecies* of the old and new testaments are such an evidence of the divine inspiration of the sacred writers, and such a proof of *Christianity*, as all the infidels in the world will never be able to overthrow, so, on the other hand, those same *prophecies* conclude, to the full, as strongly in favor of peremptory *predestination* For if events were *undecreed*, they would be *unforeknown* And, if *unforeknown*, they could not be infallibly* *predicted* To say, that ' events may be *foreknown* without falling under any ' active or permissive decree,' would be saying either *nothing* to the purpose, or *worse* than nothing For, if God can, with certainty, *foreknow* any event whatever, which he did not *previously determine* to accomplish or permit, and that event, barely foreknown, but entirely undecreed, be so *certainly future*, as to furnish positive ground for *unerring prophecy*, it would follow, 1 That God is *dependent*, for his knowledge, on the things known , instead of all things being dependent on *him* And, 2. That there are some extraneous concatenations of causes, *prior* to the will

* It is very observable, that *Wickliffe* s argument for predestination, drawn from the *prophecies* of our Lord, so puzzled the then archbishop of *Armagh* (whose name I know not, nor do I think it worth hunting out) that it furnished his grace with employment for *two years* together, to reconcile the *free will* of man with the certain completion of *prophecy* A task, however, which after all his labor, the romish prelate found too hard for him Yet, his lordship, that he might not be forced to acknowledge predestination and give up *free-will*, thought proper to give up the infallible prescience of *Christ* himself, blasphemously affirming, that ' it was possible for *Christ* to be *mistaken* in his ' prophecies, and to *misinform* his church as to future events ' The passage is so uncommon, that I will give it in the writer's own words. " Dicit adversarius [scil *Wickliffe*,] quoad istud argumentum, domi-
" num *Armachanum* per duos annos studuisse pro ejus dissolutione, &
" finaliter nescivit (ut dicit) aliter evadere, nisi CONCEDENDO, quòd
" *Christus errasse potuit, et ecclesiam decepisse* Quam conclusionem
" nullus catholicus (ut dicit *Wickliffe*) concederet Et sic videtur
" ponere dominum *Armachanum* extra numerum catholicorum " *Gulielm Wodford* contrà *Wicklefum*. Vide *Fascic. Rer.* vol. 1. p 256

and

and knowledge of God, by which his will is regulated, and on which his knowledge is founded

What he little more than intimates, in the citation given above, he delivered, it seems, more plainly and peremptorily, elsewhere. Among the sixty-two articles, laid to his charge by *Thomas Netter* (commonly called, *Thomas of Walden* who flourished about the year 1409,) and for which, that writer refers to the volume and chapter of *Wickliffe's* works, are these three: 1 That "*all things come to pass* "*by* FATAL *necessity.*" 2 That "*God could not make the* "*world otherwise than it is made.*" 3. And, that "*God* "*cannot do any thing, which he doth not do* *"

This is *fatalism* with a witness. And I cite these propositions, not to depreciate Dr *Wickliffe*, whose character I admire and revere, as one of the greatest and best since the apostolic age, nor yet with a view to recommend the propositions themselves: But, simply, to shew, how far this illustrious Reformer ran from the present Arminian system, or rather no-system, of chance and free-will. But, concerning even those of *Wickliffe's* assertions, which were the most rash and unguarded, candor (not to say, justice) obliges me to observe, with *Fuller*, that were all his works extant, ' we might therein read the *occasion, intention,* and ' *connection,* of what he spake. Together with the *limi-* ' *tations, restrictions, distinctions,* and *qualifications,* of what ' he maintained. There we might see, what was the over- ' plus of his passion, and what the just measure of his ' judgement. Many phrases, heretical in sound, would ' appear orthodox in sense. Yea, some of his [reputedly] ' poisonous passages, dressed with due caution, would prove ' not only *wholesome,* but cordial truths; many of his ex- ' pressions wanting, not *granum ponderis,* but *granum salis,* ' no weight of truth, but some grains of discretion† '

What I shall next add, may be rather styled bold truths, than indiscrete assertions. "He defined the *church* to "consist *only of persons* PREDESTINATED. And affirmed, "*That God loved* David *and* Peter *as dearly, when they*

---

* *Fuller's* church hist b 4 p 134 —What this valuable historian premises, concerning *Wickliffe,* before he enters on his account of him, deserves to be quoted ' I intend, says Dr *Fuller,* ' neither to deny, ' dissemble, defend, nor excuse, any of his faults. *We have this trea-* ' *sure,* saith the apostle, in earthen vessels. And he that shall endeavour ' to prove *a pitcher of clay* to be *a pot of gold,* will take great pains to ' small purpose. Yea, should I be over officious to run myself to ' plead for *Wickliffe's* faults, that glorious saint would sooner chide ' than thank me '

† Ibid. p. 135.

"grievously

" *grievously finned, as he doth now when they are possessed of*
" *glory** " This latter position might, possibly, have been
more unexceptionably expressed, be it, substantially, ever
so true

Wickliffe was found in the article of gratuitous pardon
and justification by the alone death and righteousness of
Jesus Christ " The merit of *Christ*," says he, " is, of
" itself, *sufficient* to redeem every man from hell   It is
" to be understood of *a sufficiency* OF ITSELF, without *any*
" *other* concurring cause   All that follow *Christ*, being
" *justified by* HIS *righteousness*, shall be saved, as his off-
" spring " Dr *Alix* observes, that *Wickliffe* ' rejects the
' doctrine of the *merit* of works, and falls upon those
' who say, that *God did not* ALL *for them*, but think that
' *their merits help* ' " *Heal us, Lord*, FOR NOUGHT, says
" *Wickliffe, that is, for no merit of ours, but for thy mercy* "
It has been already observed, and proved, that he had very
high notions of that inevitable *necessity*, by which he supposed every event is governed   Yet, he did not enthusi-
astically sever the end from the means   Witness his own
words   " Though *all* future things do happen *necessarily*,
" yet God wills that good things happen to his servants
" through the efficacy of *prayer* "   Upon the whole, it
is no wonder that such a profligate factor for popery and
arminianism, as *Peter Heylin*, should *(pro more)* indecently
affirm, that " *Wickliffe's* held had more tares, than wheat,
" and his books more heterodoxies, than found catholic
" doctrine "   See *Toplady's* Historic Proof

Whatever *Walfingham* and *Knighton* have advanced in
prejudice of *Wickliffe*, is sufficiently contradicted by letters testimonial given by the university of *Oxford*, in
1406, in his behalf, and sealed with their common seal,
wherein it is said, ' that his conversation, from his youth
' to his death, was so praise-worthy and honest in the
' university, that he never gave any offence, nor was he
' asperfed with any mark of infamy or sinister suspicion
' But that in answering, reading, preaching, and determin-
' ing, he behaved himself laudably, as a valiant champion
' of the truth, and catholicly vanquished by sentences of
' holy scripture all such as by their wilful beggary blaf-
' phemed the religion of Christ.   That this doctor was
' not convicted of heretical pravity, or by our prelates
' delivered to be burnt after his burial   For God forbid
' that our prelates should have condemned a man of so
' great probity for an heretic, who had not his equal in

* Ibid. p 134.

' all

' all the univerfity in his writings of logic, philofophy,
' divinity, morality, and the fpeculative fciences '

As doctor *Wickliffe* was very diligent and frequent in
preaching, and reading his divinity lectures, fo he wrote
and publifhed a great many tracts, of which bifhop *Bale*
has given a particular account They are two hundred
and fifty-five in all, of which thirty-two are preferved in
Trinity-college, and C C C *Cambridge*, five in *Trinity-
college*, *Dublin*, four in the *Bodleian* library, two in the
Cotton library, and three in the king's library. Moft of
them are theological, but fome are philofophical, forty-
eight are in *Englifh*, and the others are in *Latin* Befides
thefe, there is a volume of *Englifh* tracts faid to be wrote
by *Wickliffe*, fome of which are yet extant He is faid
to have wrote two hundred volumes, befides his tranflation
of the Bible into *Englifh*, a fair copy of which is in
Queen's-colleg, *Oxford*, and two more in the univerfity
library ' It was done no doubt in the moft expreffive
' language of thofe days, though founding uncouth to our
' ears, the *knave* of *Jefus Chrift* for fervant, and *Philip*
' baptized the *gelding*, for eunuch So much our tongue
' is improved in our age ' *

His opinions were mifreprefented by his adverfaries,
but he was protected by many powerful friends, and his
doctrine was embraced by the greateft part of the kingdom King *Edward* III the princefs dowager of *Wales*,
the duke of *Lancafter*, the queen of *Richard* II the earl-
marfhal, *Geoffry Chaucer* the father of *Englifh* poetry, and
lord *Cobham*, who difperfed *Wickliffe*'s works all over
Europe, were his patrons and friends From fuch a noble

---

* *Romans* ix 11,—21 Whanne thei weren not ghit borun, neither
" hadden doon ony thing of good, either of yvel, that the purpos of
" God fchulde dwell bi eleccioun, not of workis, but of God clepy-
" ing, it was feid to him, that the more fchulde ferve the laffe as it
" is writun, I louyde Jacob, but I hatide I fau What therefore
" fchulen we feie? wher wickidneffe be anentis God? God forbede.
" For he feith to Moifes, I fchal have mercy on whom I have mercy,
" and I fchal ghyve merci on whom I have mercy Therefore, it is
" not neither of man willynge, neither rennynge, but of God hauynge
" mercy And the fcripture feith to *Farao*, For to this thing have
" I ftyrrid thee, that I fchewe in thee my vertu, and that my name
" be teeld in al erthe Therefore, of whom God wole, he hath
" mercy And whom he wole, he enduruth Thanne feift thou to
" me, What is fought ghit, for who withftondith his will? Oo man,
" what art thou that anfwerift to God! Wher a maad thing feith to
" him that made it, What haft thou maad me fo? Wher a potter of
" cley hath not power to make, of the fame gobet, oo veffel into
" onoui, anothir into difpyt' ' *Lewis*'s Edition of *Wickliffe*'s Tranfl.
N. Teft.—*Lond.* 1731, Folio.

E   fountain

fountain the stream ran strong, and was soon increased, for many eminent divines, noblemen, and other persons of distinction, embraced the new doctrine, which constantly gathered ground, notwithstanding it was violently opposed by the priests, who raised bloody persecutions against the Wickliffites in the reigns of *Richard* II *Henry* IV and *Henry* V.

The number of those who believed in the doctrine of *Wickliffe* multiplied like suckers growing out of the root of a tree. After a time, the secular and ecclesiastical powers were combined to suppress its growth, and archbishop *Arundel*, in convocation, condemned eighteen of *Wickliffe's* conclusions, twelve years after his death   Acts of parliament were made against the Wickliffites, and many of them were burnt for heretics   The books of *Wickliffe* were prohibited to be read in the universities   And, in 1416, archbishop *Chichely* set up a kind of inquisition in every parish to discover and punish the Wickliffites, by which cruel and unchristian methods the great and good *John* lord *Cobham* was burnt for heresy, and he was the first nobleman whose blood was shed in *England*, on account of religion, by popish barbarity. *Fox* asserts, in his acts and monuments, that the two famous poets of that time, *Gower* and *Chaucer*, were Wickliffites, and that they covered their opinion very ingeniously, and by way of parable, in their writings, adding likewise, that, by the exposition of those writings by such as had the key, many were brought into *Wickliffe's* persuasion   *Chaucer* died in the year 1400, and *Gower* some time before

The infallibity of the pope was opposed to the doctrine of *Wickliffe*, and the council of *Constance*, on the fifth of *May*, 1415, condemned forty-five articles, maintained by *Wickliffe*, as heretical, false, and erroneous. His bones were ordered to be dug up, and cast on a dunghill   But this part of the sentence was not executed till 1428, when orders were sent by the pope to the bishop of *Lincoln* to have it strictly performed   The remains of this excellent man were accordingly dug out of the grave, where they had lain undisturbed four and forty years   His bones were burnt, and the ashes cast into an adjoining brook called the *Swift*, which springs near *Knaptoft* in *Leicestershire* Such was the resentment of the *Romish* church on the memory of him, who was called the first *English Lollard* *
                                                                    Cambden

* The sect of the *Lollards*, spread throughout *Germany*, had for their leader *Walter Lollard*, who began to disperse his doctrines about the
                                                                    year

_____ says, this was done forty-one years after his death by warrant of the council of *Sienna*. But this is a mistake, for it was done by the same council of *Constance*, which condemned *John Hass*, and *Jerom* of *Prague*, to be burnt for favoring the doctrine of *Wickliff*, and maintaining others which were also condemned as heretical. This council sat to give sanction to injustice, and to establish iniquity by law, though it inflicted an irretrievable blow upon the papal authority.

It is said, that the gown which doctor *Wickliff* wore now covers the communion-table in the church of *Lutterworth*. And, as this eminent man may justly be considered as the author of the Reformation, not only in *England*, but throughout all *Europe*, sure some decent respect should have been paid to his worth, and a public monument erected to his memory.

The Wickliffites were oppressed, but could not be extinguished. Persecution served only to establish that faith which became general at the Reformation, about a hundred years after these restraints were moderated. The whole nation then unanimously embraced the doctrine which *Wickliffe* began, and popery was abolished in *England*, that the purity of religion might increase the blessings of liberty.

His works (says Mr *Gilpin*) are amazingly voluminous, yet he seems not to have engaged in any very large work. His pieces in general may be properly called tracts. Of these many were written in Latin, and many in *English*; some on school-questions, others on subjects of more general knowledge, but the greatest part on divinity. It may be some amusement to the reader to see what subjects he hath chosen. I shall give a list therefore of the more remarkable of them, from the various collections which have been made. *Trialogorum, lib* 4.——*De religione perfectorum.*——*De ecclesiâ & membris.*——*De diabolo & membris*——*De Christo & Antichristo.*——*De Antichristo & membris*——*Sermones in epistolas.*——*De veritate scriptura.*——*De statu innocentiæ.*——*De stipendiis ministrorum.*——

year 1315. He despised the sacraments of the church, and derided her ceremonies and her constitutions, observed not the fasts of the church, nor its abstinences, acknowledged not the intercession of the saints, and believed that the damned in hell, and even the evil angels, should one day be saved. *Trithemius*, who recites their opinions, says, that *Bohemia* and *Austria* were infected with them, that there were above 24,000 persons in *Germany* which held those errors, and that the greater part defended them with obstinacy, even to death.—*De Pu*

De episcoporum erroribus ——De curatorum erroribus —— De perfectione evangelicâ ——De officio pastorali ——De simoniâ sacerdotum ——Super pænitentiis injungendis ——De seductione simplicium ——Dæmonum astus in subvertendâ religione ——De pontificum Romanorum schismate ——De ultimâ ætate ecclesiæ ——Of temptation.——The chartre of hevene ——Of ghostly battel ——Of ghostly and fleshly love —— The confession of St Brandoun ——Active life, and contemplative ——Virtuous patience ——Of pride ——Observationes piæ in Christi præcepta ——De impedimentis orationis ——De cardinalibus virtutibus ——De actibus animæ —— Expositio orationis dominicæ ——De 7 sacramentis ——De naturâ fidei ——De diversis gradibus charitatis —De defectione à Christo ——De veritate & mendacio ——De sacerdotio Levitico ——De sacerdotio Christi ——De dotatione Cæsareâ.——De versutiis pseudocleri ——De immortalitate animæ ——De paupertate Christi ——De physicâ naturali —— De essentiâ accidentium ——De necessitate futurorum ——De temporis quidditate.——De temporis ampliatione ——De operibus corporalibus ——De operibus spiritualibus ——De fide & perfidiâ ——De sermone Domini in montem ——Abstractiones logicales ——A short rule of life —The great sentence of the curse expounded.——Of good priests ——De contrarietate duorum dominorum ——Wickliffe's wicket ——De ministrorum conjugio ——De religiosis privatis ——Conciones de morte ——De vitâ sacerdotum ——De ablatis restituendis ——De arte sophisticâ ——De fonte errorum ——De incarnatione verbi ——Super impositis articulis ——De humanitate Christi ——Contra concilium terræ-motus ——De solutione Satanæ ——De spiritu quolibet.——De Christianorum baptismo.——De clavium potestate ——De blasphemiâ.——De paupertate Christi ——De raritate & densitate.——De materiâ & formâ ——De animâ ——Octo beatitudines.——De trinitate ——Commentarii in psalterium ——De abominatione desolationis ——De civili dominio ——De ecclesiæ dominio. ——De divino dominio ——De origine sectarum ——De perfidiâ sectarum ——Speculum de antichristo ——De virtute orandi——De remissione fraterna ——De censuris ecclesiæ ——De charitate fraternâ ——De purgatorio piorum —— De Pharisæo & Publicano

His great work, and what offended the church of *Rome* most highly, was his *Translation of the Scriptures into English*, which effectually exposed the sophistries and superstitions of the time, and led the people from following the traditions of men to the pure will and word of the blessed GOD.

JOHN

JOHN HUSS, D.D,

THE BOHEMIAN REFORMER.

JOHN HUSS, or Hus, whose name in the *Bohemian* language signifies *Goofe*, was born at *Huffenitz*, a village in *Bohemia* His parents were not blest with affluence, but they gave him a liberal education, which he improved by his strong mental abilities, and close application to his studies, in the university of *Prague*, where he commenced batchelor of arts in 1393, master of arts in 1395, and batchelor of divinity in 1408 *Hufs* was a man (says *Wharton* in his Appendix to *Cave's Hiftoria Literaria*) even by the confession of his enemies, illustrious and remarkable both for doctrine and piety It was in this year that *Sbynko*, or *Subinfco Lepus*, the archbishop of that city, issued two orders to suppress the doctrine of the *Wickliffites*, which had been introduced into that kingdom, and was countenanced by the greatest part of the masters and scholars of the university of *Prague*, who, by a providence we shall mention presently, had got the books of *Wickliffe* into their hands

Queen *Anne*, the wife of king *Richard* II of *England*, was daughter to the emperor *Charles* IV and sister to *Wenceslaus*, king of *Bohemia*, and *Sigismund* emperor of *Germany* She was a princess of great piety, virtue, and knowledge, nor could she endure the implicit and unreasonable service and devotion of the *Roman* church Her death happened in 1394, and her funeral was attended by all the nobility of *England* She had patronized *Wickliffe*, who speaks of her in his book " Of the three-fold Bond of Love," in these words " It is possible that the noble queen of *England*, the sister of *Cæfar*, may have the gospel written " in three languages, *Bohemian*, *German*, and *Latin*. " But to hereticate her, on this account, would be Lu- " ciferian folly " After her death, several of *Wickliffe's* books were carried by her attendants into *Bohemia*, and were the means of promoting the reformation there

The books of *Wickliffe* were carried into *Bohemia* by *Peter Payne*, an *Englishman*, one of his disciples But the archbishop of *Prague* ordered the members of that
university

univerfity to bring him the books of *Wickliffe*, that thofe in which any errors were found might be burnt. The tracts of *Wickliffe* had been fo carefully preferved, that we are affured a certain bifhop wrote out of *England*, that he had got two very large volumes of them, which feemed as large as St *Auftin*'s works. Archbifhop *Sbynko* burnt two hundred volumes of them, very finely written, and adorned with coftly covers and gold boffes, for which reafon, they are fuppofed to belong to the nobility and gentry of *Bohemia*.

, *Peter Payne* was principal of *Edmund-hall*, in the univerfity of *Oxford*, where he was diftinguifhed for his excellent parts, and his oppofition to the friars He was a good difputant, and confuted *Walden*, the *Carmelite*, about the beggary of Chrift, pilgrimages, the eucharift, images, and relicts, for which he was obliged to quit the univerfity, and fly into *Bohemia*, where he contracted an acquaintance with *Procopius*, the *Bohemian* General, and publifhed fome books written by *Wickliffe*, which were greatly efteemed by *Hufs*, *Jerom*, and the greateft part of the univerfity of *Prague* The ftudents belonging to this learned feminary were offended with their archbifhop for fuppreffing the books of *Wickliffe*, and ordering the *Bohemian* clergy to teach the people, that, after the pronunciation of the words of the holy facrament, there remained nothing but the body of *Jefus Chrift* under the ipecies or bread, and the body of *Jefus Chrift* in the cup

There was alfo, according to *Fox*, another caufe of the difperfion of *Wickliffe*'s books in *Bohemia*. A young man of an opulent and noble family of that country came over to *Oxford*, about the year 1389, for the profecution of his ftudies, and, upon his return, carried with him feveral tracts of *Wickliffe*, amongft which were his books, *De realibus univerfalibus*, *De civili jure & divino*, *De ecclefiâ*, *De quæftionibus variis contra clerum*, &c With this gentleman *Hufs* was well acquainted, and obtained from him the loan of thefe books, which were the means of bringing light into his mind, and fo much impreffed him with the conviction of their truth, that he embraced and maintained the doctrines they contained ever afterwards. He ufed to call *Wickliffe* an angel fent from heaven to enlighten mankind, and would mention among his friends his meeting with that great author's writings, as the moft happy circumftance of his life, adding, that it would be his joy in heaven to live for ever with that excellent man.

Hufs had diftinguifhed himfelf in the univerfity, where he taught grammar and philofophy. He had applied him-

self

felf to the ftudy of the holy fcriptures, and the Latin fathers He was become an excellent preacher, and was
made chaplin in the church of the *Holy Innocents*, called
Bethlehem, at *Prague* He was held in great eftimation
for his exemplary life and converfation as a divine, and
for having been one of the principal perfons who had obtained a great favor to the univerfity It fhould be obferved, that this univerfity was founded by the emperor
Charles IV who compofed it of perfons from the four
different ftates of *Bohemia*, *Bavaria*, *Saxony*, and *Poland*.
The three latter were almoft all *Germans*, and had three
voices againft one, which made them mafters of the profeffor's chair, governors of the univerfity affairs, and dif-
pofers of the beft benefices in the city While the poor
Bohemians, whofe profperity depended entirely on thofe
advantages, found themfelves utterly excluded This
was the ftate of that feminary, when doctor *Hufs*, affifted
by others, reprefented the caufe of the complaining *Bohemians* to their king *Wenceflaus* V. *Hufs* was fuccefsful,
he obtained a revocation of the privileges granted to thofe
foreigners, and the *Bohemians* were reftored to the principal places in the univerfity, which fo greatly offended
the foreigners, that they retired to *Mifnia*, and carried
with them upwards of two thoufand fcholars This increafed the reputation of doctor *Hufs*, and made him of
great confideration in the univerfity, when the archbifhop
publifhed two orders againft Wickliffitifm.

Hufs arduoufly embraced the doctrine of *Wickliffe*, and
eafily perfuaded many members of the univerfity, * that
the firft of thefe orders, made by the archbifhop, was an
infringement of the privileges and liberties of the univerfity, whofe members had a right to read all forts of
books, without any moleftation He alfo obferved, that
the fecond order contained a moft intolerable error, in
feeming to affirm that there was nothing but the body and
blood of *Chrift* under the fpecies of bread, and in the cup.
Upon this foundation, they appealed from thofe orders to
Gregory XII. at *Rimini*, who was then acknowledged pope
in *Germany*, in oppofition to *John* XXIII at *Rome*, and
Benedict XIII at *Avignon* Their appeal was received,
and the pope cited the archbifhop to *Rome* But that
prelate informed the pope, that the doctrine of *Wickliffe*
began to take root in *Bohemia* upon which the archbifhop

---

* For Dr *Hufs*'s public defence of *Wickliffe*'s opinions before the
univerfity of *Prague*, in the year 1412, fee Fox's *Acts*, &c vol 1.
temp Ric. 2.

obtained

obtained a bull, whereby the pope gave him commiſſion to prevent the publiſhing of thoſe errors in his province

This archbiſhop, we are told, was a moſt illiterate man He was ſo illiterate, that he was called, in ridicule, *Alphabetarius*, the A B C Doctor. Indeed, the clergy of thoſe times were remarkably ignorant, inſomuch that many of the prelates could not write, but directed their chaplains to ſubſcribe their very names for them to eccleſiaſtical deeds and papers.

The archbiſhop, by virtue of this bull, definitively condemned the writings of *Wickliffe*, proceeded againſt four doctors, who had not delivered up the copies of that divine, and prohibited them, notwithſtanding their privileges, to preach in any congregation. Doctor *Huſs*, with ſome other members of the univerſity, and the patron of the chapel of *Bethlehem*, made their proteſtations againſt theſe proceedings, and, on the twenty-fifth of *June*, A D 1410, entered a new appeal from the ſentences of the archbiſhop This affair was carried before pope *John* XXIII who granted a commiſſion to cardinal *Colonna* to cite *John Huſs* to appear perſonally at the court of *Rome*, to anſwer the accuſations laid againſt him of preaching both errors and hereſies Doctor *Huſs* deſired to be excuſed a perſonal appearance, and was ſo greatly favored in *Bohemia*, that king *Wenceſlaus*, the queen, the nobility, and the univerſity, deſired the pope to diſpenſe with ſuch an appearance, as alſo that he would not ſuffer the kingdom of *Bohemia* to lie under the defamation of being accuſed of hereſy, but permit them to preach the goſpel with freedom in their places of worſhip, and that he would ſend legates to *Prague* to correct any pretended abuſes, the expence of which ſhould be defrayed by the *Bohemians*

Three proctors appeared for doctor *Huſs*, before cardinal *Colonna*, who was elected pope, in 1417, and aſſumed the name of *Martin* V The proctors alledged excuſes for the abſence of *Huſs*, and declared they were ready to anſwer in his behalf But the cardinal declared *Huſs* contumacious, and excommunicated him accordingly

The proctors appealed to the pope, who appointed the cardinals of *Aquileia*, *Brancas*, *Venice*, and *Zabarella*, to draw up the proceſs of this whole affair Theſe commiſſioners not only confirmed the judgement given by cardinal *Colonna*, but carried the matter much further, for they extended the excommunication, which had paſſed againſt *Huſs*, to all his diſciples, and alſo to his friends He was declared a promoter of hereſy, and an interdict

           was

was pronounced against him. From these proceedings he appealed to a future council, and, notwithstanding the decision of the four commissioners, and his being expelled from the church of *Bethlehem*, he retired to *Hussinitz*, the place of his nativity, where he boldly continued to promulge his doctrine, both from the pulpit, and with the pen.

The letters which he wrote, about this time, are very numerous; and he compiled a treatise wherein he maintained that the reading of the books of heretics cannot be absolutely forbidden. He justified *Wickliffe*'s book on the Trinity, and defended the character of that Reformer against a charge brought by one *Stokes*, an *Englishman*, and others, who accused him of disobedience.

It is truth, and not opinion, which can travel through the world without a passport. The glorious cause of truth had been freely espoused by *Huss*, who undauntedly declaimed against the clergy, the cardinals, and even against the pope himself. He wrote a discourse to prove, that the faults and vices of churchmen ought to be reproved from the pulpit. Regarding the blood of *Jesus Christ*, which many pretended to have as a relic, he observed, that *Christ*, being glorified, took up with him all his own blood, and that there is no remain of it on earth; as also that the greatest part of the miracles, which are reported about the apparition of his blood, are the frauds and impostures of avaricious and designing men. He maintained, that *Jesus Christ* might be called bread. But he departed not from the doctrine of the church about the transubstantiation of the bread and wine into the body and blood of *Jesus Christ*. But it is of small importance with the church of *Rome*, in what particular points the judgements of men coincide with its doctrines, if the whole of the corrupt leaven be not implicitly swallowed. And perhaps no points are held more sacred by that heretical communion, than those which yield the most abundant profit to the holy see, falsly so called. To attack the virtue of papal indulgences, is striking at the most fundamental pillar of the popedom; and to deny the stock of merit, laid up in the church for public sale, is a damnable denial of the privileges of the clergy, to whom both heaven and earth belong, under the disposal of their pontiff, *Christ*'s pretended vicar here below. These monstrous abuses, some very few of that church have attempted, as far as they dared, to censure.—And with respect to *Rome* itself, a journey thither would probably

F

effect

effect more to prevent a perversion from proteftantifm to popery, than a thoufand wordy arguments The wickednefs and vices of the clergy, in that city, fpeak aloud for their principles The review of thefe caufed *Hildebert*, archbifhop of *Tours*, fo long ago as the twelfth century, to characterize that famous mart of fouls in the following words

Urbs fœlix, fi vel dominis urbs illa careret,
Vel dominis effet turpe carere fide.

That is,

' Happy city, if it had no mafters, or if it were fcan-
' dalous for thofe mafters to be unfaithful ' *Luther* ufed to fay, that ' for 1000 florins he would not but have ' been at *Rome*,' where he faw fo thoroughly into that fink of fin and fpiritual abomination, that he abhorred the place and its profeffion all his life afterwards He had been fent thither, in the early part of his life, in behalf of his convent But to proceed

About the time when *Hufs* wrote the above difcourfes, *Peter of Drefden* was obliged to fly from *Saxony*, and feek a refuge at *Prague*, where he encouraged *Jacobelle* of *Mifnia*, a prieft of the chapel of St *Michael*, to preach up the eftablifhment of the communion under the fpecies of wine. This opinion was embraced by doctor *Hufs* and his followers, who began to preach, that the ufe of the cup was neceffary to the laity, and that the facrament fhould be adminiftered under both kinds Archbifhop *Shynko* was incenfed at thefe proceedings, and applied to king *Wenceflaus* for affiftance, which that monarch refufed The prelate then had recourfe to *Sigifmund*, king of *Hungary*, who promifed to come into *Bohemia*, and fettle the affairs of the church in that kingdom But *Shynko* died in *Hungary*, before *Sigifmund* began his journey into *Bohemia* *Albicus* fucceeded to the archiepifcopal fee of *Prague*, who permitted the Huffites to continue their fermons, and their doctrine became almoft general.

Doctor *Hufs* left his retirement, and returned to *Prague*, in 1412, at the time that pope *John* XXIII. publifhed the bulls againft *Laodiflaus*, king of *Naples*, whereby he ordered a croifade againft him, and granted indulgences to all thofe who undertook this war. Thefe bulls were confuted by doctor *Hufs*, who declaimed againft croifades and indulgences. The populace became animated by his orations, and declared that pope *John* was antichrift. The magiftrates caufed fome of them to be apprehended, and the

the reft took up arms to fet them at liberty, but they were
pacified by the magiftrates, who gave them folemn affurances that no injury fhould be done to the prifoners:
however, they were privately beheaded in the judgement-
hall The blood which ran out from the place of execution difcovered the maffacre of thefe men to the common people, who took arms again, forcibly carried off the
bodies of thofe that were executed, honourably interred
them in the church of *Bethlehem*, and reverenced them as
martyrs. '*Hufs* (fays Mr *Gilpin*) difcovered, on this'
' occafion, a true Chriftian fpirit. The late riot had
' given him great concern, and he had now fo much
' weight with the people, as to reftrain them from at-
' tempting any farther violence—whereas, at the found
' of a bell, he could have been furrounded with thou-
' finds, who might have laughed at the police of the city.'

The magiftrates of *Prague* found it neceffary to publifh
their reafons for thefe rigorous proceedings againft the
Huffites. They affembled many doctors of divinity in
their city, who drew up a cenfure of forty-five of *Wickliffe's* propofitions, and, in their preface to it, they afferted
the authority of the pope, the cardinals, and the church
of *Rome*, after which, they accufed the Huffites of fedition. Doctor *Hufs* wrote many books, and other difcourfes, againft the cenfure of thefe doctors, whom he
called Prætorians He maintained fome of the articles
which they condemned, particularly thofe concerning the
liberty of preaching, the power of fecular princes over
the revenues of ecclefiaftics, the voluntary payment of
tythes, and the forfeiture that fpiritual and temporal lords
make of their power, when they live in mortal fin.

Doctor *Hufs* wrote a long treatife about the church, to
confute the preface of that cenfure, in which he maintains, that the church confifts of thofe only who are predeftinate, that the head and foundation of it is *Jefus
Chrift*, that the pope and cardinals are only members of
it, and the other bifhops are fucceffors to the apoftles as
well as they, that no one is obliged to obey them, if their
commands are not agreeable to the law of God, and that
an excommunication, which is groundlefs, hath no effect.
He particularly anfwered the writings of *Stephen Paletz*,
Staniflaus Znoima, and eight other doctors. He alfo caufed
a writing to be fixed upon the church of *Bethlehem*,
charging the clergy with thefe fix errors.

Firft, Of believing that the prieft, by faying mafs, becomes the creator of his Creator. Second, Of faying that

we ought to believe in the virgin, in a pope, and in the saints. Third, That the priests can remit the pain and guilt of sin Fourth, That every one must obey his superiors, whether their commands be just or unjust Fifth, That every excommunication, just or unjust, binds the excommunicate. The sixth relates to simony.

He also wrote three large volumes against the clergy, the first entitled, " The Anatomy of the Members of An-" tichrist." The second, " Of the Kingdom of the " People, and the Life and Manners of Antichrist " The third, " Of the Abomination of Priests, and carnal " Monks, in the Church of *Jesus Christ*." Besides these, he wrote several other tracts on Traditions, the Unity of the Church, Evangelical Perfection, the Mystery of Iniquity, and the Discovery of Antichrist With what surprizing spirit, strength of argument, and powerful judgement, he wrote on these subjects, may be well conceived by the amazing influence that his doctrines obtained

Wickliffe had advanced, ' That if a bishop or priest ' should give holy orders, or consecrate the sacrament of ' the altar, or minister baptism, whiles he is in mortal ' syn, it were nothing av*ylable ' This was vindicated by doctor *Huss*, who observes, that the article consists of three parts First, That a civil or temporal lord is no lord, while he is in mortal sin Secondly, That a prelate is no prelate, while he is in mortal sin Thirdly, That a bishop is no bishop, while he is in mortal sin. Both these divines taught subjection and obedience to princes But *Wickliffe* asserted, that ' If temporal lords do wrongs and extor-' tions to the people, they ben traytors to God and his ' people, and tyrants of antichrist ' And *Huss* corroborated this opinion, by shewing that it was held by St. *Austin.*

Though *John Huss*, and *Jerom* of *Prague*, so far agreed with *Wickliffe*, that they opposed the tyranny and corruptions of the pope and his clergy Yet they were not of the same opinion with relation to the eucharist, for neither of them ever opposed the real presence, and transubstantiation, as *Wickliffe* had done.

The great and noble Sir *John Oldcastle*, lord *Cobham*, had spoken boldly in several parliaments against the corruptions of the Christian faith and worship, and had frequently represented to the kings *Richard* II *Henry* IV. and *Henry* V. the insufferable abuses committed by the clergy. This nobleman, at the desire of doctor *Huss*, caused all the works of *Wickliffe* to be wrote out, and dis-

perſed

perfed in *Bohemia*, *France*, *Spain*, *Portugal*, and other parts of *Europe*. But that good man, who had wrote several discourses concerning a reformation of discipline and manners in the church, was abandoned by *Henry* V and fell a sacrifice to the fury of the priests. He was condemned, in 1413, by the archbishop of *Canterbury* as a heretic, and sent to the tower by the king, who had an affection for him. He escaped from his confinement, and avoided the execution of his sentence till 1418, when he was taken, and burnt hanging. His behaviour, at the time of his death, was great and intrepid. He exhorted the people to follow the instructions, which God had given them in the Scriptures; and admonished them to disclaim those false teachers, whose lives and conversations were so contrary to *Christ*, and repugnant to his religion. *England* was filled with scenes of persecution, which extended to *Germany* and *Bohemia*, where doctor *Huss*, and *Jerom* of *Prague*, were marked out to share the fate of Sir *John Oldcastle*.

The council of *Constance* was assembled on the sixteenth of *November* 1414, to determine the dispute between three persons who contended for the papacy. There were, as attendants and members of this council (says Mr *Fox*), ‘ archbishops and bishops, 346, abbots and doctors, 564, ‘ princes, dukes, earls, knights, and squires, 16,000, ‘ common women, 450, barbers, 600, musicians, cooks, ‘ and jesters, 320 ’ *Bartholomew Cossa* took the name of *John* XXIII. *Angelo de Corario* called himself *Gregory* XII. And *Pedro de Luna* was stiled *Benedict* XIII. But it was *John*, who summoned doctor *Huss* to appear at *Constance*. The emperor *Sigismund*, brother and successor to *Wenceslaus*, encouraged *Huss* to obey the summons, that he might clear the *Bohemian* nation from the imputation of heresy. And, as an inducement to his compliance, he sent him a passport, with assurance of safe conduct, whereby he gave him permission to come freely to the council, and return from it again.

Doctor *Huss* caused some placarts to be fixed upon the gates of the churches in *Prague*, wherein he declared, that he went to the council to answer all the accusations that were made against him, and that he was ready to appear before the archbishop, to hear his adversaries, and justify his innocence. He demanded of the bishop of *Nazareth*, the inquisitor, whether he had any thing to propose against him, from whom he received a favorable testimony. But when he presented himself at the court of

the

the archbiſhop, who had called an aſſembly againſt him, he was denied admiſſion When he departed from *Prague* to repair to *Conſtance*, he was accompanied by *Wences*, lord of *Dunbar*, and *John*, lord of *Chlum*. *Huſs* made public declarations, in all the cities through which he paſſed, that he was going to vindicate himſelf at *Conſtance*, and invited all his adverſaries to be preſent He arrived at *Conſtance* on the third of *November*, and ſoon after *Stephen Paletz* came there as his adverſary, who was joined by *Michael* of *Cauſis*. They declared themſelves his accuſers, and drew up a memorial againſt him, which they preſented to the pope, and prelates of the council.

Doctor *Huſs*, twenty-ſix days after his arrival, was ordered to appear before the pope and cardinals It has been obſerved, that his appearing there was by the emperor's own requeſt But, notwithſtanding the ſafe conduct, he was no ſooner come within the pope's juriſdiction, than he was arreſted, and committed priſoner to a chamber in the palace This violation of common law and juſtice was taken notice of by a gentleman, who urged the imperial ſafe conduct But the pope obſerved, that he never granted any ſafe conduct, nor was he bound by that of the emperor. This infamous ſynod acted up to the ſpirit of their own favorite maxim, THAT NO FAITH IS TO BE KEPT WITH HERETICS The emperor arrived at *Conſtance* on the twenty-third of *December*, and pope *John* fled from thence, as the council had reſolved, that he and his two rivals, *Gregory* and *Benedict*, ſhould diveſt themſelves of all authority, that their competition might be fairly decided, ſchiſm extirpated, and an univerſal Reformation of faith and manners enacted, with reſpect both to the head and members of the church. The fourth ſeſſion was held on the twenty-ſixth of *March* 1415, in which the powers of the council, independent of the pope, were re-acknowledged and ratified The eighth ſeſſion was held *May* the fifth, when the doctrines of *Wickliffe* were condemned as heretical in forty-five articles And in the twelfth ſeſſion, held the twenty-ninth of *May*, pope *John* XXIII. was depoſed.

The fathers of the council were ranged under five nations, *Italy*, *France*, *Germany*, *England*, and *Spain* All matters, propoſed in the council, were to be determined by the plurality of voices in each nation But the cardinals, and their college, had their votes And it was agreed, that after the buſineſs had paſſed through the different committees, the full ſtate of the whole ſhould be made to

the

the council, and that their decree fhould be formed upon
the plurality of the votes of the nations *Robert Halam*,
bifhop of *Salifbury*, the bifhop of *Litchfield*, and the abbot
of St *Mary's*, in *York*, were members of this council for
the *Englifh* nation

The fpirit with which the council of *Conftance* acted
againft the popes, their declaring themfelves as a council,
and all councils to be above popes, the rigour with which
they executed their decrees, and the awful form of their
proceedings, are commendable   But to what did it all
tend? To no generous principle of love to God, or benevolence to man. It only tranflated the feat of wicked
power. The people were as much flaves to ignorance;
they were as much tied down to fuperftition, and they
had as little the exercife of any one rational fentiment, is
ever   This council acted the part of inquifitors   They
ordered the remains of doctor *Wickliff* to be dug up and
burnt, ' with this charitable caution, if they might be
' difcerned from the bodies of other faithful people   His
' afhes (fays *Fuller*) were caft into the *Swift*, that brook
' conveyed them into the *Avon*, *Avon* into the *Severn*,
' *Severn* into the narrow feas, they into the main ocean
' Thus the afhes of *Wickliffe* are the emblems of his doc-
' trine, which is now difperfed all over the world '

Doctor *Hufs* was allowed to be a man of confequence,
and reputation, in *Bohemia* He was a great and good
man, and a noble martyr' to Chriftianity His accufers prefented a petition to the pope; containing
the heads of the accufation which they had to propofe
againft him, and requefted that commiffioners might be
named to draw up his procefs The patriarch of *Conftantinople*, and two bifhops, were the perfons commiffioned,
who heard many witnefles againft doctor *Hufs*, and ordered his books to be examined. While this procefs was
drawing up, pope *John* efcaped from the emperor *Sigifmund*, who delivered *Hufs* into the hands of the bifhop of
Conftance, by whofe order he was confined in a caftle beyond the *Rhine*, near to *Conftance*

The council appointed the cardinals of *Cambray*, and
St *Mark*, the bifhop of *Dol*, and the abbot of the *Cifter-
cians*, to finifh the procefs againft doctor *Hufs*, and renew
the condemnations againft the doctrine of *Wickliffe*. Soon
after, they joined to thefe commiffioners a bifhop for each
nation, and granted a commiffion to cite *Jerom* of *Prague*,
the companion and friend of doctor *Hufs*, who was one of
the principal preachers of this new doctrine. The nobility

lity of *Bohemia* and *Poland* presented a petition to the emperor and council, wherein they desired that doctor *Huss* might be set at liberty, as he had been seized and imprisoned contrary to the safe conduct of his imperial majesty. The *Bohemians* presented a writing to the council, wherein they maintained, that the propositions, which the enemies of *Huss* had drawn out of his books, were mutilated, and falsified, on purpose to put him to death. They prayed the council to set him at liberty, that he might be heard for himself, and offered to give bond for his appearance. The patriarch of *Antioch* answered, in the name of the council, that they could not set *Huss* at liberty, but would send for him, and give him a favorable hearing. The lords of *Bohemia* then addressed the emperor, who had sent him there to defend that kingdom from a charge of heresy, and was now one of his persecutors.

The fourteenth session was held on the fifth of *June*, when it was resolved, that, before they sent for doctor *Huss*, the articles drawn out of his books should be examined, and condemned, even without hearing his vindication This was so strongly opposed by the nobles of *Bohemia*, that the emperor told the council, they must hear *Huss*, before they condemned him, upon which they sent for him, ordered him to acknowledge his books, and read the first articles of his accusation These were about thirty,* drawn from the writings of *Wickliffe*, and some of them he freely admitted, such as, ' that there was one, only, ' universal church, which is a collection of all the elect ' That the apostle *Paul* was never a member of the devil, ' which he proved from the testimony of St *Augustin* ' That a predestinate person always continues a member ' of the church, because, though he may sometimes fall ' from that grace which is adventitious to him, yet never ' from the grace of predestination, That no member of ' the true church apostatizes from it, because the grace ' of God, which establishes him, never fails That St, ' *Peter* never was, nor is, the head of the catholic church, ' because this is the peculiar prerogative of *Christ* That ' the condemnation of the forty-five articles of *Wickliffe*

---

* The reader, who is desirous more particularly to examine the acts and proceedings against this good man, together with some of his letters to friends, may find them at large in the first volume of Fox's *Acts and Monuments* And for a more minute account, he may peruse an excellent history of *Huss, Jerom, Zisca,* &c. written in a very masterly manner by the Rev. Mr. *Gilpin*

' was

' was irrational and unjuſt   That there was no colour
' of reaſon, that there ſhould be a ſpiritual head always
' viſibly converſant in the church, and governing it '

Mr *Toplady*, in his very able performance, entitled,
*Hiſtoric Proof of the Doctrinal Calviniſm of the church of
England*, ſtates the following articles for which, among
others, this excellent man was put to death   " *There is*
" *but one holy, univerſal, or catholic church, which is the*
" *univerſal company of* ALL *the* PREDESTINATE   I do
" confeſs," ſaid *Huſs*, " that this propoſition is mine;
" and [it] is confirmed by St. *Auguſtin* upon St *John* "

" *St Paul was* NEVER *any member of the devil, albeit*
" *that he committed and did certain acts like unto the acts of*
" *the malignant church*" [i.e St. *Paul* prior to his converſion, acted like a *reprobate*, though he was, ſecretly, and
in reality, one of God's *elect*]   " *And likewiſe St* Peter,
" *who fell into an horrible ſin of perjury, and denial of his*
" *Maſter*, *it was by the* PERMISSION *of God, that he might*
" *the more firmly and ſteadfaſtly riſe again and be confirmed* "
To this charge, *Huſs* replied, " I anſwer, according to
" St *Auſtin*, that it is expedient that the elect and pre-
" deſtinate ſhould ſin and offend* "

" *No part or member of the church doth depart, or fall*
" *away, at any time, from the body*   *Forſomuch as the cha-*
" *rity of* PREDESTINATION, *which is the bond and chain of*
" *the ſame, doth never fall.*"   *Huſs* anſwers , " *This pro-*
" poſition is thus placed in my book   *As the reprobate of*
" *the church procede out of the ſame, and yet are not as parts*
" *or members of the ſame, forſomuch as no part or member of*
" *the ſame doth* FINALLY *fall away   Becauſe that the charity*
" *of* PREDESTINATION, *which is the bond and chain of the*
" *ſame, doth never fall away*   This is proved by 1 *Cor.*
" XIII   and *Rom.* VIII, *All things turn to good, to them that*
" *love God*   Alſo, *I am certain that neither death nor life*
" *can ſeparate us from the charity and love of God*, as it is
" more at large in the book."

Another article, objected againſt him, was, his being
of opinion that " *The* PREDESTINATE, *although he be not*
" *in the ſtate of grace according to the preſent juſtice, yet is*
" ALWAYS *a member of the univerſal church.*"   He anſwers   " Thus it is in the book, about the beginning of

---

* Let not the reader imagine (ſays Mr *Toplady*) that I *approve* of
the unguarded manner, in which Mr. *Huſs* here expreſſes himſelf   I
only give his anſwer, faithfully, as I find it   His meaning I doubt
not, was this   That, by the incomprehenſible alchymy of God's infinite wiſdom, even moral evil itſelf ſhall be finally over ruled to good "

" the

" the fifth chapter, where it is declared, that *There be*
" *divers manners or sorts of being in the church* For there
" *are* some in the church, according to the mif-fhapen
" faith, and other some *according to* PREDESTINATION
" As Christians predeftinate, now in fin, SHALL RETURN
" AGAIN *unto grace.*" The good man added " *Predef-*
" *tination* doth make a man a member of the univerfal
" church, the which [i e *Predeftination*] is a *preparation*
" *of* GRACE *for the prefent,* and *of* GLORY *to come* And
" not any degree of" [outward] " dignity, neither elec-
" tion of man" [or, one man's defignation of another to
fome office or ftation], " neither any fenfible fign" [i e
Predeftination does not barely extend to the outward figns,
or means of grace But includes fomething more and
higher] " For the traytor *Judas Ifcariot,* notwithftand-
" ing *Chrift's* election" [or appointment of him to the
apoftlefhip], " and the *temporal* graces which were given
" him for his office of apoftlefhip, and that he was *reputed*
" and *counted of men* a true apoftle of *Jefus Chrift*, yet
" was he no true difciple, but a *Wolf* covered in a fheep's
" fkin, as St *Auguftin* faith "

" *A* REPROBATE *man is never a member of the holy church*
" —I anfwer, It is in my book, with fufficient long pro-
" bation out of the xxvith *Pfalm,* and out of the vth
" chapter to the *Ephefians* And alfo by St *Bernard's*
" faying, *The church of* Jefus Chrift *is* MORE *plainly and*
" *evidently* HIS BODY, *than the body which he delivered for*
" *us to death.* I have alfo written, in the fifth chapter of
" my book, that *the holy church*" [i e the *outward, vifible*
" church of profeffing Chriftians, here on earth} " *is the*
" *barn of the Lord, in which are both good and evil, pre-*
" *deftinate and reprobate The good being as the good corn,*
" *or grain, and the evil, as the chaff* And thereunto is
" added the expofition of St *Auftin* "

" Judas *was* NEVER *a true difciple of* Jefus Chrift —I
" anfwer, and I do confefs the fame —*They came out from*
" *amongst us, but they were none of us* —*He knew, from the*
" *beginning, who they were that believed not, and fhould betray*
" *him. And therefore I fay unto you, that none* COMETH
" *unto me, except it be* GIVEN *him of my Father* "

Such were fome of the allegations, brought againft this
holy man by the council of *Conftance,* and fuch were his
anfwers, when he ftood on his public trial, as a lilly
among thorns, or a fheep in the midft of wolves How
eafy is it for a man to write in defence of thefe ineftimable
truths, which (through the goodnefs of divine providence)

have

have now, in our happy land, the function of national establishment! But with what invincible strength of grace was this adamantine saint endued, who bore his explicit, unshaken testimony to the faith, in the presence and hearing of its worst foes, armed with all the terrific powers of this world!

These are doctrines which, even in the purest ages of the church, have received countenance, and *Huss* boldly acknowledged them. But one circumstance bore more hard against him, which was, wishing his soul to be with the happy spirit of *Wickliffe*. Doctor *Huss* had too generous, too open, a nature, to deny what he thought; nor did he imagine that life was worthy prevarication. He freely confessed, he was so charmed with *Wickliffe's* books, that he wished his spirit might enjoy the same fate with his hereafter. A great many other false and frivolous objections were raised against him, which he refuted with a manly eloquence, and recommending himself, and his cause, to God, he was carried off.

He was no sooner gone, than the emperor, whose subject he was, and who shewed a peculiar zeal in his fate, rose, and told the assembly, ' That, in his opinion, every ' tenet he had then held, deserved death. That if he did ' not abjure, he ought to be burnt. And that all his fol- ' lowers, especially *Jerom* of *Prague*, should be exem- ' plarily punished.' But we are told, that the emperor and the cardinal of *Chambre*, exhorted doctor *Huss* to submit to the decision of the council. The next day, he was brought again before the assembly, where eighty-nine articles were read to him, which were said to be drawn out of his books, and he was advised to abjure them all. But he replied, that there were many of those propositions which he had never maintained, and he was ready to explain his opinion regarding the others. After many disputes, he was sent back to prison, and a resolution was then taken to burn him as a heretic, if he would not retract.

The emperor, on the tenth of *June*, sent four bishops, and two lords, to the prison, to prevail on *Huss* to make a recantation. But that pious divine, with truly Christian simplicity, called the great God to witness, with tears in his eyes, that he was not conscious of having preached, or written, any thing against the truth of God, or the faith of his orthodox church. The deputies then represented the great wisdom and authority of the council. " Let " them, said *Huss*, send the meanest person that can con-

" vince

" vince me, by arguments, from the word of God, and
" I will submit my judgement to him " This Christian
and pious answer had no effect, because he would not
take the authority and learning of the council upon trust,
without the least shadow of an argument offered, and the
deputies departed in high admiration of his obstinacy!

While this good confessor was in bonds, he wrote letters to incite his countrymen to persevere in the doctrines
he had taught, and expressed his own firm resolution of
never departing from them while he had life.

Doctor *Huss*, on the seventh of *July*, was conducted to
the place where the fifteenth session of the council was
held He was required to abjure, which he refused And
the bishop of *Londi*, in a bloody, persecuting sermon,
about the destruction of heretics, pronounced the prologue
of his fate, by exhorting the emperor, who seemed ready
enough of himself, to exterminate the growing heresy,
that (as he was pleased to pervert the scripture) *the body
of sin might be destroyed.* He told *Sigismund*, ' that he
' ought to destroy all errors and heresies, and especially
' the obstinate heretic *Huss* before him, since by his
' wickedness and mischief, many places of the world were
' infected with most pestilent and heretical poison, and,
' by his means and occasion, almost utterly subverted and
' destroyed. And that then the emperor's praises would
' be celebrated for evermore, for having overthrown such
' and so great enemies of the faith ' A most honorable
testimony for Dr. *Huss* from the traducing mouth of a
virulent adversary ! In fine, the proctor of the council
demanded that the process against *Huss* should be finished,
the condemned articles of *Wickliffe* were read, and the
thirty articles alledged against *Huss*, who explained some,
and defended others. Many other articles of accusation
were also read, which were proved by witnesses against him.
His fate was determined, his vindication disregarded, and
judgement was pronounced His books were thereby
condemned, and he was declared a manifest heretic, convicted of having taught many heresies and pernicious
errors, of having despised the keys of the church, and
ecclesiastical censures, of having seduced and given scandal to the faithful by his obstinacy; and of having rashly
appealed to the tribunal of *Christ* The council, therefore, censured him for being obstinate and incorrigible, and
ordained, ' That he should be degraded from the priest-
' hood, his books publicly burnt, and himself delivered
' to the secular power.'

Doctor

Doctor *Hufs* heard this fentence without the leaft emotion. He kneeled down, with his eyes lifted towards heaven, and faid, with all the fpirit of primitive martyrdom, " May thy infinite mercy, O my God, pardon this " injuftice of my enemies. Thou knoweft the injuftice " of their accufations. How deformed with crimes I have " been reprefented ; how I have been oppreffed by worth- " lefs witneffes, and an unjuft condemnation. Yet, O " my God, let that mercy of thine, which no tongue can " exprefs, prevail with thee not to avenge my wrongs." Thefe excellent fentences were fo many expreffions of treafon againft the trade of prieftcraft, and confidered as fuch by the narrow-minded affiftants. The bifhops appointed by the council ftript him of his prieftly garments, degraded him from his prieftly function and univerfity degrees, and put a mitre of paper on his head, on which devils were painted, with this infcription, in great letters, ' A RING-LEADER OF HERETICS.' Our heroic martyr received this mock-mitre, fmiling, and faid, " It was lefs " painful than a crown of thorns." A ferenity, a joy, a compofure, appeared in his looks, which indicated that his foul had cut off many ftages of tedious journey, in her way to the point of eternal joy and everlafting peace.

The bifhops delivered *Hufs* to the emperor, who put him into the hands of the duke of *Bavaria.* His books were burnt at the gate of the church, and he was led to the fuburbs to be burnt alive. Prior to his execution, Mr *Hufs* made his folemn *appeal* to God, from the judgement of the pope and council. In this *appeal* (the whole of which would well repay the reader's perufal,) he again repeats his affured faith in the doctrine of *election*, where he celebrates the willingnefs with which *Chrift* vouchfafed, " *By the moft bitter and ignominious death, to* REDEEM " *the* CHILDREN *of* GOD, C H O S E N BEFORE THE " FOUNDATION OF THE WORLD, *from everlafting dam-* " *nation.*" When he came to the place of execution, he fell on his knees, fang portions of pfalms, looked ftedfaftly towards heaven, and repeated thefe words. " Into " thy hands, O Lord, do I commit my fpirit, thou haft " redeemed me, O moft good and faithful God. Lord " *Jefus Chrift*, affift and help me, that with a firm and " patient mind, by thy moft powerful grace, I may un- " dergo this moft cruel and ignominious death, to which " I am condemned for preaching the truth of thy moft " holy gofpel." When the chain was put about him at the ftake, he faid, with a fmiling countenance, " My
" Lord

" Lord *Jefus Chrift* was bound with a harder chain than
" this for my fake, and why fhould I be afhamed of this
" old rufty one ?" When the faggots were piled up to
his very neck, the duke of *Bavaria* was officious enough
to defire him to abjure " No, fays *Hufs*, I never preached
" any doctrine of an evil tendency, and what I taught
" with my lips, I now feal with my blood " He faid to
the executioner, " Are you going to burn a *goofe?* In
" one century, you will have a *fwan* you can neither
" roaft nor boil," If he was prophetic, he muft have
meant *Luther*, who had a fwan for his arms   The flames
were then applied to the faggots, when the martyr fang
a hymn with fo loud and chearful a voice, that he was
heard through all the cracklings of the combuftibles, and
the noife of the multitude   At laft his voice was cut
fhort, after he had uttered, " *Jefus Chrift*, thou Son of
" the living GOD, have mercy upon me," and he was
confumed in a moft miferable manner   The duke of
Bavaria ordered the executioner to throw all the martyr's
cloaths into the flames   After which, his afhes were carefully collected, and caft into the *Rhine*

False! a
German
peasant
does not
bear arms
nor his
children.

While doctor *Hufs* was in prifon, he wrote fome treatifes about the commands of God, of the Lord's prayer,
of mortal fin, of marriage, of the knowledge and love of
God, of the three enemies of man, and the feven mortal
fins, of repentance, and of the facrament of the body and
blood of *Chrift*   He alfo drew up a little piece about the
communion in both kinds   He wrote an anfwer to the
propofitions drawn out of his books, which had been
communicated to him   And he prepared three difcourfes,
one about the fufficiency of the law of *Jefus Chrift*, another to explain his faith about the laft articles of the creed,
and the third about peace   All thefe treatifes were printed
in one volume at *Nuremburg* in 1558   As alfo a fecond
volume containing a harmony of the four evangelifts, with
moral notes, many fermons, a commentary upon the firft
feven chapters of the firft epiftle to the *Corinthians*, commentaries upon the feven canonical epiftles, the cixth
pfalm, and thofe following to the cxixth, and feveral
other pieces, which, if they were not altogether correct,
muft be imputed to the reigning darknefs of the times,
and to his inceffant conflicts with the fons of *Rome*.

This great martyr, as well as his friend *Jerom*, may be
confidered, in fome meafure, as dying for the principles
of *Wickliffe*, or rather the principles of the gofpel, tranf-
mitted to them from *England*.   To preferve the memory of

this

this excellent man, the seventh of *July* was, for many years, held sacred among the *Bohemians* In some places large fires were lighted in the evening of that day upon the mountains, to preserve the memory of his sufferings, round which the country-people would assemble, and sing hymns

As a specimen of the composed spirit of this excellent martyr, in the midst of this virulent persecution, we will subjoin one of his letters, which he wrote from the prison, to his friends in *Bohemia*

" My dear friends, let me take this last opportunity of
" exhorting you to trust in nothing here, but to give
" yourselves up entirely to the service of GOD Well
" am I authorized to warn you not to trust in princes,
" nor in any child of man, for there is no help in them.
" GOD only remaineth stedfast. What HF promiseth,
" he will undoubtedly perform As to myself, on his
" gracious promise I rest. Having endeavoured to be his
" faithful servant, I fear not being deserted by him.
" *Where I am*, says the gracious Promiser, *there shall my*
" *servant be* —May the GOD of heaven preserve you?
" —This is probably the last letter I shall be enabled to
" write. I have reason to believe, I shall be called upon
" to-morrow to answer with my life —*Sigismund* hath, in
" all things, acted deceitfully I pray, GOD forgive
" him! You have heard in what severe language he hath
" spoken of me."

There are several other letters in Fox's acts and monuments, in old *English*, to which we must refer our readers. They all breathe the same spirit of piety, firmness, and inward consolation.

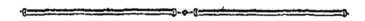

JEROM of PRAGUE.

The LAY-REFORMER.

GREAT were the commotions, which prevailed in the world, about the time of the promulgation of the gospel in *Germany* The truth had every kind of prejudice to encounter, nor did the kingdom of darkness yield to its power without violent struggles and disorder And all protestants, who are protestants indeed, and who

know the grace of GOD and his gospel, have reason to
bless that wonderful providence, by which many of the
European nations were delivered from the grossest darkness
and ignorance, and by which indeed even popish nations
have been led to the revival of knowledge, and to disd un
in part the blind submission, they once universally shewed,
to the corrupted see of *Rome.*

Jerom of *Prague* was the companion and co-martyr of
doctor *Hufs,* to whom he was inferior in experience, age,
and authority, but he was esteemed his superior in all
polite and liberal endowments   He was born at *Prague,*
and educated in that university, where he was admitted
master of arts; and promoted the doctrine of *Wickliffe* in
conjunction with *Hufs*   He travelled into most of the
states of *Europe,* and was every where esteemed for his
happy elocution, which gave him great advantages in the
schools, where he promoted what *Hufs* had advanced.
The universities of *Paris, Cologne,* and *Heidelberg,* conferred the degree of master of arts upon him   He is said
also to have had the degree of master of arts conferred
upon him at *Oxford,* but it is certain, that he commenced
doctor in divinity, in the year 1396   He began to publish
the same doctrine with doctor *Hufs* in 1408, and it is
averred, that he had a greater share of learning and subtilty than his excellent friend   However that may be,
the council of *Conftance* kept a very watchful eye upon
him, and esteemed him to be a very dangerous person to
the interests of *Rome*   While he was in *England,* and
most probably when at *Oxford,* he copied out the books
of *Wickliffe,* and returned with them to *Prague*   By that
great man's evangelical writings, it pleased GOD to
work upon him, and upon his friend doctor *Hufs,* to the
acknowledgement of his truth   *England,* therefore (as
we observed in the life of *Wickliffe*) may claim the honor
of beginning the Reformation, and may it be the last
country upon earth to lose it!   At present, it must be
owned, such is the national corruption of manners, the
prevailing luxury of the times, and the practical atheism
and irreligion of many among us, that it will be through
GOD's mercy, if we are not consumed by his judgements, and given up for a prey to our enemies.

Jerom was cited before the council of *Conftance,* on the
seventeenth of *April* 1415, when his friend doctor *Hufs*
was confined in a castle near that city   He arrived at *Conftance* in the same month, when he was informed how his
friend had been treated, and that he also would be seized.
Upon

Upon which, *Jerom* retired to *Iberlingen*, an imperial city, from whence he wrote to the emperor and council to desire a safe conduct, and one was presented to him, which gave him permission to come, but not to return. He then caused a protestation to be fixed up, wherein he declared, that he would appear before the council to justify himself, if a proper safe conduct was granted. And he demanded of the *Bohemian* lords an act of his declaration. After this, he began his journey to return into *Bohemia*. But he was stopt at *Hirschau*, by the officers of *John* the son of prince *Clement*, count *Palatine*, who had the government of *Sultzbach*. And *Lewis*, another son of the same prince, carried *Jerom* to *Constance*, where he was to answer the same accusation as had been exhibited against doctor *Hufs*, who was martyred on the seventh of *July*.

Jerom had many friends at the council, who bore him great affection, and tried all they could to bring him to a recantation, as they were convinced he had no prospect of escaping if he took his trial, because the emperor had declared that he should be exemplarily punished. His friends prevailed, and he was brought before the council, in the nineteenth session, held the twenty-third of *September*, when he read a public abjuration of his doctrines, thinking thereby to elude his prosecution.

In this retractation, he is said to have anathematized the doctrines of *Wickliffe* and *Hufs*, to have protested, that he was of the same sentiments with the *Romish* church; and to have professed, that he would follow its doctrine, particularly about the keys, the sacraments, the orders, the offices, and the censures of the apostolic see, as also concerning indulgences, the relics of saints, ecclesiastical liberty, and the ceremonies. It is further said, that he thereby approved the condemnation of the articles which the council prescribed, acknowledged they were faithfully extracted from the works of *Hufs*, and that he was justly condemned. But he was carried back to prison, notwithstanding this recantation, and was accused of insincerity. New articles of accusation were brought against him, and it was alledged, that it would be dangerous to set him at liberty. He immediately repented of his abjuration, and of condemning *Hufs*. He desired audience of the council, and was twice heard in the general congregations held in *May* 1416, when one hundred and seven heads of accusation were proposed against him, which he endeavored to answer, and made an oration, wherein he declared that he repented of his recantation, and of having approved

H   the

the condemnation of *Wickliffe* and *Huf.* *Dupin* alfo fays, that the fathers of the council were fully fatisfied of his relapfe, and fent for him to the twenty-firft feffion, held the thirtieth of *May* The bifhop of *Londi*, who preached the fermon previous to the condemnation of *Huf*, now preached another to ufher in the fate of *Jerom* When the fermon was ended, the martyr, unjuftly ftigmatized a heretic, declared he ftill perfifted in his laft retractation, and told them, that they would condemn him wickedly and unjuftly. But (fays he) after my death, I will leave a fting in your confcience and a nail in your hearts, ET CITO VOS OMNES, UT RESPONDEATIS MIHI CORAM ALTISSIMO ET JUSTISSIMO JUDICE, POST CENTUM AN-NOS That is, " I cite you all to anfwer to me before " the moft high and the moft juft Judge, within a hun- " dred years." He was then condemned as a heretic relapfed, delivered over to the fecular power, and led away to death, which he endured with great conftancy

Such is the account given by the popifh writers But the *Florentine* fecretary, *Poggius*, who was a fpectator of all he relates, and give a full account of the matter to *Aretin* the pope's fecretary, is more circumftantial and impartial in his relation of this affair He tells us, (as we fhall fee below) that as *Jerom* was returning to *Bohemia*, he was brought back to *Conftance* by the duke of *Bavaria*, and, the next day, carried as a prifoner before the council, where it foon appeared, that his abjuration had flipt from him in an unguarded hour through the weaknefs of the flefh *Poggius*, who was one of the beft judges of the age, afferts, that *Jerom* fpoke with fuch a quicknefs of fentiment, fuch a dignity of expreffion, and fuch ftrength of argument, that he feemed to equal the nobleft of the antient compofitions When fome members of the council called out to him to put in his anfwers, he told the affembly, that the objections againft him were the effects of prepoffeffion and prejudice That, therefore, in juftice, they fhould permit him to lay open the whole tenor of his doctrine, life, and converfation, whereby he could indubitably weaken and invalidate all the prepoffeffions, which ignorant zeal and open malice had rendered too ftrong againft him in his unhappy condition He was told, he could not expect fuch indulgence This exhaufted his patience, and he exclaimed to the whole affembly in thefe terms. " What barbarity " is this! For three hundred and forty days have I been " through all the variety of prifons. There is not a
" mifery

" misery, there is not a want, that I have not experienced
" To my enemies you have allowed the fulleft fcope of
" accufation To me you deny the leaft opportunity of
" defence. Not an hour will you indulge me in pre-
" paring my trial You have fwallowed the blackeft
" calumnies againft me You have reprefented me as a
" heretic, without knowing what is my doctrine, as an
" enemy to the faith, before you knew what faith I pro-
" feffed, and as a perfecutor of priefts, before you could
" have any opportunity of underftanding my fentiments
" on that head You are a general council In you
" center all that this world can communicate of gravity,
" wifdom, and fanctity But ftill you are men, and men
" are feducible by appearances The higher your cha-
" racter is for wifdom, the greater ought your care to be
" not to deviate into folly The caufe I now plead is
" not my own caufe It is the caufe of men, it is the
" caufe of Chriftians, it is the caufe which is to affect
" the rights of pofterity, however the experiment is to
" be made in my perfon " The bigotted part of the
affembly confidered this fpeech as poifon to the ears of
the auditors But many of the members were men of
tafte and learning, who were favorably inclined to the
prifoner, and pitied him in their hearts, though a reftraint was on their tongues.

Jerom was obliged to give way to their authority, and
to hear his charge read, which was reduced under thefe
heads, ' That he was a derider of the papal dignity, an
' oppofer of the pope, an enemy of the cardinals, a per-
' fecutor of the prelates, and a hater of the Chriftian
' religion ' He anfwered this charge with an amazing
force of elocution, and ftrength of argument. " Now,
" fays he, wretch that I am ! whither fhall I turn me ?
" To my accufers ! My accufers are as deaf as adders
" To you my judges ! You are prepoffeffed by the arts
" of my accufers " We are told by Poggius, that Jerom,
in all he fpoke, faid nothing unbecoming a great and wife
man And he candidly afferts, that, if what Jerom faid
was true, he was not only free from capital guilt, but
from the fmalleft blame

The trial of Jerom was brought on the third day after
his accufation, and witneffes were examined in fupport of
the charge The prifoner was prepared for his defence,
which will appear almoft incredible, when it is confidered
that he had been three hundred and forty days fhut up in
a dark offenfive dungeon, deprived of day-light, food, and

fleep.

sleep His spirit soared above these disadvantages, under which a man less enabled, must have sunk, nor was he more at a loss for quotations from fathers and antient authors, than if he had been furnished with the finest library in *Europe*.

Many of the zealots and bigots of the assembly were against his being heard, as they knew what effect eloquence is apt to have on the minds even of the most prejudiced However, it was carried by the majority that he should have liberty to proceed in his defence, which he began in such an exalted strain of moving elocution, that the heart of obdurate zeal was seen to melt, and the mind of superstition seemed to admit a ray of conviction He made an admirable distinction between evidence as resting on facts, and as supported by malice and calumny He laid before the assembly the whole tenor of his life and conduct, which he owned had been always open and unreserved. He justly observed, that the greatest and most holy men have been known to differ in points of speculation, with a view to distinguish truth, not to keep it concealed And he then expressed a noble contempt of all his enemies, who would have induced him to retract the cause of religion and truth He next entered on a high encomium upon doctor *John Huss*, and declared he was ready to follow him in the glorious tract of martyrdom He was (said *Jerom*) a good, just and holy man, and very unworthy of the death which he suffered He knew him, from his youth upward, to be neither fornicator, drunkard, nor addicted to any kind of vice, on the contrary, he was a chaste and sober man, and a faithful and true preacher of the blessed gospel. That, with respect to himself, whatsoever things *Wickliffe* and *Huss* had written, and especially against the pomp and pride of the clergy, he would affirm to his latest breath, that they were holy and blessed men, and that nothing so much troubled his conscience as the sin, which he committed by his recantation in speaking against them, which recantation he utterly abjured and abhorred from the bottom of his heart He added, that he could not help saying, with his dying breath, it was certainly impious that the patrimony of the church, which was originally intended for the purpose of charity and universal benevolence, should be prostituted to the lust of the flesh, and the pride of the eye, in whores, feasts, foppish vestments, and other reproaches to the name and profession of Christianity.

The

The prisoner received many interruptions from the impertinence of some, and the inveteracy of others. But he answered every one with so much readiness, and vivacity of thought, that, at last, they were ashamed, and he was permitted to finish his defence. His voice was sweet, clear, and sonorous, pliable to captivate every passion, and able to conciliate every affection, which he knew how to do with wonderful address. He was admired by his enemies, and compassionated by his friends. But he received the same sentence that had been passed upon his martyred friend, and, *Poggius* says, the assembly condemned him with great reluctance.

The same author tells us, that *Jerom* had two days allowed for his recantation, and that the cardinal of *Florence* used all the arguments he could for that effect, which were ineffectual. The divine was resolved to seal his doctrine with his blood, he could not be seduced to make another retractation, and he suffered death with all the magnanimity of *Hufs*. He embraced the stake to which he was fastened, with the peculiar malice of wet cords. When the executioner went behind him to set fire to the pile, "Come here, said the martyr, and kindle " it before my eyes, for if I dreaded such a sight, I " should never have come to this place, when I had a " free opportunity to escape." The fire was kindled, and he then sung a hymn, which was soon finished by the incircling flames.

He cried out several times, *In manus tuas, Domine, commendo spiritum meum*, i. e. "Into thy hands, O Lord, I " commend my spirit." His last words, which could be heard were, " O Lord GOD, the Father Almighty, " have mercy upon me, and forgive all my sins. Thou " knoweft, with what sincerity I have loved thy truth " He appeared to endure much by the fire for the space of a quarter of an hour, all the while seeming, by the motion of his lips, to pray within himself. After he was dead, his bed, cloaths, and the other things he had with him in prison, were thrown into the fire and consumed with him. Finally, the ashes were gathered together, and cast into the river *Rhine*, which runs close by the city.

We cannot conclude this account of *Jerom*, without annexing at large the most honorable testimony given of him by *Poggius* of *Florence*, an adversary and the secretary of two popes, and consequently not a more favorable testimony than truth itself compelled. We copy it from Mr. *Gilpin*'s valuable and elegant history of *Jerom*, whose life

of

of *Zifca*, the great General of the *Bohemians*, is an admirable performance

A Letter from *Poggius* of *Florence* to *Leonard Aretin*

‘ In the midft of a fhort excurfion into the country, I
‘ wrote to our common friend, from whom, I doubt not,
‘ you have had an account of me
‘ Since my return to *Conftance*, my attention hath been
‘ wholly engaged by *Jerom*, the *Bohemian* heretic, as he
‘ is called The eloquence, and learning, which this
‘ perfon hath employed in his own defence are fo extraor-
‘ dinary, that I cannot forbear giving you a fhort ac-
‘ count of him
‘ To confefs the truth, I never knew the art of fpeak-
‘ ing carried fo near the model of antient eloquence It
‘ was indeed amazing to hear with what force of expref-
‘ fion, with what fluency of language, and with what
‘ excellent reafoning he anfwered his adverfaries, nor
‘ was I lefs ftruck with the gracefulnefs of his manner,
‘ the dignity of his action, and the firmnefs, and con-
‘ ftancy of his whole behaviour It grieved me to think
‘ fo great a man was labouring under fo atrocious an ac-
‘ cufation Whether this accufation be a juft one, God
‘ knows For myfelf, I enquire not into the merits of
‘ it, refting fatisfied with the decifion of my fuperiors
‘ —But I will juft give you a fummary of his trial.
‘ After many articles had been proved againft him,
‘ leave was at length given him to anfwer each in its or-
‘ der. But *Jerom* long refufed, ftrenuoufly contending,
‘ that he had many things to fay previoufly in his defence,
‘ and that he ought firft to be heard in general, before he
‘ defcended to particulars —When this was over-ruled,
“ Here, faid he, ftanding in the midft of the affembly,
“ here is juftice, here is equity Befet by my enemies,
“ I am already pronounced a heretic I am condemned,
“ before I am examined Were you gods omnifcient,
“ inftead of an affembly of fallible men, you could not
“ act with more fufficiency —Error is the lot of mortals,
“ and you, exalted as you are, are fubject to it But
“ confider, that the higher you are exalted, of the more
“ dangerous confequence are your errors —As for me,
“ I know I am a wretch below your notice But at
“ leaft confider, that an unjuft action, in fuch an af-
“ fembly, will be of dangerous example.”
‘ This, and much more, he fpoke with great elegance
‘ of language, in the midft of a very unruly and indecent

‘ affembly :

' affembly And thus far at leaft he prevailed, the coun-
' cil ordered, that he fhould firft anfwer objections, and
' promifed that he fhould then have liberty to fpeak
' Accordingly, all the articles alledged againft him were
' publicly read, and then proved, after which he was
' afked, whether he had aught to object ? It is incredible
' with what acutenefs he anfwered, and with what
' amazing dexterity he warded off every ftroke of his ad-
' verfaries Nothing efcaped him His whole behaviour
' was truly great and pious If he were indeed the man
' his defence fpoke him, he was fo far from meriting
' death, that, in my judgement, he was not in any degree
' culpable —In a word, he endeavoured to prove, that
' the greater part of the charge was purely the invention
' of his adverfaries.—Among other things, being accufed
' of hating and defaming the holy fee, the pope, the car-
' dinals, the prelates, and the whole eftate of the clergy,
' he ftretched out his hands, and faid, in a moft moving
' accent, " On which fide, reverend fathers, fhall I turn
" me for redrefs? whom fhall I implore? whofe affiftance
" can I expect? which of you hath not this malicious
" charge entirely alienated from me? which of you hath
" it not changed from a judge into an inveterate enemy?
" —It was artfully alledged indeed ! Though other parts
" of their charge were of lefs moment, my accufers
" might well imagine, that if this were faftened on me,
" it could not fail of drawing upon me the united in-
" dignation of my judges "
' On the third day of this memorable trial, what had
' paffed was recapitulated When *Jerom*, having obtained
' leave, though with fome difficulty, to fpeak, began his
' oration with a prayer to God ; whofe divine affiftance
' he pathetically implored He then obferved, that many
' excellent men, in the annals of hiftory, had been op-
' preffed by falfe witneffes, and condemned by unjuft
' judges. Beginning with profane hiftory, he inftanced
' the death of *Socrates*, the captivity of *Plato*, the banifh-
' ment of *Anaxagoras*, and the unjuft fufferings of many
' others He then inftanced the many worthies of the
' Old Teftament, in the fame circumftances, *Mofes*, *Jo-*
' *feph*, *Daniel*, and almoft all the prophets, and laftly
' thofe of the New, *John* the *Baptift*, St. *Stephen*, and
' others, who were condemned as feditious, profane, or
' immoral men. An unjuft judgement, he faid, proceed-
' ing from a layic was bad, from a prieft, worfe, ftill
' worfe from a college of priefts, and from a general
' council,

‘ council, fuperlatively bad ——Thefe things he fpoke
‘ with fuch force and emphafis, as kept every one’s atten-
‘ tion awake.

　‘ On one point he dwelt largely　As the merits of the
‘ caufe refted entirely upon the credit of witneffes, he
‘ took great pains to fhew, that very little was due to
‘ thofe produced againft him　He had many objections
‘ to them, particularly their avowed hatred to him, the
‘ fources of which he fo palpably laid open, that he made
‘ a ftrong impreffion upon the minds of his hearers, and
‘ not a little fhook the credit of the witneffes　The
‘ whole council was moved, and greatly inclined to pity,
‘ if not to favour him.　He added, that he came uncom-
‘ pelled to the council, and that neither his life nor doc-
‘ trine had been fuch, as gave him the leaft reafon to
‘ dread an appearance before them　Difference of opi-
‘ nion, he faid, in matters of faith had ever arifen among
‘ learned men, and was always efteemed productive of
‘ truth, rather than of error, where bigotry was laid
‘ afide　Such, he faid, was the difference between *Auf-*
‘ *tin* and *Jerom*　And though their opinions were not
‘ only different, but contradictory, yet the imputation of
‘ herefy was never fixed on either

　‘ Every one expected, that he would now either retract
‘ his errors, or at leaft apologize for them　But nothing
‘ of the kind was heard from him　He declared plainly,
‘ that he had nothing to retract　He launched out into
‘ an high encomium of *Hufs*, calling him a holy man,
‘ and lamenting his cruel, and unjuft death　He had
‘ armed himfelf, he faid, with a full refolution to follow
‘ the fteps of that bleffed martyr, and to fuffer with con-
‘ ftancy whatever the malice of his enemies could inflict,
“ The perjured witneffes, (faid he) who have appeared
“ againft me, have won their caufe　But let them re-
“ member, they have their evidence once more to give
“ before a tribunal, where falfhood can be no difguife ”

　‘ It was impoffible to hear this pathetic fpeaker with-
‘ out emotion　Every ear was captivated, and every
‘ heart touched.—But wifhes in his favour were vain.
‘ He threw himfelf beyond a poffibility of mercy　Brav-
‘ ing death, he even provoked the vengeance, which was
‘ hanging over him.　“ If that holy martyr, (faid he,
“ fpeaking of *Hufs)* ufed the clergy with difrefpect, his
“ cenfures were not levelled at them as priefts, but as
“ wicked men.　He faw with indignation thofe reve-
　　　　　　　　　　　　　　　　　　　　　　“ nues,

" hues, which had been defigned for charitable ends,
" expended upon pageantry, and riot "

' Through this whole oration he fhewed a moft amaz-
' ing ftrength of memory He had been confined almoft
' a year in a dungeon The feverity of which ufage he
' complained of, but in the language of a great and
' good man In this horrid place, he was deprived of
' books and paper. Yet notwithftanding this, and the
' conftant anxiety, which muft have hung over him, he
' was at no more lofs for proper authorities, and quota-
' tions, than if he had fpent the intermediate time at
' leifure in his ftudy

' His voice was fweet, diftinct, and full His action
' every way the moft proper, either to exprefs indigna-
' tion, or to raife pity, though he made no affected ap-
' plication to the paffions of his audience Firm, and
' intrepid, he ftood before the council, collected in him-
' felf, and not only contemning, but feeming even de-
' firous of death The greateft character in antient ftory
' could not poffibly go beyond him If there is any juf-
' tice in hiftory, this man will be admired by all pofte-
' rity.——I fpeak not of his errors Let thefe reft with
' him What I admired was his learning, his eloquence,
' and amazing acutenefs God knows whether thefe
' things were not the ground-work of his ruin

' Two days were allowed him for reflection, during
' which time many perfons of confequence, and particu-
' larly my lord cardinal of *Florence*, endeavoured to bring
' him to a better mind But perfifting obftinately in his
' errors, he was condemned as a heretic

' With a chearful countenance, and more than ftoical
' conftancy, he met his fate, fearing neither death itfelf,
' nor the horrible form, in which it appeared When he
' came to the place, he pulled off his upper garment,
' and made a fhort prayer at the ftake, to which he was
' foon after bound with wet cords, and an iron chain;
' and inclofed as high as his breaft with faggots

' Obferving the executioner about to fet fire to the
' wood behind his back, he cried out, " Bring thy torch
" hither Perform thy office before my face. Had I
" feared death, I might have avoided it "

' As the wood began to blaze, he fang an hymn, which
' the violence of the flame fcarce interrupted

' Thus died this prodigious man. The epithet is not
' extravagant. I was myfelf an eye-witnefs of his whole
I   ' behaviour.

' behaviour   Whatever his life may have been, his
' death, without doubt, is a leſſon of philoſophy
    ' But it is time to finiſh this long epiſtle   You will
' ſay I have had ſome leiſure upon my hands   And, to
' ſay the truth, I have not much to do here   This will,
' I hope, convince you, that greatneſs is not wholly con-
' fined to antiquity   You will think me perhaps te-
' dious, but I could have been more prolix on a ſubject
' ſo copious.——Farewel, my dear *Leonard*.'
    Conſtance, May 20th.

Such was the teſtimony borne to an adverſary by this ingenuous papiſt. His friend *Aretin* was leſs candid   ' You
' attribute more, ſays he, to this man, than I could wiſh
' You ought at leaſt to *write* more cautiouſly of theſe
' things.' And indeed, it is probable, *Poggius* would have
written more cautiouſly, had he written a few days after
wards. But his letter is dated on the very day on which
Jerom ſuffered, and came warm from the writer's heart.
It is ſufficiently plain, what *Poggius* himſelf thought of the
council, and its proceedings. His encomium on *Jerom*,
is certainly a tacit cenſure of them.

WE may add here, as there are not materials to com-
poſe a diſtinct life, that the perſecution of JOHN de WE-
SALIA, for adopting the opinions of *Wickliffe*, followed
not many years after the martyrdom of *Huſs* and *Jerom*
He was brought before the inquiſition and treated with
great harſhneſs and ſeverity, which appear to be the more
inhuman, as the good man was advanced to decrepid old
age. However, he boldly defended the truth, and even
told his inquiſitors, upon an inſtance of their ill treatment, that " if *Chriſt* himſelf were upon the earth, they
" muſt condemn him for an heretic, if they condemned
" him for following his doctrines." He maintained, that
the ſubſtance of bread continued in the ſacrament, but
did not deny that *Chriſt*'s body was there, after a manner,
That no profeſſion of religion can ſave a man, but only
the grace of GOD, That the merits of the ſaints could
not be diſpoſed of on earth at market by the pope and his
prieſts, if even the works of the ſaints *had* any merit, becauſe it is written, that *their works do follow them*, That
pardons and indulgences were nothing better than *piæ
fraudes*, holy cheats, to impoſe upon the ignorant, * That
                                                    holy

---

* See an entertaining expoſure of theſe deluſions in a late pamphlet,
entitled, *A new Defence of the holy Roman Church againſt Heretics*
                                                    Where,

holy water had no more virtue than common water, That GOD gives his grace without the motion of our free-will, and that St *Paul* in particular did nothing of his own free-will in his conversion, That nothing is to be believed, which cannot be proved by scripture, That GOD hath from everlasting written a book, where he hath inscribed *all his elect*, and that whosoever is not already written there, will never be written there at all, but that he, who is written therein, will never be blotted out of it, That the elect are saved by the alone grace of GOD, and that what man soever GOD willeth to save, by enduing him with grace, if all the priests in the world were desirous to damn and excommunicate that man, he would still be saved, That he despised the pope, his church, and his councils, but that he loved *Christ*, and desired that his word might dwell in him abundantly.

Doctor *Wesalia* was bowed down with years and infirmities, when he underwent the above examination, which produced, in that dark age [*viz* A D 1479] this noble testimony for the truth Thus broken by age, and insulted with menaces, he was prevailed upon to sign a retractation, into which he was trepanned It is plain, that this retractation was not considered as sincere, from his being condemned to perpetual confinement and penance in a monastery of the *Augustins*, where he died soon after, about the time of the birth of LUTHER

PATRICK HAMILTON,

THE FIRST SCOTCH REFORMER.

PATRICK HAMILTON was a gentleman of *Scotland*, and, says Mr *Hugh Spence*, of royal descent, being by his father nephew to *James Hamilton*, earl of *Arran*, and by his mother nephew to *John Stewart*, duke of *Albany*, a circumstance in Providence, that was subservient to raise more attention to his excellent doctrine, holy life, and patient sufferings He had an amiable

Where, in a vein of irony, the author has shewn the most palpable absurdities and blasphemies of popery. Printed for *Mathews*, in the *Strand*.

disposition,

difposition, and was well educated, he was very early made abbot of *Ferme*, with a view to his being one day more highly preferred At the age of twenty-three, he with three companions travelled into *Germany*, in pursuit of religious knowledge, and coming to *Wittenberg* he met with *Luther* and *Melancthon*, with whom he held frequent and close conferences, and by whom he was well instructed in the doctrines of the gospel From thence he went to *Marpurg*, an university newly erected by *Philip Landgrave* of *Hesse*, he became intimately acquainted with *Lambert*, our *English* martyr, at whose instance he was the first in that university who set up public disputations concerning faith and works, the propositions and conclusions of which, are in what is entitled *Patrick's Places*, of which excellent tract we shall subjoin a specimen at the end of this article

He grew daily in grace and in the knowledge of *Jesus Christ*, and being well established in the faith, and much improved in all useful learning, he returned with one of his companions to *Scotland*, desirous to impart the knowledge of the true religion to his countrymen With a view to this, he began to preach the gospel of *Jesus Christ* with great fervency and boldness, and to lay open the errors and corruptions of the church of *Rome* This soon alarmed the whole body of the clergy, and particularly *James Beaton*, archbishop of St *Andrew's*, who labored to get Mr *Hamilton* to come to him at St *Andrew's*, where, after several days conference, he was dismissed, the archbishop seeming to approve of his doctrine, acknowledging that many things wanted reformation in the church But, at the same time, the archbishop consulted with other bishops, to put the king, (who was young and much led by them) upon going on a pilgrimage to St *Dothesse* in *Ross*, so that, during his absence, they might condemn Mr *Hamilton*, as no interest could then be made with the king to save his life Mr *Hamilton*, not suspecting their malice and treachery, remained at St. *Andrew's*, and the king being gone on his pilgrimage, he was cited to appear before the archbishop and his colleagues on the first day of *March*, 1527. The articles of accusation brought against him, which he was found guilty in holding and maintaining, and for which he was condemned to death, are the following. " That " man hath no free-will.—That there is no purgatory.— " That the holy patriarchs were in heaven before *Christ's* " passion.—That the pope hath no power to loose and " bind,

" bind Neither any pope had that power fince St *Pe-*
" *ter* —That the pope is *antichrift*, and that every prieft
" hath the power, that the pope hath —That Mr *Pa-*
" *trick Hamilton* was a bifhop —That it is not neceffary
" to obtain any bulls from any bifhop —That the vow
" of the pope's religion is a vow of wickednefs —That
" the pope's laws be of no ftrength —That all Chrif-
" tians, worthy to be called Chriftians, do know that
" they be in the ftate of grace —That none be faved, but
" thofe that are before predeftinate —Whofoever is in
" deadly fin, is unfaithful.—That God is the caufe of
" fin, in this fenfe, that is, that he withdraweth his
" grace from men, whereby they fin —That it is devilifh
" doctrine, to enjoin to any finner actual penance for fin
" —That the faid Mr *Patrick Hamilton* himfelf doubteth
" whether all children, departing incontinent after their
" baptifm, are faved or condemned —That auricular con-
" feffion is not neceffary to falvation."

Though thefe articles are inferted in their regifters,
' neverthelefs,' fays Mr. *Fox*, ' other learned men, who
' communed and reafoned with him, do teftify, that thefe
' articles following were the very articles, for which he
' fuffered '

" 1 Man hath no free-will   2 A man is only jufti-
" fied by faith in *Chrift*   3 A man, fo long as he liveth,
" is not without fin   4. He is not worthy to be called
" a Chriftian, who believeth not that he is in grace
" 5 A good man doeth good works   But good works do
" not make a good man   6 An evil man bringeth forth
" evil works   Evil works, being faithfully repented, do
" not make an evil man.   7. Faith, hope, and charity,
" be fo linked together, that one of them cannot be with-
" out another in one man in this life "

' And as touching the other articles,' adds Mr *Fox*,
' whereupon the doctors gave their judgements, as divers
' do report, he was not accufed of them before the arch-
' bifhop   Albeit in private difputation he affirmed and
' defended the moft of them '   That he did not hold the
whole of them, at leaft as they are expreffed in their re-
gifter, may eafily be learnt from his writings, where he
treats of the fame doctrines, and efpecially in his treatife
entitled *Patrick's Places*   A performance fo very judicious and truly evangelical, that it is fome concern to us,
that we cannot oblige the reader with the whole of it.

Having gone through the farce of a trial, they proceeded to pronounce fentence upon him, which, becaufe

I5

it shews his understanding, orthodoxy and innocence, as well as the ignorance and cruelty of the papists, we will lay it before the reader in their own words

His sentence, as it stands in the register of the archbishop's court, was as follows

' CHRISTI *nomine invocato* We *James*, by the mercy
' of God, archbishop of Saint *Andrew*'s, primate of *Scot-*
' *land*, with the council, decree, and authority of the
' most reverend fathers in God, and lords, abbots, doc-
' tors of theology, professors of the holy scripture, and
' masters of the university, assisting us for the time, sit-
' ting in judgement within our metropolitan church of
' Saint *Andrew*'s, in the cause of heretical pravity, against
' Mr. *Patrick Hamilton*, abbot or pensionary of *Ferme*,
' being summoned to appear before us, to answer to cer-
' tain articles affirmed, taught, and preached by him, and
' so appearing before us, and accused, the merits of the
' cause being ripely weighed, discussed, and understood
' by faithful inquisition made in *Lent* last past We have
' found the same Mr *Patrick Hamilton* many ways in-
' flamed with heresy, disputing, holding, and maintaining
' divers heresies of *Martin Luther*, and his followers, re-
' pugnant to our faith, and which are already condemned
' by general councils, and most famous universities. *
' And he being under the same infamy, we decerning be-
' fore him to be summoned and accused upon the pre-
' mises, he of evil mind (as may be presumed) passed to
' other parts forth of the realm, suspected and noted of
' heresy And being lately returned, not being admitted,
' but of his own head, without licence or privilege, hath
' presumed to preach wicked heresy

' We have found also, that he hath affirmed, published
' and taught divers opinions of *Luther*, and wicked he-
' resies, after that he was summoned to appear before us,
' and our council " That man hath no free-will That
" man is in sin so long as he liveth That children, in-
" continent after their baptism, are sinners † All Chris-
" tians, that be worthy to be called Christians, do know
" that they are in grace No man is justified by works, but
" by faith only Good works make not a good man, but
" a good man doth make good works That faith, hope,
" and charity, are so knit, that he, that hath the one, hath

---

* They do not pretend so much as to say they were condemned by the scriptures

† It may be observed, that these articles do not agree with those in their register.

" the

" the reft, and he, that wanteth the one of them, wanteth
" the reft, &c " with divers other herefies and deteftable
' opinions and hath perfifted fo obftinate in the fame,
' that by no counfel nor perfuafion he may be drawn
' therefrom to the way of our right faith

' All thefe premifes being confidered, we, having God
' and the integrity of our faith before our eyes, and fol-
' lowing the council and advice of the profeffors of the
' holy fcripture, men of law, and other affifting us for the
' time, do pronounce, determine, and declare the faid
' Mr *Patrick Hamilton*, for his affirming, confeffing, and
' maintaining of the aforefaid herefies, and his pertinacity
' (they being condemned already by the church, general
' councils, and moft famous univerfities) to be an here-
' tic, and to have an evil opinion of the faith, and
' therefore to be condemned and punifhed, like as we
' condemn, and define him to be punifhed, by this our
' fentence definitive, depriving and fentencing him to be
' deprived of all dignities, orders, offices, and benefices
' of the church, and therefore do judge and pronounce
' him to be delivered over unto the fecular power, to be
' punifhed, and his goods to be confifcate

' This our fentence definitive was given and read at
' our metropolitan church of St *Andrew's*, the laft day
' of the month of *February*, Anno 1527, being prefent the
' moft reverend fathers in *Chrift*, and lords, *Gawand*, bi-
' fhop of *Glafgow*, George, bifhop of *Dunkeldon*, *John*,
' bifhop of *Brecham*, *William*, bifhop of *Dunblane*, *Pa-
' trick*, prior of St *Andrew's*, *David*, abbot of *Abirbro-
' thoke*, *George*, abbot of *Dumfermling*, *Alexander*, abbot
' of *Caumbufkineth*, *Henry*, abbot of *Lendors*, *John*, prior
' of *Peterweme*, the dean and fubdean of *Glafgow*, Mr
' *Hugh Spence*, *Thomas Ramfay*, *Allane Meldrum*, &c. In
' the prefence of the clergy and the people '

That this fentence might have the greater authority,
they caufed it to be figned by all prefent, of any account,
whether clergy or laity, and, in order to make their number appear great, they took the fubfcription of the very
children of the nobility Being thus condemned as an
obftinate heretic, he was delivered over to the fecular
power, and after dinner, on the fame day, the fire was
prepared, and he was led to execution, whilft moft people thought it was only to terrify him, and to make him
recant But God, for his own glory, the good of the
elect, and for the manifeftation of their brutal tyranny,
had decreed it otherwife, and fo ftrengthened him, that

neither

neither the love of life, though young, nor fear of this cruel death, could in the least move him from the truth he had boldly profesed

At the place of execution, he gave his fervant, that had long attended him, his gown, coat, cap, and his other garments, faying, " Thefe are the laft things you can " receive of me, nor have I any thing now to leave you, " but the example of my death, which I pray you to bear " in mind, for, though it be bitter to the flefh, and fear- " ful before men, yet it is the entrance into eternal life, " which none fhall inherit, who deny *Jefus Chrift* before " this wicked generation " He was then bound to the ftake in the midft of wood and coal, which they attempted to fet on fire with gun-powder, but it neither killed him nor kindled the fire, only exceedingly fcorched one fide of his body and his face During the painful interval of their going to the caftle for more powder and combuf- tibles, the friars called frequently upon him to recant, and when the fire was kindled, it burnt fo flowly, that he endured great torment, which the friars endeavored to increafe by fetting fome of their own creatures to cry out in a clamorous manner, ' Turn, thou heretic, pray ' to the virgin, fay, *falve regina, &c* ' to whom he an- fwered, " Depart from me, and trouble me not, you " meffengers of *Satan* " One friar *Campbell*, who had vifited him often in prifon, was particularly officious, and continued to bellow out, ' Turn, thou heretic, ' turn, thou heretic,' whom Mr *Hamilton* thus addreffed, " Wicked man ! you know I am not a heretic, and have " confeffed the fame to me in private, but I appeal to " the juft tribunal feat of *Jefus Chrift*, and cite you to " appear there to anfwer for it to almighty GOD " And then faid, " How long, O Lord, fhall darknefs " overwhelm this realm ? and how long wilt Thou fuffer " the tyranny of thefe wicked men ?" And at length with a loud voice he cried, as he had frequently done, " Lord *Jefus*, receive my fpirit !" and died.

It is recorded, that friar *Campbell* died not long after in a phrenfy, and feemingly in defpair Which, con- fidered with the circumftance of his being cited by Mr. *Ha- milton*, made a great impreffion on the minds of the people, and caufed them to inquire more particularly into the na- ture and meaning of the articles, for which Mr *Hamilton* was burnt, and fo this event proved the means of many embracing the truth Mr. *Knox*, in his hiftory of *Scot- land*, relates the amazing effects of this great man's death,

and

and how wonderfully the Lord spread abroad the light of the gospel, by a careful examination of the articles upon which he was condemned, and of his writings

' When those cruel wolves had, as they supposed, clean
' devoured the prey, they found themselves in worse case
' than before, for then, within St *Andrew's*, yea, almost
' within the whole realm, (who heard of that tact) there
' was none found who began not to inquire, wherefore
' Mr *Patrick Hamilton* was burnt, and when his articles
' were rehearsed, question was holden, if such articles
' were necessary to be believed, under the pain of dam-
' nation? And lo, within a short space, many began to
' call in doubt, that which before they held for a certain
' verity, insomuch that the university of St. *Andrew's*
' and St *Leonard's* college, principally by the labours of
' Mr *Gavin Logy*, the novices of the abbey, and the sub-
' prior, began to smell somewhat of the verity, and to
' espy the vanity of the received superstition, yea, within
' few years after, began both black and grey friars pub-
' lickly to preach against the pride and idle life of bishops,
' and against the abuses of the whole ecclesiastical state.
' Amongst whom was one called *William Arithe*, who,
' in a sermon preached in *Dundee*, spake somewhat more
' freely against the licentious life of the bishops, than
' they could well bear   The bishop of *Berchin* having
' his parasites in the town, buffeted the friar, and called
' him heretic   The friar passed to St *Andrew's*, and did
' communicate the heads of his sermon to Mr *John Mair*,
' whose word then was held as an oracle, in matters of
' religion, and being assured of him, that such doctrine
' might well be defended, and that *he* would defend it,
' for it contained no heresy, there was a day appointed to
' the said friar, to make repetition of the same sermon,
' and advertisement was given to all such, as were of-
' fended at the former, to be present   And so, in the
' parish church of St *Andrew's*, upon the day appointed,
' appeared the said friar, and had, amongst his auditors,
' Mr. *John Mair*, Mr *George Lockhart*, the abbot of
' *Cambuskereth*, Mr. *Patrick Hepburn*, prior of St *An-
' drew's*, with all the doctors and masters of the univer-
' sities   Shortly after this, new consultation was taken
' there, that some should be burnt, for men began freely
' to speak.   A merry gentleman, called *John Lindsay*, fa-
' miliar to archbishop *Beaton*, standing by, when consul-
' tation was had, said, " My lord, if ye burn any more,
" except ye follow my counsel, ye will utterly destroy

K   " yourselves

" yourfelves, if you will burn them, let them be burnt
" in hollow cellars, for the fmoke of Mr *Patrick Hamil-*
" *ton* hath infected as many as it blew upon."

The rulers and doctors of the univerfity of *Louvain*,
hearing that the bifhops and doctors of *Scotland* had condemned and burnt this great and good man, exceedingly
rejoiced and triumphed, and in a letter written to the
archbifhop of St *Andrew's* and the other doctors, they
' highly applaud the worthy and famous defervings of
' their atchieved enterprife in that behalf ' Which letter *Fox* has given at large

We may here obferve, that the church of *Rome*, from
the very beginning of her claiming *temporal* authority,
worldly riches, and *earthly* government, has more and more
departed from the purity of the gofpel, has imbibed a
bloody and perfecuting fpirit againft all opponents, and
at length has placed itfelf entirely upon a footing with
the princes and kingdoms of this world, which come to
nought   The love of temporal dominion and authority
in the church, in which the paffions of carnal men can be
as fully fatisfied as in any other fyftem of human polity,
has been the chief ground of diffention, error, and perfecution   Nor is this love of rule to be confined to the
church of *Rome*, the fmalleft fect and party, acting upon
the fame principles, and founded upon the bottom of human aims and human authority, either exercifing dominion or defpifing dominion from worldly motives, is guilty
of the fame fpirit, and would exercife the fame conduct,
but for the prevention of fuperior force   While men act
from the world, their end will be *the world*, be their outward profeffions what they may   Thefe profeffions, in
no fenfe, make a Chriftian, whofe definition it is, to be
crucified to the world and to the *flefh, to put on Chrift* and
to be *one with him*, and to be *a ftranger and pilgrim upon
earth*, feeking *a better country and a heavenly*

In the interval between this holy man's death, and the
public miniftrations of the excellent Mr *George Wifhart*,
feveral perfons fuffered for the truth in *Scotland*, and,
among the reft, Mr. *John Rogers*, a gracious and learned
minifter, who was murdered in prifon, by the order of
cardinal *Beaton*, and thrown over the wall, with a report,
that in attempting to efcape he had broken his neck   Mr.
Thomas Forreft, another minifter, was alfo burned, for an
heretic, by the means of the popifh bifhop of *Dunkelden*.
By the writings and fermons of thefe bleffed men, a feed
of Reformation was fown in *Scotland*, which, being watered

2   and

and witnessed by their blood, soon sprung up into a flourishing tree, and gloriously overspread that whole country.

WE promised to give our readers a specimen of this excellent man's tract, called *Patrick's Places*, which have ever been esteemed by the most able and serious Christians (especially considering the time when they were written) as an admirable and invaluable performance. They were prefaced by Mr *John Frith*, the martyr, in the following manner.

'John Frith unto the *Christian Reader*.

' Blessed be the God and Father of our Lord *Jesus*
' *Christ*, which, in these last days and perilous times,
' hath stirred up in all countries witnesses unto his Son, to
' testifie the truth unto the unfaithful, to save at the least
' some from the snares of antichrist, which lead to per-
' dition, as ye may here perceive by that excellent and
' well learned young man, *Patrick Hamilton*, born in *Scot-
' land* of a noble progeny. Who to testifie the truth
' sought all means, and took upon him priesthood (even
' as *Paul* circumcised *Timothy*, to win the weak *Jews*)
' that he might be admitted to preach the pure word of
' God. Notwithstanding, as soon as the chamberlain
' and other bishops of *Scotland* had perceived, that the
' light began to shine, which disclosed their falshood that
' they conveyed in darkness, they laid hands on him, and
' because he would not deny his Saviour *Christ*, at their
' instance, they burnt him to ashes. Nevertheless, God
' of his bounteous mercy (to publish to the whole world,
' what a man these monsters have murdered) hath reserved
' a little treatise, made by this *Patrick*, which if ye list,
' ye may call PATRICK's PLACES. For it treateth ex-
' actly of certain common places, which known, ye have
' the pith of all divinity. This treatise I have turned
' into the *English* tongue, to the profit of my nation. To
' whom I beseech God to give light, that they may espie
' the deceitful paths of perdition, and return to the right
' way, which leadeth to life everlasting, Amen.'

The following are extracts from the treatise.

The doctrine of the LAW.

Proposition.
" He that keepeth not all the commandments of God,
" keepeth not one of them.

Argument.

Argument

" *He that keepeth one commandment of God, keepeth all*
" Ergo, *he that keepeth not all the commandments of God,*
" *keepeth not one of them*

Proposition

" It is not in our power to keep any one of the com-
" mandments of God

Argument.

Ba- ⎧ " *It is impossible to keep any of the commandments of*
⎪   "   *God, without grace*
ro- ⎨ " *It is not in our power to have grace*
⎪   " Ergo, *it is not in our power to keep any of the com-*
co ⎩   " *mandments of God*

" And even so may you reason concerning the Holy
" Ghost and faith; forasmuch as neither without them
" we are able to keep any of the commandments of God,
" neither yet be they in our power to have   *Non est*
" *volentis neque currentis, &c* Rom ix 16.

Proposition

" The law was given us to shew our sin
" *By the law cometh the knowledge of sin*, Rom iii 20
" I knew not what sin meant, but through the law
" *For I had not known what lust had meant, except the law*
" *had said, Thou shalt not lust Without the law, sin was*
" *dead, that is, it moved me not, neither wist I that it was*
" *sin, which notwithstanding was sin, and forbidden by the*
" *law.* Rom. vii.

Proposition

" The law biddeth us do that thing, which is impos-
" sible for us

Argument.

Da- ⎧ " *The keeping of the commandments is to us impossible*
⎪   " *The law commandeth to us the keeping of the com-*
ri- ⎨   " *mandments*
⎪   " Ergo, *the law commandeth unto us, what is impos-*
i   ⎩   " *sible*

" *Objection*   But you will say, Wherefore doth God
" bid us do that, which is impossible for us?
" *Answer.*   To make thee know, that thou art but evil,
" and that there is no remedy to save thee in thine own
" hand And that thou mayest seek a remedy at some other
" For the law doth nothing else, but condemn thee.

" The doctrine of the GOSPEL

" The GOSPEL is, in other words, good tidings*, and
" may be expressed in the following manner.

* *Luke iii*

ᵗˢ *Christ*

"Christ is the Saviour of the [elect] world[1]. Christ is
" the Saviour[2] Christ died for us[3] Christ died for our
" sins[4] Christ bought us with his blood[5]. Christ
" washed us with his blood[6] Christ offered himself for
" us[7] Christ bare our sins on his own back[8] Christ
" come into this world to save sinners[9] Christ came into
" this world to take away our sins[10] Christ was the
" price that was given for us and our sins[11] Christ was
" made debtor for us[12] Christ hath payed our debt, for
" he died for us[13] Christ made satisfaction for us and
" our sins[14]. Christ is our righteousness[15] Christ is our
" sanctification[16] Christ is our redemption[17] Christ is
" our peace[18]. Christ hath pacified the Father of heaven
" for us[19] Christ is ours, and all his[20] Christ hath
" delivered us from the law, from the devil, and from
" hell[21] The Father of heaven hath forgiven us our
" sins for Christ's sake And many other similar ex-
" pressions, equally scriptural, which declare unto us the
" mercy of God.

" *The nature and office of the* LAW *and of the* GOSPEL.

{ " The law sheweth us our sin. *Rom* iii
{ " The gospel sheweth us a remedy for it *John* i
{ " The law sheweth us our condemnation *Rom* viii.
{ " The gospel sheweth us our redemption *Col* i.
{ " The law is the word of ire [wrath] *Rom* iv
{ " The gospel is the word of grace *Acts* xiv 20.
{ " The law is the word of despair *Deut* xxvii
{ " The gospel is the word of comfort *Luke* ii
{ " The law is the word of disquietude *Rom* vii.
{ " The gospel is the word of peace *Eph.* vi

" *A disputation between the* LAW *and the* GOSPEL, *in which*
" *is shewed the difference or contrariety between them both.*

{ " The law saith, *Pay the debt*
{ " The gospel saith, *Christ hath paid it*
{ " The law saith, *Thou art a sinner, despair, and thou*
{ " *shalt be damned.*
{ " The gospel saith, *Thy sins are forgiven thee, be of good*
{ " *comfort, for thou shalt be saved*
{ " The law saith, *Make amends for thy sins*
{ " The gospel saith, *Christ hath made it for thee.*

1 *John* iv   2 *Luke* ii   3 *Rom* v   4 ibid iv   5 i *Pet* ii.
6 *Rev* i v   7 *Gal* i.   8 *Isa* liii   9 i *Tim* i   10 i *John* iii.
11 i *Tim* ii   12 *Rom* viii.   13 *Col* ii   14 i *Cor* vii   15 i *Cor* i.
16 i *Cor* i   17 *Eph.* ii.   18 *Rom.* v.   19 2 *Cor* iii.   20 *Col* iii
21 *John* i.

" The

{ " The law faith, *The Father of heaven is angry with thee*
{ " The gospel faith, *Christ hath pacified him with his blood*

{ " The law faith, *Where is thy righteousness, goodness, and*
  " *satisfaction?*
{ " The gospel faith, *Christ is thy righteousness, goodness,*
  " *and satisfaction.*

{ " The law faith, *Thou art bound and obliged to me, to the*
  " *devil, and to hell*
{ " The gospel faith, *Christ hath delivered thee from them*
  " *all.*

" *A comparison between* FAITH *and* UNBELIEF.

{ " Faith is the root of all good
{ " Unbelief is the root of all evil
{ " Faith maketh God and man good friends.
{ " Unbelief maketh them foes
{ " Faith bringeth God and man together,
{ " Unbelief separates them
{ " All that faith doth, pleaseth God
{ " All that unbelief doth, displeaseth God
{ " Faith only maketh a man good and righteous,
{ " Unbelief maketh him unjust and evil
{ " Faith maketh a man a member of *Christ*
{ " Unbelief maketh him a member of the devil
{ " Faith maketh him an inheritor of heaven
{ " Unbelief maketh a man the inheritor of hell.
{ " Faith maketh a man the servant of God
{ " Unbelief maketh him the servant of the devil.
{ " Faith sheweth us God to be a tender Father
{ " Unbelief sheweth him to be a terrible judge
{ " Faith holdeth fast by the word of God.
{ " Unbelief wavereth here and there
{ " Faith esteemeth God to be true
{ " Unbelief looketh upon him to be false and a liar.
{ " Faith knoweth God.
{ " Unbelief knoweth him not.
{ " Faith loveth both God and his neighbour,
{ " Unbelief loveth neither of them.
{ " Faith only saveth us
{ " Unbelief only condemneth us.

" *A comparison between* FAITH, HOPE, *and* CHARITY

" *Faith* cometh of the word of God, *hope* cometh of
" faith, and *charity* springeth of them both
" *Faith* believeth the word, *hope* trusteth to enjoy that,
" which is promised in the word, *charity* doeth good unto
" her

" her neighbour, through the love that it hath to God,
" and gladness that is within herself

" *Faith* looketh to God and his word, *hope* looketh
" unto his gift and reward, *charity* looketh on her neigh-
" bour's profit

" *Faith* receiveth God, *hope* receiveth his reward, *cha-*
" *rity* loveth her neighbour with a glad heart, and that
" without any respect of reward.

" *Faith* pertaineth to God only, *hope* to his reward,
" and *charity* to her neighbour "

This little treatise of Mr *Hamilton's* (continues his
editor) though short, is very comprehensive, containing
matter sufficient for several volumes, and shews us the
true doctrine of the law, of the gospel, of faith, and
of works, with their nature, properties and difference
Which difference is thus to be understood, that in the
article of salvation, and in the office of justifying, they
are distinct and to be kept asunder, the law from the gospel, and faith from works Though in the person that is
justified, and also in the order of doctrine, they ought and
do go necessarily together.

Therefore, wheresoever any question or doubt ariseth
respecting salvation, or our justification before God, there
the law and all good works must be utterly excluded, that
grace may appear to be sovereign, the promise free and
gratuitous, and that faith may stand alone, which faith
alone, without law or works, confirms to every believer
his own particular salvation For as the grace of God
is the *efficient* cause, and *Jesus Christ* the *meritorious* cause,
of our redemption, so faith is the *instrumental* cause by
which the believer applieth the merits of *Christ* particularly to his own salvation So that, in the act and office
of justification, both the law and works are entirely out
of the question, as things that have nothing to do in the
matter The reason is this, that as all our salvation is by
Christ alone, so nothing can savingly profit us, but that
with which we can apprehend *Christ* Now, as neither
the law nor works, but faith alone is that by which we
can apprehend *Christ* as an almighty and all-sufficient
Saviour, so faith alone justifieth the sinner before God,
through the object it doth apprehend, namely, *Jesus Christ*.
For the only object of our faith is *Christ*, just as the brazen serpent, lifted up in the wilderness, was the object
only of the eyes of the *Israelites* looking, and not of their
hands working, by virtue of which, through the promise
of God, immediately proceeded health to the beholders

So *Chriſt*, being the object of our faith, becomes righteouſneſs and ſalvation to our ſouls, not by works, but
by faith only

Thus we ſee how faith, being the only eye of our ſoul,
ſtandeth alone in apprehending or ſeeing *Chriſt* for juſtification to life, but yet, nevertheleſs, in the body it
ſtandeth not alone For beſides the eye, there are alſo
hands to work, feet to walk, ears to hear, and other members, every one convenient for the ſervice of the body,
and yet of them all, the eye only can ſee, So in a Chriſtian
man's life, and in order of doctrine, there is the law,
repentance, hope, charity, and the deeds of charity, all
which in life and in doctrine are joined, and neceſſarily do
concur together, and yet in the act of juſtification there
is nothing elſe in man, that hath any part or place but
faith alone apprehending the object, which is *Chriſt* crucified, in whom is all the worthineſs and fulneſs of our
ſalvation, that is, by our apprehending and receiving of
him by faith, as it is written, *Whoſoever received him, to
them gave he power to become the ſons of God, even to them
that believe on his name Which were born, nor of blood, nor
of the will of the fleſh, nor of the will of man, but of God*[*]
And alſo in *Iſaiah*[†],—*By his knowledge, ſhall my righteous
Servant juſtify many*, *&c*

Argument

Da- ⎧ " Apprehending and receiving of *Chriſt* only mak-
      " eth us juſtified before God *John* i
ti- ⎨ " *Chriſt* only is apprehended and received by faith
fi. ⎩ " *Ergo*, faith only maketh us juſtified before God.

Argument.

Ba- ⎧ " Juſtification cometh only by apprehending and
      " receiving of *Chriſt* *Iſa* liii.
ro- ⎨ " The law and works do nothing pertain to the
      " apprehending of *Chriſt*.
      " *Ergo*, the law and works pertain nothing to
co ⎩ " juſtification

Argument.

Ce- ⎧ " Nothing, which is unjuſt of itſelf, can juſtify
      " us before God, or help any thing to our juſti-
      " fying.
la- ⎨ " Every work we do is unjuſt before God *Iſa* lxiv.
      " *Ergo*, no work, that we can do, can juſtify us
      " before God, nor help any thing to our juſti-
re. ⎩ " fying

---

[*] *John* i 12, 13. [†] Chap. liii. 11.

Argument.

Argument

Ca- "If works could any thing further our juſtification,
  "then ſhould our works ſomething profit us be-
  "fore God

ne- "No works, do the beſt we can, do profit us be-
  "fore God *Luke* xvii *John* xv

  "*Ergo*, no works, that we do, can any thing fur-
ſties "ther our juſtification

Argument.

Ba- "All that we can do with God, is only by *Chriſt*
  "*John* xv

ro- "Our works and merits be not *Chriſt*, neither any
  "part of him

  "*Ergo*, our works and merits can do nothing with
co "God.

Argument

Da- "That, which is the cauſe of condemnation, can-
  "not be the cauſe of juſtification

ri- "The law is the cauſe of condemnation *Rom* iv.

1 "*Ergo*, it is not the cauſe of juſtification

A conſequent.

"We are quit and delivered *from* the law *Rom* vii.

"*Ergo*, we are not quit and delivered *by* the law

"For as much, therefore, as the truth of the ſcripture,
"in expreſs words, hath thus included our ſalvation in
"faith only, we are inforced neceſſarily to exclude all
"other cauſes and means in our juſtification, and to
"make this difference between the law and the goſpel,
"between faith and works, affirming, with ſcripture,
"that the law condemneth us, our works do not avail us,
"and that faith in *Chriſt* only juſtifieth us And this
"difference and diſtinction ought diligently to be learned
"and retained of all Chriſtians, eſpecially in conflicts of
"conſcience between the law and goſpel, between faith
"and works, grace and merits, promiſe and condition,
"God's free election and man's free-will So that the
"light of the free grace of God in our ſalvation may ap-
"pear to all conſciences, to the immortal glory of God's
"holy name *Amen.*

"*The order and difference of places*

| "The GOSPEL. | { Faith. Grace. | { Promiſe God's free election. | } |
| "The LAW | { Works Merits | { Condition Man's free-will | } |

L   "The

" The difference and repugnance of thefe forefaid
" places being well noted and expended, it fhall give no
" fmall light to every faithful Chriftian, both to under-
" ftand the fcriptures, to judge in cafes of confcience,
" and to reconcile fuch places in the *Old and New Tefta-*
" *ment*, as feem to contradict each other, according to
" St *Auguftine's* rule, which is, *Diftingue tempora, &*
" *conciliabis fcripturas*, &c ' Make diftinction of times,
' and thou fhalt reconcile the fcriptures, &c ' On the
" other hand, where men are not perfectly inftructed in
" thefe places, to difcern between the law and the gofpel,
" between faith and works, &c So long they can never
" rightly eftablifh their minds in the free promifes of
" God's grace, but walk confidently without order, in
" all matters of religion. Example of which we have
" too much in the *Romifh* church, who confounding thefe
" places together without diftinction, following no me-
" thod, have perverted the true order of Chriftian doc-
" trine, and have obfcured the fweet comfort and benefit
" of the gofpel of *Chrift*, not knowing the true ufe either
" of the law or gofpel.

" *In the doctrine of the* LAW *three things are to be noted*

" In the *law*, three things are to be confidered Firft,
" what is the true vigour and ftrength of the law, which
" is, to require full and perfect obedience of the whole
" man, not only to reftrain his outward actions, but alfo
" his inward motions, and inclinations of will and af-
" fection from the appetite of fin. And therefore faith
" St *Paul, The law is fpiritual, but I am carnal, &c.*
" Rom. vii. Whereupon rifeth this propofition, That
" it is not in our nature and power to fulfill the law.
" *Item*, The law commandeth that which is to us im-
" poffible, &c

" The *fecond* thing to be noted in the doctrine of the
" law, is, to confider the time and place of the law, what
" they be, and how far they extend. For as the furging
" feas have their banks and bars to keep them in, fo the
" law hath its times and limits, which it ought not to
" pafs. If *Chrift* had not come and fuffered, the time and
" dominion of the law had been everlafting. But now
" feeing *Chrift* hath come, and hath died in his righteous
" flefh, the power of the law againft our finful flefh doth
" ceafe. *For the end of the Law is Chrift* Rom x that is,
" the death of *Chrift's* body is the death of the law to all
" that believe in him So that whofoever repent of their
" fins, and flee to the death and paffion of *Chrift*, the

" condemnation

" condemnation and time of the law to them is expired.
" Wherefore, this is to be understood as a perpetual rule
" in the scripture, that the law, with all his sentences
" and judgements, wheresoever they are written, either
" in the *Old* or *New Testament*, do ever include a privy
" exception of repentance and faith in *Christ*, to the
" which always it giveth place, having there his end, and
" can proceed no further, according as St *Paul* saith,
" *The law is our schoolmaster until Christ, that we might be*
" *justified by faith**

" Moreover, as the law hath its time, *how long to reign*,
" so also it hath his proper place, *where to reign* By
" the reign of the law here is meant the condemnation of
" the law For as the time of the law ceaseth, when the
" faith of *Christ* in a true repenting heart beginneth, so
" hath the law no place in such, as be good and faithful;
" that is, in sinners repenting and amending, but only
" in them which be evil and wicked. Evil men are such,
" as walking in sinful flesh are not yet driven by earnest
" repentance to flee to *Christ* for succour And therefore
" saith St *Paul*, *The law is not made for a righteous man*,
" *but for the lawless and disobedient, for the ungodly and for*
" *sinners, &c†* By the *just* man here is meant, not he
" which never had disease, but he, who knowing his dif-
" ease, seeketh out the physician, and being cured, keepeth
" himself in health, as much as he may, from any more
" surfeits Notwithstanding, he shall never so keep
" himself, but that his health (that is, his new obedience)
" shall always remain frail and imperfect, and shall con-
" tinually need the physician Where, by the way, these
" three things are to be noted, first, the sickness itself
" Secondly, the knowing of the sickness Thirdly, the
" physician The sickness is sin. The knowing of the
" sickness is repentance, which the law worketh. The
" physician is *Christ* And therefore although in remif-
" fion of our sins repentance is joined with faith, yet it
" is not the dignity or worthiness of repentance that
" causeth remission of sins, but only the worthiness of
" *Christ*, whom faith only apprehendeth, no more than
" the feeling of the disease is the cause of health, but
" only the physician For else, when a man is cast and
" condemned by the law, it is not repentance that can
" save or deserve life, but if his pardon come, then is it
" the grace of the prince, and not his repentance that
" saveth.

* Gal, iii, 24,   † 1 Tim, i, 9,

L 2   " The

" The third point to be confidered in the doctrine of
" the law, is this, that we mark well the end and purpofe
" why the law is given, which is not to bring us to fal-
" vation, nor to work God's favour, nor to make us
" good　But rather to declare and convict our wicked-
" nefs, and to make us feel the danger thereof, to this
" end and purpofe, that we, feeing our condemnation,
" and being in ourfelves confounded, may be driven
" thereby to have our refuge in *Chrift* the Son of God,
" and fubmit ourfelves to him, in whom only is to be
" found our remedy, and in none other　And this end
" of the law ought to be ferioufly confidered by all Chrif-
" tians　That they do not fall into manifold errors and
" inconveniences　1　They pervert all order of doc-
" trine　2　They feek that in the law, which the law
" cannot give,　3　They are not able to comfort them-
" felves nor any other　4　They keep men's fouls in an
" uncertain doubt of their falvation　5. They obfcure
" the light of God's grace　6　They are unkind to
" God's benefits　7　They are injurious to *Chrift*'s paf-
" fion, and enemies to his crofs　8　They ftop Chrif-
" tians' liberty　9. They bereave the church, the fpoufe
" of *Chrift*, of her due comfort, as taking away the fun
" out of the world　10　In all their doings, they fhoot
" at a wrong mark　For where *Chrift* only is to be fet
" up to be apprehended by our faith, and fo freely to juf-
" tify us, they, leaving this juftification by faith, fet up
" other marks, partly by the law, partly of their own
" devifing, for men to fhoot at　And here cometh in
" the manifeft and manifold abfurdities of the bifhop of
" *Rome*'s doctrine, which (the Lord willing) we will re-
" hearfe, as in a catalogue here following "

Errors and abfurdities of the Papifts, *touching the doctrine of*
the Law *and of the* Gospel.

" 1　They erroneoufly conceive an opinion of falva-
" tion in the law, which only is to be fought in the faith
" of *Chrift*, and in no other

" 2　They erroneoufly feek God's favour by works of
" the law　Not knowing that the law, in this our cor-
" rupt nature, worketh only the anger of God　*Rom* iii

" 3. They err alfo in this, that where the office of the
" law is diverfe and contrary from the gofpel, they,
" without any difference, confound the one with the
" other, making the gofpel to be a law, and *Chrift* to be
" a *Mofes*.

" 4. They

" 4 They err in dividing the law unskilfully into
" three parts, into the law-natural, the law-moral, and
" the law-evangelical

" 5 They err again in dividing the law-evangelical
" into precepts and councils, making the precepts to
" serve for all men, the councils only to serve for them
" that be perfect.

" 6 The chief substance of all their teaching and
" preaching resteth upon the works of the law, as ap-
" pears by their religion, which wholly consisteth in
" men's merits, traditions, laws, canons, decrees, and
" ceremonies

" 7 In the doctrine of salvation, of remission, and
" justification, either they admit the law equally with
" the gospel, or else, clean secluding the gospel, they
" teach and preach the law, so that little mention is
" made of the faith of *Christ*, or none at all.

" 8 They err in thinking, that the law of God re-
" quireth nothing in us under pain of damnation, but
" only our obedience in external actions As for the in-
" ward affections and concupiscence, they esteem but
" light matters

" 9 They, not knowing the true nature and strength
" of the law, do erroneously imagine that it is in man's
" power to fulfil it

" 10 They err in thinking, that it is in man's power
" not only to keep the law of God, but also to perform
" more perfect works than be in God's law commanded,
" and these they call the works of perfection And hereof
" rise the works of supererogation, of satisfaction, of con-
" gruity and condignity, to store up the treasure-house of
" the pope's church, to be sold out to the people for money.

" 11. They err in saying, that the state monastical is
" more perfect for keeping the councils of the gospel,
" than other states be in keeping the law of the gospel.

" 12 The councils of the gospel they call the vows of
" their religious men, as profound humility, perfect chas-
" tity, and wilful poverty

" 13 They err abominably, in equalling their laws
" and constitutions with God's law, and in saying, that
" man's law bindeth under pain of damnation, no less
" than God's law

" 14 They err sinfully, in punishing the transgressors
" of their laws more sharply than the transgressors of the
" law of God, as appeareth by their inquisitions, and
" their canon-law, &c,

" 15 Finally

" 15 Finally, they err moſt horribly in this, that where
" the free promiſe of God aſcribeth our ſalvation only to
" our faith in *Chriſt*, excluding works, they, on the con-
" trary, aſcribe ſalvation only, or principally, to works
" and merits, excluding faith. Whereupon ariſeth the
" application of the ſacrifice of the maſs, *ex opere operato*,
" for the quick and dead, application of the merits of
" *Chriſt*'s paſſion, in bulls, application of the merits of
" all religious orders, and other ſuch like trumpery, as
" above mentioned.

" THREE *cautions to be obſerved and avoided in the true un-*
deiſtanding of the LAW

" *Firſt*, that we, through the miſunderſtanding of the
" ſcriptures, do not take the law for the goſpel, nor the
" goſpel for the law, but ſkilfully diſcern and diſtinguiſh
" the voice of the one from the voice of the other. Many
" there be, who reading the book of the *New Teſtament*,
" imagine that whatever they find contained in it, to be
" only and merely the voice of the goſpel And, on the
" other hand, whatever is contained in the *Old Teſtament*,
" that is, within the *law, ſtories, pſalms*, and *prophets*,
" to be only and merely the word and voice of the law
" In which they are deceived, for the preaching of the
" law and of the goſpel are mixed together in both the
" *Teſtaments*, as well in the *Old* as in the *New* Neither
" is the order of theſe two doctrines to be diſtinguiſhed
" by books and leaves, but by the diverſity of God's ſpi-
" rit ſpeaking unto us. For ſometimes in the *Old Teſ-*
" *tament* God doth comfort, as he comforted *Adam*, with
" the voice of the goſpel. Sometimes alſo in the *New*,
" he doth threaten and terrify, as when *Chriſt* threatened
" the *Phariſees*. In ſome places, again, *Moſes* and the
" *prophets* play the *evangeliſts*. Inſomuch that *Jerom*
" doubted whether he ſhould call *Iſaiah* a *prophet* or an
" *evangeliſt* In ſome places, likewiſe, *Chriſt* and the
" *apoſtles* ſupply the part of *Moſes* And as *Chriſt* him-
" ſelf, until his death, was under the law (which law he
" came not to break, but to fulfil), ſo his ſermons made to
" the *Jews*, run all for the moſt part upon the perfect doc-
" trine and works of the law, ſhewing and teaching what
" we ought to do by the right law of juſtice, and what
" danger enſueth in not performing the ſame All which
" places, though they be contained in the book of the
" *New Teſtament*, yet they are to be referred to the doc-
" trine of the law, ever having in them included a privy
" exception

" exception of repentance and faith in *Christ Jesus* As
" for example, where *Christ* thus preacheth, *Blessed are*
" *the pure in heart; for they shall see God** *Except ye be*
" *converted, and become as little children, ye shall not enter*
" *into the kingdom of heaven*† *But he, that doeth the will*
" *of my Father, shall enter into the kingdom of heaven*‡.
" Likewise the parable of the unkind servant, justly cast
" into prison for not forgiving his fellow-servant, &c §
" The casting the rich glutton into hell, &c ‖ *He, that*
" *denieth me before men, shall be denied before the angels of*
" *God* ¶ With other such like places of scripture All
" these, I say, pertaining to the doctrine of the law, do
" ever include in them a secret exception of earnest re-
" pentance and faith in *Christ*'s precious blood For
" else, *Peter* denied, and yet repented Many publicans
" and sinners were unkind, unmerciful, and hard-hearted
" to their fellow-servants, and yet many of them re-
" pented, and by faith were saved, &c The grace of
" *Christ Jesus* works in us repentance towards God, and
" faith in himself unfeigned.

" Briefly, to know when the law speaketh, and when
" the gospel speaketh, and to discern the voice of the one
" from the voice of the other, we may learn from the
" following remark. That when there is any moral
" work commanded to be done, either to avoid punish-
" ment, or upon promise of any reward temporal or eter-
" nal, or else when any promise is made with condition
" of any work commanded in the law, there is to be un-
" derstood the voice of the law On the other hand,
" where the promise of life and salvation is offered unto
" us freely, without any merits or doings of ours, and
" simply without any condition annexed, of any law,
" either natural, ceremonial, or moral All such places,
" whether they be read in the *Old Testament* or in the
" *New*, are to be referred to the voice and doctrine of
" the gospel And this promise of God, freely made to
" us by the merits of *Jesus Christ*, so long before pro-
" phesied to us in the *Old Testament*, and afterward ex-
" hibited in the *New Testament*, and now requiring no-
" thing but our faith in the Son of God, is called pro-
" perly the voice of the gospel, and differeth from the
" voice of the law in this, that it hath *no condition* ad-
" joined of our meriting, but only respecteth the merits
" of *Christ* the Son of God, by faith in whom alone we

* Matth v 8. † Ibid xviii 3 ‡ Ibid vii 21.
§ Ibid xviii. 23, &c. ‖ Luke xvi. 19, &c. ¶ Ibid xii. 9

" are

" are promised of God to be faved and juftified, accord-
" ing as we read, *The righteoufnefs of God*, which is *by*
" *faith of Jefus Chrift unto all, and upon all them that be-*
" *lieve, &c* Rom iii 22.

" The fecond caution or danger to be avoided is, that
" we now knowing how to difcern rightly between the
" law and the gofpel, and having intelligence not to
" miftake one for the other, muft take heed again that
" we break not the order between thefe two, taking and
" applying the law where the gofpel is to be applied,
" either to ourfelves or toward others. For notwith-
" ftanding the law and the gofpel many times are to be
" joined together in order of doctrine, yet it may fome-
" times fall out, that the law muft be utterly fequeftered
" from the gofpel. As when any perfon or perfons do
" feel themfelves with the majefty of the law and judge-
" ment of God fo terrified and oppreffed, and with the
" burden of their fins overweighed and thrown down in-
" to utter difcomfort, and almoft even to the pit of hell,
" as happeneth many times to foft and timorous con-
" fciences of God's good fervants When fuch mortified
" hearts do hear, either in preaching or in reading, any
" fuch example or place of the fcripture which per-
" taineth to the law, let them think, that they do not in
" the leaft belong to them, no more than a mourning-
" weed belongeth to a marriage-feaft, and therefore re-
" moving out of their minds all thoughts of the law, of
" fear, of judgement, and condemnation, let them only
" fet before their eyes the gofpel, the fweet comfort of
" God's promife, free forgivenefs of fins in *Chrift,* grace,
" redemption, liberty, rejoicing, pfalms, thanks, finging,
" and a paradife of fpiritual jocundity, and nothing elfe,
" thinking thus with themfelves, that the law hath done
" his office in them already, and now muft needs give
" place to his better, that is, muft needs give room to
" *Chrift* the Son of God, who is the Lord and Mafter,
" the Fulfiller and Finifher of the law, *for* Chrift *is the*
" *end of the law for righteoufnefs to every one that believeth*
" Rom x 4

" The third danger to be avoided is, that we do not,
" on the other hand, ufe or apply the gofpel, inftead of
" the law. For, as applying the law inftead of the gof-
" pel, is like going to a marriage-feaft in a mourning
" gown, fo to apply the gofpel inftead of the law, is to
" caft pearls before fwine In which there is great abufe
" among many For commonly it is feen, that thefe
" worldly epicures and fecure mammonifts, to whom the
I   " doctrine

" doctrine of the law doth properly appertain, do receive
" and apply to themselves most principally the sweet
" promises of the gospel So likewise it is too often the
" case, for those broken and contrite in heart, to whom
" only belong the joyful tidings of the gospel and not
" the law, to receive and retain to themselves the terrible
" voice and sentences of the law Whereby it cometh
" to pass, that many do rejoice, that should mourn, and
" many fear and mourn, that should rejoice Where-
" fore, to conclude, in private use of life, let every per-
" son wisely discern between the law and the gospel,
" and aptly apply to himself, that which he seeth con-
" venient

" And again, in public order of doctrine, let every
" discreet preacher put a difference between the broken
" heart of the mourning sinner, and the impenitent
" worldling, and so join both the law with the gospel,
" and the gospel with the law, that in throwing down
" the wicked he ever spare the weak-hearted, and again, so
" spare the weak, that he do not encourage the ungodly "

The Christian Reader will excuse the length of these
extracts, which we will conclude with remarking, that
this excellent man *Hamilton*, and his blessed commentator
Frith, lived before the establishment of the Reformation
in their respective countries of *Scotland* and *England*, and
that it is comfortable to reflect, that the same Spirit teaches
the same truth in all places and times, as appears in the
instance before us, which contains the gospel with as much
clearness (and would to GOD, it might not be said,
with *more* clearness) as among the professors of a later day.

GERARD GELDENHAUR,

SOMETIMES CALLED,

GERARDUS NOVIOMAGUS.

GERARD GELDENHAUR, a very learned
German, was born at *Nimeguen*, in the year 1482.
From his earliest youth, he was distinguished by his love

of learning, especially of history and poetry He studied classical learning at *Daventer*, and went through his course of philosophy at *Louvain* with such success, that he was chosen to teach that science there   It was in this famous university, that he contracted a very strict friendship with several learned men, and in particular with *Erasmus*, as appears from the epistles of the latter He made some stay at *Antwerp*, from whence he was invited to the court of *Charles of Austria*, to be reader and historian to that prince But not loving to change his abode often, he did not think proper to attend him into *Spain*, but disengaged himself from his service, and entered into that of *Philip* of *Burgundy*, bishop of *Utrecht* He was his reader and secretary twelve years, namely, to the year 1524, after which, he executed the same functions in the court of *Maximilian of Burgundy* He was sent to *Wittenberg* in the year 1526, in order to enquire into the state of the schools, and of the church there He faithfully reported what he had observed in that city, and confessed, he could not disapprove of a doctrine so conformable to the scriptures, as that which he heard there And upon this he forsook the popish religion, and retired towards the *Upper Rhine* He married at *Worms*, and taught youth for some time. Afterwards, about the year 1531, he was invited to *Augsburg*, to undertake the same employment , and at length, in the year 1534, he went from thence to *Marpurg*, where he taught history for two years, and then divinity to his death He died of the plague on the 10th of *January*, A. D 1542. He was a man well skilled in poetry, rhetoric, and history The most considerable of his works are—*Historia Batavica*, *Strasburg*, 1533, but *Vossius* mentions an edition of the year 1520 —*De Batavorum Insulâ*.—*Germaniæ Inferioris Historia*, *Strasburg*, 1532 —*Epistola de Zelandia* —*Satyræ Octo*, printed at *Louvain*, in 1515.—*Historiæ et Catalogus episcoporum Ultrajectinorum*, &c.

His changing his religion, and some writings which he published against the church of *Rome*, occasioned a quarrel between him and *Erasmus* *Erasmus* called him a seditious fellow, and blamed him for publishing scoffing books, which only irritated princes against *Luther's* followers He blamed him also for prefixing the name, and some notes, of *Erasmus* to certain letters, the intent of which was to shew, that the heretics ought not to be punished. This was exposing *Erasmus* to the court of *Rome*, and to the popish powers For it was saying in effect,

effect, that *Erasmus* had furnished the innovators with weapons to attack their enemies. Nothing could be more true; but *Erasmus* did not like to have such offices done him. Age had made him a coward, if he was not one naturally, and he was afraid to avow principles, which he secretly maintained. He abused *Geldenhaur*, therefore, in very severe terms, compared him to the traitor *Judas*, and, instead of assisting him in his necessity, put him off with raillery. 'But, my dear *Vultu-*
'*rius*,' for so he nick-named him, 'since you have taken
'the resolution to profess an evangelical life, I wonder
'you find poverty uneasy, when St *Hilarion*, not having
'money enough to pay his boat-hire, thought it cause of
'glory, that he had undesignedly arrived at such gospel-
'perfection. St *Paul* also glories, that he knew how
'to abound, and how to suffer need, and that, having
'nothing, he possessed all things. The same apostle
'commends certain *Hebrews*, who had received the gos-
'pel, that they took the spoiling of their goods joyfully.
'Add that, if the *Jews* suffer none to be poor among
'them, how much more does it become those, who boast
'of the gospel, to relieve the wants of their brethren by
'mutual charity. Especially, since evangelical frugality
'is content with very little? Those, who live by the
'spirit, want no delicacies, if they have but bread and
'water. They are strangers to luxury, and feed on fast-
'ing. We read, that the apostles themselves satisfied
'their hunger with ears of corn rubbed in their hands.
'Perhaps, you may imagine, I am jesting all this while,
'—very likely—but others will not think so.'——These
taunts of *Erasmus* give us another trace of his true character. He had not grace to dare the frowns of the world,
and particularly of the great, among whom were most of
his considerable friends, and these were of the *Roman* communion. Whatever he said in favor of Protestantism,
was by pure constraint of the truth. He had very little
court to make in that quarter. Hence, as he was a man
of great wit as well as learning, he was free in his jests
upon the foibles of many excellent men among the Protestants, which served his purpose, with many of the popish party, of concealing his real sentiments, or of en-
joying them without molestation. He had, in short, too
much of that wisdom, which strives to reconcile GOD
and mammon.

Under this life, *Melchior Adam* relates an anecdote of
John Weselus, a physician, as well as divine, who can-

vaffed the doctrine of the facrament full thirty years before the ventilation of that fubject by *Luther* and *Zuinglius*, and wrote notes upon thofe paffages of the New Teftament, in which it occurs. *Wefelus* was alfo firnamed *Bafil* and *Gansfort* He was efteemed of fuch uncommon learning, piety, and judgement, that he was ufually called *lux mundi,* ' The light of the world ,' and, in refpect to any controverted matter (like another *Pythagoras)* it was fufficient for determination to prove, *hoc dixit, hoc docuit, hoc fcripfit,* that *Wefelus* had faid, taught, and wrote it. He vifited moft of the univerfities of note in the Chriftian world, and was an intimate friend of *John de Wefaliâ,* whom we mentioned before, and whom the younger *Spanheim* has miftaken for the fame perfon in his ecclefiaftical hiftory He expected to have fhared perfecution with his learned friend; and probably would, but for the interpofition of *David à Burgundiâ,* then bifhop of *Utrecht,* whom he had greatly ferved in his medical capacity He wrote many tracts, which were printed at *Leipfig, Antwerp,* &c and which have been honored by being placed in the firft clafs of thofe books, piohibited by the church of *Rome* He died in his 70th year. By the writings of this excellent perfon, were the eyes of *Geldenhaur* opened, to the acknowledgement of the truth. And he relates this remarkable circumftance, that in the church of St *Levinus,* in *March* 1520, he [*Geldenhaur*] was informed by *John Oflendorp,* a man advanced in years, that *Wefelus,* long before, had, in converfation with him, when he was but a youth, addreffed him [the faid *Oflendorp,*] in thefe words " My " ftudious young friend, you will live to fee the day, " when the doctrine of our late contentious fchool-di " vines, *Thomas Aquinas, Bonaventure,* and others of the " fame leaven, fhall be exploded by all true teachers of " the Chriftian religion "—How true a prophet he was, the event amply fhewed, for, foon after that time, the Reformation began in *Germany.* — The learned Reader may fee more of this *Wefelus,* in *Bafelius*'s " Sulpitius " Belgicus," and in the writings of *Flaccus Illyricus, Wolfius,* and others.

It is proper to obferve, that *Gerard Geldenhaur* was better known by the name of his country, than by that of his family, for he was ufually called *Gerardus Noviomagus* And *Erafmus,* in his letters to him, gives him no other name.

JOHN

JOHN OECOLAMPADIUS.

THIS *German* Reformer was born at *Winſperg* in *Franconia*, in the year 1482, according to *Bayle*. *Dupin* ſays he was born at *Aufchein* in *Switzerland*, but it is certain he was of *Franconia*. His parents were of a good family and in very competent circumſtances It appears, in the preface to his innotations upon the prophecy of *Iſaiah*, that his grand-father was of *Baſil*, and that his mother was remarkable for the great ſanctity of her life, and liberality to the poor. His father, being (it is ſaid) a merchant, deſigned him for his own profeſſion, but his mother was deſirous of making him a ſcholar, and prevailed on her huſband to ſend him to the college of *Halbrun* He was ſoon removed to the univerſity of *Heidelberg*, where he received the degree of batchelor at fourteen years of age From *Heidelberg*, he was ſent to *Beulogne*, where he ſtudied the civil law ſix months, and then returned to *Heidelberg*, where he applied himſelf to the ſtudy of divinity He aſſiduouſly read the works of *Thomas Aquinas*, *Richard*, and *Gerſon*, but he deſpiſed the ſubtilties of *Scotus*, and ſcorned to follow the humour which prevailed in the univerſities He diſregarded the honorary diſtinctions in the public exerciſes, and only endeavored to obtain the character of a learned man He furniſhed his mind with uſeful knowledge, and abſtained from the diſputations of the ſchoolmen. All his converſation was remarkably ſerious and exemplary, grounded upon the maxim, *Eum, qui proficiat in literis & deficiat in moribus, non proficere, ſed deficere* That he, who increaſes in knowledge without virtue, does not increaſe, but decreaſe. 'Not long after (ſays Dr *Fuller* in his *Abel Redivivus*) he was honored with the title of maſter of arts, in the ſame academy, after which, by the advice of his parents, he went to *Bononia*, with an intent to apply himſelf to the ſtudy of the civil law, but after ſtaying half a year, and finding the air very prejudicial to his health, he returned again to his father, and remained with him till he had recovered his former ſtrength He then went again to *Heidelberg*, where, contrary to the will of his father, he quitted the ſtudy of the civil law, and gave
himſelf

himself wholly to the study of divinity, being led and guided thereto by the love of truth In the performance of which act he imitated the example of that burning lamp of the church *John Chryfoflem*, the fame act being also approved and embraced by *Martin Luther*, *John Calvin*, *Peter Martyr*, *Theodore Beza*, *Lambertus Danæus*, and others.

Here he began to make himself acquainted with fuch fchoolmen, whofe judgement in points of controverfy were moft approved of in that academy, as *Thomas Aquinas*, *Gerfon*, and others, which he ftudied with the utmoft labor day and night, defiring an explanation of fuch diftinctions, as he could not underftand

This more than ordinary induftry procured him a general approbation, together with a certain demonftration of his future worth, not only in *Heidelberg*, but in the adjacent places, infomuch, that he was recommended to that illuftrious prince *Philip*, *Elector Palatine*, who fent for him, and committed his youngeft fons to his tuition, bearing always a reverend refpect to him, for the excellency of thofe parts with which he faw he was endowed After he had been a while in this new employment, he perceived that a courtly life did not fuit his natural inclination, therefore he left it, and returned again (as one that had been long captivated) to the ftudy of divinity

His parents perceiving that his mind was altogether fet on that ftudy, and having no other child but him, they made ufe of thofe means that God had bleffed them with, in order to procure a priefthood for him, in the town where he was born, to which alfo was added the authority of preaching Unto this place he was called, but finding himfelf, after a fortnight's trial, unable to undergo fo laborious an office, he defired leave to return again to *Heidelberg*, that he might acquire a greater meafure of knowledge, and return from thence better qualified to difcharge the important duties of that facred function

Having obtained leave, he changed his refolution and fteered his courfe towards *Tubingen*, and from thence to *Stutgard*, where *Reuchlin* lived, a man famous for his excellent knowledge in the languages. Here he ftayed for a fhort fpace, during which time, he received from *Reuchlin* fome light concerning the *Greek*, in which, by daily ftudy and practice, he fo profited, that, upon his return to *Heidelberg*, he publifhed a *Greek* grammar, where he alfo learned the *Hebrew* by a *Spanifh* teacher

Finding

Finding himself better qualified by the addition of the languages, he returned to his native place, and chearfully labored in his pastoral office, preaching *Christ* so powerfully to them, that he was greatly admired of his auditors, nor did he shine only in found excellent doctrine, but also in a corresponding life and conversation, setting a good example before those to whom he preached, and always associating with such as were famous for religion or learning, especially *Wolfgang Capito*, with whom he was acquainted at *Heidelberg*. Their friendship being here renewed, it continued firm till death.

During the discharge of his holy calling in the place of his nativity, *Wolfgang Capito* was called to *Basil*, to be their public lecturer, which advancement did not cause him at all to forget his old friend *Oecolampadius*, but rather put him upon thinking, how he might be of service in promoting him to some more eminent place, shewing great concern, that so bright a lump of piety should be shut up in so narrow and unregarded a part of the country, wherefore he used all means to persuade the inhabitants of *Basil*, signifying his worth, to invite him to this city, and to confer that dignity upon him, which should correspond with his merit. *Capito* herein succeeded according to his wishes, for they readily agreed, and sent *Oecolampadius* a call to the pastoral office in that city, in 1515. Where, after he had preached, with great applause, for about a twelve-month, he was honored, in the same academy, with the title of doctor in divinity. About the same time *Erasmus Rotterodamus* came to *Basil*, to publish his annotations on the New Testament, for the perfecting of which, he used the assistance of our *Oecolampadius*, on account of the eminency of his parts, as he himself freely confesseth.

When *Erasmus's* work was finished, *Oecolampadius* left *Basil* and went to *Augsburg*, being called by the commons of the cathedral church to preach in that place unto the people. But he remained not long here, partly because of the humble opinion he had of his own abilities, thinking himself insufficient for so important and eminent a station, and, partly because of a degree of melancholy which predominated in his constitution, that disposed him to retirement and solitude. He therefore departed, and entered into the monastry of St *Bridget*, situated without the city of *Augsburg*, but used such caution in making his covenant with the monks, as that he was to have liberty to study, and to believe what he would, and to depart from

them

them when he pleafed, for, faid he, " *Etiamfi fexcentis*
" *juramentis me obftrixero, nequaquam ea fervare potero, fi*
" *quando utilis minifterio verbi fum futurus* " Although I
fhould bind myfelf by innumerable oaths, I fhall not by any
means be able to keep them, if at any time I fhall perceive
that any profit will accrue to the church by my miniftry

The monks, fenfible of their acquifition, received him
joyfully into their fociety, beftowing all things on him
that he defired moft liberally, and particularly acquainted
him with all their privileges   After a few months he was
fo well pleafed, that he purpofed to fpend the reft of his
days in this lazy manner of life   But it pleafed God to
call him out again, and for that end ftirred up his friends,
and efpecially *Capito*, who ferioufly perfuaded and earneftly exhorted him to give over that monaftical life, to
whofe entreaties he yielded, and purpofed to betake himfelf again to the labors of his calling, but, by way of
preparation to his leaving the monaftry, he firft prepared
and publifhed a book of confeffion, in which, in many
particulars, he oppofed the doctrine of the church of
Rome, and thereby rendered his life in danger   The
monks alfo were greatly afraid, left any inconvenience
fhould happen to them on account of his proceedings,
and therefore endeavored to free their monaftry of him
In the mean time, he fharply reprehended them for their
errors, perfuading them to embrace the truth, which fo
exceedingly incenfed them againft him, that they labored
privately with his friends to be more earneft with him to
leave the monaftry.'   Thus far *Fuller*.

Oecolampadius, in 1517, wrote a letter to *Erafmus*,
full of friendfhip and refpect   He had feen *Erafmus* at
Bafil, and informed him, of his own occupations at this
time, for he was collating the *Vulgate* with the *Hebrew*,
and of his connections with *Melancthon*   In 1518, *Erafmus* wrote a friendly letter to *Oecolampadius*, in which he
highly commends *Melancthon*, though, at that time, he
was difpleafed with him, for having fpoken flightly of
his New Teftament.

Oecolampadius had acquired a great reputation for his
fkill in the learned languages, and was held in great efteem
for his preaching   He was fo far from admitting any
change in religion, that he wrote a book againft *Luther*
to prove that the mafs might be called a facrifice   It was
in 1520, when he was thirty-eight years old, that he with-
drew himfelf from the world, and became a monk of the
order of St. *Bridget*, in the monaftry of St. *Laurence*, near
Augfburg.

Augsburg ' I hear, says *Erasmus*, that *Oecolampadius* is
' turned monk I wish he had thought better upon it '
Erasmus approved this step of *Oecolampadius* as little as
his friend *Bilibaldus*, and observes, that a man's discon-
tented and restless temper will pursue him even into the
retirement of a monastry. *Oecolampadius* informed *Erasmus* of his change of life, to which the latter replied,
and wished, that this learned man might find his new
situation answerable to his hopes ' If I thought, says
- *Erasmus*, it would prove so, I could be content to bear
' you company But I fear you will find your expec-
' tations disappointed ' *Oecolampadius* suspected, that
Erasmus disapproved of his entering into a monastic life
Erasmus tells him, it was not so, and that, when he
treated the monks as *Pharisees*, he only meant his own
persecutors, and those, who, under a pretence of religion,
were real foes to it He was willing to suppose, that
Oecolampadius had chosen a society less infected than some
others

Erasmus was not deceived in his conjecture, for, in
1521, *Oecolampadius* began to go over to the reformers.
He had corrected the first edition of the New Testament
published by *Erasmus*, who describes him as a person that
approved the state of life into which he had entered, and
performed his duty However, *Oecolampadius* soon altered
his judgement, and left his monastery in 1522 He retired to *Basil*, in *Switzerland*, where he was made curate,
and preacher of the church of St *Martin*, and he soon
introduced the doctrine of *Luther* Here he was again
advanced by the senate to a pastoral office, with a yearly
stipend, which he performed with great zeal and constancy
to the glory of God and the good of his church, here he
boldly discovered to his auditors those errors, which by
continuance had got firm footing in the church—he
opened up to them the perfection and sufficiency of the
merits of *Christ*—he declared to them the true nature of
faith—and explained to them the true doctrine of charity,
insomuch that they began to waver in their minds about
the authority of the popish religion Whilst he was thus
zealously occupied in these things, there were some who
labored to draw him again to the *Pseudo-Catholick* religion, especially *Johannes Cochlæus*, who, in 1524, wrote
letters to him, in which he declared himself deeply afflicted, to hear that a man, so excellently learned, should
lay aside his coul, and adhere to such heretical opinions,
and at the same time exhorted him to revoke his opinion

N   and

and return to the monaſtry, promiſing him a diſpenſation from the *Pope*, and the favor of the *Prior*, which he had formerly enjoyed   But theſe and ſuch like things were ſlighted by *Oecolampadius*, who, bringing them to the word of God, found they would not endure the trial

In the performance of his paſtoral charge, an aſſiſtant was appointed him by public authority, and now he began to ſettle a more excellent Reformation in the church, commanding the ſacrament of baptiſm to be adminiſtred in the mother tongue, and the ſacrament of the Lord's ſupper to be received in both kinds, he taught that the maſs was not a ſacrifice for the living and the dead, or for thoſe who were tormented in their feigned purgatory, but that perfect ſatisfaction was made for all believers by the paſſion and merits of *Chriſt*   He diſſuaded them from ſprinkling themſelves with holy-water, and from the conſecration of palms, and the like, declaring, that they, who attributed virtue to ſuch things, did exceedingly detract from the glory and power of God   His preachings of the doctrines of *Chriſt* took ſuch deep root in the hearts of his auditors, that they gave a period to many ſuperſtitious actions among them

The foundation of future Reformation was no ſooner laid, than the old dragon began to play his part, and to diſcover his malicious envy and hatred againſt ſuch things as make for the glory of God, either by hindering their proceedings, or by laying ſome foul aſperſion on them   For at that time brake forth that, yet continued, ſacramentary diſſenſion between *Martin Luther* and *Huldericus Zuinglius*, paſtor of the church at *Zurich*, concerning the euchariſt, which cauſed a great diſſenſion between the churches of *Switzerland* and *Saxony*   *Oecolampadius* endeavored, but with little ſucceſs, to heal theſe diſſenſions by publiſhing a book upon the true meaning of theſe words, *Hoc eſt corpus meum*, and by many ſtrong arguments affirmed, that it was a *tropial* phraſe

This intended Reformation was again hindered by *Eckius* and his followers, who taught, 1   That the ſubſtantial body and blood of *Chriſt* was in the ſacrament of the altar   2   That they were truly offered up in the maſs, both for the living and the dead   3   That the virgin *Mary* and the *Saints* were to be worſhipped as interceſſors. 4. That the images of *Jeſus* and the *Saints* were not to be aboliſhed.   5   That after this life there was a purgatory

Theſe poſitions were vehemently oppoſed by *Oecolampadius* at the public diſputation held at *Baden*   The
consequence

consequence of which was, that some of the *Helvetians* or
Switzers, subscribed the arguments of *Eckius*, and others
those of *Oecolampadius*, so that their dissension still remained, nor could it be removed by any means, although
attempted by many worthy instruments of *Christ*, who
encountered many dangers, in order to accomplish an end
so desirable However *Oecolampadius* wrought so with the
people, that liberty of conscience was granted to the citizens in matters of religion

Luther was introducing the Reformation in *Germany*;
while *Zuinglius* began to introduce it in *Switzerland*,
by publicly preaching against the corruptions of the
Roman church. *Oecolampadius* assisted *Zuinglius*, which
made *Erasmus* speak ill of them both, in 1524, and inveigh violently against the morals both of the reformed,
who then began to make a party, and of the Lutherans.
' Shall we, says *Erasmus*, shake off the domination of
' popes and prelates, to submit to worse tyrants than
' they, to scabby madmen, to the scum of the earth?'
He had in view *Otho Brunfield*, and *Farellus*, whom he
could not bear, because they had declared him is a political time-server, who durst not act according to his true
sentiments They had their faults But they applied
themselves closely to the study of the holy scriptures,
and, as far as they understood the gospel, they preached
it with great fervor, and with no less danger If there
was something in their behavior which *Erasmus* could
justly censure, there was also something which he might
have commended.

Oecolampadius and *Zuinglius* had declared openly enough,
that they followed not the sentiments of *Luther* in all
things Yet they spoke of *Luther* with respect, and these
differences were not concerning things essential and fundamental *Erasmus*, who was so well versed in ecclesiastical antiquities, knew that the antient fathers were far
enough from being all of a mind, though they agreed in
the main, and as he pardoned them, he ought to have
extended the same favor to his contemporaries, to men
equally liable to the same defects, and equally worthy of
the same regard and respect.

Erasmus, in 1525, appeared angry with *Oecolampadius*;
because, in the preface to his commentary on *Isaiah*, he
had said of *Erasmus*, *Magnus* Erasmus *noster*, " *Our* great
" *Erasmus*," which might give occasion to the enemies of
the latter to say, that he and *Oecolampadius* were of a mind.
The beginning of this epistle is not worthy of *Erasmus*

' I judge

' I judge not, says he, I leave that to the Lord, who will
' abfolve, or condemn you· But I confider what feveral
' great men think of you, the emperor, the pope, Ferdi-
' nand, the king of *England*, the bifhop of *Rochefter*, car-
' dinal *Wolfey*, and many others, whofe authority it is
' not fafe for me to defpife, and whofe favour it is not
' prudent for me to throw away' What reply this
learned and worthy Reformer made to this ftrange complaint, we know not But he might very juftly have told
Erafmus, that he had done him more honor than he deferved, and that, for the future, he would throw away
no more civilities upon him.

Whilft Lutheranifm was fettling in *Germany*, the doctrine of the new fect, founded in *Switzerland* by *Zuinglius*,
was called, ' Evangelical Truth,' and *Zuinglius* boldly
oppofed the errors of the church of *Rome* Upon this
foundation he continued preaching from the beginning
of the year 1519, not only againft indulgences, but alfo
againft the interceffion and invocation of faints, the facrifice of the mafs, the ecclefiaftical vows, the celebacy
of priefts, and the abftinence from meats However, he
attempted no alteration in the outward and public worfhip
of God till 1523, when he found the magiftrates and citizens of *Zurich* difpofed to caft off the *Romifh* doctrine, and
receive the reformed

About this time, the fect of Anabaptifts fprung up in
Germany, under *Nicholas Stork* and *Thomas Muncer*, who
had been followers of *Luther* They taught, that the
goods of all men ought to be common That all men
fhould be free, and independent That God would no
longer permit the oppreffions of kings, and the injuftice
of magiftrates That the time was come for them to be
depofed, and men of honefty and religion fet up in their
places This feditious doctrine was difperfed in *Germany*,
and caufed a rebellion among the peafants in all places
The firft commotions began in *Swabia*, which foon fpread
throughout all the ten circles of the empire, where vaft
multitudes of peafants plundered the country, robbed and
burnt the churches, monaftries, and caftles, flew the
priefts, monks, and nobility, and made a ftrange defolation in all the ftates The princes of the empire fent a
confederate army againft the rebels, who were defeated
in three battles by *George Truchfes*, count of *Walburg*, and
the elector Palatine *Muncer* ftill kept fome bands of
peafants in *Thuringia*, and made *Mulhaufen* the chief refidence of his *Utopian* kingdom. But *John* elector of
Saxony,

Saxony, *Frederic* prince of *Hesse*, and the duke of *Brunswick*, attacked *Muncer* at *Franckhusen*, where he was defeated, taken prisoner, and executed

While the *German* princes were crushing this rebellion of the peasants, there happened great disputes in *Germany* and *Switzerland* between the *Romish* priests and the Reformers, as also between the Lutherans, Zuinglians, and Anabaptists *Luther* declared himself against the doctrine of *Zuinglius* concerning the Lord's Supper But *Oecolampadius* concurred with *Zuinglius*, and taught the same doctrine at *Basil*

Erasmus resided at this time at *Basil*, and speaks of the slaughter of the peasants in *Germany* But commends the comparative moderation of the reformers of *Basil* He wrote to *Bedda*, to justify a letter which he had formerly sent to the bishop of *Basil* In it we find some remarkable things concerning the sentiments of the reformed, as to the eucharist ' *Caroloftad*, says he, hath brought a most
' formidable tragedy upon the stage He hath persuaded
' the people, that there is nothing in the Lord's Supper
' except bread and wine. *Zuinglius* hath written books
' to support this opinion And *Oecolampadius* hath de-
' fended it with such skill, and hath employed so many
' arguments, and such persuasive eloquence, that, if God
' should not interpose, even the elect may be seduced.
' This city of *Basil* wavers, but it may still be confirmed
' in the faith. I am obliged to quit all my other affairs,
' to enter into this war, although I-have not abilities
' equal to so difficult a task.' It appears not, that *Erasmus* even undertook to confute *Oecolampadius*, and this was probably a mere bragging and threatening, not intended to be put in execution, and thrown out only to please the Romanists He acted very prudently in letting *Oecolampadius* and *Zuinglius* at quiet, and in declining a combat, wherein he would infallibly have been buffeted and disgraced He was ever suspected of favoring this very sentiment, and, in another letter, he bestows the same praises upon this work of *Oecolampadius*

Oecolampadius agreed with *Zuinglius* in the nature of the doctrine, but he gave a different sense of our Lord's words *Zuinglius* placed the figure of these words, ' This
' is my body,' in the verb, ' is,' which he held to be taken for *signifies* *Oecolampadius* laid it upon the noun, *body*, and affirmed that the bread is called, *the body*, by a metonymy, which allows the name of the thing signified to be given to the sign.

The

The Lutherans, in *Swabia* and *Bavaria*, decried the doctrine of *Oecolampadius* in their sermons, which obliged him to dedicate a treatise upon the words of the institution of the Lord's Supper to them, printed at *Strasburg* in 1525, and afterwards in the *German* tongue at *Basil*, where it was at first forbidden. As soon as this formidable book appeared, the magistrates of *Basil* consulted two divines and two lawyers, to know whether the public sale of it might be permitted The divines were *Erasmus* and *Berus*, the lawyers were *Bonifacius Amerbachius* and *Claudius Canzonetta*. *Erasmus* says, that, in giving his answer upon this point, he made no invectives against *Oecolampadius*, and so the book was allowed to be sold He adds, *Zuinglius*, *Oecolampadius*, *Capito*, and *Pellican*, were alarmed at this procedure, and that *Capito* wrote from *Strasburg*, desiring that too much deference might not be paid to the judgement of these four arbitrators

Brentius answered *Occolampadius*, in the name of all the Lutheran ministers of *Swabia*, in a book intitled, *Syngramma Suevicum super verbis cœnæ*, in which he isserted, ' That *Jesus Christ* is present in the sacrament, and in ' the action of the supper That his body and blood are ' received, although in an invisible manner, by faith, as ' remission of sins is received by baptism ' Yet he intimated, that the body and blood of *Christ* are present only by faith, and are received only spiritually. The *Syngramma* was translated by *John Agricola* into the *German* language, and it was approved by *Luther*, who wrote a preface to it, wherein he says, ' The sacramentarians ' had already five or six leaders, the first, *Carolostadius*, ' who applies the pronoun *this*, to the visible body of ' *Jesus Christ*, the second *Zuinglius*, who expounds the ' word *is*, by *signifies*, the third *Occolampadius*, who places ' the figure upon the word, *body*, a fourth perverts the ' order of the words, a fifth alters their places, the sixth ' is not yet produced, who will chicane about the words, ' and, perhaps, we may soon see a seventh, who will ' overthrow all '

Oecolampadius and *Zuinglius* were obliged to defend themselves against *Luther*, who answered them, and wrote a book on purpose upon the eucharist in the *German* tongue, in which he attempted to prove the ubiquity of the body of *Jesus Christ* by this argument ' That in all ' places where the divinity of our Saviour is, there his ' humanity ought also to be present ' *Oecolampadius* and *Zuinglius* immediately replied And *Occolampadius* and

Bucer

Bucer confuted the large confeffion of *Luther* *Brentius* oppofed their opinions in his expofition upon the gofpel of St. *John*, and the other Lutherans perfifted refolutely in the condemnation of it

Erafmus, in 1526, paffed a remarkable judgement upon the fentiments of *Oecolampadius* touching the eucharift, in a letter to *Pirckheimerus*, who had written a book on the fubject againft *Oecolampadius.* ' The opinion of *Oeco-* ' *lampadius*, fays *Erafmus*, would not difpleafe me, if the ' confent of the church did not hinder me from adopting ' it For I difcern not what good an invifible fubftance ' can do there, or how it can profit any one, if it were ' difcernable ' Here the good fenfe of *Erafmus* fuggefted to him plain and ftrong arguments againft either tranfub-ftantiation, or the real and bodily prefence He thought miracles fhould be fo wrought as to be feen, and that they fhould never be wrought in vain *Pirckheimerus* ral-lied *Erafmus* for having faid, that he preferred the fenti-ment of *Oecolampadius* upon the eucharift to that of others *Erafmus* replied, ' I never faid that his fentiment was the ' beft I only faid to fome friends that I could adopt it, if ' the authority of the church had approved it, but that I ' could not quit the fentiments of the church I call the ' church, the confent of the body of Chriftian people '

The confequence of thefe difputes was a divifion among the reformers into two confiderable fects The Luthe-rans, and the Zuinglians, or Sacramentarians The *Saxons* continued firm to the doctrine of *Luther*, and that of *Zuinglius* was received by the *Switzers*, and fome cities of the upper *Germany.*

All this time, the gofpel was preached in no other of the *Swifs* cantons, than *Zurich.* The other twelve can-tons, therefore, appointed among themfelves a difputation, to be held at *Baden*, at which place were affembled the famous *Eckius*, *John Faber*, *Murner*, &c together with the bifhops' legates of *Lucern*, *Bafil*, *Laufanne*, &c The points difputed were, tranfubftantiation, the propitiation offered in the mafs, the invocation of faints, the worfhip of images, and purgatory. *Oecolampadius*, with others, difputed againft thefe thefes, but came to no other con-clufion, than to refer the decifion to the authority of the next general council, when it fhould be convened.

A conference between the Zuinglians, Lutherans, and Papifts, was held at *Bern*, on the feventh of *January*, 1528 This difputation was particularly on the propo-fition of the facrament, and *Oecolampadius*, together with

3 *Zuinglius*,

Zuinglius, *Bucer*, *Capito*, *Blauretus*, and several other Sacramentarians, maintained it against the Papists and Lutherans.   It ended in the abolition of the superstitious
ceremonies of the *Romish* church, throughout the canton
of *Bern*.   The cities of *Constance* and *Geneva* immediately
followed the example But it was not effected in the cities
of *Basil* and *Strasburgh* till 1529 *Oecolampadius* was married this year to the widow of *Cellarius* It is remarkable,
that, after the death of *Oecolampadius*, she was married to
Wolfangus Capito And lastly, to *Martin Bucer* *Erasmus*
laughed at *Oecolampadius* for his marriage, and said, ' He
' hath taken to himself a wife, a pretty girl, probably he
' designs to mortify the flesh Some call Lutheranism a
' tragedy I call it a comedy, where the distress ends in
' matrimony.' Yet he afterwards commended him as a
divine.

The troubles of *Germany* increased, and the emperor
Charles V was obliged to call a diet at *Spire*, in *March*
1529, in the first place, to require the assistance of the
princes of the empire against *Solyman*, who had taken
Buda, and threatened to conquer all *Hungary* And in
the next place, to find out some way to allay the disputes
about religion   The Anabaptists were not permitted to
come to this diet It was also intended to exclude the deputies of *Strasburgh*, and the other cities, who had, contrary to the edicts of the preceding diets, abolished the
mass, and other ceremonies, by their own authority The
Catholics labored all they could to divide the Lutherans,
and Sacramentarians , and had accomplished their design,
if the landgrave of *Hesse* had not prevented their divisions
from breaking out   The Lutheran princes *protested* against
the edict published at the diet of *Spire* , and, for that
reason, were called PROTESTANTS   In the following
year they presented to the emperor, at the diet of *Augsburg*,
their confession of faith ; and entered into a defensive
league, at *Smalcald*, for their common security.

The article of the *protestation*, which concerned the doctrine of the Sacramentarians, was particularly worded,
that the princes might take away the difference between
the Lutherans and *Zuinglians*, without approving the
doctrine of the Sacramentarians. *Oecolampadius* complained, in a letter wrote to *Melancthon*, that *Faber*, bishop of *Vienna*, attempted to procure the condemnation of
their opinions And he desired *Melancthon* to declare on
his side *Melancthon* answered him, that he could not
approve their opinion, as he found no sufficient reason to
depart

depart from the literal fenfe of the words He defired *Oecolampadius* to confider the importance of the queftion in debate And adds, it would be convenient that fome good men fhould confer together upon that head *Oecolampadius* replied to this letter of *Melancthon*, and yielded to the neceffity of fome conferences But obferved, that the perfons to be appointed fhould be men free from paffion, and not of contentious fpirits, otherwife they would be unable to difcover the truth, and only increafe their enmity

The landgrave of *Heffe*, in purfuance of thefe propofitions, invited *Zuinglius* and *Luther* to a friendly conference at *Marpurg*, in *October* following Both parties were unwilling to accept the propofal But *Oecolampadius* prevailed on *Zuinglius*, *Bucer*, and *Hedio*, to embrace it, and repair to *Marpurg*, where they were followed by *Luther*, *Melancthon*, *Juftus Jonas*, *Andreas Ofiander*, *Brentius*, and *Agricola* Before they held their public conference, there was a private meeting between *Oecolampadius* and *Zuinglius*, *Luther* and *Melancthon*. They difagreed upon the article of the Lord's Supper, and debated it before the landgrave himfelf This conference held three days, wherein *Luther* kept clofe to the words of the inftitution, which he affirmed to be full and pofitive for the corporal manducation *Oecolampadius* afferted, that they ought to be underftood metaphorically, and of a fpiritual prefence, but affirmed, that it did not exclude the corporal Many authorities and arguments were produced on both fides Though neither was convinced

Bucer endeavored to reconcile the Lutherans and Zuinglians at the diet of *Augfburg* But *Oecolampadius* difapproved of his articles, and his labours to procure an union were ineffectual In 1531, a civil war broke out between the popifh and proteftant cantons in *Switzerland*, in which *Zuinglius* was killed The fame year the book, publifhed by *Servetus* about the errors concerning the Trinity, was brought into *Switzerland*, where it difgufted feveral of the proteftant divines, as it appears from a letter of *Oecolampadius* to *Bucer*, dated the fifth of *Auguft*, 1531, wherein he fays, " I have feen our friends of *Bern*, " who are very much offended with the book intitled *De* " *Trinitatis Erroribus.* I defire you will acquaint *Luther*, " that this book was printed out of this country, and " without our knowledge. The author impudently af-" firms, that the Lutherans do not underftand the doc-" trine of juftification, and our church will be ill fpoken

O of,

" of, unlefs our divines make it their bufinefs to explode
" him. I befeech you to make an apology for our church,
" at leaft in your confutation infcribed to the emperor.
" He wrefts all the paflages of the fcripture, to prove
" that the Son is not co-eternal and confubftantial with
" the Father, and that the man *Chrift* is the Son of God "

The magiftrates of *Bafil* defired that *Oecolampadius*
would give them his opinion conceining the book of *Servetus*, and the reformei made a fhort difcouife in their
prefence, wherein he fhewed that it was a pernicious
book, but he expreffed himfelf with great moderation.
Oecolampadius alfo wrote two letters to *Servetus* about his
book, wherein he confuted him in a very civil manner,
and intreated him to renounce his errors   He blamed
Servetus for expreffing a greater efteem for *Tertullian*, than
for all the other fathers of the church.   *Servetus* continued an Anti-trinitarian, and fome are of opinion, that
the Reformation would have made a further piogrefs, if
it had not been for that fect.

After the painful fuftaining (fays Dr *Fuller*) of fo many
labors, at home and abroad, he returned to *Bafil*, where
he fpent the remainder of his life in preaching, reading,
writing, publifhing, vifiting the fick, and alfo the care of
certain adjacent churches, till 1531, when it pleafed God
to vifit him with ficknefs, that foon confined him to his
bed, with the greateft appearance of a fpeedy diffolution.
He fent for the paftors of the place, and welcomed them
with a fhort, pithy oration, in which he exhorted them
to remain conftant and firm in the puiity of the doctrine
which they profeffed, becaufe it was agreeable to the word
of God   As to other things, he wifhed them to be lefs
careful, affuring them, that the all-fufficient God would
care for them, and would not be wanting to his church

His children ftanding before him, he took them by their
right-hand, and gently ftroking their heads, he advifed
them to love God, who would be to them in place of a
father

A little before his death, one of his intimate friends coming to him, he afked him, "*What news?*" his friend anfwered, '*None*'   But (faid he) "*I will tell thee news,*" being
afked, what it was? he anfwered, "*Brevi ero apud* CHRIS-
" TUM DOMINUM "   I fhall in a *fhort* time be with
CHRIST my LORD.   And laying his hand upon his breaft,
he faid, "*Here is abundance of light.*"   In the morning before he died, he repeated the fifty-firft pfalm; at the end of
which he added, "*Salva me, Chrifte Jefu,*" fave me, O *Chrift
Jefus*,

Jefus, being the laft words he was heard to fpeak. Thofe prefent in the room praying, continued to pray till he had furrendered his fpirit to his Creator, which he did moft willingly and chearfully, on the firft day of *December*, 1531, and in the forty-ninth year of his age, and was buried, with every mark of refpect and concern, in the fame city.

He was of a meek and quiet difpofition, in the undertaking of any bufinefs, he was very circumfpect, nor was any thing more pleafing to him, than to fpend his time in reading and commenting. He left the following works behind him.

1 Annotations on *Genefis*　2. On *Job*　3 On *Ifaiah* 4 *Jeremiah*　5. *Ezekiel*　6. *Daniel*　7. *Hofea*　8 *Amos* 9 *Jonah*　10 *Micah*, chap. ii.　11 On the three laft prophets.　12 On the Pfalms　13 *Matthew*.　14 *Romans*　15 *Hebrews*　16 1 Epiftle of *John*.　17. Of the genuine fenfe of thefe words, *Hoc eft corpus meum*. 18 An exhortation to the reading of God's word.　19 Of the dignity of the eucharift.　20. Of the joy of the refurrection　21. A fpeech to the fenate of *Bafil*.　22 A catechifm　23 Annotations on *Chryfoftom*　24 Enchiridion to the Greek tongue　25 Againft Anabaptifts. 26. Annotations on the *Acts* of the apoftles, and epiftles to the *Corinthians*　27. Of alms-deeds　28 Againft *Julian* the apoftate　29. Of true faith in *Chrift*　30. Of the praifes of *Cyprian*　31 Of the life of *Mofes*　32 Againft ufury.

His learning and doctrine were fuch, that even cardinal *Sado'et*, on hearing the news of his death, wifhed that he could lawfully grieve for the lofs of him. He was fucceeded by *Ofwaldus Myconius*　*Sleidan* fays, that his grief upon the death of *Zuinglius*, whom he loved extremely, heightened his diforder, and haftened his end　*Verheiden* fays, that there was fcarce ever fuch an inftance of cordial friendfhip, as fubfifted between thefe two great men.

U L R I C U S　Z U I N G L I U S,

THE REFORMER OF SWITZERLAND.

ULRICUS ZUINGLIUS, the famous Reformer of this country, was of a good parentage, and born on the firft of *January*, 1487, at *Wildehaufen* in the county of *Tockenburg*, which is a diftinct republic, in alliance with the *Switzers*, or *Helvetic* body   He was fent to *Bafil*, when he was ten years of age, to receive the firft rudiments of his learning, and from thence he went to *Bern*, where he was taught Greek and Hebrew under *Henry Lupulus*,   He ftudied philofophy at *Vienna*, and divinity at *Bafil*, where he was made doctor in 1505, about which time he heard *Thomas Wittenbach* preach, that the death of *Chrift* is the only price of our redemption, and that indulgences were but a device of the pope   And the next year he began to preach with fuch good fuccefs, that he was elected pastor of *Glaris*, the chief town in the canton of that name   He continued there till 1516, when the reputation which he had acquired by his fermons occafioned him to be called to the *Hermitage*, a place famous for pilgrimages to the virgin *Mary*.

It is reported, that *Zuinglius*, about this time, had a remarkable conference with cardinal *Matthew*, bifhop of *Syon*, in the allied country of *Valais*, concerning the abufes which had crept into the church, and the way to work a Reformation   He had before read the conclufions of the famous *Picus* of *Mirandula*, which had gone far to determine his judgement   He then had heard nothing of *Luther*.

He was foon after invited to *Zurick*, the capital of that canton, to undertake the principal charge of that city, and to preach the word of God among the inhabitants   The method which he followed in his fermons, was to explain a text of holy fcripture, and he began with the gofpel of St. *Matthew*.

About the year 1517, *Martin Luther*, profeffor of *Wittenberg* in *Saxony*, had entered into a difpute againft the cuftom of felling indulgences by the pope, who condemned *Luther*   But he appealed to a council, and went on writing againft the errors of the church of *Rome*

Zuinglius fhewed himfelf at firft very favorable to *Luther*, and recommended his books to his auditors, though he would not preach them himfelf   *Samfon*, a francifcan of *Milan*, was fent by the pope, as general vifitor of his order, to publifh indulgences at *Zurick*   He preached, according to the ufual manner, that the pope had granted an abfolute pardon of fins to fuch as purchafed thofe indulgences, and that they might thereby infallibly deliver fouls out of purgatory.   *Zuinglius* followed the example of *Luther*, by declaiming powerfully againft this francifçan, and againft the indulgences,   *Hugh* bifhop of *Con-*

ftance

stance believed, that *Zuinglius* was displeased only with the abuse, and exhorted him to proceed under his patronage But *Zuinglius* went farther, and solicited that prelate, as also the papal legate in *Switzerland*, to favor the doctrine that he intended to settle, which he called *evangelical truth*. They refused his proposals, and he opposed the popish ceremonies from the year 1519, to 1523, when he found an opportunity of establishing his own doctrine, and of abolishing the superstition of *Rome*

Erasmus was displeased at the violent quarrels which arose about the Lord's Supper among the Reformers, the Zuinglians, and the Lutherans, for, in those days, *Zuinglius* and his adherents were the only men who talked reasonably upon that subject He informed the president of the court at *Mechlin*, in 1522, that the spirit of Reformation increased in *Switzerland*, where there were two hundred thousand who abhorred the see of *Rome* *Erasmus* was not mistaken in this, as the Reformation in *Switzerland* soon afterwards shewed.

The *Switzers* had rendered themselves a very formidable nation, and their bravery was admired in all the *European* states. *Francis* I king of *France* purchased their friendship with a great sum of money in 1515 And, in 1521, concluded a treaty with the *Switzers*, by which he was at liberty to levy any number of *Swiss* troops, from six to sixteen thousand, without asking the consent of the magistrates. The canton of *Zurick* refused to enter into this treaty, because *Zuinglius*, who was in great esteem there, represented that the suffering a foreign prince to raise troops in this manner, was, in effect, selling the blood of their allies and children.

Zuinglius conducted the Reformation in *Switzerland* with as much progress as *Luther* conducted that in *Saxony*, though he carried himself with more moderation and prudence. He propounded his doctrine in his sermons, which he preached four years successively in *Zurick*, and thereby prepared the minds of the people for its reception But he would not attempt to make any alterations in the divine worship without the concurrence of the magistrates, and he caused an assembly to be called for that purpose by the senate of *Zurick*, on the twenty-ninth of *January*, 1523, that the differences among preachers in matters of religion might be composed

The assembly met upon the day appointed, when a great number of the clergy appeared, and the bishop of *Constance* sent three deputies, among whom was *John Faber, bei*, his chief vicar The conful opened the conference by declaring, that the fermons of *Zuinglius* had raifed fo many difputes in their city, that the fenate thought it the beft way to allay thefe differences by appointing a conference before the council of two hundred, to which all the clergy both of the city and country had been fummoned *Zuinglius* replied, " That the light of the gofpel " had been obfcured, and almoft extinguifhed, by human " traditions But that feveral eminent men had lately " endeavoured to reftore it, by preaching the word of " God to the people in its purity That he was one of " that number, and, like them, had been treated as an " heretic and feducer, though he had, for five years paft, " taught only what was contained in the holy fcripture. " That it was for this reafon he had defired to give an " account of his doctrine before the fenate of *Zurick*, and " the bifhop of *Conftance*. That he thanked the fenate " for granting him this favor, and that he had drawn his " doctrines into fixty-feven propofitions, which he was " fully perfuaded were agreeable to the gofpel And he " was ready to anfwer for himfelf, if any perfon would " accufe him of error or herefy."

The doctrines contained in thofe fixty-feven propofitions, may be reduced to thefe following articles That the gofpel is the only rule of faith The church is the communion of faints We ought to acknowledge no other head of the church but *Jefus Chrift* All traditions fhould be rejected. There is no other facrifice but that of *Jefus Chrift* upon the crofs And the mafs is no facrifice, but a commemoration of the facrifice of *Chrift*. We have need of no other interceffor with God than *Jefus Chrift*. All forts of meat may be eaten at all times. The habits of monks fmell of hypocrify. Marriage is allowed to all men, and no man is obliged to make a vow of chaftity, nor are priefts at all obliged to live unmarried Excommunication ought not to be inflicted by the bifhop alone, but by the whole church, and notorious offenders only ought to be excommunicated. The power which the pope and bifhops affume to themfelves, is a piece of pride that has no foundation in the fcripture. God alone can forgive fins For confeffion of fin to a prieft, is only to beg his ghoftly advice, and works of fatisfaction proceed from human tradition The fcripture does not teach us, that there is fuch a place as purgatory. The character which the facraments are faid to imprefs is of a modern invention. The fcripture acknowledges none for priests, or bishops, but such as preach the word of God Lastly, he promised to deliver his judgement about tythes, the revenues of the church, the condition of infants not baptized, and about confirmation, if any person desired to dispute with him upon these points.

Zuinglius exhorted the magistrates of *Zurick* to leave their citizens no longer in doubt of what concerned their salvation The council then declared, that if any person present had any thing to alledge against *Zuinglius*, he had free liberty to speak. *Zuinglius* made a public challenge three times But he met with no opponent, except *Faber*, who inadvertently mentioned the intercession of saints, which gave *Zuinglius* an opportunity of opposing that doctrine, and drawing his adversary into a dispute

Faber made a very general discourse about the authority of the church and councils, which had condemned the antient heretics, and lately *Wickliffe*, *Huss*, and *Jerom* of *Prague*, whose doctrines were now revived He said, that the intercession of saints was a doctrine, which had been long settled in the church, and authorized by the practice of all nations But concluded, that such questions ought to be debated only among divines, as in the universities of *Paris*, *Cologne*, or *Louvain*

Zuinglius replied, that he desired of him only to resolve, whether the scripture made any mention of the intercession of saints? If councils were infallible? Whether traditions and customs ought not to be rejected, when they are not grounded upon the authority of holy scripture? And whether it is not clearly expressed, that *Jesus Christ* is our only Mediator?

From this question, they passed to another concerning the celibacy of priests, and these two questions were the subject of a long contest, between the deputies of the bishop of *Constance* on the one part, and *Zuinglius*, *Leo Juda*, and some other ministers on the other The former supported their opinions by tradition, the authority of the church, and the canons of the councils But the latter would abide only by the holy scripture.

The debates ended at noon, and the senate published an edict, whereby it was ordained, ' that *Zuinglius* should ' continue to teach and preach the doctrine of the gospel, ' and the word of God, in his usual manner, and all ' pastors and teachers, both in the city and country, were ' forbid to teach any thing that could not be proved by ' the gospel, and holy scripture, and they were enjoined ' to forbear all accusations of heresy, or other crimes.'

Faber

Faber entered a protestation against this edict, and said, he would demonstrate, that the doctrine of *Zuinglius* was contrary to that of St *Paul* *Zuinglius* challenged him to do it, and promised him a cheese of *hare's milk*, if he could prove any of his doctrines erroneous, by the gospel, or holy scripture.

It is easy to imagine, after the publication of this edict, that the doctrine of *Zuinglius* became general throughout all the canton of *Zurick,* under the name of ' *evangelical* ' *truth.*' The external worship was contrary to the new doctrine; for images remained, and mass was celebrated, in the churches, which could not be abolished without authority *Zuinglius* was determined to perfect his design, and engaged the senate to call a new assembly, to which they invited the bishops of *Constance, Coire,* and *Basil,* the university of *Basil,* and the other twelve cantons of *Switzerland,* to send their deputies, and make the assembly of greater authority.

The senate assembled again, on the twenty-sixth of *October,* 1523, when *Joachim Vadianus, Sebastian Hoffman,* and *Christopher Chapplerus,* were chosen arbitrators of the dispute *Zuinglius* and *Leo Judæ* were respondents And all persons present were allowed to object what they pleased The first question propounded was, ' What the ' church is, and where it is ?' *Zuinglius* distinguished, and said, " That the church was taken in two senses " First, For' the congregation of all true Christians, of " whom *Jesus Christ* is the head Secondly, For the par- " ticular congregation of Christians in one place " And he maintained, that the congregations of cardinals and bishops were not the church. He declared, his disregard of the councils, his contempt of the pope's decree, and his neglect of the emperor's edict *Leo Judæ* opposed the use of images by texts of the Old Testament, whereby it was forbidden the Jews to make or worship any graven image, and by such places of the New Testament, wherein the adoration of idols was prohibited *Zuinglius* maintained, that images were not to be tolerated, and that the law of God forbad them absolutely. The resolution of this first conference was, that no images were to be allowed among Christians

In the second conference, they discoursed about the mass, which *Zuinglius* maintained was no sacrifice The three arbitrators, appointed by the senate, gave sentence, that ' The abuses of images and masses were sufficiently ' proved by the word of God, therefore, they left it to ' the

' the fenate to enquire how they might be abolifhed with-
' out offence' This was the refult of the conference,
which was follov ed with an edict, whereby it was forbidden to the priefts and monks to make any public proceffions, to carry the holy facrament, or elevate it in the
church to be worfhipped. Relics were taken out of
churches. It was ordered, that organs fhould not be
played, or bells be rung, that palm-branches, falt, or
tapers fhould not be bleffed, and that extreme unction
fhould not be adminiftered to the fick. Thus, part of the
outward worfhip and ceremonies of the church of *Rome*
were abolifhed in the canton of *Zurich*.

The other twelve cantons were diffatisfied with this
edict, which was maintained by the canton of *Zuric*,
whofe fenators ordered all the images to be pulled down.

Zuinglius himfelf relates in his book *Coroñas de Eucha-
riftiâ, Oper part* 11 *fol* 249. that when one of his opponents, in the conference, challenged him to fhew, in
any place of fcripture, where the verb *eft* (is) ftood for
fignificat (fignifies) without an evident tropical allufion,
fuch as where *Chrift* fays, *the feed is the word of God*, in
which place, *is*, evidently means *fignifies*, or, *I* AM *the
door, the vine*, &c. which are tropical expreffions at firft
fight, but that *hoc eft corpus meum* did not neceffarily and
obvioufly imply, *this* SIGNIFIES *my body*, or that our Lord
ufed in that cafe a figurative way of fpeech. *Zuinglius*
was puzzled at the time, and (as he fays) for thirteen
days afterwards, in which he was continually revolving
the matter in his mind, and turning over his bible incef-
fantly, but without the explicit fatisfaction he defired.
At length, in his fleep, he dreamed that he was in difputation with his adverfary, who preffed him very clofe with
this circumftance, infomuch that he feemed to have given
up the point, and to be ftruck dumb before the audience.
While he was in this perplexity, he faw in his vifion a
form approaching to him, and faying, 'O thou unwife
' one, why doft not anfwer to him the word of the Lord
' in *Exod* xii 11 where it is exprefsly and pofitively
' faid of the *Lamb* that was eaten, IT IS *the Lord's* PASS-
' OVER, or *paffage out of* Egypt.'—He awoke from his
fleep, and with this proof, in the next day's difcourfe, he
refuted the objection of his adverfary, fhewing that, in
this text, the word *is* neceffarily means *fignifies*. The
elder *Spanheim* could not but believe, from the occafion,
the matter, and the ufe, that this vifion was θεόπεμπτ,
fent from God, and the excellent *Witfius* inclines to the

P   fame

fame opinion, confirming it by the modeft and fober manner in which *Zuinglius* himfelf relates the ftory. See WITSII *Mifcell. Sacr. Lib* I *c* 24

About this time, *Zuinglius* wrote feveral books in defence of his doctrine. The firft was a large explication of the propofitions, which he had delivered in the firft conference. The fecond was a difcourfe dedicated to all the cantons of *Switzerland*, exhorting them not to impede the progrefs of his doctrine, nor to be diffatisfied with the marriages of priefts. The third was an anfwer to the advice, which the bifhop of *Conftance* had given to the fenate of *Zurick*, to oppofe innovations. He alfo wrote a book about the certainty and evidence of the word of God. Two treatifes againft the canon of the mafs. A letter concerning the grace of *Jefus Chrift*. And an anfwer to a book written by *Jerom Emfer*.

The bifhop of *Conftance*, in 1524, publifhed a book in vindication of images and the mafs. This was prefented to the fenate of *Zurick*, and *Zuinglius* anfwered it in their name.

Zuinglius, Leo Judæ, Engelhardus, Megander, and *Myconius*, on the eleventh of *April*, 1525, petitioned the fenate of *Zurick* to abolifh the mafs, and the adoration of the elements in the facraments, in confequence of which, the fenate made a decree, whereby the mafs was abolifhed for ever, and the facrament was ordered to be received after another manner.

The form of celebrating the Lord's Supper prefcribed by *Zuinglius*, differed more from the church of *Rome*, than the form prefcribed by *Luther*. He ordered, " that the " table fhould be covered with a white cloth, on which " were to be fet the patin full of leavened bread, and " veffels filled with wine. That the minifter and dea- " cons fhould ftand by the table, where they were to " exhort the people to approach with reverence, after " which, one of the deacons fhould read the inftitution " of the Lord's Supper, taken out of the epiftle to the " *Corinthians*, and another fhould repeat a part of the " fixth chapter of St *John*. That the minifter fhould " then read the creed, and exhort all the communicants " to examine their own confciences, that they might not " be guilty of the body and blood of the Lord by re- " ceiving them unworthily. That the minifter and peo- " ple fhould then kneel, and fay the Lord's Prayer; " after which, the minifter fhould take the bread in his " hands, and deliver the words of the inftitution of the " Lord's

" Lord's Supper with an audible voice, then give the
" bread and wine to the deacons, who should diftribute
" them to the people, while the minifter fhould read the
" diſcourſe which our Saviour had with his diſciples be-
" fore his paſſion, as related in the goſpel of St. *John* "
This was the form of adminiftering the facrament, which
Zuinglius appointed to be uſed. He maintained, in his
doctrine concerning the facrament, that theſe words of
Jeſus Chriſt, " *This is my body, this is my blood,* are to be
" underftood thus *This ſignifies my body and blood, this*
" *bread and this wine are a figure of my body and blood;*
" *this is a teſtimony and pledge, that my body ſhall be deli-*
" *vered up, and broken for you upon the croſs, and my blood*
" *ſhall be ſhed for you* " From whence it follows, that
not only the bread and wine exift after confecration, but
alſo, that the body and blood of *Jeſus Chriſt* are not prefent in the Euchariſt, and that the bread and wine are
only a figure of the body and blood of *Jeſus Chriſt,* communicated in a ſpiritual manner by faith

In 1525, he publiſhed his book *De vera et falſa Religione,*
which was dedicated, and preſented to *Francis* I of
France

Luther declared againſt the doctrine of *Zuinglius,* which
Oecolampadius embraced *Zuinglius* was leſs concerned at
the writings of the catholics than of *Luther,* who publiſhed
a ſermon at *Wittenberg* about the body and blood of *Jeſus
Chriſt,* which he made againſt the giddy-headed ſpirits,
contra ſpiritus vertiginoſos, as he called the Zuinglians A
confutation of this ſermon was wrote by *Zuinglius,* who
ſent letters to *Nuremberg* upon that ſubject He alſo anſwered the letters which *Pelicanus,* and *Urbanus Regius,*
wrote againſt him And he compoſed a work, entitled,
The Lord's Supper In 1527, he drew up an apology
againſt a book written by *Jacobus Strauſſius,* wherein he
explained the Lord's Supper at large, dedicated to *Luther,*
and anſwered his ſermon at *Wittenberg* againſt the Sacramentarians

Bucer wrote ſeveral tracts in defence of the Zuinglians,
and aſſiſted *Oecolampadius* in confuting the large confeſſion
of *Luther* The papiſts found, that the Zuinglians were
more to be feared than the Lutherans, and exerted their
utmoſt endeavors to prevent the ſpreading of that ſect in
the popiſh cantons of *Switzerland*

The Reformation gained ground, notwithſtanding the
remonſtrances of the emperor, the biſhops of *Conſtance,
Baſil, Lauſanne,* and *Sion,* and eight of the cantons.

P 2   Another

Another general aſſembly was convened at *Bern* by *Zuinglius*, on the ſeventh of *January* 1528, when the doctrines of the church of *Rome* were condemned The opinions of *Zuinglius* were then introduced all over *Bern*, which example was imitated by the cantons of *Baſil* and *Schaffhauſen* This occaſioned ill blood But the imprudence of the inhabitants of *Underwald*, who protected the revolters from *Bern*, conduced moſt to the embroiling the cantons The *Zurickeſe* armed themſelves, and were on the point of attacking the five cantons of *Lucern*, *Uri*, *Switz*, *Zug*, and *Underwald* But, by an agreement made at *Caſſel*, it was determined, ‘ that there ſhould be ‘ liberty of conſcience throughout *Switzerland* And that ‘ the five cantons ſhould renounce their alliance with ‘ the emperor *Ferdinand*’ *Henry* VIII of *England* employed *Grynæus* to try what *Zuinglius*, *Oecolampadius*, and *Bucer*, thought of his marriage with his queen *Catharine*. *Zuinglius* and *Oecolampadius* were of opinion, that the iſſue by a marriage *de facto*, grounded upon a received miſtake, ought not to be illegitimated

There was great altercation between the Lutherans and Zuinglians, before the citizens of *Bern* aboliſhed popery. *Conſtance*, *Geneva*, *Baſil*, and *Straſburg*, alſo threw off the yoke, and pulled down the altars and images in all places But *Bucer* was embarraſſed between the Lutherans and Zuinglians, and endeavored to procure a good underſtanding between them in vain

It muſt however be obſerved, that the only principal ground of difference was upon the ſubject of the ſacrament, and that, in this reſpect alſo, both parties were far enough from the *Romiſh* opinion In the other material points, both Lutherans and Zuinglians were ſufficiently agreed, as appears by the acts of the ſynod held at *Marpurg*, under the auſpices of the landgrave of *Heſſe*, in the year 1529, where both *Luther* and *Zuinglius* were preſent, and formed an agreement upon the following articles . *viz* 1 On the Unity and Trinity of the Godhead. 2 On the incarnation of the Word. 3 On the paſſion and reſurrection of *Chriſt* 4 On the article of original ſin 5 On the article of faith in *Chriſt* 6 That this faith doth not ſpring from human merit, but only from the gift of God 7 That, through this faith, believers have righteouſneſs On ſeveral other articles, reſpecting the baptiſm of infants, on confeſſion, on good works, on the civil power, on traditions, &c And, laſtly, concerning the Lord's Supper, they mutually agreed, that it ought to be

adminiſtered

administered in both kinds, that the mass is no such work or sacrifice, as to obtain grace either for quick or dead; that the sacrament is a true sacrament of the body and blood of *Christ*, that the spiritual manducation of his body and blood is the true receiving of this sacrament and necessary for all believers, and that the Spirit of GOD confers grace in the faithful use of it. In fine, as *Martin Bucer* observed, there was a greater difference in charity between both parties, than in the true state of the doctrine. There were, indeed, warm men on both sides, who, however sincerely pious and meaning what was right, could not yield up their own formulary, though undeniably essential to the peace of the church and the spreading interest of the protestant religion.

The diet of *Augsburg* was held in 1530, to consult about matters of religion, and the war against the *Turks*. The protestant princes publicly read their confession of faith, and the catholic divines drew up a confutation of it. The protestants presented an ' apology for their ' confession to the emperor, who would not receive it, ' though it was drawn up by *Melancthon*, with his usual ' moderation.'

The Zuinglians also presented their confession of faith to the emperor, in the name of the cities of *Strasburg*, *Constance*, *Memmingen*, and *Landau*. It was drawn up by *Bucer* and *Capito*, but contained nothing about the Trinity, or Incarnation, that was contrary to the doctrine of the *Romish* church. They held, ' That men are justified ' only by the merits of *Jesus Christ*, and faith. That ' good works are necessary, and so is obedience to ma- ' gistrates. They commended fasting and prayer, but ' condemned the worship and intercession of saints, vows, ' and the monastic state. They allowed of such tradi- ' tions as are not contrary to the word of God, and de- ' fined the church to be a congregation of true believers. ' They allowed of only two sacraments, baptism, and ' the Lord's Supper, and that God unites Christians in ' an outward communion by those sacred symbols, not ' only because they are visible signs of invisible grace, but ' also because they are testimonies of our faith. They ' disapproved of private masses, and confession. And ' concluded with a long invective against the court of ' *Rome*.'

This confession of faith was more unacceptable than that of the Lutherans, and the emperor ordered *Faber* and *Eckius* to draw up an answer to it, which was read in

I   a full

a full diet, and the emperor commanded the *Zuinglians*
to renounce their doctrine *Zuinglius* foon after wrote a
letter to the proteftant princes in defence of his opinions
againft *Eckius*, and particularly concerning the facrament
of the Euchariſt, wherein he exprefsly denied the real prefence, concerning which the Lutherans had not been fo
explicit, for *Bucer* drew up this article of the Supper in
fuch ambiguous terms, that the Lutherans might not be
condemned *Melancthon* and *Brentius* publifhed a treatife,
to fhew, that the doctrine of the *Zuinglians* was entirely
different from the Lutherans, whatever ambiguity there
was in their words.

Zuinglius alfo fent to the diet a particular confeſſion of
faith, comprized in twelve articles, relating to the Trinity
and incarnation, the fall of man, and neceſſity of grace,
original fin, baptifm of infants, the church, the facraments, ceremonies, the miniſtry of the gofpel, the authority of magiſtrates, and purgatory

The emperor publifhed the decree of the diet againft the
proteftants and facramentarians, which neither obeyed
But the proteftant princes, and the reformed cantons of
Switzerland, entered into a confederacy to defend themfelves and their religion, againft the emperor and the
Roman catholic powers. This was the league of *Smalkald*, concluded in 1531, upon the fuccefs of which the
proteftant religion depended.

The fame year a civil war began in *Switzerland*, between the five catholic cantons, and thofe of *Zurick* and
Bern. The Zurickefe were defeated in their own territories, with the lofs of four hundred men *Zuinglius*,
who accompanied them, was killed in this action, in the
forty-fourth year of his age Great cruelty was fhewn
to his corpfe, and it was attempted to be burnt.

Much has been faid by the enemies of *Zuinglius*, refpecting his appearance on the field of battle, but it may
be obferved, what *Oecolampadius* and *Sleidan* have urged
in his defence, that it was the cuftom of the Zurickefe, from
time immemorial, when they engaged in war, to have the
chief miniſter of their church attendant upon them, both
to preach to the people and to pray for a bleſſing upon
their arms. And, it muſt be owned in this view, it could
be no more improper for him, than for the chaplains
who are now appointed to accompany regiments in their
campaigns, or to fail in fhips of war. Perhaps, no order of men require inſtruction in religious duties more
than foldiers, who have always, in actual fervice, the
                                              profpect

profpect of death before them, and who certainly cannot
be the worfe, either in morality or courage, for being
prepared for it. It may be added, that *Zuinglius* went
not forth of his own accord He was abfolutely enforced
and commanded by the fenate, in point of duty He did
not go forth ' as a captain or commander of the army,
' but as a good citizen and faithful paftor, who would
' not forfake his friends in their greateft peril, nay, he
' went (fays *Melchior Adam*) as a perfuader to peace. About
' three hundred and eighty of his friends fell with him '
The action was on the 11th of *October,* in the year 1531.
'The compilers of the Biographical Dictionary (fays a
' late able writer) in tranflating fome of *Zuinglius*'s dying
' words, have been guilty of an over-fight, which does
' no more honour to their precifion, than juftice to the
' Chriftian heroifm of that great man Upon receiving
' his death's wound, fay they, and falling, he was heard
' to utter thefe words, *What a misfortune is this?* &c.
' Rather, what a *misfortune* is it, when fine fentiments
' are murdered in the relating! — The fact was this.
' During the hurry of the fight, *Zuinglius,* overwhelmed
' by the prefs of the rufhing enemy, was thrice thrown
' down, and recovered his feet as often At laft, a wea-
' pon, doomed to extinguifh one of the moft valuable
' lives that ever added lufture to religion and learning,
' entering under his chin, transfixed his throat. The
' holy man, falling firft on his knees, and then finking
' to the ground, uttered thefe noble fentences *Ecquid*
' *hoc infortunii?* CAN THIS BE CONSIDERED AS A CALA-
' MITY? *Age, corpus quidem occidere poffunt, animam non*
' *poffunt* WELL! THEY ARE ABLE, INDEED, TO SLAY
' THE BODY BUT THEY ARE NOT ABLE TO KILL THE
' SOUL Could any thing be more truly Chriftian, more
' divinely triumphant, more fublimely philofophic? His
' body being found by the papifts, among the flain, they
' burned it to afhes Which occafioned thefe elegant
' verfes, confecrated to his memory by *Beza* '

> ZUINGLIUS *arderet gemino quum fanctus amore,*
> *Nempe* DEI *imprimis, deinde etiam* PATRIÆ,
> *Dicitur in folidum fe devoviffe duobus*
> *Nempe* DEO *imprimis, deinde etiam* PATRIÆ.
> *Quàm benè perfolvit fimul iftis vota duobus!*
> *Pro patriâ exanimis, pro pietate cinis!*

After this battle, matters were accommodated And it
was agreed, that the two parties, for the future, fhould
not

not moleft each other on a religious account, and that the
papifts fhould renounce then league with the emperor,
and the Zuinglians the fame with the landgrave of *Heffe*.
Their contentions were renewed in 1577, which ended in
acknowledging *Geneva* to be a free ftate by the duke of
Savoy And, by the treaty of *Weftphalia*, in 1648, the
emperors of *Germany* loft all authority in *Switzerland*.
The abbot of St *Gall* renewed the difpute in 1712, which
was ended, after the battle of *Wilmerguen*, by the treaty
of *Rofchau* in 1714.

Peace was fettled in *Germany* by the treaty of *Nuremberg*, in 1532 But thefe religious difputes broke out
again in 1612 The proteftants were affifted by *Guftavus
Adolphus* king of *Sweden*, who loft his life at *Lutzen* in
1632 And the proteftant intereft was very much ftrengthened by the treaties of *Weftphalia* and *Ofnabrug* in 1648

Zuinglius was fucceeded by *Henry Bullinger*, and his
doctrine was vindicated againft *Luther* by *Bucer* The
long difputes between the Lutherans and Zuinglians were
concluded in 1538, by a pretended treaty of accord But
this was a work of difguife and diffimulation, and as little durable as it was fincere. The *Switzers* continued in
the opinion of *Zuinglius* But the cities of *Strafburg*,
Augfburg, *Memmingen*, and *Landau*, became Lutherans,
by keeping literally to the expreffions of the articles of
agreement.

The works of *Zuinglius*, and an apology for his doctrine, were publifhed by *Rodolphus Gualterus* The *Switzers* paid the utmoft gratitude to his memory, and his
remains were interred with all the pomp of a *Grecian*
funeral, for a man who had devoted his life to the fervice
of his country

Zuinglius and *Oecolampadius* were more efteemed by the
learned men of their time, than any other of the Reformers, becaufe they had more moderation *Zuinglius*
was fuccefsful againft the enthufiafts, called Anabaptifts
And fome have confidently affirmed, that he was for putting them to death, and faid, " Let him who dippeth
" again, be dipped, that is, drowned " But it is a very
improbable ftory, fince *Minius Celfus* himfelf, namely,
Sebaftian Caftalio, whofe teftimony in points of this kind
ought to be credited, having publicly defended his pofi-
tion, ' That heretics ought not to be put to death,'
appeals to the authority of *Zuinglius*, and affirms, that the
Anabaptifts at that time never fuffered on account of their
                                                    opinions,

opinions, as heretics, but of their evil actions, as perjured and seditious rebels

The first Anabaptists shewed a surprizing mixture of folly, stupidity, wickedness, and religious frenzy An immoral fanatic is of all animals the most dangerous to the church and state, and the history of these Anabaptists is an everlasting monument of the mischief, which such people can perpetrate

Pellicanus threatened *Erasmus* with an attack from *Zuinglius*, and *Erasmus* declared that he feared not ten *Zuinglius*'s Yet he did not care to engage in combat with this one *Zuinglius* about the eucharist, and, from the manner in which he had spoken of the performance of *Oecolampadius*, it appears, that he thought it not so easy a matter to refute these divines Very true it is, that the struggles of the Reformers drew a terrible persecution upon them and their successors But it was through the fault of that church, to which *Erasmus* wanted to remain united, and which would hear of no amendments Nor is it to be forgotten, that *Erasmus* could easily have embraced the sentiments of *Zuinglius* and *Oecolampadius*, if his mother the church would have given him leave

Zuinglius had skill in music, and a love for it He always studied standing, and was always a great student. He received a most courteous letter from pope *Adrian* VI. and might have had any favors, if he had declared himself a friend to the see of *Rome*

He wrote four volumes in folio viz TOME the first, containing, 1. A work of articles 2. An exhortation to the whole state of *Switzerland* 3 A supplication to the *bishop* of CONSTANCE 4 Of the certainty and purity of GOD's word. 5. An answer to VALENTINE of the authority of the fathers 6 Institutions for youth 7. A good shepherd. 8. Of justice divine and human. 9. Of providence

TOME the second, 1. Of baptism. 2 Of original sin. 3 Of true and false religion 4 An epistle to the princes of GERMANY. 5. Of the Lord's Supper 6 Of Christian faith, written to the FRENCH king.

TOME the third, 1. Commentaries on GENESIS 2. EXODUS 3 ISAIAH 4 JEREMIAH. 5. The PSALTER out of *Hebrew* into *Latin*.

TOME the fourth, 1. Annotations on the four EVANGELISTS 2. History of our SAVIOUR's *passion* 3 Annotations on ROMANS 4 CORINTHIANS 5 PHILIPPIANS. 6. COLOSSIANS 7 THESSALONIANS 8. HEBREWS. 9 JAMES. 10. The first epistle of JOHN.

Q   BILNEY.

THOMAS BILNEY.

THOMAS BILNEY, an *Englifhman*, was brought up at the univerfity of *Cambridge* from a youth, where he became fo great a proficient in all the liberal fciences, that in a fhort time he commenced batchelor in both laws But being enlightened by the Spirit of *Chrift*, and his heart endued with the knowledge of better things, he left the ftudy of man's laws, and devoted himfelf wholly to the ftudy of divinity Mr *Bilney*, in a *Latin* letter to *Cuthbert Tonftal*, bifhop of *London*, gives the following account of his converfion Comparing the priefts and friars to the phyficians, upon whom the woman, vexed twelve years with a bloody iffue, fpent all that fhe had, and found no help, but was ftill worfe and worfe, till at laft fhe came to *Chrift*, and was healed by Him —
" O (faid he) the mighty power of the Moft High ! which
" I alfo, a miferable finner, have often tafted and felt,
" whereas before, I fpent all I had upon thofe ignorant
" phyficians, infomuch that I had little ftrength left in
" me. But, at laft, I heard of JESUS, and that was
" when the New Teftament was tranflated by *Erafmus*,
" for at that time I knew not what it meant But look-
" ing into the New Teftament, by God's fpecial provi-
" dence, I met with thofe words of the apoftle St *Paul*,
" *This is a true faying, and worthy of all acceptation, that*
" Jefus Chrift *came into the world to fave finners, whereof*
" *I am chief.* O moft fweet and comfortable fentence
" to my foul ! This one fentence, through God's in-
" ftruction and inward working, did fo exhilarate my
" heart, which before was wounded with the guilt of my
" fins, and almoft in defpair, that immediately I found
" wonderful comfort and quietnefs in my foul, fo that
" my bruifed bones leaped for joy
" After this, the fcriptures became fweeter to me than
" the honey and the honey-comb For by them I learned,
" that all my travels, faftings, watchings, redemption of
" maffes, and pardons, without faith in *Chrift*, were but,
" as St *Auguftine* calls them, A hafty running out of the
" right way, and as fig-leaves, which could not cover
" *Adam's*

" *Adam*'s nakednefs —For as *Adam* could find no reft to
" his guilty foul, till he believed in the promife of God,
" That *Chrift*, the feed of the woman, fhould tread upon
" the ferpent's head, fo neither could I find deliverance
" from the fharp ftings and bitings of my fins, till I was
" taught of God that leffon which *Chrift* fpake of in the
" third chapter of *John* As Mofes *lifted up the ferpent in*
" *the wildernefs, even fo muft the Son of Man be lifted up*
" *That whofoever believeth in him, fhould not perifh, but have*
" *everlafting life.*

" As foon as, by the grace of God, I began to tafte
" the fweets of this heavenly leffon, which no man can
" teach, but God alone, who revealed it to *Peter*, I beg-
" ged of the Lord to increafe my faith And at laft I
" defired nothing more, than that I, being fo comforted
" by him, might be ftrengthened by his holy Spirit and
" grace, that I might teach finners his ways, which are
" mercy and truth, and that the wicked might be con-
" verted unto him by me, who alfo was once myfelf a
" finner indeed And it is my only comfort in thefe my
" afflictions, that this is what I laboured at before the
" cardinal, &c when *Chrift* was blafphemed in me, whom
" with my whole power I do teach and fet forth, to be
" *made of God the Father unto us wifdom, righteoufnefs,*
" *fanctification, and redemption,* and finally our fatisfaction.
" *—Who was made fin for us* (that is to fay, a facrifice for
" fin) *that we through him fhould be made the righteoufnefs*
" *of God —Who became accurfed for us, to redeem us from*
" *the curfe of the law —Who alfo came not to call the righ-*
" *teous, but finners to repentance* The righteous, I fay,
" who falfly think themfelves fo to be, *for* ALL *have fin-*
" *ned, and come fhort of the glory of God,* all mankind was
" grievoufly wounded in him who fell among thieves
" between *Jerufalem* and *Jericho*, therefore we *are jufti-*
" *fied freely by God's grace, through the redemption that is in*
" *Jefus* Chrift.

" And therefore with all my power I teach, that all
" men fhould firft acknowledge their fins, and condemn
" them, and that they fhould then hunger and thirft after
" that righteoufnefs, of which St *Paul* fpeaks, *the righ-*
" *teoufnefs of God by faith of Jefus Chrift is unto all, and*
" *upon all them that believe, for there is no difference For*
" *all have finned, and come fhort of the glory of God,* and
" *are juftified freely by his grace, through the redemption that*
" *is in* Jefus Chrift. For which whofoever doth hunger

Q 2   " and

" and thirst, without doubt, they shall be so satisfied that
" they shall not hunger and thirst for ever

" But as this hunger and thirst used to be quenched
" with the fulness of man's righteousness, which is
" wrought through the faith of our own elect and chosen
" works, as pilgrimages, buying of pardons, offering of
" candles, elect and chosen fasts, and often superstitious,
" and indeed all kind of voluntary devotions (as they call
" them) against the express word of God, (*Deut* iv 2)
" which says, *Ye shall not add unto the word which I com-*
" *mand you, neither shall you diminish ought from it* There-
" fore, I say, often have I spoke of these works, not
" condemning them (as God is my witness) but reprov-
" ing their abuse, shewing, even unto children, how far
" they might be used lawfully, but exhorting all men
" not so to use them, as to be satisfied in them, lest they
" should loath or grow weary of *Christ*, as many do "

In another letter to the same bishop he thus writes,
" What shall we then say of that learning, which hath
" now so long time reigned and triumphed, so that no
" man hath once opened his mouth against it? Shall we
" think it sound doctrine? Truly iniquity did never
" more abound, nor charity was never so cold And
" what shall we say is the cause? Has it been for want
" of preaching against the vices of men, and exhorting
" to charity? That cannot be, for many learned and
" great clerks sufficiently can witness to the contrary
" And yet, notwithstanding, we see the life and manners
" of men do greatly degenerate from true Christianity,
" and seem indeed to proclaim, that it is fulfilled in us,
" which God in times past threatened by his prophet.
" *Amos*, saying, *Behold, the days come, saith the Lord GOD,*
" *that I will send a famine in the land, not a famine of bread,*
" *nor a thirst for water, but of hearing the words of the*
" *LORD And they shall wander from sea to sea, and from*
" *the north even to the east, they shall run to and fro to seek*
" *the word of the LORD, and shall not find it In that day*
" *shall the fair virgins and young men faint for thirst, &c.*
" But now to pass over many things, on account of
" which I am afraid the word of God hath not been
" purely preached, one (and that not the least) is, that
" they who come and are sent, and labour to preach
" *Christ* truly, are evil spoken of for his name, who is
" the rock of offence, and stumbling block unto them
" which stumble upon his word, and do not believe on
" him on whom they [say they] are built.

                              " But

" But you will afk, Who are thofe men, and what is
" their doctrine? Truly I fay, whofoever entereth in by
" the door into the fheepfold, which all fhall do, who
" feek nothing but the glory of God, and the falvation
" of fouls, and it may be truly faid of all fuch, as the
" Lord fends, that they fpeak the WORD of GOD And
" why fo? Becaufe he reprefenteth the angel of the
" church of *Philadelphia*, unto whom St *John* writeth,
" faying, *This*, faith he, *who is holy and true, who hath*
" *the keys of* David, *who openeth and no man fhutteth, fhut-*
" *teth and no man openeth.* Behold, faith he, fpeaking in
" the name of *Chrift*, (who is the Door and Door-keeper)
" *I have fet before thee an open Door,* that is to fay, of
" the fcriptures, opening thy underftanding, that thou
" fhouldeft underftand the fcriptures, and that becaufe
" thou haft entered in by Me who am the Door *I am*
" *the Door By Me if any man enter in, he fhall be faved,*
" *and fhall go in and out and find pafture* For the Door-
" keeper openeth the Door unto him, and the fheep hear
" his voice But, on the other hand, they who have
" not entered in by the Door, but have climbed in fome
" other way, by ambition, avarice, or defire of rule, they
" fhall, even in a moment, go down into hell, except they
" repent And in them is verified the faying of *Jere-*
" *miah, All beauty is gone away from the daughter of Zion,*
" *becaufe her princes are become like rams, not finding pafture*
" And why fo? Becaufe, like thieves and robbers, they
" have climbed up another way, not being called nor
" fent

" And what wonder is it, if they do not preach, when
" they are not fent, but run for lucre, feeking their own
" glory, and not the glory of God and the falvation of
" fouls? And this is the root of all mifchief in the
" church, that they are not fent inwardly of God For
" without this inward calling of God, it helpeth no-
" thing to be a hundred times confecrated by a thoufand
" bulls, either of pope, king, or emperor God be-
" holdeth the heart, whofe judgements are according to
" truth, howfoever we deceive the judgement of men for
" a time, who alfo at laft fhall fee their abomination
" This, I fay, is the original of all mifchief in the church,
" that we thruft in ourfelves into the charge of fouls,
" whofe falvation and the glory of God (which is to
" enter in by the Door) we do not thirft nor feek for, but
" altogether our own lucre and profit."

Bilney

Bilney now counted godliness his greateſt gain, and as his own heart was enflamed with a ſincere love to *Chriſt* and his goſpel, ſo his great deſire was to bring others to embrace the ſame Nor were his labors in vain, for he was inſtrumental in the converſion of many of the gownſ-men, among whom was the afterwards celebrated Mr. *Hugh Latimer*, at that time croſs-keeper in *Cambridge*, (whoſe office it was to bring it forth on proceſſion-days) and who afterwards (as will be ſhewn in his life) ſealed the truth of *Chriſt* with his blood. *Bilney* was not ſatis-fied with a narrow limit, but extended his labors beyond the univerſity, and went to ſeveral parts of the country preaching the goſpel where ever he came, ſharply reprov-ing the pride and pomp of the clergy, and ſtriving to over-throw the authority of the biſhop of *Rome*. He had for an aſſociate, Mr *Thomas Arthur*, a fellow collegian, whom he had been inſtrumental in converting from popery Cardi-nal *Wolſey*, at that time high in power, apprehenſive of the moſt fatal conſequences to the ſee of *Rome* and his own grandeur, if once the light of the goſpel ſhould ſhine openly, cauſed *Bilney* to be apprehended Accordingly, on the 25th day of *November*, in 1527, Mr *Bilney* was brought before the ſaid cardinal and many others, both biſhops and lawyers, ſitting in the chapter-houſe of *Weſt-minſter*, and there examined, ' Whether he had not pub-' licly and privately taught the opinions of *Luther*, or of ' any other, condemned by the church ?' To which Mr. *Bilney* anſwered, " That wittingly he had not preached " or taught any of *Luther*'s opinions, or any other, con-" trary to the catholic church " After many interroga-tories and anſwers, the cardinal cauſed him to ſwear, that he would anſwer plainly to the articles and errors preached and ſet forth by him in different places, againſt a certain time, and then delivered him over to the biſhop of *London* for further examination.

On the third of *December* following, the biſhop of *Lon-don*, and other biſhops his aſſiſtants, aſſembled again in the ſame place, and, after ſome examination, repeatedly exhorted *Bilney* to abjure and recant. But he anſwered, That he would ſtand to his conſcience, ſaying, " *Fiat* " *juſtitia & judicium in nomine Domini* " i. e. Let juſtice and judgement be done in the name of the Lord Then the biſhop, putting off his cap, ſaid, ' *In nomine Patris &* ' *Filii & Spiritus ſancti*, Amen *Exurgat Deus & diſſipentur* ' *inimici ejus.*' [i e. in the name of the Father, and of the Son, and of the Holy Ghoſt, Amen Let God ariſe, and

let

let his enemies be scattered] And making a cross on his forehead and breast, he then, by the counsel of the other bishops, read part of the sentence against Mr *Bilney*, withholding the rest till the next day, to see if he would recant, but he then likewise refused for some time to abjure But at the last, after four several appearances before his judges, through infirmity and the persuasion of his friends, rather than from conviction, he recanted on the seventh day of *December*, in 1529 By way of penance for his heretical lapse (as it was termed) he was remanded to prison, there to remain till cardinal *Wolsey* should be pleased to release him, and that he should lead the procession, on the next day, bareheaded to St *Paul's*, with a faggot upon his shoulder, and stand before the preacher at St. *Paul's-Cross* [the then famous place for public preaching] during the sermon

After this abjuration, *Bilney* went to *Cambridge*, but had such conflicts within himself upon the consideration of what he had done, that he was overwhelmed with sorrow, and brought to the very brink of despair *Latimer*, in a sermon preached in *Lincolnshire*, says, ' When Mr *Bilney*
' came again to *Cambridge*, for a whole year after, he was
' in such an anguish and agony, that nothing did him
' good, neither eating nor drinking, nor any other com-
' munication of God's word , for he thought that all the
' whole scriptures were against him, and sounded to his
' condemnation So that I many a time communed with
' him, (for I was familiarly acquainted with him) but all
' things, whatsoever any man could alledge to his com-
' fort, seemed to him to make against him Yet, for all
' that, afterward he came again, God indued him with
' such strength and perfectness of faith, that he not only
' confessed his faith in the gospel of our Saviour *Jesus*
' *Christ*, but also suffered his body to be burned for that
' same gospel's sake, which we now preach in *England* '

Again, *Latimer* in his first sermon before the duchess of *Suffolk*, speaking of *Bilney*, says, ' Here I have occa-
' sion to tell you a story which happened at *Cambridge*
' Master *Bilney*, or rather St. *Bilney*, who suffered death
' for God's word's sake, the same *Bilney* was the instru-
' ment by whom God called me to his knowledge. For I
' may thank him, next to God, for that knowledge that
' I have in the word of God For I was as obstinate a
' papist as any was in *England*, insomuch that when I
' should be made bachelor of divinity, my whole oration
' was against *Philip Melancthon*, and against his opinions.

Bilney.

‘ *Bilney* heard me at that time, and perceived that I was
‘ zealous without knowledge, and came to me afterward
‘ in my ſtudy, and deſired me for God's ſake to hear his
‘ confeſſion I did ſo And (to ſay the truth) by his
‘ confeſſion I learned more than afore in many years. So
‘ from that time forward I began to taſte the word of
‘ God, and forſake the ſchool-doctors and ſuch fooleries,
‘ &c.’ Being by the grace of God, and conferences with
good men, again reſtored to peace in his conſcience, after
almoſt two years’ [from 1529 to 1531] deep ſorrow and
remorſe, *Bilney* reſolved to give up his life in the ſervice
and defence of that truth which before he had renounced,
rather than renounce it again Accordingly, he took his
leave, one evening, of his friends at *Trinity-hall*, ſaying,
“ That he would go up to *Jeruſalem*, and ſo ſhould ſee
“ them no more,” alluding to *Chriſt*'s going up to *Je-*
ruſalem before his paſſion He went immediately into
Norfolk, and there preached, firſt privately in houſes,
ſtrengthening the faithful, and afterwards openly in the
fields, bewailing his former ſubſcription, and begging of
all men to take warning by him, and never to truſt to
the counſel of friends, ſo called, when their purpoſe is to
draw them from the true religion. Soon after his arrival
at *Norwich*, upon his giving away a *New Teſtament* of
Tindal's tranſlation, and *The Obedience of a Chriſtian Man*,
he was apprehended and put in priſon, and Dr *Call* and
Dr *Stokes*, and many others, were ſent both to perſuade
him to recant, and to diſpute with him, the former of
theſe, by *Bilney*'s doctrine and conduct, was in a great
meaſure drawn over to ſide with the goſpel. After many
tedious diſputes, ſeeing they could by no means draw Mr.
Bilney from the truth, they condemned him to be burned.

The night before he ſuffered, he was viſited by many
of his friends, who rejoiced to ſee him very chearful and
to eat his food with a glad heart, ſeeing he was ſhortly
to ſuffer ſuch painful torments “ O,” ſaid he, “ I
“ imitate thoſe, who, having a ruinous houſe to dwell in,
“ hold it up by props as long as they can ” In the courſe
of their converſation, one of them obſerved to him, ‘ That
‘ though the fire, which he was to ſuffer the next day,
‘ would be of great heat to his body, yet it would be but
‘ for a moment, and that the Spirit of God would refreſh
‘ and cool his ſoul with everlaſting comfort.’ *Bilney* inſtantly put his finger into the flame of a candle, as he had
often done before, and anſwered,—“ I feel, by experi-
“ ence, that the fire is hot ; yet I am perſuaded by God's
                                                    “ holy

" holy word, and by the experience of some spoken of
" in it, that in the flame they felt no heat, and in the
" fire no consumption And I believe, that though the
" stubble of my body shall be wasted, yet my soul shall
" thereby be purged, and that, after short pain, joy
" unspeakable will follow " At the same time having
turned to *Isaiah* xliii. 1, 2 he descanted so powerfully,
and with so much of comfort and edification, both with
respect to his own case, and to that of his friends, that,
it is said, many of his friends retained a comfortable remembrance of it to their dying-day

As he was led forth to the place of execution, one of
his friends spake to him, praying to God to strengthen
him, and to enable him patiently to endure his torments .
To whom Mr *Bilney* answered, with a quiet and pleasant
countenance, " When the mariner undertakes a voyage,
" he is tossed on the billows of the troubled seas, yet, in
" the midst of all, he beareth up his spirits with this
" consideration, that e'er long he shall come into his quiet
" harbour, so (added he) I am now sailing upon the
" troubled sea, but e'er long my *ship* shall be in a quiet
" *harbour*, and I doubt not, but, through the grace of
" God, I shall endure the *storm*, only I would entreat
" you to help me with your prayers "

As he went along the streets of *Norwich*, he gave his
money in alms to the poor, by the hands of one of his
friends Being come to the stake, erected in a place called the *Lollard's-Pit*, a little way out of the *Bishops-Gate*,
he there openly made a long confession of his faith, in a
most excellent manner, and gave many sweet exhortations
to the people And then earnestly called upon God by
prayer, and ended with rehearsing the 143d *Psalm* When
he had ended his devotions, he addressed himself to the
officers, and asked them, if they were ready Upon being
answered in the affirmative, he put off his jacket and
doublet, (the layman's principal apparel of that time, for
the ecclesiastics had degraded him) and in his hose and
shirt, went to the stake, and stood upon a ledge that was
prepared for him, that, as he was but a little man, he
might be seen of all the people His friend, Dr *Warner*,
who had accompanied him in prison and to the stake, now
came to take his last leave of his beloved friend, but was
so much affected at this awful parting, that he could say
but little for his tears *Bilney* accosted him with a heavenly smile, thanked him kindly for all his friendly atten-
tions, and, inclining his body towards him, with a low

R   voice

voice concluded his farewell in the following words, of which it is hard to say, whether they convey more of love to his friend or faithfulness to his Master " *Pasce* (says " he) *gregem tuum, pasce gregem tuum, ut cum venerit Do-* " *minus, inveniat te sic facientem*" i e Feed your flock, feed your flock, that the Lord, when he cometh, may find you so doing " Farewell, dear doctor, farewell, and " pray for me " His afflicted friend could make no answer, but went away overwhelmed with tears and sorrow.

Immediately afterwards, some mendicant friars, who had been present at his condemnation and degradation, and were therefore accused of promoting his death, desired him to assure the people to the contrary, ' As (said these ' pious beggars) they will otherwise withdraw their cha- ' ritable alms from us all ' *Bilney* instantly complied with their request, and assured the people of their innocence in that behalf.

The officers then placed the faggots about him, and set fire to the reeds, which presently flamed up very high, the holy martyr, all the while, lifting up his hands towards heaven, sometimes calling upon *Jesus*, and sometimes saying " *Credo*," i e I believe. The wind being high, and blowing away the flame, he suffered a lingering death   At last, one of the officers beat out the staple, to which the chain was fastened that supported his body, and so let it fall into the fire, where it was presently consumed.   He suffered in the year 1531, in the time of king *Henry* the eighth

The papists, and the famous Sir *Thomas More* at their head, who was lord chancellor, spread reports that *Bilney* again recanted, which aspersions Mr *Fox*, by the testimony of bishop *Latimer* his most intimate friend, and of Mr *Parker* (afterwards archbishop *Parker*) and several others, who were present at his suffering, has abundantly refuted.   The Lord *kept the feet of this saint*, till He lifted up his soul, though in a fiery chariot, to his kingdom of glory

Bilney appears to have been a man of learning, as well as piety, and is spoken of, by all his contemporary Reformers, with every demonstration of respect and regard.

Mr.

JOHN FRITH,

JOHN FRITH, a holy martyr, and learned preacher, was born at *Sevenoak* in *Kent*, and was the first in *England* that profeſſedly wrote againſt *Chriſt*'s corporal preſence in the ſacrament, in which doctrine he cloſely followed *Zuinglius*. He was educated at *King's-College* in *Cambridge*, and took a batchelor of arts degree there, but afterwards went to *Oxford*, and for his bright talents was choſen one of the junior canons of cardinal *Wolſey*'s new college, now called *Chriſt-Church*. Some time before the year 1525, he became acquainted with the famous *William Tindal*, who, conferring with him about the abuſes of religion, was made the happy inſtrument under God of ſowing the pure ſeed of the goſpel in his heart. *Frith*, ſhortly after, profeſſing the true religion, was ſeized and examined by the commiſſary of the univerſity, and then impriſoned within the limits of his own college, with ſeveral others, ſome of whom died with the ſevere uſage they received. Being releaſed in 1528, he went beyond ſea, where being greatly confirmed in the faith, he returned to *England* about two years after, leaving his wife and children behind him. It is ſuppoſed he had in view an exhibition of the prior of *Reading* in *Berkſhire*, and to have had the prior over with him, but coming to *Reading*, he was taken up for a vagabond, and ſet in the ſtocks. Where after ſitting a long time, and ready to die with hunger, he at laſt deſired that the ſchool-maſter of the town might come to him, who at that time was Mr. *Leonard Cox*, a learned man. *Cox*, diſcovering his merit and great abilities, by diſcourſing with him on the *Latin* and *Greek* claſſics, procured his releaſe, and ſupplied him with victuals and money. Afterwards *Frith* went to *London*, where, though he often changed both his cloaths and place, he dwelt not long in ſafety, for ſo great a perſecutor was Sir *Thomas More*, then lord chancellor, that he had his ſpies at every port and on the roads leading to them, and offered great rewards to any one that would give information of this excellent man.

It

It is probable, that Sir *Thomas More* was the more haftily led to this perfecution, in confequence of a book,
which *Frith* had written againft him   The cafe was this
The fupplication of the beggars, a book, publifhed by a Mr
Fifh, of *Gray's-Inn*, inveighing againft the impofing arts
of the *begging friars* [an order, which profeffed poverty]
and taxing the pope with extortion and cruelty, as he
granted his indulgences and remiffions from purgatory to
none but thofe who could pay for them, was received
with great attention by the public, and even approved by
king *Henry* the eighth himfelf, whofe quarrel with the
pope it highly favored   *More* anfwered this publication
by another, entitled, *The fupplication of the fouls in purgatory*, expreffing their miferies and the relief they received
by the maffes, which were faid for them, and therefore
they called upon their friends to fupport the religious
orders, which were now befet with fo many inveterate
enemies.   Though Sir *Thomas* had exerted his ufual wit
and elegance in this compofition, whether it proceeded
from the badnefs of his caufe, or the great infight which
the world at large had then obtained in thefe matters, his
apology did not meet with any encouraging reception

However, *Frith* anfwered this book of *More*'s in a very
grave manner, and fhewed that the doctrine of purgatory
was not founded on fcripture, that it was inconfiftent
with the merits of *Chrift*, and his pardon of fin, and that
it directly oppofed the great plan of his falvation   He
alfo afferted, that the fire, which was fpoken of by the
apoftle, as that which would confume the *wood*, *hay*, and
ftubble, could only be meant of the fire of perfecution.
He urged, that the primitive church held no fuch doctrine, and that, as it was not in the fcripture, fo neither
was it in *Ambrofe*, *Jerom*, and *Auguftine*, thofe great fathers
of the church,   He infifted, that it was introduced by the
monks, with innumerable fables, on purpofe to delude
the world and to amafs great riches by it   In fhort, this
book provoked the *Romifh* clergy to the higheft degree,
and they refolved, as they could not convince with other
reafoning, to ufe the irrefiftible arguments of fire and
faggot upon thofe, who thus contemned the pope's authority, lowered their own confequence, and endangered
their revenues,

Mr *Frith* not long afterwards, converfing with a familiar friend upon the nature of the body and blood of
Chrift in the facrament, was defired by his friend to commit the fubftance of his arguments to writing, for the
                                        help

help of his memory. Mr *Frith* at first was unwilling, knowing what great danger he was in, but at length he complied, and wrote down the four following arguments:

"First, That the matter of the sacrament is no necef-
"fary article of faith under pain of damnation.

"Secondly, That forasmuch as *Christ's* natural body
"in like condition hath all properties of our body, sin
"only excepted, it cannot be, neither is it agreeable unto
"reafon, that he should be in two places or more at once,
"contrary to the nature of our body.

"Thirdly, That we should not in this place (*Matth.*
"xxvi. 26, 27, 28.) understand *Christ's* words according
"to the literal fenfe, but rather according to the order
"and phrafe of speech, comparing phrafe with phrafe,
"according to the analogy of fcripture.

"Laftly, That it ought to be received according to
"the true and right institution of *Christ*, notwithstand-
"ing that the order which at this time is crept into the
"church, and is used now a days by the priefts, do never
"fo much differ from it."

At this time one *William Holt*, a taylor, profeffed great friendfhip towards the religious party, and by that means had an opportunity, like another *Judas*, to betray them, which he did, by defiring to fee Mr *Frith's* arguments, and carrying them immediately to Sir *Thomas More*, who by his means found out and feized Mr *Frith*, and fent him prifoner to the tower. He had feveral conferences there with Sir *Thomas* and others. At length, being taken to *Lambeth*, before the archbifhop, and afterwards to *Croy-don*, before the bifhop of *Winchefter*, he was at length (on the 20th of *June*, 1533) examined before an affembly of bifhops fitting in St *Paul's* cathedral, who, after in-terrogating him refpecting the facrament and purgatory, urged him to recant, but Mr *Frith* fully confuted all their arguments, and, inftead of recanting, fubfcribed his anfwers, with his own hand, in the following manner:
"Ego FRITHUS *ita fentio, & quemadmodum fentio, ita*
"*dixi, fcripfi, afferui, & affirmavi.*" That is, I *Frith* thus do think, and as I think, fo I have faid, written, taught, and affirmed, and in my books have publifhed. From the works of *Frith*, Mr *Fox* affures us, that the great archbifhop *Cranmer* collected many of his arguments in his famous book of the facrament, and that he gave more credit to *Frith* as an author, than to any other wri-ter. However, *Frith* was, upon the fcore of his writings and verbal anfwers to the bifhops, deemed incorrigible,

and

and condemned to be burnt, and accordingly was carried
to *Smithfield*, with a young man, named *Andrew Hewet*,
a martyr in the same glorious caufe, upon the 4th of *July*,
1533 When Mr *Frith* was tied to the ftake, he fhewed
amazing conftancy and courage, and, embracing the faggots and fire when put around him, evidenced how chearfully he fuffered death for the fake of *Chrift* and his
bleffed truths One Dr *Cook*, a prieft, ftanding by,
loudly admonifhed the people not to pray for them, any
more than if they were dogs At which Mr *Frith*,
fmiling, prayed the Lord to forgive him. The wind blew
away the flames to his fellow martyr, *Hewet*, which occafioned to *Frith* a very lingering and painful death, but
his mind feemed fo eftablifhed, and his patience to have
fo much of its perfect work, that it was obferved, he
feemed more to rejoice for his fellow-fufferer, than to be
careful about himfelf, and at laft chearfully committed
his foul into the hands of God He fuffered in the prime
of his life But it is never too early to follow the will of
God or to enter into heaven.

There is a circumftance refpecting this conftant martyr,
John Frith, that may be thought not unworthy the reading It was as follows The archbifhop of *Canterbury*
fent two of his fervants to bring Mr *Frith* fafe to *Croy-
don*, to be examined there, but in the way, they were fo
convinced by his judicious and pious converfation, his
humble and amiable deportment, that they concerted a
plan, between themfelves, how to let him efcape. And
then one of them thus addreffed him, ' Mr *Frith*, the
' journey I have taken in hand to bring you to *Croydon*,
' as a fheep to the flaughter, fo grieveth me, that I am
' overwhelmed with care and forrow, nor do I regard
' what hazard I undergo, fo that I may but deliver you
' out of the lion's mouth ' And then made known to
him, how they had contrived to facilitate his efcape.
To all this Mr *Frith* anfwered with a fmiling countenance, " Do you think that I am afraid to deliver my
" opinion before the bifhops of *England*, being a mani-
" feft truth?" The gentleman replied, ' I wonder that
' you was fo willing to quit the kingdom before you was
' taken, and now fo unwilling to fave yourfelf ' Mr.
Frith anfwered, " Before I was feized, I would fain have
" enjoyed my liberty for the benefit of the church of
" God, but now being taken by the higher power, and
" by the providence of God, delivered into the hands of
" the bifhops, to give teftimony to that religion and doc-

" trine

" trine, which under pain of damnation I am bound to
" maintain and defend; if, therefore, I should now start
" aside and run away, I should run away from my God,
" and from the teſtimony of his word, and should be
" worthy of a thouſand hells; therefore, added he, I be-
" ſeech you to bring me to the place appointed for me to
" be brought, or elſe I will go thither alone."—Perhaps,
in this inſtance, he is more to be admired than juſtified.
GOD's people are no where commanded to give themſelves up to their perſecutors, but to avoid them, as far
as is conſiſtent with a faithful conſcience. Mr *Frith*
imitated, in this particular, many of the primitive Chriſtians, who rather coveted than ſhunned the crown of
martyrdom, which ſeems the more extraordinary in him,
as he was eminently of a meek and quiet ſpirit, and not
of that lion-hearted temper, which appeard in *Luther* and
ſome other of the Reformers

Frith's great opponents were *Fiſher*, biſhop of *Rocheſter*,
Sir *Thomas More*, and *Raſtal*, *More*'s ſon-in-law. Theſe
he ſolidly confuted in his writings, and, for the vigor of
that confutation, moſt probably became a particular object of their reſentment. So much learning, in conjunction with ſo much grace, were certainly an overmatch
for mere human nature, inveſted only with its natural
attainments. ' He was (ſays biſhop *Bale*) a poliſhed ſcho-
' lar, as well as maſter of the learned languages.' And
he applied all his faculties to the illuſtration and glory of
that truth, which the goodneſs of God had imparted to
him

His works are theſe 1 Treatiſe of purgatory 2 An-
tatheſis between *Chriſt* and the pope. 3 Letter to the
faithful followers of *Chriſt*'s goſpel, written in the tower,
1532 4. The mirror, or glaſs to know thyſelf, written
in the tower, 1532 5 Mirror, or looking-glaſs, wherein
you may behold the ſacrament of baptiſm. 6 Articles
[for which he died] written in *Newgate*, 23d of *June*,
1533 7 Anſwer to Sir *Thomas More*'s dialogues concerning hereſies 8 Anſwer to *John Fiſher*, biſhop of
Rocheſter, &c All theſe treatiſes were reprinted at *London* in 1573, in folio.

WILLIAM

WILLIAM TINDALE.

WILLIAM TINDALE, a learn d and zalous *Englifh* Reformer, and memorable for having made the firft verl on of the bible in modern *Englifh*, was born on the borders of *Wales*, fometime before the year 1500 He was of *Magdalen-hall* in *Oxford*, where he diftinguifhed himfelf, not only by his literary abilities, but alfo by imbibing early the doctrines of the Reformation, which were begun to be fpread in many parts of *England* He applied himfelf with great diligence to the ftudy of the fcriptures, which he did not perufe as a mere fcholar or felf-fufficient fpeculatift, but in the way, which divine grace alone induces and makes profitable, namely, with a meek and humble fpirit, craving for heavenly wifdom in a fenfe of the want of it, and not bringing human wit or reafon in order to meafure the divine Nor was he fatisfied to *hide his candle under a bufhel*, and to keep what he learned by grace to himfelf He took great pains, privately, to read divinity to feveral ftudents and fellows of the *Hall*, and to inftruct them in the knowledge and truth of the fcriptures, on account of which and his upright life and converfation, he was held in the higheft eftimation.

Having taken his degrees, he afterwards removed to *Cambridge*, and from thence, after fome time, he went to live with a gentleman (Mr *Welch*) in *Gloucefterfhire*, in the capacity of tutor to his children While he continued there, he had frequent difputes with abbots and doctors, who vifited the family, both about learned men, divinity, and the fcriptures One day Mr and Mrs. *Welch* went to return a vifit, where feveral of thofe dignitaries converfed with all freedom, Mr. *Tindale* not being prefent And in the evening, they returned full of arguments againft Mr *Tindale*, all which he anfwered by fcripture, maintaining the truth and reproving their falfe opinions.

opinions Upon which Mrs *Welch* (who was, fays *Tindale*, a fenfible woman) brake out in the following exclamation, ' Well, there was doctor ****, who can fpend a hundred ' pounds, there was doctor ****, who can fpend two ' hundred pounds, and doctor ****, who can fpend three ' hundred pounds, and, what, is it reafon, think you, ' that we fhould believe you before them ?' Mr *Tindale* made no reply, and in future fpake lefs of thofe matters,

At this time he was tranflating a book of *Frafmus*, en-titled *Enchiridion militis Chriftiani*, which, when finifhed, he gave to Mr and Mrs *Welch*, who carefully perufed it, and, it feems, were fo far convinced of the truth, in op-pofition to the popifh doctrines of the abbots and priefts, that thefe gentlemen afterwards met with a very cool re-ception at their houfe, and foon declined their vifits alto-gether   This, as it was natural to fuppofe, brought upon Mr *Tindale* the wrath of all the popifh clergy in the neighbourhood, who foon had him accufed of many he-refies to the bifhop's chancellor, before whom he had been cited to appear, but nothing being proved, after railing at him and abufing him, they difmifled him   In his way home he called upon a certain doctor, who had been an old chancellor to a bifhop, and his very good friend, to him he opened his heart, and confulted him upon many paflages of fcripture   Before they parted the doctor faid to him, ' Do you not know, that the pope is very anti-' chrift, whom the fcripture fpeaketh of ? But beware ' what you fay, for if it fhould be known you are of ' that opinion, it will coft you your life ' And added, ' I have been an officer of his, but I have given it up, ' and defy him and all his works '

Not long after this affair, Mr *Tindale* fell in company with a certain divine, remarkable for his learning, with whom he difputed, and drave him fo clofe, that at length the divine blafphemoufly cried out, ' We had better be ' without God's laws than the pope's ' *Tindale*, fired at this expreffion, and filled with zeal, replied, " I defy the " pope and all his laws," and added, " That if God " fpared his life, e'er many years, he would caufe a boy " that drives the plough to know more of the fcriptures " than he did "   After this, the hatred of the priefts was fo great, that he was obliged to leave the country, which he did, with the confent and hearty wifhes of Mr *Welch* for his welfare. Mr *Tindale*, remembering the high commendations *Erafmus* had given of *Tonftal's* learning, then bifhop of *London*, hoped he fhould find favor and

S

protection

protection with him, but, as this was not the way God, in his providence, had marked out for him, the bishop excused himself, saying, 'That his house was ' full, that he had already more than he could accommo- ' date, but that he advised him to seek about in *London*, ' where he could not fail to obtain employment'

Mr. *Tindale* remained in *London* about a year, when being desirous to translate the New Testament into *Eng- lish*, as the most effectual means (in his own opinion and in that of his dear friend *John Frith*) to remedy the great darkness and ignorance of the land, but judging it could not safely be done in *England*, he, by the kind assistance of Mr. *Humphry Monmouth* and others, went into *Ger- many*, where he labored upon the work, and finished it in the year 1527 In a letter to *Frith*, he says of it, " I call GOD to recorde agaynst the daye we shall ap- " peare before our Lord *Jesus*, to geve a reckenyng of " our doynges, that I never altered one syllable of God's " word agaynst my conscience, nor would this daye, if " all that is in the earth, whether it be pleasure, honour, " or riches, might be geven me " It was the *first* trans- lation of the scripture into modern *English*. He then began with the Old Testament, and finished the five books of *Moses*, prefixing excellent discourses to each book, as he had done to those of the New Testament *Cranmer*'s Bible, or (as it was called) the GREAT BIBLE, was no other than *Tindale*'s revised and corrected, omitting the pro- logues and tables, and adding scripture references and a summary of contents, At his first going over into *Ger- many*, he went into *Saxony*, and had much conference with *Luther* and other learned men, and then returning to the *Netherlands*, made his abode at *Antwerp*, at that time a very populous and flourishing city

About the time he had finished his translation of the book of *Deuteronomy*, he had also prepared for the press a work concerning *the nature of the sacrament*, or (as it was then called) *the altar*, but wisely considering, that the people were not yet fully convinced of the absurdity of many superstitious ceremonies and gross idolatries, and that the mass was every where held in the same estimation, as the great goddess *Diana* had been amongst the *Ephe- sians*, which they thought came down from heaven, he therefore judged it might be more seasonable, and would answer the end more fully, at some future period. And he also wrote a very valuable tract upon *the obedience of a Christian man*, and likewise his *expositions of scripture*, &c.

He

He set sail in the mean time to *Hamburgh*, with a view to print his last finished translation of the scriptures, but being shipwrecked on the coast of *Holland*, he lost all his books and papers However, going in another ship to *Hamburgh*, he met with Mr. *Coverdale*, who assisted him in translating again the five books of *Moses*, both of them being entertained in the house of a widow gentlewoman, Mrs *Margaret Van Emerson* This was in the year 1529, when the sweating-sickness very much prevailed in that place.

Having finished the printing of these books, he returned again to *Antwerp*, and his translation of the scriptures, being in the mean time sent to *England*, made a great noise there as well as in *Germany*, and, in the opinion of the bishops and clergy, did so much mischief (as they were pleased to call it) that they railed against and condemned them for containing a thousand heresies, and urged—that it was impossible for the scriptures to be translated into *English*—and that it was neither lawful nor expedient for the laity to have the scriptures in their mother-tongue. Nor could they rest, till, by their interest, they had procured a royal proclamation to be issued out, prohibiting the buying or reading such translation or translations This proclamation was published in 1527, soon after the publication of *Tindale*'s New Testament, which gave the loudest alarm, and in the same edict, as well as by the public prohibitions of the bishops, several other treatises were cried down, written by *Luther*, and other Reformers. But all this only served, as is usual in such cases, to increase the public curiosity, and to occasion a more careful reading of what was deemed so extremely obnoxious. One step taken by the bishop of *London* afforded some merriment to the protestants His lordship thought, that the best way to prevent these *English* New Testaments from circulation, would be to buy up the whole impression, and therefore employed a Mr *Packington*, who secretly favored the Reformation, then at *Antwerp*, for this purpose, assuring him at the same time, that, cost what they would, he would have them, and burn them all at *Paul's Cross* Upon this, *Packington* applied himself to *Tindale*, and, upon agreement, the bishop had the books, *Packington* great thanks, and *Tindale* all the money. This enabled our Reformer instantly to publish a new and more correct edition, so ' that they came ' over (says Mr *Fox*) thick and threefold into *England* ' This occasioned extreme rage in the disappointed bishop

S 2   and

and his popish friends One *Constantine* being soon after apprehended by Sir *Thomas More*, and being asked how *Tindale* and others subsisted abroad, readily answered, That it was the bishop of *London* who had been their chief supporter, for he bestowed a great deal of money upon them in the purchase of New Testaments to burn them, and that upon that cash they had subsisted, till the sale of the second edition was received

However, *Tindale*'s persecutors, concerned for all that was dear to them, namely, their *purse* and their *belly*, did not rest here, for, as they perceived him to be a very able man, and if suffered to live, capable of doing immense harm to their craft, they sent over to *Antwerp* one *Philips*, who insinuated himself into his company, and under the pretext of friendship betrayed him into custody He was sent prisoner to the castle of *Filford*, about eighteen miles from *Antwerp*, and though the *English* merchants at *Antwerp* did what they could to procure his release, and letters were sent from lord *Cromwell* and others out of *England*, yet *Philips* bestirred himself so heartily, that *Tindale* was tried and condemned to die. He was brought to the place of execution, and while he was tying to the stake he cried with a fervent and loud voice, "Lord, open "the king of *England*'s eyes" He was first strangled by the hands of the common hangman, and then burned near *Filford-castle*, in the year 1536 And thus he, whom *Fox*, with the utmost propriety, styles ' *England*'s Apostle,' rested from his labors and troubles, and entered into the joy of his Lord.

He was a person of seraphic piety, indefatigable study, and extraordinary learning. His modesty, zeal, and disinterestedness, were so great, that he declared, before he went to *Germany*, that he should be content "to live in any county of *England*, on an allowance "of ten pounds *per annum*, and bind himself to receive "no more, if he might only have authority to in- "struct children and preach the gospel." His uncommon abilities and learning, which, joined to great warmth and firmness of nature, and to true faith and gospel-zeal, qualified him exceedingly well for the office of a Reformer Such was GOD's blessing upon his true and faithful preaching, that, during the time of his imprisonment (which lasted a year and a half) he converted his gaoler, his daughter, and many of his houshold Nay, the procurer general, or emperor's attorney, publickly said of him, that he was *homo doctus, pius, et bonus*, a

learned,

learned, pious, and good man   The good bishop *Bale* also
says of him, that for knowledge, purity of doctrine, and
holiness of life, he ought to be esteemed the next *English*
Reformer after *Wickliffe*, and that he was born for the
conversion and edification of many souls   His picture
represents him with a bible in his hand, and this distich,

Hâc ut luce tuas dispergam, Roma, tenebras,
  Sponte extorris ero, sponte sacrificium.

That light o'er all thy darkness, *Rome*,
  With triumph might arise,
An exile freely I become,
  Freely a sacrifice

The works which he wrote, besides the translation of the
scriptures, are the following, which were published in
one general volume

1 A Christian's obedience. 2. The unrighteous mammon 3 The practice of the papists. 4. Commentaries on the seventh chapter of St *Matthew* 5 A discourse of the last will and testament of *Tracii* 6 An answer to Sir *Thomas More*'s dialogues. 7. The doctrine of the Lord's Supper against *More* 8 Of the sacrament of the altar. 9 Of the sacramental signs. 10 A footpath leading to the scriptures 11 Three letters to *John Frith.*

The remains of such men, when they are but few, are the more desirable and precious   We will, therefore, insert (as they discover the spirit and temper of this good man) the three letters abovementioned, preserved by Mr Fox, and especially as his voluminous writings are not in the possession, or within the purchase, of many serious persons.

I.

" THE grace and peace of God our Father, and of
" *Jesus Christ* our Lord, be with you, *Amen.*
" Dearly beloved brother *John*, I have heard say, how
" the hypocrites, now that they have overcome that great
" business which letted them, or at the least way have
" brought it to a stay, return to their old nature again.
" The will of God be fulfilled, and that which he hath
" ordained to be ere the world was made, that come,
" and his glory reign over all

" Dearly beloved, however the matter be, commit your-
" self wholly and only unto your most loving Father, and
" most kind Lord, fear not men that threat, nor trust
" men that speak fair. But trust him that is true of pro-
" mise,

" mife, and able to make his word good　Your caufe is
" *Chrift's* gofpel, a light that muft be fed with the blood
" of faith　The lamp muft be dreffed and fnuffed daily,
" and that oil poured in every evening and morning,
" that the light go not out　Though we be finners, yet
" is the caufe right.　If when we be buffeted for well
" doing, we fuffer patiently and endure, that is accepta-
" ble with God　For to that end we are called　For
" *Chrift* alfo fuffered for us, leaving us an example that
" we fhould follow his fteps, who did no fin.　Hereby
" have we perceived love, that he laid down his life for
" us, therefore we ought alfo to lay down our lives for
" the brethren.　Rejoice and be glad, for great is your
" reward in heaven.　For we fuffer with him, that we
" may alfo be glorified with him　Who fhall change
" our vile body, that it may be fafhioned like unto his
" glorious body, according to the working whereby he
" is able even to fubdue all things unto himfelf

" Dearly beloved, be of good courage, and comfort
" your foul with the hope of this high reward, and bear
" the image of *Chrift* in your mortal body, that it may at
" his coming be made like to his immortal body, and fol-
" low the example of all your other dear brethren, which
" chofe to fuffer in hope of a better refurrection.　Keep
" your confcience pure and undefiled, and fay againft
" that nothing.　Stick at neceffary things, and re-
" member the blafphemies of the enemies of *Chrift*,
" faying, they find none but who will abjure rather than
" fuffer the extremity.　Moreover, the death of them
" that come again after they have once denied, though
" it be accepted with God, and all that believe, yet it is
" not glorious　For the hypocrites fay, he muft needs
" die, denying helpeth not　But might it have holpen,
" they would have denied five hundred times, but feeing
" it would not help them, therefore of pure pride and
" meer malice together, they fpake with their mouths
" what their confcience knoweth falfe　If you give your-
" felf, caft yourfelf, yield yourfelf, commit yourfelf
" wholly and only to your loving Father, then fhall his
" power be in you and make you ftrong, and that fo
" ftrong, that you fhall feel no pain, which fhould be to
" another prefent death　And his Spirit fhall fpeak in you,
" and teach you what to anfwer, according to his pro-
" mife　He fhall fet out his truth by you wonderfully, and
" work for you above all that your heart can imagine,
" yea and you are not yet dead, though the hypocrites

" all,

" all, with all that they can make, have fworn your
" death *Una falus victis nullam fperare falutem*, To
" look for no man's help, bringeth the help of God to
" them that feem to be overcome in the eyes of the hy-
" pocrites Yea, it fhall make God to carry you thorow
" thick and thin for his truth's fake, in fpite of all the
" enemies of his truth   There falleth not a hair till his
" hour be come, and when his hour is come, neceffity
" carrieth us hence though we be not willing   But if
" we be willing, then have we a reward and thank

" Fear not the threatning therefore, neither be over-
" come of fweet words, with which twain the hypocrites
" fhall affail you. Neither let the perfwafions of worldly
" wifdom bear rule in your heart, no, though they be
" your friends that counfel you. Let *Bilney* be a warn-
" ing to you, let not their vizor beguile your eyes   Let
" not your body faint   He that endureth to the end
" fhall be faved. If the pain be above your ftrength,
" remember, *Whatfoever ye fhall afk in my name, I will*
" *give it you*   And pray to your Father in that name,
" and he fhall ceafe your pain, or fhorten it.   The Lord
" of peace, of hope, and of faith, be with you, *Amen*

" WILLIAM TINDALE."

II.

" TWO have fuffered in *Antwerp, in die fanctæ crucis,*
"   unto the great glory of the gofpel, four at
" *Ryfels* in *Flanders,* and at *Luke* hath there one at
" leaft fuffered, and all the fame day   At *Roan* in *France*
" they perfecute. And at *Paris* are five doctors taken
" for the gofpel See, you are not alone, be cheerful
" and remember that among the hard-hearted in *England,*
" there is a number referved by grace For whofe fakes,
" if need be, you muft be ready to fuffer. Sir, if you
" may write, how fhort foever it be, forget it not, that
" we may know how it goeth with you, for our heart's
" eafe The Lord be yet again with you, with all his
" plenteoufnefs, and fill you that you flow over, *Amen*

" If when you have read this, you can fend it to
" *Adrian,* do I pray you, that he may know how that
" our heart is with you

" *George Joy* at *Candlemas* being at *Barrow* printed
" two leaves of *Genefis* in a great form, and fent one
" copy to the king, and another to the new queen, with a
" letter to *N.* to deliver them, and to purchafe licenfe,
" that

" that he might fo go through all the bible   Out of
" this is fprung the noife of the new bible, and out of
" that is the great feeking for *Englifh* books at all printers
" and book-binders in *Antwerp*, and for an *Englifh* prieft
" that fhould print

" This chanced the ninth day of *May*

" Sir, your wife is well content with the will of God,
" and would not for her fake have the glory of God
" hindred.

" WILLIAM TINDALE."

III

" The grace of our Saviour *Jefus*, his patience, meek-
" nefs, humblenefs, circumfpection, and wifdom, be
" with your heart, *Amen*

" **D**EARLY beloved brother, mine hearts defire
" in our Saviour *Jefus*, is that you arm your-
" felf with patience, and be cool, fober, wife and cir-
" cumfpect, and that you keep you a low by the ground,
" avoiding high queftions, that pafs the common capa-
" city   But expound the law truly, and open the vail
" of *Mofes* to condemn all flefh, and prove all men fin-
" ners, and all deeds under the law, before mercy have
" taken away the condemnation thereof, to be fin and
" damnable, and then, as a faithful minifter, fet abroach
" the mercy of our Lord *Jefus*, and let the wounded
" confciences drink of the water of Him   And then fhall
" your preaching be with power, and not as the doctrine
" of the hypocrites, and the Spirit of God fhall work
" with you, and all confciences fhall bear record unto
" you, and feel that it is fo.   And all doctrine that
" cafteth a mift on thofe two, to fhadow and hide them,
" I mean the law of God, and mercy of *Chrift*, that refift
" you with all your power   Sacraments without figni-
" fication refufe   If they put fignifications to them,
" receive them, if you fee it may help, though it be not
" neceffary.

" Of the prefence of *Chrift*'s body in the facrament,
" meddle as little as you can, that there appear no di-
" vifion among us   *Barnes* will be hot againft you
" The *Saxons* be fore on the affirmative; whether con-
" ftant or obftinate, I remit it to God. *Philip Melanc-*
" *thon* is faid to be with the *French* king   There be
" in *Antwerp* that fay, they faw him come into *Paris*
" with an hundred and fifty horfes, and that they fpake

" with

" with him   If the *French* men receive the word of
" God, he will plant the affirmative in them   *George*
" *Joy* would have put forth a treatife of that matter, but
" I have ftopt him as yet   What he will do if he get
" money, I wot not   I believe he would make many
" reafons little ferving to that purpofe   My mind is,
" that nothing be put forth till we hear how you fhall
" have fped   I would have the right ufe preached, and
" the prefence to be an indifferent thing, till the matter
" might be reafoned in peace at leifure of both parties
" If you be required, fhew the phrafes of the fcripture,
" and let them talk what they will   For is to believe
" that God is every where, hurteth no man that worfhip-
" peth him no where but within the heart, in fpirit and
" verity   Even fo to believe, that the body of *Chrift* is
" every where (though it cannot be proved) hurteth no
" man, that worfhippeth him no where fave in the faith
" of his gofpel   You perceive my mind   Howbeit, if
" God fhew you otherwife, it is free for you to do as he
" moveth you

    " I guefled long ago, that God would fend a dazing
" into the head of the fpiritualty, to catch themfelves in
" their own fubtilty, and truft it is come to pafs   And
" now me thinketh I fmell a counfel to be taken, little
" for their profits in time to come   But you muft un-
" derftand, that it is not of a pure heart and for love of
" the truth, but to avenge themfelves, and to eat the
" whore's flefh, and to fuck the marrow of her bones.
" Wherefore cleave faft to the rock of the help of God,
" and commit the end of all things unto him   And if
" God fhall call you, that you may then ufe the wifdom
" of the worldly, as far as you perceive the glory of God
" may come thereof, refufe it not, and ever among
" thruft in, that the fcripture may be in the mother-
" tongue, and learning fet up in the univerfities   But
" if ought be required contrary to the glory of God, and
" his *Chrift*, then ftand faft, and commit yourfelf to
" God, and be not overcome of men's perfuafions,
" which haply fhall fay, We fee no other way to bring
" in the truth

    " Brother, beloved in my heart, there liveth not in
" whom I have fo good hope and truft, and in whom
" my heart rejoiceth, and my foul comforteth herfelf, as
" in you, not the thoufand part fo much for your learn-
" ing, and what other gifts elfe you have, as becaufe you
" will creep alow by the ground, and walk in thofe

                              T   " things

" things that the confcience may feel, and not in the
" imaginations of the brain In fear, and not in bold-
" nefs In open necelfary things, and not to pronounce
" or define of hid fecrets, or things that neither help nor
" hinder, whether it be fo or no, in unity, and not in
" feditious opinions Infomuch that if you be fure you
" know, yet in things that may abide leifure you will
" defer, or fay (till other agree with you) Methinks
" the text requireth the fenfe or underftanding Yea,
" and if you be fure that your part be good, and another
" hold the contrary, yet if it be a thing that maketh no
" matter, you will laugh and let it pafs, and refer the
" thing to other men, and ftick you ftiffly and ftubbornly
" in earneft and necelfary things And I truft you be
" perfuaded even fo of me For I call God to record
" againft the day we fhall appear before our Lord *Jefus*,
" to give a reckoning of our doings, that I never altered
" one fyllable of God's word againft my confcience, nor
" would this day, if all that is in the earth, whether it
" be pleafure, honour, or riches, might be given me
" Moreover, I take God to record to my confcience,
" that I defire of God to myfelf in this world, no more
" than that without which I cannot keep his laws

" Finally, if there were in me any gift that could help
" at hand, and aid you if need required, I promife you
" I would not be far off, and commit the end to God
" My foul is not faint, though my body be weary But
" God hath made me evil favoured in this world, and
" without grace in the fight of men, fpeechlefs and rude,
" dull and flow witted, your part fhall be to fupply
" what lacketh in me Remembring, that as lowlinefs
" of heart fhall make you high with God, even fo meek-
" nefs of words fhall make you fink into the hearts of
" men Nature giveth age authority, but meeknefs is
" the glory of youth, and giveth them honour. Abun-
" dance of love maketh me exceed in babling

" Sir, as concerning purgatory and many other things,
" if you be demanded, you may fay, if you err, the
" fpiritualty hath fo led you, and that they have taught
" you to believe as you do For they preached you all
" fuch things out of God's word, and alledged a thou-
" fand texts, by reafon of which texts you believed as
" they taught you, but now you find them lyers, and
" that the texts mean no fuch things, and therefore you
" can believe them no longer, but are as ye were before
" they taught you, and believe no fuch thing . Howbeit,
" you

" you are ready to believe, if they have any other way
" to prove it, for without proof you cannot believe them,
" when you have found them with fo many lyes, &c.
" If you perceive wherein we may help, either in being
" ftill or doing fomewhat, let us have word, and I will
" do mine uttermoft

" My lord of *London* hath a fervant called *John Tifen*,
" with a red beard, and a black-reddifh head, and was
" once my fcholar, he was feen in *Antwerp*, but came
" not among the *Englifhmen* Whither he is gone am-
" baffador fecret, I wot not

" The mighty God of *Jacob* be with you, to fupplant
" his enemies, and give you the favour of *Jofeph*, and
" the wifdom and the fpirit of *Stephen*, be with your
" heart, and with your mouth, and teach your lips what
" they fhall fay, and how to anfwer to all things He
" is our God, if we defpair in ourfelves, and truft in
" him And his is the glory *Amen.*

" *January,* 1533.   WILLIAM TINDALE "

JOHN LAMBERT.

THE true name of this admirable man was *Nicholfon*,
but, in order to avoid the dangers which threatened
him in the latter part of his life on a religious account,
he iffumed the firname of *Lambert*. It does not appear
when he was born, though it may be prefumed to have
been about the end of the fifteenth or beginning of the
fixteenth century, as he fuffered for the caufe of truth
in the year 1538 We have not likewife the precife *place*
of his birth Only it is affirmed, that he was born, and
brought up for the moft part, in the county of *Norfolk*.
His academical education he received at *Cambridge*, where
he acquired the learned languages, and (what was better
than them) his converfion to GOD from popifh fuperftition and the love of this evil world. The bleffed inftrument of this happy change was the memorable and
blefled

bleffed *Bilney*, who was likewife the inftrument of conveiting many others to the knowledge of GOD and their own hearts

The fury of king *Henry* the Eighth againft Lutheranifm (or Proteftantifm, as it was afterwards more juftly called) compelled poor *Lambert*, who began to be diftinguifhed for his learning and piety, to feek a refuge upon the continent　Accordingly, he repaired to *Antwerp*, then the refidence of *Tindale* and *Frith*, who appear to have been his chofen friends, and officiated as preacher and chaplain to the *Englifh* factory in that city, (which at that time had great correfpondence with *England* on account of the woollen manufacture) for the greater part of two years.　But the tenor of his preaching was of fuch a kind, as rendered it by no means furprizing, that he fhould procure himfelf enemies among the fons of *Rome*　One *Barlow*, glad, no doubt, of fhewing his zeal, accufed him to Sir *Thomas More*, then lord chancellor of *England*, by whofe means he was brought from *Antwerp* to *London*, as an innocent lamb to fatiate the cruelty of the *Romifh* wolves, who thirfted for his blood　This event occurred in the year 1532　He was firft examined at *Lambeth* by *Warham*, then archbifhop of *Canterbury*, and afterwards at the bifhop's houfe at *Oxford*, before a multitude of his adverfaries　He was queftioned upon forty-five articles, to all of which he gave a very long, full, and learned anfwer, which does him and the caufe he profeffed exceeding great honor.　A more folid and comprehenfive apology for Proteftantifm is rarely to be found, and we fhould be happy to lay it before our readers, did not its very great length exceed the limits of our plan　The curious Reader may fee it at large in *Fox*'s Acts and Monuments, for the reign of *Henry* the Eighth.　We will, however, fubjoin an extract or two at the end of his life, as a fpecimen of his faith and doctrine

Lambert continued in cuftody at *Oxford* till the next year, 1533, in which archbifhop *Warham* died, and was fucceeded by *Cranmer*, who was (at the time of *Warham*'s death) in *Germany*, debating the affair of the king's divorce　The death of the archbifhop, and the rife of queen *Anne* of *Boleyn*, feem to have been the immediate caufes of *Lambert*'s releafe, which he had no fooner obtained than he repaired to *London*, and engaged himfelf in teaching the Greek and Latin tongues　He preferred this fecular bufinefs to the priefthood, as times went, and as he meant to marry and fettle, he purpofed to take up the freedom of the city in the grocer's company. But GOD, who appoints and disappoints the inclinations and purposes of men after his own will and wisdom, called this blessed man to a higher vocation, and to give up his life as a martyr for the testimony of *Jesus*.

Sometime in the year 1538, *Lambert* was present at a sermon, preached by a Dr *Taylor*, who, it seems, was then rather a friend to the gospel, and was afterwards made bishop of *Lincoln* in the reign of king *Edward*, and finally deprived by queen *Mary*. *Lambert*, whether he was dissatisfied with the sermon, or had a good opinion of the preacher, desired to have a friendly conference with him, and proposed, in the course of conversation, several theological points, on which he desired to be satisfied, the chief of which was the question concerning the corporal presence of *Christ* in the sacrament. *Taylor*, pressed perhaps too close, desired *Lambert* to excuse him for the present, on account of other business, and to write his mind upon the matter, which they would talk over again at their leisure.

Lambert accordingly proposed ten arguments in writing for support of his opinion, which are mostly lost except the first, which was founded upon these words, *This cup is the New Testament*, &c. "Now, says he, if these words "do neither change the cup nor the wine therein sub-"stantially into the New Testament, which nobody as-"serts, then, by parity of reason, the words, spoken of "the bread, do not turn the bread corporally into the "person of *Christ*". The other reasons are said to have been equally acute, and supported by the scriptures and by testimonies from the primitive fathers.

Taylor, out of a real wish to satisfy *Lambert*, and feeling himself unable to answer him, applied among others to Dr *Barnes*, a good man, but as yet (like many good men at the dawning of the Reformation) not sufficiently clear in the matter of the sacrament. *Barnes* advised *Taylor* to lay the matter before *Cranmer*, the archbishop, who then was an advocate for transubstantiation, and *Lambert* was obliged to defend his doctrine in open court before him and some other bishops. This published *Lambert* and his opinions to the whole court and city.

Gardiner, bishop of *Winchester*, glad of every opportunity of insinuating himself into the king's good graces, suggested to his majesty, That now an opportunity occurred to shew to all the world, that though he had renounced the supreme authority of the bishop of *Rome*, he

had

had not renounced the catholic faith (which the king had profeſſed not to do), and that therefore he would proſecute and puniſh all hereties and others, who ſhould preſume to ſet forth doctrines contrary to it That this *Lambert* might be made a proper example, and that by his puniſhment he might quiet the apprehenſions of the people, with reſpect to further innovations

The king eagerly caught the bait, and immediately iſſued a general ordinance, commanding all the nobility and biſhops of the realm forthwith to repair to *London*, in order to aſſiſt the king againſt hereties and hereſies, as he purpoſed to ſit *perſonally* in judgement upon them

Vaſt was the concourſe of people aſſembled to ſee this ſolemn buſineſs, and the apparatus for the trial was no leſs extraordinary The king himſelf came as judge, with a great guard, and ſat upon the throne prepared for him, arrayed in white On his right-hand were the biſhops, and behind them the judges and crown lawyers, cloathed all in purple, and, on his left, the peers of the realm and other officers of the crown, according to precedency Such an appearance, with the king's ſevere looks, words, and manner, would have ſufficed to daunt any man, who could not rely upon the promiſe, That GOD's people ſhould *ſpeak* in his cauſe *before kings, and not be aſhamed.*

It would be long to enter upon the cruel and unfair proceedings of this memorable day. The imperious frowns and threats of the king, and the meek and humble deportment of *Lambert*, can only be paralleled by the hiſtory of *Caiaphas* the high-prieſt, or *Pontius Pilate*, and *Lambert*'s Saviour *Cranmer*, it is to be regretted, oppoſed a cauſe on that day, for which *Cranmer* himſelf not many years afterwards ſuffered and bled *Lambert* defended himſelf with the firmneſs of a man, the learning of a ſcholar, and the humility of a Chriſtian The iſſue was predetermined in the king's mind, and all the eloquence and truth in the world would have been of no avail The king commanded *Cromwell* (the famous lord *Cromwell*, who ſo much ſupported the Reformation) to read the doleful ſentence of condemnation. It was *Lambert*'s peculiar caſe, not only to be a martyr, but to ſuffer by thoſe who, in their turn and for the ſame identical cauſe, were not long afterwards martyrs themſelves

It appears, that, upon this judgement, he was confined to lord *Cromwell*'s houſe, and that *Cromwell* beſought his forgiveneſs for what he had been compelled to do (it is ſaid, by *Gardiner*'s particular management) againſt him.

3   Upon

Upon the day of his death, he breakfasted with great chearfulness among *Cromwell's* gentlemen, saluted them with great ease and respect upon his departure, and was led out as a lamb for a burnt-sacrifice

No man was used at the stake with more cruelty than this holy martyr. They burned him with a slow fire by inches, for if it kindled higher and stronger than they chose, they removed it away When his legs were burnt off, and his thighs were mere stumps in the fire, they pitched his poor body upon pikes, and lacerated his broiling flesh with their halberts. But GOD was with him in the midst of the flame, and supported him in all the anguish of nature Just before he expired, he lifted up such hands as he had, all flaming with fire, and cried out to the people with his dying voice in these glorious words, NONE BUT CHRIST, NONE BUT CHRIST Spoken in this manner, and at such a time, there was more energy in them than could have been expressed in a volume He was at last beat down into the fire, and flew, in a chariot of flame, to heaven

During his confinement, he wrote a long treatise to the king, in which he apologized for his faith and doctrine; a part of which treatise is preserved by *Fox* in his Acts and Monuments, to which we must refer the Reader

We promised just to extract a few words from his first examination, that the Reader may see something of the evangelical doctrines of this good man In the course of his defence before archbishop *Warham*, he was asked, ' *Dost thou believe, that whatsoever is done of man, whether* ' *it be good or ill, cometh of* NECESSITY?' Mr *Lambert* easily perceived, that his being so closely questioned on the article of *predestination*, was no other than a trap laid for his life. His reply did equal honor to his prudence and faithfulness " Unto the *first* part of your riddle, I " neither can nor will give any definitive answer —Con- " cerning the *second* part, *Whether man hath free-will, or* " *no, to deserve joy or pain?* As for our *deserving of joy*, in " particular, I think it very little or none, even when " we do the very commandments and law of God *When* " *ye have done all that are commanded you*, saith our Saviour, " *say that ye be unprofitable servants* When we have done " his bidding, we ought not so to magnify neither our " *self*, nor our own *free-will* But laud HIM, with a meek " heart, through whose benefit we have done (if at any " time we do it) his liking and pleasure Hence *Austin* " prayeth, *Domine, da quod jubes, et jube quod vis* " Lord, give what thou commandest, and command what thou wilt.

" Concerning

" Concerning FREE-WILL, I mean altogether as doth St
" *Auſtin* That, of ourſelves, we have NO *liberty* nor *abi-*
" *lity* to do the will of God, but are *ſhut up* and *ſold*
" *under ſin*, as both *Iſaiah* and *Paul* bear witneſs But
" by the GRACE of God we are rid and ſet at liberty,
" according to the portion which every man" [i e every
regenerate man] " hath received of the ſame, ſome more,
" ſome leſs."

Lambert was alſo aſked, ' *Whether faith alone, without*
' *good works, may ſuffice to the ſalvation and juſtification of*
' *a man, who has fallen into ſin after baptiſm ?*' The martyr anſwered, in the words of St *Auſtin*, " *Opera bona*
" *non faciunt juſtum, ſed juſtificatus facit bona opera* The
" PERFORMANCE of GOOD WORKS does not *juſtify* a
" man, but the man who IS JUSTIFIED *performs* GOOD
" WORKS."

URBANUS REGIUS.

U RBANUS REGIUS was born in *Arga Longa*,
in the territories of the counts *de Montfort* His
family name was *Rex*, or *King*, which was changed by the
family, as it was often applied in ridicule Having given
early proofs of his genius, he received a liberal education,
firſt at the ſchool of *Lindau*, and afterwards at *Friburg*,
where he lived with *Zaſius*, an excellent civilian, who had
the greateſt regard for him on account of his diligence and
induſtry Indeed, his application was very extraordinary,
for he buried himſelf in the library of his learned friend,
and frequently ſat up whole nights in reading authors and
tranſcribing the remarks, which *Zaſius* and other ſcholars
had made upon them, inſomuch that his kind hoſt jocu-
larly told him, ' that he certainly meant to rob him of
' his profeſſion and knowledge ' 'Tis ſaid, that *Zaſius*
loved him as a ſon, both for his delight in learning and
ſweetneſs of manners And *Urban* did not fail to anſwer
all the expectations, which had been conceived of him.

From

From *Friburg* he went to *Bafil* for further improvement, and from *Bafil* to *Ingolftadt*, which univerfity was under the direction of the famous *John Eckius* Here, after a while, he read privately to feveral noblemen's fons, whofe parents defired him to furnifh their children with books and other neceffaries, for which they would take care to remit him the money quarterly, but neglecting to fulfil their promife, he was obliged to give up his books and furniture to be divided amongft his creditors, and in de-fpair went to a captain, who was recruiting for the war againft the *Turks*, and lifted himfelf for a foldier It foon happened, that his friend *Eckius*, walking abroad to fee the foldiers, fpied poor *Urban* amongft them. *Eckius* with aftonifhment enquired the caufe of this fudden change *Urban* prefently told him the behavior of thofe noblemen, whofe children he had tutored And *Eckius* foon took the means of procuring his difcharge from the captain, as well as the money due to him from the noblemen

Urban then returned to his ftudies, and growing famous for his great erudition and ingenuity, the emperor *Maximilian*, paffing through *Ingolftadt*, made him his poet-laureat and orator Afterwards, he was made profeffor of poetry and oratory in that univerfity He then applied himfelf clofely to the ftudy of divinity, and, a while after, the controverfy growing hot between *Luther* and *Eckius*, *Urban* favoring *Luther*'s doctrine, yet unwilling to offend *Eckius*, who had been his very good friend in many in-ftances, he left *Ingolftadt* and went to *Augfburgh*, where, at the importunity of the magiftrates and citizens, he undertook the government of the church As he began to fee more and more of the purity of the gofpel, he could not but be offended at the grofs idolatry and corruptions of the papifts, and foon joined with *Luther* in preaching againft them. He alfo wrote to *Zuinglius* to know his judgement about the facrament and original-fin, from whom he received fo much fatisfaction, that he agreed with him entirely in thefe particulars ' Wherever (fays ' *Melchior Adam*) he faw the truth, he openly embraced ' and boldly confeffed it ' At that time, the enthufiaftic Anabaptifts (who followed *John* of *Leyden*, *David George*, and the other ranting cut-throats) crept into *Augfburgh*, and held private conventicles to the difturbance of the public peace, but the magiftrates imprifoning the chief of them, and punifhing the incorrigible, put an end to their difturbance in that city.

U He

He went on preaching againſt purgatory, indulgences, and the other corruptions, till the papiſts were ſo enraged, that they drove him out of the city But, after a while, through the entreaties of ſome principal citizens, he was called back again to his charge He then married a citizen's daughter, by whom he had thirteen children His friend *Eckius* wrote to him, on his return, a ſevere letter, dated *March* 21ſt, 1527, which *Urban* anſwered with equal meekneſs and faithfulneſs, recapitulating his great obligations to him on the account of his learning and friendſhip, and aſſuring him that nothing but the truth had led him to his preſent profeſſion, which by no means tended to promote his worldly intereſt or glory *Eckius* could not reſt here, but endeavored by all means, though in vain, to turn him away from the truth; and ſent *Faber* and *Cochlæus* with flatteries and large promiſes, who prevailed as little as himſelf

There was a diet held at *Augſburgh*, in the year 1530, for quieting the controverſies about religion, at which was preſent the duke of *Brunſwick*, who much importuned and at laſt prevailed with *Urban* to go to *Lunenburg* in his dominions, to take care of the church there *Urban* in his way thither, viſited *Luther* at *Coburg*, and ſpent a whole day with him in familiar conferences about the principal doctrines; and in his writings mentions this as one of the moſt comfortable days of his life " Such and ſo great " a divine is *Luther* (ſays he) that I think no age has ſeen " his equal. I always thought him a great man, but he " now appears to me the greateſt of all I ſaw him and " heard him, the manner of which cannot be deſcribed " by the pen " *Erneſt*, duke of *Brunſwick*, loved him dearly, and eſteemed him as a father, and when the city of *Augſburgh* ſent to the duke in the year 1531, deſiring him to permit *Urban*'s return to them, the duke gave for anſwer, ' That he would as ſoon part with his eyes ' as with him,' and preſently after made him chief paſtor of all the churches in his dominions, with an ample ſalary for his ſupport

Here he ſpent the reſt of his moſt uſeful life, in preaching, writing, and religious conferences, confuting gainſayers and confirming the faithful. Some years afterwards going with his prince to *Haguenau*, he fell ſick by the way, and in a few days, with much cheerfulneſs, yielded up his ſoul into the hands of God, on the 23d of *May*, in 1541 He often deſired of the Lord, if it were his will, that he might die a ſudden and eaſy death, which

which requeſt the Lord was pleaſed to grant him He was a man of an excellent underſtanding, of uncommon learning, holy and upright in his life and converſation, and moſt indefatigable in the labors of his ſacred function.

Sleidan mentions his writings againſt the Anabaptiſts, in conjunction or at the ſame time with *Melancthon* and *Juſtus Menius* His ſon *Ernſt* collected and publiſhed his works, after his deceaſe, by the deſire of his affectionate patron the duke of *Brunſwick* His common-places of the fathers, &c were printed afterwards in a ſeparate volume by *John Fred* Our excellent martyrologiſt, Mr *Fox*, is ſaid to have tranſlated one of *Regius's* treatiſes, upon faith and hope (if not more) from the original *Latin* into *Engliſh*.

WOLFGANG FABR. CAPITO.

WOLFGANG FABRICIUS CAPITO was born at *Haguinau* in *Alſace*, in the year 1478 His father was of the ſenatorian rank, who gave him a good education, and ſent him to *Baſil*, where he ſtudied phyſic till he had taken his doctor's degree, and likewiſe attained a very great proficiency in the other liberal ſciences. At his father's death, in 1504, he ſtudied divinity, and entered into the logic of thoſe times, with all the idle ſubtilties and metaphyſical jargon of the ſchools After this courſe of ſtudy, he read the civil law under *Zaſius*, an eminent civilian, for four years, and finally took his doctor's degree in that line. He was a great admirer and ſupporter of godly miniſters. At *Heidelberg* he became acquainted with *Oecolampadius*, with whom there ever afterwards ſubſiſted the ſtrongeſt tie of friendſhip and mutual communication. He ſtudied *Hebrew* with his friend *Oecolampadius* under the tuition of one *Matthew Adrian*, a converted *Jew*, and then became a preacher, firſt in *Spire*, and afterwards at *Baſil*, where he continued for ſome years

From thence he was ſent for by the *Elector Palatine*, who made him his counſellor, and ſent him on ſeveral embaſ-

ſies

fies And *Charles* the fifth conferred upon him the order of knighthood From *Mentz* he followed *Bucer* to *Strasburgh*, where he aftonished the world by preaching the reformed religion, at St *Thomas's Church* in that city, beginning his miniftry by expounding St *Paul's* epiftle to the *Coloffians* The fame of *Capito* and *Bucer* fpread fo wide, that *James Faber* and *Gerard Rufus* were fent privately from *France* to hear him, by *Margaret* queen of *Navarre*, fifter to the *French* king, and thus the proteftant doctrine was introduced into *France* *Capito* was a very prudent and eloquent man, a great critic in the *Hebrew* tongue, and mafter of the whole circle of human knowledge. This, with the endowment of the higheft wifdom—the knowledge of God and his truth, furnished him in the moft eminent manner for the facred function And God bleffed him accordingly Next to his love of the purity of the gofpel, he was very earneft that the gofpel fhould be received in mutual love and peace among its profeffors

His opinion (following that of *Oecolampadius*) concerning the facrament was, *Mittendas effe contentiones, & cogitandum de ufu ipfius coenae Viz fidem noftram pane, & vino Domini, per memoriam carnis, & fanguinis illius, pafcendam.* i. e. Difputes about the Lord's Supper fhould, as much as poffible, be avoided, and the chief point to be defired was its ufe and benefit, namely, that our faith may be ftrengthened and nourished by the Lord's bread and wine, in memory of his flesh and blood.

In the year 1525, he received a call to return to his own country, where he preached the gofpel in purity, and adminiftered the Lord's Supper, according to *Chrift's* inftitution, to his fellow citizens, and baptized without the popish ceremonies. He frequently made excurfions into the neighboring parts of *Switzerland*, and confirmed the fouls of the faithful by his doctrine. He was alfo prefent and difputed at *Bern*, in 1528, againft the popish mafs, &c He was, with feveral others, chofen by the proteftants to go to the *diet* at *Ratifbon*, in the year 1541, for the fettling of religion, and was much diftinguished in that controverfy Returning home, in a great and general infection, he died of the plague, about the end of the year 1541, in the fixty-third year of his age.

Capito was a very great fcholar himfelf, and a great promoter of learning in others. He was convinced, that true knowledge and true grace conjoined would give the fevereft fhock to the devil's kingdom And for the honor of the proteftant religion it may be faid, that it not only
introduced

introduced the revival of science throughout *Europe*, but has cherished it ever since in the most remarkable manner

Capito was ever importunate with *Erasmus*, to throw of his Nicodemean disguise, and to embrace the protestant religion openly, but *Erasmus* had neither the grace nor the zeal of *Capito* *Oecolampadius* was his principal and dearest friend, though he corresponded with all the other great divines of his time

He married the widow of his friend *Oecolampadius*, and by her had several children He had before married another lady, a literary woman, who lived but a short time, as it seems, with him before her death.

Among other works, he left behind him, two books upon the *Jewish* œconomy, expositions upon the prophets *Habakkuk* and *Hosea*, the life of *John Oecolampadius*, a tract upon the best mode of education for a divine, &c &c.

SIMON GRYNÆUS.

SIMON GRYNÆUS, a most able and learned man, was the son of a peasant of *Swabia*, and born at *Veringen*, in the county of *Hokenzollern*, in the year 1493. He pursued his studies in *Pfortsheim* at the same time with *Melancthon*, which gave rise to a friendship between them of long continuance. He pursued them at *Vienna*, and there taking the degree of master in philosophy, was appointed Greek professor Having embraced the protestant religion, he was thereby exposed to many dangers, and particularly in *Baden*, where he was some years rector of the school. He was thrown into prison at the instigation of the monks, but, at the solicitation of the nobles of *Hungary*, he was set at liberty, and retired to *Wittenberg*, where he had a conference with *Luther* and *Melancthon* Being returned to his native country, he was invited to *Heidelberg*, to be Greek professor in that city in 1523 He exercised this employment till the year 1529, when he was invited to *Basil* to teach publicly

in

in that city In 1531, he took a journey into *England*, and carried with him a recommendatory letter from *Erasmus* to *William Montjoy*, dated *Fribourg*, *March* the 18th, 1531. After defiring *Montjoy* to affift *Grynæus* as much as he could, in fhewing him libraries, and introducing him to learned men, *Erasmus* adds ' *Est homo Latine Græ-* ' *ceque ad unguem doctus, in philosophia et mathematicis* ' *disciplinis diligenter versatus, nullo supercilio, pudore penè* ' *immodico Pertraxit hominem istuc Brittanniæ visendæ* ' *cupiditas, sed præcipuè Bibliothecarum vestrarum amor.* ' *Rediturus est ad nos, &c* ' That is, He is a man perfectly fkilled in the Latin and Greek tongues, a good philofo- pher, and mathematician, without the leaft affectation, and modeft almoft to excefs The defire of feeing *Eng- land*, and efpecially the love of your libraries, has drawn him over But he muft return to us again, &c *Bibli- ander* alfo called him ' an incomparable man, in whom ' every Chriftian grace and virtue, with all learning and ' politenefs, feemed to have taken up their habitation ' *Erasmus* recommended him alfo to the lord chancellor Sir *Thomas More*, from whom he received great civilities. This appears by an epiftle of *Grynæus*, prefixed to his Greek edition of *Plato*, in 1534 In the year 1534, he was employed, in conjunction with other perfons, to reform the church and fchool of *Tubingen* He returned to *Bafil* in 1536, and in 1540 was appointed to go to the conferences at *Worms* with *Melancthon*, *Capito*, *Bucer*, *Calvin*, &c He died of the plague at *Bafil* on the firft of *Auguft* in 1541

He did great fervice to the republic of letters, and the learned are obliged to him for the editions of feveral an- tient authors He was the firft who publifhed the *Alma- geft* of *Ptolemy* in Greek, which he did at *Bafil* in 1538, and added a preface concerning the ufe of that author's doctrine. He publifhed a Greek *Euclid*, with a preface, in 1533, and *Plato*'s works, with fome commentaries of *Proclus* in 1534. He corrected in fome places *Marfilius Ficinus*'s Latin verfion of *Plato* Yet it fhould feem, as if he did not excel as a tranflator, for *Huetius* calls him ' verbofe, and more like a paraphraft ' He wrote a trea- tife upon the ufe of hiftory, and a difputation upon comets His edition of *Plato* was addrefsed to *John More*, the chancellor's fon, as a teftimony of gratitude for fa- vor's received from the father, and as the following paf- fage in the dedication fhews Sir *Thomas*, as well as *Grynæus*, in a very amiable light, we think it not amifs

to

to infert it here Our Readers will remember, that it is
in a *dedication*, in which, we are forry to fay, that good
men too often render truth itfelf hyperbolical, and fometimes fancy that men *are*, what indeed they *ought to be*
We do not mean, by this remark, to detract from the
perfonal worth of Sir *Thomas More*, which was certainly
very great, though we confefs it not a little extraordinary,
that this great man fhould perfecute, or at leaft approve
the perfecution of, fome proteftants to death only for
their religion, while he could at the fame time pafs over
this terrible fault in others, merely for a literary recommendation As to *Grynæus*, we value him as a fcholar
and promoter of fcience, which indeed is a fecondary
promotion of true religion, but we give him a place here
chiefly becaufe he was a good man, a lover of the Reformation, and confidentially employed by the Reformers

" It is you know (fays *Grynæus*) three years fince my
" arriving in *England*, and being recommended moft
" aufpicioufly by my friend *Erafmus* to your houfe, the
" facred feat of the mufes, I was there received with
" great kindnefs, was entertained with greater, was dif-
" miffed with the greateft of all For that great and
" excellent man your father, fo eminent for his high rank
" and noble talents, not only allowed to me, a private
" and obfcure perfon, (fuch was his love of literature)
" the honor of converfing with him in the midft of
" many public and private affairs, but gave me a place at
" his table, though he was the greateft man in *England*,
" took me with him when he went to court or returned
" from it, and had me ever by his fide, but alfo with
" the utmoft gentlenefs and candour enquired, in what
" particulars my religious principles were different from
" his, and though he found them to vary greatly, yet
" he was fo kind as to affift me in every refpect, and even
" to defray all my expences He likewife fent me to
" *Oxford* with one Mr *Harris*, a learned young gentle-
" man, and recommended me fo powerfully to the uni-
" verfity, that, at the fight of his letters, all the libraries
" were open to me, and I was admitted to the moft inti-
" mate familiarity with the ftudents "

He had a fon, *Samuel Grynæus*, born at *Bafil* in 1539;
who was made profeffor of oratory there at the age of
twenty-five, and afterwards of civil law, and who died
there in *April* 1599 He was uncle to *Thomas Grynæus*,
the account of whofe life will follow in its place.

LEO

LEO JUDÆ.

THIS great and good divine was born in *Alface*, in 1482, was brought up in the fchool of *Sleftadt*, and from thence was fent to *Bafil*, about the year 1502, where he joined in ftudy with the famous *Zuinglius* under the tuition of Dr. *Wittenbafh*, a very learned man, by whom he received the firft principles of the evangelical doctrine concerning *Chrift*'s fatisfaction for fin and the leading truths of the gofpel   In this univerfity he made a great proficiency in letters, and in the year 1512 took his degree of mafter of arts and profeffed philofophy.   There alfo he was made a deacon, and from this miniftration was called into *Switzerland*, where he devoted himfelf to the ftudy of the oriental languages, and to the reading of the fathers, particularly of *Jerom* and *Auguftine*   He likewife diligently read the books of *Luther*, *Erafmus*, and *Reuchlin* the famous *Hebræan*

By the writings of thefe excellent men he more plainly difcovered, and afterwards utterly abhorred the idolatrous fuperftitions of the church of *Rome*.   At length, being called to a paftoral charge at *Zurich*, he openly oppofed the popifh doctrine, both from the pulpit and prefs, and became diftinguifhed among the great and burning lights of the Reformation   At *Zurich* he continued eighteen years, and fpent much of that time in expounding the Old Teftament out of the *Hebrew*, in the knowledge of which having made uncommon progrefs, he was folicited by his brethren in the miniftry, to undertake the tranf-lation of the Old Teftament, with which requeft he complied, and was affifted by other learned men   He diligently collated all the *Hebrew* copies, which he could command, for the interpretation of the moft difficult places, and made great ufe of the *Greek* and *Latin* tranf-lations, without entirely depending upon them   But he profecuted this work with fuch intenfenefs of application, that he deftroyed his health, and died with all the debility of extreme age at fixty, on the 9th of *June*, in the year 1542;

1542, leaving unfinished *Job*, the forty laſt *Pſalms*, *Proverbs*, *Eccleſaſtes*, *Canticles*, and the eight laſt chapters of *Ezekiel*, which he commended to *Theodore Bibliander* to finiſh, who accordingly did it. And he left all to *Conrade Pellican* to peruſe, and put to the preſs, which he carefully performed. This tranſlation *Robert Stephens* afterwards in a great meaſure pirated, without once making mention of the names of theſe worthies, by whoſe learning and labor it had been accompliſhed.

Four days before his death, he ſent for the paſtors and profeſſors of *Zurich*, before whom he made a confeſſion of his faith concerning GOD, the ſcriptures, the perſon and offices of CHRIST, and the ſufficiency of his ſalvation, concluding with theſe words, " To this, my Lord
" and Saviour *Jeſus Chriſt*, my hope, and my ſalvation,
" I wholly offer up my ſoul and body. I caſt myſelf
" wholly upon His mercy and grace. Utterly abandon-
" ing all that is in myſelf, I entirely caſt myſelf upon
" his promiſes for eternal life, and in this confidence I
" fear not to die, firmly truſting, that I ſhall enjoy that
" moſt bleſſed Saviour, whom I have now ſo long preached
" to others, and whoſe face I have ſo long deſired to ſee,
" in that ſtate, where is the fullneſs of joy for ever and
" ever."

Having ſaid this, he moſt devoutly gave thanks to God for all the mercies he had received, deſired his bleſſing upon the church and people of the country where he had lived, and finally commended his dear wife, now about to become a widow, with his orphan children, to the tender mercies of his heavenly Father.

Beſides the tranſlation abovementioned, *Leo Judæ* wrote annotations upon *Geneſis* and *Exodus*, in which he was aſſiſted by *Zuinglius*, likewiſe upon the four goſpels, and upon the epiſtles to the *Romans*, *Corinthians*, *Philippians*, *Coloſſians*, *Theſſalonians*, and of *James*. He alſo compoſed a larger and ſmaller catechiſm, and tranſlated ſome of *Zuinglius*'s works into *Latin*.

Our Dr *More*, in his *Exercitationes de Scripturâ ſacrâ*, ſays of *Leo*, that he was extremely learned in the *Hebrew* tongue, and remarks likewiſe that his bible was printed at *Paris* by *Robert Stephens*, with the notes of *Vatablus* and others, under another name.

X

PETER

PETER BRULIUS.

ABOUT the year 1538, a college or fchool was opened at *Strafburg*, a free imperial city upon the *Rhine*, chiefly by the endeavors and procurement of the celebrated *James Sturmius*, one of the principal citizens and a fenator By the care and attention of this learned and worthy man, and by the learning and abilities of the mafters appointed through his recommendation, this feminary quickly arrived to the firft degree of eminence, and became famous all over *Germany* and the neighbouring countries. Proteftantifm and true knowledge at that time florifhed together. Invited by this and other favorable circumftances, great numbers of *French* and *Flemings*, driven from their native country upon the account of religion, fettled at *Strafburg*, where the fenate of the city affigned them a church for public worfhip, and allowed them the privilege of incorporating themfelves into a diftinct body. One of thefe was the famous *John Sleidan*, author of the hiftory of the Reformation, who died there on the 31ft of *October*, 1556. Of this church *Calvin* was paftor for fome years, and was fucceeded by *Brulius*, very much to the comfort and fatisfaction of the people

Throughout all the provinces, belonging to the emperor, in the *Netherlands*, there prevailed at this period among the people the moft earneft defire to be inftructed in the reformed religion, fo that in places where the truth was not, or dared not to be, preached, private invitations were fent to the minifters, who refided in towns, where the pure gofpel was preached openly Some people in *Tournay*, accordingly, invited *Brulius* from *Strafburg*. Ready to every good word and work, this excellent man complied with their requeft, and arrived at *Tournay* in the month of *September*, 1544, and was moft joyfully received by thofe who had invited him. After ftaying fometime, he made an excurfion to *Lifle* in *Flanders*, upon

the

the fame account, and returned to *Tournay* about the end of *October* following   But, by fome means, his bufinefs and profeffion were divulged to the papiftical governors of the city, who ordered ftrict fearch to be made for him, and the gates to be fhut for the purpofe   In this imminent danger, as there was no poffibility of concealing him longer, his friends, on the fecond of *November*, in the night, let him down over the wall by a rope.   When he had reached the ground, he fat down to take a little reft, but one of thofe, who affifted in his efcape, leaning as far as he could over the wall, that he might foftly bid him farewell, forced out a loofe ftone with his foot, which fell upon *Brulius*'s leg and broke it   The pain occafioned by this wound and the fevere cold of the night, extorted fuch loud groans from the good man, as alarmed the watch, who foon feized their prey and committed him to prifon   The afflicting news was not long in reaching *Germany*, nor was the fenate of *Strafburg* flow in interceding for his releafe by the moft preffing letters.   The deputies of the proteftants, then affembled at *Worms*, alfo fued in his behalf, though unhappily too late, for before the letters, which were fent in the name of the duke of *Saxony* and the landgrave of *Heffe*, were delivered, he was on the 19th of *February*, 1545, put to death, to the great grief of all good men

The manner of his execution was fevere, his body being burnt by a flow-fire, for his greater torment. But nothing could triumph over his faith, for he ftood to the truth of GOD to his laft breath, and exhorted, by his letters, many of his friends to do fo, who were imprifoned for the fake of the gofpel.   When he was examined in prifon, the monks, in prefence of the magiftrates, afked him the queftion, ' What he thought ' of the facrament of the altar, of the mafs, confecration, ' adoration of the hoft, of purgatory, of the worfhipping ' of faints, free-will, good works, juftification, images, ' vows, confeffion, and the like.'   To thefe he made anfwer, " That the body and blood of *Chrift* were re-" ceived, not by the mouth, but fpiritually by faith; " and that the fubftance of the bread and wine was not " changed   That, when according to *Chrift*'s inftitu-" tion, the Lord's Supper is given to the church in the " vulgar tongue, fo that all may underftand the ufe and " benefit of it, that then the elements are duly confe-" crated, and that by the words of *Chrift*, whereas the " whifpers and mutterings, ufed by the mafs-priefts over " the bread and wine, better became conjurers and jug-

" glers,

" glers, than Chriſtian miniſters That the popiſh maſs
" had nothing to do with the Lord's Supper, but was a
" worſhip invented by man, to the diſparagement of the
" inſtitution of *Chriſt* That the adoration of the wafer
" was idolatry, becauſe a creature was there worſhipped
" inſtead of the Creator That he neither knew, nor
" cared for, any other purgatory, than the blood of *Chriſt*,
" which alone remits both the guilt and puniſhment of
" our ſins That, therefore, maſſes and prayers for the
" dead, were not only uſeleſs, but impious, as having no
" warrant from the word of GOD That ſaints cannot
" be more truly reſpected, than by imitating their faith
" and virtues, and that, if more be done, it is impious,
" and what they themſelves, were they in the world,
" would tremble at and abhor That, therefore, they are
" not to be invoked as interceſſors, which would be giv-
" ing them a glory which belongs to *Chriſt* alone That,
" by the fall of *Adam*, the nature of man is wholly cor-
" rupted, and the freedom of his will forfeited, ſo that
" he can do no good, without the grace of GOD, but
" that a regenerated man, moved by GOD, like a good
" tree brings forth good fruits That nothing deſerves
" the name of faith, but what bringeth us ſalvation,
" namely, when we believe the divine promiſes, and cer-
" tainly conclude, that through *Chriſt Jeſus* our ſins are
" forgiven us . That traditions, by which the minds of
" men are enſlaved, are not to be received That it was
" very dangerous to have ſtatues and images in churches,
" for fear of idolatry That baptiſm is the outward ſign
" of GOD's covenant, whereby he teſtifies that he will
" pardon our ſins, and likewiſe a ſign of perpetual mor-
" tification and a new life, which ought to accompany
" baptiſm That this ſacrament is to be received by all,
" and children not to be barred from it, ſeeing they alſo
" are partakers of the divine promiſes That no vow is
" to be made, which either the word of GOD doth not
" allow, or that cannot be performed by man That
" every one ought to confeſs his ſins to GOD, and im-
" plore his mercy and forgiveneſs That, if the conſcience
" be diſquieted, counſel is to be taken of a miniſter of the
" church, for advice and comfort, but that auricular
" confeſſion and a particular enumeration of ſins to a
" prieſt, has no warrant in ſcripture, nor can be of any
" poſſible uſe."

Some days before he was brought to a tryal, he wrote
of all theſe things to his wife and to his other friends,

I   who

who had earneftly requefted an account of his treatment from him His fifter, who appears to have vifited him conftantly in his confinement, found means privately to convey this correspondence to the parties The laft letter this excellent man wrote muft have been a moft afflicting one indeed It was written to his wife the day before he fuffered He gave her an account of the kind of death he was to endure on the enfuing day, and filled his letter with pious exhortations and confolations to her, concluding that fhe ought not to be grieved for his fake but to rejoice, fince this whole difpenfation was an honor that his heavenly Father conferred upon him, that *Jefus Chrift* had fuffered infinitely more for him, and that, however, " The fervant's condition ought not to be better than his " Lord's "—What a proof is here, among a multitude of others, of the omnipotent efficacy of divine grace, which can make the nature of man, always fhrinking from pain, defy the power of torment, and which can give the human heart, when it is ftripped of all worldly comfort, fuch a flood of joy, as to bear it up over death, and all the other evils which wicked men or wicked fpirits can inflict upon it!

From this time for many years afterwards, the hiftory of pious men and women, profeffing the proteftant doctrine, who fuffered in *Germany, France, Flanders,* and indeed all over *Europe,* would be too voluminous in itfelf, and beyond the bounds we have prefcribed ourfelves in this work, to be detailed The minifters alone who preached or fuffered for the truths of the gofpel cannot be fpecified by us, without exceeding the purpofe of our plan We wifh to give the Reader the moft remarkable of thefe for life, learning, and doctrine, though it is hard to determine fometimes, not whom to infert (for, bleffed be GOD, their number is abundantly large) but whom, on account of their excellency, to omit without feeming to flight thofe excellent endowments, which God had vouchfafed them If the *martyrs* themfelves make up a *noble army,* what will the other eminent fervants of *Chrift* compofe, who only had the honor of preaching his gofpel ? And if *martyrs* and *preachers* would form fo immenfe an affembly, we may well fay, in the words of the fcripture, of the reft of GOD's people, that they are *a great multitude, which no man can number, of all nations, and kindreds, and people, and tongues.* Even fo, Amen Hallelujah !

MARTIN

MARTIN LUTHER,

The GREAT REFORMER.

IN the order of time, we come now to treat of a moſt wonderful man, whom GOD raiſed up in theſe laſt ages of the world, to break the chain of ſuperſtition and ſpiritual ſlavery, with which the biſhops of *Rome* and their dependents had, for many centuries, caſt over the conſciences of all men. He was an inſtrument truly prepared for this great work, and yet but a mean and obſcure monk, to ſhew us, that HE, who ruleth all things, efſected himſelf the important deſign, in which the greateſt prince upon earth would have undoubtedly failed.

The conduct of the dignified clergy throughout all *Europe*, had long given ſcandal to the world. The biſhops were groſsly ignorant. They ſeldom reſided in their dioceſes, except to riot at high feſtivals · And all the effect their reſidence could have, was to corrupt others, by their ill example. Nay, ſome of them could not ſo much as *write*, but employed ſome perſon, or chaplain who had attained that accompliſhment, to ſubſcribe their names for them. They followed the courts of princes, and aſpired to the greateſt offices. The abbots and monks were wholly given up to luxury and idleneſs, and it appeared, by the unmarried ſtate both of the ſeculars and regulars, that the reſtraining them from having wives of their own, made them conclude they had a right to all other men's. The inferior clergy were no better, and, not having places of retreat to conceal their vices in, as the monks had, they became more public In ſum, all ranks of churchmen were ſo univerſally deſpiſed and hated, that the world was very apt to be poſſeſſed with prejudice againſt their doctrines, for the ſake of the men whoſe intereſt it was to ſupport them. And the worſhip of God

was

LVTHER.

From an original Painting presented by Count Rennof a Bohemian Nobleman to the Lutheran Chapel in th ...

was so defiled with gross superstition, that, without great enquiries, all men were easily convinced, that the church stood in great need of a Reformation. This was much increased when the books of the fathers began to be read, in which the difference between the former and later ages of the church very evidently appeared. They found, that a blind superstition came first in the room of true piety, and when, by its means, the wealth and interest of the clergy were highly advanced, the popes had upon that established their tyranny, under which, not only the meaner people, but even the crowned heads, had long groaned. All these things concurred to make way for the advancement of the Reformation.

Wickliffe, Huss, Jerom of *Prague*, and others, had laid the seeds of the Reformation, which *Luther* nourished with great warmth. The scandalous extolling of indulgences gave the first occasion to all the contradiction that followed between *Luther* and the church of *Rome*, in which, if the corruptions and cruelty of the clergy had not been so visible and scandalous, so small a matter could not have produced such a revolution. But any crisis will put ill humours into a ferment.

As protestants, we are certainly much obliged to *Erasmus*, yet we are far more obliged, under God, to those great instruments of the Reformation, viz *Luther, Zuinglius, Oecolampadius, Bucer, Melanthon, Cranmer,* and others. The greatest enemies of *Luther* cannot deny, but that he had eminent qualities, and history affords nothing more surprizing than what he had done. For a simple monk to be able to give popery so rude a shock, that there needed but such another entirely to overthrow the *Romish* church, is what we cannot sufficiently admire, and marks the hand of providence conducting the whole. It was said, with reason, that *Erasmus*, by his railleries, prepared the way for *Luther*, and *Simon Fontaine* the popish historian, complained, that *Erasmus* occasionally had done more mischief than *Luther*, because *Luther* only opened the door wider, after *Erasmus* had picked the lock, and half opened it. Notwithstanding all this, says *Bayle*, there must have been eminent gifts in *Luther* to produce such a Revolution as he has done.

Martin Luther was born at *Isleben*, a town in the county of *Mansfield*, in the circle of *Upper Saxony*, on the tenth of *November*, 1483, at nine o'clock at night, being St. *Martin*'s eve, which made his parents name him *Martin*. His father was called *John Luther*, or *Luder*, because he

was

was a refiner of metals, for Luder, in the *German* language, has that fignification It is agreed that his bufinefs was about the mines, and that he was the chief magiftrate of the city of *Mansfield* His mother's name was *Margaret Lindeman*, who was remarkable for her piety

Among the falfhoods which have been publifhed concerning *Martin Luther*, no regard has been had to probability, or to the rules of the art of flandering The authors of them have affumed all the confidence of thofe who fully believe that the public will blindly adopt all their ftories, however abfurd They have dared to publifh, that an *Incubus* begat him, and have even falfified the day of his birth, to frame a fcheme of nativity to his difadvantage Father *Maimbourg* has been fo equitable as to reject this ridiculous ftory But *Gauricus* has made himfelf contemptible for his aftrology

When *Martin Luther* was fourteen years of age, he was fent to the public fchool of *Magdeburg*, where he continued one year, and was then removed to that of *Eyfenach*, where he ftudied four years The circumftances of his parents were at that time fo very low, and fo infufficient to maintain him, that he was forced, as *Melchior Adam* relates, *mendicato vivere pane*, to live by begging his bread When he had finifhed his grammar ftudies, he was fent to the famous fchool at *Eyfenech* in *Thuringia*, for the fake of being among his mother's relations, where he applied himfelf very diligently to his books for four years, and began to difcover all that force and ftrength of parts, that acutenefs and penetration, that warm and rapid eloquence, which afterwards were attended with fuch amazing fuccefs. In the year 1501, he was entered at the univerfity of *Erford* or *Erfurt*, in *Thuringia*, where he went through a courfe of philofophy, and was admitted mafter of arts, in 1503, being then twenty years old He was foon after made profeffor of phyfic, and ethics But he chiefly applied himfelf to the ftudy of the civil law, and intended to advance himfelf to the bar, from which he was diverted by this uncommon accident As he was walking in the fields with a friend, he was ftruck by a thunderbolt, which threw him to the ground, and killed his companion · Whereupon *Luther* refolved to withdraw from the world, and enter into the order of the hermits of St *Auguftine*. He made his profeffion in the monaftry of *Erfurt*, where he took prieft's orders, and celebrated his firft mafs in the year 1507.

It

It is reported, that there was an old man in this monastry, with whom *Luther* had several conferences upon many theological subjects, particularly concerning the article of remission of sins. This article was explained by the old monk to *Luther*, ' That it was the express ' commandment of God, that every man should believe ' his sins to be forgiven him in *Christ*.' *Luther* found this interpretation was confirmed by the testimony of St. *Bernard*, who says, ' That man is freely justified by ' faith.' He then perceived the meaning of St. *Paul*, when he repents, ' We are justified by faith.' He consulted the expositions of many writers upon that apostle, and saw through the vanity of those interpretations, which he had read before of the schoolmen. He compared the sayings and examples of the prophets, and apostles. He also studied the works of St. *Augustine*. But still consulted the sententiaries, is *Gabriel* and *Cananeus*. He likewise read the books of *Occam*, whose subtilty he preferred before *Thomas Aquinas* and *Scotus*.

In 1508, the university of *Wittenberg*, in the duchy of *Saxony*, was established under the direction of *Staupitius*, whose good opinion of *Luther* occasioned him to send for him from *Erfurt* to *Wittenberg*, where he taught philosophy, and his lectures were attended by *Mellanstad*, and many other wise and learned men. He expounded the logic and philosophy of *Aristotle*, in the schools, and began to examine the old theology, in the churches.

Mellanstad usually said, that *Luther* was of such a wonderful spirit, and of such ingenious parts, as to give apparent signification, that he would introduce a more compendious, easy, and familiar manner of teaching, as also alter and abolish the order that was then used.

In the year 1512, he was sent to *Rome*, to take up some controversies which happened among his order, and he conducted himself so well as to obtain the character of a prudent man. This is represented to have happened before he came to *Wittenberg*, which is a mistake. For it was three years after he was at that university. The occasion was this. Seven convents of the *Augustines* quarrelled with their vicar-general, and *Luther* was chosen by the monks to maintain their cause at *Rome*. He was of an active spirit, a bold declaimer, was endued with a most firm and steady temper, and had a prodigious share of natural courage, which nothing could break or daunt. In short, he succeeded in his business, for which he was made doctor and professor of divinity, upon his

Y

return to *Wittenberg* At *Rome* he faw the pope and the
court, and had an opportunity alfo of obferving the manners of the clergy, whofe hafty, fuperficial, and impious
way of celebrating mafs, he has feverely noted " I
" performed mafs, fays he, at *Rome*, I faw it alfo per-
" formed by others, but in fuch a manner, that I never
" think of it without the utmoft horror " He often
fpoke afterwards of his journey to *Rome*, and ufed to fay,
that " He would not but have made it for a thoufand
" florins " A monkifh poet himfelf, upon the view of
the barefaced iniquity of the pope s pretended holy city,
could not help finging

Vivere qui cupitis fanctè, difcedite Româ:
Omnia cùm liceant, non licet effe bonum '

' If you would live righteoufly, keep clear of *Rome* ·
' For though her priefts can licenfe every thing elfe,
' they allow of nothing good '

The degree of doctor was forced upon him, againft his
will, by *Staupitius*, who faid to him, ' That God had
' many things to bring to pafs in his church by him.'
Thefe words were carelefsly fpoken, yet they proved
true, like many other predictions before a great change.
Luther was graduated doctor at the expence of *Frederic*
elector of *Saxony*, who ' had heard him preach, well
' underftood the quietnefs of his fpirit, diligently con-
' fidered the vehemency of his words, and had in fingular
' admiration thofe profound matters which in his fer-
' mons he ripely and exactly explained '

After this, he began to expound the epiftle to the *Romans*, and the *Pfalms*, where he fhewed the difference
between the law and the gofpel He refuted the error that
was then predominant in fchools and fermons, that men
may merit remiffion of fins by their own proper works.
As *John Baptift* demonftrated the Lamb of God which
took away the fins of the world So *Luther*, fhining in
the church as a bright ftar after an obfcure fky, exprefsly
fhewed, that fins are freely remitted for the love of the
Son of God, and that we ought faithfully to embrace
this bountiful gift

His life was correfpondent to his profeffion, and thefe
happy beginnings of fuch important matters procured
him great authority. However, he attempted no alteration in the ceremonies of religion, and interfered in no
doubtful opinions But contented himfelf with opening
and declaring the doctrine of repentance, of remiffion of
fins,

fins, of faith, and of true comfort in times of adverfity His doctrine was generally approved by the learned, who conceived high pleafure to behold *Jefus Chrift*, the prophets, and apoftles, to emerge into the light out of darknefs, whereby they began to underftand the difference between the law and the gofpel, between fpiritual righteoufnefs and civil things, which certainly could not have been found in *Aquinas*, *Scotus*, and other fchoolmen *Erafmus* revived learning while *Luther* was teaching divinity at *Wittenberg* The former brought the monk's barbarous and fophiftical doctrine into contempt by his elegant work Which induced *Luther* to ftudy the *Greek* and *Hebrew* langunges, that, by drawing the doctrine from the very fountains, he might pafs his judgement with more authority

We come now to turbulent and tempeftuous times between the Reformed and the Romanifts The monks loudly complained of *Erafmus*, whofe bold and free cenfures of their pious grimaces and fuperftitious devotions, had opened the way for *Luther* *Erafmus*, as they ufed to fay, ' Laid the egg, and *Luther* hatched it.' The ridiculous *Maimbourg* tells us, that the catholic church enjoyed a fweet peace in the fixteenth century, and held the popes in profound veneration, till *Luther* raifed commotions A ftory which was only fit to be told to boys and girls at *Paris* It is hard to name two perfons, who were more generally, and more deſervedly abhorred, than *Alexander* VI and *Julius* II And as to *Leo* X all the world knows, that he fat very loofe to religion and morality

The year 1517, was the 356th from the Reformation of religion in *France* by the *Waldenfes* The 146th from the firft confutation of popifh errors in *England* by *John Wichliffe* The 116th from the miniftry of *John Hufs*, who oppofed the errors of popery in *Bohemia* And the 36th year from the condemnation of *John de Wefalia*, who taught at *Worms*.

The papal power was re-eftablifhed, and carried further than ever All the weftern world, except the *Waldenfes*[*] in *France*, and a few *Haffites* in *Bohemia*, having
embraced

* The rife of the *Waldenfes* was from *Waldus* or *Valdo*, a man of eminence and property at *Lyons* in *France*, about the year 1160 He was brought to ferioufnefs by the fudden death of one of his friends, and, having fome learning, he read the fcriptures, probably in the vulgate tranflation, which he rendered into *French*, and expounded to others.

embraced the communion, and submitted to the authority
of *Rome* When all of a sudden, and from a most inconsiderable accident, as it might seem, a strange discontent
arose, which ended in the revolt of great part of *Europe*,
and the pope, who might, just before, have been considered in all the meridian of his glory, was in danger
of losing all The divine providence delights to accomplish the greatest purposes by the smallest means, that
the hand of God might appear rather than the hand of
man, and the great Governor of the universe have all the
glory.

Leo X succeeded *Julius* II in 1513 He was of the
rich and powerful family of the *Medici* of *Florence*, naturally proud and lofty But it is also said, that he was
of a courteous disposition, very generous to men of learning and integrity And would, if he had been tolerably
well skilled in divinity, or shewn any regard to piety,
although but feigned, have passed for a very good pope
The magnificent church of St *Peter* was begun by *Julius* II and required very large sums to finish But *Leo*
was desirous of having it completed, notwithstanding he
had contracted many debts before his pontificate, and the
treasure of the apostolic chamber was exhausted To bear
the great expence of finishing that superb edifice, *Leo*
found himself obliged to have recourse to some extraor-

others This alarmed the clergy, who threatened him with excommunication if he persisted, but he, persuaded of the truth and utility
of what he had done, regarded not men, but God He was, therefore, driven out of the city, with his friends and followers, who were
stripped of their property, for which reason they were called not only
Waldenses, but *the poor of Lyons*, having nothing but the scanty subsistence which they could pick up on the mountains of *Savoy*, where
they remained for several ages They were joined by some men of
learning, who hated the clergy, and maintained, that the bishop of
Rome, and the priests, had corrupted the holy scriptures by their tenets
and glosses They paid no tithes, made no offerings, observed no
festivals, and celebrated no fasts They believed, that prayers for the
dead were useless and superstitious, they denied the authority of priests,
and despised confession They led pure and holy lives, and asserted,
that they only were the true church, and that the church of *Rome* was
a prostitute, which taught an infinite number of errors The *Romish*
priests called the *Waldenses*, hereticks, and their priests, who were
called *Barbes*, were persecuted But their posterity now inhabit the
vallies of *Piedmont*, called the *Vaudois* *Peter Gilles*, minister of the
reformed church of *la Tour*, in the vale of *Lucerne*, composed by
order of his superiors, an ecclesiastical history of the churches of the
Vaudois, and published it at *Geneva* in 1644 And *Claudius Seysselius*,
archbishop of *Turin* wrote a treatise against the *Vaudois*, with the
hopes of converting them to popery.

dinary

dinary means for raising money, which he was advised, by cardinal *Pucci*, to do by selling indulgences, as the court of *Rome*, upon several occasions, had formerly experienced to her advantage in raising troops and money against the *Turks* *Leo*, therefore, in 1517, published general indulgences throughout all *Europe*, in favor of those who would contribute any sum to the building of St *Peter's*

Some say, that these indulgences were published under the pretence of making war upon the *Turks*, and that the pope sent a Jubilee, with his pardons, through all Christian realms, whereby he collected an immense treasure

Several persons were sent into different countries, to preach up these indulgences, and to receive money for them The collectors persuaded the people, that those who gave to the value of about ten shillings sterling, should at their pleasure deliver one soul from the pains of purgatory But, if the sum was less, they preached, that it would profit them nothing.

The pope employed the *Dominicans* in this dirty work in *Germany*, at which the *Augustines* were irritated, and pretended that the office of retailing indulgences belonged to them   As all the money, raised this way in *Saxony* and thereabouts, was granted to *Magdalen,* sister to the pope, she, to make the most of it, appointed *Archimbald*, a bishop, by habit and title, but as well versed in the tricking part of trade as a *Genoese*, to manage for her   But we are told, that *Albert of Brandenburg*, archbishop of *Mentz* and *Magdeburg*, who was soon after made a cardinal, had a commission for *Germany* That, instead of employing the *Augustine* friars, who had labored above all the religious orders to make them pass, he gave his commission to *John Tetzelius*, a *Dominican*, and to other friars of the same order, because he had lately collected great sums for the knights of the *Teutonic* order, who were at war against the *Muscovites*, by preaching up the like indulgences, which the pope had granted to these knights *Tetzelius*, or *Iccelius* as he is called by some, boasted that ‘ He had so ample a ‘ commission from the pope, that, though a man should ‘ have deflowered the virgin *Mary*, for a proper sum of ‘ money he could pardon him,’ and assured the people, that ‘ He did not only give pardon for sins past, but also ‘ for sins to come.’

John Staupitius was the vicar-general of the *Augustines* in *Saxony*, and he was greatly esteemed by the elector,

3

who

who was one of the most opulent and potent princes in *Germany* *Staupitius* informed the elector of the pernicious consequences of these indulgences　On this occasion, *Luther*, who was of the *Augustine* order, and professor of divinity at *Wittenberg*, began to examine the doctrine of indulgences, which the *Dominicans* sold in the most open, and in the most infamous manner, and having found it full of errors, he refuted it publicly in 1517. It is said, he was naturally passionate, and zealous for the interest of his order, which made him declaim against the abuses of indulgences, and maintain doctrinal theses about them contrary to the common notions of divines. But it seems not to have been any spleen against the *Dominicans* that set *Luther* to work　It was only his dislike to such practices.　Some say, that *Leo* X whose sordid traffic, to which he reduced the distribution of indulgences, gave birth to *Luther's* Reformation, spoke honorably of this Reformer in the beginning　*Silvester Prierio*, master of the sacred palace, shewed *Leo* the doctrine which *Luther* had vented in his book concerning indulgences　But pope *Leo* answered, that friar *Martin* had a fine genius, and that these surmises were monkish jealousies

Tetzelius, or *Tecellius*, impudently sold the pope's indulgences about the country　*Luther* was greatly exasperated at the blasphemous sermons of this shameless *Dominican*, ‘ And having his heart earnestly bent with
‘ ardent desire to maintain true religion, published cer-
‘ tain propositions concerning indulgences, which are to
‘ be read in the first tome of his works, and set them
‘ openly on the temple that joineth to the castle of *Witter-*
‘ *berg*, the morrow after the feast of *All-saints*, in 1517 ’
He challenged any one to oppose them, either by writing or disputation.

John Hilten, a *German* franciscan, of *Eysenach*, pretended to ground some predictions upon the book of *Daniel* in 1485　*Melancthon*, who had seen the original of that work, says, the author foretold, that, in 1516, the power of the pope should begin to decay.　We are informed, that *Hilten* was put into prison, for having reproved some monastical abuses, and that being very sick, he sent for the guardian, and told him, ‘ I have spoke no
‘ great matter against the monkery, but there shall come
‘ one, in 1516, who shall overturn it ’　*Du Plessis* adds, that *Luther* began to preach that year, in which he was mistaken, for the æra of Lutheranism began not till 1517.

The first thesis published by *Luther* contained ninety-five propositions, in which he plainly declared his opinion about indulgences. He maintained, " that the pope " could release no punishments, but what he inflicted ; " and so indulgences could be only a relaxation of eccle- " siastical penalties That Christians are to be instruct- " ed, that the purchase of a pardon is not to be com- " pared to works of mercy, and that it is better to give " to the poor, than to buy pardons That no confidence " should be placed in indulgences, which cannot remit " the least venial sin in respect of the guilt That those " who believe they shall be saved by indulgences only, " shall be damned with their masters, and that it is a " matter of indifference whether men buy or not buy any " indulgences " He also condemned several propositions which he attributed to his adversaries, and reproved several abuses, of which he declared them guilty. He pronounced an anathema upon those who spoke against the truth of apostolic indulgences, but hoped for all blessing upon those, who should be vigilant in stopping the licence and zeal of the preachers up of papal indulgences

Luther vindicated his thesis in a letter to the archbishop of *Mentz*, who promoted the sale of these indulgences, and told him, " he could not keep silence, when he saw " the souls entrusted to the care of such an illustrious " person so ill instructed, and for which he must one day " give an account," assuring him at the same time, that what he did in opposing this monstrous traffic, was entirely from a principle of conscience and duty, and with a faithful and submissive temper of mind

Tetzelius assembled the monks and sophistical divines of his convent, whom he commanded to write something against *Luther*, while he cried out from the pulpit, that *Luther* was a heretic, and worthy to be prosecuted with fire In a public dispute at *Francfort* upon the *Oder*, he laid down a thesis, in which he opposed that of *Luther*, and he also published a piece in *German* against a sermon which *Luther* had preached on indulgences. This preaching friar, who was an inquisitor in *Germany*, maintained, ' that the ministers of the church may im- ' pose a punishment to be suffered after death, and that ' it is better to send a penitent, with a small penance ' into purgatory, than to send him into hell by refusing ' absolution That heretics, schismatics, and wicked ' men are excommunicated after death, and the dead ' are subject to the laws of the church That the pope,

by

' by granting plenary indulgences, intends to remit all
' punishments in general And that indulgences remit
' punishment more readily than works of charity '

Tetzelius also composed fifty other propositions about
the authority of the pope, which he said was supreme,
and above the universal church, and a council That
there are many catholic truths, which are not in the holy
scriptures, that the truths defined by the pope are catholic, and that his judgement in matters of faith is
infallible

These famous positions of *Luther* and *Tetzelius* were
like the challenge and defence of the dispute set on foot
by both parties. *Luther* wrote with great moderation in
the beginning of this important dispute But *Tetzelius*
treated him as an heresiarch. The former trusted to the
goodness of his cause, which he defended by his parts and
knowledge The latter was so ignorant, that he could
not write his own answer, which was drawn up for him
by *Conradus Wimpina*, the divinity-professor at *Francfort*
Luther was protected by the elector of *Saxony* But *Tetzelius* had more authority by his offices of commissioner
and inquisitor, though he was a man of such very profligate morals, that he had been condemned to die for
adultery at *Infpruck*, and was pardoned at the intercession
of the elector of *Saxony*

The emperor *Maximilian*, being at *Infpruck*, was so
offended at the wickedness and impudence of *Tetzelius*,
who had been convicted of adultery, that he intended to
have him seized upon, put in a bag, and flung into the
river, and would have done it, if he had not been hindered by the solicitations of *Frederic* elector of *Saxony*
Tetzel, or *Tezelius*, was a person too mean and worthless,
to be compared on any account with *Luther* And *Seckendorf* tells a pleasant tale of a gentleman of *Leipsic*, who
bought an indulgence of *Tezelius*, only by way of absolution for robbing and cudgelling him afterwards.

Tetzelius caused the propositions of *Luther* to be burnt,
which inforced *Luther* to treat more amply of the cause,
and to maintain his matter Thus arose this controversy,
' wherein *Luther*, (says *Fox*) neither suspecting, nor
' dreaming of any change that might happen in the cere-
' monies, did not utterly reject the indulgences, but
' required a moderation in them And, therefore, they
' falsely accuse him, which blaze that he began with
' plausible matter, whereby he might get praise, to the
' end, that he might change the state of the common-
                                                ' weal.

' weal, and purchase authority either for himself or
' others '

As it was not expected, and perhaps *Luther* did not
think at first of falling off from the pope, many divines,
some cardinals, and *George* duke of *Saxony*, pleased with
the justice of his cause, and his manner of defending it,
sided with him, and the emperor *Maximilian* said, that
he ought to be protected Nor had *Luther* any enemies,
while he confined himself to writing against the abuse of
indulgences, except the monks and their agents, whose
interest was at stake   These, indeed, raised a great clamour against him But their malice, without argument,
increased, instead of lessening, his party.

John Eckius, professor, and vice-chancellor, of the
university of *Ingoldstadt*, also opposed *Luther*, in which
he was joined by *Silvester Prierias*, professor in the university of *Padua*, vicar-general of the Dominicans, and
master of the sacred palace under pope *Leo* X *Luther*
opposed the indulgences by reasons But *Eckius* and
Prierias, not finding themselves sufficiently strong to
answer him, had recourse to common places, and laid
down for a foundation, the authority of the pope, and
consent of the schoolmen, concluding, that indulgences
ought to be received as an article of faith, since they
proceeded from the pope, who had approved the doctrine
of the schoolmen, and was infallible in matters of faith.
Eckius wrote his obelisks against *Luther's* thesis, without
intending to publish it, and *Luther* published it together
with his own refutation As for *Prierias*, nothing can
make us better understand the success of his writings,
than to know, that he was commanded by the pope to
write no more on matters of controversy *Luther* answered *Eckius* in another thesis, about repentance, and
asserted, " that the just man lives, not by the work of the
" law, but by faith " He also answered, *Prierias*, who
had treated him with threats, and imperious reflections.
He had a fourth adversary in *Jacobus Hogostratus*, a friar-
preacher, who wrote against some of his propositions, and
advised the pope to condemn *Luther*, and burn him, if
he would not retract *Luther* made a kind of manifesto
against this author, in which he reproached him with
cruelty and ignorance.

The Christian world, at that time, was overwhelmed
with ceremonies. Divinity was mere chicanery, or sophistry New and absurd notions were every day advanced
in the schools And the clergy of all orders, by lording

Z

it over men's confciences, rendered themfelves hated and
defpifed The turbulent humour, infidelity, and ambition of the two laft popes were not forgotten Bifhops,
in general, were without integrity, or capacity, and the
inferior clergy, befides being grofsly ignorant, and no-
torioufly immoral, were become intolerable, on account
of their infatiable avarice The clergy, for a long time,
had been vicious and illiterate But thefe things were
taken notice of, now learning began to revive in *Europe*,
Priefts and monks, whofe actions would not bear the
light, were highly incenfed againft the reftorers of literature, and fcrupled not to accufe them of herefy, when
they found they had no fhare with them in argument.
On this account, they commenced a difpute with *John
Reuchlin*, commonly called *Capnio*, the great Hebraian,
becaufe he oppofed the deftruction of the Talmuds, the
Targums, and the writings of the *Rabbins*, which fome
wifhed to annihilate becaufe oppofite to Chriftianity
Reuchlin fhewed, that thefe weapons might be turned
againft the *Jews*, and that it would look but ill, if, inftead of anfwering, we fhould burn the arguments of our
adverfaries Thefe ignoramufes maintained their caufe
fo very poorly, that it was no wonder it ended in their
confufion, and gave the learned *Ulric Van Hutten* a fine
handle to expofe them, in a book called, *Epiftolæ obfcu-
rorum Virorum*. *Erafmus* alfo efpoufed the caufe of *Luther*, though he afterwards, in a treatife *de libero arbitrio*,
ftarted fome objections to his opinions It was obvious,
that this was done rather at the folicitation of others, than
of his own inclination· But the main point was not
affected by them, and they were fufficiently refuted by
Luther

As *Luther* oppofed the fcandalous fale of pardons and
indulgences, fo in the countries where the Reformation
had got an entrance, or in the neighborhood of them,
this was no more heard of, and it has been taken for
granted, that fuch an infamous traffic was no longer
practifed

Seckendorf, in his hiftory of Lutheranifm, hath confuted the falfhoods and calumnies of *Varillas*, *Maimbourg*, *Palavicini*, *Boffuet*, and others of the fame ftamp.
But we will now felect a few things, from various authors, which characterife *Luther*

It is faid, he was rough in controverfy, and that his
reply to *Henry* VIII. was difrefpectful But he had a
very unfavorable opinion of fovereign princes, which

is evident from the smart remark that he made on *Charles* V snatching up spiritual livings, as a dog did meat from the shambles He used to say, that the pope and his partizans were such incorrigible reprobates, that they ought to be treated in the severest manner , and that *Erasmus* spoiled all, by shewing them too much courtesy and respect. As he thus lashed the papists, so he did not greatly spare his own brethren of the Reformation, if they departed from his sentiments. He accounted matrimony to be not only lawful, but a duty incumbent upon all who were capable of entering into that state.

Bellarmin, and the abbé *Richard*, have accused *Luther* of Arianism Their accusation hath no better foundation than this, that *Luther* declared his dislike of the word *consubstantial*, and said, that the Arians, though otherwise in the wrong, were in the right to reject unscriptural terms, introduced by men, who thought they could speak better upon the subject, than the Spirit of God But it appears, from *Luther*'s works, that he was not at all in the sentiments of the Arians

Luther was an enemy to the allegorical and mystical way of expounding the scriptures, as being precarious, and dangerous, tending to fanaticism, and exposing religion to the scoffs of infidels. He also blamed those, who pretended to interpret the Apocalypse to the people He abhorred the schoolmen, and called them sophistical locusts, caterpillars, frogs, and lice He declared himself against persecution, compulsion, and violence, in matters of religion.

Luther said, " When my first positions concerning indulgences were brought before the pope, he said, *a* " *drunken* German *wrote them*, when he hath slept out " his sleep, and is sober again, he will be of another " mind " But *Luther* often apologized for his roughness. " I am accused, says he, of rudeness and immodesty, particularly by adversaries, who have not a " grain of candour or good manners. If, as they say, " I am saucy and impudent, I am however simple, open, " and sincere, without any of their guile, dissimulation, " or treachery "

The pope, and the emperor, were equally concerned, that *Luther* was allowed to propagate his opinions in *Saxony*, where the great number of his followers, and the resolution with which he defended his opinions, made it evident, that it would become troublesome both to the church and empire, if a stop was not put to his proceed-

ings.

ings. *Luther* defended his propofitions by reafon and
fcripture againft *Tetzel's*, who had recourfe to the authority of the pope and church. This made it neceffary
for *Luther* to examine upon what foundation one was
founded, and in what ftate the other remained In the
courfe of this enquiry, monftrous errors and abufes were
difcovered, the cheats and fcandalous lives of monks and
priefts were brought to light, and *Luther*, for fecuring
to himfelf the affiftance of temporal princes, took care to
explain the nature and extenfivenefs of civil power

Temporal government is founded on the higheft reafon,
as well as on divine inftitution, for, without it, men
would be conftantly expofed to rapine and confufion
But it has never yet been proved, that a fpiritual monarchy is either neceffary or ferviceable to Chriftianity
It is an artificial fabric, which muft be fupported by
arts, and the views of popes will be always different
from thofe of temporal princes If the pope's partizans
fay, his authority is founded upon the pofitive command
of God That fhould be proved clearly from fcripture
If they fay, it is derived from St *Peter*, it ought to be
proved, not only that fuch an authority was invefted in
him, but that he was bifhop of *Rome*, exercifed it there,
conveyed it down to his fucceffors, and that fucceffion
has not been interrupted Inftead of proving thefe
things, the popifh doctors declined meddling with them,
and filled the heads of their people with things foreign
to the main point They talked of a long fucceffion of
popes, of the great antiquity and univerfality of the
church, and laid great ftrefs upon the promife, that ' the
' gates of hell fhall never prevail againft it " Fathers,
councils, and miracles, were alfo appealed to And if
any one was ftill diffatisfied, he was branded with the
name of heretic, without fo much as hearing his reafons,
and he had good luck, if he efcaped burning

The papal conftitution was admirably contrived upon
the foundation of a fingular kind of monarchy Princes
have formerly ftrengthened their authority, by giving out
that they were defcended from the gods, or that their government was founded by their exprefs command, and if
fuccefs attended them, which was looked upon as a mark
of divine favor, they were after death reckoned among the
deities. But the pope calls himfelf the lieutenant of *Jefus
Chrift*, arrogates to himfelf, while living, all power in heaven
and earth, and would have it believed, that fuch as refufe
to acknowledge his authority cannot be faved If thefe

points

points are well settled, the whole business is done For
what is more proper to draw the veneration of men, than
the notion that the Majesty of God resides in him ? Or,
what stronger motive can there be, to the most absolute
submission, than the fear of damnation ?

The pope does not, like other sovereigns, bind himself
to any terms, on his entering upon the government And,
indeed, it would be absurd for him, who is said to be
guided by the Holy Ghost, to be laid under any restrictions The subjects of this monarchy may be divided
into clergy and laity The first, which comprehends all
ecclesiastics, may be considered as his standing army.
The second, which takes in all else of the *Roman* communion, are no better than slaves, on whom large contributions are raised for the support of the others The
clergy are not allowed to marry, under a pretence, that
worldly cares would prevent a faithful discharge of their
duty But the true reason is, that they may be free from
the ties of paternal or conjugal affection, and be ready
on all occasions to promote the interest of the church

Pope *Paul* IV. boasted of having 288,000 parishes, and
44,000 monasteries, under his jurisdiction What a
prodigious number of ecclesiastics were then under the
papal power ? As a blind submission of the laity to the
clergy was absolutely necessary for supporting this spiritual tyranny, they were forbid to read the scriptures
For if these had been well understood, it would have
been obvious, that no one was authorized to lord it over
the conscience of another , and, by keeping these among
the clergy, they had an opportunity of mixing something
with every doctrine they taught, that might promote the
interest or power of the pope and themselves In order
to make way for tradition, the holy scripture was represented as imperfect , and whatever could serve the cause
of *Rome* was imposed upon tne poor deluded people under
that name

As the first decay and ruin of the church began through
ignorance, and want of knowledge in teachers So, to
restore the church again by doctrine and learning, it
pleased God to open to man the art of printing, shortly
after the burning of *John Hufs* and *Jerom* The art
of printing being found, the grace of God immediately
followed, which stirred up men of better parts to receive
the light of knowledge and of judgement , whereby darkness began to be espied, and ignorance to be detected ,
truth to be discerned from error, and religion from superstition

ftition. The firft puth and affault againft the *Romifh*
church, about this period at leaft, was given by *Picus*
Mirandula, *Valla*, *Petrarch*, *Wefalia*, *Revelinus*, *Grocin*,
Colet, *Rhenanus*, and *Erafmus*, whofe learned writings
opened a window of light to the world, and made a way
more ready for others to come after. Immediately, according to God's gracious appointment, followed *Martin*
Luther, with others after him; by whofe miniftry it
pleafed the Lord to work a more full Reformation of his
church. The Lord ordained and appointed *Luther* to be
the principal organ and minifter under him, to reform
religion, and fubvert the popifh fee.

Tetzelius ftirred up the archbifhop of *Magdeburg* and
others againft *Luther*, who boldly anfwered all their
writings. The emperor *Maximilian*, on the fifth of
Auguft, 1518, wrote to pope *Leo* X and required him to
ftop thefe dangerous difputes by his authority, affuring
him, that he would execute in the empire, whatever his
holinefs fhould appoint. The pope ordered *Hieronymus de*
Genutiis, bifhop of *Afcoli*, and auditor of the apoftolic chamber, to cite *Luther* to appear at *Rome* within fixty days,
that he might give an account of his doctrine to the
auditor, and *Prierias* mafter of the palace, to whom he
had committed the judgement of the caufe. The pope,
on the twenty-third of *Auguft*, wrote a letter to the elector of *Saxony*, defiring him to give *Luther* no protection,
but to put him into the hands of cardinal *Cajetan*, his
legate in *Germany*, affuring him, that if *Luther* was innocent, he would fend him back abfolved, and if guilty,
he would pardon him upon his repentance. At the fame
time, the pope likewife fent a brief to cardinal *Cajetan*,
in which he ordered him to bring *Luther* before him as
foon as poffible, and to hinder the princes from being
any impediment to the execution of this order, he denounced the ordinary punifhments of excommunication,
interdiction, and privation of goods againft thofe that
fhould receive *Luther* and give him protection, and promifed a plenary indulgence to thofe, who fhould affift
in delivering him up.

The elector of *Saxony* was unwilling that *Luther* fhould
appear perfonally at *Rome*, and the univerfity of *Witten-*
berg interceded with the pope, who confented that the
matter fhould be tried before cardinal *Cajetan* in *Ger-*
many. This prelate was a Dominican, yet *Luther* met
him at *Augfburg* in *October*. *Cajetan* afferted the authority
of the pope, and faid he was above a council. *Luther*

denied

denied it, and alledged the authority of the univerfity of
Paris Luther delivered *Cajetan* a formal proteftation, in
the prefence of four imperial councellors and a notary,
wherein he declared, " that he had only fought after
" truth, and would not retract, without being convinced
" he was wrong That he was fatisfied, he had ad-
" vanced nothing contrary to the holy fcripture, the
" doctrine of the fathers, decretals of the popes, and
" right reafon That he had advanced nothing but
" what was found, true, and catholic And that he
" would fubmit himfelf to the lawful determination of
" the church "

The legate threatened *Luther* with the cenfures of the
church, if he would not retract, and bring his recantation *Luther* knew that *Cajetan* had orders to feize him,
if he would not fubmit And, therefore, on the fixteenth
of *October*, he made an *act of appeal*, before a notary,
wherein he vindicated himfelf, and declared, that he was
oppreffed and injured, and obliged to appeal from the
pope, for which purpofe, he demanded letters of miffion,
and protefted he would purfue his appeal *Luther* told
the legate, that as he had not deferved his cenfures, fo
he difregarded them, and then returned to *Wittenberg*,
where he was fafe under the protection of the elector of
Saxony Luther was powerfully fupported by the univerfity of *Wittenberg*, where he continued to teach the
fame doctrines, and fent a challenge to all the inquifitors
to difpute with him there, under the fanction of a fafe
conduct from his prince, and the moft refpectable hofpitality from the univerfity

The cardinal, mortified at *Luther's* efcape, wrote to
the elector on the twenty-fifth of *October*, 1518, defiring
him to give him up, to fend him to *Rome*, or to banifh
him from his dominions To this letter the elector anfwered, on the eighteenth of *December* following, and
told the cardinal, that ' he hoped he would have dealt
' with *Luther* in another manner, and not have infifted
' upon his recanting, before his caufe was heard and
' judged, that there were feveral able men in his own
' and in other univerfities, who did not think *Luther's*
' doctrine either impious or heretical, that, if he had
' believed it fuch, there would have been no need of
' admonifhing him not to tolerate it, that *Luther* not
' being convicted of herefy, he could not banifh him
' from his ftates, nor fend him to *Rome*, and that, fince
' *Luther* offered to fubmit himfelf to the judgement of
' feveral

' several universities, he thought they ought to hear him,
' or, at least, shew him the errors which he taught in his
' writings '

While these things passed in *Germany*, pope *Leo* attempted to put an end to these disputes about indulgences, by a decision of his own, and for that purpose, upon the ninth of *November*, published a brief, directed to cardinal *Cajetan*, in which he declared, that ' the
' pope, the successor of St *Peter*, and vicar of *Jesus*
' *Christ* upon earth, hath power to pardon, by virtue of
' the keys, the guilt and punishment of sin, the guilt by
' the sacrament of penance, and the temporal punish-
' ments due for actual sins by indulgences, that these
' indulgences are taken from the overplus of the merits
' of *Jesus Christ* and his saints, a treasure at the pope's
' own disposal, as well by way of absolution as suffrage,
' and that the dead and the living, who properly and
' truly obtain these indulgences, are immediately freed
' from the punishment due to their actual sins, according
' to the divine justice, which allows these indulgences to
' be granted and obtained ' This brief ordains, ' that
' all the world shall hold and preach this doctrine, under
' the pain of excommunication reserved to the pope, and
' enjoins cardinal *Cajetan* to send it to all the archbishops
' and bishops of *Germany*, and cause it to be put in ex-
' ecution by them ' *Luther* knew very well, that after this judgement by the pope, he could not possibly escape being proceeded against, and condemned at *Rome*, and, therefore, upon the twenty-eighth of the same month, published a new appeal from the pope to a general council, in which he asserts the superior authority of the latter over the former The pope foreseeing, that he should not easily manage *Luther*, so long as the elector of *Saxony* continued to support and protect him, sent the elector a golden rose, such an one, as he used to bless every year, and send to several princes, as marks of his particular favor to them *Miltitius*, his chamberlain, whom we have before observed to have been a *German*, was intrusted with this commission, by whom the pope sent also letters, dated the beginning of *January*, 1519, to the elector's counsellor and secretary, in which he prayed those ministers to use all possible interest with their master, that he would stop the progress of *Luther*'s errors, and imitate therein the piety and religion of his ancestors It appears by *Seckendorf*'s account of *Miltitius*'s negotiation, that *Frederick* had long solicited for

this

this bauble from the pope, and that three or four years before, when his electoral highness was a bigot to the court of *Rome*, it had probably been a most welcome present. But, *post est occasio calva*. It was now too late. *Luther's* contests with the see of *Rome* had opened the elector's eyes, and enlarged his mind, and, therefore, when *Miltitius* delivered his letters, and discharged his commission, he was received but coldly by the elector, who valued not the consecrated rose, nor would receive it publicly and in form, but only privately and by his proctor.

As to *Luther*, *Miltitius* had orders to require the elector to oblige him to retract, or to deny him his protection. But, things were not now to be carried with so high a hand, *Luther's* credit being too firmly established. Besides, the emperor *Maximilian* departed this life upon the twelfth of this month, whose death greatly altered the face of affairs, and made the elector more able to determine *Luther's* fate. *Miltitius* thought it best therefore to try, what could be done by fair and gentle means, and to that end came to a conference with *Luther*. He poured forth many commendations upon him, and earnestly entreated him, that he would himself appease that tempest, which could not but be destructive to the church. He blamed, at the same time, the behavior and conduct of *Tetzelius*, and reproved him with so much sharpness, that he died of melancholy a short time after. *Luther*, amazed at all this civil treatment, which he had never experienced before, commended *Miltitius* highly, and owned, that if they had behaved to him so at first, all the troubles, occasioned by these disputes, had been avoided, and did not forget to cast the blame upon *Albert* archbishop of *Mentz*, who had increased these troubles by his levent. *Miltitius* also made some concessions, as, that the people had been seduced by false opinions about indulgences, that *Tetzelius* had given the occasion, that the archbishop had set on *Tetzelius* to get money, that *Tetzelius* had exceeded the bounds of his commission, &c. This mildness and seeming candor, on the part of *Miltitius*, gained so wonderfully upon *Luther*, that he wrote a most submissive letter to the pope, dated the thirteenth of *March*, in 1519. *Miltitius*, however taking for granted, that they would not be contented at *Rome* with this letter of *Luther's*, written, as it was, in general terms only, proposed to refer the matter to some other judgement, and it was agreed between them, that the elector of *Triers*

A a   should

should be the judge, and *Coblentz* the place of conference But this came to nothing, for *Luther* afterwards
gave some reasons for not going to *Coblentz*, and the pope
would not refer the matter to the elector of *Triers*.

During all these treaties, the doctrine of *Luther* spread,
and prevailed greatly, and he himself received great encouragement at home and abroad   The *Bohemians* about
this time sent him a book of the celebrated *John Huss*,
who had fallen a martyr in the work of Reformation,
and also letters, in which they exhorted him to constancy
and perseverance, owning, that the divinity, which he
taught, was the pure, the sound, and orthodox divinity
Many great and learned men had joined themselves to
him, among the rest *Philip Melancthon*, whom *Frederic*
had invited to the university of *Wittenberg* in *August* 1518,
and *Andrew Carolostadius* archdeacon of that town, who
was a great linguist   They desired, if possible, to draw
over *Erasmus* to their party, and to that end we find
Melancthon thus expressing himself in a letter to that great
man, dated *Leipsic, January* the fifth, in 1519 ' *Martin*
' *Luther*, who has a very great esteem for you, wishes of
' all things, that you would thoroughly approve of him.'
Luther also himself wrote to *Erasmus*, in very respectful,
and even flattering terms   " *Itaque, mi* Erasme, *vir*
" *amabilis, si ita tibi visum fuerit, agnosce & hunc frater-*
" *culum in* CHRISTO, *tui certè studiosissimum & aman-*
" *tissimum, cæterum pro inscitiâ suâ nihil meritum, quàm ut*
" *in angulo sepultus esset*"   The elector of *Saxony* was
desirous also to know *Erasmus*'s opinion of *Luther*, and
might probably think, that as *Erasmus* had most of the
monks for his enemies, and some of those, who were
warmest against *Luther*, he might easily be prevailed on
to come over to their party.   And indeed they would have
done something, if they could have gained this point,
for the reputation of *Erasmus* was so great, that if he had
once declared for *Luther*, almost all *Germany* would have
declared along with him.

But *Erasmus*, whatever he might think of *Luther*'s
opinions, had neither his impetuosity, nor his courage.
He contented himself therefore with acting and speaking
in his usual strain of moderation, and wrote a letter to
the elector *Frederic*, in which he declared ' His dislike of
' the arts, which were employed to make *Luther* odious,
' that he did not know *Luther*, and so could neither ap-
' prove nor condemn his writings, because indeed he had
' not read them, that however he condemned the railing

' at him with so much violence, because he had sub-
' mitted himself to the judgement of those, whose office
' it was to determine, and no man had endeavoured to
' convince him of his error, that his antagonists seemed
' rather to seek his death, than his salvation, that they
' mistook the matter in supposing, that all error is he-
' resy, that there are errors in all the writings of both
' antients and moderns, that divines are of different opi-
' nions, that it is more prudent to use moderate, than
' violent means, that the elector ought to protect inno-
' cency, and that this was the intent of *Leo X.*'

Erasmus wrote also a friendly letter in answer to *Luther*'s, and tells him, that ' *His* books had raised such
' an uproar at *Louvain*, as it was not possible for him to
' describe, that he could not have believed divines could
' have been such madmen, if he had not been present,
' and seen them with his eyes, that, by defending him,
' he had rendered himself suspected, that many abused
' him as the leader of this faction, so they call it, that
' there were many in *England*, and some at *Louvain*, no
' inconsiderable persons, who highly approved his opi-
' nions, that for his own part he endeavoured to carry
' himself as evenly as he could with all parties, that he
' might more effectually serve the interests of learning
' and religion; that, however, he thought more might
' be done by civil and modest means, than by intempe-
' rate heat and passion, that it would be better to inveigh
' against those, who abuse the pope's authority, than
' against the popes themselves, that new opinions should
' rather be promoted in the way of proposing doubts and
' difficulties, than by affirming and deciding perempto-
' rily, that nothing should be delivered with faction and
' arrogance, but that the mind, in these cases, should be
' kept entirely free from anger, hatred, and vain-glory
' I lay not this,' says *Erasmus*, with that great address
of which he was master, ' as if you wanted any admo-
' nitions of this kind, but only that you may not want
' them hereafter, any more than you do at present *Hæc
' non admoneo ut facias, sed ut quod facis perpetuò facias.*'
When this letter was wrote, *Erasmus* and *Luther* had
never seen each other It is dated *Louvain, May* the thirtieth, in 1519, and it is hardly possible to read it without
suspecting, that *Erasmus* was intirely of *Luther*'s sentiments, if he had had but the courage to have declared it.
Only observe, how he concludes it ' I have dipped
' into your *commentaries* upon the *Psalms*, they please me

' prodigiously,

' prodigiously, and I hope will be read with great advan-
' tage   There is a prior of the monastry of *Antwerp*,
' who says he was your pupil, and loves you most affec-
' tionately   He is a truly Christian man, and almost the
' only one of his society who preaches *Christ*, the rest
' being attentive either to the fabulous traditions of men,
' or to their own profit   I have written to *Melancthon*
' The Lord *Jesus* pour upon you his Spirit, that you may
' abound more and more, every day, to his glory and the
' service of the church   Farewell '

Frederic elector of *Saxony* was the patron and protector
of *Luther*   But *George*, a prince of the same house, opposed *Luther* to the utmost of his power   The former
desired *Erasmus* to give him his opinion concerning
Luther, and *Erasmus* gave it jocosely   But gravely told
the archbishop of *Mentz*, that the monks condemned
many things in the books of *Luther* as heretical, which
were esteemed as orthodox in *Bernard* and *Austin*.   *Erasmus* wrote also to cardinal *Wolsey*, that the life and conversation of *Luther* were universally commended, and it
was no small prejudice in his favor, that his morals were
unblameable, and that no reproach could be fastened
upon him by calumny itself   ' If I had really been at
' leisure, says *Erasmus*, to peruse his writings, I am not
' so conceited of my own abilities, as to pass a judge-
' ment upon the performance of so considerable a divine
' Though even children, in this knowing age, will
' boldly pronounce, that this is erroneous, and that is
' heretical '

Claude has spoken judiciously of *Luther*, when he
wishes he had been more temperate in his way of writing, and that, with his great and invincible courage,
with his ardent zeal for the truth, with that unshaken
constancy he ever manifested, he could have shewed a
greater reserve and moderation.   But the divine providence had a great work to effect by *Luther*, in which
strength and even roughness of spirit were requisite to
encounter every kind of difficulty and to bear up against
the rage, in a manner, of the whole world   When men
would fell a wood, they employ a heavy rough axe, and
not a smooth and polished razor.   *Melancthon* said very
justly of him, upon seeing his picture, in this *extempore*
line

' *Fulmina erant linguæ singula verba tuæ* '

Thy single words were piercing thunder-bolts.

The

The monks took upon them to rail most violently, and even seditiously, in their sermons, against the Reformers ' Whence, says *Erasmus*, came this new race ' of deities? They call every one an heretic whom they ' dislike, and stir heaven and earth when they are called ' calumniators' He owns, that *Luther* had given them good advice on many points, and that it would be an impiety to leave him undefended, where he had the truth on his side, for then who would ever dare to stand up for the truth? Hitherto, adds *Erasmus*, *Luther* has certainly been useful to the world He hath set men upon studying the fathers, some to satisfy their own minds, and others to plague him by hunting out arguments and objections against him

If *Erasmus* had not the same impetuous acrimony in his style, which predominated in the writings of *Luther*, yet the monks were equally offended at him, because the abuses which he attacked were the source of their best revenues

Erasmus, in 1519, wrote to *Melancthon*, that all the world agreed in commending the moral character of *Luther*, and wished that God might grant him success equal to the liberty which he had taken *Melancthon* was always mild and moderate, and had a sincere affection for *Luther*, but sometimes could not refrain from complaining of his bold and impetuous temper However, *Erasmus* entertained hopes, that the attempts of *Luther*, and the great notice which had been taken of them, might be serviceable to true Christianity. In this he was not mistaken, as the event proved, for, from this period, *Luther*'s writings and the cause of Reformation spread all over the Christian world, and brought into full blaze the glimmering light, which had before been introduced by *Wickliffe*, *Huss*, and other learned and good men

Frederic of *Saxony*, one of the most virtuous and illustrious princes of that century, was a friend both to *Luther*, and to the Reformation, and the protestants have great reason to reverence and bless his memory. When he might have been chosen emperor, he declined it, and gave the crown to *Charles* V *Erasmus* wrote a letter to him, which was very favorable to *Luther* *Andrew Bodestine*, from his native place called *Carolostadius*, defended the writings of *Luther* *Bucer* was present, when *Luther* maintained his doctrine before the *Augustine* friars

3   at

at *Heidelberg*, and told *Rhenanus*, ' That his fweetnefs
' in anfwering was admirable, and his patience in hear-
' ing incomparable That the acutenefs of St *Paul*, in
' refolving doubts, might have been feen in *Luther*, fo
' that he brought them all into admiration of him, by
' his concife and nervous anfwers, taken out of the ftore-
' houfe of the holy fcriptures.'

Luther was honorably entertained at *Heidelberg*, by
Wolfgang the count palatine And *Erich* duke of *Calem-
berg* efpoufed his caufe *Erich* fhared in the danger and
glory of all the undertakings of the emperor *Maximilian*,
and was a great ornament to the houfe of *Brunfwick
Lunenberg* He faved the life of that emperor in 1504,
who perpetuated the memory of his valour, by adding a
bright ftar to his coat of arms, on the very field of battle,
with this explanation ' That as the morning ftar ex-
' ceeds all the others in luftre, fo duke *Erich* was as
' much fuperior to all other princes of his time.' This
ftar has ever fince continued in the coat of arms of the
houfe of *Brunfwick*, and is placed upon the helmet in
the middle of the peacock's train. *Erneft* duke of *Lunenberg* was educated under the infpection of his uncle
Frederic, firnamed the *wife*, elector of *Saxony*, who fent
him early to the univerfity of *Wittenberg*, where he made
a great progrefs in learning, and had an opportunity to
converfe with *Luther*, when he began to difcover his
fentiments about the hierarchy, and the doctrines of the
fee of *Rome* *Erneft* boldly embraced the doctrine of
Luther And his example was followed by his brothers
Otho and *Francis*, as alfo by *Philip* of the line of *Gru-
benhagen* Thefe princes made the neceffary preparations
to introduce the Reformation into the circle of *Lower
Saxony*, as the elector their uncle was doing in that of
the *Upper Saxony* *Erneft* was determined to purfue the
glorious fcheme he had formed, gradually to abolifh the
errors and abufes that had crept into the church His
concern was fo great for extending the knowledge of the
pure faith, that he generoufly fent learned men to the
county of *Hoya*, *Eaft-Friefeland*, and other parts of *Germany*, to preach the gofpel in its native fimplicity. Such
was his zeal in the caufe of the Reformation, fo many
were the difficulties and oppofitions he met with on that
account, that he juftly merited the firname which was
given him of *confeffor*. It fhould be obferved, that the
emperor *Otho* IV one of the moft illuftrious anceftors of
the houfe of *Brunfwick*, fo early as in the beginning of
the

the thirteenth century, notwithstanding the ignorance and bigotry of those times, endeavored with uncommon resolution to lay open the abuses of the see of *Rome*, even in defiance of its excommunications His endeavors were not attended with the success they deserved, yet they have rendered his name sacred to posterity, as he was the first prince who ventured to oppose the encroachments of the papacy, whereby others were afterwards incited thoroughly to examine the title, which the popes pretended they had, to impose arbitrary laws on Christendom

Eckius had wrote some notes upon the first thesis of *Luther*, which were answered by *Coroloftadius*, and a conference was agreed on at *Leipfic*, by the consent of prince *George* of *Saxony*, uncle to the elector *Frederic*. *Eckius* appeared, and was met by *Luther*, who was accompanied by *Melancthon* and *Coroloftadius* Both parties were well received by the prince, the senate, and university, who appointed a great hall in the castle for the place of the conference, which was solemnly opened on the twenty-seventh of *June*, 1519 The first disputation was concerning free-will, which *Eckius* undertook to prove by a passage in *Ecclesiasticus*, and was opposed by *Coroloftadius*, who denied that free-will had a distinct operation from grace This dispute continued a whole week, in which time, *Luther* preached a sermon, in the chapel of the castle, upon the feast of St *Peter* and St, *Paul*, wherein he declaimed against the authority of the pope The dispute was then carried on between *Luther* and *Eckius*, upon thirteen propositions extracted by the latter out of the writings of the former, the last, and principal of which, was against the supremacy of the pope. *Luther* alledged, against it, the canon of the council of *Afric*, which ordained, that the bishop of the first see should not be called the prince of bishops, or supreme bishop And he maintained, that *Wickliffe* and *Hufs* ought not to have been condemned, as many of their articles were orthodox, and that he could oppose the tradition and usage of the *Greek* church for 1400 years, to the condemnation of the *Bohemians* *Eckius* attempted to prove the doctrine of indulgences, by the authority of the general councils of *Vienna, Lateran*, and *Conftance* He said, that St *Gregory* had published them 900 years before; that they were approved by the consent of the universal church, and that all the Christian world had acknowledged them by receiving the jubilees,

Luther

Luther replied, that he preferred works of charity before indulgences, and supported his opinion by the authority of St *Paul* and St *Augustine*, who say, we can do no good without charity and grace. *Eckius* seemed to make this question a matter of nothing. But *Luther* had the advantage of the argument. He knew, ' That the Chri-
' stian princes had been tired of making expeditions to
' the *Holy Land*, which were only specious pretences,
' invented by the popes, to drain them of their blood
' and treasure. And that another scheme was then set
' on foot to allure them and their subjects to part with
' their money. That frequent jubilees were kept at
' *Rome*, though, according to their first institution, they
' were to take place but once in a century. That the
' popes perceived the advantages which arose from bring-
' ing people together to their market from all parts of the
' Christian world, and shortened the time, by ordering
' a jubilee to be kept every fifty years. And afterwards
' appointed one to be celebrated every thirty years. That
' immense sums were brought into the pope's coffers by
' these jubilees at *Rome*, where all that resorted received
' absolution of their sins for a particular sum. And that
' indulgences being found so beneficial, they were sold
' all over *Europe*, and no more confined to certain times
' and jubilees.'

The conference at *Leipsic* continued fourteen days, and the dispute was left to the decision of the universities of *Paris* and *Erfurt*. But *Luther* opened the whole to the world, by publishing a tract, entitled, " Resolutions of " the propositions disputed at *Leipsic*," and addressed to *Spalatinus*, in which he said, that *Eckius* had no cause to boast of the dispute, and had acknowledged that no trust ought to be put in indulgences. *Melancthon* wrote with great moderation upon these conferences. And *Eckius* told *Hogostratus*, that the Lutherans had great advantages over him, because they were many against a single man. *Jerom Emser* owned, that the dispute at *Leipsic* was rather sharp than edifying. But the two universities never give their judgements about the contests in these conferences.

Zuinglius began, about this time, to write against pardons and indulgences. *Luther* wrote a book " Of Chri-
" stian liberty," which he dedicated to the pope. He also addressed another book to the nobility of *Germany*, wherein he shook the three principal bulwarks of popery, by opposing the doctrine, ' That temporal magistrates
' were

' were subject to the spiritualty, that the pope is the
' only judge of the scripture, and that he only can call
' a council.' *Luther* shewed what things should be
handled in councils, and asserted, that the pope yearly
drained *Germany* of three millions of florins He pointed
out the necessity of reforming schools and universities;
declared that heretics should be convinced by scripture,
and not awed by fire, imputed the misfortunes of the
emperor *Sigismund* to his breach of faith with *Huss* and
Jerom, and exposed the inconveniences, resulting from
the council of *Constance*

What the divines of *Paris* and *Erfurt* neglected, those
of *Louvain* and *Cologne* attempted. The former consulted
with the cardinal de *Tortosa*, afterwards pope *Adrian* VI.
and condemned twenty-two propositions extracted from
Luther as heretical, or approaching to heresy, and declared that his writings ought to be burnt. Those of
Cologne concurred; and agreed, that *Luther* ought to be
obliged to make a public recantation *Luther* declared,
he disregarded the censures of these two universities, and
that *Occam*, *Stapulensis*, *Huss*, and other eminent men,
were unjustly condemned after the same manner. He
accused the universities of rashness, of want of charity,
and contempt of justice, after which, he sharply confuted their censures, without any respect to their persons.

The emperor *Maximilian* was so far from suffering
himself to be persuaded to proceed against *Luther*, that
he used to say, ' If the clergy would lead pious lives,
' *Luther* would have no room for a Reformation.' But
his successor was of a different disposition, and gave
occasion to the violent measures that were taken to nip
the Reformation in its very bud *Luther* wrote a letter
to the new emperor, on the fifteenth of *January*, 1520,
before his arrival in *Germany*, to vindicate his conduct,
and intreat his protection from the power of his numerous
adversaries, who had persecuted him for three years, and
were resolved that he should perish with the gospel He
told the emperor, he would not desire his protection, if
he was convicted of impiety or heresy But desired, he
would not let him be condemned without hearing, and
declared, he would either be silent, or refer himself to
the judgement of any impartial universities, before which
he was ready to appear.

It was a great mistake in *Leo* X to decide in favour of
the indulgence-merchants, by his bull in 1518, since
thereby all hopes of an accommodation were cut off For

it would have been much more political in him to have enjoined filence to both parties, and to have contrived fome way to fatisfy *Luther*, who offered *Cajetan* to drop the controverfy, if his adverfaries would do the fame But they would be fatisfied with nothing lefs than a recantation. The elector of *Saxony* was again folicited to give up *Luther*, who was compelled to fall upon the pope, to vindicate himfelf, by appealing to a general council, the calling whereof was delayed upon various pretences, whereby the caufe of *Rome* became more and more fufpected. About the fame time, the pope's quarrel with *Henry* VIII made way for the introduction of the Reformation in *England* And the houfe of *Navarre*, in revenge for the pope's fiding with *Ferdinand* the catholic, encouraged the proteftant religion to the utmoft of their power in *France*. Befides all this, many fenfible honeft men, even among the *Roman-catholics*, were quite unconcerned at the rough treatment which *Luther* fhewed the papal fee, becaufe they knew it deferved his refentment

Luther alfo wrote to the elector of *Mentz*, who anfwered him, and commended his difpofition But defired him to treat of religious matters with moderation and refpect, for he obferved with grief, that the profeflors difputed upon frivolous opinions, and queftions of little confequence, with intolerable pride

While *Luther* was vindicating himfelf to the emperor, and the bifhops of *Germany*, judgement was paffed upon his writings at *Rome*, where *Eckius* and *Ubricus* went on purpofe to folicit his condemnation, which was refolved upon, notwithftanding he had obediently reverenced the perfon of the pope *Luther*, at the requeft of the *Auguftines*, wrote a long epiftle to his holinefs, full of fubmiffion and refpect, wherein he told him, " That the " court of *Rome* was vifibly more corrupt than either " *Babylon* or *Sodom*, but that his holinefs was a lamb in " the midft of wolves, a *Daniel* among lions, and an " *Ezekiel* among fcorpions That there were not above " three or four cardinals, who had any learning or piety, " and that it was againft thefe diforders of the court of " *Rome*, that he was obliged to appear "

The writings of *Luther* were examined in a congregation of cardinals, who diftinguifhed his doctrine, writings, and perfon They condemned forty-one propofitions taken out of his works, ordered him to appear in perfon, and agreed that his writings fhould be burnt In confequence of this refolution, the bull was drawn up by

the

the cardinal of *Ancona*, and publifhed by the pope, who invoked the aid of *Jefus Chrift*, the apoftles, and all the faints, againft the new errors and herefies, and to preferve the faith, peace, and unity of the church This bull was dated the fifteenth of *June*, 1520, and condemned the forty-one articles, extracted from the writings of *Luther*, as heretical, falfe, and fcandalous Indulgences, the papal fupremacy, free-will, purgatory, and the begging friars, were the principal things vindicated in this bull, and all Chriftians were forbid, under the pain of excommunication, to defend any of the propofitions that were thus condemned *Luther* was admonifhed to revoke his errors by fome public act, and caufe his books to be burnt within fixty days, otherwife he, and his adherents, fhould incur the punifhments due to heretics.

Luther, now perceiving that all hopes of an accommodation were at an end, threw off all referve, and anfwered this bull, which he called " The execrable bull of " antichrift," by publifhing a book called " The cap-" tivity of *Babylon*," in which he abfolutely rejected indulgences, and afferted, that the papacy was the kingdom of *Babylon*. He denied there were feven facraments, and faid, there was properly only one, in three facramental figns, the Lord's Supper, baptifm, and penance. He affirmed, that the facrament of the altar is the teftament of *Jefus Chrift*, which he left when he died, to be given to all thofe who fhould believe in him That this teftament is a promife of forgivenefs of our fins, confirmed by the death of the Son of God, that it is only faith in this promife which juftifies, and the mafs is entirely ufelefs without that faith He declared, that the effect of baptifm depended alone upon faith in the promife of *Jefus Chrift*, of which the outward baptifm is only a fign, fupplied in infants by the faith of the church. He maintained, that the remiffion of fins, which is the effect of penance, depends upon faith in the promife of *Jefus Chrift*, and allowed no effect to the other parts of penance. He wondered that confirmation, and ordination, fhould be facraments, when they are no more than ecclefiaftical ceremonies Neither would he allow marriage to be a facrament, becaufe there is no promife annexed to it, and the marriage of infidels is as binding as that of Chriftians And he rejected the ufage of the extreme unction, built upon the authority of the epiftle of St. *James*, becaufe he thought there was not any promife of grace annexed to that unction.

B b 2 *Luther*

Luther was fully perfuaded of the neceffity of " Jufti-
" fication by faith alone " Which he looked upon as
the bafis of the whole Chriftian religion   When he fii ft
preached againft indulgences, he intended no feparation
from the church of *Rome* But the violence of his opponents, and the heat of the controverfy, drew him fo far
into the difpute, that he carried it on with unparalleled
fpirit, and came at laft to fix upon that fcheme, which
has been fince adhered to by the Lutheran churches, with
little variation.

As the pope had condemned *Luther* at *Rome*, *Luthei*
degraded the pope in *Germany*. He compiled a hiftory of
the wars raifed by the popes againft the emperors, and
maintained, that the *German* princes had the fame power
over the clergy as over the laity. He advifed the *Germans* to fhake off the yoke of popery, and propofed a
Reformation, that fhould fubject the pope and bifhops to
the power of the emperor, and take away from the pope
the authority of interpreting fcripture, or calling a general council. He declaimed againft the manners and
practice of the court of *Rome*, the pride of the pope, and
the avarice of the cardinals He afferted, that annates and
papal months, fhould be abolifhed, and that the canon-
law ought to be entirely deftroyed He even affembled
the ftudents of *Wittenberg* together, and flung the pope's
bull and decretals into a fire prepared for that purpofe,
faying, " Becaufe thou haft troubled the Holy One of
" God, let eternal fire trouble thee." This ceremony
was performed by *Luther*, upon the tenth of *December*,
1520, The next day he expounded the *Pfalms*, and earneftly charged his auditors, *that, as they loved the falvation
of their fouls, they fhould take heed of the pope's decrees* He
alfo defended what he had done in writing, and publifhed, among other errors in the papal doctrine, the
following thirty .

I.
' The pope and his clergy are not bound to obey the
' commandments of God.

II.
' It is not a precept, but a counfel of St. *Peter*, when
' he teaches, *That all men ai e to be fubject to kings.*

III.
' That in a ftate, the fun fignified the papal power, the
' moon meant the imperial or fecular,

IV.

IV

' That the pope and his chair are not to be held sub-
' ject to the councils and decrees

V.

' That the pope has in the fecret of his own breaft all
' laws, and plenary power over all laws.

VI.

' Whence it follows; That the pope hath power to
' difannul, change, and determine, all councils, and all
' conftitutions and ordinances, as he daily practifes.

VII.

' That the pope hath a right to demand an oath of all
' bifhops, and an obligation upon them for their palls.

VIII

' That if the pope be fo negligent of his own and his
' brethren's falvation, and fo unprofitable and carelefs in
' his function, as to carry with him (like the chief fac-
' tor for hell) innumerable people to their everlafting
' damnation, no man ought to reprove him or blame his
' faults

IX.

' That the falvation of all the faithful, next to God,
' depends upon the pope.

X.

' That no man upon earth can judge the pope, or
' cenfure his determinations, but the pope is judge of
' all men.

XI.

' That the *Roman* fee giveth to all laws and rights
' their due force, but is itfelf fubject to none of them.

XII.

' That the fee of *Rome* is the rock, on which *Chrift*
' built his church, according to *Matth* xvi —*Diftinct.* 19.

XIII

' That the keys were given to St. *Peter* only.

XIV.

' That the priefthood of *Chrift* was tranflated from
' Him to St. *Peter*. *De conftit.* c. *tranflato.*

XV

' That the pope hath power to make laws and ordi-
' nances for the catholic church.

I   XVI.

XVI

' That this fentence, *Whatfoever thou bindeft on earth,*
' *fhall alfo be bound in heaven,* eftablifhes this point, That
' the pope hath power to impofe even his unadvifed laws
' upon the whole catholic church.

XVII

' That his injunction to abftain from flefh, butter, &c.
' on particular days, is not to be difobeyed without fin,
' or danger of excommunication

XVIII

' That no prieft can marry, becaufe he hath forbid-
' den it

XIX.

' That pope *Nicholas* the 3d or 4th, hath well decreed,
' that *Chrift,* by giving the keys, gave him power both
' over the heavenly and earthly kingdom.

XX.

' That *Conftantine* the great gave to popes the power
' over all the provinces and kingdoms of this lower
' world.

XXI.

' That the pope is the rightful heir of the holy *Roman*
' empire.

XXII.

' That it is lawful for a Chriftian to avenge himfelf

XXIII.

' That fubjects may rebel againft their princes, and
' that the pope may depofe kings

XXIV.

' That the pope can overturn and diffolve all oaths,
' covenants, and obligations.

XXV.

' That the pope hath power to diffolve and compound
' for all vows made to God.

XXVI.

' That he, that doth not pay his vow to God, is not
' guilty of breaking it.

XXVII

' That no married man or woman can truly ferve
' God.

XXVIII.

XXVIII

' That the pope's injunctions are of equal force and
' weight with the scriptures.

XXIX

' That the pope hath power to explain the scripture,
' at his own will and pleasure, and that no man can dare
' to explain it in a contrary sense.

XXX.

' That the pope doth not receive his authority from
' the scripture, but the scripture from the pope
' In short, the sum of the whole canon law is this
' *The pope is God on earth, supreme in all heavenly, earthly,*
' *spiritual, and secular matters All things are the pope's,*
' *and there is none who can say unto him, What doest thou ?*'
Melch Adam in vit Luth.

This publication gave (as it may be supposed) the
highest offence to the *Romanists*, and the pope resolved
to crush him at once by his bulls, which commanded all
secular princes to destroy him

Eckius carried the bull against *Luther* into *Germany*,
and was entrusted by the pope to carry it into execution,
which was a smart blow given him by his mortal enemy,
who was his adversary, accuser, and executioner

Charles V was crowned emperor, at *Aix-la-Chapelle*,
the twenty-first of *October* 1520, and appointed a diet to
be held at *Worms*, on the sixth of *January*, 1521. The
nuncios, *Martinus Caracciolus* and *Jerom Alexander*, presented the elector of *Saxony* the brief which the pope had
sent him, to inform him of the decree which he had made
against *Luther*, who was then more than ever protected
by the elector, and the university of *Wittenberg* *Luther*
renewed his appeal to a future council, and called the
pope a tyrant, and heretic. *Erasmus*, and several other
divines, foresaw that the fire, which was to burn the books
of *Luther*, would put all *Germany* into a flame, and were
for referring the whole cause to a general council But
the nuncios prevailed, and *Luther*'s books were burnt
at *Mentz* and *Cologne*. *Ulricus Hultenus*, a satirical poet,
ridiculed the papal bull, which *Luther* called the execrable bull of antichrist, and caused it (as we have just
observed) to be burnt at *Wittenberg*. *Catharinus* wrote
five books in defence of the papal supremacy, which
Luther refuted, and *Alexander* obtained a new bull from
Rome, wherein *Luther* was declared contumacious, and
to have incurred the penalty denounced by the pope.

The

The diet of *Worms* aſſembled on the day appointed, when *Alexander* exerted all his intereſt and eloquence, to perſuade the emperor, and the princes of the empire, to put the bull againſt *Luther* into execution, without ſuffering him to appear, or hear his vindication. The diet reſolved, that *Luther* ſhould be ſummoned, and have a ſafe conduct, which was granted by the emperor, who ſent with it a private letter, directed ' To the honour- ' able, beloved, devout, doctor *Martin Luther*, of the ' order of St. *Auguſtine*.' This letter was dated the ſixth of *March*, and *Luther* was thereby ordered to appear at *Worms* within twenty one days. The tragical end that *John Huſs* had met with at *Conſtance*, in 1415, was remembered by the friends of *Luther* on this occaſion But he anſwered thoſe, who diſſuaded him from appearing, that " he would go, though there ſhould be as many " devils at *Worms* as there were tiles upon the houſes " He was accompanied from *Wittenberg* by ſome divines, and one hundred horſe But he took only eight horſemen into *Worms*, where he arrived on the ſixteenth of *April* And, when he ſtept out of the coach, he ſaid, " God ſhall be on my ſide," in the preſence of a great multitude of people, whom curioſity had brought together to ſee the man, who had made ſuch a noiſe in the world

Luther had his apartments in the houſe belonging to the knights of the *Teutonic* order, near thoſe of the elector of *Saxony* He was viſited by many princes, noblemen, and divines, and the next day appeared before the diet. *Eckius* acted as prolocutor, and told *Luther*, that the emperor had ſent for him, ' to know whether he owned ' thoſe books that bore his name, and if he intended to ' retract, or maintain, what was contained in them?" *Luther* is ſaid to have had as much courage, as *Alexander* and *Julius Cæſar* put together. He anſwered, he owned the books But deſired time to conſider the other queſtion " So that he might make a ſatisfactory anſwer, " without prejudice of the word of God, and prejudice " of his own ſoul." The emperor granted him a day to conſider the matter And ſome of his principal friends encouraged him with this ſentence, *When thou art before kings, think not what thou ſhalt ſpeak, for it ſhall be given to thee in that hour.*

Luther appeared again before the diet the following day, when *Eckius* repeated the ſame queſtion, to which *Luther* replied with modeſty and conſtancy. He proteſted,

that

that all he had wrote, was for the glory of God, and the
inftruction of the faithful But defired the affembly to
obferve, that his books were of three kinds ‘ That in
‘ fome, he treated only of piety and morality, in fuch
‘ a plain and evangelical manner, that his adverfaries
‘ acknowledged, they were innocent, profitable, and
‘ worthy to be read by all Chriftians That in others,
‘ he had wrote againft popery And in a third fort againft
‘ thofe private perfons, who oppofed the truths which he
‘ taught ’ He afferted, that the bull itfelf had condemned nothing in particular which was taken out of
thofe books , though all his books in general were condemned And declared, “ that, as a man, he might err;
“ and if any one could convince him, by holy fcripture,
“ of any error, he was ready to revoke it, and burn his
“ writings ” Eckius paffionately faid, he had not anfwered the queftion, therefore, he infifted that Luther
would give a plain and direct anfwer, ‘ whether he would
‘ retract, or not ?’ Luther replied, “ that he was not
“ obliged to believe the pope, or his councils, becaufe
“ they erred in many things, and contradicted them-
“ felves That his belief was fo far fettled by the texts
“ of fcripture, and his confcience engaged by the word
“ of God, that he neither could, nor would, retract any
“ thing, becaufe it was neither fafe, nor innocent, for
“ a man to act againft his confcience ” Eckius then
faid, that Luther had revived the errors condemned in the
council of Conftance And the emperor declared he would
proceed againft him as a heretic , which was prejudging
the caufe, and contrary to the eftablifhed rules of the
diet

As Luther undauntedly refufed to recant at Worms, as
he had done three years before at Augfburg , the clergy
infinuated to the emperor, ‘ that faith was not to be kept
‘ with heretics ’ They wanted him to revoke the fafe-
conduct he had granted to Luther But Charles made this
generous anfwer, ‘ that if no faith was to be found in
‘ the reft of the world, it ought at leaft to be feen in a
‘ Roman emperor ’ The elector Palatine alfo oppofed
the violation of the fafe-conduct, as had been done at
the council of Conftance The electors of Brandenburg
and Triers, with Eckius, Cochlæus, and others, had a
private conference with Luther, to perfuade him to defift
from his enterprize But he declared, he was refolved
to die, rather than recede from the word of God The
elector of Triers defired Luther to propofe fome means of

C c

ending this matter himself, to which *Luther* answered
he had no other way than the council of *Gamaliel*, " If
" this work be of men, it will come to nought, and
" fall of itself, but, if it be of God, ye cannot hinder
" the execution of it "

The emperor, on the twenty-sixth of *April*, ordered
Luther to depart immediately from *Worms*, under a safe-
conduct for twenty-one days, and the elector of *Saxony*
imagined, that *Charles* would issue a severe edict against
Luther, but the elector was resolved to protect him from
the prosecution of the emperor and pope. *Luther* was
purposely seized on the road by a troop of masked horse-
men, and carried, as if by violence, to the castle of
Wartburg, near *Eisenach*, where the elector concealed him
ten months *Luther* called this retreat his *Patmos*, and
wrote several useful treatises there While his enemies
employed reputed wizards to find out the place of his
concealment. Here he held a constant correspondence
with his friends at *Wittenberg*, and employed himself in
composing several of his works. He frequently made
excursions into the neighborhood, though always in
disguise Weary, however, of this confinement, he appeared at the end of ten months at *Wittenberg*, on the
sixth of *March*

The emperor published an edict against *Luther*, on the
twenty-sixth of *May*, when the electors of *Saxony* and
Palatine were absent from the diet He declared, ' it
' was his duty to extinguish heresies, that *Luther* was a
' schismatic and heretic, that the sentence of the pope
' should be put in execution against him, and that no per-
' son should revive, defend, maintain, or protect him, under
' the penalty of high treason, and being put to the ban
' of the empire.' This edict was drawn up with all
possible rancor and malice by *Aleander*. However, whilst
Luther attended at *Worms*, and pleaded his cause, he
was treated with much affability and civility by that
illustrious assembly He shewed a sufficient presence of
mind, and a noble intrepidity, in the opinion of every
one but himself, for he afterwards lamented, that he had
not been still bolder in the cause of God

Some are of opinion, that the emperor connived at the
spreading of *Luther*'s doctrine in *Germany*, that he might
make himself absolute there by such divisions Else, say
they, he might easily have suppressed it, by putting *Luther*
to death, when he had him in his power at *Worms*
However, it is far from being clear, that if he had been
                                        murdered,

murdered, contrary to the function of the safe-conduct, his opinions would have died with him And it would have been very imprudent in *Charles* to have thereby disobliged the elector of *Saxony*, who had placed him on the imperial throne, and whose authority in *Germany* was great, while he had a war upon his hands against *Turkey* and *France*

The tenets of *Luther* became now to be received, not only in *Upper* and *Lower Saxony*, but also in other parts of *Germany*, and in the *North* *Erasmus*, and the learned *Agrippa* of *Cologne*, looked upon this Reformer as a hero, who would put a stop to the tyranny which the mendicant friars, and the rest of the clergy, exercised over the minds and consciences of men Being ignorant and voluptuous, they encouraged a thousand paltry superstitions, and would neither emerge from their barbarity, nor suffer others to do it Insomuch, that to be witty, and polite, was sufficient to expose a man to their hate and indignation *Agrippa, Erasmus*, and some other great geniuses, were pleased that *Luther* had broke the ice They expected the critical hour for the deliverance of honest men from oppression But when they saw that things did not take the turn they expected, they were the first to cast a stone at *Luther* *Agrippa* wrote to *Melancthon* in these words, ' Pay my compliments to the invincible heretic ' *Martin Luther*, who, as St *Paul* says in the *Acts*, ' worships God after the way which they call heresy.' But the divines of *Louvain* censured *Agrippa* for writing ' the vanity of sciences,' though that book convinced *Erasmus*, its author was of a fiery genius, extensive reading, and great memory But *Jovius*, and *Thevet*, ridiculously charge *Agrippa* with being a magician Though this did not hinder the famous *John Colet* from lodging *Agrippa* in his house at *London*, nor the emperor *Maximilian* from employing him in *Italy*.

Jerom Savonarola, a Dominican at *Florence*, had distinguished himself by the austerity of his life, and by the fervent eloquence with which he preached against immorality, without sparing the disorders of the clergy, nor even the court of *Rome* *Philip de Commines*, the celebrated historian of *France*, saw *Savonarola* at *Florence*, and says, ' that no preacher ever had a greater influence ' over a city ' Some authors maintain, that his conduct was the effect of a great zeal for truth, and for the Reformation of the church Others pretend that he was an impostor, and a hypocrite It is certain, that this divine had acquired such a great power over the Florentines, by his singular sanctity, and the reputation of his virtue, that, in the opinion of all, he deserved to be canonized alive But he lost his credit, was excommunicated, degraded from his ecclesiastical order, hanged and burnt in the year 1498. Friar *Jerom* had been considered as a prophet sent by God for the Reformation of manners, and he had preached, that the state of the church should be reformed by the sword He foretold many things before they came to pass But the pope excommunicated him, on a charge that his doctrine was not catholic, and the Franciscan friars undertook to prove it heretical. The truth is, *Savonarola* had earnestly wished to be the instrument of calling a general council, in which the corrupt manners of the clergy might be reformed, and the state of the church of God, which had deviated so far, might be reduced to as great a resemblance as possible of those days that were nearest to the times of the apostles The general of the Dominicans, and the bishop of *Romolino*, were appointed commissaries by the pope to punish *Savonarola*, whom they put to the torture, and delivered him over to the secular arm to be hanged and burnt His trial was falsified in the most unjust and scandalous manner But he suffered death courageously, and many persons considered him as a martyr His ashes were thrown into the *Arno*, that his adherents might not have any relic left of him But books were written for his justification, and the protestants have revered his memory.

Beza, Vigner, Cappel, Du Plessis Mornay, and the other Reformers, considered *Jerom Savonarola* as a martyr like *Jerom* of *Prague* They looked on him as one of the forerunners of the evangelical Reformation, and called him the *Luther* of *Italy* The popish writers also defended his character, particularly the learned prince of *Mirandula* But pope *Clement* VIII forbade the sermons of *Savonarola* to be read till they had undergone a purgation.

Luther quoted *Savonarola*, and prefixed a preface to his meditations, because he considered him as an author that is very orthodox upon the subject of justification, and the merit of good works. The tools of *Rome* were for putting *Luther* to death, as well as *Savonarola* But *Erasmus* was greatly dissatisfied, when *Luther* was proscribed, and said, ' that they, who condemned him, de-' served to be condemned themselves; That the pope's

' unmerciful

' unmerciful bull was difapproved by all honeft men,
' and that *Luther*, being a man void of ambition, was
' the lefs to be fufpected of herefy.' One of the ecclefiaftical electors faid, ' Would to God that *Luther* had
' written in Latin, and not in *German* ' Mention being
made of *Luther* at the emperor's table, *Ravenftein* faid,
' here is one Chriftian arifen among us, at laft, after
' four hundred years, and the pope wants to kill him '

The emperor had performed the conditions of the fafe-
conduct to *Luther*, and the pope had tried him before a
council ' But the Lutherans would have been fools and
' mad, to have trufted themfelves and their caufe, to
' fuch a pontiff, and to fuch an emperor,' notwithftanding *Erafmus* faid, ' we have a pope, who in his temper
' is much difpofed to clemency, and an emperor who is
' alfo mild and placable ' *Erafmus* judged very wrong
of both thefe perfons *Leo* was a vain, voluptuous, and
debauched man, who had no religion, and no compaffion
for thofe, who could not fubmit entirely to his pleafure,
as he fhewed by the haughty manner in which he treated
Luther, without admitting the leaft relaxation in any of
the difputed points *Charles* V was only twenty years
of age, at this time, and made a confcience of nothing
to accomplifh any of his projects He faid fo himfelf,
and we may take his word for it. This emperor, dif-
courfing of paft events with the prior and the monks of
St *Juftus*, told them, that he repented of having fulfilled the promife of fafe-conduct which he gave to *Luther*.
This regret is afcribed to his pious zeal for the caufe
of God But the examples of *Gregory* the Great, who
kept his faith given to heretics, of *Jofhua*, who kept it
to the idolatrous *Gibeonites*, and of *Saul*, whom God
punifhed for doing the contrary, might have quieted his
royal confcience And if he had any caufe to repent, it
fhould have been for plighting his faith to a heretic, and
not for keeping it However, *Charles* in his old age
feemed inclined to proteftant principles And, if reports
may be credited, his fon *Philip* intended to have made
his father's procefs, and to have had his bones burnt for
herefy, being only hindered from doing it by this confideration, that if his father was an heretic, he had forfeited all his dominions, and by confequence he had no
right to refign them to his fon If thefe things are true,
the emperor muft have been the greateft hypocrite that
ever lived, or we have been greatly impofed upon by
hiftorians.

At

At the time the diet of *Worms* was held, a treatise was published, in which were the following among other anecdotes The count of *Naſſau*, governor of *Flanders*, *Brabant*, and *Holland*, ſaid to the divines at the *Hague*, ' Go, and preach the goſpel in ſincerity and ' truth, like *Luther* ' The academics of *Louvain* complained to *Margaret* the emperor's ſiſter, governeſs of the *Netherlands*, that *Luther* was ſubverting Chriſtianity by his writings ' Who, ſaid ſhe, is this *Luther?* ' They replied, he was an illiterate monk ' Is he ſo, ſaid the ' princeſs? Then you, who are very learned and nu- ' merous, write againſt this illiterate monk And ſurely ' the world will pay more regard to many ſcholars than ' to one blockhead '

As the pope and emperor had publiſhed ſuch a furious bull, and violent edict, againſt *Luther*, *Eraſmus* began to be in pain for the Reformer, though the elector of *Saxony* had taken him under his protection ' I fear, ' ſays he, for the unfortunate *Luther* So violent is the ' conſpiracy, and ſo ſtrongly have the pope and the ' prince been inſtigated againſt him Would to God he ' had followed my counſel, and had abſtained from ' violent and ſeditious proceedings ! He would then have ' done more good, and have incurred leſs hatred '

But if *Luther* had followed the advice of *Eraſmus*, and conducted the affair with all moderation and reſerve, he would ſtill have had leſs ſucceſs, becauſe his ſyſtem paſſed, in the opinion of the divines, for a moſt peſtilent hereſy, tending to overſet the authority of the pope and the monks, and to deſtroy the credit of certain opinions and doctrines, from which they drew an immenſe profit If *Luther* had recanted after he had been condemned, all the benefit, that his doctrine was capable of producing, would have been loſt And if he reſiſted, a ſeparation from thoſe who had excommunicated him muſt enſue

Eraſmus declined the taſk of refuting *Luther* , ' be- ' cauſe it was a work above his abilities, and he would ' not deprive the univerſities, which had undertaken to ' confute him, of their honour and glory.' He wiſhed that *Luther* had been ſolidly confuted before his books were burnt Becauſe it is the duty of divines to per- ſuade, and the practice of tyrants to compel But this was not the language of the inquiſition, and of the monks, who breathed nothing beſides revenge, and the deſtruction of heretics To pleaſe them, he ought to have cried out, that ' *Luther* deſerved to be hanged, for ' what

2

' what he had done, whether he fubmitted or not He
' ought to have infulted and abufed him upon all occa-
' fions, if he hoped for any favour from men, who ac-
' counted moderation and equity to be capital crimes,
' when they extended to a man accounted by them the
' leader of the heretical armies.' *Luther* was fometimes
cenfured by *Erafmus* for writing with fuch fpirit, but in
this, *Luther* acted more like an apoftle, or primitive
Chriftian, than *Erafmus*

Luther alfo made a tranflation of the New Teftament
into the *German* language, and wrote feveral books, during his retirement, which he called his hermitage He
was immediately accufed of corrupting the gofpel in
feveral places, but none of his adverfaries ventured to
condemn the tranflation of the New Teftament into the
vulgar tongue On the contrary, *Jerom Emfer* criticifed
upon this verfion, and made another The king of *England* wrote to the princes of *Germany* upon that fubject,
and faid, it was ufeful to have the fcripture in feveral
languages, that corrupt verfions might be prevented

However, it is acknowledged, that *Luther*, in tranflating the bible, was affifted by the difciples of *Reuchlin*,
and hath hit off many places very happily That he was
mafter of the *German* language, and that there is much
to be learned from this work But the Sieur de St *Al-
degonde*, in 1594, wrote to *John Drufius*, who was employed by the ftates-general to make a new tranflation of
the bible into the *Dutch* tongue, that, ' among all the
' verfions he had met with, he had feen none that dif-
' fered fo widely from the true *Hebrew*, as that of
' *Luther* '

Luther wrote againft private confeffion, private maffes,
and monaftic vows, in confequence of which, *Carolof-
tadius*, and the Auguftine friars at *Wittenberg*, abolifhed
the ufe of the mafs Vows of celibacy very little promoted continence The monks left their cloifters at
Wittenberg, and the priefts married, after *Carloftadius*
and *Juftus Jonas* had fet them the example, which was
afterwards followed by *Luther*

The adverfaries of *Luther* affirmed, ' that he uttered
' a thoufand blafphemies, and particularly againft *Mofes*
' They went fo far as to maintain, that he got *Amadis de*
' *Gaul* tranflated into *French*, to put people out of con-
' ceit with the fcripture, and all books of devotion
' They obferved fo little meafures in the calumnies they
' publifhed againft him, as to accufe him of having faid,
' that

‘ that he believed nothing of what he preached ’ Moſt
of theſe calumnies were grounded upon ſome words in
a book publiſhed by *Luther*'s friends, to which his
enemies gave a very malicious interpretation, and very
remote from this miniſter's thoughts

He was even accuſed of Atheiſm But this, as well as
what was ſaid of *Amadis*, was an egregious falſhood, and
proved ſo by *Bayle*, from the journal of *Leipſic*, *October*
1684, where it is ſaid, that ‘ this ridiculous calumny
‘ cannot excite indignation, but laughter, for the honeſt
‘ catholics themſelves muſt be aſhamed of it They can-
‘ not be ignorant that, by the indefatigable pains of
‘ *Luther*, the ſacred writings were once more put not
‘ only into the hands of the clergy, but into thoſe of
‘ the middle rank, nay, even of thoſe of the meaneſt ſort,
‘ he having, for that purpoſe, with incredible ſtudy and
‘ toil, tranſlated the holy bible into the vulgar tongue,
‘ and not *Amadis* ’ What is not a man capable of, in
point of groſs calumnies, ſo diametrically oppoſite to
all probability, when there are thoſe who dare affirm,
that *Luther* deſired to bring the ſcriptures into diſcre-
dit *Luther* had no greater reproach to bear, with all
the Reformers, from the popiſh clergy, than that of too
much recommending to laymen the reading of the bible
in the vulgar tongue

The doctrine of *Luther* was not prevented by the edict
of the emperor, which was contemned by the princes and
magiſtrates. *Henry* VIII king of *England*, ſtopt the
new doctrine from ſpreading in his dominions He did
ſomething more, for he cauſed to be made, in his own
name, a treatiſe about the ſeven ſacraments, againſt
Luther's book of “ the Captivity of *Babylon* ” Some
have thought that *Edward Lee*, afterwards archbiſhop of
York, was the author of that work But the king preſented it to the pope, who received it very favorably,
and was ſo well pleaſed with *Henry*, that he rewarded
him with the glorious title of ‘ Defender of the Faith ’
Henry was the ſlave of *Rome* for the firſt eighteen years of
his reign Delighted with the flatteries of the pope and
the clergy, he drew his pen in their defence The papal
compliments induced *Henry* to order all *Luther*'s books
to be called in, and forty-two articles, taken from
his doctrine, were condemned *Luther* had made very
free with *Aquinas*, the favorite author of king *Henry* VIII.
who had a great opinion of his learning and talents for
diſputation, and ſtepped forth as the champion of the
church,

church, to defend her against the danger she was in from
the spreading of *Luther*'s heresy. But *Luther* was not to
be silenced by the power of his adversary. And con-
ceiving himself to be used too contemptuously by the
king, he replied with more acrimony than was thought
decent towards the person of a sovereign prince. He answered *Henry* with sharpness, and without any respect to
his royal dignity, for *Luther* spared no man in the cause
of God. Many divines thought it an honor to defend
the king of *England*, by confuting the book which *Luther*
wrote against him. In *Germany*, it was answered in
Latin by *Eckius*, and in High Dutch by *Muncer*. In
England, *John Fisher*, bishop of *Rochester*, wrote a book
to maintain the doctrine which the king had vindicated;
and Sir *Thomas More* wrote another, under the name of
William Rofs, in which he gave a character of *Luther*.
But *Luther*'s magnanimous spirit was not to be depressed
by the words of a king, whose treatment of *Lambert*, the
martyr, discovered an heart full of rancor against the
truth, because he condemned it without investigation,
and a mind full of meanness, because he insulted and
threatened an humble subject and inferior. *Luther* defended his sharp style in answering the king, after this
manner, " If my asperity towards the king has offended
" any body, let them take this answer. In that book I
" had to do with unfeeling monsters, who have despised
" my best and gentlest writings, who have trampled
" upon my most humble submissions, and who only seem
" the more insolent, in proportion to my calmness and
" temperance. Let it be remembered too, that I en-
" tirely omitted all threats of virulence and falshoods,
" with which the king has filled his book against me
" from beginning to end. Nor ought it to be considered
" as a great affair, if I affront and treat sharply an
" earthly prince, who has dared to blaspheme the King
" of heaven in his writings, and to insult his holy name
" with the bitterest lies —But GOD will judge the
" people in his equity."——*Luther* had indeed written a
very humble letter to *Henry* the Eighth, by the persuasion
of *Christiern*, the banished king of *Denmark*, to which the
king returned a very harsh and unbecoming answer in his
book, which probably induced *Luther* to treat this haughty
prince with the more tartness. His submissive letters to
cardinal *Cajetan*, *George* duke of *Saxony*, and others, were
all served in the same contemptuous strain, which determined *Luther* to take up a different conduct with his

D d

adversaries,

adverfaries, in which his bravery of foul was equal to all their infolence

If we would know what was the ground of this wonderful man's magnanimity, it cannot be better expreſſed than it is by himſelf in a letter to *Spalatinus*, during the buſineſs of *Augſburgh* "That kings, and princes, and " people, (ſays he) rage againſt *Chriſt*, the Lord's " Anointed, I eſteem a good ſign, and a much better one " than if they flattered For it follows upon this, that " he, who dwelleth in heaven, laughs them to ſcorn " And if our Head laugh, I fee no reaſon why we ſhould " weep before the faces of ſuch beings. He does not " laugh for his own ſake, but for our's, that we, putting " the more truſt in him, might deſpiſe their empty de- " ſigns, of ſo great need is faith, that the cauſe and " ground of it is not to be perceived without faith He, " who began this work, began it without our advice and " contrivance, he hath hitherto protected it, and hath " ordered the whole above and beyond our counſels and " imaginations. He alſo, I make no doubt, will carry " on and complete the ſame, without and above all our " conceptions and cares I know and am aſſured of this, " for I reſt the whole upon him, who is able to do above " all that we can aſk or think. Yet our friend *Philip* " *Melanſthon* will contrive and deſire, that God ſhould " work according to and within the compaſs of his puny " notions, that he may have ſomewhat whereof to glory ' Certainly (he would ſay) thus and thus it ought to be ' done, and thus and thus would I do it' But this is " poor ſtuff 'Thus I *Philip* would do it' This (I) " is mighty flat. But hear how this reads, I AM " THAT I AM, *this is his name* JEHOVAH HF, " *even* HE, *will do it* ——But I have done. Be ſtrong " in the Lord, and exhort *Melanſthon* from me, that he " aim not to ſit in God's throne, but fight againſt that " innate, that deviliſhly implanted ambition of our's, " which would uſurp the place of God, for that am- " bition will never further our cauſe It thruſt *Adam* " and *Eve* out of paradiſe, and this alone perplexes us, " and turns our feet from the way of peace We muſt " be men, and not gods" The proteſtant champion knew full well where his ſtrength lay—not in himſelf, but in his Sovereign. If deſerted by his Covenant-head, he felt the deep conviction, that every reed might make him tremble, and every blaſt of trial caſt him down He knew (to uſe the words of a late writer) that 'if

' God

' God changed from his purpose of saving a man, when-
' ever the man, left to his own will, would change from
' the desire of being saved, he must renounce the strongest
' believer upon earth, in five minutes after he had com-
' mitted him to himself '*—But *Luther* had *not* so *learned
Christ*

Leo X called *John de Medicis*, was elected pope on the
eleventh of *March*, 1513, and it is thought, that nothing
contributed more to his elevation to the popedom, than
his intrigues and connexions with some dissolute women
of great influence   He made a league with the emperor
against *France*, to recover the places which the *French*
held in *Italy*   He took that affair so much to heart, that
having received the news of the misfortunes of the
French, he died, it is said, of mere joy   Not but there
are writers who affirm, that he was poisoned.   He died,
on the second of *December*, 1521, in the forty-sixth year
of his age, and the ninth of his pontificate   He might
justly be termed the father of revived and restored learning, which claims from history a tribute perhaps not due
to his other virtues as a man, or to his piety as a prelate.
His encouraging arts and sciences, his boundless libe-
ality to the poor, to wits, poets, artists, and men of
letters, is what his apologists have to oppose to abundance
of scandalous defects, and grievous faults in his character.   Even the failings of his character were productive
of some public use, for he seems to have had a contempt
for the understanding of other nations, which led him
to trespass upon them too far in the matter of indulgences, and other ecclesiastical propositions, that paved
the way for the Reformation

After the death of *Leo*, the several factions of the con-
clave terminated in the election of *Adrian* VI which
highly displeased the people of *Rome*   He was born at
Utrecht in 1459, and his father got his living by barge-
making   But the university of *Louvain* supplied his domestic indigence, and educated the son, who made a
great progress in all kinds of sciences, and was appointed
preceptor to the archduke *Charles* in 1507.   The new
pope refused to change his name   And in every thing
expressed his aversion to pomp and pleasures.   He was
thought fit to be raised to the papacy, which had need, at
that time, of a man learned in divinity, to oppose *Luther*,
and also of one capable of governing a state, because of

* See ' *Horæ Solitariæ*, or Essays upon the Names of *Christ* p 379
Mathews, Strand.

D d 2   the

the troubles in *Italy* But he thought it neceffary, in the firft place, to reform the difcipline of the church, and particularly the abufes of the court of *Rome*, which he obferved, and publicly acknowledged, in a very ftrong manner. He began with revoking all the privileges granted to the Francifcans, by the promulgation of indulgences Next, he abolifhed part of the refervations, acceffions, regreffes, and fuch inventions, which were called the fnares of the court of *Rome* And afterwards he attempted to reform the difcipline of the church, as alfo the manners of the clergy and laity But his laudable views were prevented by the cardinals, and priefts, who could not endure the thoughts of a Reformation, which was fo contrary to their intereft *Erafmus* entertained fome hopes, that his old friend and fchool-fellow, *Adrian* VI would do fome good The new pope deplored the fad life of the clergy, and the corruption of morals which had appeared in fome popes But his reign was fhort, and troublefome, which made him fay, he had more fatisfaction in governing a college of *Louvain*, than in governing the whole Chriftian church

Luther was now at open war with the church of *Rome*, and wrote againft the excommunication iffued by the pope He alfo attacked the bifhops, and ecclefiaftical princes, in a work, entitled, " Againft the order, falfely " called, the order of bifhops " And he exhorted the ftates of *Bohemia* to continue in their feparation from the *Roman* church He wrote his rough anfwer to *Henry* VIII. in Latin, and afterwards tranflated it into *German* *Emfer* wrote the life of *Benno*, bifhop of *Mifnia* in the eleventh century, whofe principal merit was, that he had been a rebel and a traitor, yet he was canonized by pope *Adrian* VI. for his miracles. *Luther* wrote againft this canonization, and treated *Benno's* miracles as human frauds, or diabolical operations Every thing co-operated with the decree of heaven, in fpreading the doctrines of *Luther*, and the fpiritual monarchy of *Rome* was on the brink of ruin.

As the diet of *Worms* had not fettled the tranquillity of the empire, another diet was appointed by the emperor to be held at *Nuremberg* in *November*, 1522 The emperor was not prefent, and his brother *Ferdinand* fupplied his place The pope fent his nuncio, *Cheregatus*, to this diet, with letters, in manner of a brief, to the princes, and inftructions how to proceed againft *Luther* The pope informed the diet, that *Luther* continued to difturb

and

and replenish the world with new books, which grieved
him the more, because he was his countryman He exhorted the members to reduce *Luther*, and his adherents,
to a conformity of faith with the church But, ' if this
' pestiferous canker cannot be cured with gentle medi-
' cines, sharper salves must be proved, and fiery searings
' The putrified members must be cut off from the body,
' lest the sound parts should be infected ' Yet the
nuncio was instructed to declare, ' that God suffered this
' persecution to be inflicted upon his church for the sins
' of men, especially of priests and prelates of the clergy '
The cardinals strongly resented these reflections cast
upon them in such an assembly, and it is imagined that
the life of *Adrian* was shortened on that account.

The diet answered the nuncio by writing, that they
had not put the papal sentence, nor the imperial edict, into
execution against *Luther*, for fear of raising civil commotions But they particularly desired he would apply a
remedy to the abuses and grievances of which they would
give him a memorial, as this would be the only way to
re-establish peace and concord between the ecclesiastical
and secular orders They thought it would be necessary,
as soon as possible, to call a free council in *Germany*, to
extirpate all errors and abuses And that all controversy
should cease, till the determination of such a council
should be known The nuncio replied, that the negli-
gence which they had shewn concerning *Luther*, was
offensive to God, to the pope, the emperor, and the empire That they should observe the imperial edict, and
also put in execution the decree of the council of *Lateran*, which inhibits the printing of any book about
religious matters, without being licensed by the ordinary

The diet, in the reign of *Maximilian*, proposed ten
grievances against the court of *Rome* But this diet of
Nuremberg sent one hundred heads of complaint, or
grievances, to the pope, with a protestation, that they
neither could nor would endure such oppressions and
extortions The principal of the *centum gravamina* were
against the great number of human constitutions, indulgences, ecclesiastical causes, collation of benefices, annates, exemption of ecclesiastics in criminal causes,
excommunication, and many others which they reserved
to be proposed, when justice was done them in these

This resolution of the diet was published, on the sixth
of *March*, 1523, in the form of an edict, but both the
Papists and Lutherans interpreted it in favor of themselves.

felves *Luther* continued to publish feveral new tracts, and undertook to compofe a new form of celebrating the communion in the church of *Wittenberg.* He would have none admitted to the communion, but fuch as could give an account of their faith, and who knew the nature, ufe, and benefit of the Lord's Supper. He appointed, that both kinds fhould be given, and that thofe, who would take only in one, fhould have neither.

Jodocus Clichtovæus, and *Joannes Cochlæus,* anfwered *Luther,* againft whom, and the Reformation, the writings of *Cochlæus* have been the fund of virulent abufe, for all thofe who have flandered the Proteftant religion ever fince. But *Luther* anfwered, and confuted, both thefe antagonifts, as alfo two others, *John Faber,* afterwards bifhop of *Vienna,* and *Conradus Collinus,* a Dominican. *Luther* was defirous of totally fuppreffing the monaftic orders, and wrote a book called, " The common Trea- " fury," for blending them with the public, which made his enemies fay, he fet himfelf up as a fupreme legiflator, and difpofer of the revenues of the church.

Zuinglius, at this time, was eftablifhing his doctrine in *Switzerland.* But differed from *Luther* in the doctrine of the facrament. Pope *Adrian* VI died on the twenty-fourth of *October,* 1523, in the fixty-fifth year of his age, without being able to reform the church. He was fucceeded by the cardinal *Julius de Medicis,* who affumed the name of *Clement* VII. The new pope fent cardinal *Campegius* to the diet of *Nuremberg,* in *February,* 1524, when he had an audience of the affembly, and vainly endeavored to ftop their complaints by promifes. The diet declared for a free council, to allay the difputes of *Luther.* But the legate procured a private affembly to be held at *Ratifbon* in *July,* where it was agreed, that the edict of *Worms* fhould be put into execution, and that thirty-five articles of certain conftitutions, made for the Reformation of the *German* clergy in purfuance of the late complaints, fhould be publifhed. The doctrines of *Luther* were generally favored by the imperial cities, whofe deputies held an affembly at *Spires,* and explained the decrees of *Nuremberg* in their favor, while the other fat at *Ratifbon.*

Luther expofed the contradictions in the two laft edicts; and the popifh princes oppofed Lutheranifm, by putting thofe edicts in execution. *Luther* was certainly right, in afferting, that the edicts of *Nuremberg* and *Spires* contradicted each other. For if the edict of *Worms,* which
         condemned

condemned *Luther* as a heretic, was to be obeyed, why
should the diet of *Nuremberg*, which ordered that edict to
be executed, also order his books to be examined at
Spires? And if an examination was to be made of his
writings, why was he to be condemned as a heretic, before such examination was made?

Luther published a book " Of the Duty and Dignity
" of the civil Magistrate," and wrote in elegy upon
two Augustine monks, who were burnt for Lutheranism
at *Brussels* Their names were *Henry Voes*, and *John
Esch* The greatest error they were accused of, was,
' that men ought to trust only in God ' They suffered
with heroic constancy, and *Luther* composed a hymn in
their praise, which was sung in the reformed churches
The charitable catholics rejoiced at their death, and
called them ' the devil's martyrs ' But *Erasmus* had the
courage to declare his dislike of such barbarous and unchristian proceedings, and observed, that the sufferings
of these men had brought over multitudes to Lutheranism About this time *Luther* wrote a consolatory
epistle to three noble ladies at *Misnia*, who were banished
from the duke of *Saxony*'s court at *Friburg* for reading
his books The disputes between *Luther* and *Carolstadius* increased, and the latter retired from *Wittenberg* to
Ortamunden, where he was followed by *Luther*, who
accused him of making innovations in the public worship
without the consent of the magistrate, and the elector
banished *Carolstadius* out of his dominions He settled
at *Strasburgh*, where he published two books upon the
Lord's Supper, to maintain that " the body of *Jesus
" Christ* is not in the sacrament." *Zuinglius* would not
absolutely condemn his opinion But he censured his
conduct, and rejected his interpretation.

About this time, the Anabaptists sprang up under
Muncer and *Stork*, who were discovered to be fanatics,
and were banished *Saxony*. A rebellion ensued, which
the popish writers attribute to the rise of Lutheranism
But it has been fully proved, that these tumults were
occasioned by grievances of a civil nature The peasants refused to pay obedience to their superiors, and
desolated whole countries in a most barbarous manner,
but they were reduced, and returned to their duty, after
more than one hundred thousand of their associates had
been killed during this commotion, and their leaders had
received the punishment they deserved Their principal
tenets were these,

I ' That

1 ‘ That every man hath the fpirit.

2 ‘ That the fpirit was nothing more than our natural
‘ reafon and underftanding

3 ‘ That every man believes, or may believe

4. ‘ That there is no hell to torment fouls, but that
‘ the body only is condemned

5 ‘ That every foul fhall be faved

6 ‘ That we are taught by the law of nature to do to
‘ others, as we would have them do to us, and that this
‘ principle is all we are to underftand by the term *faith*.

7 ‘ That we do not fin againft the law by concupif-
‘ cence, if in the will we do not follow that concupif-
‘ cence

8. ‘ That a man not having the holy Spirit hath no
‘ fin, becaufe he is without reafon, which is only another
‘ name for the holy Spirit

9. ‘ That infants are not to be baptized.

10 ‘ That all things are to be held in common ’

Luther exerted himfelf againft thefe fanatical people,
and fet forth a treatife, wherein he admonifhed them to
lay down their arms, and proved the neceffity of obeying
their magiftrates. Thefe Anabaptifts were enemies to
popery, and a fcandal to the Reformation. The exhortations of *Luther* on this occafion, both to the rebellious
peafants, and to the tyrannical nobles, were excellent,
and gave a high idea of his probity, plain-dealing, and
good fenfe Lutheranifm increafed, and was eftablifhed
in feveral cities, even before thefe feditions were fuppreffed in *Germany* It was publicly profeffed by the
elector of *Saxony*, the landgrave of *Heffe*, and the duke
of *Brunfwick*. It was received at *Strafburgh*, *Francfort*,
Mentz, and *Cologne*. And it prevailed in almoft all the
ftates of the empire, except in the hereditary countries
fubject to the emperor

Erafmus had been frequently folicited by the pope,
and the popifh princes, to write againft *Luther* But he
avoided the difpute, till he was fufpected of being a
Lutheran, and then he undertook to oppofe him, in a
book entitled, ‘ A Diatribe, or Confcience about Free-
‘ will,’ againft the opinion of *Luther* concerning liberty
The Lutherans themfelves have rejected that opinion.
But *Luther* and *Erafmus* were in the fame condition and
fituation in one refpect They had innumerable adverfaries, and for the moft part extremely contemptible.
Le Clerc fuppofes that *Luther* was a Thomift But we
find, that he abhorred *Ariftotle*, and defpifed the fchoolmen

men in general, particularly both the Thomists and Scotists If he was a favorer of any scholastic sect, it was that of *Occam*, whom he esteemed Therefore, a judicious divine thinks, that *Luther* first received his doctrine of predestination from *Augustine*, of whom he was a great admirer Certain it is, that scarce any man ever carried the doctrine of predestination to greater lengths, or wrote more positively in defence of it* If
there

* Witness his book *de servo arbitrio*, written against *Erasmus*, who had attacked the doctrine of predestination *Erasmus* had said ' What can be more useless, than to publish this paradox to the ' world? namely, that whatever we do, is done, not by virtue of ' our own free-will, but in a way of necessity, &c What a wide ' gap does the publication of this tenet open among men, for the ' commission of all ungodliness' What wicked person will reform ' his life? Who will dare to believe himself a favourite of heaven? ' Who will fight against his own corrupt inclinations? Therefore, ' where is either the need, or the utility, of spreading these notions, ' from whence so many evils seem to flow?"

To which, LUTHER replies " If, my *Erasmus*, you consider these " paradoxes (as you term them) to be no more than the inventions of " men, why are you so extravagantly heated on the occasion? In " that case, your arguments affect not *me* For there is no person, " now living in the world, who is a more avowed enemy to the doc- " trines of men, than myself But, if you believe the doctrines, in " debate between us, to be (as indeed they are) the doctrines of God, " you must have bid adieu to all sense of shame and decency, thus " to oppose them I will not ask, Whither is the *modesty* of *Erasmus* " fled? but, which is much more important, Where, alas! are your " *fear* and *reverence* of the Deity, when you roundly declare, that " this branch of truth, which He has revealed from heaven, is, at " best, *useless*, and *unnecessary* to be known? What! shall the glo- " rious Creator be *taught*, by *you* his creature, what is fit to be " preach'd, and what to be suppress'd? Is the adorable God so " very defective in wisdom and prudence, as not to know, till *you* " instruct him, what would be useful, and what pernicious? Or " could not HE, whose understanding is infinite, foresee, previous to " his revelation of this doctrine, what would be the *consequences* of " his revealing it, till those consequences were pointed out by *you?* " You cannot, you dare not say this If, then, it was the divine " pleasure to make known these things in his word, and to bid his " messengers publish them abroad, and leave the consequences of their " so doing to the wisdom and providence of Him, in whose name they " speak, and whose message they declare, *who art thou, O Erasmus,* " *that thou shouldest reply against God,* and say, to the Almighty, *What* " *doest thou?* St PAUL, discoursing of God, declares peremptorily, " *Whom he will he hardeneth* And again, *God willing to shew his* " *wrath,* &c And the Apostle did not write this, to have it stifled " among a few persons, and buried in a corner, but wrote it to the " Christians at *Rome* Which was, in effect, bringing this doctrine " upon the stage of the whole world, stamping an *universal impri-* " *matur* upon it, and publishing it to believers at large, throughout
E e " the

there was any difference between *Luther* and the Thomists of the church of *Rome*, it was this, that *Luther* spake more simply, sincerely, and openly than they, for

he

" the earth —What can sound harsher, in the uncircumcised ears of
" carnal men, than those word of *Christ*, *Many are called, but few*
" *are chosen?* and elsewhere, *I know whom I have chosen* Now,
" these and similar assertions of *Christ* and his Apostles, are the very
" positions which you, O *Erasmus*, brand as useless and hurtful
" You object, *If these things are so, who will endeavour to amend his*
" *life?* I answer, Without the Holy Ghost, no man *can* amend his
" life to purpose Reformation is but varnish'd hypocrisy, unless it
" proceed from *grace* The elect and truly pious are amended by
" the Spirit of God And those of mankind, who are not amended
" by Him, will perish.—You ask, moreover, *Who will dare to be-*
" *lieve himself a favourite of heaven?* I answer, It is not in man's
" own power to believe himself such, upon just grounds, till he is
" enabled from above But the Elect shall be so enabled They
" shall believe themselves to be what indeed they are As for the
" rest, who are not endu'd with faith, they shall perish, raging and
" blaspheming, as you do now But, say you, *These doctrines open*
" *a door to ungodliness.* I answer, Whatever door they may open to
" the *impious* and *prophane*, yet, they open a door of righteousness
" to the *elect* and *holy*, and show them the way to heaven, and the
" path of access unto God. Yet you would have us *abstain from the*
" *mention* of these grand doctrines, and leave our people in the dark,
" as to their election of God The consequence of which would be,
" that every man would bolster himself up with a delusive hope of a
" share in that salvation, which is suppos'd to lie open to all, and,
" thus, genuine humility, and the practical fear of God, would be
" kick'd out of doors This would be a pretty way indeed of *stopping*
" *up the gap*, *Erasmus* complains of! Instead of closing up the door
" of licentiousness, as is falsely pretended, it would be, in fact,
" opening a gulph into the nethermost hell Still you urge, *Where*
" *is either the necessity, or utility of preaching predestination?* God him-
" self teaches it, and commands *us* to teach it And that is answer
" enough We are not to arraign the Deity, and bring the motives
" of his will to the test of human scrutiny, but simply to revere both
" *Him* and *It* He, who alone is all-wise and all-just, can, in reality
" (however things appear to us), do wrong to no man, neither can
" he do any thing unwisely or rashly And this consideration will
" suffice, to silence all the objections of truly religious persons How-
" ever, let us, for argument's sake, go a step farther I will venture
" to assign, over and above, *Two very important reasons*, why these
" doctrines should be publicly taught 1 For *the humility of our*
" *pride*, and the manifestation of divine grace God hath assuredly
" promis'd his favour to the truly humble By truly humble, I mean,
" those who are endu'd with repentance, and despair of saving them-
" selves For a man can never be said to be really penitent and
" humble, 'till he is made to know that his salvation is not sus-
" pended, in any measure whatever, on his own strength, machi-
" nations, endeavours, free-will, or works But entirely depends on
" the free pleasure, purpose, determination, and efficiency of another,
" even of God alone. Whilst a man is persuaded, that he has it

" is

he absolutely denied there was any such thing as free-will, whilst they admitted it in words. This, perhaps, deceived *Erasmus*, who imagined he was only disputing against *Luther*, whilst he was really disputing as much against *Thomas Aquinas* and his followers, as against the Reformers. To attack *Luther* upon the single point of liberty and necessity, was, in an oblique and indirect way, to allow him superior to his adversaries in other respects. *Erasmus* very dextrously and artfully chose this point of disputation, that he might appear to the *Romanists* to write against *Luther*, and yet that he might avoid censuring his other doctrines opposite to the *Roman* church.

Erasmus insisted, that the human will co-operates with the grace and assistance of God, and that a man should use all his endeavors to attain to perfection. He shews

" in his power to contribute any thing, be it ever so little, to his
" own salvation, he remains in carnal confidence. He is not a self-
" despairer, and therefore he is not duly humbled before God. So
" far from it, that he hopes some favourable juncture or opportunity
" will offer, when he may be able to lend an helping hand to the
" business of his salvation.—On the contrary, whoever is truly con-
" vinced that the whole work depends singly and absolutely on the
" will of God, who alone is the *author* and *finisher* of salvation, such
" a person despairs of all *self assistance.* He renounces his own will,
" and his own strength. He waits and prays for the operation of
" God. Nor waits and prays in vain. For the *Elect's* sake, therefore,
" these doctrines are to be preach'd. That the chosen of God, being
" humbled by the knowledge of his truths, felt empty'd, and sunk,
" as it were, into nothing in his presence, may be saved in *Christ,*
" with eternal glory. This, then, is one inducement to the publi-
" cation of the doctrine, that the penitent may be made *acquainted*
" with the promise of grace, *plead* it in prayer to God, and *receive*
" it as their own. 2. The *nature of the Christian faith* requires it.
" Faith has to do with things not seen.—And this is one of the highest
" degrees of faith, stedfastly to believe that God is infinitely *merciful,*
" tho' he saves (comparatively) but few, and condemns so many,
" and that he is *strictly just,* tho', of his own Will, he makes such
" numbers of mankind necessarily liable to damnation. Now, these
" are some of the unseen things, whereof faith is the evidence.
" Whereas, was it in my power to *comprehend* them, or clearly to
" make out, *how* God is both inviolably just, and infinitely merciful,
" notwithstanding the display of wrath and seeming inequality in his
" dispensations respecting the reprobate, *faith* would have little or
" nothing to do. But now, since these matters cannot be adequately
" comprehended by us, in the present state of imperfection, there is
" room for the exercise of faith. The truths, therefore, respecting
" *predestination* in all its branches, should be taught and publish'd.
" They, no less than the other mysteries of Christian doctrine, being
" proper objects of faith, on the part of God's people." See Top-
" lady's *Zanchius,* p. 97, &c.

that

that man was created a free agent, but took a middle
way between thofe who deftroy free-will entirely, and
thofe who attribute too much to it He would have
fomething afcribed to it, but more to grace

Erafmus fent his treatife againft *Luther* to the king of
England, to *Wolfey, Warham*, and many more *Luther*
anfwered *Erafmus* in his book " *De fervo arbitrio*", to
which *Erafmus* replied in two books, entitled, *Hyperafpiftæ*

Luther had wrote a letter to *Erafmus*, full of life, fire,
and fpirit, which vexed him not a little He begins in
the apoftolical manner, " Grace and peace to you from
" the Lord *Jefus* " After modeftly reproving him, for
keeping fair with the papifts, he fays, " We faw that
" the Lord had not conferred upon you the difcernment,
" courage, and refolution to join with us, and freely
" and openly to oppofe thofe monfters, and therefore we
" dared not to exact from you, that which greatly fur-
" paffeth your ftrength and your capacity We have even
" borne with your weaknefs, and honoured that portion
" of the gift of God which is in you " Then having
beftowed upon him his due praifes, as he had been the
reviver of good literature, by means of which the holy
fcriptures had been read and examined in the originals,
he tells *Erafmus*, that he had with-held fome perfons from
attacking him, and that he had reftrained himfelf, though
provoked " What, fays he, can I do now? Things
" are exafperated on both fides, and I could wifh, if it
" were poffible, to act the part of a mediator between
" you, that they might ceafe to attack you with fuch
" animofity, and fuffer your old age to reft in peace in
" the Lord They would fhew their moderation towards
" you fo much the more, fince our affairs are advanced
" to fuch a point, that our caufe is in no peril, although
" even *Erafmus* fhould attack it with all his might "
He defires of *Erafmus*, if he cannot or will not defend
their fentiments, to let them alone, and concludes with
a high compliment on his authority and reputation

Erafmus anfwered this letter, and fpeaks ambiguoufly
of the Lutheran doctrine *Luther* wrote another againft
the *Hyperafpiftæ*, wherein he accufes *Erafmus* of Arianifm.
The Minorite brethren had faid, that ' *Erafmus* laid the
' egg, and *Luther* hatched it ' But, fays *Erafmus*, ' I
laid a hen-egg, and *Luther* hath hatched a very different
' bird.' It is to be lamented that thefe two eminent men
had any mifunderftanding, as they had both tranflated
the

the holy fcriptures, and were both inclined for a Reformation in the church. *Erafmus* afterwards wrote fome
other treatifes againft the Reformers. Yet he honeftly
diffuaded the *German* princes from hanging and burning
the poor Lutherans, and declared himfelf againft the
cruel and fanguinary methods of defending the caufe of
Rome. The *Italians* thought him a Lutheran, and the
Germans called him a *Romanift.* But every man pafled
for an heretic at *Rome,* who did not join in every article
with the pope againft *Luther.* About this time, the
violent and unhappy controverfy, concerning the eucharift, was excited among the proteftants. As many books
were written upon the fubject as would load feveral wag-
gons, and were of no fmall harm to the Reformation,
which, like the growth of the *Roman* commonwealth,
flourifhed in the midft of violent and continual divifions.

Luther was this year occupied in tranflating the book
of *Job,* which he was inclined to think was wrote by
Solomon. He complained of the difficulty of the tafk, and
obferved, fomewhat jocofely, that *Job* chofe to fit on his
dunghill, and to admit of no interpreters.

Luther's memorable proteftation, upon the article of
juftification, muft not be omitted. " I *Martin Luther,*
" an unworthy preacher of the gofpel of our Lord *Jefus*
" *Chrift,* thus profefs, and thus believe, that this article,
" THAT FAITH ALONE, WITHOUT WORKS, CAN JUS-
" TIFY BEFORE GOD, fhall never be overthrown neither
" by the emperor, nor by the *Turk,* nor by the *Tartar,*
" nor by the *Perfian,* nor by the pope, with all his
" cardinals, bifhops, facrificers, monks, nuns, kings,
" princes, powers of the world, nor yet by all the
" devils in Hell. This article fhall ftand faft, whether
" they will or no. This is the true gofpel. *Jefus*
" *Chrift* redeemed us from our fins, and he only. This
" moft firm and certain truth is the voice of fcripture,
" though the world and all the devils rage and roar.
" If *Chrift* alone take away our fins, we cannot do this
" with our works, and as it is impoffible to embrace
" *Chrift* but by faith, it is, therefore, equally impoffible
" to apprehend him by works. If then faith alone muft
" apprehend *Chrift, before* works can *follow,* the conclu-
" fion is irrefragable, that faith alone apprehends him,
" before and without the confideration of works. And
" this is our juftification and deliverance from fin. Then,
" and not till then, good works follow faith, as its ne-
" ceffary and infeparable fruit. This is the doctrine I
" teach,

" teach, and this the Holy Spirit and church of the
" faithful have delivered. In this will I abide Amen "

The judgement of this great man, upon synods and
councils, is very remarkable " I do not think it (says
" he) very safe to call a council of our friends, for the
" settlement of a unity in ceremonies, for it will occa-
" sion a bad example, though it be attempted with the
" best zeal, as all councils of the church from the be-
" ginning may serve to shew us Thus, as in the
" synod of the apostles, matters of action and tradition
" were much more treated of than matters of faith, so,
" in succeeding councils, were opinions and questions
" always agitated, without entering upon faith, for
" which reasons I have a greater suspicion and detes-
" tation of the very shadow of a council, than I have
" of free-will itself If one church will not follow
" another in those external things, what need is there
" to compel it by the decrees of councils, which soon
" are perverted into institutions and traps for the in-
" tanglement of souls? Let one church, therefore, be
" at liberty either to follow or not to follow another,
" principally regarding, above all indifferent circum-
" stances, the unity of the spirit, founded upon one
" common faith in the word of God, which being main-
" tained, the difference of outward rites is only to be
" considered as a difference in the flesh and the elements
" of the world."—It would be happy for the cause of
Christianity, if all its professors were like-minded, and
it would save the gospel much of that reproach, which
infidels in all ages, upon this very account, have cast
upon it

Luther laid aside the friar's habit in *October*, 1524, and
married *Catharine de Bore*, a lady of noble descent, who,
with eight other nuns, was taken out of the nunnery at
Nimptschen in 1523, and carried to *Wittenberg*, by *Leonard Coppen*, of *Torgau* *Luther* vindicated that action,
and intended to marry *Catharine* to *Glacius* minister of
Ortamunden, whose person she disliked, and so *Luther*
married her himself, on the 13th of *June*, 1525, without
consulting his friends But *Luther* says, he took a wife
in obedience to his father's command *Luther* was then
forty-two, and his wife was twenty-six. He was so far
from being ashamed of entering into the holy state of
matrimony, that he exhorted the elector of *Mintz*, and
the grand master of the Teutonic order, to follow his
example, which was done by the latter, notwithstanding
the

the censure of the *Romanists*. This grand master was *Albert* margrave of *Brandenburgh*, for whom that part of *Prussia* which belonged to the Teutonic order was to be made into a secular duchy. He embraced the Lutheran religion, renounced his vow of celibacy, and married *Anna Maria* of *Brunswick*. He afterwards conformed to the *Augsburg* confession, and founded an university at *Konigsberg*, in 1544, that the protestant religion might be introduced and established in *Prussia*, and all the professors were to be Lutherans. In those times, marriage soon became a recommendation among the Reformers, and was a certain proof that they had abjured popery, for if a converted clergyman did not marry, he caused a suspicion that he had not renounced the doctrine of celibacy.

Luther was very fond of his wife, and used to call her his *Catharine*. She was handsome and modest. *Luther* did not pretend she was without faults, but he believed she was less faulty than other women; and when she had borne him a son a little after, he said he would not change his condition for that of *Crœsus*. He was heard to say, that he would not exchange his wife for the kingdom of *France*, nor for the riches of the *Venetians*, because she had been given him by God, at a time when he implored the assistance of the Holy Ghost in finding a good wife, and had strictly regarded her conjugal fidelity. But he professed himself, that one great reason which induced him to marry was, to give an example of the doctrine he preached against celibacy, and to shew, that he was not afraid or ashamed to do himself, what he exhorted and enjoined in others.

Erasmus sent word to *Nicholas Everard*, president of the court of *Holland*, that the Lutheran tragedy would end, like the quarrels of princes, in matrimony. He says, ‘ If the common story be true, that antichrist ‘ shall be born of a monk and a nun, as they pretend, ‘ how many thousands of antichrists are there in the ‘ world already? I was in hopes that a wife would have ‘ made *Luther* a little tamer. But he has published a book ‘ against me more virulent than ever.’ *Erasmus* was not well instructed in this affair, or he was too prone to give credit to the scandal which was published against *Luther*.

Luther had answered the king of *England* in a rough way, and was now persuaded by his friends to write him a very humble letter, with some hope that his majesty would favor the Reformation. *Henry* returned him a very haughty and churlish answer. Upon which *Luther*, (as we have observed) ferved) who had too much fpirit to bear affronts even from crowned heads, declared publicly that he was very forry for having demeaned himfelf fo far And that he would never more throw away any civilities and fubmiffions upon *Henry* VIII cardinal *Cajetan*, prince *George* of *Saxony*, or *Erafmus*, who had all paid his humility with infults The king of *England* was chiefly angry, becaufe *Luther* had faid, that his book upon the facrament was made by another, and put out in his name. *Luther* believed it was written by *Lee*, who was a zealous Thomift, and had been engaged in difputes with *Erafmus*, and was afterwards made archbifhop of *York*. Therefore, *Luther* wrote another book, entitled, " An anfwer to the abu-" five and flanderous book of the king of *England* " None fufpect the king wanted learning for fuch a defign. ' But it is probable fome other gardener gathered the ' flowers, though king *Henry* had the honour to wear ' the pofie, carrying the credit in the title thereof.' The king was affifted by bifhop *Fifher* and Sir *Thomas More*, in return for which, he afterwards cut off their heads

The difturbances in *Germany* increafed every day, and the emperor called another diet, which was held at *Spires* on the twenty-fifth of *June*, 1526 *Ferdinand*, and fix other deputies, acted for the emperor, and were for executing the edict of *Worms* But the elector of *Saxony*, and landgrave of *Heffe*, were for holding a general council, and laid the foundation of an union for the defence of thofe who followed the new doctrine The emperor had a quarrel with the pope, who entered into a league againft him with the *French* king, and the *Venetian* republic *Charles* V told *Clement* VII. he would appeal to a general council, and vindicate himfelf The next year his troops invaded *Italy*, plundered *Rome*, and took the pope prifoner, who was obliged to fubmit to fome hard conditions before he was fet at liberty

A motion was made in the confiftory at *Rome* to tempt *Luther* with a great fum of money, and buy him off from oppofing popery But one of the cardinals cried out, ' *Hem l Germana illa beftia non curat aurum, fed auram* '

The difputes between the Lutherans and Zuinglians, about the facrament, continued till the emperor affembled another diet at *Spires* in *March*, 1529, when long and warm debates were held about religion. The *Romanifts* again infifted, that the ban fhould be executed upon the Lutherans, which was oppofed by the electors of *Saxony* and *Brandenburgh*, the dukes of *Lunenberg*, the landgrave of of *Heffe*, and the prince of *Anhalt*, who declared again for a council, either general or national. But the *Romanifts* prevailed, and confirmed the decree of the former diet of *Spires*, againft which the Lutheran princes, and fourteen cities, joined in a formal proteft, whereby they appealed, from all that fhould be done, to the emperor, a future council, or to unfufpected judges, and accordingly they fent deputies to the emperor, with a petition that this decree might be revoked. This was the remarkable proteftation, which gave the name of PROTESTANTS to the Lutherans in *Germany*. The protefters acted with fo much fteadinefs and refolution, that the emperor was much ftartled at it, and determined to ufe moderation for the prefent.

The fame year, the landgrave of *Heffe* brought *Luther* and *Zuinglius* to a conference at *Marpurg*, when the Lutherans produced fuch articles as they objected againft in the doctrine of the Zuinglians. After fome debates, articles were drawn up, in which they agreed about the Trinity, original fin, juftification by faith, the efficacy of baptifm, and the authority of the magiftrates. But they difagreed about the facrament, in the fenfe and meaning of the words, though they affented, that the communion fhould be adminiftered in both kinds, and they denied tranfubftantiation, as alfo the facrifice of the mafs.

At this time, *Solyman* the Magnificent invaded *Germany*, and befieged *Vienna*. But foon retired with great lofs. The emperor *Charles* returned to *Germany*, and appointed another diet to be held at *Augfburg*, which was opened on the twentieth of *June*, 1530. It was given out, that the emperor would tread the gofpellers under his feet, which made the proteftant princes inclined to meet him in arms. But *Luther* prevailed on them to meet in peace. The princes appointed *Luther*, *Melancthon*, *Juftus Jonas*, and *Pomeran*, to draw up their form of doctrine, to lay before the diet, where *Luther* was too obnoxious to appear, and was left in the caftle of *Coburg*, near at hand, that he might be confulted on occafion. *Erafmus* excufed himfelf from appearing at this diet, becaufe he knew upon whofe judgement the emperor relied, upon divines, in whofe opinion whofoever fhould dare to open his mouth in favor of piety, was a Lutheran, and worfe than a Lutheran.

The imperial chancellor opened the diet by declaring, that the emperor had fummoned this affembly, that every

F f   one

one might confult upon fuch propofitions as fhould be made, and offer in writing what he thought convenient, concerning religion. The proteftant princes petitioned the emperor to permit their confeffion of faith to be read in a full diet, which he refufed, but granted them leave to read it in his prefence before a fpecial affembly of princes, and other members of the empire This con-feffion of faith, which was afterwards called, ' The ' AUGSBURG CONFESSION,' was delivered to his impe-rial majefty both in *Latin* and *German*, with the authority whereon each article was founded It was figned by the elector of *Saxony*, *George* margrave of *Brandenburgh*; *Erneft* and *Francis*, dukes of *Brunfwick* and *Lunenberg*, *Philip* landgrave of *Heffe*, and the princes of *Anhalt*, as alfo by the deputies of *Nuremberg* and *Ruthlingen*

The emperor fhed tears when this confeffion was read; which were doubtlefs owing to the truth of the doctrines contained in it, and the moderation that *Melancth on* had fhewn in revifing the whole. It was divided into two parts The one contained twenty one articles upon the principal points of religion And the other was con-cerning the ceremonies of the church The emperor difmiffed the affembly, when they had heard the confef-fion, and the *Romanifts* agreed to draw up a confutation of it, which was undertook by *Faber, Eckius, Cochlæus, Conradus de Wimpina, Conradus Collinus*, and other popifh divines, who examined the proteftants confeffion of faith ftep by ftep, and anfwered all the articles, fome of which were approved, and others condemned, but fome were partly received, and partly rejected, as will be feen in the life of *Melancthon*.

Luther, in his retirement, was not a little afraid to what lengths the pacific fpirit of *Melancthon* might induce him to yield to the papifts, and therefore wrote to him to be careful of what conceffions he fhould make them, " for (fays he) they will take them in the large, the " larger, and largeft fenfe, but hold their own in the " ftrict, ftricter, and ftricteft In fhort, I have but a " fmall opinion of this projected concord in doctrine · " I believe it truly impoffible, unlefs the pope will " renounce his popedom " With regard to the *Romifh* confutation of the proteftant articles, he faid, " I " thank God, who fuffered our adverfaries to compofe " fo wretched a confutation *Chrift* will reign for-" ever. Let the devils, if they will, turn monks and " nuns, for truly no fhape would better become them
" than

" than that, in which they have fo long held forth
" themſelves, for the adoration of the world "

This confutation, however, was read before the diet,
and the *Romaniſts* ſaid they hoped the proteſtants would
return to the communion of the church, as they agreed
in ſeveral points which had been formerly conteſted.
The elector of *Saxony* anſwered, that the proteſtants
were always ready to come to an union in religion, in
any thing which was not prejudicial to their conſciences.
In conſequence of this, the *Romaniſts* appointed ſeven-
teen perſons to treat about religion with the proteſtants,
and this conference was held at *Augſburg* on the ſeventh
of *Auguſt* The popiſh deputies ſaid, that *Luther* would
not ſubmit to the judgement of a council But the
proteſtants declared, they would refer themſelves to the
determination of a council, to which they appealed, and
alſo preſented to the emperor an apology for their confeſſion, which put an end to the diet at *Augſburg*, and the
proteſtant princes returned home in *October*, without an
accommodation with the *Romaniſts*

The ſacramentarians alſo preſented their confeſſion of
faith to the emperor at this diet, which was drawn up
by *Bucer* and *Capito* But this confeſſion was more unacceptable than that of the Lutherans, and was anſwered
by *Faber* and *Eckius*, in conſequence of which, the emperor commanded the Zuinglians to renounce their errors,
and threatened to compel them by his authority, if they
refuſed

A ſymbolical repreſentation was exhibited before the
emperor and his brother *Ferdinand* at *Augſburg*, when the
Lutherans preſented their confeſſion of faith to that aſſembly. As the princes were at table, a company of
perſons offered to act a ſmall comedy for the entertainment of the company They were ordered to begin, and
firſt entered a man in the dreſs of a doctor, who brought
a large quantity of ſmall wood, of ſtraight and crooked
billets, and laid it on the middle of the hearth and retired On his back was written the name of *Reuchlin*.
When this actor went off, another entered, apparelled
alſo like a doctor, who attempted to make faggots of the
wood, and to fit the crooked to the ſtraight, but having
labored long to no purpoſe, he went away out of humour,
and ſhaking his head On his back appeared the name
of *Eraſmus* A third, dreſſed like an Auguſtinian monk,
came in with a chafing-diſh full of fire, gathered up the
crooked wood, clapped it upon the fire, and blew till he

made

made it burn, and went away, having upon his frock the name of LUTHER   A fourth entered dreſſed like an emperor, who, ſeeing the crooked wood all on fire, ſeemed much concerned, and to put it out drew his ſword, and poked the fire with it, which only made it burn the briſker   On his back was written *Charles* V   Laſtly, a fifth entered, in his pontifical habit and triple-crown, who ſeemed extremely ſurprized to ſee the crooked billets all on fire, and by his countenance and attitude betrayed exceſſive grief   then looking about on every ſide, to ſee if he could find any water to extinguiſh the flame, he caſt his eyes on two bottles in a corner of the room, one of which was full of oil, and the other of water, and in his hurry, he unfortunately ſeized on the oil, and poured it upon the fire, which made it blaze ſo violently that he was forced to walk off   On his back was written *Leo* X. This farce wanted no commentary

Luther wrote ſome books againſt popery, during the ſitting of the diet, particularly a treatiſe upon the ſecond *Pſalm*, in which he applied to the princes met at *Augſburg*, what was ſaid in that *Pſalm* concerning the aſſembly and conſpiracy of the princes of the world againſt *Jeſus Chriſt*.   The emperor procured a decree in the diet, which allowed the proteſtant princes till the fifteenth of *April* following, to conſult about their ſubmiſſion to it, and his imperial majeſty promiſed to iſſue out his ſummons for a council to begin the next year   The proteſtant princes remained firm to their confeſſion of faith, and the emperor publiſhed the decree of the diet on the ſixteenth of *November*, which ordered, that no alterations or innovations ſhould be made in the faith or religious worſhip of the church, and that none ſhould be admitted to the imperial chamber, who diſobeyed this decree.

The elector of *Saxony* was ſummoned by the emperor to be preſent at *Cologne*, on the twenty-ninth of *December*, at the election of *Ferdinand* to be king of the *Romans*   But the elector appointed the other proteſtant princes to meet him at *Smalkald*, on the twenty-ſecond of the ſame month, where they entered into a confederacy to defend themſelves againſt the emperor and the *Romaniſts*, who were determined to put the decree, made at the diet of *Augſburg*, rigorouſly into execution

The court of *Rome* was greatly diſturbed at what had been tranſacted at the diet at *Augſburg*, and the pope employed his nuncios to diſſuade the emperor from holding a council. But the emperor urged the neceſſity of it, and the pope, on the firſt of *December*, 1530, wrote a circular letter to all the Chriſtian princes, informing them, that a council ſhould be held, and deſiring them to countenance ſo holy a cauſe by their perſonal attendance. The proteſtant princes alſo wrote circular letters to the European ſovereigns, and particularly to the kings of *England* and *France*, requeſting their intereſt and protection in obtaining a Reformation, which had been attempted by *John Colet* in *England*, by *John Gerſon* and *Nicholas Clemangis* in *France*, and by *Luther* in *Germany* The kings of *England* and *France*, declared for a general council, peace, and Reformation, which encouraged the confederate princes to meet again at *Smalkald* on the twenty-ninth of *March*, 1531, when they renewed their league, and *Luther* compoſed a treatiſe againſt the diet of *Augſburg*, to prove that it was lawful to reſiſt the magiſtrates, if they commanded any perſons to aſſault thoſe who would not ſubmit to the decree

The proteſtant princes held another aſſembly at *Francfort* on the fourth of *July*, and the emperor, on the thirteenth of *July*, 1532, by the treaty of *Nuremberg*, agreed that all the diſputes concerning religion ſhould ceaſe, until a free general council was held, which was to be within a year. The proteſtants inſiſted, that no innovation in doctrine ſhould be made from their *confeſſion*, nor any ceremonies introduced contrary thereto, which was granted by the emperor, and the proteſtant princes agreed to aſſiſt him in the war againſt the *Turks*.

The elector of *Saxony* died in *Auguſt*, and was ſucceeded by his ſon *John Frederic* in his dominions, and zeal for the proteſtant cauſe. The pope ſent his nuncio, in *January*, 1531, to the new elector, to ſettle with him the conditions of holding a council And the proteſtant princes met upon this occaſion at *Smalkald*, on the twenty-fourth of *June*, when they deſired that the council might be free, and be held in *Germany*, where theſe differences in religion firſt began But the pope refuſed to comply with their requeſt

Luther diſſuaded the elector of *Saxony* from making an alliance with the *Switzers*, and perſiſted to unite more zealouſly than ever againſt the ſacramentarians But *Bucer* undertook to reconcile the Lutherans and Zuinglians *Luther* met *Bucer* and *Capito* at *Wittenberg*, on the twenty-ſecond of *May*, 1536, when they entered into a long debate upon their faith and doctrine concerning the ſacrament, and they delivered to *Luther* the confeſfion of faith of the churches of *Switzerland*, but they could not agree in their articles of *the form of union* about the facrament. *Luther* explained himfelf concerning the Lord's Supper, by faying, he had never taught that *Jefus Chrift* came down from heaven to the earth, either vifible or invifible, and that he left it to the almighty power of God to effect how the body and blood of *Chrift* are offered in the Lord's Supper, keeping himfelf entirely clofe to the words of the fcripture, *This is my body, this is my blood.* He obferved, that as they could not underftand each other, it was convenient they fhould be friends, and entertain a good opinion reciprocally of themfelves, till the fpirit of contention fhould ceafe among them, and fo he committed to the care of *Bucer* and *Capito* to finifh what they had begun.

About the beginning of the year 1527, *Luther* was attacked by a very fevere illnefs, which brought him near to his grave. He applied himfelf to prayer, made a confeffion of his faith, and lamented grievoufly his unworthinefs of martyrdom, which he had fo often and fo ardently defired. In this fituation he made a will, for he had a fon and his wife was again with child, in which he recommended his family to the care of heaven. " Lord God, fays he, I thank thee, that thou wouldeft " have me poor on earth and a beggar. I have neither " houfe, nor land, nor poffeffions, nor money, to leave. " Thou haft given me a wife and children. Take them, " I befeech thee, under thy care and preferve them, as " thou haft preferved me." He bequeathed his deteftation of popery to his friends and brethren, agreeably to what he often ufed to fay, " *Peftis eram vivus, moriens* " *ero mors tua, papa*", i. e. Living, I was the plague of the pope, and dying, I fhall be his death.

Luther, from about this period, having laid the great foundation of the Reformation, was chiefly employed in raifing and completing the fuperftructure. The remainder of his life was fpent, in exhorting princes, ftates, and univerfities, to confirm the great work, which had been brought about through him, and in publifhing from time to time fuch writings, as might encourage, direct, and affift them in doing it. The emperor threatened temporal punifhment with armies, and the pope eternal pains with bulls and curfes, but *Luther*, armed with the intrepidity of grace, over and above his own courageous nature, regarded neither the one nor the other. His friend and affiftant *Melancthon* could not be fo indifferent,

for

for *Melancthon* had a great deal of softness, moderation and diffidence in his constitution, which made him very uneasy and alarmed at these formidable appearances. Hence we find many of *Luther's* letters were written on purpose to comfort him under these anxieties " I am (says " he, in one of these letters) much weaker than you in " private conflicts, if I may call those conflicts private, " which I have with the devil, but you are much weaker " than me in public   You are all distrust in the public " cause, I, on the contrary, am very confident, because " I know it is a just and true cause, the cause of God " and of *Christ*, which need not tremble or be abashed " But the case is different with me in my private con-" flicts, feeling myself a most miserable sinner, and there-" fore have great reason to look pale and tremble   Upon " this account it is, that I can be almost an indifferent " spectator amidst all the noisy threats and bullyings of " the papists, for if we fall, the kingdom of *Christ* falls " with us   And if it should fall, I had rather fall with " *Christ* than stand with *Cæsar*." So again a little far-ther " You, *Melancthon*, cannot bear these disorders, " and labour to have things transacted by reason, and " agreeably to that spirit of calmness and moderation, " which your philosophy dictates. You might as well " attempt *cum ratione insanire*, to be mad with reason. " Don't you see, that the matter is entirely out of your " power and management, and that even *Christ* himself " forbids your measures to take place ? If the cause be " bad, indeed, let us renounce it   But if it be good, " why do we make God a liar, who hath promised to " support us ? Does he make his promises to the wind, " or to his people ?"

About the year 1533, he had a terrible controversy with *George* duke of *Saxony*, who had such an aversion to *Luther's* doctrine, that he obliged his subjects to take an oath, that they would never embrace it   However, sixty or seventy citizens of *Leipsic* were found to have deviated a little from the catholic way, in some point or other, and they were known previously to have consulted *Luther* upon it   Upon which duke *George* complained to the elector *John*, that *Luther* had not only abused his person, but also preached up rebellion among his subjects   The elector ordered *Luther* to be acquainted with this, and to be told at the same time, that if he did not clear himself from the charge, he could not possibly escape punishment   But *Luther* easily refuted the accusation by proving, that

he

he had been fo far from ftirring up his fubjects againft him, on the fcore of religion, that, on the contrary, he had exhorted them rather to undergo the greateft hard-fhips, and even fuffer themfelves to be banifhed Indeed, it appears from all his conduct and writings, that no man more abhorred that impious principle of fubverting kingdoms and ftates, under a pretence of advancing the caufe of God or his gofpel. The Almighty is furely able to effect his own will in this cafe And it is the duty of Chriftians to fuffer and obey it

In this year, 1533, *Luther* wrote a confolatory letter to the citizens of *Ofchatz*, who had been banifhed for the gofpel; in which letter he ufes thefe words, " The devil " is the hoft in the world; and the world is his inn. " Go where you will in the world, you will be fure to " find this ugly hoft walking up and down in it "

In the year 1534, he printed, and in the next year publifhed, his tranflation of the bible into *German*, in which latter year, he began publicly to preach upon the book of *Genefis*, which tafk he ended with his life, as he is faid to have foretold.

In the year 1538, arofe the vile fect of the Antino-mians, who taught that it mattered not how wicked a man was, if he had but faith The principal perfon amongft them was *Joannes Iflebius Agricola Luther* had the honor not only of confuting, but of converting this man, and of bringing him back to his fenfes and his duty.

In the year 1540, *Luther* printed and prefaced the confeffion of *Robert Barres*, his intimate friend, and a learned divine, who was burnt this year at *London* for the gofpel. They became acquainted through *Barnes's* com-ing to *Wittenberg* about the bufinefs of king *Henry* the Eighth's divorce

Luther was continually baited at by a world of furies; and he was particularly fet up by providence to effect a Reformation. He publifhed feventy-five propofitions againft the divines of *Louvain*, and alfo a fhort confeffion of faith, after which he was fent for to his native country, to compofe a difference between the counts of *Mansfield*. He preached his laft fermon at *Wittenberg* on the feventeenth of *January*, 1546, and, on the twenty-third, fet out for *Ifleben*, where he was honorably enter-tained by the count, who efcorted him to his apartments with one hundred horfe. *Luther* attended the bufinefs upon which he came from the twenty-ninth of *January*,

to

to the seventeenth of *February*, when he sickened a little
before supper of his usual illness. This was an oppression of humors in the opening of the stomach, with
which *Melancthon*, who was with him, had seen him frequently afflicted His pain increased, and he went to
bed, where he slept till midnight, when he awaked in
such anguish that he found his life was near at an end.
He then prayed in these words " I pray God to pre-
" serve the doctrine of his gospel among us; for the
" pope and the council of *Trent* have grievous things in
" hand " After which, he said, " O heavenly Father,
" my gracious God, and Father of our Lord *Jesus Christ*,
" thou God of all consolation, I give thee hearty thanks,
" that thou hast revealed to me thy Son *Jesus Christ*,
" whom I believe, whom I profess, whom I love, whom
" I glorify, and whom the pope and the multitude of
" the wicked do persecute and dishonor —I beseech thee,
" Lord *Jesus Christ*, receive my soul O my heavenly
" Father, though I be taken out of this life, and must
" lay down this frail body, yet I certainly know, that
" I shall live with thee eternally, and that I cannot be
" taken out of thy hands *God so loved the world, &c*
" Lord, I render up my spirit into thy hands, and come
" to thee. Lord, into thy hands I commend my spirit
" Thou, O God of truth, hast redeemed me !'" *Albert*
count of *Mansfield*, *Melancthon*, *Justus Jonas*, and several
other friends, attended him in his last moments, joining
him in prayer, that God would preserve the doctrine of
his gospel among them *Melancthon* says of *Luther*, that
having frequently repeated his prayers, he was called to
God, ' unto whom he so faithfully commended his spirit,
' to enjoy, no doubt, the blessed society of the patriarchs,
' prophets, and apostles, in the kingdom of God the Fa-
' ther, the Son, and the Holy Ghost '

Luther died on the eighteenth of *February*, 1546, in the
sixty-fourth year of his age A thousand fables have
been invented concerning his death, nor would his enemies forbear publishing lies on this subject long after he
had left this world Some have said, that he died suddenly, others that he killed himself, and some have impudently proceeded so far as to give out that he was
taken away by the devil. Nor are they people of mean
figure or credit, who vent these calumnies, but the most
famous writers, as *Cochlæus*, *Bessæus*, *Bozius*, *Fabianus*,
Justinian, and *Bellarmine*. This, says *Bayle*, reflects on
the whole body of popery, for such fables ought not to

pass

pass the press. Father *Maimbourg* has rejected all these
foolish stories, but he has been mistaken in a notable
fact. Speaking of *Luther*, he says, the elector of *Saxony*
caused his body to be conveyed with a most magnificent
pomp to *Wittenberg*, where he erected for him a monument of white marble, surrounded with the statues of
the twelve apostles, as if he had been the thirteenth,
with respect to *Germany* He was honorably interred
at *Wittenberg* But *Seckendorf* has shewn that no such
statues were placed round his tomb

The virulent partizans of the church of *Rome* tell us,
that *Luther* was not only no divine, but even an out-
rageous enemy and calumniator of all kinds of science,
and that he committed gross, stupid, and abominable
errors against the principles of divinity and philosophy.
They accuse him of having confessed, that after strug-
gling for ten years together with his conscience, he at
last became a perfect master of it, and fell into Atheism.
And add, that he frequently said, he would renounce his
portion in heaven, provided God would allow him a pleasant life for a hundred years upon earth. And lest we
should wonder, that so monstrous and such unheard-of
impiety should be found in a mere human creature, they
make no scruple to say, that an Incubus begat him
These, and many more such scandalous imputations, Mr
Bayle has been at the pains to collect, under the article
LUTHER, in his dictionary, and has treated them
with all the contempt and just indignation they deserve
But let us leave these impotent railers, and attend a little
to more equitable judges. *Luther*, says Mr *Warton*, in
his appendix to Dr *Cave's Historia Literaria*, was ' a man
' of prodigious sagacity and acuteness, very warm, and
' formed for great undertakings, being a man, if ever
' there was one, whom nothing could daunt or intimi-
' date. When the cause of religion was concerned, he
' never regarded whose love he was likely to gain, or
' whose displeasure to incur He treated the pope's
' bulls, and the emperor's edicts, just alike, that is, he
' heartily despised both In the mean time, it must be
' owned, that *Luther* often gave a greater loose to his
' passions than he ought, and did not in his writings pay
' that deference to crowned heads which it is always
' necessary to pay But every man has his foible, and
' this was *Luther*'s However, he was very diligent in
' his application to letters, and very learned, considering
' the times he lived in. His chief pursuit was in the

3 ' study

' study of the scriptures, upon a great part of which he
' wrote commentaries. He reformed the Christian reli-
' gion from many errors and superstitions, with which
' it had been long corrupted, and reduced it, as well as
' he could, to its primitive purity. It in some places
' he appears not quite so orthodox, we must impute it
' to the times, and not to him; for it is no wonder, that
' one who attempts to cleanse such a stable of *Augeus* as
' the church of *Rome*, should not escape free from spots
' and blemishes. He kept primitive antiquity constantly
' before his eyes, as his guide and rule; and, as *Erasmus*
' has observed, many things are condemned as heretical
' in the writings of *Luther*, which are thought very or-
' thodox and pious in the books of *Augustine* and *Ber-*
' *nard*. *Erasmus* also says, that *Luther* wrote many
' things rather imprudently than impiously. His stile
' was rough and harsh; for in those days every body
' could not write like *Erasmus*, *Politian*, *Bembus*, &c
' who were always reading *Tully*, *Livy*, and *Terence*. Yet
' how uncouth and inelegant soever his style may be, it
' every where breathes a genuine zeal and piety, which
' is more solicitous about things than words.'

Luther left a widow, three sons, and two daughters. His family was not extinct, when *Seckendorf* published his history, towards the latter end of the last
century. Whilst the troops of *Charles* V. were at *Wittenberg*, in the year 1547, the *Spaniards* solicited the
emperor to pull down *Luther*'s monument, and wanted to
dig up his bones. But the emperor had more generosity
and prudence, than to consent to a procedure so base and
infamous.

Luther had a very sharp and satirical stile. But his
commentary on the epistle to the *Galatians*, was his
favorite work, which he used to call his wife, his *Cotha-
rine de Bore*. It was a very great imprudence to publish
such a collection as the *Sermones Mensales*, or *Colloquia
Mensalia*, for *Luther*'s table-talk is the subject of the
book. It was published, in 1571, by *Henry Peter Re-
benstock*, minister of *Eischersheim*. But *Luther* was not the
author of that book, the publication of which was the
effect of an inconsiderate zeal.

His favorite doctrine was justification by faith alone,
and not by works, moral, legal, or evangelical. But we
must do him the justice to observe, that he perpetually
inculcated the absolute necessity of good works. Accord-

ing to him, a man is justified only by faith, but he cannot be justified without works, and where those works are not to be found, there is assuredly no true faith He was once somewhat inclined to the opinion, that souls after death sleep till the resurrection But he afterwards said, that the souls of the faithful are in a state of felicity, and this seems to have been his last and settled opinion. He thought that the *Jewish* nation would never be converted, and that St *Paul's* expressions concerning this subject were misunderstood

Luther was a magnanimous person even by the confession of his enemies, and undertook such things as the world may reasonably admire, having opposed himself alone to the whole earth. His followers called themselves Lutherans much against his mind But they recede from him in many things, as may be seen by their writings

Melancthon says, ' *Pomeranus* is a grammarian, I am a ' logician, and *Justus Jonas* is an orator But *Luther* ' is good at every thing, the wonder of mankind, for ' whatever he says, or writes, it penetrates the heart, and ' makes a lasting impression.'

It has also been said of *Luther*, that it was a great miracle a poor friar should be able to stand against the pope It was a greater that he should prevail And the greatest of all, that he should die in peace, as well as *Erasmus*, when surrounded by so many enemies

The doctrine of this eminent divine, and great Reformer, was soon extended through all *Germany*, *Denmark*, *Sweden*, *England*, and other countries, under different modifications.

Luther's works were collected after his death, and printed at *Wittenberg* in seven volumes folio *Catharine de Bore* survived her husband a few years, and continued the first year of her widowhood at *Wittenberg*, though *Luther* had advised her to seek another place of residence. She went from thence in the year 1547, when the town was surrendered to the emperor *Charles* V. Before her departure, she had received a present of fifty crowns from *Christian* III. king of *Denmark*, and the elector of *Saxony*, and the counts of *Marsfelt*, gave her good tokens of their liberality With these additions to what *Luther* had left her, she had scarce wherewithal to maintain herself and her family. She returned to *Wittenberg*, when the town was restored to the elector, where she lived in a very devout and pious manner, till the plague obliged her to leave it again in the year 1552. She fold what she had at *Wittenberg*, and retired to *Torgau*, with a refolution to end her life there. An awful providence befel her in her journey thither, which proved fatal to her. The horfes growing unruly, and attempting to run away, she leaped out of the vehicle she was conveyed in, and, by leaping, got a fall, of which she died about a quarter of a year after, at *Torgau*, upon the twentieth of *December*, 1552. She was buried there in the great church, where her tomb and epitaph are still to be feen, and the univerfity of *Wittenberg*, which was then at *Torgau*, becaufe the plague raged at *Wittenberg*, made a public programma concerning the funeral pomp.

Upon *Luther*'s tomb the univerfity of *Wittenberg* directed the following infcription

MARTINI LUTHERI S THEOLOGIÆ
D. CORPUS H L. S E. QUI ANNO
CHRISTI MDXLVI XII CAL
MARTII EISLEBII IN PA-
TRIA S M O C V AN.
LXIII M III D. X.

TRANSLATION

' In this place lies buried the body of MARTIN LU-
' THER, doctor of divinity, who died at *Ifleben*, his
' birth-place, on the twelfth of the calends of *March*,
' in the year 1546, when he had lived fixty-three years,
' three months, and ten days.'

Beza's epigram upon *Luther* has been much admired; and therefore we will prefent it to our Readers

Roma orbem domuit; Romam fibi papa fubegit:
 Viribus illa fuis, fraudibus ifte fuis
Quantò ifto major Lutherus, major et illâ
 Iftum illamque uno qui domuit calamo!
I nunc! Alciden memorato, Græcia mendax;
 Lutheri ad calamum ferrea clava nihil.

The learned Reader will excufe the following unequal tranflation.

Rome

Rome tam'd the world, yet *Rome* the pope hath aw'd:
She rofe by force, but he by holy fraud
Greater than both how much was *Luther*, when
He vanquifh'd both with nothing but a pen!
Go, fabling *Greece*, and bid *Alcides* know,
His club, as *Luther*'s pen, gave no fuch blow.

Our ferious Readers will, perhaps, be pleafed with the infertion of fome remarkable fayings and obfervations of this great man, which we will extract from that able and faithful biographer, *Melchior Adam. Erafmus* confeffed, ' that there was more folid divinity contained in one leaf ' of *Luther*'s commentaries, than could be found in many ' prolix treatifes of fchoolmen, and fuch kind of authors '

Speaking of the pope's ufing the mafs for departed fouls, *Luther* obferved, that " he with his mafs was not " fatisfied to thruft himfelf into all corners of the earth, " but he muft needs go tumbling down into the very " bofom of hell "

He ufed to call the indulgence-merchants, *purfe-threfhers.*

There were many plots laid againft his life, which the bloody papifts fought after by all means   Poifon, daggers, piftols, were intended, when fire and faggot could not be ufed, through the elector's protection. A *Polifh Jew* was hired for 2000 crowns to poifon him   " The " plot (fays *Luther*) was difcovered to me by the letters " of my friends   He is a doctor of phyfic, and dares to " attempt any thing   He would go about this bufinefs " with incredible craft and agility.   He is juft now ap- " prehended "——Howe/er, God preferved him from the malice of his enemies   It fhews, however, what papifts can attempt (fays *Melchior Adam*), and if we wanted further proof of it, the words of *Aleander*, the pope's legate, are quite fufficient. ' Though you *Ger* ' *mans* (faid he), who pay the leaft of all people to the ' *Roman* fee, have fhaken off the pope's yoke, yet we ' will take care, that ye fhall be devoured with civil ' wars, and perifh in your own blood.'——A pious refo-lution indeed!

When *Luther*'s bold manner of expreffing himfelf was cenfured, he replied, " Almoft all men condemn my tart- " nefs of expreffion, but I am of your opinion, (fays he " to his friend) that God will have the deceits of men " thus powerfully expofed.   For I plainly perceive, that " thofe things, which are foftly dealt with in our cor-
" rupt

" rupt age, give people but light concern, and are pre-
" fently forgotten —If I have exceeded the bounds of
" moderation, the monſtrous turpitude of the times has
" tranſported me   Nor do I tranſcend the example of
" *Chriſt*, who, having to do with men of like manners,
" called them ſharply by their own proper names, ſuch
" as, *an adulterous and perverſe generation, a blood of*
" *vipers, hypocrites, children of the devil*, who could *not*
" *eſcape the damnation of hell* "——*Eraſmus*, with all his
refinement, could own, ' That God had ſent in *Luther*
' a ſharp phyſician, in conſideration of the immenſity of
' the diſeaſes, which had infected this laſt age of the
' world '

Luther cauſed the *Pſalms*, uſed in worſhip, to be tranſlated into *German*   " We intend (ſays he to *Spalatinus*),
" after the example of the prophets and primitive fathers
" of the church, to turn the *Pſalms*, for ſpiritual ſing-
" ing, into the vulgar tongue for the common people,
" ſo that the word of God may remain among the people
" even in their ſinging.   Upon this account, we ſeek
" for ſome poets   And as you poſſeſs the copiouſneſs
" and elegance of the *German*, which you have greatly
" cultivated, I would requeſt your aſſiſtance in this
" buſineſs, in tranſlating ſome of the *Pſalms* into *Ger-*
" *man* verſe, according to the incloſed example.   My
" wiſh is, to avoid all difficult and courtly terms, and
" to uſe the ſimpleſt and moſt common phraſes, ſo that
" they are fit and proper, for the edification of the
" loweſt among the people   Let the ſenſe be clear,
" and as cloſe as poſſible to the original   To preſerve
" the ſenſe, when you cannot render word for word, it
" may be right to uſe ſuch a phraſe as will moſt per-
" fectly convey the idea.   I confeſs, I am not ſuffi-
" ciently qualified myſelf, and therefore would requeſt
" you to try how near you can approach to *Heman*,
" *Aſaph*, and *Jeduthun* "

He uſed to ſay of himſelf and the other miniſters;
" We are only planters and waterers, in adminiſtring
" the word and ſacraments, but the *increaſe* is not in our
" power "

Concerning our righteouſneſs, he obſerved, " Thou,
" Lord *Jeſus*, art my righteouſneſs, but I am altoge-
" ther ſin   Thou haſt taken what was mine, and haſt
" given me what was thine, thou haſt taken what thou
" waſt not, and haſt given me what I was not before "

Reſpecting

Refpecting ceremonies, he faid, " I condemn no cere-
" monies, but fuch as oppofe or obfcure the gofpel "

With regard to human learning, he thus exprefled himfelf, " I am perfuaded, that true divinity could not well
" be fupported without the knowledge of letters Of
" this we have fad proof, for while learning was decayed
" and in ruins, theology fell too, and lay moft wretchedly
" obfcured I am fure, that the revelation and mani-
" feftation of the word of God would never have been
" fo extenfive and glorious as it is, if preparatorily, like
" fo many *John Baptifts* fmoothing the way, the know-
" ledge of languages and good learning had not rifen up
" among us ——They are moft exceedingly miftaken,
" who imagine, that the knowledge of nature and true
" philofophy is of no ufe to a divine "

He advifed, in the cafe of temptations, in this manner;
" I would comfort thofe, that are tried in their faith
" and hope towards God, in this way, firft, let them
" avoid folitarinefs, keep always in good company, fing
" the *Pfalms,* and converfe upon the holy fcriptures
" Secondly, Though it be the moft difficult point to
" work upon the mind, yet it is the moft prefent remedy,
" if they can, through grace, perfuade themfelves, that
" thefe grievous thoughts are not their own, but *Satan's*;
" and that, therefore, they fhould earneftly endeavour to
" turn the heart to other objects, and quit thefe evil
" fuggeftions. For to dwell upon them, or fight with
" them, or to aim to overcome them, or to wait for an
" end of them; is only to irritate and ftrengthen them,
" even to perdition, without relief."

It is well known, that *Luther* earneftly defended *Chrift's*
corporal prefence in the facrament, but it is faid, that
he was of a contrary fentiment a little before his death,
and owned it. For as he was preparing to make his laft
journey to *Ifleben,* he confeffed to *Melancthon,* on the
twenty-third of *January,* 1546, " that he had gone too
" far in the facramentarian controverfy." *Melancthon*
perfuaded him to explain himfelf by fome public writing;
but to this he objected, " that by fo doing he fhould
" make all his doctrine doubtful; but that he [*Melanc-*
" *thon*] might do as he thought fit, after his deceafe."
This fpeech was made before feveral witneffes.

Luther frequently faid, " That a preacher fhould take
" care not to bring three little fly dogs into his pro-
" feffion, viz PRIDE, COVETOUSNESS, and ENVY."
To which he added to preachers, " When you obferve
" the

' the people hear moſt attentively , be aſſured, they will
" return the more readily.   Three things make a divine,
" *meditation, prayer,* and *temptation* And three things
" are to be remembered by a miniſter , *turn over and over*
" *the bible , pray devoutly, and be never above learning* —
" They are the beſt preachers for the common people,
" who ſpeak in the meaneſt, loweſt, humbleſt, and moſt
" ſimple ſtyle "

In private life, *Luther* was an example of the ſtrickeſt
virtue   At dinner or ſupper, he would often dictate
matter of preaching to others, or correct the preſs , and
ſometimes amuſe himſelf with muſic, in which he took
great delight   Though a large man, he was a very moderate eater and drinker, and not at all delicate in his
appetite, for he uſually fed upon the ſimpleſt diet   He
much delighted in his garden, and was very fond of cul-
tivating it with all kinds of plants   In ſhort, he was
never idle.

Though he had not much himſelf, he very freely beſtowed of what he had upon others   A poor ſtudent,
aſking money of him, he deſired his wife to give ſome,
who excuſing herſelf on account of their poverty, he
took up a ſilver cup and gave it to the ſcholar, bidding
him to ſell it to the goldſmith, and keep the money for
his occaſions   When a friend ſent him two hundred
pieces of gold, he beſtowed them all on poor ſcholars
And when the elector gave him a new gown, he wrote in
anſwer, " That too much was done, for if we receive
" all in this life, we ſhall have nothing to hope for in
" the next."   He took nothing of printers, for his works,
to his own uſe, ſaying, " 'Tis true, I have no money,
" but am indeed poor, yet I deal in this moderate man-
" ner with printers, and take nothing from them for my
" variety of labours, except ſometimes a copy or two
" This, I believe, may be due to me, when other au-
" thors, even tranſlators, for every ſheet have their ſtipu-
" lated price "   When he had ſome money ſent him, he
wrote thus to a friend , " I have received by *Taubenheim*
" an hundred pieces of gold , and at the ſame time *Sehart*
" has ſent me fifty, ſo that I begin to fear, leſt God ſhould
" give me my portion here   But I ſolemnly proteſt,
" that I would not be ſo ſatisfied from Him I will
" either preſently return, or get rid of them   For what
" is ſo much money to me ? I have given half of it to
" *Prior*, and made him very happy "

H h   He

He had great tendernefs for his family When he faw *Magdalen* his eldeft daughter at the point of death, he read to her this paffage from the xxvith of *Ifaiah*, *Thy dead men fhall live, together with my dead body fhall they arife Awake and fing, ye that dwell in the duft, for thy dew is as the dew of herbs, and the earth fhall caft out the dead Come, my people, enter thou into thy chambers and fhut thy doors about thee Hide thyfelf as it were for a little moment, until the indignation be overpaft* " My daughter, " do thou enter (fays he) into thy chamber with peace " I fhall foon be with thee, for God will not permit me " to fee the judgements, that hang over *Germany* " And upon this he poured forth a flood of tears. Yet afterwards, when he attended the funeral, he contained himfelf, fo as not to appear to weep

What he faid of the covetoufnefs of the *Germans* and of the prevailing fcarcity in his time, may be applied to fome other profeffing people befides them. " We are " in dread of famine, and famine we fhall feel, without " remedy And as we, without neceffity, and like im- " pious and faithlefs heathens, have been diftracted with " carefulnefs, folicitous left we fhould be deftroyed by " famine, and utterly neglecting the word and work of " God fo he will permit the evil day fhortly to come, " which will bring with it a moft heavy load of forrows, " beyond our power either to fuftain or remove "

Being once afked, *Whether we fhould know each other in heaven?* he anfwered, " How was it with *Adam?* He " had never feen *Eve*, for when God formed her, he " was in a deep fleep, yet when he awaked and faw her, " he did not afk, Who fhe was? or from whence fhe " came? but immediately faid, that fhe was flefh of his " flefh, and bone of his bone. How, then, did he know " this? Being filled with the Holy Spirit, and endued " with the true knowledge of God, he was able to de- " termine upon the nature of things —In like manner, " we fhall be perfectly renewed hereafter through *Chrift*, " and fhall know, with far greater perfection than can " be conceived of here, our deareft relations, and indeed " whatever exifts, and in a mode too much fuperior to " that of *Adam* in paradife."

He was of a proper ftature and of a robuft body, with fuch a piercing vivacity in his eyes, that but few could look upon him directly, when he intentively looked upon them. He had but a foft voice, and that not very clear, fo that when mention was made, one day at table, of

Paul's

Paul's voice, that it was rather weak, he obferved of his own, that it could not deliver his words but with a low pronunciation ' Yes, (faid *Melancthon*) but that feeble ' voice of thine is powerfully perceived both far and ' near '

Sturmius fays, that he faw a letter written by *Luther* to *Wolfgang Capito*, in which he affirmed, that fcarce any of his writings pleafed himfelf, except his catechifm, and his book *de fervo arbitrio*, " or free-will a flave " Of this laft work the late Mr *Toplady* had begun a tranflation, and indeed carried it on a confiderable way, but being prevented from finifhing it by his death (it having been long delayed through other avocations), we are deprived of this valuable companion to *Zanchius* in an *Englifh* drefs.

We will conclude this account of *Luther* with the high encomium, paid to his memory by *Wolfgang Severus*, preceptor to the emperor *Ferdinand* ·

> *Japeti de gente prior majorque Luthero*
> *Nemo fuit. Sed nec credo futurus erit.*

GEORGE WISHART.

-

GEORGE WISHART, or *Georgius Sophocardus*, as *Buchanan* tranflated it, was born in *Scotland*, and brought up at a grammar-fchool From whence he went to the univerfity After which he travelled into feveral countries, and at laft came to *Cambridge*, where he was admitted into *Bennet-College*

He was a moft famous and fuccefsful preacher of the gofpel, and in many places of *Scotland*, through which he preached, he was blefled with many feals of his miniftry And though he was much perfecuted by the cruel cardinal *Beton*, he ftill continued to preach in public, and perfeveringly to go about doing good.

H h 2 He

He was (says the excellent Mr *Robert Fleming*) one of the moſt extraordinary ambaſſadors of *Jeſus Chriſt*, that can be inſtanced. He was alſo the great friend, and (it is believed) ſpiritual father of the famous *John Knox*, to whom we are chiefly indebted for the memorials of *Wiſhart's* life, that have been tranſmitted down to us.

Wiſhart ſpent a conſiderable time abroad for his improvement in literature, and diſtinguiſhed himſelf for his great learning and abilities both in philoſophy and divinity. His deſire to promote true knowledge and ſcience among men, as is uſually the caſe, accompanied the poſſeſſion of it in himſelf. He was very ready to communicate what he knew to others, and frequently read various authors both in his own chamber and in the public ſchools.

He appears to have left *Cambridge* in the year 1544, and to have returned into his own country with the ambaſſadors of *Scotland*, who came into *England* to treat with *Henry* the eighth, about the marriage of his ſon prince *Edward* with their young queen *Mary*, who was afterwards the mother of *James* the firſt, and put to death by queen *Elizabeth*. *Wiſhart* firſt preached at *Montroſe*, and then at *Dundee*, to the admiration of all that heard him. In this laſt place, he made a public expoſition of the epiſtle to the *Romans*, which he went through with ſuch grace and freedom in ſpeaking the truth, that the papiſts began to be exceſſively alarmed. At length, upon the inſtigation of cardinal *Beton*, one *Robert Miln*, a principal man at *Dundee*, and formerly a profeſſor of religion, prohibited his preaching, forbidding him to trouble their town any more for he would not ſuffer it. This was ſpoken to him in the public place. Whereupon he muſed a ſpace, with his eyes lifted up to heaven, and afterwards, looking ſorrowfully on the ſpeaker and people, he ſaid, " God is my witneſs, that I never minded " your trouble, but your comfort, yea, your trouble is " more dolorous to me than it is to yourſelves. But I " am aſſured, to refuſe God's word, and to chaſe from " you his meſſenger, ſhall not preſerve you from trouble, ' but ſhall bring you into it. For God ſhall ſend you " miniſters that ſhall neither fear burning nor baniſh- " ment. I have offered you the word of ſalvation. " With the hazard of my life I have remained among " you. Now ye yourſelves refuſe me, and I muſt leave " my innocence to be declared by my God. If it be " long proſperous with you, I am not led by the Spirit

" of

" of truth   But if unlooked-for trouble come upon
" you, acknowledge the caufe, and turn to God, who is
" gracious and merciful   But if you turn not at the
" firft warning, he will vifit you with fire and fword."
And then he came down from the pulpit

After this he went into the weft of *Scotland*, where he
preached God's word, which was gladly received by
many, till the archbifhop of *Glafgow*, at the inftigation
of the aforefaid cardinal, came with his train to the town
of *Air* to refift *Wifhart*, and would needs have the church
himfelf to preach in.   Some oppofed it, but *Wifhart* faid,
" Let him alone, his fermon will not do much hurt.
" Let us go to the market-crofs "   And fo they did,
where he made fo notable a fermon, that his very enemies themfelves were confounded.

Wifhart remained with the gentlemen of *Kyle*, preaching fometimes in one place, fometimes in another, but
coming to *Macklene*, he was by force kept out of the
church   Some would have broken in, upon which he
faid to one of them, " Brother, *Jefus Chrift* is as mighty
" in the fields as in the church, and himfelf often
" preached in the defert, at the fea-fide, and other places.
" The like word of peace God fends by me   The blood
" of none fhall be fhed this day for preaching it "

Then going into the fields, he ftood upon a bank,
where he ftayed in preaching to the people above three
hours, and God wrought fo wonderfully by that fermon, that one of the moft wicked men in all the country,
the laird of *Sheld*, was converted by it, his eyes flowing
with fuch abundance of tears that all men wondered
at it.

Soon after news was brought to *Wifhart*, that the
plague was broke out in *Dundee*, which began within
four days after he was prohibited to preach there, and
raged fo extremely, that it is almoft beyond credit how
many died in the fpace of twenty four hours.   This
being related to him, he would needs, notwithftanding
the importunity of his friends to detain him, go thither;
faying, " They are now in troubles and need comfort
" Perhaps this hand of God will make them now to
" magnify and reverence the word of God, which be-
" fore they lightly efteemed "

There he was with joy received by the godly   He
chofe the *Eaftgate* for the place of his preaching, fo that
the healthy were within, and the fick without the gate
His text was, *He fent his word and healed them*, &c. Pfalm

cvii 30. In this sermon he chiefly dwelt upon the advantage and comfort of God's word, the judgements that ensue upon the contempt or rejection of it, the freedom of God's grace to all his people, and the happiness of those of his elect, whom he takes to himself out of this miserable world. The hearts of his hearers were so raised by the divine force of this discourse, as not to regard death, but to judge them the more happy who should then be called, not knowing whether they might have such a comforter again with them. After this, the plague almost quite ceased, though, in the midst of it, *Wishart* constantly visited those that lay in the greatest extremity, and comforted them by his exhortations.

When he took his leave of the people of *Dundee*, he said, " that God had almost put an end to that plague, " and that he was now called to another place." He went from thence to *Montrose*, where he sometimes preached, but spent most of his time in private meditation and prayer, in which he was so earnest that night and day he frequently continued in it.

It is said, that before *Wishart* left *Dundee*, and while he was engaged in the labors of love to the bodies as well as to the souls of those poor afflicted people, the cardinal corrupted a desperate popish priest, called *John Weighton*, to slay him. And on a day the sermon being ended, and the people departed, the priest stood waiting at the bottom of the stairs, with a naked dagger in his hand under his gown. But Mr *Wishart* having a sharp piercing eye, and seeing the priest as he came down, said to him, " My friend, what would you have ?" And immediately clapping his hand upon the dagger, took it from him. The priest being terrified, fell down upon his knees, and confessed his intention, and craved pardon. A noise being hereupon raised, and it coming to the ears of those who were sick, they cried, ' Deliver the traitor ' to us, or we will take him by force,' and they burst in at the gate. But *Wishart* taking the priest in his arms, said, " Whatsoever hurts him shall hurt me, for he hath " done me no mischief, but much good, by teaching me " more heedfulness for the time to come." And so he appeased them, and saved the priest's life.

Soon after his return to *Montrose*, the cardinal again conspired his death, causing a letter to be sent to him as if it had been from his familiar friend, the laird of *Kinnier*, in which he was desired with all possible speed to come to him, because he was taken with a sudden sickness.

nefs In the mean time the cardinal had provided fixty
men armed, to lie in wait within a mile and a half
of *Montrofe*, in order to murder him as he paffed that
way

The letter coming to *Wifhart*'s hand by a boy, who
alfo brought him a horfe for the journey, *Wifhart*, accompanied by fome honeft men his friends, fet forward;
but fuddenly ftopping by the way, and mufing a fpace,
he returned back, which they wondering at, afked him
the caufe, to whom he faid, " I will not go I am for-
" bidden of God. I am affured there is treafon Let
" fome of you go to yonder place, and tell me what you
" find " Which doing, they made the difcovery, and
haftily returning, they told Mr *Wifhart* Whereupon he
faid, " I know I fhall end my life by that blood-thirfty
" man's hands, but it will not be in this manner."

The time approaching when he fhould meet the gentlemen at *Edinburgh*, he took his leave and departed By
the way he lodged with a faithful brother, called *James
Watfon*, of *Inner-Goury* In the night-time he got up,
and went into a yard, which two men hearing, they
privately followed him There he walked in an alley
for fome fpace, breathing forth many groans Then he
fell upon his knees, and his groans increafed Then he
fell upon his face, when thofe that watched him heard
him lamenting and praying And thus he continued near
an hour Then getting up he went to his bed again
Thofe who attended him, appearing as though they were
ignorant of all, came and afked him where he had been?
But he would not anfwer them The next day they importuned him to tell them, faying, ' Be plain with us,
' for we heard your mourning, and faw your geftures.'
Then he, with a dejected countenance, faid, " I had
" rather you had been in your beds." But they ftill
preffing upon him to know fomething, he faid, " I will
" tell you · I am affured that my warfare is near at an
" end, and therefore pray to God with me, that I fhrink
" not when the battle waxeth moft hot."

When they heard this they fell a weeping, faying,
' This is fmall comfort to us.' Then faid he, " God
" fhall fend you comfort after me This realm fhall be
" illuminated with the light of *Chrift*'s gofpel, as clearly
" as any realm fince the days of the apoftles. The houfe
" of God fhall be built in it, yea, it fhall not lack, in
" defpite of all enemies, the top-ftone, neither will it
" be long before this be accomplifhed. Many fhall not
" fuffer

" fuffer after me, before the glory of God fhall appear
" and triumph in defpite of Satan. But alas, if the
" people afterwards fhall prove unthankful, then fearful
" and terrible will the plagues be that fhall follow "

He then went forward upon his journey and came to
Leith, but hearing nothing of the gentlemen, who were
to meet with him, he kept himfelf retired for a day or
two. He then grew penfive, and being afked the reafon
of it, he anfwered, " What do I differ from a dead
" man ? Hitherto God hath ufed my labours for the
" inftruction of others, and to the difclofing of dark-
" nefs And now I lurk as a man afhamed to fhew his
" face." His friends perceived that his defire was to
preach, whereupon they faid to him, ' It's moft com-
' fortable to us to hear you, but becaufe we know the
' danger wherein you ftand, we dare not defire it ' But,
faid he, " If you dare hear, let God provide for me as
" beft pleafeth him ," and fo it was concluded that the
next day he fhould preach in *Leith* His text was of the
parable of the fower, *Matt* xiii. The fermon ended, the
gentlemen of *Lothian*, who were earneft profeffors of
Jefus Chrift, would not fuffer him to ftay at *Leith*, becaufe the governor and cardinal were fhortly to come to
Edinburgh, but took him along with them, and fo he
preached at *Brunftone*, *Longniddry*, and *Ormiftone*, then
was he requefted to preach at *Inverefk* near *Mufelburgh*,
where he had a great confluence of people, and amongft
them Sir *George Douglas*, who after fermon faid publicly,
' I know that the governor and cardinal will hear that
' I have been at this fermon But let them know that
' I will avow it, and will maintain both the doctrine,
' and the preacher, to the uttermoft of my power.' This
much rejoiced thofe that were prefent.

Among others that came to hear him preach, there
were two gray-friars, who, ftanding at the church-door,
whifpered to fuch as came in Which *Wifhart* obferving,
faid to the people, " I pray you make room for thefe
" two men, it may be they come to learn ," and turning
to them, he faid, " Come near, for I affure you, you
" fhall hear the word of truth, which this day fhall feal
" up to you either your falvation or damnation ," and
fo he proceeded in his fermon, fuppofing that they would
be quiet , but when he perceived that they ftill continued
to difturb all the people that ftood near them, he faid to
them the fecond time, with an angry countenance, " O
" minifters of Satan, and deceivers of the fouls of men,
" will

" will ye neither hear God's truth yourſelves, nor ſuffer
" others to hear it ? Depart and take this for your por-
" tion, God ſhall ſhortly confound and diſcloſe your
" hypocriſy within this kingdom, ye ſhall be abomin-
" able to men, and your places and habitations ſhall be
" deſolate." This he ſpake with much vehemency, and
turning to the people, he ſaid, " Theſe men have pro-
" voked the Spirit of God to anger," and then he proceeded to the end of his ſermon.

He preached afterwards at *Branſtone, Languedine, Or-
miſtone,* and *Inveresk,* where he was followed by a great
confluence of people. And he preached alſo in divers
other places, the people much flocking after him, and
he, in all his ſermons, foretold the ſhortneſs of the time
that he had to travel, and the near approach of his death.

Being come to *Haddington,* his auditory began much to
decreaſe, which was thought to happen through the influence
of the earl of *Bothwel,* who was moved to oppoſe him
at the inſtigation of the cardinal.   Soon after, as he was
going to church, he received a letter from the weſt-coun-
try gentlemen, and having read it, he called *John Knox,*
who had diligently waited upon him ſince he came into
Lothian, to whom he ſaid, " That he was weary of the
" world, becauſe he ſaw that men began to be weary of
" God For, ſaid he, the gentlemen of the weſt have
" ſent me word, that they cannot keep their meeting at
" *Edinburgh*" *John Knox,* wondering that he ſhould
enter into conference about theſe things immediately before his ſermon, contrary to his cuſtom, ſaid to him;
' Sir, ſermon-time approaches, I will leave you for the
' preſent to your meditations '

Wiſhart's ſad countenance declared the grief of his
mind   At laſt he went into the pulpit, and his auditory
being very ſmall, he began in this manner, " O Lord,
" how long ſhall it be, that thy holy word ſhall be de-
" ſpiſed, and men ſhall not regard their own ſalvation ?
" I have heard of thee, O *Haddington,* that in thee there
" uſed to be two or three thouſand perſons at a vain and
" wicked play, and now, to hear the meſſenger of the
" eternal God, of all the pariſh can ſcarce be numbered
" one hundred preſent. Sore and fearful ſhall be the
" plagues that ſhall enſue upon this thy contempt. With
" fire and ſword ſhalt thou be plagued, yea, thou *Had-
" dington* in ſpecial, ſtrangers ſhall poſſeſs thee, and you,
" the preſent inhabitants, ſhall either in bondage ſerve
" your enemies, or elſe you ſhall be chaſed from your

I i   " own

" own habitations, and that becaufe you have not known,
" nor will know, the time of your vifitation."

This prophecy was accomplifhed not long after, when
the *Englifh* took *Haddington*, made it a garrifon, enforced
many of the inhabitants to fly, oppreffed others, and
after a while, a great plague breaking forth in the town,
whereof multitudes died, the *Englifh* were at laft forced
to quit it, who at their departure burnt and fpoiled great
part of it, leaving it to be poffeffed by fuch as could firft
feize upon it, which were the *French* that came as auxi-
liaries to *Scotland*, with a few of the antient inhabitants;
fo that *Haddington*, to this day, never recovered her former beauty, nor yet men of fuch wifdom and ability as
did formerly inhabit it

That night was *Wifhart* apprehended in the houfe of
Ormefton, by the earl of *Bothwel*, fuborned thereto by the
cardinal. The manner was thus After fermon he took
his laft farewel of all his friends in *Haddington*, *John
Knox* would fain have gone with him, but he faid, " Re-
" turn to your children, and God blefs you One is
" fufficient for one facrifice " Then went he to the laird
of *Ormefton*'s with fome others that accompanied him.
After fupper he had a comfortable difcourfe of God's
love to his children, then he appointed the 51ft *Pfalm*
to be fung, and fo retired to his chamber.

Before midnight the houfe was befet, and the earl of
Bothwel called for the laird of the houfe, and told him
that it was in vain to refift, for the governor and cardinal
were within a mile, with a great power, but if he would
deliver *Wifhart* to him, he would promife upon his honor
that he fhould be fafe, and that the cardinal fhould not
hurt him *Wifhart* faid, " Open the gates, the will of
" God be done," and *Bothwel* coming in, *Wifhart* faid
to him, " I praife my God that fo honourable a man as
" you, my lord, receive me this night, for I am per-
" fuaded that for your honour's fake you will fuffer no-
" thing to be done to me but by order of law I lefs
" fear to die openly, than fecretly to be murdered "
Then faid *Bothwel*, ' I will not only preferve your body
' from all violence that fhall be intended againft you
' without order of law, but I alfo promife in the pre-
' fence of thefe gentlemen, that neither the governor nor
' cardinal fhall have their will of you, but I will keep
' you in mine own houfe, till I either fet you free, or
' reftore you to the fame place where I receive you'.
Then faid the lairds, ' My lord, if you make good your
' promife,

' promife, which we prefume you will, we ourfelves will
' not only ferve you, but we will procure all the profef-
' fors in *Lothian* to do the fame, &c.' Thefe promifes
being made in the prefence of God, and hands being
ftricken by both parties, the earl took *Wifhart*, and fo
departed

Wifhart was carried to *Edinburgh*, but gold and women
eafily corrupt flefhly men, for the cardinal gave *Bethwel*
gold, and the queen, that was too familiar with him,
promifed him her favor, if he would deliver *Wifhart* into
Edinburgh caftle, which he did, and fhortly after he was
delivered to the blood-thirfty cardinal. Who, becaufe it
was forbidden by their canon-law for a prieft to fit as a
judge upon life and death, fent to the governor, re-
quefting him to appoint fome lay-judge to pafs fentence
of death upon *Wifhart*.

The governor would eafily have yielded to his requeft,
if *David Hamilton*, a godly man, had not told him, that
he could expect no better an end than *Saul*, if he perfecuted the truth which formerly he had profeffed, &c.
Hereupon the governor fent the cardinal word, that he
would have no hand in fhedding the blood of that good
man   The cardinal, being angry, returned this anfwer,
that he had fent to him of mere civility, and that he
would proceed without him, and fo to the great grief of
the godly, the cardinal carried *Wifhart* to Saint *Andrew's*,
and put him into the tower there, and, without any long
delay, he caufed all the bifhops, and other great clergy-
men to be called together to Saint *Andrew's*

On *February* the twenty-eighth, 1546, *Wifhart* was
brought before them, to give an account of his feditious and
heretical doctrine, as they called it.   The cardinal caufed
all his retinue to come armed to the place of their fitting,
which was the abby-church, whither when *Wifhart* was
brought, there was a poor man lying at the door, that
afked his alms, to whom he flung his purfe   When he
came before the cardinal, there was a dean appointed to
preach, whofe fermon being ended, *Wifhart* was put up
into the pulpit to hear his charge   And one *Lawder*, a
prieft, ftood over againft him, and read a fcroll full of
bitter accufations and curfes, fo that the ignorant people
thought that the earth would have opened and fwallowed
up *Wifhart* quick   But he ftood with great patience,
without moving or once changing his countenance. The
prieft, having ended his curfes, fpat at *Wifhart's* face,
faying, ' What anfwereft thou ? thou runagate, traitor,

' thief,

' thief, &c ' Then *Wishart* fell upon his knees, making his prayer unto God, after which he said, " Many and " horrible fayings unto me a Christian man, many words " abominable to hear, have ye spoken here this day; " which not only to teach, but even to think, I ever " thought a great abomination, &c." Then did he give them an account of his doctrine, answering every article, as far as they would give him leave to speak.

But they, without any regard to his fober and godly answers, presently condemned him to be burnt. After which fentence, he, falling upon his knees, said,

" O immortal God, how long wilt thou fuffer the " rage, and great cruelty of the ungodly to exercife " their fury upon thy fervants, which do further thy " word in this world, whereas they on the contrary feek " to deftroy the truth, whereby thou haft revealed thyfelf " to the world, &c O Lord, we know certainly that " thy true fervants muft needs fuffer, for thy name's " fake, perfecutions, afflictions, and troubles in this " prefent world, yet we defire, that thou wouldeft pre- " ferve and defend thy church, which thou haft chofen " before the foundation of the world, and give thy peo- " ple grace to hear thy word, and to be thy true fervants " in this prefent life "

Then were the common people put out, the bifhops not defiring that they fhould hear the innocent man fpeak, and fo they fent him again to the caftle, till the fire fhould be made ready In the caftle came two friars to him, requiring him to make his confeffion to them, to whom he faid, " I will make no confeffion to you, " but fetch me that man who preached even now, and I " will fpeak with him " Then was the fub-prior fent for, with whom he conferred a pretty while, till the fub- prior wept, who, going to the cardinal, told him that he came not to intercede for *Wishart*'s life, but to make known his innocency to all men; at which words the cardinal was very angry, faying, ' We knew long ago ' what you were '

The captain of the caftle with fome friends, coming to *Wishart*, afked him if he would break his faft with them. " Yea, faid he, very willingly, for I know you be " honeft men " In the mein time he defired them to hear him a little, and fo he difcourfed to them about the Lord's Supper, his fufferings and death for us, exhort- ing them to love one another, laying afide all rancor and malice, as becomes the members of *Jefus Chrift*, who

continually

continually intercedes for us with his Father. Afterwards he gave thanks, and blessing the bread and wine, he took the bread and brake it, giving it to every one, saying, " eat this, remember that *Christ* died for us, and " feed on it spiritually," so taking the cup, he bad them " remember that *Christ's* blood was shed for them, &c." Then he gave thanks and prayed for them, and so retired into his chamber.

Presently came two executioners to him from the cardinal, one put on him a black linen coat, the other brought him bags of powder, which they tied about several parts of his body, and so they brought him forth to the place of execution, over against which place, the castle windows were hung with rich hangings, and velvet cushions laid for the cardinal and prelates, who from thence were to feed their eyes with the torments of this innocent man   The cardinal, fearing lest *Wishart* should be rescued by his friends, caused all the ordnance in the castle to be bent against the place of his execution, and commanded his gunners to stand ready all the time of his burning.   Then were his hands bound behind his back, and so he was carried forth   In the way some beggars met him, asking him his alms for God's sake   To whom he said, " My hands are bound wherewith I was wont " to give you alms   But the merciful Lord, who of his " bounty and abundant grace feeds all men, vouchsafe " to give you necessaries both for your bodies and " souls."   Then two friars met him, persuading him to pray to our lady to mediate for him, to whom he meekly said, " Cease, tempt me not, I entreat you "   And so with a rope about his neck, and a chain about his middle, he was led to the fire, then falling upon his knees, he thrice repeated, " O thou Saviour of the world, have " mercy upon me, Father of heaven, I commend my " spirit into thy holy hands "   Then turning to the people, he said, " Christian brethren and sisters, I be- " seech you, be not offended at the word of God for the " torments which you see prepared for me, but I exhort " you that ye love the word of God for your salvation, " and suffer patiently, and with a comfortable heart, for " the word's sake, which is your undoubted salvation " and everlasting comfort. I pray you also shew my " brethren and sisters, who have often heard me, that " they cease not to learn the word of God, which I " taught them according to the measure of grace given " me, for no persecution or trouble in this world what-

I   " soever,

" foever, and fhew them, that the doctrine was no old
" wives fables, but the truth of God, for if I had
" taught men's doctrine, I fhould have had greater
" thanks from men. But for the word of God's fake I
" now fuffer, not forrowfully, but with a glad heart and
" mind. For this caufe I was fent, that I fhould fuffer
" this fire for *Chrift's* fake, behold my face, you fhall
" not fee me change my countenance I fear not the
" fire, and if perfecution come to you for the word's
" fake, I pray you *fear not them that can kill the body, and*
" *have no power to hurt the foul, &c*" Then he prayed
for them, who accufed him, faying, " I befeech thee,
" Father of heaven, forgive them that have, of ignorance
" or of an evil mind, forged lies of me. I forgive them
" with all my heart, I befeech *Chrift* to forgive them,
" that have condemned me this day ignorantly." Then
turning to the people again, he faid, " I befeech you,
" brethren, exhort your prelates to learn the word of
" God, that they may be afhamed to do evil, and learn
" to do good, or elfe there fhall fhortly come upon them
" the wrath of God which they fhall not efchew"
Then the executioner upon his knees, faid, ' Sir, I pray
' you forgive me, for I am not the caufe of your death,'
Wifhart, calling him to him, killed his cheeks, faying,
" Lo here is a token that I forgive thee My heart, do
" thine office." And fo he was tied to the ftake, and the
fire kindled.

The captain of the caftle, coming near him, bade him
be of good courage, and to beg for him the pardon of his
fin, to whom *Wifhart* faid, " This fire torments my body,
" but no whit abates my fpirits" Then, looking towards the cardinal, he faid, " He, who, in fuch ftate
" from that high place, feeds his eyes with my tor-
" ments, within few days fhall be hanged out at that
" fame window, to be feen with as much ignominy, as
" he now leans there with pride" And fo his breath
being ftopped, he was confumed by the fire, near the
caftle of St. *Andrew's*, in the year 1546

This prophecy was fulfilled, when, after the cardinal
was flain, the provoft, raifing the town, came to the caftle
gates, crying, ' What have you done with my lord car-
' dinal ? Where is my lord cardinal ?' To whom they
within anfwered, ' Return to your houfes, for he hath
' received his reward, and will trouble the world no
' more' But they ftill cried, ' We will never depart till
' we fee him.' Then did the *Leflies* hang him out at

that window to fhew that he was dead, and fo the people departed

But we will relate more particularly, from the *Scotch*
hiftorian, the circumftances of the cardinal's death   God
(fays he) left not the death of this holy man long un-
revenged   For the people generally exclaimed againft the
cruelty ufed upon him, efpecially *John Lefley*, brother
to the earl of *Rothes*, and *Norman Lefley* his coufin, fell
foul upon the cardinal for it   But he thought himfelf
ftrong enough for all *Scotland*, faying, ' Tufh, a fig for
' the fools, and a button for the bragging of heretics.
' Is not the lord governor mine, witnefs his eldeft fon
' for a pledge at my table? Have I not the queen at my
' devotion? Is not *France* my friend? Why fhould I
' fear any danger?' Yet he had laid a defign to cut off
fuch as he feared and hated, which was difcovered after
his death by letters and memorials found about him. He
kept himfelf for his greater fecurity in his caftle, and on
a *Friday* night there came to the town of Saint *Andrew's*,
Norman Lefley, *William Kircaldy*, *John Lefley*, and fome
others, and on the *Saturday* morning they met together
not far from the caftle, waiting till the gate was opened,
and the draw-bridge let down, for the receiving in fome
lime and fand, to repair fome decays about the caftle;
which being done, *Kircaldy*, with fix more, went to the
porter, falling into difcourfe with him, till the *Leflies*
came alfo with fome other company   The porter, feeing
them, would have drawn up the bridge, but was prevented, and whilft he endeavored to keep them out at
the gate, his head was broken, and the keys taken from
him.   The cardinal was afleep in bed, for all night he
had for his bedfellow, Mrs *Mary Ogleby*, who was a
little before gone from him out at the poftern gate, and
therefore the cardinal was gone to his reft.

There were about one hundred workmen in the caftle,
who, feeing what was done, cried out, but, without hurt,
they were turned out at the wicket gate   Then *William
Kircaldy* went to fecure the poftern, left the cardinal
fhould make an efcape that way   The reft, going to the
gentlemen's chambers, who were above fifty, without
hurting them, turned them all out at the gate   They,
who undertook this enterprize, were but eighteen men.
The cardinal, being awakened with the noife, afked out at
the window, ' what was the matter?' Anfwer was
made, that *Norman Lefley* had taken his caftle   Then
did he attempt to have efcaped by the poftern, but finding

ing that to be kept, he returned to his chamber, and, with the help of his chamberlain, fell to barricadoing the door with chests, and such things   Then came up *John Lesley*, and commanded him to open the door   The cardinal asked, ‘who was there?’   He answered, *John Lesley*. The cardinal said, ‘I will have *Norman*, for he is my ‘ friend ’   ‘ Content yourself, said the other, with those ‘ that are here ’   And so they fell to breaking open the door.   In the mean time, the cardinal hid a box of gold under some coals in a secret corner   Then he said to them, ‘ Will ye save my life?’   *John Lesley* answered, ‘ It may be, that we will ’   ‘ Nay, said the cardinal, ‘ swear unto me by God’s wounds that you will; and ‘ then I will open the door ’   Then said *John*, ‘ that ‘ which was said, is unsaid,’ and so he called for fire to burn down the door; whereupon the door was opened, and the cardinal sat him down in his chair, crying, ‘ I ‘ am a priest, I am a priest; ye will not slay me !’   Then *John Lesley* and another struck him once or twice   But Mr. *James Melvin*, a man that had been very familiar with *Wishart*, and of a modest and gentle nature, perceiving them both to be in choler, plucked them back; saying, ‘This work and judgement of God, although it ‘ be secret, ought to be done with great gravity ’   And so presenting him the point of his sword, he said, ‘ Re- ‘ pent thee of thy former wicked life, but especially of ‘ shedding the blood of that noble instrument of God, ‘ Mr. *George Wishart*, who, though he was consumed by ‘ the fire before men, yet cries it for vengeance upon ‘ thee, and we from God are sent to revenge it, for ‘ here, before my God I protest, that neither the hatred ‘ of thy person, the love of thy riches, nor the fear of ‘ any hurt thou couldst have done me, moveth me to ‘ strike thee, but only because thou hast been, and still ‘ remainest, an obstinate enemy against *Jesus Christ*, and ‘ his holy gospel,’ and so he thrust him through the body, who falling down, spake never a word, but ‘ I ‘ am a priest, I am a priest   Fie, fie, all is gone.’

The death of this tyrant was grievous to the queen mother, with whom he had too much familiarity, as with many other women, as also to the *Romanists*, though the Reformed were freed from their fears in a great measure thereby.

The conduct, however, of these *Lesleys* is, by no means, to be justified, for killing men without law, is undoubtedly *murder*, and a defiance of all civil institutions

And,

And, in a Christian view, it is still more unjustifiable, for we are taught to *suffer, and not to revenge, but to commit ourselves to* HIM, *who judgeth righteously* It was also what *Wishart* himself would have condemned, as evidently appears by his meek and tender conduct to the prieft, who would have ftabbed him, as we have above related *Vengeance is mine, I will repay, faith the Lord.* The judgement was certainly juft upon the cardinal, but God, in the difpenfations of his juftice, ufually lets wicked inftruments loofe, and even *Satan* himfelf, to accomplifh his awful defigns Chriftians have a better bufinefs allotted them

The *Scotch* hiftorian's account of *Wishart's* perfon and manner of life is fo extraordinary, that we flatter ourfelves it will not be unacceptable to our Readers

‘ *Wishart,* fays he, was tall of ftature, and of a me-
‘ lancholy conftitution He had black hair, a long beard,
‘ was comely of perfonage, and well-fpoken, courteous,
‘ lowly, lovely, willing to teach, defirous to learn As
‘ for his habit, he wore a frize gown, a black fuftian
‘ doublet, plain hofe, coarfe canvafs for his fhirts, fall-
‘ ing bands, &c all which apparel he gave to the poor,
‘ fome weekly, fome monthly, fome quarterly, faving a
‘ *French* cap that he wore, which he kept a twelvemonth
‘ He was modeft, temperate, fearing God, hating
‘ covetoufnefs His charity was extraordinary, he for-
‘ bore his food one meal in three, and one day in four,
‘ that he might the better relieve the poor His lodging
‘ was upon ftraw, and he had coarfe new canvafs fheets,
‘ which, when once foul, he gave away He had by his
‘ bedfide a tub of water, in which in the dark night he
‘ bathed himfelf. He taught with great modefty and
‘ gravity.’

FREDERIC MYCONIUS.

FREDERIC MYCONIUS was born at *Lich-tenfeldt*, in *Franconia*, *December* the twenty-fixth, in the year 1491, of religious parents, and bred up at fchool there till he was thirteen years of age, and then was fent to *Annaberg*, where he ftudied till he was twenty About that age he entered into a monaftry of Francif-cans, without the knowledge of his parents. To this ftep he was led, by the fuperftition of the times, not for the love of eafe, (fays *Melchior Adam*) and much lefs for the fake of his belly or pleafures, but with a view to ferve God, and to obtain, by his own righteoufnefs, the remiffion both of his own fins and of others For the monks perfuaded men, ' That their vow was equivalent ' to baptifm, that it was the ftate of perfection, that ' the monaftic rules and ordinances [*verbo* DEI *multis* ' *parafangis anteire*] were very far to be preferred to the ' word of God, that the habit of their order was much ' holier than all other garments, and that whofoever ' fhould be buried in the cowl of a monk, would infal-' libly obtain the remiffion of one-third part of all his ' fins,' with much other goodly doctrine of the fame profitable kind.

The firft night after his entry, *Myconius* had a remark-able dream, which proved prophetical, but is too long for infertion here. In this monaftry he read the fchoolmen and *Auguftine's* works. He read alfo, at meal-times, the bible with *Lyra's* notes, which he continued for feven years together, and with fuch exactnefs, that he had it almoft by heart But at length, defpairing of making any confiderable attainments in learning, he turned himfelf to the mechanical arts. About which time the arrant vagabond *Tetzelius* brought his indulgences into *Germany*, boafting of the virtue of them, and exhorting all men,

as

as they loved their own falvation, and the falvation of their deceafed friends, that they fhould buy them, &c. *Myconius* had been taught, by his father, the Lord's prayer, the creed, the decalogue, and had been admonifhed to pray often, that the blood of *Chrift* only could cleanfe us from fin, that if only three perfons were to be faved by this blood, he fhould endeavor to be one of them, and that pardon of fin and eternal life could not be bought with money, &c From this circumftance, it has been fuppofed that *Myconius*'s father had fecretly embraced the doctrine of the *Waldenfes* *Myconius*, however, was greatly troubled, not knowing whether to believe his father or the priefts, but underftanding, that there was a claufe in the indulgences, that they fhould be *freely given to the poor*, he went to *Tetzelius*, and begged him to give him one, for that he was a poor finner, and one that needed a free pardon of his fins, and a participation of the merits of *Chrift* *Tetzelius* wondered to hear him fpeak Latin fo well, which was what few priefts could do in thofe days, and he therefore confulted with his colleagues, what was beft to be done, who advifed him to give *Myconius* a pardon But, after a long debate, *Tetzelius* concluded, 'That the pope wanted money, with-' out which he could not part with an indulgence' *Myconius* urged the above-mentioned claufe in the bull; upon which *Tetzelius*'s colleagues defired he might have one given him, pleading his learning, ingenuity, poverty, &c and that it would be a difhonor both to God and the pope to deny him one But ftill *Tetzelius* abfolutely refufed. Upon this one of them whifpered to *Myconius*, to give a little money for one, which he refufed to do. They fearing the event, and believing that he was fuborned by others, offered him money to buy one with, but he would not accept of it, faying, "That, if he " chofe to buy one, he could fell a book for that pur- " pofe, but he defired one for God's fake, which if they " denied him, he wifhed them to confider how they could " anfwer it to God, &c" But prevailing nothing, he went away rejoicing, that there was yet a God in heaven to pardon finners freely, &c according to that promife, *As I live, faith the Lord, I defire not the death of a finner*, &c

A little time after this [*viz* in the year 1516] he took orders, and read privately *Luther*'s books with *John Voit*, till he made profeffion of the truth, which gave great offence to the other friars, who feverely threatened him

for

for it About this period, while *Luther* was attacking the errors and blafphemies of the church of *Rome* at *Wittenberg*, and the light of the gofpel began to fhine, he received a call to be a preacher at *Vinaria*, which he accepted of, and where at firft he mixed fome popifh errors with the truth, but being further enlightened by the SPIRIT's teaching in reading the fcriptures and *Luther*'s works, he at length began to preach boldly againft popery, and to hold forth the truth clearly, which fpread with fuch incredible fwiftnefs, not only through *Saxony*, but through all *Europe*, ' as if,' fays our biographer, ' the angels had been the carriers of it ' Afterwards, in the year 1524, he was called to *Gotha*, to teach and govern the *Thuringian* churches, where he lived with his colleagues twenty-two years in much peace and concord, of which himfelf fays, " *Cucurrimus, certavimus, laboravimus, pugnavimus, vicimus, & viximus femper conjunctiffime, &c* " i e. " We ran, we ftrove, we fought, we conquered, and we lived together always in the greateft harmony and love " He was remarkable for the great pains he took to pacify and keep quiet the boors, or common people, and is faid to have made fuch an oration to great numbers of them, that were pulling down fome noblemen's houfes, that they all went away in peace The fame year he married; and, by the blefsing of God, had a numerous pofterity.

At this early period, the found of the gofpel was happily fpread over moft parts of *Germany*, and the following illuftrious perfons were fcattered over it and the bordering countries; *Luther, Zuinglius, Melancthon, Pomeran, Amsdorf, Urbanus Regius, Snepfius, Brentius, Vitus Theodorus, John Alpin, Herman Bonn, John Hefs, Ambrofe Moiban, Brifman, Speratus, Poliander, P. Rhodius, Hausmann, N. Medlerus, J Cæfius, J. Langus*, and many others.

He accompanied the elector of *Saxony* in many of his journies into the *Low Countries*, and other places, where he preached the gofpel openly and faithfully, though often at the hazard of his life. About this time, our king *Henry* VIII had fallen out with the pope, for not divorcing him from his wife *Catharine*, aunt to *Charles* V emperor of *Germany*, and king of *Spain*, becaufe of whofe greatnefs the pope durft not do it The king then fent over to the *German* princes, efpecially to the duke of *Saxony*, to confederate againft the pope, and to join with him in an agreement refpecting religion, upon which account *My-*

conius

conius was sent over to *England*, partly about religious
matters, but principally about a match between king
Henry and *Anne* of *Cleve*. *Myconius* upon his arrival
soon discovered the king's hypocrisy respecting religion,
not only by the six articles about that time established,
but also by his imprisoning of *Latimer*, beheading lord
Cromwel, burning Dr *Barnes*, &c and by his seizing all
the abbey-lands, all which gave him such offence that
he left *England* Upon his return home, he was called
by *Henry* of *Saxony* to visit and reform, (in conjunction
with *Luther*, *Jonas*, *Cruciger*, and others) the churches
of *Misnia* The occasion of this reformation-visit was;
George duke of *Saxony*, laying on his death-bed, sent to
his brother *Henry* (all his own sons being already dead)
desiring him, as he was to be his successor, not to make
any innovations in religion, at the same time he promised him, by his ambassadors, golden mountains if he
would comply with his request To whom *Henry* answered, ' This embassage of your's is just like the devil's
' dealing with *Christ*, when he promised him all the
' world if he would fall down and worship him But,
' for my own part, I am resolved not to depart from th.
' truth which God hath revealed unto me.' But before
the return of the ambassador, duke *George* was dead
Upon which *Henry*, notwithstanding all the oppositions
of the papists, carried on the Reformation in the churches
This reformation-work being finished, *Myconius* visited
all the churches in *Thuringia*, and, with the help of
Melancthon and some others, he provided them pastors and
schoolmasters, and procured stipends to be settled upon
them for their maintenance.

In the year 1541, he fell into a consumption, of which
he wrote to *Luther*, " That he was sick, not to death, but
" unto life " Which interpretation of the text pleased
Luther exceedingly, who wrote for answer, ' I pray
' *Christ* our Lord, our salvation, and our health, &c
' that I may not live to see thee and some others of our
' colleagues to die, and go to heaven, and leave me here
' amongst the devils alone I pray God, that I may first
' lay down this dry, exhausted, and unprofitable taber-
' nacle· Farewel, and God forbid, that I should hear of
' thy death while I live, but may God grant thee to out-
' live me This is my prayer, and my wish, and may it
' be granted me, amen, for I ask it for the glory of
' God's holy name, and not for my own ease or profit.'
Awhile after, *Myconius* recovered according to this

prayer, though his difease feemed to be defperate, and outlived it fix years, even till the year after *Luther's* death, upon which *Juftus Jonas* remarks, in fpeaking of *Luther*, *Ifte vir potuit quod voluit*, That man could have of God whatever he pleafed. *Myconius*, a little before his death, wrote an excellent letter to *John Frederic* elector of *Saxony*; in which he praifed God for raifing up three fucceffively in that family, namely, *Frederic, John,* and *John Frederic*, to undertake the patronage of *Luther*, &c. He was a man of fingular piety, of folid learning, of an excellent judgement, of a burning zeal, and of an admirable candor and gravity. He died of a relapfe into his former difeafe, on the feventh of *April*, in 1546, having lived fifty-five years, three months, and feventeen days. And he died as he had lived, glorifying God for all the mercies which had been received by him and by the church in the blefled Reformation. He was a dear friend to *Luther*, and *Luther* was not lefs fo to him. In their lives, they were united, and, in their deaths, they were not long divided, for *Myconius* furvived his magnanimous friend only feventy-feven days.

Stigelius wrote the following epitaph for his tomb.

> *Quo duce, Gotha, tibi monftrata eft gratia* CHRISTI;
> *Hic pia Myconii contegit offa lapis.*
> *Doctrinâ et vitæ tibi moribus ille reliquit*
> *Exemplum. Hoc ingens, Gotha, tuere decus.*

He is faid to have publifhed the following works: *Expofitio in Evang. Marci. Enarrationes in Pfalmum ci. Expofitiones in Evang. fecundùm Matthæum, Lucam, & Johannem. Commentaria in Efaiam, Jeremiam, & Jonam. Narratio de vitâ & morte Zuinglii. Sermo de liberis rectè educandis. De crapulâ, & Ebrietate. De fænore & ufurâ, &c.*

J O H N D I A Z I U S.

THIS learned, pious, and conftant fufferer, in the caufe of God and truth, was born and educated in *Spain*, and from thence was fent to *Paris*

to complete his studies, but it pleafed God, in the reading of the books of *Luther* and fome other proteftant
divines, fo to enlighten his mind and to teach him the
knowledge of the truth from the fcripture, that he began
to fee and abhor the herefies and abominations of the
church of *Rome*. In order therefore to further himfelf in
the knowledge and ftudy of the gofpel, he went to *Geneva*,
where he became intimately acquainted with *Calvin*, and
was very dear to him From *Geneva* he went to *Strafburgh*, where *Bucer*, obferving his learning, piety, and
diligent application to ftudy, obtained leave of the fenate
for him to be joined with him to go to the difputation
at *Ratifbon*. When he came thither, he vifited *Peter
Malvinda a Spaniard*, the pope's agent in *Germany*, who,
finding that he came in company with *Bucer* and other
proteftant divines, was much furprized, but more upon
obferving the great change that had taken place in him
fince he knew him at *Paris* *Malvinda* was alfo exceedingly uneafy that the proteftants had got a *Spaniard*
amongft them, prefuming they would triumph more in
him than in many *Germans*, and therefore tried all ways
and means to draw him back to the church of *Rome*,
fometimes making large proffers and promifes to him, at
other times threatening him with fevere punifhments,
and mixing both with earneft intreaties. But when he
found he was unfuccefsful in all his endeavors, he fent
for his brother *Alphonfus Diazius*, one of the pope's
lawyers, from *Rome*, who, hearing that his brother was
turned proteftant, came with all fpeed into *Germany*,
bringing a notorious cut-throat with him, refolving either
to draw him back to popery, or to deftroy him

When *Alphonfus* came to *Ratifbon*, his brother *John*
was gone to *Newberg* about the printing of *Bucer*'s book,
to which place *Alphonfus* followed him, and there they
maintained many difputations upon religious matters
But *Alphonfus*, finding his brother *John* fo ftedfaft in the
belief of the truths of the gofpel, that neither the pope's
agent by his promifes or threats could terrify him, nor
he, by his perfuafions and pretenfions of brotherly love,
could prevail upon him, to return to popery, he feigned
to take a moft friendly and affectionate leave of him,
and departed. But, foon after, he returned with his
ruffianly murderer, and, by the way, they bought an
hatchet of a carpenter *Alphonfus* fent the ruffian in firft,
difguifed, with letters to his brother, himfelf following
behind. And while *John Diazius* was reading the letters,
th s

this bloody murderer cleft his head with the hatchet, and taking horse they both rode away. This cruel act was perpetrated in the year 1546. *Alphonfus*, another inhuman *Cain*, was highly applauded by the papifts for his deed. But God did not fuffer this unnatural cruelty to go unpunifhed, for, not long after, he was fo exceedingly tormented with horrors and dread of confcience, that being at *Trent*, when the general council was held there, he died, like *Judas*, by hanging himfelf.

We thought this account of a *Spaniard*, though fhort, might be the more defirable, as the country of his birth was ever famous for bigotry and fuperftition, and hath been remarkably barren in the real profeffion of the gofpel. Indeed, it hath not, of late ages, been much diftinguifhed for men of great liberality or learning, and, at this day, partakes lefs of civil and religious liberty than any other kingdom in *Europe*. The people there know ftill lefs of that fpiritual and heavenly liberty, with which *Chrift* makes his people free. And their bloody and horrid inquifition will do what it can to keep them ignorant of it. All the *acts of faith* (as they fhamefully call the executions of this abominable tribunal) are begun in ignorance and infamy, and end in cruelty and blood.

Spain has, however, produced fome few learned men of the *firft* clafs, within the three paft centuries. But thefe have, almoft without exception, been bigots of the church of *Rome*, and employed their talents in fupporting the papal jurifdiction. It is a pleafure to fee an example to the contrary, and, therefore, our Readers will not think it an impertinent digreffion to relate, that *Cyprian de Valera* was of this country, became a fincere as well as learned proteftant, made a voyage to *England* for improvement, and returned with the bible tranflated into *Spanifh*, copies of which, with copies of a *Spanifh* tranflation of *Calvin's* inftitutes, he difperfed among his countrymen ——The word of God is indeed a *pearl of great price*, but the grace of God alone can make it *precious* to the foul, and render thofe, who read it, *wife unto falvation*. Happy for his countrymen, if the fame light, which bleffed his mind, had illuminated their's!

CASPAR

CASPAR CRUCIGER.

CASPAR CRUCIGER, was born at *Leipfick* in *Mifnia*, 1504, of religious parents, who brought him up in the nurture and admonition of the Lord, as well as in all useful learning. He was naturally inclined to melancholy, loved retirement, was much in meditation, and of few words. In the midst of company he was frequently abfent, and collected within himfelf. The difcovery of this temper in him, in his childhood, gave his parents occafion to conclude, that he would be dull in underftanding, and of a flow capacity. But judgements of this kind have been very frequently erroneous, for fome, who have promifed but little in their infancy, have turned out the firft of men, while others, who have made an early fhew, have yielded only difappointment to the fond expectation of their friends. *Cruciger*, when put under the tuition of an able mafter, foon afforded proofs of a reach and ftrength of genius, which furprized every body who knew him. Nothing was too difficult, in human fcience, for his comprehenfion, and his induftry equalled the clearnefs of his judgement, and the penetration of his mind. Having acquired the *Latin* language, he ftudied the *Greek*, together with *Camerarius*, under *Richard Croke*, an *Englifhman*. At this time it was faid of him, ' That though he feemed dull to every body, he ' acquired more knowledge than all his fellow-ftudents ' put together.' Yet, with all his attainments, he was meek, modeft, and humble in his deportment, tinctured with no arrogance or oftentation, patient, chafte and pious. He was beloved by his tutor, as though he had been his fon, and indeed had the affection and efteem of the whole academy, where he ftudied.

Having made great proficiency in letters, he went to the univerfity of *Wittenberg*, to ftudy divinity, with a view of being more useful to the church. There he

acquired

acquired the *Hebrew* language, and became very skilful in it, for whatever he studied, he studied profoundly He then was called from *Wittenberg* to govern the school at *Magdeburg*, where he taught with great success and applause till the year 1527, when he was invited back again to *Wittenberg*, to preach and expound the scriptures, which he did with so much judgement and use, that they conferred upon him the degree of doctor in divinity At that university, he also studied and practised physic and botany, both of which he greatly delighted in He was very helpful to *Luther* in his translation of the bible To *Luther* he was extremely dear, both for the probity of his manners, and the soundness of his doctrine. He is said to write so swiftly, that he was requested to take down the disputation at *Worms*, in 1540; which he did with so much ease and exactness, that, at the same time, he suggested to *Melancthon* many things which he had not answered to his adversary, and several hints with which he confuted the arguments of *Eckius* his opponent. This being observed by *Granvel Bane*, who there personated the emperor, it caused him to say, ' That the Lutherans ' had a clerk that was more learned than all the papists ' And the following lines of *Martial* were frequently applied to him, upon account of this extraordinary faculty.

> *Cui rant verba licet, manus est velocior illis.*
> *Nondum lingua suum, dextra peregit opus.*

' Though words can swiftly run,
' His pen could move more fast
' The tongue had scarcely done,
' But hand the work had past.'

He frequently made notes of *Luther's* sermons, while he was preaching them, and could recite them *per extensum*, or as they were delivered, afterwards

He always opposed the errors of the fanatical Anabaptists of that day, and was very careful to preserve the truth from corruption He had a great aversion to sophistical and ambiguous phrases, which had often caused much trouble in the church, and he took such frequent delight in contemplating the foot-steps of God in the creation, that he would often say with St. *Paul*, ' That God was ' so near unto us, that he might be almost felt with our ' hands.' In the latter part of his time he studied the mathematics, in which he made so great a progress that few excelled him. He was also a most accomplished op-

tician

tician In short, he mastered almost the whole compass of human learning, and, what was better, applied all he learned to the use of those about him. To the sick, he was a physician, under God, both for body and soul; and a friend to all men At length, by intense and incessant application to study, he brought upon himself a disease, which, though it wasted his body away, did not impair his intellects He laid sick three months, all which time he gave the most lively demonstrations of his faith, patience, and piety Every thing he said spoke the deepest resignation to the divine will, and that full assurance of faith, with which he waited for glory. Nor did he give up his studies during his sickness, but turned into *Latin Luther*'s books concerning the last words of *David*, and often read the *Psalms*, and sometimes other authors His common conversation with his friends was upon the principles of religion, the affairs of the church, immortality, and our sweet communion in heaven.

A little before his death he called to him his two young daughters, and caused them to repeat their prayers before him, and then himself prayed with great fervency, for himself, the church, and these his orphans, earnestly and often repeating these words, " I call upon thee, O om-
" nipotent God, eternal and only Father of our Lord
" *Jesus Christ*, maker of heaven and earth, of mankind
" and of thy church, and upon thy co-eternal Son our
" Lord *Jesus Christ* and upon the Holy Spirit, thou only
" wise, faithful, just, true, merciful and holy God,
" have mercy upon me, and forgive me all my sins for
" *Christ*'s sake, who was crucified and raised again for
" us, the Word and everlasting image of thy person, whom
" thou madest to be a propitiation, and also mediator
" and intercessor for thy people, by thy wonderful and
" unspeakable covenant, O sanctify me by thy Holy
" Spirit, and preserve the remnant of thy church in these
" lands, nor suffer the light of thine own gospel to be
" put out Make my dear orphans vessels of mercy.
" Lord, I call upon thee, and though it be with a languid
" and feeble faith, yet with faith notwithstanding I
" trust in thy promise, O thou Son of God, which thou
" didst seal by thy blood and by thy resurrection. Help,
" help me, Lord *Jesus*, and support and warm my bosom
" with faith to the end !" Having repeatedly uttered these words, he inculcated upon his children his paternal advice, respecting the welfare of their souls, and spent the remainder of his time in prayer, and so quietly ended his

L l 2

days

days at *Wittenberg*, on *November* the fixteenth, in 1548, and in the forty-fifth year of his age. Confidering the mutability of all fublunary things, he ufed often to fay,

" *Omnia prætereunt, præter amare deum.*"

All things muft perifh, but God's love
That only, nothing can remove

He publifhed fome theological commentaries, upon the gofpel of St *John*, upon the firft epiftle of St. *Paul* to *Timothy*, upon the *Pfalms*, and upon two controverted articles in the *Nicene* creed He wrote a tract of the " Method of teaching," which has been afcribed to *Melancthon* And the Chriftian church is obliged to *Crucigo*'s nimble pen for many remains of *Luther*, which had otherwife been loft.

P A U L U S   F A G I U S.

PAULUS FAGIUS, in the *German* language, called *Buchlin*, a learned divine, was born at *Reinzahern* in *Germany*, in the year 1504, and received the foundation of his learning in that town, under his father *Peter Buchlin*, who was chief fchoolmafter there He was fent to *Heidelberg* at eleven years of age, and at eighteen to *Strafburgh*, where not being properly fupported, by reafon of his parents narrow circumftances, he had recourfe to teaching others, in order to find himfelf books and neceffaries The ftudy of the *Hebrew* growing into vogue in *Germany*, *Fagius* applied himfelf to it, and by the help of *Capito*'s two books of rules and inftructions for learning the *Hebrew*, and of *Elias Levita* a learned *Jew*, became a very great proficient in it This branch of learning led him into a ftrict acquaintance with *Capito*, *Hedio*, *Bucer*, *Zellius*, and other learned Reformers In the year 1527, he took upon him the care of a fchool at *Ifna*, where he married a wife, and had feveral children.

Afterwards,

From an Original Engraving published under the Inspection of P.

Afterwards, quitting the schoolmaster, he entered into the ministry, and became a sedulous preacher. This was about the year 1537. *Petrus Bufflerus*, one of the senators of *Isna*, being informed of his perfect knowledge in the holy tongue, and of the natural bias which he had to learning, erected a printing-house at his own cost and charge, to the end that *Fagius* might publish, whatever he might deem useful to religion and to posterity. But the event did not answer the charges *Bufflerus* had been at. *Fagius*, however, prosecuted his studies with continued zeal, and was allowed to be one of the greatest *Hebræans* of his time. He often employed his knowledge to the confutation of the *Jews*, with whom he had strenuous debates. Mr. *Leigh* notes of him, that, as the *Jews* say of *Moses Ben Maimon* (or *Maimonides*), from *Moses* to *Moses* not one has risen up like this *Moses*, so the *Germans* might add of *Paulus Fagius*, that from *Paul* to *Paul* not one, in this way, has appeared like this *Paul*.

In the year 1541, the plague began to spread at *Isna*; when *Fagius* understanding, that the wealthiest of the inhabitants were about to leave the place, without having any regard to the poorer sort, he rebuked them openly, and admonished them of their duty, that they should either continue in the town, or liberally bestow their alms before they went, for the relief of those they left behind; adding that, during the time of their visitation, he would himself in person visit those that were sick, would administer spiritual comfort to them, pray for them, and be present with them day and night. All which he did, and yet escaped the distemper. At the same season, the plague was hot in *Strasburgh*, and, among many others, took off *Wolfgang Capito*, upon which *Fagius* was called by the senate to succeed him, and here he continued preaching till the beginning of the *German* wars. Then *Frederic* the second, the prince elector palatine, intending a Reformation in his churches, called *Fagius* from *Strasburgh* to *Heidelberg*, and made him public professor there. But the emperor prevailing against the elector, the Reformation was put a stop to. During his residence there, he published many books for the promotion of *Hebrew* learning, which were greatly approved by *Bucer*, *Hedio*, *Zellius*, and others, who were the first planters of the gospel in those parts, and who also employed him to read divinity lectures on week-days, and to officiate for them in other parts of their

I   pastoral

paftoral function, when they were hindered themfelves by
ficknefs or other important avocations. Even *Scaliger*
confeffed him to be the moft learned of all the Chriftians
of his time in the *Hebrew* tongue

His father dying in the year 1548, and the perfecution
in *Germany* threatening pains, penalties and banifhments
to all, who did not profefs the doctrine of the church of
Rome, he and *Bucer* came over to *England*, upon receiving letters from archbifhop *Cranmer*, in which they had
repeated affurances of a kind reception and a handfome
ftipend, if they would continue there   They arrived in
April, 1549, were cordially entertained for fome time in
the palace at *Lambeth*, and were deftined at length to
refide at *Cambridge*, where they were to perfect a new
tranflation and illuftration of the fcriptures, *Fagius* taking the Old Teftament, and *Bucer* the New, for their
feveral parts.   But this was all put an end to, by the
fudden illnefs and death of both thefe gracious and learned
profeffors   *Fagius* fell ill at *London* of a quartan fever,
but would be removed to *Cambridge*, upon a prefumption
of receiving benefit from the change of air.   He died
there upon the 13th of *November*, 1550, aged 45, and
Bucer did not live above a year after him   See *Bucer's*
life.   *Melchior Adam* fays, that *Fagius* flept with great
refignation in *Chrift*, not without fufpicion of having
been poifoned, which laft circumftance is not mentioned
by any of the *Englifh* hiftorians

Both their bodies were dug up and burnt in the reign
of queen *Mary*, both becaufe they had maintained the
doctrine of predeftination with the other Reformers, and
becaufe they, in their writings, had highly commended
thofe Reformers.   *Fagius* was tall in ftature, fomewhat
black-vifaged, his countenance appeared ftern, yet fuch
as commanded reverence, he was of an affable and courteous difpofition, affectionate, meek, and lowly, an excellent orator, and a great ftudent, as appears by his
works, which are, 1. A tranflation of *Thefbites Elias*.
2 Apothegms of the *Hebrew* fathers. 3. Moral fentences
of *Ben Syra*, alphabetically digefted, with notes. 4 The
tranflation of *Tobias Hebraicus*. 5. *Hebrew* prayers ufed
by the *Jews* on their folemn feftivals 6. An expofition
of the *Hebrew* fayings on the four firft chapters of *Genefis*,
with the *Chaldee* paraphrafe of *Onkelos*   7. Tranflation of
a book called, of the truth of faith, compiled by a converted *Jew*, to prove the verity of the Chriftian religion.
8. Commentaries on certain Pfalms by *Kimchi*. 9. An
Hebrew

Hebrew preface to *Elias Levita's Chaldee* lexicon 10 The Targum, with notes 11 An introduction to the *Hebrew* tongue And many others

Melchior Adam has preserved the heads of his valedictory sermon, when *Fagius* left *Strasburgh*, in which, among other exhortations, he desired his hearers, " not to raise " a disturbance, nor attempt by human force, to keep " the ministers of the gospel among them, now attacked " by persecution, but to read their bibles, to edify one " another, and to continue in the doctrine which had " been faithfully preached to them, to honour the mini- " sters for their work's sake, who were not sent to serve " their own bellies, nor to please men, that the causes " of the present evil were, 1. That wherever God raised " a church, the devil would build a chapel by it 2. " That the professors of the gospel had been too remiss " and secure, so that the devil had sown his tares 3. " That they had been too little thankful for the divine " blessing of God's word 4 That God would try his " own, and, by the trial, separate the chaff from the " grain." He added concerning himself " I hear the " trumpet of sedition, upon this occasion; but, I bless " God, I have instigated no man to follow it This " cannot truly be said of me What I would confess is, " that I have been too little diligent in preaching the " gospel among you, for which I implore pardon of my " God Pray for me, that I may abide faithful in all " afflictions. I am *but* a man And even *Peter* fell "— Thus humbly did this gracious man think and speak of himself! He knew his own heart, and knew too, that nothing but almighty grace could keep that heart from falling This is a point of wisdom, which comes alone from heaven, and which is given to all the faithful in leading them thither.

MARTIN

MARTIN BUCER,

THE MODERATE REFORMER.

THIS proteſtant divine was born at *Scheleſtadt*, in *Alſace*, in 1491, and died at *Cambridge* in 1551 He was one of the ableſt miniſters of that century, and there were but few eccleſiaſtical negociations in which he was not employed. He wrote ſeveral books, and compoſed many lectures, in which he labored with great zeal, and much dexterity, to pacify the differences between the Lutherans and Zuinglians. He wiſhed that both parties had been leſs rigid, and that great affair might have happily ſucceeded, if all the heads had been perſons of a reconciling temper like himſelf.

Bucer was a man of immenſe learning From his earlieſt youth he applied himſelf to acquire a thorough knowledge of the *Greek* and *Hebrew* He read *Erasmus's* books with great attention. Meeting afterwards with ſome of *Luther's* treatiſes, and comparing the doctrine there delivered with the ſcripture, he began to doubt of his *Romiſh* principles His uncommon learning and eloquence, which was aſſiſted by a ſtrong and muſical voice, recommended him to the elector palatine, who made him one of his chaplains

Bucer met *Luther* at the diet of *Worms* in 1521, when they paſſed ſeveral days in familiar converſation, after which *Bucer* embraced the doctrine of *Luther*, and openly profeſſed it from that time Two years after, he was admitted into the number of the reformed preachers in *Straſburgh*, and he ſubſcribed a book with them, which they publiſhed in 1524, ſetting forth the reaſons that induced them to renounce popery But he wrote ſome tracts in 1527, in defence of the Zuinglians againſt *Brentius* and *Pomeranus*, who were Lutherans. He aſſiſted,

in

From an original Engraving published under the inspection of the

in 1529, as deputy of the church of *Strasburgh*, in the conferences of *Marpurg*, where they endeavored to pacify the diflentions between the Lutherans and the Zuinglians But it was falfe, that he begun by being a facramentarian, for he followed *Luther* as the inftrument of his converfion from the beginning

The bishop of *Meaux* endeavors to make *Bucer* pafs for a diffembler, and alledges the teftimony of *Calvin* for it ' Whether *Bucer* had a formal defign to trifle with the ' world by affected equivocations, or whether any con- ' fufed idea of reality made him believe, that he might ' fincerely fubfcribe to expreffions fo evidently contrary ' to the figurative fenfe, is left to the judgement of the ' proteftants. It is certain that *Calvin*, his friend, and ' in fome meafure his difciple, when he would expref a ' blameible obfcurity in a profeffion of faith, faid, that ' there was nothing fo perplexed, fo obfcure, fo ambigu- ' ous, fo winding in *Bucer* himfelf ' It was faid by *Juftus Jonas*, that there was in *Zuinglius* fomething ruftic, and a little arrogant In *Oecolampadius* a wonderful good nature and clemency In *Hedio* no lefs humanity and good nature. In *Bucer* a fox-like cunning, imitating prudence and fagacity But the bishop of *Meaux* would not rely on the difadvantageous judgement that this divine of *Saxony* made of *Bucer*, after the conferences of *Marpurg* in 1529.

All the works of *Bucer* were very moderate But, it is faid, by one who was an Arminian in his heart, that *Calvin* caftrated fome of them at his pleafure at *Geneva*. However, we are told, that ' *Bucer* ufed, as often hap- ' pens among learned men as long as they live, to revife ' his lucubrations, to add, or take away, and even to ' retract fome things ' *Bucer* declares this concerning himfelf, in his preface to his commentaries on the gofpels, in thefe words " This difturbs fome, becaufe they make " no doubt but many will be offended, that I now feem " not very confiftent with myfelf Becaufe the Lord " has given me to underftand fome places more fully " than I formerly did, which as it is fo bountifully given " to me, why should I not impart it liberally to my " brethren, and ingenuoufly declare the goodnefs of the " Lord ? What inconfiftency is there in profiting in the " work of falvation ? And who, in this age, or in the " laft, has treated of the fcripture, and has not experi- " enced, that, even in this ftudy, one day is the fcholar " of another ?" Afterwards he produces the example of

M m   *Auguftine*

Augustine in his retractions, and wishes that more books of retractions were published If *Bucer* himself declares that he retracted many things of his former meditations, by what consequence, or even with what conscience, can any one assert, that the later editions of his works are corrupted, if every thing, in some places of them, is not found expressed in the very same words? *David Paraeus* made a confession like this of *Bucer*, for which he was insulted by a jesuit of *Mentz*

Luther did not admire *Bucer*, and yet *Bucer* has been ranked with *Luther*, *Zuinglius*, *Calvin*, and *Cranmer*, as one of the promoters of the Reformation, to whom the protestants are more obliged than to *Erasmus*, whose timidity offended the Reformers, by his obstinately adhering to the interpretations of the church, upon whose authority he founded his faith and belief of the canonical scriptures In a civil letter to *Bucer*, in 1527, *Erasmus* sets forth his reasons why he could not join with the reformed, and gives them a very bad character, though he declares his esteem for *Bucer*, who, like *Erasmus*, endeavored to pacify the religious disputants, and bring things to an accommodation, and, like *Erasmus*, was insulted by both parties

Bishop *Burnet* says, that ' *Bucer* was a very learned, ' judicious, pious, and moderate person Perhaps, he ' was inferior to none of all the Reformers for learning ' But for zeal, true piety, and a most tender care of ' preserving unity among the foreign churches, *Me-* ' *lancthon* and he, without any injury done to the rest, ' may be ranked apart by themselves At *Ratisbon* he ' had a conference with *Gardiner*, who was then ambas- ' sador from king *Henry* VIII in which *Gardiner* broke ' out into such a violent passion, that, as he spared no ' reproachful words, so the company thought he would ' have fallen on *Bucer* and beat him He was in such ' disorder, that the little vein between his thumb and ' fore-finger did swell and palpitate, which *Bucer* said he ' had never before that observed in any person in his life ' Even *Cochlaeus* acknowledged, that *Bucer* and *Melancthon* were very learned men And cardinal *Contarene*, on his return out of *Germany* from the disputation at *Ratisbon*, being asked his judgement of the *German* divines, answered, ' They have, among others, *Martin Bucer*, ' endowed with that excellency of learning both in the- ' ology and philosophy, and, besides, of that subtlety ' and happiness in disputation, that he alone may be set

' against

'against all our learned men' *John Gropper*, likewise, imbassador of the archbishop of *Cologne*, said of him, after the assembly at *Regensburg*, 'That he was the fittest 'man in the world to reform religion, because he was 'not only very learned and exemplary in his life, but a 'great lover of peace and concord'

The Sacramentarians presented their confession of faith at the diet of *Augsburgh*, in 1530. It was drawn up by *Bucer* and *Capito*, and approved by the senate of *Strasburgh*. They held, that men are only justified by the merits of *Jesus Christ*, and faith, but that faith ought to be attended with charity. And they allowed only of two sacraments, Baptism, and the Lord's Supper.

The Lutherans and Zuinglians differed about the Lord's Supper, and were separated as to communion. The Lutherans denied having any union with the Sacramentarians, and *they* were not able to bear the opinion of *Luther*. But there was a third party gathered out of both, who were sensible that they were not obliged to hold up their divisions, and labored to persuade them that their opinions were not so different, as was commonly thought, and that they might easily re-unite. *Bucer*, then a minister at *Strasburgh*, was at the head of this party, and undertook, purely out of a desire of uniting the Lutherans and Zuinglians, to draw up a confession of faith, which both sides might approve. The task was difficult to perform. *Luther*, and his followers, had always asserted, that the body and blood of *Christ* were really with the bread and wine in the Eucharist. *Zuinglius*, and his adherents, on the contrary, held, that the bread and wine were only signs of the body and blood of *Christ*.

These two propositions were directly contrary. *Bucer* found out a medium, which he thought might satisfy both parties, namely, that the bread and wine remained the same substance, that they ever were, without any alteration, but, by receiving them, they received the substance of the real body and blood of *Jesus Christ*, spiritually, and by faith. He made use of the same sort of expressions, as were made by the four imperial cities, *Strasburgh*, *Constance*, *Memminghen*, and *Lindau*, and presented to the diet of *Augsburg*. He made also the same declaration to *Luther*, to persuade him that the Sacramentarians were not of a contrary opinion to him about the Eucharist. But *Luther* knew the opinion of the Zuinglians, and gave no credit to *Bucer*. He wrote a letter to the senate of *Francfort* upon this occasion, in which hav-

ing clearly shewn the difference between his own doctrine
and the Zuinglian, he says, that the Zuinglians play after
a strange manner with the words of *Jesus Christ* That
they are a double-tongued generation, who say that the
body and blood of *Jesus Christ* are really in the sacra‑
ment, but, when they explain themselves, say, that it is
spiritually, not corporeally, and so continue in the error,
that there is nothing but bread and wine in the Lord's
Supper. The ministers of *Francfort* made an apology
against this letter, and made use of *Bucer's* expressions,
affirming that believers receive the true body and blood
of *Jesus Christ* in the Lord's Supper, and do really eat
and drink it for the nourishment of their souls That
though the bread and wine are not changed in their own
nature, yet it cannot be said, that there is nothing in the
Lord's Supper except the bread and wine, but that it is
the sacrament of the true body and blood, which God
has given us for the nourishment of our souls The
Zuinglians suspected, on the other side, that *Bucer* was
departed from their opinion, so that in his journey to
Zurick, which he made in *May*, 1533, he was forced to
remove that suspicion, by assuring them, that he was of
the same opinion which he maintained in the conference
of *Bern.* He added, that he certainly knew, and could
prove, that the opinion of *Luther* did not differ from
Zuinglius, but in terms, and that the presence of the body
of *Jesus Christ*, which he asserted in the Lord's Supper,
was not contrary to the doctrine of *Zuinglius*

　　The ministers of *Augsburg* also complained of *Bucer*,
and accused him of having changed his opinion, by
acknowledging that the body of *Jesus Christ* was eat
corporeally and substantially in the Lord's Supper, and
exhorting others to subscribe the confession of *Augsburg*,
and the apology. They plainly told him, that they would
acknowledge no other presence of *Jesus Christ* in the
Lord's Supper, than that of which he speaks in the sixth
chapter of St. *John* *Bucer* replied, that the imperial
cities had not, in the assembly of *Schweinfort*, departed
from the confession of faith, which they had given into
the diet at *Augsburg*, and that, by subscribing to the
confession of *Augsburg*, they had not asserted a corporeal
eating, but only promised to teach nothing contrary to
that confession, which, in the article of the Lord's Sup‑
per, might agree with the doctrine of *Zuinglius*

　　The ministers of *Strasburgh* importuned the *Switzers*
to draw up a confession of their faith about the Lord's
Supper.

Supper. It was compofed at *Bafil* in thefe words. ‘ We
‘ acknowledge, that our Lord *Jefus Chrift* inftituted his
‘ holy Supper in remembrance of his paffion, to publifh
‘ his death with thankfgiving, to fhew our Chriftian
‘ charity, and union in the true faith. And as in bap-
‘ tifm the water retains its own nature, fo in the Lord’s
‘ Supper, in which the true body and true blood of *Jefus*
‘ *Chrift* is fignified and tendered to us with the bread and
‘ wine by the minifter of the church, the bread and the
‘ wine remain. Now we firmly believe, that *Jefus Chrift*
‘ is the nourifhment of faithful fouls to eternal life, and
‘ that our fouls are nourifhed and watered by true faith in
‘ *Jefus Chrift*, with his flefh and his blood.’ They added,
in the margin of that confeffion, fome words, by which
they reftrained what they feemed to fay, in favor of the
real prefence, to a facramental and fpiritual prefence by
faith.

What oppofition foever there was between the Lutherans and Zuinglians, *Bucer* would not defpair of effecting
an union, and, to that end, he obtained that a fynod of
the minifters of the cities of *Upper Germany* fhould meet
at *Conftance*, in 1534 The minifters of *Zurick* were
invited, but not being able to come, they fent a confeffion of their faith, in which they expreffed their fenfe
of the facrament in the fame words they had ufed at the
conference at *Bern*, where they had declared, that they
could not re-unite with *Luther*, unlefs he would acknowledge that they eat the flefh of *Jefus Chrift*, no otherwife,
than by faith, for, according to his human nature, he
is only in heaven, and is only in the eucharift by faith
after a facramental manner, which makes things prefent
not carnally and fenfibly, but fpiritually, and to be received by faith This form, approved by the churches
of *Bafil*, *Schaffhaufen*, and *Gall*, was received by the fynod
of *Conftance*, and put into the hands of *Bucer* for him to
communicate to *Luther* and *Melancthon*. *Bucer* had a
conference with the latter at *Caffel*, in the prefence of
the landgrave, and told him, “ that we received truly
“ and fubftantially the body and blood of *Jefus Chrift*,
“ when we receive the facrament That the bread and
“ wine are exhibiting figns, and, by receiving them,
“ the body and blood of *Jefus Chrift* are given to us,
“ and received by us That the bread and body of *Jefus*
“ *Chrift* are united, not by a mixture of fubftance, but
“ becaufe it is given with the facrament ” *Melancthon*
was inclinable enough to accept this expofition But,

3

becaufe

becaufe he acted in the names of others, he would not conclude any thing, and obliged himfelf to give a fair account of *Bucer*'s words. *Luther* alfo began to be more tractable, after *Bucer* had made this declaration, and, in feveral letters, fhewed great inclination for an agreement, and to confer about the means of coming to an union

The minifters and magiftrates of the reformed cantons of *Switzerland*, met at *Bafil* in *January*, 1536, to draw up a confeffion of faith. *Bucer* and *Capito* went thither and propounded an union with the Lutherans, affuring them that *Luther* was much mollified as to the Zuinglians, and defired nothing more than to come to an agreement with them, and therefore prayed them, fo to moderate the expreffions of their confeffion of faith, which they were about to draw up, efpecially in the articles about the eucharift, and the efficacy of the facraments, as that they might forward the union, by omitting fuch words, as might occafion a conteft This they partly obtained of the minifters of *Switzerland*, from the confeffion of faith which they had compofed They owned, that the facraments of baptifm and the Lord's Supper were not mere figns, but made up of figns, and things fignified. That the water was the fign in baptifm, and the thing fignified was regeneration and adoption That, in the eucharift, the bread and wine are the figns, and the thing fignified is the communion of the body of *Chrift* received by faith That the body and blood of *Chrift* is offered to the faithful in the Lord's Supper, that *Jefus Chrift* may live in them, and they in *Jefus Chrift*, not that the body and blood of *Jefus Chrift* are naturally united to the bread and wine, or included in the elements, or carnally prefent, but becaufe they are fymbols, by which we have a real communion with the body and blood of *Jefus Chrift* to nourifh the foul fpiritually. This confeffion of faith was alfo approved in a fecond affembly of the magiftrates and minifters of the proteftant cantons of *Switzerland*, held at *Bafil* in *March* of the fame year

The minifters of *Strafburgh* gave notice to thofe of *Bafil* and *Zurick*, that they had appointed a fynod to meet at *Eifenach*, on the fourteenth of *May*, where *Luther* would be prefent to treat of an union about the article of the Lord's Supper, and intreated them to fend fome of their divines. The *Switzers* thought it inconfiftent to fend any perfons from them, but fent their confeffion of faith to *Bucer* and *Capito*, that they might prefent it to the fynod. *Bucer* and *Capito* carried it to *Eifenach*, where the

the minifters, fent by the chiefs of *Upper Germany*, were
affembled *Luther* could not be there, and therefore
they went to him at *Wittenberg*, where they arrived on
the twenty-fecond of *May*, and had a conference with
him. *Luther* required of them, that they would plainly
acknowledge, that the bread and wine in the facrament
were the body and blood of our Lord, and that the good
and bad receive them alike   When they met again, the
next day, *Luther* afked them whether they would not revoke their opinion ? *Bucer* anfwered him, that their faith
and doctrine concerning the facrament was, that, by the
inftitution, and the operation of our Lord, and according
to the natural fenfe of the words, the true body and true
blood of *Jefus Chrift* were made prefent, given, and received, with the vifible figns of bread and wine   That
they alfo believed, that the body and blood of *Jefus Chrift*
are offered by the minifters of the church to all thofe that
receive them   And that they are not only received by the
heart and mouth of the godly for falvation, but by the
mouth of the unworthy for their condemnation, which
they yet defire may be underftood of the members of the
church. *Luther* replied, he did not believe the body and
blood of *Chrift* were united with the bread and wine by
any natural union, nor that they were locally included
in the bread and wine, but he admitted a facramental
union of the bread and body, and wine and blood   Then
having confulted privately with the *Saxon* divines, he
returned to *Bucer* and his brethren, and told them, that
if they did believe, and would teach, that the true body
and true blood of *Jefus Chrift*, were offered, given, and
taken in the Lord's Supper, and not mere bread and
wine, and that this perception and exhibition were made
really, and not after an imaginary manner, they were
agreed among themfelves, and he would acknowledge and
embrace them as brethren in *Jefus Chrift*.

This confeffion of faith was figned by the minifters of
the cities of *Upper Germany*. Afterwards, on the twenty-
fifth of *May*, they conferred with *Pomeranus* about images,
the ceremonies of the mafs, priefts veftments, tapers, the
elevation and adoration of the facrament, which were yet
ufed in *Saxony*. *Pomeranus* faid, that *Luther* confeffed
thefe things were amifs   But that he had hitherto continued them up on account of the weak, and was thinking
to abolifh them on the twenty-feventh of the fame month.
Bucer and *Capito* delivered to *Luther* the confeffion of faith
of the churches of *Switzerland*, that he might examine it

He

He took notice of fome words, which, as he faid, might offend the weak. Neverthelefs he declared, that he would acknowledge them for his brethren, if they would fign the form of the union, which had been drawn up. *Bucer*, having undertaken to caufe it to be received by them, returned to *Strafburgh*, and made fuch an explication of the words, by foftening them, that he reduced them to a fenfe, which was not contrary to the doctrine of the Sacramentarians. Thefe articles were fuccefsful at *Straf-burgh*, yet they had not the fame fate in *Switzerland*, where *Bucer* had fent this form of union. It was there thought obfcure, doubtful, and captious, and they would not fubfcribe to it, fo that *Bucer* and *Capito* were obliged to go themfelves to an affembly of the proteftant cantons, which was held at *Bafil* in *September*. *Bucer* there related, that *Luther* had not difapproved the confeffion of the *Switzers*. But both parties judged it convenient to draw up a form of union, and he undertook to fhew, that the doctrine of it was not different from their confeffion of faith, and he exhorted them to fign it, that the union might be complete. The *Switzers* could not be prevailed on to do it, and all that *Bucer* could obtain was, that they would draw up a declaration of the opinions of the churches of *Switzerland*, in which they would explain the articles of the agreement, and fend them to *Luther*.

In this declaration, which is very long, the articles of the form of union about the Lord's Supper are delivered in fuch expreffions, as wholly favor the judgement of *Zuinglius*, and are oppofite to the real prefence. They there fay, that *Jefus Chrift* is the food of our fouls, and that his body is really eaten, and his blood really drank, not carnally, fubftantially, and corporeally, but fpiritually, and by faith, by believing the promifes of God, that the elements of the bread and wine, in the adminiftration of the Lord's Supper, are figns which reprefent *Jefus Chrift* to us, and put us in mind of his myfteries. That his prefence in the Supper is not a corporeal prefence, but a coeleftial one, and that his body is united to the bread only in a facramental manner. That the bread and wine are figures of the body of *Chrift*, which is difcerned by the mind in the facrament. That thofe who eat the bread at the Lord's Supper, by a fincere faith, receive the benefits which God hath promifed, but that they, who eat without faith, receive their own judgement and condemnation. This declaration was compofed in a fynod at *Zurick*, held in *October*, and approved in
another

another affembly, which met in *November* following at
Bafil, from whence it was fent to *Luther*, and prefented
by *Bucer* at the affembly at *Smalkald*, in 1537 *Luther*
approved all the articles, excepting that which contained
the Lord's Supper

The *Switzers* called a fynod on purpofe, in *March*,
1538, to confult about an anfwer to *Luther*'s letter, and
Bucer and *Capito* were fent thither, to deliver his judgement. The minifters of *Zurich* alledged, that *Luther*, in
his writings, and in the confeffion of *Augfburg*, had
maintained the real prefence, and pofitively condemned
the opinion of the Zuinglians That thefe writings of
Luther were public, and the words clear, nor could they
allow of his doctrine, unlefs they were certain he had
altered his opinion, and embraced the truth. *Bucer* was
much amazed at this objection, and anfwered, that it
was very unfit to prefs it at this time, fince they had long
known what was contained in *Luther*'s writings, and had
never urged it before in the whole courfe of the treaty.
That, now things were near an end, they had contrived
to propound it, and revive the old quarrel to prevent the
conclufion of the whole affair The minifters of *Zurick*
replied, they never defired the minifters of *Strafburgh* to
concern themfelves with the treaty That *Bucer* and
Capito came to find them, and affured them, that *Luther*'s
opinion about the facrament agreed with theirs, and that
they might unite with him, if they would frame a confeffion of faith, which fhould contain their opinion, and
the conditions on which they would come to an agreement with *Luther* That they had drawn up a confeffion
at *Bafil*, and delivered their opinion about the Lord's
Supper fully That if *Luther* had approved of their confeffion of faith, there would have needed no more to be
done towards an agreement, but, inftead of that, *Bucer*
had brought them other articles from *Wittenberg*, and
prayed them to fign thereto That they had offered to do
it, provided *Luther* liked the explication which *Bucer*
gave of them That at laft, they had fent a declaration
of their opinions, which they were refolved to abide by,
and would not confent to any thing new or obfcure.
Bucer, the next day, made a long difcourfe, in which he
labored to prove, that there was no other difference between the Lutherans and Zuinglians, about their opinion
concerning the Lord's Supper, but in words, and expreffions. However, the minifters of *Zurick* continued
to declare, that they would keep clofe to the confeffion

N n   of

of *Bafil*, and the difpute at *Bern*, that the words, which *Luther* had always ufed, were directly contrary to their opinions, that they could not explain themfelves in any other terms without force, becaufe they were clear and without ambiguity That it was not reafonable to judge of the opinion of any man, rather by the declaration of another, than from his own words That *Luther*, in his laft letter, had named *Bucer* and *Capito*, for his interpreters, but it was to be feared that in the iffue he would blame them for being too eafy, and going too far, and fo would not confent to the declaration they fhould make. Then the minifters of *Zurick* came to debate the matter with *Bucer*, and brought him to grant, that thefe words, *this is my body*, were figurative That the facramental union of the body of *Chrift* with the bread, confifted only in this, that the bread fignified the body That the body of *Jefus Chrift* is effentially at the right-hand of the Father, and after a fpiritual manner in the facrament. They difputed upon this queftion Whether the prefence of *Jefus Chrift*, in the Lord's Supper, was miraculous? *Luther* had faid, in his laft letter, that the prefence was inexplicable, and an effect of the divine omnipotence. The minifters of *Zurick* would not allow any miracle to be in the Lord's Supper, and maintained that it was eafy to explain after what manner *Jefus Chrift* was fpiritually prefent by operation and efficacy They urged *Bucer* to fign the articles, on which they were agreed But he defired time, and drew up a long inftrument, in form of a verbal procefs, containing what had been faid on both fides, which was difapproved by the affembly

The chancellor of *Zurick*, being fenfible if they went on difputing there would be no end, turned his fpeech to the minifters of *Zurick*, and faid, 'Do you believe that ' we receive the body and blood of *Jefus Chrift* in the ' facrament, or no?' They all anfwered, 'We believe ' it.' Then turning himfelf to *Bucer* and *Capito*, he faid to them, 'Do you own that the body and blood of *Jefus* ' *Chrift* is received into the fouls of believers by faith ' and fpirit?' They anfwered, "We believe, and con- " fefs it" 'To what purpofe then, (replied the chan- ' cellor) are all your difputes, which have lafted thefe ' three days?' The minifters of *Zurick* added, that they held no other doctrine, than that which they had ex- preffed in their confeffion of faith, and their declaration And the minifters of *Strafburgh* folemnly declared, that they would not oblige them to embrace any thing con-

I　　　　　　　　　　　　trary

trary to it, much less draw any person from that doctrine

Upon these declarations it was agreed, that an answer should be sent to *Luther*, which was drawn up and read two days after in the assembly The *Switzers* were very careful it should be expressed, that, in their joining with *Luther*, they would not change their opinion about the Lord's Supper, for they declared, they did not enter into that union, till they were assured, by *Bucer* and *Capito*, that *Luther* approved their confession of faith made at *Basil*, with the exposition they had given of it; and because he had declared to them, that *Jesus Christ* was at the right-hand of his Father, and did not come down in any manner into the Lord's Supper, and that he did not grant any presence of *Jesus Christ* in the eucharist, nor any manducation contrary to the Christian faith They also declared, that the body and blood of *Jesus Christ* were received and eaten in the Lord's Supper but only so far as they were truly taken and received by faith, and that they would not recede from their confession of faith, and their declaration That as *Luther* was of the same opinion, they were filled with extreme joy, that they might live in peace and union with him, and keep up this agreement, and avoid all discord. This letter was dated the fourth of *May*, 1538

Bucer was embarrassed between the opinions of *Luther* and *Zuinglius* concerning the eucharist One appeared to him too strong, the other too weak The doctrine of the Lutherans seemed to him to attribute too much reality to the presence of *Jesus Christ* in the sacrament of the eucharist He could not digest the consequences of it: But he also thought, that the opinion of the Zuinglians was too narrow, and did not come up to the ideas, which the scripture and antient tradition imprint on our minds They gave him great uneasiness, and he wrote to *John à Lasco*, overseer of the churches of *East Friesland*, to enquire, whether *à Lasco*, besides a power of signifying, acknowledged a power of exhibiting *Christ* himself, and that the Lord, in the communion of his body and blood, is given and received, whereby we are members of him in part, and flesh of his flesh, and bone of his bone, whereby we abide in him, and he in us, and that it is given and perceived, when the Lord himself operates in his ministry, and when the words and symbols are received as the Lord's, and as it were from the Lord himself, by free dispensation through his ministers, which

they

they call an union, not fenfual, local, or natural, but facramental, and of the covenant on account of thefe texts of fcripture, which fpeak of the myftery of the incorporation of the church, and of the communion, and eating and drinking of the flefh and blood of *Chrift*

Bucer alfo faid, that *Luther* was fatisfied, if the Zuinglians owned in the holy fupper any thing more than bare figns of *Chrift* abfent. " I am grieved, fays he, and " not without reafon, that we, to whom the Lord hath " fo bountifully revealed the other myfteries of his " kingdom, have not been able, now in thirty-four " years, to agree concerning this moft facred and moft " general myftery, which all Chriftians ought to under- " ftand, as well as ufe "

The Lutherans faid, that *Bucer* died in the Calviniftical faith. *Jofias Simler*, profeffor at *Zurick*, in an oration on the life and death of *Peter Martyr*, teftifies that *Bucer* ftudied fuch expreffions throughout the whole conteft, as nothing certain could be concluded from, that fo, pleafing both parties, he might gradually compofe the difference. However, *Bucer* and *Martyr* continued good friends, and were fully perfuaded of each other's oxthodoxy

Bucer has been accufed of approaching too near the papiftical doctrine of the merit of good works*, but this

does

* The late Mr *Toplady*, in his *Hiftoric Proof*, has defended *Bucer* from this imputation See p 363 His words are ' It has been ' affirmed, that *Bucer* held the doctrine of juftification by works, and ' believed human obedience to be meritorious in the fight of God. ' That he was once of this opinion, is not at all wonderful, when ' we confider that he was born and educated in the bofom of the ' *Romifh* church, with whom the tenet of legal juftification is a fun- ' damental principle And, for a confiderable time after God had ' called him out of papal darknefs, his improvements in divine know- ' ledge were progreffive His fpiritual growth refembled the gradual ' vegetation of an oak, not the rapid proficiency of a mufhroom. ' *Bucer* feems to have expreffed himfelf the moft incautioufly, in the ' difputation at *Leipfic*, A D 1539, yet, even then, he roundly de- ' clared, that " thofe GOOD WORKS, to which fo great a reward is " given, ARE THEMSELVES THE GIFT OF GOD." And that ' paffage, which *Voffius* quotes from *Bucer*, falls extremely fhort of ' proving that the latter was, even at the early period in which he ' penned it, an affertor of juftification by performances of our own. ' Impartiality obliges me to fubjoin that celebrated paffage, which fo ' many Arminians and merit mongers have fince caught at, as if it ' made for the popifh doctrine of juftification "I cannot but wifh," ' faid *Bucer*, in the year 1529, "a more found judgement to fome " perfons, who have difturbed many in this our age with this para- " dox,

does not appear in his dispute with *Malvenda* and other
popish divines at the conference at *Ratisbon* in 1546,
where (according to *Sleidan*) he maintained, " That a
                                                " man

" dox, That we are saved by faith only Though they saw the thing
" was carried so far, as to confine righteousness only to the opinion
" of the mind, and excluding good works Where is then charity,
" who refuse to cure this evil, by one word or two? It is only to say,
" that, when FAITH is formed, we are JUSTIFIED, and that,
" through faith, we obtain a disposition to GOOD WORKS, and, con-
" sequently, a righteousness Or, that FAITH IS THE FOUNDA-
" TION AND ROOT OF A RIGHTEOUS LIFE, as *Augustine* said'
' Is there a single sentence, in this paragraph, to which the strictest
' Calvinist would not consent? Observe the order, in which *Bucer*
' arranges faith, justification, and obedience Faith goes before,
' *justification* follows faith, and practical *obedience* follows justifica-
' tion We first *believe*, we no sooner believe, than we are *justified*;
' and the faith, which justifies, disposes us to the after performance of
' *good works* Or, in other words, *justifying faith* " is the root and
" *foundation* of a *righteous life* " Says not every Calvinist the same?
' As *Bucer* advanced in years and experience, he learned to express
' his idea of justification with still greater clearness and precision,
' than he had done on some past occasions Finding that the enemies
' of grace had greedily laid hold of some inadvertent phrases, and
' taken ungenerous advantage of some well-meant concessions, which
' he had made, before his evangelical light was at the full, he
' deemed it necessary, to retract such of his positions as countenanced
' the merit of works, and to place justification on the scriptural basis
' of the Father's gratuitous goodness, and the Son's imputed righte-
' ousness Still, however, taking care to inculcate, that the *faith*, by
' which we receive the grace of God and the righteousness of *Christ*,
' is the certain source of all *good works* —For being thus honest to his
' convictions, he was loaded, by his adversaries, with accumulated
' slander and reproach How modestly, and forcibly, he vindicated
' his conduct, may be judged from the following passage " The
" Lord, (says *Bucer*) has given me to understand some places [*of*
" *scripture*) more fully than I formerly did Which, as it is so boun-
" tifully given to me, why should I not impart it liberally to my
" brethren, and ingenuously declare the goodness of the Lord? What
" inconsistency is there, in profiting in the work of salvation? And
" who, in this age, or in the last, has treated of the scripture, and
" has not experienced, that, even in this study, one day is the scho-
" lar of another?"
' Indeed, no stronger proof need be given, of *Bucer's* soundness in
' the article of justification, than the rapture and admiration with
' which he mentions the *English* book of HOMILIES No sooner,
' says Mr *Strype*, were the homilies composed, and sent abroad, but
' the news thereof (and the book itself, as it seemed, already trans-
' lated into *Latin*) came to *Strasburgh*, among the protestants there.
' Where it caused great rejoicing And *Bucer*, one of the chief mi-
' nisters there, wrote a gratulatory epistle hereupon to the church of
' *England*, in *November*, 1547, which was printed in the year after
' Therein, that learned and moderate man shewed, " How these
" pious sermons were come among them, wherein the people were so
                                                " godlily

" man is not juftified before God through his own
" works or merits, but that he is freely juftified through
" *Chrift* by faith, when he believeth, both that he is
" received into grace, and that his fins are pardoned
" through *Chrift* That *Chrift*, by his death, made fatis-
" faction for our fins, and that God doth impute faith
" for righteoufnefs " All which he proved and illuftrated by teftimonies from fcripture, and confuted the
arguments of *Malvenda*

That *Bucer* was alfo, in the other points, a ftrict Reformer, let his own words teftify " Predeftination,
" (fays he) is neither more nor lefs than pre-limitation,
" or fore-appointment And God, who configns every
" thing to its proper ufe, worketh all things agreeably
" to its pre-determination, and, accordingly, feparates
" one thing from another, fo as to make each thing
" anfwer to its refpective ufe If you defire a more
" extenfive definition of this predeftination, take it thus,
" predeftination is an appointment of every thing to its
" proper ufe, by which appointment, God doth, before
" he made them, even from eternity, deftine all things
" whatever to fome certain and particular ufe Hence
" it follows, that even wicked men are predeftinated
" For, as God forms them out of nothing, fo he forms
" them to fome determinate end For he does all things,
" knowingly, and wifely *The Lord hath made all things*
" *for himfelf, even the wicked for the day of evil* [Prov.
" xvi. 4] Divines, however, do not ufually call this
" *predeftination*, but, *reprobation* ——'Tis certain, that
" God makes a good ufe of evil itfelf And every fin we
" commit, hath fomething in it of the good work of
" God.——Scripture does not hefitate to affirm, that
" there are fome perfons, whom God delivers over to a

" godnily and effectually exhorted to the reading of the holy fcrip-
" tures, and FAITH was fo well explained, whereby we become
" Chriftians, JUSTIFICATION, whereby we are faved, and the
" other chief heads of Chriftian religion are foundly handled And
" therefore, (as he added) thefe foundations being rightly laid, there
" could nothing be wanting in our churches, requifite towards the
" building hereupon found doctrine and difcipline " ' He com-
' mended much the homilies of FAITH, the nature and force of which
' was fo clearly difcuffed, and wherein it was fo well diftinguifhed
' from the faith that was dead He much approved of the manner
' of treating concerning the mifery and death, we are all lapfed into,
' by the fin of our firft parent, and how we are refcued from that
' perdition, ONLY by the GRACE of GOD, and by the MERIT and
' refurrection of his Son.'

" reprobate

" reprobate fenfe, and whom he forms for deftruction:
" Why, therefore, fhould it be deemed derogatory from
" God, to affert, that he not only does this, but refolved
" beforehand to do it?"

Nothing can be more plain and nervous, than the following remarks of *Bucer*, refpecting God's obduration of
Pharaoh Whether the remarks be, or be not, carried
too far, is beyond my province to enquire   " The
" apoftle fays, *Who may refift the will of God?* By the
" word *will*, Paul gives us to underftand, that God
" actually willeth thofe very things, unto which men
" are hardened by him. When *Paul* adds, *Who may*
" *refift?* he, in fact, points out the neceffity, which
" they, whom God hardens, are under of doing thofe
" things. When God would harden *Pharaoh*, in order
" that he might not obey the commandment, it was the
" actual will of God that *Pharaoh* fhould not obey.
" Yea, God himfelf wrought in *Pharaoh* to oppofe the
" commandment fent to him. *Pharaoh* therefore did
" what in reality he willed him to do, yea, he did no more
" than what God himfelf had wrought in him Nor
" was it in *Pharaoh's* power, to act otherwife than he
" did " Such was the doctrine taught by this able
and indefatigable divine   Willing, however, to ob-
viate any exceptions, which thofe perfons might raife,
who had not ftudied thefe deep points fo carefully and
fo extenfively as he had been enabled to do, he, prefently after, fhelters both his doctrine and himfelf under
the following words, and the correfpondent practice, of
the great apoftle whom he had quoted before " *Nay but,*
" *O man, [Who art thou that repliest against God?]* St.
" *Paul* does not accommodate, nor foften down, a fingle
" fyllable of what he had juft afferted The facred pen-
" man does not deny, that they, who are hardened by
" God, perifh according to the will of God The
" apoftle does not admit it to be even poffible, that a
" perfon, who is hardened from above, can perform what
" is good *Paul* [inftead of fetting himfelf to anfwer
" our reafonings on the matter] contents himfelf with
" merely giving us a folemn caution, not to fit in judge-
" ment on the decrees of God Affuring us, that we
" cannot arraign the Deity at our own bar, without
" being guilty of the uttermoft boldnefs and impiety "
If *Bucer* was not a Calvinift, where fhall we find one?
I cannot prevail on myfelf to defraud the Readers of a
few more citations, which may be found in another
                                                        moft

moſt valuable work of *Bucer*, entitled, " A continued
" Interpretation of the Four Goſpels " And they
are the rather ſubjoined, as the book itſelf is exceeding ſcarce, and poſſibly may be in the hands of very
few of our Readers. " They, who are at any
" time able to fall quite away from *Chriſt*, did never
" really belong to him Conſequently, they never truly
" believed, nor were indeed pious, nor had the holy
" Spirit of adoption On the contrary, all their per-
" formances were nothing but hypocriſy, how ſanctified
" and ready ſoever unto good works they, for a time,
" pretended to be They, whom *Chriſt* loves, are loved
" by him even unto the end And he doth not caſt away
" thoſe whom the Father giveth him, neither can any
" ſnatch them from his hand Therefore, admitting
" that theſe may fall, yet they cannot fall utterly, for
" they are elect unto life And God's election cannot
" be made void by any creature whatever Seeing, then,
" that *the purpoſe of God, according to election, may ſtand,*
" *not of works, but of him that calleth* [Rom ix 2.]
" He not only elected his own people, *before they were*
" *born, and had done either good or evil,* [Rom ix 11]
" but even *before the very foundation of the world* [Eph.
" i 4] Hence, our Lord ſaid, concerning his apoſtles,
" *I pray not for the world, but for them whom thou haſt*
" *given me, for they are thine* That is, they were choſen
" by thee unto life

   " As, therefore, on the one hand, *Chriſt never knew*
" [i e never loved] the reprobate, whatever deceitful
" appearance of virtue they might have, ſo, on the
" other, he *always knew* [i e always loved] the elect,
" how ungodly ſoever they might ſeem for a time.
" Conſequently, as theſe [i. e the elect] are predeſti-
" nated and called, they ſhall, ſooner or later, be
" formed anew, according to the likeneſs of *Chriſt*
" While thoſe [i e the reprobate] ſhall be ſtripped of
" that artificial maſk, under which they paſſed for chil-
" dren of God, and be made to appear in their own
" proper colours "—On thoſe words of *Chriſt, ye believe*
not, becauſe ye are not of my ſheep, *Bucer* thus remarks ·
" They were not of our Lord's ſheep, i e they were
" not in the number of thoſe who were given to him by
" the Father, they were not elected unto life There-
" fore it was, that they were totally deſtitute of God's
" good Spirit, and were utterly immerſed in fleſh.
" Neither were they able to believe in our Lord, nor to
" embrace him as a Saviour "—A little farther on, we
find

find this admirable commentator observing as follows.

" *My sheep hear my voice, &c.* In these words, our Lord
" expresly teaches, that all good things are dependent
" on God's election And that they, to whom it is once
" given to be sheep, can never perish afterwards *Christ*
" here tells us, that they alone *hear his voice.* That is,
" they, who are indeed his sheep, are made partakers of
" faith Now, whence is it, that some people are
" *Christ's* sheep, or susceptible of his doctrine, while
" others are not? Undoubtedly, because the former are
" inspired by the good Spirit of God, whereas the latter
" are not inspired at all —But whence is it, that the
" former are indued with the Holy Spirit, and not the
" latter? For this reason Because the former were
" given to *Christ*, to be saved by him, but the latter
" were not given to him Let us therefore allow
" God the honour of being the bestower of his own
" Spirit, without supposing him to need or receive any
" of our assistance *Christ* adds, *And I know them* &c
" They are committed to my trust, I have them in spe-
" cial charge. And doubtless, from hence it is, that
" his sheep follow him, and live the life which never
" ends The Father gave them to him, that he might
" endue them with life eternal And they can no more
" be *plucked from Christ's* hand, than from the hand of
" the Father, who is mightier and *greater than all Christ*
" and the Father are *one* Their power and strength are
" the same Consequently, as none can pluck the elect
" from the Father's hand, so neither from the hand of
" *Christ* ——We are to observe moreover, that it flows
" only from God's election, that we are the sheep of
" *Christ* and follow him We must observe, too, that
" such can never entirely fall away For, the Father
" and the Son being undivided, their hand, that is, their
" power, must be undivided also And, out of their
" hand, none shall never snatch those whom that hand
" has once laid hold on for salvation Now, unto
" whomsoever it shall be given to hear the voice of
" *Christ*, and to follow him, they may be said to be
" thus lain hold on [by the hand, or power, of divine
" grace], seeing, none but the sheep are able to hear and
" follow the Redeemer And, if they are sheep now,
" they are so held in the hand of *Christ* and of the Fa-
" ther, as never to perish, but to have eternal life '

Bucer was at the diet of *Ratisbon*, in 1541, with *Melancthon* and *Pistorius* And he also accompanied *Brentius*,

Major,

Major, and *Schneppius*, at the conference of *Ratisbon* in
1545 He greatly distinguished himself on both occasions
against *Cochlæus*, and the other disputants for the Romanists But he was much troubled to see the dispute
between the Lutherans and Zuinglians hotter than ever.
He wrote to *Luther*, to pacify him. He told him, that
these divisions would not advance the Reformation, and
assured him, that the ministers of the imperial cities and
Switzerland held to the terms of the act of agreement

Bucer, at the same time, drew up a new confession of
faith about the eucharist, in which he asserted, that we
ought to acknowledge, that the body and blood of *Jesus
Christ* are given us in the Lord's Supper, for our nourishment and drink, and that the eucharist bread and
wine are the communion of his body and blood, so that
we not only receive the Holy Spirit, or the virtue of the
body of *Jesus Christ*, but *Jesus Christ* himself After
this explication, he added several other considerations, to
let us know, that manducation is not real, and is only
done by faith But he acknowledged, that the body and
blood of *Jesus Christ* are really and truly given in the
Lord's Supper, if it is celebrated according to the institution of *Christ*, and we have a firm faith in the words
in which it was given.

Bucer, in his discourses and writings, always made profession of Lutheranism, accommodated to the establishment in *England*. It is false, that he made a separate
sect. He continued always united with one of the Protestant communions, though the stricter part of each
party did not approve his remissness.

He offended *Luther*, by inserting some things in his
ecclesiastical postill, which made for the Helvetic opinion, concerning the Holy Supper, therefore *Luther*, in
his book ' *de verbis institutiones*,' vehemently complained
of *Bucer*, that he had corrupted his book of homilies,
which, he said, was the best of all that he had wrote,
and which even pleased the papists *Bucer* was at no loss
for an excuse, and might have alledged the maxim which
Erasmus attributed to him, " That a deceit which hurts
" nobody, and is useful to many, is an action of piety "
Erasmus endeavored to refute him in this, on occasion of
a work, which *Bucer* had dedicated to the dauphin under
a fictitious name.

Bucer had a great quarrel with *Pomeranus*, for having
caused *Luther*'s commentary on the *Psalms* to be printed
with alterations. He was desirous to have his own commentaries

mentaries on the *Psalms* read by the Romanists, and published them under the name of *Arethius*, which is a
Greek word, answering to *Martin*, and *Felinus*, a German word, expressing the signification of *Bucer* in *Latin*
If he had put his true name to them, which was hated
by the monks, the reading of them would have been forbidden in the popish countries. The priests, in the inquisition in *Spain*, imagined that *Bucer*'s book " *adversus*
" *merita bonorum operum*," was published as a work of
the bishop of *Rochester*, *de misericordia Dei*

It is said, the first Reformers clamored loudly against
the peripatetic philosophy, which was founded by *Ariftotle*, commonly called the prince of philosophers We
are told, that *Thomas Aquinas* made use of *Aristotle's*
method, with such great success, in explaining the doctrines of the church of *Rome*, that *Bucer*, one of the
greatest enemies to the *Roman* church, used to say,
" Suppress *Thomas's* works, and I will destroy the church
" of *Rome* " If he said this, he said it with but very
little reason, as a cursory examination of *Aquinas* is sufficient to shew.

It is well known, that the doctrine of the sacraments
was purified from the *Romish* idolatry, and from scho-
lastical phrases, by *Zuinglius* and *Oecolampadius*, and that
the loss, which the canton of *Zurick* sustained in the fight,
wherein *Zuinglius* was killed, broke the league lately
concluded between the cantons of *Switzerland*, the city
of *Strasburgh*, and the landgrave of *Hesse* Whereupon
Martin Bucer, being too timorous, was afraid that the
whole party would sink, unless he strengthened, with a
new alliance, the towns of *Upper Germany*, and particularly *Strasburgh*, where he taught. He cast his eye
upon the potent duke of *Saxony*, and the better to gain
him, he endeavored to make every body believe, that the
opinions of *Luther* and *Zuinglius*, concerning the Lord's
Supper, were the same in the main, and that a mere difpute about words had prevented their agreement He
further said, that it was better to use the expressions of
Luther, than of *Zuinglius*, because the latter spoke too
meanly of the eucharist, and the other in a sublime manner. He inspired the same thoughts into *John Calvin*,
who had gone from *France* to *Strasburgh* This intrigue
of *Bucer* introduced the Lutheran expressions into the
towns of *Upper Germany*, especially after the fatal concordate of *Wittenberg* The divines, who taught in
Saxony, under the elector *Christian*, used themselves to

those

those phrases of confubftantiation, *phrafibus illis fynufaf-*
ticis affueverant, fo that being expelled after that prince's
death, and retiring into the palatine, they took the minifters who ufed *Zuinglius's* expreffions in that country
to be heterodox, which occafioned a diffenfion, but it
was fo happily, and fo quickly, fuppreffed, that from that
time forward there was vifibly a better underftanding
between the divines of the univerfity and the reft

We are told, that *Bucer* repented of having mediated
the formulary of concord in 1536 " *Bucerus dixit fe*
" *poœnas dare qued caufam publicam homo privatus voluiffet*
" *comperer , & tam multa prava dogmata conciliare.*"
Peter *Martyr*, who heard him fay fo in *England*, told
Bullinger of it, *Daniel Toffanus* had it from *Bullinger*,
and *Pozelius* from *Daniel Toffanus*, in the prefence of
Scultetus, who inferted it in the hiftory of his life   *Cal-*
vin's friends accufed *Bucer* of introducing a new kind of
popery, which they called Bucerifm, in oppofition to
Calvinifm, This Bucerifm confifted principally in his
approving epifcopacy But *Calvin* denied, that he ever
laid this to *Bucer's* charge, and wifhed that he would
not give a handle for calumny, while he followed the
middle way, which was manifeft from his writings,
efpecially from the form of Reformation, preferibed to
Herman, archbifhop of *Cologne*, and what he wrote for
the Reformation of *England* As *Bucer* came nearer the
church of *Rome* than *Luther*, *Calvin* departed farther
from it than *Luther*, fo that there arofe two denominations befides Lutheranifm, that is, Bucerifm, and Calvinifm *Calvin* confeffed that Bucerifm was more tolerable than Calvinifm, if the matter was not to be tried
by the fcriptures, and that *Bucer* ftudied peace too
much But he himfelf meafured all things by truth,
Thefe are *Calvin's* words to *Bucer* . ' You have no oc-
' cafion to make any excufe to me, that you are not
' erecting a new popery, but I would have your inte-
' grity fo well known to all the world, that no room
' might be left for fufpicion It is alfo unneceffary for
' you to endeavour not to take in any thing of Calvin-
' ifm If we might vary from the fcripture, I know
' very well how much more tolerable Bucerifm is than
' Calvinifm '

Herman de Wida, archbifhop of *Cologne*, having a mind
to fettle the Reformation in his diocefe, fent for *Martin*
Bucer in the year 1542 Moft of the canons oppofed the
enterprize, and publifhed a work, wherein they mixed
a great

a great many invectives against *Bucer Melancthon*, in confuting that piece, did not forget this article. He maintained, that the nun, whom *Bucer* had married for his first wife, did well in forsaking the church of *Rome*, after she had discovered the idolatry of its worship. He added, that she had led a very exemplary life, by her chastity, modesty, and piety, that she had been brought to-bed thirteen times, and that she died of the plague, which she might have escaped, if she would have left her husband. It would have been a pity so fruitful a woman should have remained in a nunnery. And as there are many others as fit to people the world, who are hindered by monastries, one may easily judge of what prejudice these monastical vows are to the temporal good of the state. *Bucer* married a second time to a widow, which gave the canons of *Cologn* occasion to reproach him with another irregularity, because, according to St *Paul*, a bishop ought to be the husband of one wife only, that is, as they pretended, that he ought not to marry a second time, nor to marry a widow.

The word of God, say they, directs, that he, who is called to the ministry, should be the husband of one wife, 1 *Tim.* iii. and *Titus* i. which the canons of the apostles, and apostolical fathers, have ever to this day understood in this sense, that he who, enters into a second marriage, or marries a widow, cannot be one of those that serve in the holy ministry. *Melancthon* easily confuted this objection. But we are told, that *Bucer* was married a third time.

Martin Bucer, and *Paulus Fagius*, at the instance of archbishop *Cranmer*, were sent for by king *Edward* VI. from *Strasburgh*, to become professors in *Cambridge*. My author, a *German*, makes them to depart thence, *Magistratus Argentinensis voluntate et consensu*, whom the Jesuit *Parsons* will have both banished by that state. If so, the disgrace is none at all, to be exiled for no other guilt than preaching the gospel, and opposing the *Ausburg* confession, which that imperial city embraced. Besides, the greater the providence, if, when commanded from one place, instantly to be called to another. They came to *England*, and were fixed at *Cambridge*, where *Bucer* was made professor of divinity, *Fagius* of *Hebrew*. The former had the ordinary stipend of his place tripled unto him, as well it might, considering his worth, being of so much merit, his need, having wife and children, and his condition, coming here a foreigner, and fetched from a far country

country　So it was ordered, that *Fagius* fhould in *He-brew* read the evangelical prophet *Ifaiah*, and *Bucer* in *Greek* the prophetical evangelift St *John* —But, alas! the change of air and diet fo wrought on their temper, that both fell fick together. *Bucer* hardly recovered, but *Fagius*, that flourifhing tree (nature not agreeing with his tranfplanting) withered away in the flower of his age, at fcarce forty-five, and was buried in the church of St. *Michael*.

Calvin exhorted *Bucer* to order matters in fuch a manner, that the Reformation of *England* might be well purged of all remains of popery　He lets him know, that if he does not take pains, he will never be able to wipe out the ill fufpicions, which feveral had conceived of his inclining to both fides.

Calvin writes to him thus ' I fhall endeavour, ac-
' cording to your defire, to advife the lord protector as
' the prefent ftate of affairs require　It will be your
' bufinefs to prefs him every way, if you can but gain
' audience, as I am perfuaded you do, but chiefly, that
' all ceremonies may be abolifhed, which any way favour
' of fuperftition　This, particularly, I recommend to
' you, that you free yourfelf from envy, which you
' know you labour under, without caufe, among feveral
' perfons, for they always call you the author or approver
' of indifferent [or, moderate] councils　I know that
' this fufpicion is fo deeply rooted in the minds of fome
' people, that you will fcarce be able to remove it, though
' you omit nothing　And fome there are who flander you,
' not out of miftake, but mere malice　In fhort, this evil
' is, as it were, deftined for you, and you will hardly be
' able to efcape it, but you muft take care not to give
' the ignorant occafion to think ill of you, or a handle to
' the wicked to reproach you '　It does not appear that *Bucer* took any notice of thefe admonitions　Yet *Calvin* teftifies, that he expected great things from him, if death had not taken him away fo foon

Archbifhop *Cranmer*, who had fettled *Bucer* at *Cambridge*, wrote to him, for his opinion upon the point in difpute between his grace and doctor *Hooper*, who accepted the king's nomination to the bifhopric of *Gloucefter*, yet refufed to be confecrated in the epifcopal habit, and *Cranmer* would not confecrate him without it　The archbifhop fufpended *Hooper* from preaching till he would conform himfelf to the laws.　The king was then moved to write to *Cranmer*, and to difcharge him from

all

all penalties, and forfeitures, which his grace might otherwise be liable to, in difpenfing with all these usual rites, to which *Hooper* had an objection But as the archbifhop could not comply with the king's requeft without violating the laws, and incurring a praemunire, so it was pushed no farther by his majefty, till *Hooper* had fatisfied himself by confulting with *Bucer* and *Peter Martyr*, who told him, that, in the bufinefs of religious rites, they were for keeping as clofe as possible to the holy fcriptures, and the moft uncorrupt ages of the church But, however, they could not go fo far as to believe, that the fubftance of religion was affected by the clothes we wear, and they thought things of this nature altogether indifferent, and left to our liberty by the word of God *Hooper* continued obftinate; and *Martyr* tells *Bucer*, in one of his letters, his bufinefs was now at that pafs, that the beft and moft pious difapproved of it, and many were much provoked *Hooper* afterwards died a martyr in the proteftant caufe, and more of this affair will be mentioned in the life of *Peter Martyr*

Martin Bucer ended his life, at the age of fixty-one years, and was buried at St. *Mary's* in *Cambridge*, feveral authors affigning fundry dates of his death *Martin Crufius*, part. 3, annal. Suev lib. 11, cap 25, makes him to die in 1551, on the fecond of *February* *Sleidan*, on the 27th of *February*, 1551 *Pantaleon, de Viris Illuftribus Germaniæ*, makes him expire about the end of *April* of the fame year. Mr. *Fox*, in his reformed Almanack, appoints the twenty-third of *December*, for *Bucer's* confefforfhip A printed table, of the chancellors of *Cambridge*, fet forth by doctor *Perne*, figneth *March* the tenth, 1550, for the day of his death. Nor will the diftinction of old and new ftile, had it been in ufe, help to reconcile the difference It feems, by all reports, that *Bucer* was incontestably dead in or about this time *Parfons*, the Jefuit, tells us, that fome believed he died a Jew, merely, perhaps, becaufe he lived a good Hebræan, citing *Surius, Genebrand*, and *Lindan*, for this report. But it is certain, none of them were near him at his death, as Mr *Bradford*, and others were Who, when they admonifhed him in his ficknefs, that he fhould arm himself against the affaults of the devil, anfwered, " that he had nothing to do with the devil, be-" caufe he was wholly in CHRIST God forbid, fays " he, that I fhould not now have experience of the

3   " fweet

" fweet confolations of *Chrift* "——He likewife faid,
" Caft me not off, O my God, in my old age, now
" when my ftrength faileth me," adding—" He hath
" afflicted me fore, but he will never caft me off " And
when Mr *Bradford* came to him, and told him that he
muft die, he anfwered, " *Ille, ille, regit, & moderatur*
" *omnia ,*" i e The Lord, the Lord alone rules and dif-
pofes all things, and fo quietly yielded up his foul. He
was a plain man in perfon and apparel, and therefore, at
his own requeft, privately created doctor, without any folemnity A fkilful linguift, whom *Voffius*, a great critic,
and of palate not to be pleafed with a common guft,
ftileth, " *Ter Maximum Bucerum*," a commendation which
he juftly deferved *Calvin*, whofe teftimony is equal at
leaft to any of *Bucer*'s contemporaries, faid of him, in a
letter to *Vinetus*, that ' he never thought of the lofs which
' the church of God had felt in *Bucer*, but his heart was
' rent with forrow'—*cor meum prope lacerari fentio*

Boffuet fays, that *Bucer* was a man pretty well learned,
of a flexible fpirit, and more fertile in diftinctions, than
the moft refined fcholaftics. A fine preacher, fomewhat
heavy in his ftyle, but was refpected for his ftature, and
the found of his voice He had been a Jacobin, and
married as others did, and, as one may fay, more than
others, for his wife dying, he married a fecond and a
third time —This is calm for a papift. *Burnet* fays, ' that
' *Bucer* was inferior to none of all the Reformers in learn-
' ing, but fuperior to moft of them in an excellent tem-
' per of mind, and great zeal for preferving the-unity of
' the church——a rare quality in that age, in which *Me-
' lancthon* and he were moft eminent He had not that
' nimblenefs of difputing, for which *Peter Martyr* was more
' admired, and the popifh doctors took advantage from
' that to carry themfelves more infolently towards him '

Bucer's writing was fo very bad, that the printers and
he himfelf could hardly read it But *Mufculus* read it
eafily, and copied it elegantly He tranfcribed for him,
among many other things, his expofition of the prophet
Zephaniah, which is in print In the beginning of this
are his verfes, and that whole Pfalter, which he publifhed
under the name of *Aretius Felinus Erafmus, Lipfius,*
and feveral other great authors, had the fame defect as
Bucer, and there were few learned men who could write
fo well as *Mufculus*.

There is nothing more abfurd, than to impute to him
as particular errors, that the body of *Jefus Chrift* is prefent

sent in the eucharist, only in the act of receiving. That baptism does not procure salvation to children. And that there is no sin in not believing, that priests are not obliged to celibacy. The first of these propositions is the common doctrine of the Lutherans. The second and fourth are the common doctrine of all protestants.

'When I consider, says *Calvin*, with myself, what a ' loss the church of God has suffered by the loss of this ' one man, I cannot but every now and then renew my ' grief. He would have done great service in *England*, ' and I hoped for something greater from his writings ' hereafter, than what he has hitherto published.'

Cardinal *Pole* kept a visitation in *Cambridge*, by his power legatine, whereby the bones of *Bucer* and *Fagius* were burnt to ashes, and many superstitions established. This cardinal was of the blood royal, and obtained the see of *Canterbury* when *Cranmer* was martyred. He was at enmity with the pope, and the *English* clergy wished him at *Rome* again, because he was not willing to indulge queen *Mary*, and the persecuting prelates, in their cruelties against the protestants. For he was a modest, humble, good-natured, and learned man. However, the next year, *Pole* sent his *Italian* friend *Ormaneto*, and several bishops, on a visitation to the university of *Cambridge*, of which he was chancellor in the room of *Gardiner*. The first thing which they did, was to put two churches under an interdict, because the bodies of *Bucer* and *Fagius*, two *German* heretics, were laid in them. They entered on a ridiculous process against the two dead bodies, of which sensible men, whose understanding was not devoured by their bigotry, must have been ashamed. The process being finished by the visitors, and a writ from the queen having been sent in consequence of their sentence, the bodies were taken out of their graves, tied to stakes with many of their books, and all the heretical writings they could find, and burnt all together.

Beza composed some excellent verses in celebration of his memory, and the duke of *Suffolk* wrote his epitaph, both of which are in *Melchior Adam*, but require too much room for insertion.

P p   SEBASTIAN

SEBASTIAN MUNSTER.

SEBASTIAN MUNSTER, an eminent *German* divine, was born at *Inghelheim* in the year 1489, and at the age of fourteen, was sent to *Heidelberg* to study Two years after, he entered the convent of the Cordeliers, where he labored assiduously, yet did not content himself with the studies relating to his profession, but applied himself also to mathematics and cosmography. He was the first who published a *Chaldee* grammar and lexicon, and gave the world, a short time after, a *Talmudic* dictionary He went afterwards to *Basil*, and succeeded *Pellicanus*, of whom he had learned *Hebrew*, in the professorship of that language He was one of the first who attached himself to *Luther*, yet he seems to have done it with little or none of that zeal which distinguished the first Reformers, for he never concerned himself with their disputes, but shut himself up in his study, and busied himself in such pursuits as were most agreeable to his humor, and these were the *Hebrew* and other oriental languages, the mathematics, and natural philosophy He published a great number of works on these subjects, of which the principal and most excellent is a *Latin* version from the *Hebrew* of all the books of the Old Testament, with learned notes, printed at *Basil* in 1534 and 1546 His version is thought much better, more faithful, and more exact, than those of *Pagninus* and *Arias Montanus*, and his notes are generally approved, though he dwells a little long upon the explications of the rabbins For this version he was called the *German Esdras*, as he was the *German Strabo*, for an universal cosmography, in six books, which he printed at *Basil* in 1550 *Munster* was a sweet-tempered, pacific, studious, retired man, who wrote a great number of books, but never meddled in controversy all which considered, his going early over to *Luther*, may justly seem somewhat extraordinary He died of the plague at *Basil* in 1552, aged sixty-three years

CASPAR

CASPAR HEDIO.

THIS truly excellent and learned man was born at *Etling*, in the marquisite of *Baden*, and educated at *Friburg*, where he took his master of arts degree, from thence he went to *Basil*, where he studied divinity, and commenced doctor about the year 1520. He was called from this last station to the principal church at *Mentz*, but some of his hearers, not liking his plain and close preaching, were easily induced by the enemies of the faith to persecute him. Upon this account, he left *Mentz*, and went to *Strasburgh*, in the year 1523, and there afforded, under God, great assistance to *Capito* and *Bucer* in the Reformation of religion, by the command of the senate. And there also he married in 1533. *Gerbelius*, a writer of that time, said of him in a letter to a friend, that *Hedio's* success in preaching the gospel was wonderful, and that he was of vast service to his colleagues, and to the cause of truth, not only by the solidity of his discourses, but also by the integrity and purity of his life. The papists there likewise greatly persecuted him, notwithstanding which he preached and wrote boldly against masses, indulgences, auricular confession, and the other flagrant enormities of the church of *Rome*. In the year 1543, *Herman* archbishop of *Colen*, set on foot a Reformation, and sent for *Bucer* and *Hedio* to assist him in it, as both these excellent men were remarkable for their popular way of preaching, and consequently most likely, through the divine blessing, to succeed in the instruction of the people. But being exceedingly persecuted, and at length driven away by the emperor and the *Spaniards* who were then at *Bonn*, he escaped through many difficulties and dangers, and returned to *Strasburgh*. All the time he could spare from his ministerial employments, he spent in writing commentaries upon the holy scriptures, or in compiling histories. For the latter he

was

was exrremely well qualified, being thoroughly verfed in antiquities, and in almoft every branch of human learning

He had a great correfpondence and ftrict concord with moft of the great and good men of his time He was remarkable for the fincerity of his attachments And (as one of his deareft friends obferved, in writing of him) the devil hates nothing more than cordial friendfhip and mutual love He was particularly intimate with *Oeco-lampadius*

This great man calmly refigned his breath on the 17th of *October*, in the year 1552, and was fucceeded by the famous *Jerom Zanchius* in his paftoral duties at *Strafburgh*

Hedio's writings were both theological and philological And he was a great editor of the writings of others, having tranflated, from the learned languages into *German*, the works of many of the fathers and other ufeful authors Upon the whole, though we can furnifh our readers with no longer account of him, we may fafely fay, confidering the great ufefulnefs afcribed to him in promoting the Reformation, that he is one of thofe, who will furely be had *above*, and ought to be had *below*, in perpetual remembrance.

Boiffard (according to Mr. *Leigh*) enumerates *Hedio*'s works in his *Icones*

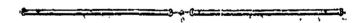

GEORGE, PRINCE of ANHALT, &c.

AND

BISHOP of MERSBURG.

WE are told by the apoftle, *that not many wife men after the flefh, not many mighty, not many noble are called*, 1 *Cor* 1 26 And the truth of this obfervation is confirmed by the experience of paft and prefent ages.
However,

However, bleffed be God, it is not fud—*not any* A *few* of thefe, though *but a few*, in moft generations, have been called to the enjoyment of a better treafure than that of earth, and have, with difciples of a lower order in the world, found the fame *mercy to be faithful*, to be *rich in good works*, and to be *wife unto falvation*

This excellent perfon was defcended from the dukes of *Saxony*, and had in his family (what the world at large is glad to boaft of) many great princes and honorable men He was born on the 14th of *Auguft*, in the year 1507 His immediate parent was prince *Erneft* of *Anhalt*, who gave him a very fober as well as liberal education. His father feems to have been a religious man by his conduct towards his fon, for he gave fuch perfons the charge of his education, as were not only eminent for their knowledge of letters, but for religion and facred learning He ftudied at the univerfity of *Leipfig* under *George Forcheme*, who had been the preceptor of *Camerarius*, *Cruciger*, and other eminent perfons. Under this able tutor, the prince made a rapid progrefs in every branch of fcience, both human and divine

His rank and probable deftination in life made the ftudy of the civil law highly expedient and neceffary; and accordingly he was led to devote much attention to the attainment of it But he abhorred the quibbles and fophiftries practifed by the profeffors of law, and difcovered the utmoft candor and ingenuoufnefs of temper in his legal refearches Truth was his object in all things, and he ufed to fay, with the wife prince of *Ifrael*, that *lying lips do not become a prince* above all men *Panormitan*, the great civilian, was his favorite author in this branch of ftudy

He had made fuch attainments in every kind of knowledge, that, when he was fcarce twenty two years of age, he was chofen by *Albert*, elector of *Mentz*, to be one of his council, and, being very eloquent, was much employed and attended to by that prince in the difcuffion of ftate-affairs.

" About this time, the great bufinefs of the Reformation attracted the attention of all men, and *Luther*'s writings,
' concerning the difference between the law and the gof-
' pel—of true repentance—of grace—of faith—of true
' prayer—of the ufe of the facraments—of the diftinction
' between divine and human laws, and between the dif-
' penfation of the gofpel and the civil power'—were difperfed and read every where, Prince *George* was no idle
ſpectator.

fpectator He fought truth like a philofoph r, and loved
it like a Chriftian But, diftrufting his own judgement
upon matters of fuch immenfe and important controverfy,
he begin his inveftigations with prayer *Melchior Adam*
fays, that he moft conftantly and ardently begged of God
to incline his heart *only* to the truth, and frequently with
tears ufed to repeat thefe pathetic words, *Deal with thy*
fervant according to thy mercy, and teach, O teach me thy
righteoufnefs From this period, he fought for truth t
the fountain of truth,—in the HOLY SCRIPTURES, and,
for affiftance in difficult paffages, he read *Auguftine, from*,
and *Peter Lombard*, ufing at the fame time the learned
conferences of his friend *Forcheme* For this end he alfo
perfected himfelf in *Greek* and *Hebrew*, and is faid to have
been fo great a mafter in the latter language, as to equal
the moft learned profeffors Nor did he omit, in converfation with the ableft divines, not only to feek the truth
for himfelf, but to induce and confirm it in others

At length, not without the moft mature confideration
and hearty prayers, he openly embraced and profeffed the
doctrines of the Reformation, and renounced all com-
merce with papifts and popery He lived upon the moft
-affectionate terms with the princes his brothers, who
concurred with him in planting the Reformation in the
territories that belonged to them He pulled down ignorant fuperftition, and fet up feminaries of learning—the
fureft way, under God, of exterminating error and darknefs from the earth All this he accomplifhed without
the leaft difpute or tumult, brought multitudes to the
light of the gofpel, and eftablifhed many, through the
divine grace, in the happy enjoyment of that light in
their fouls

Such a burning and fhining lamp was this pious and
learned prince, that, by the perfuafion of *Luther*, who
wrote a book about this time upon Chriftian epifcopacy,
he was induced to accept of an ecclefiaftical function, and
became bifhop of *Merfourg* in *Saxony*, in the year 1545;
at which time *Nicholas Amfdorf* was made bifhop of *Neo-*
burg His letter of epifcopal ordination was dated on
the third of *Auguft*, in the forementioned year, and his
ftyle runs thus, ' The moft reverend and illuftrious
' GEORGE, prince in *Anhalt*, count of *Afcania*, and lord
' in *Bernburg*, &c. bifhop of *Merfourg*,' and he is therein
exhorted to comfort himfelf by feveral texts of fcripture,
and to be affured, ' that though his facred office was
' attended with many and great dangers, to fuftain which

' all

' all human capacity is utterly unequal, yet God is truly
' prefent with and dwells in his church, and the voice
' of the gofpel is under the protection and defence of
' God '—His was an episcopate of danger and difficulty
for the truth of God, which no worldly man would covet,
and no good man could condemn.

He entered upon this holy office with humble prayer,
and he difcharged it with the utmoft care and affiduity
His whole time was from thence forward wholly employed,
in preaching, writing, reading, and fettling the affairs of
the church Knowingly, he never hurt any man, but
profited all to the utmoft of his power, both in public
and private He was a great promoter of peace among
princes, fettled many of their difputes, and, being fri
above all low ambition and revenge himfelf, he endeavored to remove it from others He bare many and
very great infults with true Chriftian magnanimity, and
fhewed that he lived *with* God in his heart, and *for* God
in his intercourfe with men. He ufed frequently to fay
to people of agitated tempers, *Submit yourfelf to God,
and pray to him, for the Lord is nigh unto them who are
broken in heart, and will fave thofe that are of an humble
fpirit.*

Moft of his time, difengaged from the duties of his
function, was paffed with learned and pious men With
thefe he converfed, according to their feveral faculties,
whether of law, phyfic, or divinity For this laft profeffion, his great colleagues were, *Luther*, *Juftus Jonas*,
Bugenhagius, and *Camerarius*, with whom he conferred
freely upon the moft profound and interefting topics in
theology.

As his life, fo his death, befpoke an heart full of refignation, faith, and love He lingered under a painful
difenfe for half a year, in which time he fettled the affairs
of his church, and gave himfelf up, in conftant prayer,
to fuch preparations, as became a Chriftian removing to
his heavenly manfion He frequently dwelt upon the
divine promifes, and particularly thefe, *God fo loved the
world, that he gave his only begotten Son, that whofoever believeth in him, fhould not perifh, but have everlafting life;
and, My fheep hear my voice, and I know them, and they
follow me, and I give unto them eternal life, and they fhall
never perifh, neither fhall any pluck them out of my hand,
and, Come unto me all ye that labour and are heavy laden,
and I will refrefh you* He fweetly difcourfed with his
brethren and friends upon the bleffings of *Chrift*, upon the
hope

hope of eternal life, upon the wonderful gathering in of God's church from the race of mankind, and other heavenly doctrines, all demonstrating where his heart and treasure was, and where his spirit would shortly be. He ceased to breathe in this world, at *Dessau*, on the seventeenth of *October*, in the year 1553, and in the 47th year of his age.

Melancthon wrote two elegies upon his death, and speaks of him in terms of the highest esteem and respect. He held two synods of his clergy twice in every year, and delivered to them a proper charge in *Latin*, according to the exigencies of the church

He wrote many tracts and sermons, which were published, either at the time they were written, or soon after his death They are said to have been composed in a plain and perspicuous style The principal of them were as follow A consolatory oration upon the promise of *Christ* in *John* x 29 —A sermon preached upon the marriage of *Augustus* duke of *Saxony*, with *Anne* daughter of the king of *Denmark*. Our prince-bishop united their hands at *Torgau* on the 14th of *October*, 1548 —Four sermons upon the two species of bread and wine in the sacrament.—A consolatory letter to his brother *Wolfgang* in his sickness —Two sermons upon false prophets and the true use of Christian doctrine —And several others, preached in the reformed churches, which were translated from the *German* into *Latin*

JOHN ROGERS,

THE PROTO-MARTYR UNDER Q MARY

THIS brave champion for the truth, who had the honor of being PROTO-MARTYR, or the first that was burned for the gospel, in the reign of queen *Mary*, was educated at the university of *Cambridge*, where he at-

tained

tained to a great proficiency in learning From thence
he was chosen by a company of merchants to be their
chaplain at *Antwerp*, to whom he preached many years.
He there happily became acquainted with *William Tindale*
and *Miles Coverdale*, who fled thither from the persecution of the papists under king *Henry* VIII in *England*,
and, by their means, coming to the true knowledge of
Jesus Christ, he joined heartily with them in the laborious and commendable work of translating the bible
into *English*, and was thereby so much enlightened in the
doctrines of the gospel, that he cast off the futile and
idolatrous worship of the church of *Rome* At *Antwerp* he
married his wife, and from thence went to *Wittenberg*, daily
increasing in knowledge, and became such a proficient in
the *Dutch* language, that he was chosen pastor of a congregation there, which office he discharged with great
diligence and faithfulness for some years. In king *Edward's* time, he was sent for home by bishop *Ridley*, and
made prebendary and divinity-lecturer of St *Paul's*,
where he preached faithfully and zealously till the coming in of queen *Mary* In the beginning of her reign, in
a sermon at *Paul's* cross, he exhorted the people stedfastly and perseveringly to adhere to that doctrine, which
they had been taught, and to beware of pestilent popery,
idolatry, and superstition His zeal could not long be
unnoticed, and accordingly he was soon called before the
privy council, where he answered so scripturally, sensibly,
and boldly, and at the same time in so becoming a manner, that, for that time, he was dismissed But, after the
queen's proclamation against the preaching of the truth
came forth, he was again called before the popish bishops
(who thirsted for his blood) and committed prisoner to his
own house, from whence he might easily have escaped, and
to which indeed he had many inducements, viz. his wife
and ten children, his many friends in *Germany*, and the
undoubted preferment he would there have met with, but
being once called to answer in *Christ's* cause, he would
not depart, though he stayed at the hazard and (as will
be seen) to the loss of his life.

After being confined a prisoner in his own house about
six months, he was removed to *Newgate*, and there kept
for a long time among thieves and murderers At length,
on the twenty-second, and several other days, of *January*,
in 1555, he was examined before Dr *Gardiner*, bishop
of *Winchester*, and others, in a very illiberal and cruel
manner, they not permitting him to speak or answer for

Q q

himself,

himself, nor yet to defend his doctrines in writing And on the twenty-ninth of the same month, *Gardiner* and others pronounced sentence against him in th following manner, ‘ In the name of God, Amen We *Stephen*, ‘ by the permission of God, bishop of *Winchester*, &c do ‘ find that thou hast taught, holden, and affirmed, and ‘ obstinately defended divers errors, heresies, and dam- ‘ nable opinions, contrary to the doctrine and determi- ‘ nation of the holy church, as namely these, “ That “ the catholic church of *Rome* is the church of anti- “ christ *Item*, that, in the sacrament of the altar, there “ is not, substantially nor really, the natural body and “ blood of *Christ* ” We do therefore judge thee and ‘ condemn thee, *John Rogers*, otherwise called *Matthews* ‘ (thy demerits and faults being aggravated through thy ‘ damnable obstinacy) as guilty of most detestable here- ‘ sies, and as an obstinate impenitent sinner, refusing ‘ to return to the lap and unity of the HOLY MOTHER ‘ CHURCH, and that thou hast been and art by law ex- ‘ communicate, and do pronounce and declare thee to ‘ be an excommunicate person. Also we pronounce and ‘ declare thee, being an heretic, to be cast out from the ‘ church, and left unto the judgement of the secular ‘ power, by this our sentence definitive, which we here ‘ lay upon and against thee, with sorrow of heart ’

When this sentence was read, Mr *Rogers* again at- tempted to speak, but was not suffered He then asked of them, to permit his wife, a poor stranger, to see him before he suffered, but this also was denied, and she was absolutely forbidden, When he was taken back to pri- son, after this and every preceding day’s examination, he wrote down the questions put to him, and his answers, as far as they would allow him to speak, and also what he would have said, had he been permitted, which, be- cause of their length, we cannot, consistent with our plan, insert, but must refer those who wish to see them at large to *Fox*’s martyrology Yet, on account of their excellency, we presume it will be acceptable to our Readers in general to see so much of them, as may serve for a specimen of the true wisdom, piety, and zeal of this great and good man

    “ But here (says he) they will cry out, Lo, these men “ will be still a *John Baptist*, an apostle, a prophet, &c “ —I answer, We make not ourselves like unto them, “ in the gifts and power of God bestowed on them to “ the working of miracles, and the like, but that we

                  “ are

" are like them in believing the same doctrine, and in
" suffering persecution and shame for the same We
" preach their very doctrine, and none other This we
" are able to prove from their writings, which I have
" proferred to do again and again by writing And, for
" this cause, we suffer the like reproach, shame, and
" rebuke of the world, suffering the same persecution,
" to the loss of our goods, and even of our lives, and
" to the forsaking (as our master *Christ* commandeth)
" father, mother, sister, brethren, wives, children, &c
" being assured of a joyful resurrection, and to be crowned
" in glory with them, according to the infallible pro-
" mises made unto us in *Christ*, our only and all-sufficient
" Mediator, Reconciler, Priest, and Sacrifice Who, for
" us, is well as them, hath pleased the Father, quieted
" and pacified his wrath against our sins, and, by impu-
" tation, hath made us without spot or wrinkle in his
" sight, although we, of and in ourselves, are polluted
" with many filthy sins, which if the measureless, un-
" speakable mercy and love of God in *Christ* did not put
" away, by not imputing them to us, would have brought
" us to everlasting damnation, and death perpetual—In
" this, and in no other sense; do we affirm ourselves to
" be like *Christ* our head, his apostles, prophets, martyrs,
" and saints And so far ought *all* Christians to be like
" them, according to the measure of faith, and the di-
" versity of the gifts of the Spirit, that God hath given
" unto them.

" But let us now consider, that, if it be God's good
" will and pleasure to give the members of his beloved
" church into the hands of their enemies; it is to chasten,
" try, and prove them, to bring them to an unfeigned
" acknowledgement of their natural perverseness and dis-
" obedience towards God and his commandments, as
" touching their love of God, their brethren and neigh-
" bours, and to shew them their natural inclination and
" readiness to seek their own ease and pleasure, and to
" desire that good from the creature which God has for-
" bid, as only to be found in himself And in order,
" that having fallen into gross outward sins, like *David*,
" *Peter*, and others, they may be brought to a true and
" earnest repentance; and to sigh and cry for the forgive-
" ness of the same, and for the aid of the Spirit, duly
" to mortify and subdue all evil desires and affections in
" future. And many other wise and gracious purposes
" of the Lord concerning his people are answered by

Q q 2 " their

" their being often put into the furnace of affliction.
" But let us also consider what he doth with those ene-
" mies into whose hands he giveth his tender darlings
" to be chastened and tried   In truth, he does but chas-
" ten and crofs them for a little while, according to his
" fatherly love and good pleasure, as all fathers do their
" children (*Heb* xii and *Prov* iii), but he utterly
" destroyeth, yea and everlastingly damneth their impe-
" nitent enemies

   " Let *Herod* tell me what he got by killing *James*, and
" by persecuting *Peter*, and *Christ*'s tender darlings and
" beloved spouse, his church ? Verily God thought him
" not worthy to have death ministered by men or angels,
" or any other creature, than those small, filthy vermin,
" lice and worms, which were ordained to destroy his
" beastly, tyrannous body. *Pharaoh* and *Nebuchadnezzar*,
" with all their pride and might, must at length let
" God's favourite people go freely out of their land,
" from their bands and cruelty For when they could
" obtain nothing but counterfeit mercies, like those of
" our day*, namely, extreme cruelties and death, then
" did God arise, as one awoke out of sleep, and destroyed
" those enemies of his flock with a mighty hand, and
" stretched-out arm. When *Pharaoh* grievously oppressed
" the poor *Israelites* with intolerable labours and heavy
" burdens, his courtiers noised abroad his tender mercies
" towards them, in suffering them to live in the land,
" and in setting them to work, that they might get their
" livings, for, if he should thrust them out of his land,
" they must be no better than vagabonds and runagates.
" Have we not the like examples now a-days ? O that
" I had now time to write certain things pertaining to
" the bishop of *Winchester*'s mercy ! I have not time to
" speak how *merciful* he hath been to me and to my good
" brethren, and to the duke of *Suffolk*'s most innocent
" daughter, and her innocent husband O that I had
" time to paint it in it's proper colours ! but there are
" many that can do it better than I, who shall live when
" I am dead *Pharaoh* had his plagues, and his once
" most flourishing land utterly destroyed, on account of
" hypocrisy and counterfeit mercy, which was no other
" than cruelty and abominable tyranny And think ye,
" that the bloody, butcherly, bishop of *Winchester* and

---

* Alluding to their frequent expressions of great sorrow and concern for him in the course of his examination, and in the sentence
pronounced against him.

3   " his

" his bloody brethren, fhall efcape? Or that *England*,
" for their offences, and efpecially for the maintenance
" of their idolatry, and wilful following of them in it,
" fhall not abide as great brunts? yes, undoubtedly.

" If God look not mercifully upon *England*, the feeds
" of utter deftruction are already fown in it by thefe
" hypocritical tyrants, and antichriftian prelates, papifts,
" and double traytors to their country And yet they
" fpeak of mercy, of bleffing, of the catholic church,
" of unity, of power, and of ftrengthening the realm
" This double diffimulation will appear in the day of the
" Lord's vifitation, when thofe crown-fhorn captains,
" who have fhewn no mercy to the poor godly fufferers
" of this realm, fhall have judgement without mercy*."

Mr.

---

* In the courfe of Mr *Rogers's* firft day's examination, *Gardiner*,
bifhop of *Winchefter*, afked him, ' What fayeft thou? Make us a direct
' anfwer, whether thou wilt be one of this catholic church or not,
' with us, in the ftate in which we are now ' To which Mr *Rogers*
anfwered, " My Lord, I cannot believe, that ye yourfelves do think
" in your hearts that he [the pope] is fupreme head in forgiving of
" fin, &c as ye have now faid, feeing you and *all* the bifhops of the
" realm have now for twenty years long preached, and fome of you
" alfo written, to the contrary, and the parliament hath fo long ago
" condefcended unto it,"—Here he was interrupted, and not allowed
to fay any more If men could fubfcribe to, and preach and write,
proteftant doctrines for twenty years together, and after that flaughter
proteftants in the manner thefe men did, may it not from hence be
juftly inferred, that it is a very great miftake which at this time feems
but too generally to prevail, viz That the *Roman* catholics may in
time, (and thofe even *now* in *England*) have little or no bigotry,
and nothing of a perfecuting fpirit, notwithftanding they ftedfaftly
believe the fame doctrines that their anceftors did, whofe bigotry,
cruelty and thirft for the blood of the proteftants, are beyond expreffion? Similar caufes will always produce fimilar effects This may be
illuftrated by a comparifon of the experience of thofe that truly believe
in the Lord *Jefus Chrift* at this day, with all true believers in every
age and place under the like circumftances They of old believed in
the Lord *Jefus Chrift*, as reported in the word—they loved God—they
kept his commandments as obedient children—they feared to offend
their heavenly Father—they loved one another—they fought under the
banner of *Chrift* againft the world, the flefh and the devil—they endured, feeing Him who is invifible—when called to it they took chearfully the fpoiling of their goods—and many (of whom the Lord
thought the world not worthy) fealed the truths of the gofpel with
their blood, and witneffed a good confeffion of their faith in the flames.
Do not thofe, who, with the faith of God's elect, believe the fame glorious truths with them, difcover the fame happy difpofitions, which
under the like circumftances, bring forth the fame bleffed fruits? If
the believing of the doctrine of *Jefus Chrift* does uniformly influence
the heart and life of all true believers in every place and different
period, and that contrary to flefh and blood, and all temporal intereft
and natural inclination Can we reafonably fuppofe, that the papifts
of

Mr *Rogers*, being sentenced to be burned, and remanded back to prison, was on *Monday* morning, the fourth day of *February*, 1555, awakened out of a very found sleep, with great difficulty, by the keeper's wife, who suddenly warned him to make haste and prepare himself for the fire "If it be so, said he, I need not tie "my points"—He was then had down to bishop *Bonner*, who degraded him, of whom (he said) he had one favor to ask Bonner asked what that should be "Nothing, "answered Mr *Rogers*, but that I may speak a few "words to my wife before my burning" This request not being granted, he added, "You declare your cha-"rity, what it is" The time being come, he was brought out of *Newgate*, and delivered up to the sheriffs of *London* to be taken to *Smithfield*, one of whom said, ' Mr *Rogers*, will you revoke your abominable doctrine, ' and your evil opinion of the sacrament of the altar?' Mr. *Rogers* answered, "That, which I have preached, "I will seal with my blood" ' Then, (said the sheriff) ' thou art an heretic' "That shall be known, (replied "Mr *Rogers*,) at the day of judgement." ' Well, (said ' the sheriff,) I will never pray for thee ' "But I will "pray for you," said Mr *Rogers*, and so they proceeded towards *Smithfield*, Mr *Rogers* saying the 51st Psalm, and the people exceedingly rejoicing and giving thanks to God for his constancy His wife and ten children by her side, with one at her breast, met him by the way, being the only opportunity they had even of seeing one another any more in the flesh, but neither did this very affecting scene seem in the least to shake his confidence, so graciously was he supported, in the trying hour, by HIM, who hath promised, *I will never, never, leave thee, never, never, forsake thee.* When he came to the stake, he shewed great constancy and patience, but, not being suffered to speak many words, he briefly exhorted the people steadily to remain in that faith and true doctrine, which he had before taught them, and for the confirmation of which he was not only content patiently

of the present day, who announce the same creed with their bloody fore fathers, will not, whenever it is in their power, be found in their fore father s cruel practices, especially when, through ignorance and superstition, they believe, *that while they kill you, they do God service?* In short, almost every doctrine, they hold, is framed to sooth the pride and flatter the vanity of fallen man, and calculated to gratify those sensual passions and desires, which rule in a heart deceitful above all things and desperately wicked.

to fuffer all fuch bitternefs and cruelty, as had been already fhewn him, but alfo moft gladly to refign up his life, and to give his flefh to the confuming fire, for a teftimony of the fame. They then again brought him a pardon, upon condition that he would recant, but he, with the magnanimity of a true martyr, refufed it, not preferring life upon fuch terms to the cruel death of burning, which he fuffered with the greateft patience and fortitude, wafhing as it were his hands in the flames, and ejaculating with his laft breath, "Lord, receive my "fpirit!"

It is remarked of Mr. *Rogers*, that, during the year and a half that he was imprifoned, he was always chearful, but very earneft and intent upon every thing he did. He wrote much, efpecially his examinations, which were wonderfully preferved. For they frequently made diligent fearch for his writings, and it is fuppofed, that they refufed his wife vifiting him, left fhe fhould convey them away. And when he was taken out of *Newgate* and led to *Smithfield*, they again fearched his room, but found nothing. They, therefore, readily admitted his wife and fon *Daniel* into his apartment, upon their return from *Smithfield*, who looked in every corner, as they thought, and were coming away, fuppofing others had been before hand with them, when *Daniel* fpied fomething black in a dark corner under a pair of ftairs, which proved to be his examinations and writings, to which the Reader has been already referred in *Fox's* martyrology, where they are inferted at large. He was charitable to the poor prifoners, agreeing with Mr *Hooper* and others, to take but one meal a day, and to give the reft to thofe on the other fide of the prifon that were ready to die for hunger, but the cruel keeper withheld it from them. The *Sunday* before he fuffered, he drank to Mr *Hooper*, being then underneath him, and defired them to commend him unto him, and to tell him, "There was never a little fellow "would better ftick to a man, than he would ftick to "him," fuppofing, contrary to what happened, that they fhould have been both burned together.—Thus died, triumphant in the faith, this bleffed proto-martyr, and proved the reality of the antient obfervation, 'that the ' blood of the martyrs is the feed of the church,' for, inftead of being intimidated, multitudes were encouraged by his example, and thofe, who had no religion before, were put upon inquiries, *What was the caufe, for which fuch pious and learned men were contented to die*; and fo,

from

from being athiests or papifts, they were led, by God's blefling, to a knowledge and profeffion of that gofpel, the darkening of which was the main ond and defign of all this bloody perfecution.

LAURENCE SAUNDERS.

THIS gracious man, defcended from an opulent family, and eminent as a fcholar, but ftill more refpectable for the grace given him of God, was educated at *Eaton*, and from thence chofen to *King's-College*, in *Cambridge*, where, for three years, he applied himfelf clofely to ftudy, and made a confiderable proficiency in learning But his mother, with a view to increafe his plentiful fortune, bound him to a capital merchant, in the city of *London*, to be inftructed in trade The merchant, being a religious man, foon perceived that *Saunders*'s natural bias was to learning, rather than trade, and, from his ferioufnefs, prefuming that the Lord had fome employment for him, far more important than that of merchandize, he gave him his indentures Upon this, *Saunders* returned again to *Cambridge*, where he made a further progrefs in his ftudies. He was a man, exercifed with very fevere temptations and inward conflicts, but gracioufly fupported, and much comforted Thefe trials wrought in him fuch experience, as qualified him afterwards, in his minifterial labors, to adminifter comfort to others. He remained fome confiderable time in the univerfity, after he had taken his mafter of arts degree, and in the reign of king *Edward*, he entered into holy orders, and was made lecturer of *Fotheringhay*, about which time he married. He was next made a reader in the cathedral of *Litchfield*, where he was very fuccefsful in winning fouls to God, and, by his holy life and converfation, obtained a good report, even of his adverfaries. He was from thence removed to *Church-Langton* in Lei-
ceifterfhire,

cefterſhire, and, laſtly, to the rectory of *Allhallows*, in *Bread-ſtreet*, *London*

He went down frequently to *Church-Langton*, intending to reſign it, but, queen *Mary* coming to the throne, he changed his mind, knowing that none but a papiſt would ſucceed him. In his way thither, he preached at *Northampton*, and, being filled with zeal for the truth, he bore a noble teſtimony againſt the errors of popery. Which (ſaid he) are likely to ſpring up again, as a juſt viſitation of God, for the little love that *England* hath borne to the truths and privileges of the goſpel, ſo plentifully afforded her. He was apprehenſive of the troubles that afterwards came to paſs, and therefore applied himſelf, with all diligence, to confirm his people in the truth (notwithſtanding the proclamation to the contrary) and to arm them againſt all falſe doctrines, but he was at length oppoſed, and finally hindered by open violence. He was then much adviſed to leave the kingdom, which he poſitively refuſed, and went ſtraight for *London* to viſit his flock in *Bread-ſtreet*. In his way, pretty near to town, he was overtaken by *Mordaunt*, the queen's counſellor, who aſked, If he did not preach at ſuch a time in *Bread-ſtreet*. He anſwered, yes. And will you, ſaid *Mordaunt*, preach ſo again? Yes, ſaid he, to-morrow you may hear me there, where I will confirm, by God's word, all I then preached. I would adviſe you, ſaid *Mordaunt*, to forbear. Mr *Saunders* ſaid, If you will forbid me by lawful authority, I muſt then forbear.—Nay, ſaid the other, I ſhall not forbid you. So they parted. The next day being *Sunday*, he expounded the eleventh chapter of the ſecond epiſtle to the *Corinthians*, and in the afternoon, deſigning to give his people another exhortation, he went again to church, but when he came there, the biſhop of *London's* officer prevented him, by taking him before his lordſhip [*Bonner*], *Mordaunt*, and ſome of the biſhop's chaplains.

The biſhop charged him with treaſon, hereſy, and ſedition, and required of him his opinion about tranſubſtantiation in writing, which being obliged to comply with, he ſaid, "You ſeek my blood, and you ſhall have "it. I pray God you may be ſo baptized in it, that you "may hereafter loathe blood-ſucking, and become a "better man." Biſhop *Bonner* ſent him to biſhop *Gardiner*; where he was kept ſtanding uncovered four hours at the door of the room, in which were ſitting *Mordaunt* and ſome others, till at length the biſhop returning

R r

from court, ordered him into a proper place for examination, and then interrogated him in the following manner 'How dare you to preach, notwithstanding 'the queen's proclamation to the contrary?' Mr *Saunders* answered, "he was moved in his conscience so to "do from the apostle's command, *to obey God rather than* "*man*." 'A goodly conscience surely, said the bishop, 'which could make our queen a bastard, or misbegotten, 'is it not, I pray?' Mr *Saunders* said, "I do not say, "or go about to make the queen base or misbegotten, "but let those be careful about that matter, who have "published the same to the world, to their shame and re-"proach" (For it seems the bishop had prefaced the book of *true obedience*, in order to curry favor with *Henry* VIII in which queen *Mary* was openly declared to be a bastard) Mr *Saunders* added, "We do only preach in sincerity "the purity of the word, which although we are now "forbid to do with our mouths, yet I doubt not, but "that our blood hereafter shall more fully manifest the "same" Upon which the bishop cried out, to take away the frantic fool to prison To which Mr *Saunders* said, "I thank God, who has at last given me a place of "rest and quietness, where I may pray for your lord-"ship's conversion."

Mr *Saunders* being sent to prison, and there confined a year and three months, wrote a letter to the bishop of *Winchester*, by way of answer to several particulars, with which the bishop had charged him The following is all of the letter that has been preserved

"Touching the cause of my imprisonment, I doubt "whether I have broken any law or proclamation. In "my doctrine I did not, for at that time it was per-"mitted by the proclamation to use, according to our "consciences, such service as was then established "My doctrine was then agreeable to my conscience and "the same service then used. The act which I did "(alluding to his expounding the scriptures in his own "church in *Bread-street*) was such, as being indifferently "weighed, founded to no breaking of the proclamation, "or at least no wilful breaking of it, as I caused no "bell to be rung, neither occupied I any place in the "pulpit, after the order of sermons or lectures. But "be it, that I did break the proclamation, this long "imprisonment may be thought more than a sufficient "punishment for such a fault.

"Touching

" Touching the charge againſt me is to my religion,
" I ſay with S. *Paul, this I confeſs, that after the way*
" *which they call hereſy, ſo worſhip I the God of my fore-*
" *fathers, believing all things which are written in the law*
" *and the prophets, and have hope towards God, &c.* And
" herein I ſtudy to have always a clear conſcience to-
" wards God and towards man. So that I call God to
" witneſs, I have a conſcience. And this my conſcience
" is not grounded upon vain fantaſy, but upon the in-
" fallible verity of God's word, with the teſtimony of
" his choſen church agreeable to the ſame.

" It is eaſy for them that take *Chriſt* for their true
" paſtor, and are the true ſheep of his paſture, to diſcern
" the voice of their true ſhepherd, from the voice of
" wolves, hirelings, and ſtrangers. For *Chriſt* ſaith,
" *My ſheep hear my voice.* And are thereby given to
" know the voice of the true ſhepherd, and to follow
" him, as our Saviour alſo ſaith. The ſheep follow the
" ſhepherd, for they know his voice. A ſtranger they
" will not follow, but will flee from him, for they
" know not the voice of a ſtranger. Such inward in-
" ſpiration doth the Holy Ghoſt put into the children
" of God, being indeed taught of God, but otherwiſe
" unable to underſtand the true way of their ſalvation.
" And although (as *Chriſt* ſaith) the wolf cometh in
" ſheeps cloathing, he likewiſe adds, by their fruits ye
" ſhall know them. For there are certain fruits by
" which the wolf is bewrayed, notwithſtanding, in out-
" ward appearances of holineſs, he ſeems to be ever ſo
" true a ſheep. That the *Romiſh* religion is ravening
" and wolliſh, is evident from a variety of conſider-
" ations, and eſpecially from theſe three.

" Firſt, it robbeth God of his due and only honour.

" Secondly, it taketh away the true comfort of con-
" ſcience, in obſcuring, or rather burying, of *Chriſt* and
" his office of ſalvation.

" Thirdly, it ſpoileth God of his true worſhip and
" ſervice in ſpirit and truth, which he requires and
" commands, and driveth men to that inconvenience,
" againſt which both *Chriſt* and the prophet *Iſaiah* ſpeak
" very ſharply, *This people honoureth me with their lips,*
" *but their heart is far from me. In vain do they worſhip*
" *me, teaching, for doctrines, the commandments of men.*
" And in another place, *Ye caſt aſide the commandments of*
" *God, to maintain your own traditions.*

    " Wherefore

" Wherefore I in confcience, weighing the *Romiſh*
" religion, and by a candid difcuſſion thereof, finding
" the foundation unftedfaſt, and the building upon it
" but vain And on the other hand, having my con-
" fcience framed after a right and uncorrupt religion,
" ratified and fully eſtabliſhed by the word of God, and
" the confent of his true church, I neither may, nor do
" intend, by God's gracious aſſiſtance, to be pulled one
" jot from the fame, no, though an angel out of heaven
" fhould preach another gofpel than that, which I have
" received of the Lord

" And though I have neither that deep knowledge nor
" profound judgement, nor that eloquence to utter what
" I know and judge, as may be required in an excellent
" clerk, in order fufficiently to infwer and convince
" the gainfayer Yet neverthelefs this my proteſtation
" fhall be premifed, that with refpect to the grounds and
" caufes before confidered, notwithſtanding I cannot
" *explicitâ fide*, as they call it, conceive all that is to be
" conceived, neither can difcufs all that is to be dif-
" cuſſed, nor exprefs all that can be expreſſed, in the
" difcourfe of the doctrine of this moſt true religion
" which I profefs Yet do I bind myfelf, as by my
" humble fincerity, fo by my *fidem implicitam*, that is,
" by faith in general (as they call it) to wrap up my
" belief in the credit of the fame, that no authority of
" that *Romiſh* religion, repugnant thereunto, fhall by any
" means remove me from the fame, though it may come
" to pafs that our adverfaries will labour to beguile us
" through philofophy and deceitful vanity, after the
" traditions of men, and after the ordinances of the
" world, and not after *Chriſt*, &c "

When Mrs *Saunders* went firſt to the prifon to fee
her hufband, the keeper told her he had ſtrict charge
not to fuffer any body to fpeak to him, but that, if ſhe
chofe to ſtay at the gate, he would take the child, which
fhe had in her arms, to its father She confented, and
the father rejoiced to fee his fon, and faid, " He had
" rather have fuch a boy than two thoufand pounds "
And to fome that ſtood by, who admired the child, he
faid, " What man, that fears God, would not rather
" lofe his life, than baſtardize fuch a child, make his
" wife a whore, and himfelf a whore-monger? If there
" were no other reafon, why a man of my eſtate fhould
" lofe his life, yet who would not give it, to avouch
" this

" this child to be legitimate, and his marriage to be law-
" ful and holy?"

Mr *Saunders*, being confined a year and a quarter in
prison, was at length sent for and examined, before the
queen's council, bishop *Gardiner*, *Bonner*, and others, in
the following manner

Gard 'It is well known that you have been a pri-
' soner for the abominable heresies and false doctrine that
' you have sown, and now it is thought good, that
' mercy be shewed to such as seek for it   Wherefore,
' if you will now conform, and come home again,
' mercy is ready   We must say, that we have all fallen,
' but now are we risen again, and returned to the ca-
' tholic church   You must therefore rise with us, and
' come home unto it   Give us then a direct answer'

Saund " My lord, if it please your honours, give me
" leave to speak with deliberation '

Gard 'Leave off your painting and pride of speech;
' for such is the fashion of you all, to please yourselves
' in your glorious words.   Answer yea, or nay.'

Saund " My lord, it is not a time for me now to
" paint   And as for pride, I have no cause to be proud,
" my learning I confess to be but little, and is for
" wealth I have now none at all   Nevertheless, it be-
" hoves me to answer your demand cautiously, seeing that
" one of these two extreme perils are likely to befal me
" The losing of a good conscience, or my life   And I
" tell you the truth, I love both life and liberty, if I
" could enjoy them without the hurt of my conscience "

Gard ' Conscience ! you have none at all, but pride
' and arrogancy, dividing yourselves by singularity from
' the church '

Saund " The Lord knows all men's consciences   And
" as to the charge of separation from the church, as I
" understand your lordship's meaning, I assure you I
" live in the faith in which I have been brought up ever
" since I was fourteen years of age, being taught, that
" the power of the bishop of *Rome* is but usurped, with
" many consequent abuses   Yea, this have I received
" from YOUR hands that are here present, as a thing
" agreed   upon   by the catholic church   and public
" authority."

Gard ' Yea, marry, but I pray you, have you received
' by consent and authority all your heresies of the blessed
' sacrament of the altar?'

Saund.

Saund "My lord, it is less offence to cut off an arm,
"hand, or joint of a man than to cut off the head, for
"a man may live with the loss of any one of these, but
"he cannot live without his head. But you, all the
"whole sort of you, have agreed to cut off the su-
"premacy of the bishop of *Rome*, whom now you will
"have again to be head of the church."

Bishop of *London* 'My lord, I have his own hand-
'writing against the blessed sacrament What say you
'to that, *Saunders?*'

Saund "What I have written, I have written, and
"further I will not accuse myself. You can lay no-
"thing to my charge, for having broke any of your
"laws, since they were in force."

Gard 'Well, you are obstinate, and refuse liberty'

Saund. "My lord, I may not buy liberty at such a
"price But I beseech your honours to obtain of the
"queen such a pardon for us, that we may live and
"keep our consciences unclogged, and we shall live as
"most obedient subjects. Or else, I must say for my-
"self, that, by God's grace, I will abide the greatest
"extremity that man can do against me, rather than to
"act against my conscience."

Gard. 'Ah, sirrah! you will live as you list The
'*Donatists* desired to live in singularity, but indeed they
'were not fit to live upon the earth No more are you,
'and that you shall know within these seven days, and
'therefore away with him'

Saund "Welcome be it, whatsoever the will of God
"shall be, either life or death And I tell you truly, I
"have learned to die But I exhort you to beware of
"shedding innocent blood Truly it will cry aloud
"against you The Spirit of God rest upon all your
"honours! amen."

Mr *Saunders* was then taken into an adjoining room
till some others were examined, that they might be all
led to prison together And where finding a great number of people, he spake to them freely, declaring what
they deserved on account of their falling from *Christ* to
antichrist, and exhorted them to repent and turn, and
with a stronger faith embrace *Christ*, and confess him to
the end, in defiance of antichrist and sin, death and the
devil, and so live in the love and favor of God. He
was afterwards taken to the prison in *Bread-street*, out
of which he preached to his parishioners, as he had formerly done out of the pulpit.

2

On

On the fourth day of *February*, the bishop of *London* went to him in the prison, and degraded him, upon which he said, " I thank God, I am none of your " church " The next morning the sheriff of *London* delivered him up to some of the queen's guard, who were appointed to take him to *Coventry* to be burned there. They travelled no further than St *Alban*'s the first night, where they were met by Mr. *Grimoald*, a man of greater gifts than constancy, to whom Mr. *Saunders* said, after giving him a lesson suitable to his revolting state, " Will " you pledge me out of this cup which I will begin to " drink of to you?" *Grimoald*, shrugging up his shoul- ders, answered, ' I will pledge you out of that cup, ' which is in your hand, with all my heart, but of that ' other which you mean, I will not promise you ' " Well, replied Mr *Saunders*, my dear Lord *Jesus Christ* " hath drank to me of a more bitter cup, and shall I " not pledge my most precious Saviour? Yes, I hope I " shall." At *Coventry*, he was put into the gaol amongst the common prisoners, where he slept very little, spend- ing the night in prayer and in instructing others, and where to a friend he said, " Pray for me, for I am the " most unfit for this high office of any one that was " ever appointed to it, but my gracious God and dear " Father is able to make me strong enough "

The next day, the eighth of *February*, 1555, they led him away to the place of execution, without the city, which when they were within sight of, the officer, appointed to see the execution done, said to Mr *Saunders*, that he was one of the people that marred the queen's realm with false doctrine and heresy, and that therefore he deserved death However, if he would revoke his heresies, he had orders with him for his pardon, but if not, added he, yonder is fire prepared for thee. To which Mr. *Saunders* answered, " It is not I, nor my fellow-preachers of God's truth, " that have hurt the queen's realm, but it is yourself, " and such as you are, that have always resisted God's " holy word, that marr the queen's realm I hold no " heresies, but the doctrine of God, the blessed gospel " of *Christ*, it is *that* I hold, it is *that* I believe, it is " *that* I have taught, and it is *that* I will never revoke " Upon this, the other rejoined, ' Away with him ' And M. *Saunders* proceeded with much apparent comfort and resolution When he came to the place, he fell to the ground and prayed, and then arose, and took the stake in his arms, to which he was to be chained, and kiffed it, saying, " Welcome the crofs of *Chrift*, welcome ever- " lafting life " He was faftened to the ftake, and the fire was kindled , but the wood being green, they cruelly tormented him for a long time Which gave an oppor- tunity for a further proof of the covenant-faithfulnefs and love of HIM, who hath promifed, that his grace *fhall be fufficient*, and where afflictions abound, caufeth the confolations of his Spirit much more to abound This holy man, with the utmoft fortitude and patience, endured his torments, and at length fweetly *fell afleep in* JESUS.

In the beginning of Q *Mary*'s reign, Mr *Saunders* met with Dr *Pendleton*, a man of learning and feeming zeal in preaching the gofpel, and their converfation turning upon the times, and the probability of a very fevere perfecution, Mr *Saunders* appeared weak in faith, and very fearful that he fhould not remain ftedfaft But *Pendleton*, with an air of courage and zeal, faid ' What, ' man! there is much more caufe for me to fear than ' you, for I have a very big, fat body, yet will I fee ' the utmoft drop of this greafe of mine melted away, ' and the laft gobbet of this flefh of mine confumed ' to afhes, before I will forfike *Jefus Chrift*, and his ' truth which I have profefled.'—It was not long after, that they were both put to the trial , when poor feeble, faint-hearted *Saunders*, always jealous of himfelf, by the power of divine grace, fealed the truth with his blood, and proud, felf-fufficient *Pendleton* fell away and turned papift.——So true is it, that the moft confident *in them- felves*, are the neareft to apoftacy, and that nothing can fupport the foul in trials, and carry it happily through them, but the omnipotent grace of an almighty Redeemer

It has been obferved, that nothing difcovers the temper and mind of a perfon more than his letters. The letters of Mr *Saunders* eminently difcover the frame of his fpirit, for which reafon, we will add three or four of them.

A letter,

A letter, written on the thirty-first of *January*, 1555, after his condemnation, addressed to his wife, and other faithful friends

" THE grace of *Christ*, with the consolation of the
" Holy Ghost, to the keeping of the faith and a
" good conscience, confirm and keep you for ever vessels
" to God's glory, amen

" Oh! what worthy thanks can be given to our gra-
" cious God for his unmeasurable mercies plentifully
" poured upon us! And I, most unworthy wretch, can-
" not but pour at this present, even from the bottom
" of my heart, the bewailing of my great ingratitude
" and unkindness towards so gracious so good a God and
" loving Father I beseech you all, as for my other
" many sins, so specially for that sin of my unthankful
" ness, crave pardon for me in your earnest prayers,
" commending me to God's great mercies in *Christ*

" To number these mercies in particular, were to
" number the drops of water which are in the sea, the
" sands on the shore, and the stars in the sky   O my dear
" wife, and ye the rest of my friends, rejoice with me;
" I say, rejoice with thanksgiving for this my present
" promotion, in that I am made worthy to magnify my
" God, not only in my life, by my slow mouth and un-
" circumcised lips, bearing witness unto his truth, but
" also by my blood to seal the same, to the glory of my
" God, and confirming of his true church   And as yet
" I testify unto you, that the comfort of my sweet *Christ*
" doth drive from my fantasy the fear of death   But if
" my dear husband *Christ* doth for my trial leave me
" alone a little to myself, alas! I know in what case I
" shall be then   But if for my proof he do so, yet I am
" sure he will not be long or far from me   Though he
" stand behind the wall and hide himself, (as *Solomon*
" saith in his mystical song,) yet will he peep in by a
" cleft to see how I do   He is a very tender-hearted
" *Joseph*, though he speak roughly to his brethren, and
" handle them hardly, yea, threaten grievous bondage
" to his best-beloved brother *Benjamin* Yet can he not
" contain himself from weeping with us and upon us,
" with falling on our necks, and sweetly kissing us.
" Such, such a brother is our *Christ* unto all. Where-
" fore hasten to go unto him as *Jacob* did with his sons
" and family, leaving their country and acquaintance.
" Yea, this our *Joseph* hath obtained for us, that *Pha-*

S f   " raoh

" *raob* the infidel fhall minifter unto us chariots, wherein
" at eafe we may be carried to come unto him As we
" have experience how our very adverfaries do help us
" unto our everlafting blifs by their fpeedy difpatch,
" yea, and how all things have been helpings thereunto,
" bleffed be our God Be not afraid of fray-bugs which
" lie in the way Fear rather the everlafting fire Fear
" the ferpent which hath that deadly fting, of which by
" bodily death they fhall be brought to tafte which are
" not grafted in *Chrift*, wanting faith and a good con-
" fcience, and fo are not acquainted with *Chrift*, the
" killer of death But oh, my dear wife and friends!
" we, we whom God hath delivered from the power of
" darknefs, and hath tranflated us into the kingdom of
" his dear fon, by putting off the old man, and by faith
" putting on the new, even our Lord *Jefus Chrift*, his
" wifdom, holinefs, righteoufnefs, and redemption, we,
" I fay, have to triumph againft the terrible, fpiteful
" ferpent the devil, fin, hell, death, and damnation.
" For *Chrift* our brazen ferpent hath pulled away the
" fting of this ferpent, fo that now we may boldly, in
" beholding it fpoiled of its fting, triumph, and with our
" *Chrift*, and all his elect, fay, *Death, where is thy fting?*
" *Hell, where is thy victory? Thanks be to God, who hath*
" *given (us) the victory, through our Lord* Jefus Chrift

  " Wherefore be merry, my dear wife, and all my dear
" fellow heirs of the everlafting kingdom, always re-
" member the Lord. Rejoice in hope, be patient in
" tribulation, continue in prayer, and pray for us now
" appointed to the flaughter, that we may be unto our
" heavenly Father a fat offering, and an acceptable fa-
" crifice I may hardly write to you Wherefore let
" thefe few words be a witnefs of my commendations to
" you and all them which love us in the faith, and
" namely, unto my flock, among whom I am refident
" by God's providence, but as a prifoner

  " And although I am not fo among them, as I have
" been, to preach to them out of a pulpit, yet doth God
" now preach unto them by me, by this my imprifon-
" ment and captivity which now I fuffer among them
" for *Chrift*'s gofpel fake, bidding them to beware of the
" *Romifh* antichriftian religion and kingdom, requiring
" and charging them to abide in the truth of *Chrift*,
" which is fhortly to be fealed with the blood of their
" paftor Who, though he be unworthy of fuch a mi-
" niftry, yet *Chrift* their high paftor is to be regarded,
          " whofe

" whose truth hath been taught them by me, is witnessed
" by my chains, and shall be by my death, through the
" power of that high pastor Be not careful, good wife,
" cast your care upon the Lord, and commend me unto
" him in repentant prayer, as I do you and our *Samuel*,
" whom, even at the stake, I will offer as myself unto
" God Fare ye well all in *Christ*, in hope to be joined
" with you in joy everlasting This hope is put up in
" my bosom, Amen, Amen, Amen, pray, pray

Another letter to his wife, &c.

" GRACE and comfort, &c Wife, you shall do best
"   not to come often unto the grate where the porter
" may see you Put not yourself in danger where it
" needs not You shall, I think, shortly come far enough
" into danger by keeping faith and a good conscience
" Which, dear wife, I trust you do not slack to make
" reckoning and account upon, by exercising your in-
" ward man in meditation of God's most holy word,
" being the sustenance of the soul, and also by giving
" yourself to humble prayer For these two things be
" the very means how to be made members of our *Christ*,
" meet to inherit his kingdom
"   Do this, dear wife, in earnest, and not leaving off,
" and so we two shall, with our *Christ* and all his chosen
" children, enjoy the merry world in that everlasting
" immortality, whereas here will nothing else be found
" but extream misery, even of them which most greedily
" seek this worldly wealth And so, if we two continue
" God's children grafted in our *Christ*, the same God's
" blessing which we receive shall also settle upon our
" *Samuel* Though we do shortly depart hence and leave
" the poor infant (to our seeming) at all adventures, yet
" shall he have our gracious God to be his God For
" so hath he said, and he cannot lye, *I will be thy God*,
" saith he, *and the God of thy seed* Yea, if you leave
" him in the wilderness, destitute of all help, being called
" of God to do his will, either to dye for the confes-
" sion of *Christ*, or any work of obedience That God
" which heard the cry of the little poor infant of *Agar*,
" *Sarah's* hand-maiden, and did succour it, will do the
" like to the child of you or any other fearing him, and
" putting your trust in him
"   And if we lack faith, as we do indeed many times,
" let us call for it, and we shall have the increase both

" of

" of it, and alfo of any other good grace needful for us
" And be merry in God, in whom alfo I am very merry
" and joyful O Lord, what great caufe of rejoicing
" have we, to think upon that kingdom which he vouch-
" fafeth for his *Chrift's* fake freely to give us, forfaking
" ourfelves and following him Dear wife, this is truly
" to follow him, even to take up our crofs and follow
" him, and then, as we fuffer with him, fo fhall we
" reign with him everlaftingly, fhortly. Amen "

To his wife, a little before his burning.

" GRACE and comfort in *Chrift*, Amen Dear wife,
" be merry in the mercies of our *Chrift*, and alfo
" ye my dear friends. Pray, pray for us every body
" We be fhortly to be difpatched hence unto our good
" *Chrift*, Amen, Amen Wife, I would you fent me
" my fhirt, which you know whereunto it is confecrated.
" Let it be fewed down on both fides, and not open
" O my heavenly Father, look upon me in the face of
" thy *Chrift*, or elfe I fhall not be able to abide thy coun-
" tenance, fuch is my filthinefs He will do fo, and
" therefore I will not be afraid what fin, death, hell and
" damnation can do againft me O wife, always re-
" member the Lord God blefs you, yea, he will blefs
" thee, good wife, and thy poor boy alfo Only cleave
" thou unto him, and he will give thee all things. Pray,
" pray, pray."

To Mr *Robert* and Mr *John Glover*, his laft letter,
  written on the morning, in which he was burnt.

" GRACE and confolation in our fweet Saviour *Chrift*.
" Oh my dear brethren whom I love in the Lord,
" being loved of you alfo in the Lord, be merry and
" rejoice for me, now ready to go up to that mine in-
" heritance, which I myfelf indeed am moft unworthy
" of, but my dear *Chrift* is worthy, who hath purchafed
" the fame for me with fo dear a price. Make hafte my
" dear brethren to come unto me, that we may be merry,
" *eo gaudio quod nemo tollet à nobis*, i e with that joy
" which no man fhall take from us O wretched finner,
" that I am not thankful unto this my Father, who hath
" vouchfafed me to be a worthy veffel unto his honour.
" But, O Lord, now accept my thanks, though they
" proceed out of a not-enough circumcifed heart. Sa-
" lute my good fifters your wives, and good fifters, fear

" the

"the Lord. Salute all other that love us in the truth.
"God's blessing be with you always, Amen Even now
"towards the offering of a burnt sacrifice. O my *Christ*
"help, or else I perish"

<hr />

J O H N H O O P E R,

BISHOP of GLOUCESTER.

THIS great Divine, who was born in 1495, was a native of *Somersetshire*, and received his academical education at *Merton-College* in *Oxford*, where he was sent in 1514, and placed under the tuition of his uncle *John Hooper*, who was made master-fellow of that house in 1513, and was also principal of St *Alban's-Hall* In 1518, *John Hooper*, the nephew, was admitted bachelor of arts, which was the highest degree he took in this university, and about the same time completed it by determination. What became of him afterwards is not justly known But it is reported, that he was one of the number of *Cistercians*, commonly called white monks, and continued so for some years, till he grew weary of a monastic life, and returned to *Oxford*, where he was converted by books brought from *Germany*, and soon became a zealous protestant

In 1539, when the statute of the six articles was put in execution, he left *Oxford*, and got into the service of Sir *Thomas Arundel*, a *Devonshire* gentleman, to whom he became chaplain and steward of his estate. This gentleman was a *Roman* catholic knight, and was afterwards put to death with the protector, duke of *Somerset*, in the reign of *Edward* VI. He soon discovered that *Hooper* was a protestant, who thereby lost his protection, and was obliged to fly into *France*, where he continued some time among the reformed, till his dislike of some of their proceedings made him return to *England* On his arrival in his native country, he lived with a gentleman of the name

of

of *Saintlow*, where he became known, and was fought
after to be apprehended. Upon this, he difguifed himfelf
like a failor, hired a boat, and went to *Ireland*, from
whence he went to *Holland*, and fo on to *Switzerland*.
Bullinger was then at *Zurick*, where he fucceeded *Zuinglius* in the chair. He likewife had been obliged to forfake his country on account of religion, and therefore
gave a very friendly reception to *Hooper*, who was remarkable for his knowledge in the *Greek* and *Hebrew* languages, and who, by *Bullinger*'s advice, married a *Burgundian* lady during his refidence in that country.

Edward VI. came to the crown, in 1547, and *Hooper*
came to *England* again, when he fettled in *London*, where
he frequently preached to the people on feveral reformed
doctrinal heads, and particularly againft pluralities. He
had a great fweetnefs of temper, and was much regarded
by all the party of the Reformed, who inclined to a purity
of church government. He refided fo long in foreign
parts, under the difcipline of Reformers, who had abrogated every thing that appeared like the church of *Rome*
in their conftitution, that he came home with predilections
lefs in favor of the eftablifhment under *Cranmer*, than
many other pious men of his time. He abhorred the
very name and appearance of fuperftition, and confcientioufly believed, that our Reformation fhould have gone
many degrees farther from *Rome* even in its rites, than it
actually did. He thought, that to do lefs, was only to
temporize. The others, that is *Cranmer* and *Ridley*, believed, that if they could fecure the main points of doctrine, other things might be borne as pardonable weaknesses, if not neceffary forms at that time, when they had
to do with a great and powerful oppofition, and a very
critical life to hope for in the king, with all the profpect
of a popifh fucceffor. All of them undoubtedly acted
from motives of piety; but fome wifhed to mix greater
portions of human prudence with it, than others could
confider to be either right or religious. *Hooper* had all
the qualifications of a gracious and great divine, and was
loved and revered even by thofe who differed from him in
leffer things. He was confidered as a great acquifition to
the Reformation. His learning, piety, and character would
give ftrength and honor to any profeffion. He was now appointed chaplain to the duke of *Somerfet*, and, perhaps, was
more feverely treated on that account, when his great patron loft the protectorfhip. In 1549, he became an accufer of bifhop *Bonner*, when he was to be deprived of his
bifhopric,

bishopric, which made him fare the worse when queen *Mary* came to the crown.

After *Hooper* had practised himself in his popular and common kind of preaching, he was called to preach before the king, who, in 1550, made him bishop of *Gloucester*, and, about two years after, he had the bishopric of *Worcester* given him to keep in commendam with the former. The earl of *Warwick* recommended *Hooper* to this preferment, as a man who had all those virtues and qualities required by St. *Paul* in a good bishop, in his epistle to *Timothy*. But some disputes having arisen about the vestments or habits proper for the clergy, and *Hooper* among others wishing to proscribe as much as possible whatever had the appearance of *Romish* superstition, an unhappy controversy arose between other good men and himself upon the subject. It was customary to wear such garments and apparel as the popish bishops used. First a chymere, and under that a white rochet, then a mathematical cap with four angles, dividing the whole world into four parts. *Hooper* was a man of learning, and of great parts, as well as piety. He thought that all these were mere human inventions, brought into the church by custom or tradition, and invented chiefly for celebrating the mass, and consecrated for that use, and that they were therefore among the ceremonies condemned by the apostle as beggarly elements. In answer to this, it was told him by archbishop *Cranmer*, and bishop *Ridley*, that though tradition in matters of faith was justly to be rejected, yet in rites and ceremonies which were indifferent, custom alone was a good argument for the continuance of that which had been long used. The archbishop therefore required *Hooper* to conform himself to the law. But he persisted in refusing a rochet, and *Cranmer* persisted in refusing to consecrate him without it. The earl of *Warwick*, who was then prevalent at court, wrote a letter to the archbishop, desiring him not to insist upon these ceremonies from the bishop elect of *Gloucester*, nor to ' charge ' him with an oath burthensome to his conscience.' It is said by some writers, that this was the oath of supremacy; but others, with more reason, conceive it the oath of canonical obedience to the archbishop, which consequently commanded such ceremonies as *Hooper* was willing to decline, for it is improbable, that the king would dispense with any person from taking the oath of supremacy, wherein his own dignity was so nearly concerned. *Warwick*

wick also prevailed on the king to write a letter to *Cranmer* in favor of *Hooper*, wherein his majesty told his grace, that ' he had chosen *Hooper* to be bishop of *Gloucester*, as
' well for his great learning, deep judgement, and long
' study, both in the scriptures, and other profound learn-
' ing, as also for his good discretion, ready utterance, and
' honest life for that kind of vocation. From consecrat-
' ing of whom, says the king, we understand you do stay,
' because he would have you omit, and let pass certain
' rites and ceremonies offensive to his conscience, whereby
' ye think, you should fall in præmunire of laws We
' have thought good to dispense, and discharge you of all
' manner of dangers, penalties, and forfeitures, you should
' run into, and be in any manner of way, by omitting any
' of the same.' This letter was dated the fifth of *August*
1550, and was signed by *Somerset*, and five other lords of
the council But *Cranmer* insisted that *Hooper* should conform himself in all points, and denied him the liberty of
the pulpit, while the council confined him to his house.
Cranmer consulted *Bucer* and *Martyr* upon this occasion,
who were also consulted by *Hooper*. *Hooper* continued
strong in his prepossession, and many arguments were urged
on both sides, which later ages have more amply enlarged
and explained. *Hooper* then published a confession of his
faith, in which he complained of the privy council. Upon this he was committed to the custody of the archbishop,
who used all his endeavors to bring *Hooper* off from his
opinion, but without effect. His grace then informed the
council, that his prisoner was not content with his non-
conformity, but had offered to prescribe rules on this head
to the public, whereupon the council ordered his grace to
send him to the Fleet, and he continued there till the
next year.

At last the earl of *Warwick* deserted his chaplain, and
the affair of *Hooper*, which had slept from *August* to *March*
whilst he remained in the Fleet, was resumed. He was
brought before the council, to explain himself on the difficulties which he had started. The objection he made to the
oath was, the " swearing by God, the saints, and the holy
" gospels," when none but God himself ought to be appealed to in an oath. Upon this the king struck out those
words with his own hand, and allowed that no creature
ought to be sworn by. As to the point about the vestments, it was compromised on these conditions He
was to wear the episcopal habit which was prescribed,
when he was consecrated, and when he preached before

the

the king, or in his cathedral, and in any public place, and on other occasions he was dispensed with. On these terms he was consecrated in the usual form, by which he lost much of the popularity he had gained by his declamation against the established rites. Both parties had violently contended about this matter, which was the means of introducing a contention into *England*, that hath been pernicious to the interests of religion and the church.

Thus *Hooper* was consecrated bishop of *Gloucester*, on the eighth of *March*, 1551, and then preached before the king, in his episcopal habit. When he entered into his diocese, ' he left no pains untaken, nor ways unsought, ' how to train up the flock of *Christ* in the true word ' of salvation, continually labouring in the same.' He 'preached often, kept good hospitality for the poorer sort of people, and was beloved by all.

The see of *Gloucester* was looked upon as a poor pittance for so great a divine, and, on the twentieth of *May*, 1552, he was declared bishop of *Worcester*, in the room of *Heath*, who was then a prisoner in the *Fleet*, for refusing to agree with the book of ordinations. *Hooper* was permitted to hold *Worcester* in commendam with *Gloucester*, for which he was censured by the papists. ' But let such know, that the diocesses of *Gloucester* and ' *Worcester* lie contiguous. That many single bishoprics ' in *England* are larger than both, for extent in land, ' and number of parishes. That *Dunstan* had the bi- ' shoprick of *Worcester* and *London* with it at the same time, ' being far more remote. That it is not having two bi- ' shoprics together, but the neglecting of one, is the ' sin; whereas *Hooper*, in preaching and visiting, afforded ' double diligence in his double diocese.'

The compliance of *Hooper* with the established religion was, at this time, of great service to the public. But this plurality conferred upon one prelate, is a proof how far the government began to deviate from the strict maxim it had laid down, of not suffering a bishop to keep even a parsonage in commendam. *Hooper* made a very good use of his power. He visited both sees, and did great services both to the church and state of *England*. He made to the king a deed of gift of his bishopric of *Glou- cester*, and of all the lands and annuities he enjoyed by the same. Soon after, that bishopric was dissolved, or rather united with the see of *Worcester*, so that the juris- diction of *Gloucester* ceased. In the act of his translation

T t

to *Worcester*, he was made bishop of the same, during his natural life, ' provided he behaved so long well ' But it is probable, the new bishop enjoyed only a small part of the revenues, considering the daily growing practice of courtiers begging for ecclesiastical revenues

When king *Edward* died, in 1553, religion was subverted, and this good bishop was one of the first that was sent for by queen *Mary* to be at *London*, to answer *Heath* the deprived bishop, and *Bonner* bishop of *London*, for being one of his accusers Hooper was seasonably advised to make his escape But he was determined to bear the storm, and said, " once I fled, and took me to " my feet, now I will continue to live and die with my " sheep " He was brought up to *London* by a pursuivant in *August*, and was very opprobriously received by the bishop of *Winchester*, who committed him prisoner to the *Fleet* on the first of *September* following He remained there several months, during which time he was examined many times, and required to recant his opinions But he stood constant and resolute to the articles of his faith *Cranmer* *Ridley*, *Latimer*, and *Ferrar*, were also imprisoned The archbishop of *York*, and the bishops of *Bristol*, *Chester*, and St *David's*, were deprived of their bishoprics, for having been married The sees of *Lincoln*, *Hereford*, and *Gloucester*, were declared void, because those bishops had misbehaved themselves. Thus were seven bishops turned out all at once, by an authority which the bigotted queen herself thought sinful and schismatical, and their sees were filled with men in whom she confided.

The council proceeded with vigor in matters of heresy, and removed *Cranmer*, *Ridley*, and *Latimer*, to dispute with some members of the convocation at *Oxford*, where they all suffered martyrdom. There was a design of the same nature to be executed at *Cambridge*, over some other bishops and eminent clergy, who were in the several prisons of *Newgate*, the *Fleet*, and the *King's-bench* But the prisoners set forth a declaration, signed by *Hooper*, *Ferrar*, *Coverdale* bishop of *Exeter*, and seven divines, that they would not dispute unless in writing, except it were before the queen and her council, or one of the houses of parliament. To this declaration they added a summary of their belief, for which, they said, they were ready to offer up their lives to the halter, or the fire, as it should please God to appoint This prevented any farther public conferences in religion, and it was determined

mined to silence the protestants more effectually in another manner

It would be disagreeable to particularize the numerous deprivations, hardships, expulsions, and imprisonments, which the protestants, both clergy and laity, women as well as men, underwent. The government had the parliament on its side, and drove on as furiously as could be wished. Nothing was to be heard but declamations, from their most florid preachers, in favor of their religion. Nothing was to be seen in the streets, but pageants exposed by papists, and pilleries occupied by protestants. Yet no pomp could amuse, no severity could damp the spirit of the people.

Gardiner chearfully undertook to put the laws in execution against heretics. But as the people could not be intimidated by his threats, or worked upon by his promises, the council sent for the most popular preachers that were in custody, to begin the severities upon them, according to *Gardiner's* plan. It was resolved that *Hooper*, as the most obnoxious to the government, if not the most popular, should be the leading sacrifice to popery. They called him before them on the twenty-first of *January*, 1555, and offered him a pardon by the name of *John Hooper* clerk, not acknowledging him to have been a bishop, if he would confess his heresies, and return to the church, which he absolutely refused. Three articles were then exhibited against him, for marrying, for allowing a divorce and second marriage in the case of fornication, and for denying the corporal presence of *Christ* in the sacrament. *Hooper* owned himself guilty of the accusation, but offered to defend himself against all who should maintain the contrary. He behaved with all humility to the bishops, who treated him with the utmost insolence, and remanded him back to prison.

The two bloody bishops of *London* and *Winchester* had a personal hatred to *Hooper*, who behaved with all the constancy of a primitive martyr. He had kept up a correspondence with *Bullinger*, and others of the reformed abroad, to whom he sent his wife *Anne*, and her children, who was herself a foreigner, and he was at very little pains to conceal his sentiments, none having been more active, or more successful, than he was in the cause of Reformation. *Bullinger* wrote him a long letter from *Zurich*, dated the tenth of *October*, 1554, wherein he desires *Hooper* to commend him to the most reverend fathers and holy confessors of *Christ*, *Cranmer*, *Ridley*,

and

and *Latimer* He exhorts them all to be strong in the
Lord, to fight a good fight, and to be faithful unto the end;
as *Chrift* was their captain, and all the prophets, apoftles,
and martyrs, their fellow foldiers

The commiffioners had declared that *Hooper* ought to
be deprived of his bifhopric, and he was brought before
them again, on the twenty-fecond of *January*, at the
bifhop of *Winchefter*'s houfe at St *Mary Overy*'s He
was then afked to acknowledge the pope to be head of the
church, which he denied, as the pope taught a doctrine
directly contrary to the doctrine of *Chrift* Therefore,
he would not condefcend to any fuch ufurped jurifdiction, neither efteemed he the church, of which they call
him head, to be the catholic church of *Chrift* "For
" the church only heareth the voice of her fpoufe *Chrift*,
" and fleeth the ftrangers" He was commanded back
to the fleet, and brought before the commiffioners again
on the twenty-eighth of *January*, together with Mr *John
Rogers*, vicar of St. *Sepulchre*'s and reader of St *Paul*'s.
They were both examined, and fent away to be brought
into court the next morning, to fee if they would relent
They were conducted to the *Compter* in *Southwark*, by
the fheriffs of *London*, and *Hooper* faid to *Rogers*, as they
walked through the ftreet furrounded by the populace,
" Come, brother *Rogers*, muft we two take this matter
" firft in hand, and begin to fry thefe faggots?" *Rogers*
anfwered 'Yes, fir, by God's grace' "Doubt not,
" replied *Hooper*, but God will give grace"

The next morning they were brought again before the
commiffioners, who fat in judgement in St *Mary Overy*'s
church *Hooper* would by no means condefcend to the
commiffioners, who condemned him, to be degraded, and
ordered him to be carried to the *Clink*, a prifon near the
bifhop of *Winchefter*'s houfe, from whence he was removed to *Newgate* the fame night

The people prayed for him as he was guarded through
the ftreets, and he was kept clofe prifoner in *Newgate* fix
days During this time he was frequently vifited by
Bonner and his chaplains, who vainly endeavored to
make him a convert to their church They offered him
wealth and preferment, which he defpifed, and then they
fpread a report that he had recanted. This report foon
came to his ears, at which he was greatly grieved, and,
on the fecond of *February*, wrote a letter to difprove that
falfe and malicious ftory, and to affure the world that he
was more than ever confirmed in the proteftant faith,

faying,

ſaying, "I have taught the truth with my tongue and "with my pen heretofore, and hereafter ſhortly ſhall "confirm the ſame, by God's grace, with my blood"

The biſhop of *London* came to *Newgate*, and degraded *Hooper*, after reading the ſentence of his degradation, wherein *Hooper* is called a Preſbyter, under the juriſdiction of the biſhop of *Wincheſter*, by whoſe definitive ſentence he was pronounced, 'an open, obſtinate, and 'incorrigible heretic,' and, as ſuch, was to be degraded from his order, and for theſe demerits to be delivered to the ſecular power 'In degrading this bleſſed biſhop, 'they did not proceed againſt him as a biſhop, but only 'as againſt a prieſt, as they termed him, for ſuch as he 'was, theſe Balaamites accounted no biſhop'

Rogers was degraded at the ſame time, and died a martyr in *Smithfield* But *Hooper* was impolitically ſent by the government to die at *Glouceſter*, that the hearers of his doctrine might be the witneſſes of his ſufferings By the order that was ſent to burn him at *Glouceſter*, the ſheriff was directed to call in ſome of reputation in the county to aſſiſt at his execution And becauſe he was, ſays the order, 'a vain-glorious perſon, as all heretics 'are,' he was neither ſuffered to ſpeak at large in going to his execution, nor at the place, for avoiding further infection He was much pleaſed at being carried to *Glouceſter*, that he might confirm with his death the truth which he had taught there in his life, not doubting but the Lord would give him ſtrength to perform the ſame to his glory.

On the fifth of *February*, before daylight, he was brought by the ſheriffs from *Newgate*, to a place appointed near St *Dunſtan's* church in *Fleet-ſtreet*, where he was received by a body of the queen's guards, who were to carry him to *Glouceſter* He eat a hearty breakfaſt, and leapt chearfully on horſeback without help. On the ſeventh he arrived at *Glouceſter*, where he found all the citizens aſſembled to ſee him, who cried and lamented for his condition.

The next morning ſome of his friends were permitted to ſee him, among whom was Sir *Anthony Kingſton*, who found the good biſhop at his prayers, and burſt forth into tears, as he ſpoke in this manner 'I underſtand 'you are come here to die But, alas! conſider that life 'is ſweet, and death is bitter Therefore, ſeeing life 'may be had, deſire to live, for life hereafter may do 'good,' The biſhop anſwered, "Indeed, I am come

3 "here

" here to end this life, and to fuffer death, becaufe I
" will not gainfay the former truth that I have taught
" in this diocefe, and elfewhere. I do not fo much re-
" gard this death, nor efteem this life, but have fettled
" myfelf, through the ftrength of God's Holy Spirit,
" patiently to pafs through the torments and extremities
" of the fire now prepared for me, rather than deny the
" truth of his word" The fame night he was committed by the guard to the cuftody of the fheriffs of
Gloucefter, who, with the mayor and aldermen, attended
him with great refpect He thanked them for their civility, and requefted the fheriffs, that " there might be
" quick fire, fhortly to make an end" He told them,
" he was not come there is one compelled to die, for it
" was well known he might have had his life with
" worldly gain But as one willing to offer and give his
" life for the truth, rather than confent to the wicked
" papiftical religion of the bifhop of *Rome*, received and
" fet forth by the magiftrates in *England*, to the high
" difpleafure and difhonour of God And he trufted,
" by God's grace, the next day to die a faithful fervant
" of God, and true obedient fubject to the queen" He
was not carried to the common jail of the city called
North-gate, but lodged in the houfe of Mr *Robert Ingram*,
where he fpent the night in devotion.

About eight the next morning, the commiffioners, appointed to fee the execution, came to the houfe, and at
nine the bifhop was brought down from his chamber by
the fheriffs, and led to the ftake between them like a
lamb going to the flaughter It was market-day, and
about feven thoufand people were affembled on the occafion, which made him fay, " Alas! why are thefe people
" here? Perhaps they think to hear fomething of me
" now, as they have in times paft, but, alas! fpeech is
" prohibited me Notwithftanding the caufe of my death
" is well known unto them When I was appointed
" here to be their paftor, I preached unto them true and
" fincere doctrine out of the word of God Becaufe I
" will not now account the fame to be herefy and un-
" truth, this death is prepared for me."

He was dreft in a gown of his hoft's, a hat on his
head, and a ftaff in his hand to fupport him, as the
fciatica which he had contracted in prifon, made him
halt The people mourned for him all the way, and he
looked very chearfully upon fuch as he knew He frequently lifted up his eyes towards heaven as he paffed
along,

along, and he was never known, since his being then bishop, to look with so lively and ruddy a countenance as he did at that time.

When he came to the stake, which was opposite the college of priests, where he used to preach, he beheld the preparation for his death with a composed and smiling countenance. When the iron work was brought to fasten him to the stake, he took an iron hoop and put it about his waist, and, bidding them take away the rest, he said, " I doubt not but God will give me strength to abide " the extremity of the fire without binding." The place was surrounded with spectators, and the priests of the college were in the chamber over the college-gate As the bishop was not permitted to speak to the people, he kneeled down to prayer, and beckoned to Mr *Bridges*, whom he knew, to hear it, which he did with great attention, and reported that the prayer was made upon the whole creed, wherein the bishop continued about half an hour, and declared his faith in the form of a prayer. When he was in the middle of this prayer, a box was brought, and laid before him on a stool, with his pardon from the queen, if he would recant When he saw it, he cried, " If you love my soul, away with it, if you " love my soul, away with it " He was then permitted to proceed in prayer, which he concluded in these words " Lord, I am hell, but thou art heaven Thou " art a gracious and merciful Redeemer Have mercy " therefore upon me, a most miserable and wretched " offender, after thy great mercy, and according to thy " inestimable goodness. Thou art ascended into hea- " ven, receive me to be a partaker of thy joys there, " where thou sittest in equal glory with thy Father " For well thou knowest wherefore I am come hither to " suffer, and why the wicked do persecute thy poor " servant, not for my sins and transgressions committed " against thee, but because I will not allow of their " wicked doings, to the contaminating of thy blood, and " the denial of the knowledge of thy truth, in which it " pleased thee, by thy Holy Spirit, to instruct me " With as much diligence as so poor a creature could, " being thereto called, I have set forth thy glory Thou " well feest, O Lord my God, what terrible torments " and cruel pains are prepared for thy poor creature, " even such, Lord, as, without thy strength, no one is " able to bear or patiently to pass. But that which is

" impossible

" impoſſible with man, is poſſible with thee There-
" fore, ſtrengthen me of thy goodneſs, that in the fire I
" break not the rules of patience, or elſe aſſuage the
" terror of the pains, as ſhall ſeem fitteſt for thy glory "

When prayer was done, he prepared himſelf for the
ſtake, and was undreſt to his ſhirt, which he truſſed between his legs, where he had a pound of gunpowder in
a bladder, and under each arm the like quantity delivered
him by the guard A flood of tears burſt from the
eyes of the ſpectators as he was faſtened to the ſtake,
from whence he directed the executioner where to place
the fire, which was ſoon kindled But the wood burning
ill, and the wind blowing away the flame that it did not
riſe up and ſuffocate him, nor deſtroy his vitals, he was
for a long time in the utmoſt torment He frequently
called to the people, for the love of God, to bring him
more fire, which, though it was renewed, was prevented
by the wind from putting him out of his miſery, till he
had been near three quarters of an hour in burning.
During this ſpace, he frequently ſaid, " O Jeſus, thou
" ſon of *David*, have mercy on me, and receive my
" ſoul !" The laſt words, he was heard to utter, were,
" Lord *Jeſus*, receive my ſpirit !" The account given
by *Fox* of his long excruciating torments is terrible to
hear, who ſays, he patiently bore the extremity of the
fire, ' neither moving forwards, backwards, or to any
' ſide, but having his nether parts burnt, and his bowels
' fallen out, he died as quietly as a child in his bed
' And he now reigneth as a bleſſed martyr in the joys of
' heaven, prepared for the faithful in *Chriſt* before the
' foundations of the world For whoſe conſtancy all
' Chriſtians are bound to praiſe God '

This learned and pious prelate was thus cruelly martyred, like *Polycarp*, biſhop of *Smyrna*, to whom he has
been juſtly compared, on the ninth of *February*, 1555,
and in the ſixtieth year of his age

In one of his letters, whilſt he was in priſon, he uſed
theſe words, " Impriſonment is painful, but liberty
" upon evil conditions is worſe The priſon ſtinks, yet
" not ſo much as the ſweet houſes, where the fear of
" God is wanting. I muſt be alone and ſolitary It is
" better ſo to be, and have God with me, than to be in
" company with the wicked Loſs of goods is great,
" but the loſs of grace and God's favour is greater. I
" cannot tell how to anſwer before great and learned
           " men.

" men Yet it is better to do that, than to ſtand naked
" before God's tribunal I ſhall die by the hands of
" cruel men He is bleſſed, that loſeth his life, and
" findeth life eternal There is neither felicity nor ad-
" verſity in this world, that is great, if it be weighed
" with the joys and pains of the world to come " Soon
after he added, " I am a precious jewel now, and dain-
" tily kept, never ſo daintily before, for neither my
" own man, nor any of the ſervants of the houſe, may
" come to me, but my keeper only, who is a ſimple rude
" fellow But I am not troubled thereat "

He wrote twenty-four books and treatiſes when in
priſon Beſides he wrote of the Sacraments, the Lord's
Prayer, and the Ten Commandments His writings are
moſtly theſe Anſwer to *Gardiner*'s book, entitled, A
Detection of the Devil's Sophiſtry A Declaration of
Chriſt and his Office Leſſon of the Incarnation of *Chriſt*
Sermons on *Jonas* · A godly Confeſſion and Proteſtation
of the Chriſtian Faith . *Homily* to be read in the time
of the Peſtilence. All theſe were wrote from 1549, to
1553 And he afterwards wrote, *Epiſtola ad Epiſcopos*,
&c An Exhortation to Patience, ſent to his wife Sentences wrote in Priſon Comfortable Expoſitions on the
twenty-third, ſixty-ſecond, ſeventy-third, and ſeventy-
ſeventh *Pſalms* Annotations on the thirteenth Chapter
to the *Romans* Twelve Lectures upon the Creed Declaration of the Ten Holy Commandments of Almighty
God And he alſo tranſlated *Tertullian*'s ſecond book to
his wife, concerning the choice of a huſband or wife

The manner of his death being ſo very ſevere, very
uncharitable reflexions were made upon it, as though he,
who had kindled the fire of diſſention about the veſt-
ments, had ſuffered thus uncommonly for that reaſon.
Ridley and *Hooper* were not fully reconciled till the reign
of *Mary*, when *Hooper* had the honor to offer the firſt
agreement, which *Ridley* embraced with a brotherly love,
and ſeveral letters paſſed between them on that occaſion.
They acknowledged their mutual faults in carrying
things of ſuch indifference to ſo great a length, and
aſſured each other of their ſincere love and affection.
Happy would it have been for *England*, and much to the
intereſt of religion, if the fires which conſumed theſe
pious men had put an end to ſuch frivolous and idle
conteſts l And if thoſe who have ſince engaged in them
with a furious zeal, would reflect more on the ſenſe which

U u   theſe

thefe good bifhops had of them when they were on the verge of another world, than on the heats into which they put them, while they were in cafe and fecurity, it is probable they might be perfuaded to a little more humility and moderation.

ROWLAND TAYLOR, D.D.

' OF whom the world was not worthy'—is an obfervation made by the Divine Spirit of God's people in general, but it is particularly faid of thofe, who have had the invincible courage to fuffer for his truth It is eminently applicable to the excellent martyr, fome account of whom we are now to fubmit to the Reader

Rowland Taylor, doctor both in civil and canon laws, was a very uncommon man both for grace and gifts He had the piety of *Calvin*, the intrepidity of *Luther*, and what was orthodox in both. He was rector of *Hadley*, in *Suffolk*, which was one of the firft towns in *England* that received the gofpel, by the preaching of Mr. *Thomas Bilney* ' By whofe induftry, fays Mr *Fox*, the gofpel of ' *Chrift* had fuch gracious fuccefs, and took fuch root ' there, that a great number in that parifh became ex-' ceedingly well learned in the holy fcriptures, as well ' women as men ' So that one might have found amongft them many, who had often read the whole bible through, and who could have faid great part of St *Paul's* epiftles by heart, and very well and readily have given a fcriptural and judicious anfwer in any matter of controverfy. Their children and fervants were alfo brought up with fuch care, and fo diligently inftructed in the right knowledge of God's word, that the whole town feemed rather an univerfity of the learned, than a town of clothmaking, or laboring, people. And, what is moft to be commended, they were, for the moft part, faithful followers of God's word in holinefs of life and converfation.

Dr *Taylor* was no fooner prefented to this benefice of *Hadley*, than he went and refided upon it, though he had the happinefs of living at *Lambeth* with archbifhop *Cranmer* He not only labored abundantly in preaching the
pure

pure doctrines of the gospel of *Jesus Christ*, but, as becomes every true pastor, he was an example to the believers, in word, in conversation, in charity, in spirit, in faith, in purity, that in a little time, the people resorted to him as a father. 'To the poor, says Mr *Fox*, 'that were blind, lame, sick, bed-rid, or that had many 'children, he was indeed a father, a careful patron, and 'diligent provider, and stirred up such parishioners, as 'had it in their power, to make a general provision for 'them, while he himself (beside the continual relief they 'always found at his house) gave most liberally every 'year to the common alms-box. His wife also was an 'honest, discreet, and sober matron, and his children well 'nurtured, and brought up in the fear of God and good 'learning.' He was of a meek and humble spirit, yet bold and faithful in reproving sin, even in the greatest. And thus he continued, as a faithful and good shepherd, feeding, governing, and leading his flock through the wilderness of this evil world, all the days of good king *Edward*.

When queen *Mary* ascended the throne, one *Foster*, a steward and keeper of courts, and *John Clerk*, of *Hadley*, two papists, agreed together, by violence, to build up an altar in Dr *Taylor*'s church, and to have mass said in it, and accordingly engaged *John Averth*, minister of *Aldam*, a dissembling papist, to come with all the popish implements and garments, and to be their priest, having a band of papists with drawn swords to defend them. They proceeded to *Hadley* church in a body, and rang the bell, which Dr *Taylor* hearing, as he sat at his studies, thought it was some parish-business that required his attendance, and therefore went to church, where, to his great surprize, he saw *Averth*, in all his popish vestments, with a broad new shaved crown, ready to begin his popish sacrifice, and surrounded with armed men, lest any body should approach to disturb him, whom he thus addressed:

" Thou devil, who made thee so bold to enter into this " church, to prophane and defile it with this abominable " idolatry? I command thee, thou popish wolf, in the " name of God, to avoid hence, and not to presume " thus to poison *Christ*'s flock." Then said *Foster*, ' Thou traitor, what doest thou here, to let and disturb ' the queen's proceedings?' Doctor *Taylor* answered, " I am no traitor, but I am the shepherd, that God my " Lord *Christ* hath appointed to feed his flock, there- " fore I have very good authority to be here." Mrs

Taylor, who had followed her hufband into the church, kneeled down, and lifting up her hands, cried with a loud voice, ' I befeech God, the righteous judge, to ' avenge this injury, which this popifh idolater doth this ' day to the blood of *Chrift*.' They then thruft both the Doctor and her out of the church, and, in a day or two after, wrote to *Gardinei*, bifhop of *Winchefter* and lord chancellor, lodging in his court many falfe and heavy charges againft him.

The bifhop no fooner heard of it, than he fent letters miffive to Dr *Taylor*, commanding him within a certain time to come and appear before him, upon his allegiance, to anfwer fuch complaints as were made againft him When his friends knew this, they earneftly entreated him to fly, for there was no reafon to expect he would meet either with juftice or favor, but, on the contrary, imprifonment and death To thefe he anfwered, " I " know my caufe to be fo good and righteous, and the " truth fo ftrong on my fide, that I will, by God's " grace, appear before them, and to their face refift their " falfe doings, for I believe I fhall never be able to do " God fo good fervice as now, and that I fhall never " have fo glorious a calling, nor fo much of the mercy " of God proferred me, as I have now Therefore, pray " for me, and I doubt not but God will give me " ftrength, and his Holy Spirit, that all my adverfaries " fhall be afhamed of their doings." And when they further urged, that he had fufficiently done his duty, and borne witnefs to the truth, both in his fermons and in refifting the popifh prieft, that our Saviour *Chrift* fays, *when they perfecute you in one city, flee unto another*, and that, in fleeing from the prefent perfecution, he might referve himfelf for better times, he replied, " I am old, " and have already lived too long to fee thefe terrible " and wicked days You may act according to your " confciences, but I am refolved not to fly God fhall " hereafter raife up teachers, who fhall teach with more " diligence and fruitfulnefs than I have done, for God " will not forfake his church, though for a time he trieth " and correcteth us, and that not without juft caufe."

Dr *Taylor* fet out for *London*, attended by his own fervant, *John Hull*, who, by the way, labored to perfuade his mafter to fly, proffering him his fervice, though at the hazard of his life, in all the perils and dangers that might attend his flight " Oh *John!* (anfwered the " good Doctor) fhall I give place to this thy counfel
" and

" and worldly perfuasion, and leave my flock in this
" danger? Remember the good shepherd *Chrift*, who not
" only fed his flock, but also died for it Him I muft,
" and, by the grace of God, will follow Therefore,
" good *John*, pray for me, and if, at any time, thou feeft
" me weak, comfort me, but difcourage me not in this
" my godly enterprize and purpofe "

Dr. *Taylor*, upon his arrival at *London*, waited on the
bifhop, who, according to cuftom, reviled him, calling
him *knave*, *traitor*, *heretic*, and much more of the fame
kind of language, which was ufual with him, all which
the doctor heard with great patience, and then faid,
" My lord, I am neither a traitor nor a heretic, but a
" true fubject, and a faithful Chriftian man, and am
" come, according to your command, to know your
" lordfhip's pleafure in fending for me " Then faid the
bifhop, ' Art thou come, thou villain? How dareft thou
' look me in the face for fhame? Knoweft thou not who
' I am?'—" Yes, (anfwered the doctor) I know who
" you are. You are Dr *Stephen Gardiner*, bifhop of
" *Winchefter*, and lord chancellor, and yet but a man, I
" trow. But (continued the doctor) if you expect that
" I fhould be afraid of your lordly looks, why do you
" not fear God, the Lord of us all? How dare you for
" fhame look any Chriftian man in the face, feeing you
" have forfaken the truth, denied our Saviour *Chrift* and
" his word, and have done contrary to your own oath
" and writing? With what countenance will you appear
" before the judgement-feat of *Chrift*, and anfwer to
" your oath made, firft unto king *Henry* VIII. and after-
" ward unto king *Edward* his fon?"—' Tufh, tufh,
' (cried the bifhop) that was an *Herod*'s oath, unlawful,
' and therefore worthy to be broken I have done well
' in breaking it,—and, I thank God, I am come home
' again to our mother, the catholic church of *Rome*, and
' fo I would thou fhouldeft do '

" But (faid Dr. *Taylor*) you will not be difcharged
" before *Chrift*, who doubtlefs will require it at your
" hands, as a lawful oath made to our liege and fove-
" reign lord the king, from whofe obedience the pope
" nor any other man can abfolve you."—' I fee, (faid
' the bifhop) thou art an arrogant knave, and a very
' fool '—" My lord, (faid the doctor) leave your un-
" feemly railing at me, it is unbecoming a man in
" authority as you are I am a Chriftian man, and
" you know, that *he that faith to his brother, Racha, is in*
" *danger*

" danger of the council, and he that faith, Thou fool, is in
" danger of hell-fire "—' Ye are false, (said the bishop)
' and liars all the fort of you '—" Nay, my lord, we
" are true men, (replied *Taylor*) and know that it is
" written, *The mouth that lieth, slayeth the soul* And
" again, *Thou Lord God shalt destroy all that speak lies*
" And therefore we abide by the truth of God's word,
" which you, contrary to your consciences, deny and
" forsake "

' Thou art a married man,' said the bishop " Yes,
" my lord, (said the doctor) I thank God I am, and
" have had nine children, all in lawful matrimony,
" and blessed be God who has ordained matrimony, and
" commanded that every man, that had not the gift of
" continency, should marry a wife of his own, and not
" live in adultery or whoredom "—' But thou hast re-
' fisted the queen's proceedings, in not suffering the
' minister of *Aldam* to say mass in *Hadley* '—" My lord,
" I am the minister of *Hadley* And it is against all
" right, conscience, and law, that any man should come
" into my charge, and presume to infect the flock, com-
" mitted to my care, with the venom of the popish
" idolatrous mass " With that, the bishop grew very
angry, and said, ' Thou art a blasphemous heretic in-
' deed, that blasphemest the blessed sacrament, [and put
' off his cap] and speakest against the holy mass, which
' is made a sacrifice for the quick and the dead '—" Nay,
" (says *Taylor*) I blaspheme not the blessed sacrament,
" which *Christ* instituted, but I reverence it as a Chris-
" tian ought to do, and confess, that *Christ* ordained
" the holy communion in remembrance of his death and
" passion, which, when we keep according to his ordi-
" nance, we, through faith, eat the body of *Christ*, and
" drink his blood, giving thanks for our redemption.
" That sacrifice, oblation, and atonement, which *Christ*
" made and offered in his own person once for all, was
" full, perfect, and sufficient for all them that believe in
" him, so that no priest can offer him again, nor need
" we any more propitiatory sacrifice Therefore I say,
" with *Chrysostom*, and all the doctors, ' Our sacrifice is
' only memorative, in the remembrance of *Christ*'s death
' and passion, a sacrifice of thankgiving,' and therefore
" the fathers called it *eucharistia* And any other sacrifice
" the church knows nothing of "—' True, (said the
' bishop) the sacrament is called *eucharistia*, a thankf-
' giving, because we there give thanks for our redemp-
' tion,

' tion, but it is also a sacrifice propitiatory for the quick
' and dead, which thou shalt confess e'er thou and I
' have done '—Then the bishop called his men, and said,
' Have this fellow hence, and carry him to the *King's*
' *Bench*, and charge the keeper that he be close confined '
Upon which Dr *Taylor* kneeled down, and holding up
both his hands, said, " Good Lord, I thank thee, and
" from the tyranny of th bishop of *Rome*, and all his
" detestable errors, idolatries, and abominations, good
" Lord deliver us,"—and added, " God be praised for
" good king *Edward !*"

Dr *Taylor*, being sent to prison, was confined almost
two years; during which time he was frequently examined respecting his faith, and as often witnessed a good
confession before his adversaries But, as his examinations are substantially the same, we will lay before the
Reader the following letter, written by the doctor to a
friend, in which he gives an account of his examination
on the twenty-second of *January*, before the chancellor
and other commissioners.

A letter of Dr. Taylor, *containing a conversation between
him and the lord chancellor and other commissioners, the
twenty-second of* January

" WHEREAS you would have me to write the
"   talk between the king and queen's most ho-
" nourable council and me on *Tuesday* the twenty-second
" of *January*, so far as I remember First, my lord
" chancellor said, ' You among others are at this present
' time sent for, to enjoy the king and queen's majesties
' favour and mercy, if you will now rise again with us
' from the fall which ye generally have received in this
' realm, from the which (God be praised) ye are now
' clearly delivered, miraculously If you will not rise
' with us now, and receive mercy now offered, you shall
' have judgement according to your demerit ' To this I
" answered, that so to rise, should be the greatest fall
" that ever I could receive For I should so fall from
" my dear Saviour *Christ* to antichrist For I do believe,
" that the religion set forth in king *Edward's* days, was
" according to the vein of the holy scripture, which
" containeth fully all the rules of our Christian religion,
" from the which I do not intend to decline so long as I
" live, by God's grace.
" Then master secretary *Bourn* said, ' Which of the
' religions mean ye of in king *Edward's* days ? For ye

3   ' know

' know there were diverſe books of religion ſet forth in
' his days   There was a religion ſet forth in a cate-
' chiſm by my lord of *Canterbury.* Do you mean that
' you will ſtick to that "

" I anſwered, my lord of *Canterbury* made a catechiſm
" to be tranſlated into *Engliſh,* which book was not of
" his own making   Yet he ſet it forth in his own name,
" and truly that book for the time did much good.   But
" there was, after that, ſet forth by the moſt innocent king
" *Edward* (for whom God be praiſed everlaſtingly) the
" whole church-ſervice, with great deliberation, and the
" advice of the beſt learned men in the realm, and
" authoriſed by the whole parliament, and received and
" publiſhed gladly by the whole realm   Which book was
" never reformed but once, and yet by that one refor-
" mation it was ſo fully perfected, according to the rules
" of our Chriſtian religion in every behalf, that no
" Chriſtian conſcience could be offended with any thing
" therein contained, I mean of that book reformed.

" Then my lord chancellor ſaid, ' Didſt thou never
' read the book that I ſet forth of the ſacrament?'

" I anſwered, that I had read it.

" Then he ſaid, ' How likeſt thou that book?' With
" that one of the council (whoſe name I know not) ſaid,
' My lord, that is a good queſtion   For I am ſure, that
' book ſtoppeth all their mouths'   Then ſaid I, My
" lord, I think many things be far wide from the truth
" of God's word in that book.

" Then my lord ſaid, ' Thou art a very varlet'   To
" that I anſwered, That is as ill as *racha* or *fool.*
" Then my lord ſaid, ' Thou art an ignorant beetle-
' brow.'

" To that I anſwered, I have read over and over
" again the holy ſcriptures, and *S. Auguſtine's* works
" through, *S. Cyprian, Euſebius, Origen, Gregory Nazi-*
" *anzene,* with divers other books through once, there-
" fore, I thank God, I am not utterly ignorant.   Beſides
" theſe, my lord, I profeſſed the civil laws, as your lord-
" ſhip did, and I have read over the canon law alſo.

" Then my lord ſaid, ' With a corrupt judgement
' thou readeſt all things · Touching my profeſſion, it is
' divinity, in which I have written divers books.'   Then
" ſaid I, My lord, ye did write one book, *De verâ obe-*
" *dientiâ,* I would you had been conſtant in that   For
" indeed you never did declare a good conſcience that I
" heard of, but in that one book,

" Then

" Then my lord faid, ' tut, tut, tut, I wrote againft
' *Bucer* in priefts marriages But fuch books pleafe not
' fuch wretches as thou art, which haft been married
' many years '

" To that I anfwered, I am married indeed, and I
" have had nine children in holy matrimony, I thank
" God And this I am fure of, that your proceedings
" now at this prefent in this realm againft priefts mar-
" riages, is the maintenance of the doctrine of devils,
" againft natural law, civil law, canon law general
" councils, canons of the apoftles, antient doctors, and
" God's laws

" Then fpake my lord of *Durham*, faying, ' you have
' profeffed the civil law, as you fay Then you know
' that *Juftinian* writeth, that priefts fhould at their tak-
' ing of orders fwear, that they were never married, and
' he bringeth in to prove that, *Canones Apoftolorum* '

" To that I anfwered, that I did not remember any
" fuch law of *Juftinian* But I am fure, that *Juftinian*
" writeth in *Titulo de vidicta viduitate*, in cod that if
" one would bequeath to his wife in his teftament a
" legacy, under a condition that fhe fhould never marry
" again, and take an oath of her for accomplifhing the
" fame, yet fhe may marry again if he die, notwithftand-
" ing the aforefaid conditions, and oath taken and made
" againft marriage And an oath is another manner of
" obligation made to God, than is a papiftical vow made
" to man.

" Moreover, in the pandects it is contained, that if a
" man doth manumit his handmaid, under a condition
" that fhe fhall never marry, yet fhe may marry, and her
" patron fhall lofe *Jus patronatus*, for his adding of the
" unnatural and unlawful condition againft matrimony

" Then my lord chancellor faid, ' thou fayeft that
' priefts may be married by God's law How proveft
' thou that ?'

" I anfwered, by the plain words and fentences of St
" *Paul*, both to *Timothy*, and to *Titus*, where he fpeaks
" moft evidently of the marriage of priefts, deacons and
" bifhops And *Chryfoftom*, writing upon the epiftle to
" *Timothy*, faith, it is an herefy to fay that a bifhop may
" not be married

" Then faid my lord chancellor, ' thou lyeft of *Chry-*
' *foftom* But thou doft, as all thy companions do, bely
' ever without fhame both the fcriptures and the doctors.
' Didft thou not alfo fay, that by the canon law priefts

X x   ' may

' may be married' which is most untrue, and the con-
' trary is most true'

" I answered, we read in the decrees, that the four
" general councils, *Nicene*, *Constantinopolitan*, *Ephesine*,
" *Chalcedone*, have the same authority that the four evan-
" gelists have. And we read in the same decrees (which
" is one of the chief books of the canon law) that the
" council of *Nice*, by the means of one *Paphnutius*, did
" allow priests and bishops marriages   Therefore, by the
" best part of the canon law, priests may be married

" Then my lord chancellor said, ' thou falsifiest the
' general council, for there is express mention in the
' said decree, that priests should be divorced from their
' wives, which be married '

" Then said I, if those words be there, as you say,
" then am I content to lose this great head of mine.
" Let the book be fetched.

" Then spake my lord of *Durham*, ' though they be
' not there, yet they may be in *Ecclesiastica Historia*,
' which *Eusebius* wrote, out of which book the decree
' was taken '

" To that said I, it is not like that the pope would
" leave out any such sentence, having such authority,
" and making so much for his purpose

" Then my lord chancellor said, ' *Gratian* was but a
' patcher, and thou art glad to snatch up such a patch
' as maketh for thy purpose,'

" I answered, my lord, I cannot but marvel that you
" do call one of the chief papists that ever was, but a
" patcher

" Then my lord chancellor said, ' nay, I call thee a
' snatcher and patcher   To make an end, wilt thou not
' return again with us to the catholick church?'' And
with that he rose

" And I said, by God's grace I will never depart
" from *Christ*'s church.   Then I required that I might
" have some of my friends to come to me in prison
" And my lord chancellor said, thou shalt have judge-
" ment within this week, and so was I delivered again
" unto my keeper.   My lord of *Durham* would that I
" should believe as my father and my mother did   I
" alledged St. *Augustine*, that we ought to prefer God's
" word before all men "

On the last day of *January*, Dr *Taylor* was examined,
for the last time, before the bishops of *Winchester*, *London*,
Norwich, *Salisbury*, and *Durham*, who charged him with,
herefy

herefy and fchifm, requiring at the fame time a determinate anfwer, whether he would fubmit himfelf to the *Roman* bifhop, and abjure his errors, or elfe they would proceed according to their laws [*ex poft facto*, made fince his confinement] to his condemnation. Dr. *Taylor* anfwered, with a great deal of courage and ftedfaftnefs, that he would not depart from the truth which he had preached in king *Edward*'s days, neither would he fubmit himfelf to the *Romifh* antichrift, but thanked God, who had fo honored him, as to call him to fuffer for his word and truth's fake. When the bifhops faw him fo bold, conftant and immoveable, they read the fentence of death upon him, which when he had heard, he faid, with a remarkable degree of fortitude, " I doubt not, but that God, the " righteous judge, will require my blood at your hands, " and that the proudeft of you all fhall repent this re- " ceiving again of antichrift, and the tyranny you now " fhew againft the flock of *Chrift* "

He was remanded to prifon, and the keeper was charged to confine him clofer than ever. In his way back, the people crouded to fee him, to whom he faid, " God be " praifed, good people, I am come away from them " undefiled, and will, by God's grace, confirm the truth " with my blood "

After he had been condemned about a week, *Bonner*, bifhop of *London*, went to the prifon to perform upon him the ceremony of degradation, and becaufe the Dr refufed to put on the popifh veftments, the bifhop ordered thofe, who accompanied him, to put them on him by force, which done, he fet his hands on his fides, and walking up and down the room faid, " How fay you, " my lord, am I not a goodly fool? How fay you, my " mafters, if I were in *Cheapfide*, fhould I not have boys " enow to laugh at thefe apifh toys, and toying trum- " pery?" Upon which the bifhop fell to fcraping his fingers, and thumbs, and the crown of his head, and curfed him again and again. " Though you curfe me " (faid the doctor) God doth blefs me. I have the wit- " nefs of my confcience, that ye have done me wrong " and violence. Neverthelefs, I pray God, if it be his " will, to forgive you. But from the tyranny of the " bifhop of *Rome*, and his deteftable enormities, good " Lord deliver us."

After his degradation he was fent to the *King's Bench*, where he foon experienced (what at that time was remarkable) the difference between the keepers of the bifhop's

prifons,

prisons, and those of the king's, the former were wicked
and cruel, like their merciless masters, but the latter
were humane, and generally shewed all the favor in their
power. Therefore Dr *Taylor* obtained leave, through
the courtesy of his new keeper, to have his wife, his son
Thomas, and his servant *John Hull*, to sup with him the
evening before he suffered They came to him before
supper-time, when he prayed with them, beginning with
the litany After supper, walking up and down the room,
he gave God thanks for his grace, and for his effectual
calling, and that he had given him strength to abide by
his holy word And then turning to his son *Thomas*, he
thus addressed him ,

    " My dear son, (said he) almighty God bless thee, and
" give thee his Holy Spirit, to be a true servant of *Christ*,
" to learn his word, and constantly to stand by his truth
" all thy life long And, my son, see that thou fear
" God always Flee from all sin and wicked living Be
" virtuous, serve God with daily prayer, and apply thy
" book. In any wise see that thou be obedient to thy
" mother, love her and serve her Be ruled by her now
" in thy youth, and follow her good counsel in all things.
" Beware of lewd company, of young men that fear not
" God, but follow their lewd lusts and vain appetites
" Fly from whoredom, and hate all filthy living, remem-
" bering, that I thy father do die in the defence of holy
" marriage Another day, when God shall bless thee,
" love and cherish the poor people, and count that thy
" chief riches is, to be rich in alms And when thy
" mother is waxed old, forsake her not , but provide for
" her to thy power, and see that she lack nothing For
" so will God bless thee, and give thee long life upon
" earth and prosperity Which I pray God to grant
" thee "

    Then turning to his wife, " my dear wife, (said he)
" continue stedfast in the fear and love of God, keep
" yourself undefiled from their popish idolatries and su-
" perstitions. I have been unto you a faithful Yoke-
" fellow, and so have you been unto me , for the which
" I pray God to reward you, and doubt not, dear wife,
" but God will reward it.

    " Now the time is come that I shall be taken from
" you, and you discharged of the wedlock-bond towards
" me, therefore I will give you my counsel what I think
" most expedient for you You are yet a child-bearing
" woman, and therefore it will be most convenient for

                                                         " you

" you to marry For doubtless you shall never be at a
" convenient stay for yourself and our poor children, nor
" out of trouble till you be married, therefore, as soon
" as God will provide it, marry with some honest faith-
" ful man that feareth God, Doubt you not, God will
" provide an honest husband for you, and he will be a
" merciful father to you and to my children Whom I
" pray you to bring up in the fear of God, and in learn-
" ing, to the uttermost of your power, and keep them
" from this *Romish* idolatry "

Having thus finished his last, parting advice, with the
utmost tenderness and affection, they prayed together,
embraced, and wept over each other, in a very affecting
manner He then gave his wife a book of *Common Prayer*
published by king *Edward*, which he had taken with him
to prison and occasionally used And to his son *Thomas*
he gave a *Latin* book of remarkable sayings of the antient
martyrs, gathered out of ecclesiastical authors, and in
the end of it wrote his last will And so they took their
leave of him.

The next morning, at two o'clock, came the sheriff
and his officers, and led the doctor away to the sign of
the *Woolpack*, without *Aldgate*. His wife, suspecting that
in the night they would take him away somewhere or
other, had watched all night in St *Botolph's* church-porch
beside *Aldgate*, with two children, one called *Elizabeth*,
thirteen years of age, an orphan that they had brought
up as their own from three years old, the other *Mary*,
their own daughter When the sheriff with his prisoner
came opposite the church, *Elizabeth* cried, ' O my dear
' father, mother, mother, here is my dear father led away.'
Then cried Mrs *Taylor*, ' *Rowland*, *Rowland*, where art
' thou ?' [for it was very dark, being in the month of
February] Dr *Taylor* answered, " Dear wife, I am here,"
and stood The sheriff's men were for making him go
on, but the sheriff said, ' stay a little, and let him speak
' to his wife ' He then took up his little daughter *Mary*
in his arms, and kneeled down with his wife and *Elizabeth*, and prayed, saying the Lord's Prayer, &c which
was so affecting a scene, that the sheriff and his officers
melted into tears.

When they rose up from prayer, the doctor kissed his
wife, and shook her by the hand, saying, " farewel, my
" dear wife, be of good comfort; for I am quiet in my
" conscience —God will raise up a father for my chil-
" dren " He then kissed his daughter *Mary*, and said,
" God

" God blefs thee and make thee his fervant " And kifs-
ing *Elizabeth*, he faid, " God blefs thee   I pray you all
" ftand ftrong and ftedfaft unto *Chrift* and his word, and
" keep you from idolatry "   Then faid his wife, ' God
' be with thee, dear *Rowland*, I will, with God's help,
' meet thee at *Hadley*,'   But fhe following them to the
inn, and the fheriff, feeing her there, ordered her to be
taken away and confined, till he returned from the execution   So that fhe faw not her fuffering hufband, nor
he her, any more in this vale of tears

The doctor was put into a chamber, with a guard of
four men, where he gave himfelf wholly to prayer, till
eleven o'clock, when they put him on horfeback in the
inn yard, and then opened the gates and led him forth.
At the gates ftood waiting his trufty fervant *John Hull*,
with his fon *Thomas*, whom, when the doctor faw, he
faid, " come hither, my fon *Thomas*," and fetting the
child before him on his horfe, and taking off his hat, he
faid to the numerous fpectators, " Good people, this is
" my own fon, begotten of my body in lawful matri-
" mony, and God be bleffed for lawful matrimony "
He then lifted up his eyes to heaven and prayed for his
fon, and bleffed him, and delivered him to *John Hull*,
whom he took by the hand and faid, " Farewel *John*
" *Hull*, the faithfulleft fervant that ever man had "

At *Burntwood*, by the way, they ftopped and had a clofe
hood made for him, with holes for his eyes and one for
his mouth   This was done to him and many others,
becaufe it was underftood that the meeknefs, patience and
fortitude, which appeared in their countenances, tended
very much to ftrengthen the proteftants in the faith of
God's word, and to increafe their abhorience of the cruelties of popery

Notwithftanding this kind of treatment, the doctor was
exceeding chearful on the road, more like one going to a
marriage-fupper, than one going to be burnt alive   He
exhorted the fheriff and his men to repent and forfake
their wicked courfes of life in fo earneft and pathetic a
manner, that they frequently wept   In the evening they
were met by the fheriff of *Suffolk*, at *Chelmsford*, where
they all fupped together   After fupper, the fheriff of
Effex, fuppofing he could perfuade Dr. *Taylor* by fair
words to abjure, thus addreffed him

' Good mafter doctor, we are right forry for you, con-
' fidering what the lofs is of fuch a perfon as you are,
' and might be, if you would. God hath given you great
                                                              ' learning

'learning and wisdom, wherefore you have been in great
'favour and reputation in times past with the council,
'and people of the highest rank, in this realm. Besides
'this, you are a man of goodly personage, in your best
'strength, and by nature like to live many years, and
'without doubt, you would, in time to come, be in as
'good reputation as ever you was, or rather better. For
'you are well-beloved of all men, as well for your vir-
'tues as for your learning, and methinks it were great
'pity you should cast away yourself willingly, and so
'come to such a painful and shameful death. You would
'do much better to revoke your opinions, and return to
'the catholic universal church of *Rome*, acknowledge the
'pope to be head of the church, and reconcile yourself
'to him. You may do well yet, if you will. Nor need
'you doubt, but you will find favour at the queen's
'hands, and I and all these your friends will be suitors
'for your pardon. This counsel I give you good master
'doctor, of a good heart, and a good will towards you,
'and thereupon I drink to you '—' Upon that condition
'(said the others) we will all drink to you '

When it came to the doctor's turn to drink, he took
the cup, and, after pausing a little, he said, " Master
" sheriff, and my masters all, I heartily thank you for
" your good will, I have hearkened to your words, and
" marked well your counsels. And to be plain with you,
" I do perceive, that I have been deceived myself, and
" am like to deceive a great many at *Hadley* of their ex-
" pectation " The sheriff, hoping these words referred,
to a recantation, said, ' God's blessing be on your heart,
' that is the most comfortable word we have heard you
' speak yet—but pray explain yourself.' The doctor did
so, by saying, " I am a man of a very great carcase,
" which, I hoped, would have been buried in *Hadley*
" church-yard, but I see, I am deceived. And there is
" a great number of worms there, which should have
" had jolly feeding upon this carrion. But now both I
" and they shall be deceived of our expectation, for this
" carcase shall be burnt to ashes." The sheriff was astonished at such an instance of fortitude in the approach of
so shocking a death.

The sheriff of *Suffolk* stopped two days at *Lanham*, and
was met by the magistrates and principal gentlemen of
the county, who all labored to bring Dr *Taylor* over to
the *Romish* religion, promising him great promotion, even
a bishopric, if he would accept of it. But he had not *so*

learned

learned *Chriſt* Within two miles of *Hadley*, he deſired
to alight, and being accordingly permitted, he fetched a
leap or two, as men do in dancing, which was obſerved
by the ſheriff, who ſaid, ' Well, maſter doctor, how do
' you do now ?' " Very well, never better"—and added,
" God be praiſed, I am now almoſt at home, and have
" not more than two ſtiles to go over, before I am at my
" father's houſe" Being told he ſhould go through
Hadley, he ſaid, " O good Lord, I thank thee, I ſhall
" yet once, e'er I die, ſee my flock, whom, thou Lord
" knoweſt, I have moſt heartily loved, and truly taught
" Good Lord, bleſs them, and keep them ſtedfaſt in thy
" word and truth !"

The ſtreets of *Hadley* were lined with men and women,
both of the town and from the country round about,
weeping, and lamenting their loſs, and praying to God
to ſtrengthen and comfort him in the trying hour, to
whom he frequently ſaid, is he rode along, " I have
" preached to you God's word and truth, and am come
" this day to ſeal it with my blood" Paſſing the alms-
houſes, where he was well-known, he diſtributed what
little money he had left, taking his leave of them, with
his prayers to God for them

When he was come to *Aldham-common*, the place where
he was to ſuffer, he ſaid, " thanked be God, I am even
" at home," and alighting from his horſe, with both
hands rent the hood from his head, when it appeared that
he, who, with the utmoſt propriety, is called BLOODY
Bonner, when he degraded Dr *Taylor*, had with feminine
envy endeavored to disfigure him by clipping off in places
his fine hair, and by tying other parts of it into knots,
which notwithſtanding when the people ſaw again his
venerable countenance with his long white beard, they
burſt out into tears and prayers, that God, for *Chriſt's*
ſake, would ſtrengthen, help, and comfort him. He then
attempted to ſpeak to the people, but as ſoon as he opened
his mouth, immediately one or other thruſt a tipſtaff into
it He aſked leave of the ſheriff, but he denied him,
bidding him remember his promiſe. " Well, ſaid the
" doctor, promiſe muſt be kept*" He then put off his
cloaths to his ſhirt, and gave them away, and with a
loud voice cried out, " Good people, I have taught you
" nothing but God's holy word, and thoſe leſſons that I

---

* The promiſe was ſuppoſed to be given in conſequence of a threat
to cut out his tongue, if he attempted to ſpeak.

" have

" have taken out of God's blessed book, the holy bible "
With that, *Holmes*, one of the guard, who had behaved
the most cruelly to the doctor all the way down, gave
him a severe blow on the head with a waster, [or bludgeon], and said, ' Is this the keeping thy promise, thou
' heretic ?'

He then saw, that they would not allow him to speak;
and therefore he kneeled down and prayed Rising from
prayer, he went to the stake and kissed it, and stood in
a pitch-barrel, set for that purpose, with his back upright
against the stake, with his hands clasped together, and
his eyes lifted up to heaven, and so continued praying
One of the men, employed to make the fire, threw a figgot at him, which so wounded him that the blood ran
down his face To whom the doctor said, " Friend, I
" have harm enough What need of that ?" Another,
hearing him say the Psalm *Miserere*, in *English*, struck
him on the mouth, saying, ' Knave, speak *Latin*, or I
' will make thee ' The fire being kindled, he continued
in the same posture, without moving at all, praying unto
God, and saying, " Merciful Father of heaven, for *Jesus*
" *Christ* my Saviour's sake, receive my soul into thy
" hands !" At last, one with a halbert struck out his
brains, and his body fell into the fire. Thus did this
gracious man render his soul into the hands of his merciful God and Saviour, whom he most dearly loved, faithfully and zealously preached, obediently followed in his
life, and constantly glorified in his death

The last will and testament of doctor *Rowland Taylor*,
parson of *Hadley*

" I Say to my wife, and to my children, the Lord gave
"   you unto me, and the Lord hath taken me from you,
" and you from me Blessed be the name of the Lord.
" I believe that they are blessed which die in the Lord.
" God careth for sparrows, and for the hairs of our heads.
" I have ever found him more faithful and favourable,
" than is any father or husband Trust ye therefore in
" him by the means of our dear Saviour *Christ's* merits ·
" Believe, love, fear, and obey him Pray to him, for he
" hath promised to help Count me not dead, for I shall
" certainly live, and never die I go before, and you
" shall follow after, to our long home I go to the rest
" of my children, *Susan, George, Ellen, Robert* and *Zachary*. I have bequeathed you to the only Omnipo-
" tent.

Y y   " I

" I say to my dear friends of *Hadley*, and to all others
" which have heard me preach, that I depart hence with
" a quiet conscience, as touching my doctrine, for the
" which I pray you think God with me For I have,
" after my little talent, declared to others those lessons
" that I gathered out of God's book, the blessed bible
" Therefore if I or an angel from heaven should preach
" to you any other gospel than that ye have received,
" God's great curse upon that preacher

" Beware for God's sake that ye deny not God, neither
" decline from the word of faith, left God decline from
" you, and so ye do everlastingly perish. For God's sake
" beware of popery, for though it appear to have in it
" unity, yet the same is vanity and antichristianity, and
" not in *Christ*'s faith and verity

" Beware of the sin against the Holy Ghost, now after
" such a light opened so plainly and simply, truly, tho-
" roughly and generally to all *England*

" The Lord grant all men his good and holy Spirit,
" increase of his wisdom, contemning the wicked world,
" hearty desire to be with God and the heavenly company,
" through *Jesus Christ*, our only mediator, advocate,
" righteousness, life, sanctification, and hope Amen,
" Amen Pray, pray "

ROBERT FERRAR,

BISHOP OF St. DAVID's

WE cannot omit, in these memoirs of illustrious
champions for the truth, some account of this
great and good man, though history furnishes us with
but little more of him, than the circumstances which occasioned, or immediately preceded, his death

Mr *Ferrar* received his education at *Oxford*, and was
a canon regular of St *Mary's*, in that university He
also proceeded to the degree of batchelor in divinity.

It appears, that the great duke of *Somerset*, lord protector in the reign of *Edward* the sixth, and friend to the
Reformation, was the patron of Mr. *Ferrar*, and thought
him a proper instrument to assist in carrying on that im-
                                                    portant

potent work Accordingly, he procured for him the bifhopric of St *David*'s, in *Wales*, to which he was confecrated on the ninth of *September*, 1547, where his zeal foon procured him many enemies among the papifts and their adherents. And his patron foon after falling by the defigns of an oppofite party, thefe people gave him a great deal of trouble, and artfully and villainoufly (by means of two ungrateful officers of his own fee) procured an attachment againft him, by which, fome time before the king's death, he was committed to prifon under a debt, pretended to be due from his bifhopric to the crown

It may eafily be fuppofed, that *fuch* a man could not expect a releafe in *fuch* a reign, as immediately followed On the contrary, inftead of the pretence of a *præmunire*, with which he had been before charged by thofe, who wifhed to difplace him from his bifhopric, he was now attacked upon the fcore of herefy by others, who hunted for his life

On the fourth of *February*, 1555, he was brought, in the company of bifhop *Hooper*, Mr *Bradford*, Mr *Rogers*, Mr *Saunders*, and others, before that zealous perfecutor, *Gardiner*, bifhop of *Winchefter* and lord chancellor, who, according to his cuftom, treated him and them with great afperity and very ill manners He frequently taunted at this venerable man, though of his own rank and order in the church, and defcended to fuch grofs vulgarities, as to call him by the names of—*froward-fellow*—*falfe-knave*—*froward-knave*, &c—terms, more fcandalous to thofe who ufe them, than to thofe, to whom they are given. He alfo threatened to make *fhort work with him*, and, in this cafe, he was as good as his word, for the fuffering bifhop was hurried away to death, with very little formality or examination

Under the liberty, both civil and religious, which we now enjoy, it may feem furprizing, that men were fuffered to be condemned fo arbitrarily and uniformally, as we find them, in particular, throughout the fhort and bloody reign of queen *Mary*. But religious bigotry fwallowed up all other confiderations, and the powers of the crown were not fo bounded and curtailed, as they have been in fucceeding reigns The general liberties of the fubject were far lefs underftood than they are at prefent, and the fhackles of ecclefiaftical tyranny were not thoroughly broken The *abufe* of power led (as it always leads) to the due examination of its *foundation* And men never fuffer extremities, but they fet their wits, at leaft, to work for the difcovery of fome relief. Thus, the fevere perfecution by the papifts tended much more to the deftruction of popery, than to the demolition of tn proteftant doctrine. Where brutal force is thought neceffary, there muft be a very low apprehenfion of the exiftence and power of truth.

To complete their enormous proceedings, Gardner and his colleagues fent this worthy bifhop down to his diocefe, in order to be condemned—and can it be read without furprize?—by his *fucceffor*, whofe *intereft* it was to condemn him. This new bifhop's name was *Morgan*, and he feconded his friend's ideas of making *fhort work* with *Ferrar*, by all the diligence in his power. He condemned him, after two or thrice fhort examinations (for the fake of a plaufible pretence) upon the articles—" of allowing " the marriage of priefts—of denying *Chrift's* corporal " prefence in the facrament—of affirming, that the mafs " is not a facrifice propitiatory for the quick and dead— " of declaring, that the hoft ought not to be elevated or " adored—and, of afferting, that man is juftified by faith " alone", all which *Morgan* pronounced to be damnable errors, herefies, and falfe opinions. He next degraded him from his ecclefiaftical functions, and then delivered him to the fecular power, the fcandalous tool of their abominable malice and perfecution.

The fecular power, ready to follow the fpiritual direction of the popifh authority, foon brought this martyr forth, as a lamb to the flaughter. He was burned, on the fouth-fide of the market-crofs at *Carmarthen*, on *Saturday* the thirtieth of *March*, in the year 1555.

A little before this good bifhop fuffered, a Mr *Richard Jones*, a young gentleman of family in the country, lamented to him the feverity and painfulnefs of the kind of death, which he was to undergo. The bifhop, with all the firmnefs which was celebrated in the primitive martyrs of the church, immediately anfwered in thefe words, " If " you fee me once to ftir, while I fuffer the pains of burn- " ing, then give no credit to the truth of thofe doctrines, " for which I die."—Undoubtedly, it was by the grace and fupport of God, he was enabled to make good this affertion, ' for (fays Mr *Fox*) fo patiently he ftood, that ' he never moved, but even as he ftood holding up his ' ftumps, fo ftill he continued, till one *Richard Gravell*, ' with a ftaff, dafhed him upon the head, and fo ftruck ' him down.'

Bifhop

Bishop *Ferrar* was one of the committee (according to bishop *Burnet*) nominated to compile the *English* liturgy* He also signed the brief *confession of faith*, in conjunction with other protestant bishops and martyrs imprisoned in *London*, which is composed in the following words

' First, We confess and believe all the canonical books ' of the Old Testament, and all the books of the New ' Testament, to be the very true word of God, and to ' be written by the inspiration of the Holy Ghost, and ' are therefore to be heard accordingly, as the judge in ' all controversies and matters of religion

' Secondly, We confess and believe, that the catholic ' church, which is the spouse of *Christ*, as a most obedient ' and loving wife, doth embrace and follow the doctrine ' of these books in all matters of religion, and therefore ' is she to be heard accordingly So that those who will ' not hear this church, thus following and obeying the ' word of her husband, we account as heretics and schis- ' matics, according to this saying, *If he will not hear the* ' *church, let him be unto thee as a heathen*

' Thirdly, We believe and confess all the articles of ' faith and doctrine set forth in the symbol of the apostles, ' which we commonly call the creed, and in the symbols ' of the council of *Nice*, kept A D 432, of *Constantinople*, ' A D. 384, of *Ephesus*, kept A. D. 432, of *Chalcedon*, ' kept A D 454, of *Toletum*, the first and fourth Also ' in the symbols of *Athanasius*, *Irenæus*, *Tertullian*, and of ' *Damasus*, which was about the year of our Lord 376 ' We confess and believe (we say) the doctrine of the

---

* Probably the *correction* of the liturgy in the time of *Henry* the Eighth, about the year 1540 For as to the composition of a *new* liturgy, in 1547, in the first year of *Edward* the Sixth, the committee appointed were, 1 *Thomas Cranmer*, archbishop of *Canterbury*, 2 *Thomas Goodrich*, bishop of *Ely*, 3 *Henry Holbech*, bishop of *Lincoln*, 4 *George Day*, bishop of *Chichester*, 5. *John Skip*, bishop of *Hereford*, 6 *Thomas Thirlby*, bishop of *Westminster*, 7 *Nicholas Ridley*, bishop of *Rochester*, 8 Dr *William May*, dean of St *Paul's*, 9. Dr *John Taylor*, dean of *Lincoln*, 10. Dr *Simon Haynes*, dean of *Exeter*, 11 Dr *John Redmayne*, master of *Trinity College, Cambridge*; 12 Dr *Richard Cox*, dean of *Christchurch, Oxon*, 13 Mr *Thomas Robertson*, archdeacon of *Leicester* This liturgy was revised in the first year of Q *Elizabeth*, by 1 Dr *Matthew Parker*, afterwards archbishop of *Canterbury*, 2 Dr *Richard Cox*, afterwards bishop of *Ely*, 3 Dr *May*, 4 Dr *Bill*, 5 *James Pilkington*, afterwards bishop of *Durham*, 6 Sir *Thomas Smith*, 7 Mr *David Whitevead*, 8 Mr *Edmund Grindall*, afterwards bishop of *London*, and then archbishop of *Canterbury*, 9 Dr *Edwin Sandys*, bishop of *Worcester*, 10 and the learned *Edward Guest*, afterwards a bishop See *Whately*'s Illustration of the Common Prayer, p 25 4th edit

' symbols

' symbols, generally, and particularly, so that whosoever
' doth otherwise, we hold the same to err from the truth

' Fourthly, We believe and confess, concerning justi-
' fication, that as it cometh only from God's mercy
' through *Christ*, so it is perceived and had of none, who
' be of years of discretion, otherwise than by faith only
' Which faith is not an opinion, but a certain persuasion
' wrought by the Holy Ghost in the mind and heart of
' man, where through, as the mind is illuminated, so the
' heart is suppled to submit itself to the will of God un-
' feignedly, and so sheweth forth an *inherent* righteous-
' ness, which is to be discerned in the article of justifi-
' cation from the righteousness which God endueth us
' withal in justifying us, although inseparably they go
' together And this we do, not for curiosity, or con-
' tention sake, but for conscience sake, that it might be
' quiet, which it can never be, if we confound, without
' distinction, forgiveness of sin and *Christ's* justice im-
' puted to us, with regeneration and inherent righteous-
' ness. By this, we disallow the papistical doctrine of
' free-will, of works of supererogation, of merits, of the
' necessity of auricular confession, and satisfaction to
' God-ward

' Fifthly, We confess and believe, concerning the
' exterior service of God, that it ought to be according
' to the word of God And therefore in the congrega-
' tion all things public ought to be done in such tongue
' as may be most to edify And not in *Latin*, where the
' people understand not the same

' Sixthly, We confess and believe, that God only,
' through *Jesus Christ*, is to be prayed unto and called
' upon And therefore we disallow invocation or prayer
' to saints departed this life

' Seventhly, We confess and believe, that as a man
' departeth this life, so shall he be judged in the last day
' generally, and in the mean season is entered, either into
' the state of the blessed for ever, or damned for ever
' And therefore is either past all help, or else needeth no
' help of any in this life By reason whereof we affirm
' purgatory, masses of *Scala Cœli*, trentals, and such suf-
' frages, as the popish church doth obtrude as necessary,
' to be the doctrine of antichrist

' Eighthly, We confess and believe the sacraments of
' *Christ*, which be Baptism and the Lord's Supper, that
' they ought to be ministered according to the institution
' of *Christ*, concerning the substantial parts of them.

' And

' And that they be no longer facraments than they be
' held in ufe, and ufed to the end for which they were
' inftituted

' And here we plainly confefs, that the mutilation of
' the Lord's Supper, the fubtraction of one kind from the
' lay people, is antichriftian And fo is the doctrine of
' tranfubftantiation of the facramental bread and wine
' after the words of confecration, as they be called. Item,
' the adoration of the facrament with the honour due unto
' God, the refervation and carrying about of the fame
' Item, the mafs to be a propitiatory facrifice for the quick
' and dead, or a work that pleafeth God All thefe we
' confefs and believe to be antichrift's doctrine As is
' the inhibition of marriage, as unlawful, to any ftate

' And we doubt not, by God's grace, but we fhall be
' able to prove all our confeffion here, to be moft true by
' the verity of God's word, and confent of the catholic
' church, which followeth, and hath followed the go-
' vernance of God's Spirit, and the judgement of his
' word And this through the Lord's help we will do,
' either in difputation by word before the queen's high-
' nefs and her council, either before the parliament
' houfes (of whom we doubt not to be indifferently
' heard), either with our pens, whenfoever we fhall be
' thereto, by them that have authority, required and
' commanded.

' In the mean feafon, as obedient fubjects, we fhall
' behave ourfelves toward all that be in authority, and
' not ceafe to pray to God for them, that he would go-
' vern them all, generally and particularly, with the
' fpirit of wifdom and grace And fo we heartily defire,
' and humbly pray all men to do, in no point confenting
' to any rebellion or fedition againft our fovereign lady
' the queen's highnefs But, where they cannot obey,
' but they muft difobey God, there to fubmit themfelves
' with all patience and humility, to fuffer as the will and
' pleafure of the higher powers fhall adjudge The Lord
' of mercy endue us all with the fpirit of his truth, and
' grace of perfeverance therein unto the end Amen '

This remarkable confeffion was dated the eighth day of
May, in the year 1554, and fubfcribed by
ROBERT FERRAR, late bifhop of St. *David*'s
ROWLAND TAYLOR, JOHN PHILPOT,
JOHN BRADFORD, LAURENCE SAUNDERS,
JOHN HOOPER, late bifhop of *Worcefter* and *Gloucefter*.
EDWARD CROME, JOHN ROGERS,
EDMUND LAWRENCE And J P.—T M.

1

To which was annexed the following declaration ·

' To thefe things aboveſaid, do I, *Miles Coverdale*,
' late biſhop of *Exeter*, conſent and agree with theſe mine
' afflicted brethren, being priſoners. Mine own hand.

M C

JOHN BRADFORD.

DIVINE grace works in the ſouls of the faithful,
and particularly of faithful miniſters, a great variety of gifts and qualifications, ſuited to the work and
buſineſs in the world, which they are appointed to fulfil.
Though, perhaps, it gives no new faculty to the animal
nature, yet it certainly corrects and improves whatever
is bad in it, according to the meaſure of the heavenly gift
And if it does not abſolutely deſtroy perverſe diſpoſitions
and wrong habits, it keeps them down and will not ſuffer them to triumph and prevail Some have boldneſs
of natural ſpirit, as *Luther* had, which will appear even
in the life of grace, and carry the man the more ſtrenu-
ouſly onward in what he conceives to be his duty Others
have a ſoftneſs and meekneſs of heart, which ſeem more
calculated to conciliate friends and build up profeſſors in
the faith, than to war againſt the powers of darkneſs or
attack the ſtrong holds of error Both have their uſe,
under the divine agency, and God makes uſe of both to
accompliſh his deſigns of ſalvation towards his people
Of this laſt character was the ſubject of the preſent
memoir For the kindneſs and benevolence of his ſpirit,
and for the circumſpect purity of his life, he obtained the
name of *Holy John Bradford* His worſt enemies could
object nothing to his life and converſation, and they were
obliged to give almoſt as poor an account of their fury
againſt him, as the *Jews* had given before againſt his Saviour, *That they had a law, and by their law he ought to die.*
They had indeed a *power*, but as to law, or the right uſe
of that power, in ſlaying men like *Bradford*, we muſt
examine ordinances very different from the word and will
of God,

BRADFORD

From an original Painting in the Possession of W. Blyth

John Bradford was born at *Manchester*, in *Lancashire*
His parents brought him up in learning from his infancy,
and when he had attained to good knowledge in the *Latin*
tongue, being apt and ready at his pen, he became fit for
such business as might procure him an honest livelihood
He soon afterwards was employed by Sir *John Harring-
ton*, knight, who was treasurer to the king's camps and
buildings, in the reigns of king *Henry* VIII and *Edward*
VI Sir *John* had such early proofs of the dexterity and
faithfulness of *Bradford*, both at home and abroad, that
he trusted him with the management of the most weighty
affairs, and owned they were better done than he could
have transacted them himself

Mr *Bradford* continued in this situation for several
years, in which he prospered, and gave such general satisfaction, that he was in the way to get an estate easily
and honestly But God set his heart upon the things of
another world, and he had no sooner tasted that the Lord
was gracious, than he was for publishing the gospel-sal-
vation to all people And therefore after he had given a
just and clear account to his master of all he was intrusted
with, he forsook all worldly affairs and the fair prospect
of getting riches, and went from the *Temple*, in *London*,
(where he had begun the study of the law) to the university of *Cambridge*, to meditate upon the word of God, and
to study divinity, where he made such an uncommon
progress in learning, and so pleased all by his godly and
blameless conversation, that in less than a year the university thought proper to confer the degree of master of
arts upon him

Immediately after, the master and fellows of *Pembroke-
hall* chose him to a fellowship in their college And, that
great and good man *Martin Bucer* so highly valued him,
that he used many persuasions with him to preach, but
Mr *Bradford* for some time declined it, saying, that he
had not learning enough. To which *Bucer* replied, ' If
' you have not fine manchet-bread, yet give the poor
' people barley-bread, or such as thou hast ' And while
Mr *Bradford* was thus persuaded to enter into the ministry, Dr *Ridley*, bishop of *London*, made him a prebend
of St. *Paul*'s He continued three years preaching in a
most pathetic and godly manner, in reproving sin sharply,
yet sweetly preaching *Christ* crucified, and defending the
truth against errors and heresies And even after queen
Mary came to the crown, he still went on preaching as

before,

before, till thofe in power unjuftly perfecuted him, and fent him prifoner to the tower of *London*

On *Sunday*, the thirteenth of *Auguft*, in the firft year of queen *Mary*'s reign, Dr *Bourne*, then bifhop of *Bath* and *Wells*, made a fermon at *Paul's-crofs*, in which he railed againft pious king *Edward*, then deceafed, and fo reviled the Reformation and Reformers, that the common people began to lofe their patience, and from a great murmuring there arofe a greater uproar among the multitude, in fo much that the lord mayor and all his officers could not filence the tumult, which was fo enraged, that one of the people threw a dagger at the preacher's head, which narrowly miffed him, and, we are told, that the mob would certainly have torn him in pieces, had not this Mr *Bradford*, who then fat behind him, ftood up at the earneft intreaty of Dr *Bourne* himfelf, to appeafe the people And the people heard him gladly, while *Bourne* was glad to fit down, and hide his head to fave his life. Mr *Bradford* preached fo long upon peace and quietnefs, that the multitude became quiet, and when the fermon was ended, they went peaceably away Yet, notwithftanding the mob was greatly difperfed, Dr. *Bourne* was ftill afraid to fhew his head, till Mr. *Bradford*, and Mr. *Rogers*, vicar of St *Sepulchre*'s, undertook to conduct him, at the hazard of their own lives, to the grammarfchool, which was hard by, which they did by fcreening him with their gowns For which charity they were foon afterwards rewarded by popifh gratitude, with fire and faggot

Among the company at St. *Paul's-crofs* at that time, there was one who faid thefe words, ' Ah, *Bradford*, ' *Bradford*, thou faveft him that will burn thee, I give ' thee his life If it were not for thee, I would, I affure ' thee, have run him through with my fword ' The fame day in the afternoon, Mr. *Bradford* preached at *Bow-church* in *Cheapfide*, and fharply reproved the people for their feditious behaviour

Yet, notwithftanding this benevolent conduct, about three days after, he was fent to the tower of *London*, where the queen then refided, and was ordered to appear before the council. He was charged with fedition at *Paul's-crofs*, though he had been the means of faving *Bourne*, and alfo for preaching. He was firft committed to the *Tower* as aforefaid, and was afterwards harraffed about almoft two years, from prifon to prifon, till the

flames

times deprived him of his body, and dismissed his soul to heaven.

Mr *Bradford* was sent from the *Tower* to the *King's-Bench* in *Southwark* And after his condemnation he was sent to the *Poultry-Compter* in *London* And while he remained in each of these two last places he preached twice a day, unless prevented by sickness In the same places, he would often celebrate the Lord's Supper, and the keepers were so kind as to permit many people to come both to the sermon and the sacrament, so that his chamber was on these occasions commonly filled with serious Christians Preaching, reading, and praying, was the chief business of his whole life. He did not eat more than one meal a-day, and that a sparing one, and his continual study was upon his knees In the midst of his dinner he was wont to meditate with his hat over his eyes, from whence would often shed abundance of tears Very gentle he was both to man and child, and in so good credit with his keeper, that he had liberty to go abroad any evening without any guard, on his promise that he would return again the same night; which he always punctually did, and rather before than after the hour appointed

He was of person somewhat tall and slender, spare of body, of a faint sanguine color, with a dark-brown beard He would seldom sleep above four hours in the night He would never waste his time in any sort of gaming, but his chief recreation was in Christian conversation with his family, wherein he usually spent some time after dinner at his table, and then to prayer and his book again He accounted that time lost which was not spent in doing good, either with his pen, study, or in exhorting of others, &c. He was no niggard of his purse, but would liberally communicate a part of what he had to his fellow-prisoners. And commonly once a week he visited the thieves, pick-pockets, and such others as were with him in prison, to whom he would give pious exhortations, and afterwards distribute money among them for their subsistence.

While he was in the *King's-Bench*, and Mr *Laurence Saunders* in the *Marshalsea*, both prisoners, and afterwards martyrs, on the back-side of these two prisons they met many times, and conferred together as often as they would And Mr *Bradford* was so trusted by his keeper, and had such liberty in the back-side of the prison, that any day he might eafily have efcaped if he would, but the Lord had another work for him to do

One of his old friends once came to him in prifon, and faid, 'Suppofe I fhould make interceffion for you, ' and get you out of prifon, what would you do, or whi- ' ther would you go?' To which he anfwered, as though he did not care whether he had his liberty or no But being further preffed to know what he would do, if fuch a thing fhould be brought about, he then faid that he would marry, and ftill abide in *England*, teaching the people fecretly, till the Lord's providence fhould fo order it, that he fhould do it in a more public manner.

He was fo well refpected by all good men, that many, who knew no more of him than the report only, much lamented his death Yea, and great numbers of the papifts themfelves alfo heartily wifhed, that he might have been fpared Bifhop *Ridley* fpoke of him in thefe terms, 'In my confcience, fays he, I judge Mr. *Brad-* ' *ford* more worthy to be a bifhop, than many of us, who ' are bifhops already, to be parifh-priefts,'—This cha- racter was given of him by *Ridley* in the days of king *Ed-ward*, upon recommending him to preferment.

The Lord was pleafed fo to blefs his company to others, that there were but few to be found in the prifons where he had been, who had not received fome advantage from his pious converfation A fingular and eminent inftance of which here follows Bifhop *Ferrar* being prifoner in the *King's-Bench*, was prevailed upon by the papifts to receive the facrament in one kind. But, by the providence of God, Mr *Bradford* was brought to the fame prifon the very day before he was to have done it; and he was made inftrumental in faving the good bifhop from fuch a bafe and unworthy action

The night before he was removed to *Newgate*, he was fomewhat difturbed in his fleep, by dreaming, that the chain for his burning was brought to the *Compter-gate*, that the next day he muft go to *Newgate*, and, that the day after he was to be burnt in *Smithfield*. Which came to pafs accordingly.

One afternoon, as he and his bedfellow were walking together in the keeper's chamber, the keeper's wife came up in much grief, and faid, 'Oh Mr. *Bradford*, I come ' to bring you heavy news!' "What is that?" faid he, ' Indeed, quoth fhe, to-morrow you are to be burned. ' Your chain is now preparing And you muft prefently

' go

' go to *Newgate*.' On this Mr *Bradford* put off his cap, and lifting up his eyes to heaven, said, " I thank God " for it, I have looked for this a long time, and there- " fore it cometh not unexpectedly, but as a thing waited " for daily and hourly, the Lord make me worthy of " it !" And, after thanking her for her good-will, he repaired to his chamber, and prayed in secret for a long time, which when he had done, he came to his friend, and took several writings and papers, and told him what he would have to be done with them, and having thus settled his affairs in the afternoon, at night half-a-dozen of his friends came to see him, with whom he spent all the evening in prayer, and devout exercises

A little before he went out of the *Compter*, he prayed very affectionately, which produced a number of tears, and greatly affected the hearts of the hearers And when he stripped himself to his shirt, in which he was to suffer, he made another excellent prayer upon the wedding-garment When he went out of the chamber, he prayed again, and gave money to every servant and officer in the house, exhorting them all to serve and fear the Lord. And the prisoners, to all of whom he had been profitable in one shape or other, were in tears on their parting with him

About eleven or twelve o'clock in the night, when they thought no body would be stirring, the officers carried him to *Newgate*, but, contrary to their expectations, the streets between the *Compter* and *Newgate* were crouded with people, who waited to see him, and bid him farewel with prayers and many tears, and he took his leave of them in the same affectionate manner, praying that the Lord would bless them and keep them in his truth

Whether it was a command from the queen and her council, or from *Bonner* and his adherents, or whether it was devised by the lord mayor, aldermen, and sheriffs of *London*, or not, there was a strong rumour all over the city the night before, that Mr *Bradford* was to be burnt the next morning at four o'clock in *Smithfield* There were different opinions about this report Some thought that it was for fear of a tumult, others conjectured, that the papists were afraid that his behaviour would so work upon the minds of the people, as to do their cause much damage However the true cause of this contrivance never came to light.

At four o'clock in the morning *Smithfield* was full of people, though Mr. *Bradford* was not brought thither

before

before nine. Going through *Newgate*, he espied an old friend, to whom he called, and gave him his velvet-cap, an handkerchief, &c. And when he departed, one Mr *Roger Beswick*, brother-in-law to Mr *Bradford*, came up and shook him by the hand, for which Mr *Woodrooffe* the sheriff, like a rough rude man, broke Mr. *Beswick's* head, so that the blood flew about, and as they could not change many words together, Mr. *Bradford* took his leave of him, desiring to be recommended to his mother and his friends, and advised him to go directly to a surgeon.

He was taken into *Smithfield* with a strong guard of armed men When he came to the place, where he was to suffer, he fell on his face and prayed. After which he took a faggot and kissed it, and the stake likewise. Then having put off his clothes, he stood by the stake, and lifting up his eyes and hands towards heaven, said, " O " *England, England*, repent of thy sins, repent of thy " sins, beware of idolatry Beware of antichrists, take " heed they do not deceive thee!" Then he turned his face to *John Leaf*, a young man about twenty years old, who suffered with him, and said, " Be of good comfort, " brother, for we shall sup with the Lord this night " He then embraced the reeds, and said, " Strait is the " gate, and narrow is the way, that leadeth to life eter- " nal, and few there be that find it." After which he was fastened to the stake and burnt, on the first of *July*, in the year of our Lord 1555. He ended his life like a lamb, without the least alteration of countenance, and in the prime of his days.

We shall now give some farther account of the troubles and examination of this worthy martyr, Mr *John Brad- ford*, which began on the twenty-second of *January*, 1555, when he was commanded to appear before *Stephen Gardiner*, bishop of *Winchester*, and other commissioners appointed by the queen for that purpose.

When he came into the presence of the council, the lord chancellor told him, ' that he had been a long time ' in prison for his seditious behaviour at *Paul's-cross*, and ' for his false preaching and arrogancy, in taking upon ' him to preach without authority. But the time of ' mercy is come, if you will accept it on the queen's ' terms If you will do as we have done, you shall find ' as we have found, I warrant you '

After reverent and lowly obedience first made, Mr. *Bradford* thus answered. " My lord, and lords all, I
" confess

" confess that I have been long imprisoned, and, with
" humble reverence be it spoken, unjustly, in so much
" that I did nothing seditiously, falsely, or arrogantly,
" by word or fact, by preaching or otherwise, but
" rather sought truth, peace, and godly quietness, as
" an obedient faithful subject, both in saving the life
" of him who is now bishop of *Bath*, namely Dr *Bourne*,
" who was then preacher at the cross, and in preaching
" for quietness accordingly."

At these words the lord chancellor, the famous *Gardiner*, bishop of *Winchester*, gave him the lye, ' for, said
' he, the fact was seditious, as my lord of *London* can bear
' witness.'

Bonner. ' You say true, my lord, I saw him with my
' own eyes, when he took upon him to rule and head the
' people impudently, thereby declaring that he was the
' author of the sedition '

Bradford " My lords, notwithstanding my lord bi-
" shop's seeing and saying, yet the truth I have told, as
" one day the Lord God Almighty shall reveal to all the
" world, when we shall all stand before him. In the
" mean season, because I cannot be believed by you, I
" must and am ready to suffer as now your sayings be,
" whatsoever God shall permit or licence you to do
" to me "

Lord Chancellor. ' I know thou hast a glorious tongue,
' and goodly shews thou makest, but all is lies thou
' speakest. And again, I have not forgot how stubborn
' thou wast, when thou wast before us in the *Tower*,
' whereupon thou wast committed to prison concerning
' religion I have not forgotten thy behaviour and talk,
' for which cause thou hast been kept in prison, as one
' who would have done more hurt than I will speak on '

Bradford " My lord, as I said, I say again, that I
" stand, as before you, so before God, and one day we
" shall all stand before him The truth then will be
" the truth, though we will not so take it. Yea, my
" lord, I dare say that my lord of *Bath*, Dr *Bourne*,
" will witness with me, that I sought his safeguard with
" the peril of mine own life I thank God therefore "

Bonner ' That is not true For I myself did see thee
' take upon thee too much.'

Bradford " No, I took nothing upon me undesired,
" and that of Dr *Bourne* himself, as, if he were present,
" I dare say he would affirm. [However *Bourne* had the
" ingratitude to keep out of the way] For he desired
" me

" me to help him, to pacify the people, and alfo not to
" leave him till he was in fafety　And as for my behi-
" viour in the *Tower*, and talk before your honours, if I
" did or faid any thing that did not befeem me, if your
" lordfhip would tell me wherein it was, I would fhortly
" make you an anfwer."

Lord Chancellor. ' Well, to leave this matter　How
' fayeft thou now? wilt thou return again, and do as we
' have done, and thou fhalt receive the queen's mercy
' and pardon?'

Bradford　" My lord, I defire mercy with God's
" mercy, but mercy, with God's wrath, God keep me
" from　Although, I thank God therefore, my con-
" fcience doth not accufe me, that I did fpeak any thing
" that I fhould not receive the queen's mercy or pardon.
" For all that ever I did or fpake, was both agreeable to
" God's laws, and the laws of the realm at prefent, and
" did make much to quietnefs "

Lord Chancellor. ' Well, if thou make this babbling,
' rolling thy eloquent tongue, and yet being altogether
' ignorant and vain-glorious, and wilt not receive mercy
' offered to thee; know for truth, that the queen is
' minded to make a purgation of all fuch as thou art '

Bradford　" The Lord, before whom I ftand, as well
" as before you, knoweth what vain-glory I have fought,
" and feek in this behalf　His mercy I defire, and alfo
" would be glad of the queen's favour, to live as a fub-
" ject without a clog of confcience　But otherwife, the
" Lord's mercy is better to me than life, and I know to
" whom I have committed my life, even into his hands
" who will keep it, fo that no man may take it away
" before it be his pleafure.　There are twelve hours in
" the day, and as long as they laft no man fhall have
" power thereon.　Therefore, his good-will be done, life
" in his difpleafure is worfe than death, and death, with
" his true favour, is true life."

Lord Chancellor. ' I know well enough, that we fhall
' have glorious talk enough with thee　Be fure, that as
' thou haft deceived the people with falfe and devilifh
' doctrine, fo fhalt thou receive '

Bradford　" I have not deceived the people, nor taught
" any other doctrine, than by God's grace I am, and
" hope fhall be, ready to confirm with my life　And
" as for the devilifhnefs and falfenefs of the doctrine, I
" fhould be very forry if you could prove it."

Durham.

Durham. ' Why, tell me, what say you by the minis-
' tration of the communion, as now you know it is ?'

Bradford " My lord, here I must desire of your lord-
" ship and all your honours a question, before I dare make
" you an answer to any interrogatory or question, where-
" with you now begin I have been six times sworn,
" that I shall in no wise consent to the practising of any
" jurisdiction, or any authority, on the bishop of *Rome's*
" behalf, within this realm of *England.* Now, before
" God, I humbly pray your honours to tell me, whether
" you ask me this question by his authority, or no ? If
" you do, I dare not, nor may answer you any thing in
" his authority, which you shall demand of me, except
" I would be forsworn, which God forbid !"

Secretary *Bourne* ' Hast thou been sworn six times ?
' what office hast thou borne ?'

Bradford " Forsooth, I was thrice sworn in *Cambridge,*
" when I was admitted master of arts, when I was ad-
" mitted fellow of *Pembroke-hall,* and when I was there,
" the visitors came thither and sware the university
" Again, I was sworn when I entered into the ministry,
" when I had a prebend given me, and when I was sworn
" to serve the king a little before his death."

Lord Chancellor ' Tush, *Herod's* oaths a man should
' make no conscience at '

Bradford " My lord, these were no *Herod's* oaths, no
" unlawful oaths, but oaths according to God's word,
" as you yourself have well affirmed in your book, *De*
" *verâ obedientiâ* *"

Secretary *Bourne* ' Yea, it was reported this parlia-
' ment time, that he hath done more hurt by letters, and
' exhorting those that have come to him in religion, than
' ever he did when he was abroad by preaching In his
' letters, he curseth all that teach any false doctrine (for
' so he calleth that, which is not according to that he
' taught), and most heartily exhorteth them, to whom
' he writeth, to continue still in that they have received
' by him, and such like as he is ' All which words several
of the council affirmed, to which he added, saying , ' How
' say you, sir, have you not thus seditiously written and
' exhorted the people ?'

* This book, *Of true Obedience,* was written by *Gardiner* in the
time of Henry VIII against the pope's supremacy, and prefaced with
a recommendation by *Bonner* —Both these gentlemen perceived, that,
at that time, such opinions opened the way for preferment

Bradford.

Bradford. " I have not written nor fpoken any thing
" feditioufly, neither (I thank God therefore) have I ad-
" mitted any feditious thought, nor I truft ever fhall do "

Secretary *Bourne* ' Yea, thou haft written letters '

Lord Chancellor ' Why fpeakeft thou not ? haft thou
' not written as he faith ?'

Bradford " That I have written, I have written "

Southwell ' Lord God, what an arrogant and ftubborn
' boy is this, that thus ftoutly and dallyingly behaveth
' himfelf before the queen's council !'

Bradford " My lords and mafters, the Lord God, who
" is, and will be judge to us all, knoweth, that as I am
" certain, I now ftand before his majefty, fo with re-
" verence in his fight I ftand before you, and to you
" accordingly in words and gefture I defire to behave
" myfelf If you otherwife take it, I doubt not but God
" in his time will reveal it In the mean feafon, I fhall
" fuffer with all due obedience your fayings and doings
" too, I hope "

Lord Chancellor. ' Thefe be gay and glorious words of
' reverence, but as in all other things, fo herein alfo thou
' doft nothing but lye '

Bradford " Well, I would God the author of truth
" and abhorror of lyes, would pull my tongue out of
" my mouth before you all, and fhew a terrible judge-
" ment on me here prefent, if I have purpofed, or do
" purpofe to lye before you, who either can lay my
" letters to my charge or no If you lay any thing to
" my charge that I have written, and if I deny it, then
" I am a lyar "

Lord Chancellor ' We fhall never have done with thee,
' I perceive now Be fhort, be fhort, wilt thou accept
' of mercy now ?'

Bradford " I pray God give me his mercy, and if
" therewith you will extend yours I will not refufe it,
" but otherwife I will have none "

Here arofe a great noife, fome faid one thing, and fome
another, while others again accufed him of arrogancy in
refufing the queen's pardon, which her majefty in her
great clemency had reached towards him.

To this propofal of life, Mr *Bradford* anfwered meekly
and plainly thus " My lord, if I may live as a quiet
" fubject without clog of confcience, I fhall heartily
" thank you for your pardon, if I behave myfelf other-
" wife, then am I in danger of the law In the mean
" time, I afk no more than the benefit of a fubject till I

be

" be convinced of tranfgreffions, if I cannot have this,
" as hitherto I have not had, God's good will be done "

Upon thefe words, the lord chancellor began a tedious
tale about the falfe doctrine in king *Edward*'s days, and
how the people were deceived thereby, and at the conclufion he turned to Mr *Bradford* and faid, how fayeft thou?

Bradford. " My lord, the doctrine taught in king *Ed-*
" *ward*'s days was God's pure religion, [the firft book
" of homilies in the church of *England* was then made
" and confirmed] which, as I then believed, fo do I now
" more believe it than ever I did, and therein I am more
" confirmed, and ready to declare it by God's grace,
" even as he will, to the world, than I was when I firft
" came into prifon "

Durham ' What religion mean you in king *Edward*'s
' days? What year of his reign?'

Bradford " Forfooth even the fame year, my lord,
" that the king died, and I was a preacher "

After fome fmall paufe, the lord chancellor began again
to declare, that the doctrine taught in king *Edward*'s days
was herefy, though he pretended not to prove his affertion
either by fcripture or reafon, but cunningly made ufe of
this obfervation, that it ended with treafon and rebellion,
fo that, faid he, the very end were enough to prove that
doctrine to be naught

Bradford " Ah, my lord ! that you could enter into
" God's fanctuary, and mark the end of this prefent doc-
" trine that you fo magnify "

Lord Chancellor ' What meaneft thou by that? I am
' of opinion we fhall have a fnatch of rebellion even now '

Bradford. " My lord, I mean no fuch end as you
" would gather I mean an end which no man feeth,
" but fuch as enter into God's fanctuary It a man
" look on prefent things, he will foon deftroy himfelf "

Here my lord chancellor offered mercy, and Mr *Brad-*
ford anfwered as before " Mercy, with God's mercy,
" fhould be welcome, but otherwife he would have none "
Whereupon the chancellor rang a little bell to call fomebody in, for there were but very few prefent at that time
befides the bifhop of *Worcefter* —And when one was come
in, Mr fecretary *Bourne* faid, ' it is beft for you, my
' lord, to give the keeper an extraordinary charge of this
' fellow ' Then the under-marfhal was called in.

Lord Chancellor ' Ye fhall take this man to you, and
' keep him clofe without conference of any man, but by
' your knowledge, and fuffer him not to write any letters,

    ' &c.

' &c for he is of another manner of charge to you than
' he was before '

And so they departed, *Bradford* looking as chearful as
any man could do, declaring thereby how willing he was
even to give his life for the confirmation of his faith and
doctrine.

On the twenty-ninth of *January*, 1555, the lord chancellor and other bishops were in St *Mary-Overy*'s church
in *Southwark*, when Mr *Bradford* was sent for, and they
proceeded to a second examination of him, but he by his
proper answers manifested, that he was well established in
the truths of the gospel. Mr *Bradford* was several times
examined by the lord chancellor and the bishops, by two
Spanish friars who came to him in the *Compter*, and by
Dr *Weston*, dean of *Westminster*, who came to visit Mr.
Bradford in prison, and had much conversation with him;
but in his conferences with them all he answered in a
steady and uniform manner, becoming a man, who knew
in whom he believed, and like a Christian champion for
the truths of God, though, naturally, he was (as Mr.
Edward Leigh says of him) ' a man of a humble, melting
' spirit '

He lived under so strong a sense of his corruptions,
that he subscribed some of his letters from prison in the
following words —" The most miserable, hard-hearted,
" unthankful sinner, *John Bradford* The sinful *John*
" *Bradford* "

We are informed by Mr. *Fox*, that he wrote many
treatises, especially during his confinement, of which the
following have been published —Two sermons, the first
of repentance, on *Matth.* iv 17. the second of the Lord s
Supper 2 Letters to his fellow martyrs 3. An answer
to two letters, upon the lawfulness of attending mass.
4 The danger of attending mass. 5. His examination
before the officers. 6 Godly meditations made in prison,
called his short prayers 7 Truth's complaints 8 A
translation of *Melancthon* upon prayer. 9 A dialogue of
predestination and free-will

It is no wonder that *Bradford*'s letters made such a
noise among the papists, since they were highly spiritual,
and tended to establish the people of God under the severity of their persecution They are so truly excellent,
that, notwithstanding the rude style of those times, they
are read with delight and edification even to this day.
We will select two or three of them for our Readers, to
shew his manner and spirit, and refer them for the rest to
Fox's Acts and Monuments,

" To

" To my dear fathers, D₁ *Cranmer*, D₁ *Ridley*, and
" Dr. *Latimer*

" *JESUS Emmanuel!* My dear fathers in the Lord,
" I beseech God, our sweet Father through *Christ*, to
" make perfect the good he hath begun in us all. Amen
" I had thought that every of your staves had stood next
" the door, but now it is otherwise perceived. Our dear
" brother *Rogers* hath broken the ice valiantly, as this
" day (I think) or to-morrow at the uttermost, hearty
" *Hooper*, sincere *Saunders*, and trusty *Taylor*, end their
" course, and receive their crown. The next am I, which
" hourly look for the porter to open me the gates after
" them, to enter into the desired rest. God forgive me
" mine unthankfulness for this exceeding great mercy,
" that amongst so many thousands it pleaseth his mercy
" to chuse me to be one, in whom he will suffer For
" although it be most true, that *just patior*, i e I justly
" suffer (for I have been a great hypocrite, and a griev-
" ous sinner, the Lord pardon me, yea, he hath done it,
" he hath done it indeed) yet *hic autem quid mali fecit?*
" i e what evil hath he done? *Christ*, whom the prelates
" persecute, his verity which they hate in me, hath done
" no evil, nor deserveth death Therefore ought I most
" heartily to rejoice of this dignation and tender kindness
" of the Lord's towards me, who useth remedy for my
" sin as a testimonial of his testament, to his glory, to
" my everlasting comfort, to the edifying of his church,
" and to the overthrowing of antichrist and his kingdom.
" Oh what am I, Lord, that thou shouldest thus magnify
" me, so vile a man and wretch, as always I have been?
" Is this thy wont, to send for such a wretch and an hy-
" pocrite as I have been, in a fiery chariot, as thou didst
" for *Helias?* Oh dear fathers, be thankful for me, that
" I still might be found worthy in whom the Lord would
" sanctify his holy name. And for your part, make you
" ready For we are but your gentlemen-ushers. *Nuptiæ*
" *Agni paratæ sunt, venite ad nuptias* i e the marriage of
" the Lamb is prepared, come unto the marriage I now
" go to leave my flesh there, where I received it I shall
" be conveyed thither, as *Ignatius* was at *Rome, Leopar-*
" *dis*, by whose evil I hope to be made better God
" grant, if it be his will that I ask, it may make them
" better by me. Amen.
" For my farewel therefore, I write and send this unto
" you, trusting shortly to see you where we shall never
" be

" be feparated In the mean feafon I will not ceafe, as
" I have done, to commend you to our Father of heaven,
" and that you would fo do by me, I moft heartily pray
" every one of you You know now I have moft need
" But *fidelis eft Deus, qui nunquam finet nos tentari fuprà id*
" *quod poffumus*, i. e faithful is God, which will not
" fuffer us to be tempted above our ftrength. He never
" did it hitherto, nor now, and I am affured he will
" never. Amen. *A dextris eft mihi, non movebor. Propter*
" *hoc lætabitur cor meum, quia non derelinquet animam meam*
" *in inferno, nec dabit me, fanctum fuum, per gratiam in*
" *Chrifto, videre corruptionem E carcere raptim, expectans*
" *omni momento carnificem*, i e he is on my right hand,
" therefore I fhall not fall Wherefore my heart fhall
" rejoice, for he fhall not leave my foul in hell, neither
" fhall fuffer me his holy one, by his grace in *Chrift*, to
" fee corruption Out of prifon in hafte, looking for the
" tormentor, the eighth of *February*, 1555 "

To a faithful woman in her heavinefs and trouble

" GOD our good Father, for his mercies fake in *Chrift*,
" with his eternal confolation fo comfort you, as I
" defire to be comforted of him in my moft need Yea,
" he will comfort you (my dear fifter) only caft your care
" upon him, and he never can nor will forfake you For
" his calling and gifts be fuch, that he can never repent
" him of them Whom he loveth, he loveth to the end,
" none of his chofen can perifh Of which number I know
" you are, my dearly beloved fifter. God increafe the
" faith thereof daily more and more in you, may he give
" unto you to hang wholly on him and on his providence
" and protection For whofo dwelleth under that fecret
" thing, and help of the Lord, he fhall be cock-fure for
" evermore He that dwelleth, I fay, for if we be flit-
" ters and not dwellers, as was *Lot* a flitter from *Segor*,
" where God promifed him protection, if he had dwelled
" there ftill, we fhall remove to our lofs, as he did into
" the mountains.
" Dwell therefore, that is, truft, and that finally unto
" the end, in the Lord, (my dear fifter) and you fhall be
" as mount *Sion*. As mountains compafs *Jerufalem*, fo
" doth the Lord all his people. How then can he forget
" you, which are as the apple of his eye, for his dear
" Son's fake ? Ah dear heart, that I were now but one
" half hour with you, to be a *Simon* to help carry your
" crofs

" cross with you   God send you some good *Simon* to be
" with you, and help you

" You complain in your letters of the blindness of your
" mind, and the troubles you feel   My dearly beloved,
" God make you thankful for that which God hath given
" unto you, may he open your eyes to see what and how
" great benefits you have received, that you may be less
" covetous, or rather impatient, for so (I fear me) it should
" be called, and more thankful   Have you not received
" at his hands fight to see your blindness, and thereto a
" desirous and seeking heart to see where he lieth in the
" mid-day, as his dear spouse speaketh of herself in the
" *Canticles?* Oh *Joyce*, my good *Joyce*, what a gift is this?
" Many have some light, but none this sobbing and sigh-
" ing, none this seeking which you have, I know, but
" such as he hath married unto him in his mercies   You
" are not content to kiss his feet with the *Magdalen*, but
" you would be kissed even with the kiss of his mouth,
" *Canticles*, I   You would see his face with *Moses*, for-
" getting how he biddeth us seek his face, *Psalm* xxvii.
" Yea, and that for ever, *Psalm* cv   Which signifieth
" no such fight, as you desire to be in this present life,
" which would see God now face to face, whereas he
" cannot be seen, but covered under something, yea,
" sometime in that which is (as you would say) clean
" contrary to God, as to see his mercy in his anger   In
" bringing us to hell, faith seeth him to bring us to
" heaven, in darkness it beholdeth brightness   In hid-
" ing his face from us, it beholdeth his merry counte-
" nance.   How did *Job* see God, but (as you would say)
" under Satan's cloak? For who cast the fire from heaven
" upon his goods? Who overthrew his house, and stirred
" up men to take away his cattel, but Satan? and yet
" *Job* pierced through all these, and saw God's work, say-
" ing, *the Lord hath given, the Lord hath taken away*, &c

" In reading of the *Psalms*, how often do you see that
" *David* in the shadow of death saw God's sweet love?
" And so, my dearly beloved, I see that you in your
" darkness and dimness by faith do see clarity and bright-
" ness   By faith, I say, because faith is of things absent,
" of things hoped for, of things which I appeal to your
" conscience, whether you desire not   And can you de-
" sire any thing which you know not ? And is there of
" heavenly things any other true knowledge than by
" faith ?

" Therefore

" Therefore (my dear heart) be thankful, for (before
" God I write it) you have great cause Ah, my *Joyce*,
" how happy is the stay wherein you are? Verily you
" are even in the blessed state of God's children, for they
" mourn, and do not you so? And that not for worldly
" weal, but for spiritual riches, faith, hope, charity, &c
" Do you not hunger and thirst for righteousness? And
" I pray you, saith not *Christ*, who cannot lye, that happy
" are such? How should God wipe away the tears from
" your eyes in heaven, if now on earth ye shed no tears?
" How could heaven be a place of rest, if on earth ye
" find it? How could ye desire to be at home, if in your
" journey you found no grief? How could you so often
" call upon God, and talk with him, as I know you do,
" if your enemy should sleep all the day long? How
" should you elsewhere be made like unto *Christ*, I mean
" in joy, if in sorrow you sobbed not with him? If you
" will have joy and felicity, you must first needs feel
" sorrow and misery. If you will go to heaven, you
" must sail by hell. If you would embrace *Christ* in his
" robes, you must not think scorn of him in his rags.
" If you would sit at *Christ*'s table in his kingdom, you
" must first abide with him in his temptations If you
" will drink of his cup of glory, forsake not his cup of
" ignominy.

" Can the head corner-stone be rejected, and the other
" more base stones in God's building be in this world set
" by? You are one of his lively stones, be content there-
" fore to be hewn and snagged at, that you might be made
" more meet to be joined to your fellows which suffer
" with you Satan's snatches, the world's wounds, con-
" tempt of conscience, and threats of the flesh, where-
" through they are enforced to cry, Oh wretches that we
" are, who shall deliver us? You are of God's corn,
" fear not therefore the flail, the fan, millstone, nor oven
" You are one of *Christ*'s lambs, look therefore to be
" fleeced, haled at, and even slain.

" If you were a market-sheep, you should go in more
" fat and grassie pasture. If you were for the fair, you
" should be stall-fed, and want no weal. But because
" you are of God's own occupying, therefore you must
" pasture on the bare common, abiding the storms and
" tempests that will fall Happy, and twice happy are
" you (my dear sister) that God now haleth you whither
" you would not, that you might come whither you would.
" Suffer a little and be still. Let Satan rage against you,

3

" let

" let the world cry out, let your confcience accufe you,
" let the law load you and prefs you down, yet fhall
" they not prevail, for *Chrift* is *Emmanuel*, that is, God
" with us. *If God be with us, who can be againft us?*
" The Lord is with you, your Father cannot forget you,
" your Spoufe loveth you If the waves and furges arife,
" cry with *Peter, Lord, I perifh*, and he will put out
" his hand and help you.   Caft out your anchor of hope,
" and it will not ceafe for the ftormy furges, till it take
" hold on the rock of God's truth and mercy

" Think not that he who hath given you fo many
" things corporally, as inductions of fpiritual and hea-
" venly mercies, and that without your deferts or defire,
" can deny you any fpiritual comfort, defiring it   For
" if he give to defire, he will give you to have and en-
" joy the thing defired.   The defire to have, and the
" going about to afk, ought to certify your confcience,
" that they be his earneft of the thing which, you afking,
" he will give you; yea, before you afk, and whilft you
" are about to afk, he will grant the fame, as *Ifaiah* faith,
" to his glory and your eternal confolation   He that
" fpared not his own Son for you, will not nor cannot
" think any thing too good for you, my heartily beloved

" If he had not chofen you, (as moft certainly he hath)
" he would not have fo called you, he would never have
" juftified you, he would never have fo glorified you
" with his gracious gifts, which I know, praifed be his
" name therefore, he would never have fo exercifed your
" faith with temptations, as he hath done and doth, if
" (I fay) he had not chofen you   If he hath chofen you
" (as doubtlefs, dear heart, he hath done in *Chrift*, for
" in you I have feen his earneft, and before me and to
" me you could not deny it, I know both where and
" when) if, I fay, he hath chofen you, then neither can
" you, nor ever fhall you perifh   For if you fall, he put-
" teth under his hand   You fhall not lie ftill, fo care-
" ful is *Chrift* your keeper over you.   Never was mother
" fo mindful over her child, as he is over you   And
" hath not he always been fo?

" Speak, woman, when did he finally forget you?
" And will he, now trow you, in your moft need do
" otherwife, you calling upon him, and defiring to pleafe
" him? Ah (my *Joyce*) think you God to be mutable?
" Is he a changling? Doth not he love to the end them
" whom he loveth? Are not his gifts and calling fuch,
" that he cannot repent him of them? For elfe were he

" no

" no God If you should perish, then wanted he power;
" for I am certain his will towards you is not to be
" doubted of Hath not the Spirit, which is the Spirit
" of truth, told you so? And will you now hearken with
" *Eve* to the lying spirit which would have you not to
" despair (no, he goeth more craftily to work, howbeit
" to that end, if you should give ear unto it, which God
" forbid) but to doubt and stand in a mammering, and
" so should you never truly love God, but serve him of
" a servile fear, lest he should cast you off for your un-
" worthiness and unthankfulness, as though your thank-
" fulness or worthiness were any cause with God, why
" he hath chosen you, or will finally keep you

" Ah mine own dear heart, *Christ* only, *Christ* only,
" and his mercy and truth In him is the cause of your
" election This *Christ*, this mercy, this truth of God,
" remaineth for ever, is certain for ever, I say, for ever
" If an angel from heaven should tell you the contrary,
" accursed be he Your thankfulness and worthiness are
" fruits and effects of your election, they are no causes
" These fruits and effects, shall be so much more fruitful
" and effectual, by how much you waver not

" Therefore (my dearly beloved) arise, and remember
" from whence you are fallen. You have a shepherd
" who never slumbereth nor sleepeth, no man nor devil
" can pull you out of his hands Night and day he com-
" mandeth his angels to keep you Have you forgotten
" what I read to you out of the Psalm, *The Lord is my*
" *shepherd, I can want nothing* Do you not know that
" God spared *Noah* in the ark on the outside, so that he
" could not get out? So hath he done to you (my good
" sister) so hath he done to you Ten thousand shall fall
" on your right hand, and twenty thousand on your left
" hand, yet no evil shall touch you Say boldly there-
" fore, *Many a time from my youth up have they fought*
" *against me, but they have not prevailed*, no, nor never
" shall prevail, for the Lord is round about his people
" And who are the people of God, but such as hope in
" him? Happy are they that hope in the Lord, and you
" are one of those, my dear heart, for I am assured you
" have hoped in the Lord, I have your words to shew
" most manifestly, and I know they were written un-
" feignedly Indeed not to say, that even before God
" you have simply confessed to me, and that oftentimes
" no less And if once you had this hope, as you doubt-
" less had it, though now you feel it not, yet shall you
" feel

" feel it again For the anger of the Lord lasteth but a
" moment, but his mercy lasteth for ever   Tell me (my
" dear heart) who hath so weakened you? Surely not
" a perſuaſion which came from him who called you
" For why ſhould you waver, and be ſo heavy hearted?
" Whom look you on? On yourſelf? On your worthi-
" neſs? On your thankfulneſs? On that which God
" requireth of you, as faith, hope, love, fear, joy, &c?
" Then can you not but waver indeed For what have
" you as God requireth? Believe you, hope you, love
" you, &c as much as you ſhould do? No, no, not ever
" can in this life   Ah, my dearly beloved, have you ſo
" ſoon forgotten that which ever ſhould be had in me-
" mory? Namely, that when you would and ſhould be
" certain and quiet in conſcience, then ſhould your faith
" burſt throughout all things not only that you have in
" you, or elſe are in heaven, earth or hell, until it come
" to *Chriſt* crucified, and the eternal ſweet mercies and
" goodneſs of God in *Chriſt?* Here, here is the reſting
" place, here is your Spouſe's bed, creep into it, and in
" your arms of faith embrace him Bewail your weak-
" neſs, unworthineſs, your diffidence, &c and you ſhall
" ſee he will turn to you   What ſaid I, you ſhall ſee?
" Nay, I ſhould have ſaid, you ſhall feel he will turn to
" you   You know that *Moſes*, when he went to the
" mount to talk with God, he entered into a dark cloud,
" and *Helias* had his face covered when God paſſed by.
" Both theſe dear friends of God heard of God, but they
" ſaw him not, but you would be preferred before them
" See now (my dear heart) how covetous you are. Ah
" be thankful, be thankful But God be praiſed, your
" covetouſneſs is *Moſes's* covetouſneſs   Well, with him
" you ſhall be ſatisfied But when? Forſooth when he
" ſhall appear. Here is not the time of ſeeing, but is it
" were in a glaſs *Iſaac* was deceived, becauſe he was
" not content with hearing only

    " Therefore to make an end of theſe many words,
" wherewith I fear me I do but trouble you from better
" exerciſes, inaſmuch as you are indeed the child of God,
" elect in *Chriſt* before the beginning of all times, inaſ-
" much as you are given to the cuſtody of *Chriſt*, as one
" of God's moſt precious jewels, inaſmuch as *Chriſt* is
" faithful, and hitherto hath all power, ſo that you ſhall
" never periſh, no, one hair of your head ſhall not be
" loſt I beſeech you, I pray you, I deſire you, I crave
" at your hands with all my very heart, I aſk of you with

" hand

" hand, pen, tongue and mind, in *Chrift*, through *Chrift*,
" for *Chrift*, for his name, blood, mercies, power, and
" truth's fake, (my moft entirely beloved fifter) that you
" admit no doubting of God's final mercies towards you,
" howfoever you feel for yourfelf, but to complain to
" God, and crave of him, as of your tender and dear
" father, all things, and in that time which fhall be
" moft opportune, you fhall find and feel far above that
" your heart or the heart of any creature can conceive,
" to your eternal joy   Amen, Amen, Amen

 " The good Spirit of God always keep us as his dear
" children, may he comfort you, as I defire to be com-
" forted, my dearly beloved, for evermore   Amen.

 " I break up thus abruptly, becaufe our common prayer
" time calleth me.   The peace of *Chrift* dwell in both
" our hearts for ever.   Amen

 " As for the report of *W Po.* if it be as you hear,
" you muft prepare to bear it   It is written on heaven's
" door, *Do well, and hear evil*   Be content therefore to
" hear whatfoever the enemy fhall imagine to blot you
" withal   God's holy Spirit always comfort and keep
" you   Amen, Amen.   This eighth of *Auguft*, by him
" that in the Lord defireth to you, as well and as much
" felicity as to his own heart "

His laft letter to his mother, a little before he was burned.

 " GOD's mercy and peace in *Chrift*, be more and more
 " perceived of us.   Amen.

 " My moft dear mother, in the bowels of *Chrift* I
" heartily pray and befeech you to be thankful for me
" unto God, who thus now taketh me unto himfelf
" I die not, my good mother, as a thief, a murderer, an
" adulterer, &c. but I die as a witnefs of *Chrift*, his gof-
" pel and verity, which hitherto I have confeffed (I thank
" God) as well by preaching, as by imprifonment, and
" now even prefently I fhall moft willingly confirm the
" fame by fire.   I acknowledge that God moft juftly might
" take me hence fimply for my fins (which are many,
" great, and grievous   But the Lord for his mercy in
" *Chrift*, hath pardoned them all, I hope) but now dear
" mother, he taketh me hence by this death, as a con-
" feffor and witnefs, that the religion taught by *Chrift*
" *Jefus*, the prophets, and the apoftles, is God's truth.
" The prelates do perfecute in me *Chrift* whom they hate,
" and his truth which they may not abide, becaufe their
" works are evil, and may not abide the truth and light,
            " left

" left men fhould fee their darknefs Therefore, my good
" and moft dear mother, give thanks for me to God, that
" he hath made the fruit of your womb to be a witnefs
" of his glory, and attend to the truth, which (I thank
" God for it) I have truly taught out of the pulpit of
" *Manchefter*. Ufe often and continual prayer to God
" the Father, through *Chrift*. Hearken, as you may, to
" the fcriptures · Serve God after his word, and not after
" cuftom Beware of the *Romifh* religion in *England*;
" defile not yourfelf with it Carry *Chrift*'s crofs as he
" fhall lay it upon your back Forgive them that kill
" me Pray for them, for they know not what they do .
" Commit my caufe to God the Father Be mindful of
" both your daughters, and help them as you can.

" I fend all my writings to you and my brother *Roger*;
" do with them as you will, becaufe I cannot as I would .
" He can tell you more of my mind I have nothing to
" give you, or to leave behind me for you Only I pray
" God my Father, for his *Chrift*'s fake, to blefs you, and
" keep you from evil May he give you patience, may he
" make you thankful, as for me, fo for yourfelf, that he
" will take the fruit of your womb to witnefs his verity :
" Wherein I confefs to the whole world, I die and depart
" this life, in hope of a much better Which I look for
" at the hands of God my Father, through the merits of
" his dear Son *Jefus Chrift*.

" Thus, my dear mother, I take my laft farewel of you
" in this life, befeeching the almighty and eternal Father
" by *Chrift*, to grant us to meet in the life to come, where
" we fhall give him continual thanks and praife for ever
" and ever Amen. Out of prifon the twenty-fourth
" of *June*, 1555 Your fon in the Lord."

JUSTUS JONAS.

THIS famous *German* divine, was born at *Northaufen*
in *Thuringia*, on the fifth of *June*, 1493, where
his father was chief magiftrate, who, falling fick of the
plague, and having applied an onion to the fore, took it
off and laid it by, which young *Jonas*, coming in, took
up and eat, but, through the goodnefs of God, received

no hurt He applied himself first to the study of the civil law, and made good proficiency in it, but, quitting that study, he devoted his whole attention to theology, and proceeded to the degree of doctor immediately. This was about the first dawning of the true light of the gospel, of which *Jonas* was not only an hearer and observer, but soon afterwards a principal instrument in promoting For he was almost always present at the several synods and meetings of divines, which were held to settle the matters of religion, in those days He united in one person the characters of a most able divine and learned civilian , and as the state of religion at that time was unavoidably connected with human politics, he became a very necessary man to the protestants, in being a skilful politician He assisted *Luther* and *Melancthon* in the assembly at *Marpurg*, in 1529, and was afterwards with *Melancthon* at the famous convention at *Augsburg*, in which he was a principal negotiator. With these two great men he was extremely intimate, and particularly with *Melancthon*

In the year 1521, he was called to a pastoral charge at *Wittenberg*, and made principal of the college and professor in that university He, with *Spalatinus* and *Amsdorf*, was employed by the elector of *Saxony* to refoint the churches in *Misnia* and *Thuringia* From thence he was called to *Hall* in *Saxony*, where he also exceedingly promoted the work of the Reformation *Luther* sometimes resorted thither to him, and took him with him in his last journey to *Isleben*, where he died in his arms.

After *Luther's* death, he continued some time in the duke of *Saxony's* court, and was a constant companion of *John Frederick's* sons in all their afflictions. He was at length set over the church in *Eisfield*, where he ended his days in much peace and comfort, on the ninth of *October*, in the year 1555, and in the sixty-third year of his age

He was one of those, who might be called moderate Reformers, wishing to make no further alteration in the established modes of worship, and even doctrine, than was absolutely necessary for the introduction of piety and truth. Hence the Lutheran churches have departed least of any, in external ceremonies, from the corruptions of the church of *Rome* The motive of *Luther*, *Jonas*, and other Reformers of that cast, was undoubtedly good, but the effect was not answerable The danger, in such cases, is, that the great bulk of the people, seeing such stress laid upon outward observances, will fall into the error of leaning entirely upon them, and so make that, which

perhaps

perhaps might be originally intended for an *help* to devotion, the whole *end* and *purpose* of their attention

Jonas's death was exceedingly regretted by all the good men of that time, for such a loss to the church of *Christ* was not easily to be repaired None but almighty grace could effect it, which has promised not to leave the church without faithful witnesses to the end of time *Siberus*, in his epitaph, said of him

——————*flent ademtum*
Omnes judicii elegantioris,
Et bonique viri pique cœlo
Ille, colloquio Dei, receptus,
Et Christi fruitur beatus ore.

——————' the heavy loss
' All men bewail'd of pious mind,
' All men of sentiments refin'd
' To heav'n he flew, at God's behest;
' And joyful there, among the blest,
' He views his Saviour face to face,
' And triumphs in redeeming grace '

He wrote, among other treatises, in defence of the marriage of priests, against *Faber*, upon the study of divinity; notes upon the acts of the apostles, upon the death of *Luther*, against *Wicelius*, and he translated into *Latin* several of *Luther*'s works.

About this period, the gospel flourished in what is now called *Prussia*, under the ministry of three very great and excellent divines, *Paulus Speratus, Poliander*, and *Brismann* This last was a particular friend of *Luther*, and with the other two, his colleagues, fed the flock of *Christ*, and superintended the churches in *Prussia*, above twenty years. About the latter end of their ministry, *Osander*, who during *Luther*'s life harmonized in all the great points with the other Reformers, left *Noremberg*, where he had long preached, and came into *Prussia* Here he started some opinions of his own upon the doctrine of justification, asserting, that man is not justified by faith, but by the righteousness of *Christ* dwelling in us Matters were carried so high, that *Albert*, duke of *Prussia*, who had embraced *Osander*'s opinion, banished the other Reformers from his dominions Osander was justly censured by most of the protestants for making this breach in a most unseasonable time, and particularly for his ill treatment of *Melancthon*, to whom he returned abuse and harshness

nefs for mildnefs and reafon. The truth is, that *Ofian-*
der, with all his learning and abilities, appears to have
been a very vain and intemperate man, affecting high-
flown language and manners, inftead of that fimplicity
which becomes the gofpel. He died at *Koningfberg*, in
Pruffia, on the very fame day that the excellent *Cafpar
Hedio* departed this life at *Strafburgh* After his death,
duke *Albert*, whether from a wifh to heal the differences
occafioned by *Ofiander* and his fectaries, or from the fuggeftions of fome great and good men, caufed a public
agreement to be made about the year 1556, and fo the
church in that part of the world was fettled in peace.

H U G H　L A T I M E R,

BISHOP of WORCESTER.

OF this plain and pious, as well as moft zealous,
divine, it may be faid, that he was one of the firft
and moft ufeful Reformers of the church of *England*.
He was defcended of mean but honeft parents at *Thurkeffon*,
or *Thurcafton*, near *Mount Sorrel*, in *Leicefterfhire*, where
his father lived in good reputation, and though he had no
land of his own, but rented a fmall farm of four pounds
a year at the utmoft, yet, by frugality and induftry, and
the advantage of a good bargain, he brought up a large
family of fix daughters, befides this his only fon. *

* In one of his court fermons, in king *Edward*'s time, our author,
inveighing againft the nobility and gentry, and fpeaking of the moderation of landlords a few years before, and the plenty in which their
tenants lived, tells his audience, in his familiar way, that upon a
farm of four pounds a year, at the utmoft, his father tilled as much
ground as kept half a dozen men, that he had it ftocked with a hundred fheep and thirty cows, that he found the king a man and horfe,
himfelf remembering to have buckled on his father's harnefs, when he
went to *Blackheath*, that he gave his daughters five pounds a piece at
marriage, that he lived hofpitably among his neighbors, and was not
backward in his alms to the poor. " And all this (faid he) he did of
" the faid farm Whereas he, that now hath it, pays fixteen pounds
" by the year, or more, and is not able to do any thing for his prince,
" for himfelf, nor for his children, or give a cup of drink to the
" poor "—What would *Latimer* have faid of our prefent rack-renting
landlords, who not only do not relieve, but procure means to grind
the face of, the poor?

Hugh,

BISHOP LATIMER

Hugh, who was born in the farm-house about the year 1470, in the eleventh year of king *Edward* the Fourth, and put to the grammar-school at *Thurcafton*, and afterwards at *Leicefter*, took his learning so well, that it was determined to breed him to the church. With this view, as soon as he was fit, he was sent to *Cambridge*, in 1484, where, at the ufual time, he took his degrees in arts, and, entering into prieft's orders, behaved with remarkable zeal and warmth in defence of popery, his religion, againft the reformed opinions, which had lately difcovered themfelves in *England*. He heard thofe new teachers with high indignation. He inveighed, publicly and privately, againft the Reformers. He looked upon them in fo bad a light, that he declared he was of opinion, the laft times, the day of judgement, and the end of the world, were now approaching. "Impiety, he "faid, was gaining ground apace, and what lengths may "not men be expected to run, when they begin to quef- "tion even the infallibility of the pope." If any, inclined to the Reformation, and particularly good Mr *Stafford*, divinity-lecturer in *Cambridge*, read lectures in the fchools, Mr *Latimer* was fure to be there to drive out the fcholars, and, when he commenced batchelor of divinity, (which was in the year 1515, when he was fortyfive years of age) he took occafion to give an open teftimony of his diflike to their proceedings, in an oration, which he made againft *Philip Melanchon*, whom he treated with great feverity, for his "impious innovations ('as he "called them) in religion." His zeal was fo much taken notice of in the univerfity, that he was elected, in the next year, into the office of crofs-bearer in all public proceffions, an employment which he accepted with reverence, and difcharged with becoming folemnity for the fpace of feven years.

Among thofe, who about this period favored the Reformation, the moft confiderable was Mr *Thomas Bilney*, whofe life we have related to our Readers.

It was Mr *Latimer*'s happinefs to be well acquainted with this good man, who had indeed long conceived very favorable fentiments of him. He had known *Latimer*'s life in the univerfity to be a life ftrictly moral and devout, he afcribed his failings to the genius of his religion, and, notwithftanding his more than ordinary zeal in the profeffion of that religion, he could obferve in him a very candid temper, prejudiced by no finifter views, and an integrity, which gave him great hopes of his refor-

3 C   mation

mation　Induced by thefe favorable appearances, Mr. *Bilney* failed not, as opportunities offered, to fuggeft many things to him about corruptions in religion in general, whence he ufed frequently to drop a hint concerning fome in the *Romifh* church in particular, till having prepared the way by degrees, he at length made an earneft perfuafion, that his friend would only endeavor to diveft himfelf of his prejudices, and place the two fides of the queftion before him.　How Mr *Latimer* at firft received thefe few declarations, and by what fteps he came to be fettled in the truth of the gofpel, we have no particular account, only we find in general, that his friend's application had its defired effect.　This was in the year 1523, when *Latimer* had nearly attained the fifty-third year of his age

Mr *Latimer* no fooner ceafed from being a zealous papift, than he became, with the fame zeal and integrity, a zealous proteftant, very active in fupporting and propagating the reformed doctrine, and affiduous to make converts both in the town and univerfity　He preached in public, exhorted in private, and every-where preffed the neceffity of true faith and holinefs, in oppofition to thofe outward performances, which were then efteemed the very effentials of religion.　A behavior of this kind was immediately taken notice of, *Cambridge*, no lefs than the reft of this kingdom, was entirely popifh, every new opinion was watched with the utmoft jealoufy, and Mr. *Latimer* foon perceived, how obnoxious he had made himfelf　The firft remarkable oppofition he met with from the popifh party, was occafioned by a courfe of fermons he preached, during the Chriftmas holidays, before the univerfity, in which he fpoke his fentiments with great freedom upon many opinions and ufages maintained and practifed in the *Romifh* church, and particularly infifted upon the great abufe of locking up the fcripture in an unknown tongue　Few of the tenets of popery were then queftioned in *England*, but fuch as tended to a relaxation of manners, tranfubftantiation, and other points rather fpeculative, ftill held their dominion, Mr. *Latimer* therefore chiefly dwelt upon thofe of immoral tendency. He fhewed what true religion was, that it was feated in the heart, and that, in comparifon with it, external appointments were of no value.　Great was the outcry occafioned by thefe difcourfes.

The ftate of religion at that time is well defcribed, in the following words, gathered from the ecclefiaftical hiftorians

torians of the reign of king *Henry* the Eighth. ' The
' cathedral clergy (fay they) throughout the kingdom
' gave themfelves up wholly to idlenefs and pleafure,
' they decried and difcouraged learning, affirming, that
' learning would bring in herefy and all manner of mif-
' chief. The rural and parochial clergy were univerfally
' ignorant, flothful, idle, fuperftitious, proud, and vicious,
' preaching, moft of them, but once a quarter on a *Sun-*
' *day*, and, but few; more than once a month, on the
' firft *Sunday* thereof In Lent, fermons were more fre-
' quent, but thefe ufually turned on abftinence, con-
' feffion, the neceffity of corporal feverities, pilgrimages,
' the enriching of the fhrines, and the relics of the faints,
' and the great ufe of indulgences No pains were taken
' to inform the people of the hatefulnefs of vice, the
' excellency of holinefs, or the wonderful love of *Chrift*.
' It was far otherwife on the holy or faints' days, for on
' them the monks, and the friars, and others, would afcend
' the pulpit, and, inftead of fermons, harangue the peo-
' ple on the merits, fupererogations, and miracles, of the
' faints, to the memory of whom the days were dedicated;
' magnifying their relics, which they always took care to
' inform them were laid up in fuch and fuch places ——
' The clergy in general were fo proud and infolent, that,
' if any man denied them any part of that refpect, or of
' thofe advantages to which they pretended, he was pre-
' fently brought under the fufpicion of herefy, and vexed
' with imprifonments, and articles in the fpiritual courts
' were exhibited againft him '
Learning was at a very low ebb, in both the univerfities, in the year 1526 *Cambridge* was then the feat and
afylum of ignorance, bigotry, and fuperftition, and every
reformed opinion and perfon was perfecuted with the moft
inveterate hatred and zeal *Latimer* had, by this time,
through his daily and indefatigable fearching of the fcriptures of the Old and New Teftaments, made himfelf a
complete mafter of all the fcriptural arguments, proper
to confute the reigning errors of the church of *Rome* —
He fpoke largely againft the abominable fuperftition and
idle ufage of faying mafs in an unknown tongue, and
gave the moft folid reafons, why the fcriptures of the
Old and New Teftaments fhould be tranflated into *Eng-*
lifh, printed, and put into the hands of the moft illiterate.
This preaching of his had a very great effect, and, with
great truth; it may be faid, that we greatly owe, under

3 C 2　　　　　　　　God,

God, to Mr *Latimer* the inestimable blessing of reading the bible in our own tongue

Mr *Latimer* now became a preacher of particular eminence, and displayed a remarkable address in adapting himself to the capacities of the people. The orthodox clergy, observing him thus followed, thought it high time to oppose him openly. This task was undertaken by Dr *Buckingham*, or *Buckenham*, prior of the *Black-Friars*, who appeared in the pulpit against him, and with great pomp and prolixity, shewed the dangerous tendency of Mr *Latimer*'s opinions, particularly, he inveighed against his heretical notions of having the scriptures in *English*, laying open the ill effects of such an innovation. 'If 'that heresy, said he, prevail, we should soon see an end 'of every thing useful among us. The plough-man, 'reading that if he put his hand to the plough, and 'should happen to look back, he was unfit for the king-'dom of God, would soon lay aside his labour, the 'baker likewise reading, that a little leaven will corrupt 'his lump, would give us very insipid bread. The simple 'man also finding himself commanded to pluck out his 'eyes, in a few years we should have the nation full of 'blind beggars.' Mr. *Latimer* could not but smile at this ingenious reasoning, and promised to balance accounts with the prior on the next *Sunday*, and to expose this solemn trifler. The whole university accordingly met together on the next *Sunday*, as the news was generally spread, that Mr. *Latimer* would preach. That vein of pleasantry and humour which ran through all his words and actions, would here, it was imagined, have its full scope. And, to say the truth, the preacher was not a little conscious of his own superiority. To complete the scene, just before the sermon began, prior *Buckingham* himself entered the church with his cowl about his shoulders, and seated himself with an air of importance, before the pulpit. Mr *Latimer*, with great gravity, recapitulated the learned doctor's arguments, placed them in the strongest light, and then rallied them with such a flow of wit, and at the same time with so much good humour, that, without the appearance of ill-nature, he made his adversary in the highest degree ridiculous. He then, with great address, appealed to the people, descanted upon the low esteem in which their holy guides had always held their understandings, expressed the utmost offence at their being treated with such contempt, and wished his honest countrymen might only have the

use

use of the scripture, till they shewed themselves such absurd interpreters, as the prior had seemed to make them. He concluded his discourse with a few observations upon scripture metaphors. "A figurative manner of speech, "he said, was common in all languages." Representations of this kind were in daily use, and generally understood "Thus, for instance, continues he, (addressing "himself to that part of the audience where the prior "was seated) when we see a fox painted preaching in a "friar's hood, no body imagines that a fox is meant, but "that craft and hypocrify are deſcribed, which are so "often found diſguiſed in that garb"——This pointed ridicule expoſed the poor prior to the laughter and contempt of every body, and, though we do not approve of humor or drollery in such places, and upon such ſolemn occaſions, as the profeſſed worſhip of God, yet certainly he deſerved it. And it is probable, Mr *Latimer* himſelf thought this levity unbecoming. For when one *Venetus*, a foreigner, not long after, attacked him again upon the ſame ſubject, and in a manner the moſt ſcurrilous and provoking, we find him uſing a graver ſtrain. He anſwers, like a ſcholar, what is worth anſwering, and, like a man of ſenſe, leaves the abſurd part to confute itſelf. Whether he ridiculed, however, or reaſoned, with ſo much of the ſpirit of true oratory, conſidering the times, were his harangues animated, that they ſeldom failed of their intended effect. His raillery ſhut up their *Buckingham* within his monaſtry, and his arguments drove *Venetus* from the univerſity.

Theſe advantages increaſed the credit of the proteſtant party in *Cambridge*, of which *Bilney* and *Latimer* were at the head. The meekneſs, gravity, and unaffected piety of the former, and the cheartulneſs, good-humour, and eloquence of the latter, wrought much upon the junior ſtudents.

Theſe things greatly alarmed the popiſh clergy. Of this ſort were all the heads of colleges, and indeed the ſenior part of the univerſity. Frequent convocations were held, tutors were admoniſhed to have a ſtrict eye over their pupils, and academical cenſures of all kinds were inflicted. But academical cenſures were found inſufficient. Mr *Latimer* continued to preach, and hereſy (as they called it) to ſpread. The heads of the popiſh party applied to the biſhop of *Ely*, as their dioceſan, but that prelate was not a man for their purpoſe, he was a papiſt indeed, but moderate. He came to *Cambridge*, however,

however, examined the ftate of religion, and, at their
intreaty, preached againft heretics, but he would do nothing farther. Only indeed he filenced Mr. *Latimer*.
This occurred in the year 1529 But it gave no great
check to the Reformers. There was at that time a proteftant prior in *Cambridge*, Dr *Barnes**, of the *Auftin-
Friars* His monaftry was exempt from epifcopal jurifdiction, and being a great admirer of Mr *Latimer*, he
boldly licenfed him to preach there Hither his party
followed him, and the late oppofition having greatly
excited the curiofity of the people, the friars chapel was
foon incapable of containing the crouds that attended.
Among others, it is remarkable that the aforefaid bifhop
of *Ely* was often one of his hearers, and had the inge-
fiuoufnefs to declare, that Mr *Latimer* was one of the
beft preachers he had ever heard, and that he wifhed, he
had the fame grace and abilities for himfelf

The credit to the proteftant caufe, which our preacher
had thus gained in the pulpit, he maintained by a holy
life out of it Mr. *Bilney* and he did not fatisfy themfelves with acting unexceptionably, but were daily giving
inftances of goodnefs, which malice could not fcandalize,
nor envy mifinterpret. They vifited the prifoners, re-
lieved the poor, and fed the hungry They were always
together concerting their fchemes. The place where they
ufed to walk, was long afterwards known by the name of
the *Heretics-Hill*. *Cambridge*, at that time, was full of
their good works; their charities to the poor, and friendly
vifits to the fick and unhappy, were common topics of
difcourfe.

But thefe ferved only to increafe the heat of perfecution from their adverfaries. Impotent themfelves, and
finding their diocefan either unable or unwilling to work
their purpofes, they determined upon an appeal to the
higher powers, and heavy complaints were carried to
court of the increafe of herefy, not without formal depofitions againft the principal abettors of it.

The principal perfons, at this time concerned in ecclefiaftical affairs, were cardinal *Wolfey*, *Warham*, archbifhop
of *Canterbury*, and *Tunftal*, bifhop of *London*, and as
Henry VIII. was now in expectation of having the bufinefs of his divorce ended in a regular way at *Rome*, he
was careful to obferve all forms of civility with the

---

* We have mentioned this excellent perfon in the life of *Luther*,
p. 224. He loved the truth, and fuffered for it with great boldnefs
and conftancy.

pope.

pope   The cardinal therefore erected a court, confifting
of bifhops, divines, and canonifts, to put the laws in
execution againft herefy   Of this court *Tunftal* was made
prefident, and *Bilney*, *Latimer*, and one or two more,
were called before him   *Bilney* was confidered as the
herefiarch, and againft him chiefly the rigor of the court
was levelled, and they fucceeded fo far that he was prevailed upon to recant, accordingly he bore his faggot (a
token of recantation and penance), and was difmiffed.
As for Mr. *Latimer*, and the reft, they had eafier terms.
Tunftal omitted no opportunities of fhewing mercy, and
was dextrous in finding them.   The heretics, upon their
difmiffion, returned to *Cambridge*, where they were received with open arms by their friends   Amidft this
mutual joy, *Bilney* alone feemed unaffected, he fhunned
the fight of his acquaintance, and received their congra-
tulations with confufion and blufhes.   In fhort, he was
ftruck with remorfe for what he had done, grew melancholy, and after leading a life for two years in all the
feverity of an afcetic, he refolved (as we have feen above)
to acknowledge the truth unto death.

Bilney's fufferings, far from fhocking the Reformation
at *Cambridge*, infpired the leaders of it with new courage.
Mr *Latimer* began now to exert himfelf more than he
had yet done, and fucceeded to that credit, which Mr.
Bilney had fo long fupported.   He conftantly preached in
Dr, *Barnes*'s church, and affifted him in the difcharge of
his paftoral duty.   Among other inftances of his zeal and
refolution, he gave one which was indeed very remarkable:
He had the courage to write to the king againft a proclamation then juft publifhed, forbidding the ufe of the bible
in *Englifh*, and other books on religious fubjects.   He
had preached before his majefty once or twice at *Windfor*,
and had been taken notice of by him in a more affable
manner, than that monarch ufually indulged towards his
fubjects   But whatever hopes of preferment his fovereign's favor might have raifed in him, he chofe to put
all to the hazard, rather than omit what he thought his
duty   He was generally confidered as one of the moft
eminent of thofe, who favored proteftantifm, and therefore thought it became him to be one of the moft forward in oppofing popery   His letter is the picture of an
honeft and fincere heart, it was chiefly intended to point
to the king the bad intention of the bifhops in procuring
the proclamation, and concluded in thefe terms   " Ac-
" cept, gracious fovereign, without difpleafure, what I
" have

" have written, I thought it my duty to mention those
" things to your majesty No personal quarrel, as God
" shall judge me, have I with any man, I wanted only
" to induce your majesty to consider well what kind of
" persons you have about you, and the ends for which
" they counsel Indeed, great prince, many of them,
" or they are much slandered, have very private ends.
" God grant your majesty may see through all the de-
" signs of evil men, and be in all things equal to the
" high office with which you are intrusted. Wherefore,
" gracious king, remember yourself, have pity upon
" your own soul, and think that the day is at hand,
" when you shall give account of your office, and of
" the blood that hath been shed by your sword In the
" which day, that your grace may stand stedfastly, and
" not be ashamed, but be clear and ready in your reckon-
" ing, and have your pardon sealed with the blood of
" our Saviour *Christ*, which alone serveth at that day, is
" my daily prayer to HIM, who suffered death for our
" sins. The Spirit of God preserve you!"

Though the influence of the popish party then prevailed so far, that this letter produced no effect Yet the
king, no way displeased, received it not only with temper, but with great condescension, graciously thanking
him for his well-intended advice The king loved sincerity and openness, and Mr *Latimer's* plain and simple
manner had before made a favorable impression upon him,
which this letter contributed not a little to strengthen;
and the part he acted in promoting the establishment of
the king's supremacy, in 1535, rivetted him in the royal
favor Dr *Butts*, the king's physician, being sent to
Cambridge on that occasion, and upon the affair of the
king's divorce, began immediately to pay his court to the
protestant party, from whom the king expected most
unanimity in his favor Among the first, he made his
application to Mr *Latimer*, as a person most likely to
serve him, begging that he would collect the opinions
of his friends in the case, and do his utmost to bring
over those of most eminence, who were still inclined to
the papacy Mr *Latimer*, being a thorough friend to
the cause he was to solicit, undertook it with his usual
zeal, and discharged himself so much to the satisfaction
of the doctor, that, when that gentleman returned to
court, he took Mr *Latimer* along with him, in the
design, no doubt, of procuring him a proper consideration,

About

About this time a perfon was rifing into power, who became his chief friend and patron—the lord *Cromwell*, who, being a friend to the Reformation, encouraged of courfe fuch churchmen, as moft inclined towards it. Among thofe was Mr *Latimer*, for whom his patron very foon obtained the benefice of *Weft-Kingfton*, in *Wiltfhire*, whither he refolved, as foon as poffible, to repair, and keep a conftant refidence. His friend Dr *Butts*, furprized at this refolution, did what he could to diffuade him from it. ' You are deferting, faid he, the faireft op-' portunities of making your fortune The prime minifter ' intends this only as an earneft of his future favours, and ' will certainly in time do great things for you. But it ' is the manner of courts to confider them as provided ' for, who feem to be fatisfied, and, take my word for ' it, an abfent claimant ftands but a poor chance among ' rivals, who have the advantage of being prefent.' Thus the old courtier advifed. But thefe arguments had no weight. He was heartily tired of the court, where he faw fo much debauchery and irreligion, without being able to oppofe them; having neither authority nor talents, he thought, to reclaim the great. The great defign, however, of lord *Cromwell* and Dr. *Butts* in procuring *Latimer* this provifion was, to encourage him in affifting them by his oratory among the people, in their bufinefs of rendering the king's fupremacy and divorce acceptable to the public. He was then the moft diligent and popular preacher in the kingdom, and they wifhed for the exercife of his talents in and about *London*. But *Latimer*'s views were of another kind. He thirfted for the falvation of fouls; and, next to that confideration, he wifhed to retire from the buftle of a court, where he had with the deepeft concern beheld every vice triumphant, and malice, envy, detraction, and vanity, carrying all before them.

He left the palace, therefore, and entered immediately upon the duties of his parifh. Nor was he fatisfied within thofe limits, he extended his labors throughout the county, where he obferved the paftoral care moft neglected, having for that purpofe obtained a general licence from the univerfity of *Cambridge*. As his manner of preaching was very popular in thofe times, the pulpits every where were gladly opened for him, and at *Briftol*, where he often preached, he was much countenanced by the magiftrates. But this reputation was too much for the popifh clergy to fuffer; and their oppofition firft broke out at *Briftol*. The mayor had appointed him to preach

there

there on *Easter-day* Public notice had been given, and all people were pleased, when suddenly there came out an order from the bishop, prohibiting any one to preach there without his licence. The clergy of the place waited upon Mr *Latimer*, informed him of the bishop's order, and, knowing that he had no such licence, ' were ex-
' tremely sorry, that they were, by that means, deprived
' of the pleasure of hearing an excellent discourse from
' him ' Mr *Latimer* received their compliment with a smile, for he had been apprized of the affair, and well knew, that *these* were the very persons who had written to the bishop against him

Their opposition became afterwards more public, the pulpits were made use of to spread their invectives against him, and such liberties were taken with his character, that he thought it necessary to justify himself, and accordingly called upon his maligners to accuse him publicly before the mayor of *Bristol* And, with all men of candor, he was justified, for when that magistrate convened both parties, and put the accusers upon producing legal proof of what they had said, nothing of that kind appeared, but the whole accusation was left to rest upon the un-certain evidence of some hearsay information

His enemies however were not thus silenced The party against him became daily stronger, and more in-flamed. It consisted, in general, of the country priests in those parts, headed by some divines of more eminence. These persons, after mature deliberation, drew up articles against him, extracted chiefly from his sermons, in which he was charged with speaking lightly of " the worship of " saints," with saying, " there was no material fire in " hell," and that " he would rather be in purgatory " than in *Lollard*'s tower " This charge being laid be-fore the bishop of *London*, that prelate cited Mr *Latimer* to appear before him, and, when he appealed to his own ordinary, a citation was obtained out of *Warham*'s (the archbishop's) court, where the bishop of *London* and some other bishops were commissioned to examine him

An archiepiscopal citation brought him necessarily to a compliance His friends would have had him fly from it, but their persuasions were in vain He set out for *London* in the depth of winter, and under a severe fit of the stone and cholic, and in the sixty-sixth year of his age, but he was more distressed at the thoughts of leaving his parish exposed to the popish clergy, who he feared might undo in his absence and detention, what he had

hitherto

hitherto done. On his arrival at *London*, a court of bishops and canonists were ready to receive him, where, instead of being examined, as he expected, about his sermons, a paper was put into his hands, which he was ordered to subscribe, declaring his belief in the efficacy of masses for the souls in purgatory, of prayers to the dead saints, of pilgrimages to their sepulchres and relics, the pope's power to forgive sins, the doctrine of merit, the seven sacraments, and the worship of images And, when he refused to sign it, the archbishop, with a frown, begged he would consider what he did 'We intend not, 'says he, Mr *Latimer*, to be hard upon you, we dismiss 'you for the present, take a copy of the articles, examine 'them carefully, and God grant that, at our next meet- 'ing, we may find each other in better temper' The next and several succeeding meetings, the same scene is acted over again. *He* continued inflexible, and *they* continued to distress him Three times every week they regularly sent for him, with a view either to draw something from him by captious questions, or to teize him at length into compliance. Of one of these examinations he gives us the following account " I was brought out, " says he, to be examined in the same chamber as be- " fore, but, at this time, it was somewhat altered For, " whereas, before, there was a fire in the chimney, now " the fire was taken away, and an arras hanged over the " chimney, and the table stood near the chimney's end. " There was, among these bishops that examined me, one " with whom I have been very familiar, and whom I took " for my great friend, an aged man, and he sat next the " table-end Then, among other questions, he put forth " one, a very subtle and crafty one, and when I should " make answer 'I pray you, Mr *Latimer*, said he, ' speak out, I am very thick of hearing, and there be ' many that sit far off' I marvelled at this, that I was " bidden to speak out, and began to misdeem, and gave " an ear to the chimney, and there I heard a pen plainly " scratching behind the cloth —They had appointed one " there to write all my answers, that I should not start " from them. God was my good Lord, and gave me " answers, I could never else have escaped them " At length he was tired out with such usage, and, when he was next summoned, instead of going himself, he sent a letter to the archbishop, in which, with great freedom, he tells him, that the treatment he had of late met with, had fretted him into such a disorder, as rendered him unfit

to attend that day—that, in the mean time, he could not
help taking this opportunity to expoftulate with his grace,
for detaining him fo long from the difcharge of his duty—
that it feemed to him moft unaccountable, that they, who
never preached themfelves, fhould hinder others—that,
as for their examination of him, he really could not
imagine what they aimed at, they pretended one thing
in the beginning, and another in the progrefs—that, if
his fermons were what gave offence, which he perfuaded
himfelf were neither contrary to the truth, nor to any
canon of the church, he was ready to anfwer whatever
might be thought exceptionable in them—that he wifhed
a little more regard might be had to the judgement of
the people, and that a diftinction might be made between
the ordinances of God and man—that if fome abufes in
religion did prevail, as was then commonly fuppofed, he
thought preaching was the beft means to difcountenance
them—that he wifhed all paftors might be *obliged* to perform their duty, but that, however, liberty might be
given to thofe who were *willing*—that, as for the articles
propofed to him, he begged to be excufed from fubfcribing
them, while he lived, he never would abet fuperftition;
and that, laftly, he hoped the archbifhop would excufe
what he had written—he knew his duty to his fuperiors,
and would practife it; but, in that cafe, he thought a
ftronger obligation laid upon him.

The bifhops ftill continued their perfecution, till their
fchemes were fruftrated by an unexpected hand. The
king being informed, moft probably by lord *Cromwell*'s
means, of Mr. *Latimer*'s ill ufage, interpofed in his behalf, and refcued him out of the hands of his enemies
A figure of fo much fimplicity, and fuch an apoftolic
appearance as his at court, did not fail to ftrike queen
Ann Boleyn, who was the favorite wife of *Henry*, and a
great friend to the reformed religion. This unfortunate
queen mentioned him to her friends, as a perfon, in her
opinion, as well qualified, as any fhe had feen, to forward
the Reformation, the principles of which fhe had imbibed
from her youth Lord *Cromwell* raifed our preacher ftill
higher in her efteem, and they both joined in an earneft
recommendation of him for a bifhopric to the king, who,
remembering probably the fincerity of his letter to him,
did not want much folicitation in his favor. It happened
that the fees of *Worcefter* and *Salisbury* were at that time
vacant, by the deprivation of *Ghinuccii* and *Campegio*,
two *Italian* bifhops, who fell under the king's difpleafure,

3

upon

upon his rupture with *Rome*. The former of thefe was
offered to *Latimer*, and, as he had been at no pains to
procure this promotion, he looked upon it as the work
of providence, and accepted it without much perfuafion.
Indeed he had met with fo very rough a check already, as
a private clergyman, and faw before him fo hazardous a
profpect in his old ftation, that he thought it neceffary,
both for his own fafety, and for the fake of being of more
fervice to the gofpel, to avail himfelf of fuch an acquifition of refuge and of power. Accordingly, his
enemies were difconcerted in their malevolence, and *Latimer* being out of their power, they quitted all thoughts
of moleftation for the prefent.

All the hiftorians of thefe times mention him as a perfon remarkably zealous in the difcharge of his new office,
and tell us, that, in overlooking the clergy of his diocefe,
he was uncommonly active, warm and refolute, and prefided in his ecclefiaftical court in the fame fpirit In
writing, he was frequent and obfervant, in ordaining
ftrict and wary, in preaching indefatigable, in reproving
and exhorting fevere and perfuafive. Thus far he could
act with authority, but in other things he found himfelf
under difficulties. The popifh ceremonies gave him great
offence, and he neither durft, in times fo dangerous and
unfettled, lay them entirely afide, nor, on the other hand,
was he willing entirely to retain them. In this dilemma,
his addrefs was admirable; he inquired into their origin,
and when he found any of them, as fome were, derived
from a good meaning, he took care to inculcate their
original, though itfelf a corruption, in the room of a
more corrupt practice Thus, he put the people in mind,
when holy bread and water were diftributed, that thefe
elements, which had long been thought endowed with a
kind of magical influence, were nothing more than ap-
pendages to the two facraments of the Lord's Supper and
Baptifm. The former, he faid, reminded us of *Chrift*'s
death, and the latter was only a fimple reprefentation of
being purified from fin. By thus reducing popery to its
firft principles, he improved in fome meafure, a bad ftock,
by lopping from it fome fruitlefs excrefcenfes

While his endeavors to reform were thus confined to
his diocefe, he was called upon to exert them in a more
public manner, by a fummons to parliament and convocation, in 1536. This feffion was thought a crifis by the
proteftant party; at the head of which ftood the lord
Cromwell, whofe favor with the king was now in its meridian

ridian. Next to him in power was *Cranmer*, archbishop of *Canterbury*, after whom our bishop of *Worcester* was the most considerable man, to whom were added the bishops of *Ely, Rochester, Hereford, Salisbury*, and St *David's* On the other hand, the popish party was headed by *Lee*, archbishop of *York, Gardiner, Stokesley*, and *Tunstal*, bishops of *Winchester, London*, and *Durham*

The convocation was opened on the ninth of *June*, and, as usual, by a sermon, or rather an oration, spoken at the appointment of *Cranmer* by our good bishop of *Worcester*, whose eloquence was at this time every where famous Many warm debates passed in this assembly, the result whereof was, that four facraments out of the seven were concluded to be insignificant But, as the bishop of *Worcester* made no figure in them, for debating was not his talent, it is beside the purpose of this memoir to enter into a detail of the several transactions of it We shall only add, that an animated attempt was at this time made to get him and *Cromwell* stigmatized by some public censure, but they were too well established to fear any open attack from their enemies

In the mean while, the bishop of *Worcester*, highly satisfied with the prospect of the times, repaired to his diocese, having made no longer stay in *London* than was absolutely necessary He had no talents, and he knew he had none, for state affairs, and therefore he meddled not with them. It is upon that account, that bishop *Burnet* speaks in a very slight manner of his public character at this time But it is certain, that he never desired to appear in any public character at all. His whole ambition was to discharge the pastoral functions of a bishop, neither aiming to display the abilities of a statesman, nor those of a courtier. How very unqualified he was to support the latter of the characters, will sufficiently appear from the following story —It was the custom in those days for the bishops to make presents to the king on new-year's-day, and many of them would present very liberally, proportioning their gifts to their expectancies Among the rest, the bishop of *Worcester*, being at this time in town, waited upon the king with his offering, but, instead of a purse of gold, which was the common oblation, he presented a New Testament, with a leaf doubled down, in a very conspicuous manner, to this passage *Whoremongers and adulterers God will judge*

Henry VIII. made as little use of a good judgement, as any man ever did. His whole reign was one continued rotation of violent paffions, which rendered him a mere machine in the hands of his minifters, and he among them, who could make the moft artful addrefs to the paffion of the day, carried his point. *Gardiner*, bifhop of *Winchefter*, was juft returned from *Germany*, having fuccefsfully negotiated fome commiffions, which the king had greatly at heart. In 1539, when the parliament was called to confirm the feizure and furrendry of the monafteries, that fubtle minifter took his opportunity, and fucceeded in prevailing upon his majefty to do fomething towards reftoring the old religion, as being moft advantageous for his views in the prefent fituation of *Europe*.

In this ftate of affairs, the bifhop of *Worcefter* received his fummons to parliament, and, foon after his arrival in town, he was accufed before the king of preaching a feditious fermon. The fermon was preached at court, and the preacher, according to his cuftom, had been unqueftionably fevere enough (or rather confcientioufly faithful) againft whatever he obferved amifs. The king had called together feveral bifhops, with a view to confult them upon fome points of religion. When they had all given their opinions, and were about to be difmiffed, the bifhop of *Winchefter* (for it was moft probably he) kneeled down and accufed the bifhop of *Worcefter* as above mentioned. The bifhop being called upon by the king, with fome fternnefs, to vindicate himfelf, was fo far from denying, or even palliating, what he had faid, that he boldly juftified it, and turning to the king, with that noble unconcern, which a good confcience infpires, made this anfwer "I never thought myfelf worthy, nor did I ever "fue to be a preacher before your grace, but I was called "to it, and would be willing, if you miflike it, to give "place to my betters, for I grant there be a great many "more worthy of the room, than I am. And if it be "your grace's pleafure to allow them for preachers, I "could be content to bear their books after them. But "if your grace allow me for a preacher, I would defire "you to give me leave to difcharge my confcience, and "to frame my doctrine, according to my audience. I "had been a very dolt indeed, to have preached fo at the "borders of your realm, as I preach before your grace." The greatnefs of this anfwer baffled his accufer's malice; the feverity of the king's countenance changed into a gracious fmile, and the bifhop was difmiffed with that obliging freedom, which this monarch never ufed but to thofe whom he efteemed.

In

In the year 1538, the bible was published, by the royal authority, in *English*, and as our bishop daily preached up the necessity of a translation in the vulgar tongue, we may justly conclude, he had no little hand in it   The king commissioned only *Grafton* the printer to print it, and he printed fifteen hundred of them at his own charge; and the king by proclamation, according to the advice of archbishop *Cranmer*, and also of *Latimer*, allowed every one to read it. *Cromwell* procured this great privilege, and ' *Cranmer* publicly rejoiced to see this day of Refor-
' mation, which he concluded was risen now in *England*,
' since the light of God's word did shine over it without
' any cloud.' This he declared in a letter to *Cromwell*.

Latimer was a true bishop indeed ! for he not only preached the gospel of *Christ* faithfully and diligently, but he watched over his diocese, and took care, if possible, to right all those poor persons who were imposed upon or hardly used by their great and wealthy overbearing neigh-bors   It seems, says *Fox*, there lived a certain gentle-man in *Warwickshire*, in that part of it which lies within the diocese of *Worcester*, who had wronged a poor man his neighbor, though he had kept within the literal sense of the law.   The gentlemen had a large estate in the county, and his brother was also in the commission of the peace; and these two over-awed and cowed the whole neighborhood, for many miles round.   The poor man, not knowing what to do, at length applied to his own diocesan, told him the whole story, and the manner in which he was oppressed. *Latimer* heard, pitied the poor man's case, and promised him he would, if possible, see him redressed. Whereupon *Latimer* wrote a very long letter to the parties, reproved them sharply for the injury they had done the man, and required them speedily to do him justice   They replied to the bishop, and told him,
' They had done only what was right, and would abide
' by it. That as for the sufferer the law was open, and
' as for his lordship, they could not but think he inter-
' fered very impertinently in an affair which did not con-
' cern him.' *Latimer* never espoused a cause but he would go through with it, and therefore, finding that the gentlemen did not proceed readily to right his client, as we may call the poor man, he sent them a second letter, acquainting them in few words . " That if the cause of
" complaint was not forthwith removed, he certainly
" would himself lay the whole affair before the king."
This *Latimer* certainly would have done, (as he was then

going to *London* on the following occasion) if he had not been prevented, by their making the poor man that restitution and satisfaction he required

As *Latimer* was the champion of the doctrine of the king's supremacy, he was, about this time, sent for to *London*, in order to reclaim one *Forrest*, an observant friar, who had denied the king's supremacy, and also the gospel. *Latimer* did all that lay in his power, and studied every way he could imagine to cause the friar to recant, for, it seems, *Henry* had, till he denied his supremacy, a very great respect for him. However, *Forrest* could not by any arguments or persuasions be induced to recant, and therefore the day came when he was to be put to death in *Smithfield*. The lords of the council came thither, on the day, to offer *Forrest* his pardon, if he would abjure. *Latimer* also, on this occasion, preached a sermon, wherein he endeavored to confute his errors, and begged of him to recant, but he continued still in his former opinions. He was hanged to the stake with a great chain about his middle, and so was burnt.

About this time *Latimer*, together with eighteen other bishops, all that were then in *England*, drew up and signed a declaration against the pope's ecclesiastical jurisdiction, which concludes with these words ' That the ' people ought to be instructed, that *Christ* did expressly ' forbid his apostles or their successors to take to them- ' selves the power of the sword, or the authority of ' kings, and that if the bishop of *Rome*, or any other ' bishop, assumed such power, he was a tyrant and an ' usurper of other men's rights, and a subverter of the ' kingdom of *Christ*.'

Soon after another declaration was drawn up and signed by our bishop and seven others, to shew, ' That, by the ' commission which *Christ* gave to churchmen, they were ' only ministers of his gospel, to instruct the people in ' the purity of the faith. But that, by other places of ' scripture, the authority of Christian princes, over all ' their subjects, as well bishops and priests as others, ' was also clear. And that the bishops and priests have ' charge of souls within their cures, power to administer ' sacraments, and to teach the word of God. To the ' which word of God, Christian princes acknowledge ' themselves subject, and that in case the bishops be neg- ' ligent, it is the Christian prince's office to see them do ' their duty.'

This

This year alfo the priory of *Great Malverne* (now written *Malvern* major in *Efton*) in *Worcefterfhire*, was fuppreffed At the fuppreffion, *Latimer* with an earneft defire recommended to *Cromwell*, who was the king's vicar-general, that that houfe might ftand, not in monkery, but fo as to be converted to preaching, ftudy and prayer And the good prior was willing to compound for his houfe by a prefent of five hundred marks to the king, and of two hundred to *Cromwell* He is commended for being an old worthy man, a good houfe-keeper, and one that daily fed many poor people To this *Latimer* adds, his farther defire and recommendation to the vicar-general, " Alas, my good Lord ! fhall we not fee two or three in " every fhire, changed to fuch remedy." He wifhed, but in vain, the monaftries were diffolved, and the money mifapplied. Indeed *Cranmer* and *Latimer* wanted their lands and riches to be applied to found feminaries in every cathedral, for the training up youth for the miniftry, under the eye and tuition of every bifhop, to be tranf-planted into the feveral cures in each diocefe as occafion ferved.

In this parliament paffed the famous act, as it was cal-led, of the fix articles, which was no fooner publifhed, than it gave an univerfal alarm to all favorers of the Re-formation*, and, as the bifhop of *Worcefter* could not give his vote for the act, he thought it wrong to hold any office in a church, where fuch terms of communion were required He therefore refigned his bifhoprict, and re-tired into the country, where he refided during the heat of that perfecution which followed upon this act, and thought of nothing for the remainder of his days but a fequeftered life He knew the ftorm, which was up, could not foon be appeafed, and he had no inclination to truft himfelf in it But, in the midft of his fecurity, an un-happy accident carried him again into the tempeftuous

---

* Thefe articles were, 1 In the facrament of the altar, after the confecration, there remains no fubftance of bread and wine, but the natural body and blood of *Chrift* 2 Vows of chaftity ought to be obferved 3. The ufe of private maffes is to be continued 4. Com-munion in both kinds is not neceffary 5 Priefts muft not marry 6 Auricular confeffion is to be retained in the church

† It is related of him, that when he came from the parliament-houfe to his lodgings, he threw off his robes, and leaping up, declared to thofe who ftood about him, that he thought himfelf lighter than ever he found himfelf before The ftory is not unlikely, as it is much in character, a vein of pleafantry and good humour accompanying the moft ferious actions of his life.

3

weather that was abroad He received a bruise by the fall of a tree, and the contusion was so dangerous, that he was obliged to feek out for better affistance than could be afforded him by the unfkilful furgeons of thofe parts With this view he repaired to *London*, where he had the forrow to fee the fall of his patron, the lord *Cromwell*, a lofs which he was foon made fenfible of *Gardiner*'s emiffaries quickly found him out in his concealment, and *fomething*, that *fomebody* had *fomewhere* heard him *fay* againft the fix articles, being alledged againft him, he was fent to the tower, where, without any judicial examination, he fuffered, through one pretence or another, a cruel imprifonment for the remaining fix years of king *Henry*'s reign.

He was now in the feventy-firft year of his age. Here *Latimer* was confined, together with the bifhop of *Chichefter*, but not fo ftrictly as that his friends might not come and fee, and converfe with him Neither *Henry*, nor *Gardiner*, had any defign on his life, but the king had done with him, that is to fay, *Latimer* had ferved his majefty's purpofe in eftablifhing the grand and fundamental doctrine of his fupremacy in *England* over all perfons as well ecclefiaftical as civil, and this prince was of fo ungrateful a temper that he cared not afterwards for the man who had faithfully ferved him, and this doth moft flagrantly appear in his beheading Sir *Thomas More*, his cruel ufage of *Wolfey*, and his barbarous, illegal and unjuft treatment of *Cromwell*

Our good bifhop therefore, confidering the difpofition of king *Henry*, had mild ufage, but here he lived himfelf, he fays, " in the daily expectation of being called " to be put to death, becaufe at this time there was held " a feffion in *Newgate* once every three weeks, and exe- " cutions were as frequent " This he tells us in his fourth fermon preached before king *Edward* VI at which time he begs of the king, that as there was then no particular perfon, as he whom we now call ordinary, to inftruct and pray with the unhappy criminals, there might be fome one appointed thereto of learning and diligence, for, continues he, " many of them are caft away for " want of inftruction, and die in mifery for lack of " preaching " And on this occafion, and in this reign, a chaplain was appointed to do the abovementioned duties, and therefore it may juftly be concluded, that this office was conftituted purfuant to his advice.

In

In the difcharge of his epifcopal duty, we are told by the hiftorians of this time, that he was remarkably and exemplarily zealous He was a right bifhop, a *Paul*, a *Timothy*, a *Titus*, and as fuch he continually overlooked his clergy, exciting them to perform the duties of their functions, and he took care, at leaft, to oblige them to a legal performance of preaching, adminiftration of the facraments, vifitation of the fick, and prifoners, &c — There was no part of his diocefe but he vifited, not in a fuperficial and cuftomary manner, but rather in the primitive and apoftolic mode. With the fame refolution he prefided in his own courts, and he either rooted out fuch crimes as were there cognizable, or drove them into holes and corners He never ordained any perfon to the facred offices, but fuch as he examined himfelf, and knew to be duly qualified

Immediately upon the change of government under king *Edward* VI he and all others, who were imprifoned in the fame caufe, were fet at liberty , and bifhop *Latimer*, whofe old friends were now in power, was received by them with every mark of affection , and he would have found no difficulty in difpoffeffing *Heath*, in every refpect an infignificant man, who had fucceeded to his bifhopric. But he had other fentiments , he neither would make fuit himfelf, nor fuffer his friends to make any for his reftoration However, this was done by the parliament, who, after fettling the national concerns, fent up an addrefs to the protector to reftore him The protector was very well inclined, and propofed the refumption to Mr *Latimer*, as a point which he had very much at heart , but *Latimer* perfevered in the negative, alledging his great age, and the claim he had from thence to a private life. And it may be readily believed, that no man ever faid *Nolo epifcopari*, with more fincerity

Having thus rid himfelf of all entreaty on this head, he accepted an invitation from his friend archbifhop *Cranmer*, and took up his refidence at *Lambeth*, where he led a very retired life, being chiefly employed in hearing the complaints and redreffing the injuries of poor people, And indeed his character, for fervices of this kind, was fo univerfally known, that ftrangers from every part of *England* would refort to him, fo that he had as crouded a levee as a minifter of ftate And fure no one was better qualified to undertake the office of redreffing injuries · His free reproofs, joined to the integrity of his life, had a great effect upon thofe in the higheft ftations, while

his

his own independence and backwardness of asking any favor for himself, allowed him greater liberty in asking for others

In these employments he spent more than two years, interfering as little as possible in any public transaction, only he assisted the archbishop in composing the homilies which were set forth by authority in the first year of king *Edward* He was also appointed to preach the lent sermons before his majesty, which office he performed during the three first years of his reign

As to his sermons, which are still extant, they are indeed far enough from being exact pieces of composition; yet his simplicity and low familiarity, his humor and gibing drollery, were well adapted to the times, and his oratory, according to the mode of eloquence at that day, was exceedingly popular. His action and manner of preaching too were very affecting, and no wonder, for he spoke immediately from his heart His abilities, however, as an orator, made only the inferior part of his character as a preacher What particularly recommends him is that noble and apostolic zeal, which he exerts in the cause of truth

But in the discharge of this duty a slander passed upon him, which being taken up by a low historian of those times, hath found its way into these The matter of it is, that, after the lord high admiral's attainder and execution, which happened about this time, he publicly defended his death in a sermon before the king, that he aspersed his character, and that he did it merely to pay a servile compliment to the protector The first part of the charge is true, but the second and third are false As to his aspersing the admiral's character, his character was so bad, there was no room for aspersion His treasonable practices too were notorious, and though the proceeding against him by a bill in parliament, according to the custom of those times, may be deemed inequitable, yet he paid no more than a due forfeit to the laws of his country However, his death occasioned great clamour, and was made use of by the lords of the opposition (for he left a very dissatisfied party behind him) as a handle to raise a popular odium against the protector, for whom Mr. *Latimer* had always a high esteem He was mortified, therefore, to see so invidious and base an opposition, thwarting the schemes of so public-spirited a man, and endeavored to lessen the odium, by shewing the admiral's

character

character in its true light, from some anecdotes not commonly known.

Upon the revolution which happened at court, after the death of the duke of *Somerset*, *Latimer* seems to have retired into the country, and made use of the king's licence as a general preacher in those parts, where he thought his labors might be most serviceable He was thus employed during the remainder of that reign, and continued in the same course, for a short time, in the beginning of the next*; but as soon as the introduction of popery was resolved on, the first step towards it was the prohibition of all preaching throughout the kingdom, and a licensing only such as were known to be popishly inclined Accordingly, a strict inquiry was made after the more forward and popular preachers, and many of them were taken into custody The bishop of *Winchester*, who was now prime minister, having proscribed Mr. *Latimer* from the first, sent a message to cite him before the council He had notice of this design, some hours before the messenger's arrival, but he made no use of the intelligence The messenger found him equipped for his journey; at which expressing his surprize, Mr *Latimer* told him, that he was as ready to attend him to *London*, thus called upon to answer for his faith, as he ever was to take any journey in his life, and that he doubted not but that God, who had enabled him to stand before two princes, would enable him to stand before a third, either to her comfort or discomfort eternally. The messenger then acquainting him, that he had no orders to seize his person, delivered a letter, and departed Hence some have imagined, that the secret design of thus serving on him a citation was to drive him out of the kingdom, that so they might get rid of him, ' left (says Mr. *Fox*) his ' firmness and constancy should deface them in their po- ' pery, and confirm the godly in the truth.'

---

* Mr *Fox* says, that in all king *Edward* s days, he travelled up and down, preaching for the most part twice every Sunday, to the no small shame of all other loitering and unpreaching prelates, who occupy great rooms, and do little good He took little ease and care of sparing himself, to do the people good. And notwithstanding his great age, he would, in the pursuit of his private studies, every morning, commonly through winter and summer, arise and most diligently apply himself thereto At king *Edward*'s death, which occurred on the sixth of *July*, 1553, *Latimer* was in the country preaching there as opportunity and occasion led him, going about, in imitation of the apostles, strengthening the people every where in the protestant faith and principles.

Mr.

Mr. *Latimer*, however, opening the letter, and finding it to contain a citation from the council, refolved to obey it He fet out therefore immediately, and as he paffed through *Smithfield*, where heretics were ufually burnt, he faid chearfully, " *Smithfield* hath long groaned for me " The next morning he waited upon the council, who, having treated him rudely, and loaded him with many fevere reproaches, fent him to the *Tower*.

This was but a repetition of a former part of his life; only he *now* met with harfher treatment, and had more frequent occafion to exercife his refignation, which perhaps few men poffeffed in a larger meafure, nay, even the ufual chearfulnefs of his difpofition did not now forfake him, of which we have one inftance ftill remaining A fervant leaving his apartment in the *Tower*, Mr *Latimer* called after him, and bade him tell his mafter, that unlefs he took better care of him, he would certainly efcape him Upon this meffage, the lieutenant, with fome difcompofure in his countenance, came to Mr *Latimer*, and defired an explanation " Why, you expect, " I fuppofe, fir, replied Mr. *Latimer*, that I fhould be " burnt, but if you do not allow me a little fire this " frofty weather, I can tell you, I fhall be ftarved to " death with cold "

Cranmer and *Ridley* were alfo prifoners in the fame caufe with *Latimer*, and when it was refolved to have a public difputation at *Oxford*, between the moft eminent of the popifh and proteftant divines, thefe three were appointed to manage the difpute on the part of the proteftants. Accordingly, they were taken out of the *Tower*, where they had lain all the winter of 1553, and fent to *Oxford*, in the fpring of 1554, where they were clofely confined in the common prifon, and they might eafily imagine how free the difputation was likely to be, when they found themfelves denied the ufe even of books and pen and ink

Mr *Fox* has preferved a conference, afterwards put into writing, which was held at this time between *Ridley* and *Latimer*, which fets out author's temper in a ftrong light. The two bifhops are reprefented fitting in their prifon, ruminating upon the folemn preparations then making for their trial, of which, probably, they were now firft informed. *Ridley* firft ' The time (faid he) is now ' come, we are now called upon, either to deny our ' faith, or to fuffer death in its defence You, Mr. ' *Latimer*, are an old foldier of *Chrift*, and have fre-
' quently

' quently withstood the fear of death, whereas I am raw
' in the service and unexperienced ' With this preface
he introduces a request, that Mr *Latimer*, whom he calls
his father, would hear him propose such arguments, as
he thinks it most likely his adversaries would urge against
him, and assist him with providing himself with proper
answers to them.

To this, Mr *Latimer*, in his usual strain of good humour, replied, that he fancied the good bishop was treating him, as he remembered Mr *Bilney* used formerly to
do; who, when he wanted to teach him, would always
do it under colour of being taught himself. " But, in
" the present case, (said he) my lord, I am determined
" to give them very little trouble, I shall just offer them
" a plain account of my faith, and shall say very little
" more, for I know any thing more will be to no pur-
" pose: They talk of a free disputation, but I am well
" assured their grand argument will be, as it once was
" their forefathers, *We have a law, and by our law ye*
" *ought to die* "—Bishop *Ridley* having afterwards desired
his prayers; that he might trust wholly upon God " Of
" my prayers, (replied the old bishop) you may be well
" assured; nor do I doubt but I shall have yours in re-
" turn And indeed prayer and patience should be our
" great resources. For myself, had I the learning of
" St *Paul*, I should think it ill laid out upon an elabo-
" rate defence Yet our case, my lord, admits of com-
" fort Our enemies can do no more than God permits;
" and God is faithful, who will not suffer us to be
" tempted above our strength. Be at a point with them;
" stand to that, and let them say and do what they please.
" To use many words would be vain Yet it is requisite
" to give a reasonable account of your faith, if they
" will quietly hear you For other things, in a wicked
" judgement-hall, a man may keep silence after the ex-
" ample of *Christ* As for their sophistry, you know
" falshood may often be displayed in the colours of truth.
" But, above all things, be upon your guard against the
" fear of death This is THE GREAT ARGUMENT you
" must oppose.—Poor *Shaxton!* it is to be feared, this
" argument had the greatest weight in his recantation.
" But let us be stedfast and unmoveable, assuring our-
" selves, that we cannot be more happy, than by being
" such *Philippians*, as not only believe in *Christ*, but dare
" to suffer for his sake." Agreeably to this noble fortitude did our martyr behave himself, through this dispute,
wherein,

wherein, though much artifice was used for the purpose, he never could be drawn into any formal reasoning with his adversaries. Mr *Addison* greatly admires his behavior on this occasion, but does not assign the true cause of it ' This remarkable old man (says he) knowing how his ' abilities were impaired by age, and that it was impos- ' sible for him to recollect all those reasons which had ' directed him in the choice of his religion, left his com- ' panions, who were in the full possession of their parts ' and learning, to baffle and confound their antagonists ' by the force of reason As for himself, he only repeated ' to his adversaries the articles in which he firmly be- ' lieved, and in the profession of which he was determined ' to die '—The truth is, he knew it would answer no end to be more explicit

However, he answered their questions as far as civility required, and in these answers it is observable he managed the argument much better than either *Ridley* or *Cranmer*, who, when they were pressed in defence of transubstan- tiation, with some passages from the fathers, instead of disavowing an insufficient authority, weakly defended a good cause, evading and distinguishing after the manner of schoolmen Whereas, when the same proofs were mul- tiplied upon *Latimer*, he told them plainly, that such proofs had no weight with him, that the fathers, no doubt, were often deceived, and that he never depended upon *them*, but when *they* depended upon scripture. ' Then ' you are not of St *Chrysostom*'s faith, (replied his anta- ' gonist) nor of St *Austin*'s '—" I have told you (says " Mr. *Latimer*) I am not; except they bring scripture " for what they say." The dispute being ended, sen- tence was passed upon him in the beginning of *October*, and he and *Ridley* were executed on the sixteenth When they came to the stake, *Latimer* lift up his eyes with a sweet and amiable countenance, saying, *Fidelis est Deus, &c.* i e God is faithful, who will not suffer us to be tempted above that which we are able. When they were brought to the fire, on a spot of ground on the north side of *Baliol College*, where, after an abusive sermon, being told by an officer they might now make ready for the stake, Mr. *Latimer*, having thrown off his prison attire, appeared in a shroud prepared for the purpose, ' and ' whereas before (says Mr *Fox*) he seemed a withered ' and crooked old man, he stood now bolt upright, as ' comely a father as one might lightly behold ' Being thus ready, he recommended his soul to God, and deli-

vered

vered himfelf to the executioner, faying to the bifhop
of *London*, "We fhall this day, brother, light fuch a
" candle in *England*, as fhall never be put out"

It is faid, that as he was burning, the blood ran from
his heart in fuch abundance, that it aftonifhed the fpectators, and brought to mind what he had before wifhed,
that he might be fo happy as to fhed his heart's blood for
the truth When the fire was firft kindled, he cried,
" O Father of heaven, receive my foul," and fo receiving the flame, and (as it feemed) embracing it, and having ftroked his face with his hands and bathed them a
little in the fire, he foon died without the leaft appearance of fuffering pain

Such was the death of *Hugh Latimer*, bifhop of *Worcefter*, one of the leaders of that noble army of martyrs,
who introduced the Reformation in *England*. He had a
happy temper, improved by the beft principles, and fuch
was his chearfulnefs, that none of the circumftances of life
were feen to difcompofe him. Such was his Chriftian
fortitude, that not even the fevereft trials could unman
him, he had a collected fpirit, and on no occafion wanted
a refource, he could retire within himfelf, feel the fupport of a gracious Mafter, and hold the world at defiance

And, as danger could not daunt, fo neither could ambition allure him Though converfant in courts, and
intimate with princes, he preferved to the laft a rare
inftance of moderation in his original plainnefs In his
profeffion he was indefatigable And, that he might beftow as much time as poffible on the active part of it, he
allowed himfelf only thofe hours for his private ftudies,
when the bufy world is at reft, conftantly rifing, at all
feafons of the year, by two in the morning. How confcientious he was in the difcharge of the public parts of
his office, we have many examples No man could perfuade more forcibly, no man could exert, on proper oc-
cafions, a more commanding feverity The wicked, in
whatever ftation, he rebuked with dignity, and awed vice
more than a penal law

He was not efteemed a very learned man, for he cultivated only ufeful learning, and that he thought lay in
a very narrow compafs He never engaged in worldly
affairs, thinking that a clergyman ought to employ himfelf *only* in his profeffion Thus he lived, rather a good,
than what the world calls a great man. He had not thofe
commanding talents which give fuperiority in bufinefs,
but, for honefty and fincerity of heart, for true fimplicity

of

BISHOP RIDLEY.

From an original Painting

of manners, for apostolic zeal in the cause of religion, and for every virtue, both of a public and private kind, that should adorn the life of a Christian, he was eminent and exemplary beyond most men of his own or of any other time, well deserving that evangelical commendation, *with the testimony of a good conscience in simplicity and godly sincerity, not with fleshly wisdom, but by the grace of God, he had his conversation in the world.*

NICHOLAS RIDLEY,

BISHOP OF LONDON

THIS most learned of all our *English* martyrs, was born, of an antient and worthy family at *Wilymondswyke*, in *Northumberland* He was educated in grammatical learning at *Newcastle* upon *Tyne*, from thence he was removed to *Pembroke-Hall* in *Cambridge*, at the expence of his uncle Dr. *Robert Ridley*, about the year 1518, when *Luther* was preaching against indulgences in *Germany* Here he acquired a great proficiency in the *Latin* and *Greek* tongues, and in the other learning of that time His reputation was such, as to procure him the esteem of the other university, as well as of his own, for in the beginning of 1524, the master and fellows of *University College*, in *Oxford*, invited him to accept of an exhibition, founded by *Walter Skyrley*, bishop of *Durham*, which he declined The next year he took his master's degree, and was appointed by the college their general agent in some causes relating to it.

His uncle was now willing to add to his attainments, the advantages of travel, and the improvement of foreign universities, and as his studies were now directed to divinity, he sent him to spend some time among the doctors of the *Sorbonne* at *Paris*, (which was then the most celebrated university in *Europe*) and afterwards among the professors of *Louvain* Having staid three years abroad, viz the years, 1527, 1528, 1529, he returned to *Cambridge*, and pursued his theological studies, and as his safest guide in them, diligently applied himself to the read-

ing

ing of the scriptures in the original, and in a walk in the orchard at *Pembroke-Hall*, which is to this day called *Ridley's-Walk*, he got to repeat without book almost all the epistles in *Greek*

His behavior here was very obliging, and very pious, without hypocrisy or monkish austerity. For very often he would shoot in the bow, or play at tennis. And he was eminent for the great charities he bestowed. He was senior proctor of the university, when the important point of the pope's supremacy came before them to be examined upon the authority of scripture. And their resolution, after mature deliberation, 'That the bishop of *Rome* had ' no more authority or jurisdiction derived to him from ' God, in this kingdom of *England*, than any other fo-' reign bishop,' was signed in the name of the university by *Simon Heynes*, vice chancellor, *Nicholas Ridley*, *Richard Wilkes*, proctors. He lost his uncle in 1536, but the education he had received, and the improvements he had made, soon recommended him to another and greater patron, *Cranmer*, archbishop of *Canterbury*, who appointed him his domestic chaplain, and collated him to the vicarage of *Herne* in *East Kent*. He bore his testimony in the pulpit here against the act of the six articles, and instructed his charge in the pure doctrines of the gospel, as far as they were yet discovered to him; but transubstantiation was at this time an article of his creed. During his retirement at this place, he read a little treatise written seven hundred years before, by *Ratramus* or *Bertram*, a monk of *Cerbey*. This first opened *Ridley's* eyes, and determined him more accurately to search the scriptures on this article, and the doctrine of the primitive fathers. His discoveries he communicated to his patron, and the event was the conviction of them both, that this doctrine was novel and erroneous.

After he had staid about two years at *Herne*, he was chosen master of *Pembroke-Hall*, and appointed chaplain to the king, and the cathedral church of *Canterbury* being made collegiate, he obtained the fifth prebendal stall in it; and such was his courage and zeal for the Reformation, that, next to the archbishop, he was thought to be its greatest support among the clergy. In the succeeding reign of *Edward* VI. when a royal visitation was resolved on through the kingdom, he attended the visitors of the northern circuit as their preacher, to instruct that part of the nation, in the principles of religion. 'His cha-' racter, at this time, (says his biographer Dr. *Ridley*)

3   ' was

' was that of a celebrated difputant, a favourite preacher,
' undoubting in the article of tranfubftantiation, a zeal-
' ous fcripturift, and particularly well acquainted with
' the fathers.'

It was not before the year 1545, that *Ridley* was convinced of the error, which prevailed, concerning *Chrift's*
corporal prefence in the facrament. The fufferings and
arguments of *Frith*, *Tindale*, *Lambert*, and others, made
fuch ftrong impreffions, during his retirement at *Herne*
about this time, that, by the grace of God, they ended in
his conviction of the truth of their doctrine

He was made chaplain to king *Edward* VI. confecrated
bifhop of *Rochefter* in 1547, and tranflated to *London* on
the deprivation of *Bonner* in 1550 But he died in the
flames at *Oxford* in 1555

Ridley, of all the reforming divines of that time, ap-
proached the neareft to the church of *England* in her prefent doctrines and difcipline His notions of ecclefiaftical
polity were high, but in general juft, and, in the œconomy of the church, he allowed an equitable regard to
the authority of the ftate He faw, and avoided, but
could bear with the errors of all parties among the reformed, while the dignity, the affability, and the modefty
of his behavior, gave him a general efteem with all ranks
of men

The church of *Rome* had laid fuch a ftrefs on the indif-
penfible neceffity of the facraments, that the people were
taught to believe; that by the very action itfelf, without
the inward grace, they were fufficient to juftification,
unlefs the receiver himfelf prevented it, and this feems
to have given rife to the homilies about juftification.
Public difputations were held in both univerfities, between
the Reformers and the papifts, concerning the real prefence of *Chrift* in the facrament *Ridley* was fent to
Cambridge, with fome other delegates, where a difputation
was held for three days together, to prove, that tranfubftantiation was not to be found in the plain and manifeft
words of fcripture, nor could neceffarily be collected from
it, nor confirmed by the confent of the antient fathers,
and that there is no other facrifice and oblation in the
Lord's Supper, than of a remembrance of *Chrift's* death,
and of thankfgiving The debate was fummed up with
a great deal of temper and learning by bifhop *Ridley*, in
a ftrong determination againft the corporal prefence The
truth is, he was then mafter of that fubject more than
any man of the age, for having met with a book of *Ber-*

tram's in the ninth century, in which he, who was much esteemed, had confuted this notion of the presence of *Christ*'s real flesh and blood in the sacrament, the bishop concluded (as we have observed before) that it was not the antient doctrine of the church, but had been introduced with other errors and superstitions in the later centuries He communicated this discovery to his friend archbishop *Cranmer*, soon afterwards, and they set themselves to examine it with more than common care, making great collections out of the fathers, and other antient writers, to prove the novelty and the absurdity of the opinion They shewed, that all the high expressions which were to be found in *Chrysostom*, and other antient writers on this subject, were only strains and figures of eloquence, to raise the devotion of the people in this holy ceremony, though the following ages had built their opinion on these expressions, and were disposed to believe every thing the more readily as it appeared above all belief But this opinion of the real presence having been so generally received in *England*, above three hundred years, these eminent Reformers proceeded gradually in discussing it, that the people might be better disposed to receive what they intended afterwards to establish.

The lord protector had a design of suppressing *Clare-Hall* in *Cambridge*, and unite it with *Trinity-Hall*, to augment the number of fellows there to twenty, in order to found a new college for Civilians For this purpose a commission was granted to the bishops of *Ely* and *Rochester*, *William Paget*, Sir *Thomas Smith*, *John Cheeke*, Dr *May*, dean of St *Paul*'s, and *Thomas Wendy*, M D When the commission passed, the bishop of *Rochester* was in his diocese, ignorant of the design. Thither Mr. secretary *Smith* and the dean of St. *Paul*'s sent to acquaint him that he was in commission to visit the university of *Cambridge*, and that he was appointed to preach the sermon at the opening of it Upon which the bishop immediately dispatched a servant to *London* to Dr *May*, desiring information to what ends the visitation and commission were intended, that he might frame his sermon accordingly The dean returned for answer, that it was only to remove some superstitious practices and rites, and to make such statutes as should be needful The instructions themselves by which they were to proceed were not shewn him till after they had acted in the commission

Presently after the passing of this, he was again put into commission with the archbishop, the bishops of *Ely*,
Worcester,

Worcester, *Westminster*, *Chichester*, and *Lincoln*, Sir *William Petre*, Sir *Thomas Smith*, Dr *Cox*, Dr *May*, and others, to fearch after all Anabaptifts, Hereticks, and contemners of the common prayer. For complaint had been brought to the council, that, with the ftrangers who were come into *England*, fome Anabaptifts were mingled, who were difleminating their errors and making profelytes. Under this general name were comprehended men of various opinions, driven out of *Germany* with the more fober proteftants, who were in danger from the emperor, for not complying with the *interim*. Thefe, is bifhop *Burnet* informs us, building upon *Luther's* principles, that fcripture was to be the only rule of truth, rejected all deductions from it, how obvious or certain foever, and among thefe the baptifm of infants was one, whom therefore, when adults, they baptized again, and from thence were called Rebaptizers, or Anabaptifts. Some were more modeft and moderate, others extravagant and fierce. The opinions of the latter may be learned from fome tradefmen in *London*, who abjured before thefe commiffioners in *May*, fuch as, That a man regenerate could not fin, that though the outward man finned, the inward man finned not, that there was no trinity of perfons, that *Chrift* was only a holy prophet, and not God at all, that all we had by *Chrift* was, that he taught us the way of heaven, that he took no flefh of the virgin, and that the baptifm of infants was not profitable, becaufe it goeth before faith. Among the people who held thefe and fuch like heretical opinions was *Joan Bocher*, commonly called *Joan* of *Kent*. She appearing before the commiffioners behaved with extreme obftinacy there, perfifting in the maintenance of her error, namely, that the Son of God penetrated through the virgin *Mary* as through a glafs, taking no fubftance of her, as *Latimer* reports, who fat in the commiffion. Her own words diftinguifhing betwixt *Chrift* and the *word*, and betwixt the *outward* and *inward* man of the virgin, allowing the *word* to have taken flefh by the confent of the virgin's *inward* man, but denying that *Chrift* took flefh of her *outward* man, becaufe it was finful, are not very intelligible. She treated with fcorn all the means made ufe of to recover her to a better mind, and fentence paffed upon her, pronouncing her an heretic, and delivering her over to the fecular arm. *Ridley* was ftill at *Rochefter*, for only the archbifhop, Sir *John Smith*, *William Cook*, dean of the arches, *Hugh Latimer*, and *Richard Lyel*, LL. D were named in the fentence. The king was hardly prevailed upon

by

by *Cranmer* to fign the warrant for her burning But the archbifhop diftinguifhing betwixt errors in other points, and the open fcornful rejecting an exprefs article of the creed, *born of the virgin* Mary, thinking that thefe latter, always efteemed heretics from the firft eftablifhment of Chriftianity, deferved not the lenity with which others might be treated And reprefented, that it betrayed an indifference towards religion to neglect putting in execution the laws eftablifhed for maintaining God's honor, while they were diligent in thofe that were enacted to maintain the king's honor, and the peace or property of the fubject. However, the archbifhop was not fo earneft to get the warrant executed, as figned. He labored much to convince and fave her from the fire. In which charitable office, *Ridley*, when he came to *London*, joined; they both of them vifited her, they feverally took her home with them to their own houfes, and earneftly endeavored to recover her from her errors But fhe refifted with great ftubbornnefs and indecency all their kind pains to recover her After their unfuccefsful attempts for a whole year, fhe was at laft burned the fecond of *May*, 1550, perfifting obftinately in her opinion, and behaving with great infolence to the laft The like fentence was executed upon *George Van Parre*, a *Dutchman*, for denying the divinity of our Saviour. Which is mentioned here, though it happened not till the twenty-fifth of *April*, 1551, on the fixth of which month *Ridley*, who was a commiffioner, figned the fentence of excommunication. Mild and gentle as his nature was to every modeft enquirer, though in error, he would not break the laws in being, in indulgence to obftinate blafphemers. The reproach caft on the Reformers as enemies to all religion, and the divifions and difturbances raifed in the kingdom by emiffaries from the church of *Rome*, under the name of Anabaptifts, called for punifhment, which the feverity of the laws then in being determined in thefe cafes to be by burning

One occafion of this feverity was, probably, that in the preceding winter, there had been a defign of uniting the proteftants abroad, and at home under the *Englifh* difcipline. The churches abroad, who, not from choice, but neceffity, were under the government of prefbyters (becaufe reformed in places where all the bifhops were papifts) were very ready to come into epifcopal government And great confultations had been held, not only concerning the Reformation of *this* church, but alfo of the

the other foreign churches in *Germany*, *Switzerland*,
France, *Italy*, and *Spain*, for uniting them together in
one uniform doctrine *Bullinger* and *Calvin*, with others,
in a letter to king *Edward*, offered to make him their
defender, and to have bishops in their churches as there
were in *England*, with the tender of their service to assist
and unite together This alarmed the *Roman* fathers,
who came to the knowledge of it by some of their private
intelligencers, for they verily thought that all the heretics (as they called them) would now unite among themselves, and become one body, receiving the same discipline exercised in *England* Whereupon they sent two
of their emissaries from *Rotterdam* hither, who were to
pretend themselves Anabaptists, and preach against bap-
tizing infants, and recommending rebaptizing, and inculcate a fifth monarchy upon earth Besides this one D G,
authorised by these fathers, dispatched a letter written in
May, 1549, from *Delf* in *Holland* to two bishops, (of
which *Winchester* was one) signifying the coming of these
pretended Anabaptists, and that they should receive and
cherish them, and take their parts, if they should receive
any checks Telling them that it was left to them to
assist in this cause, and to some others whom they well
knew to be well affected to the mother church This
letter was found by Sir *H Sidney* in queen *Elizabeth*'s
closet among some papers of queen *Mary*'s Some knowledge or suspicion of these intrigues might occasion the
using greater severity to the officious and irreclaimable
Anabaptists, who were heretics in the strictest sense, than
would otherwise have been exercised against them And
if *Bonner* was the other bishop, as none more likely, both
from his zeal and situation, it may account for his and
Winchester's sufferings in this reign But if neither the
bold contradicting the articles of the creed drawn from
scripture, and confirmed by the four first general councils,
nor the laws of the country then in force, nor the reproach cast on the Reformers, as careless of the truths
of Christianity, except in opposition to the *Romish* church,
nor the disturbances occasioned both in church and state
by these real or pretended Anabaptists, can excuse the
commissioners for passing this sentence, when the facts
were open and notorious, and their endeavors to reclaim
the offenders were earnest and unwearied, we must leave
them to the censure of the Reader.

And now, sometime in *May*, the bishop of *Rochester*
repaired to *Cambridge* with his fellow commissioners to

3 G   hold

hold the vifitation for the abolifhing ftatutes and ordinances which maintained popery and fuperftition (as he
was informed,) not knowing the further end propofed,
which was the fuppreffion of *Clare-Hall* He defired to
fee the inftructions But was put off by his affociates,
who feemed afraid to fhew them unto him, till they had
engaged him in the action, by opening it with a fermon,
and proceeding two days in the bufinefs of it They
then ventured to fhew him their inftructions, in which
he found the fuppreffion of *Clare-Hall* was the thing
intended, under a cover of uniting it to *Trinity-Hall*,
and erecting there a new college of Civilians However
the bifhop might difrelifh this defign, he found it was his
duty now to concur with the other commiffioners in
laboring for two days together with the mafter and fellows *voluntarily* to furrender their college into the king's
hands But the fociety could not be induced to confent
to fuch a furrender The commiffioners fat fecretly by
themfelves, confulting how to proceed The majority
determined that they might proceed to the union of the
two colleges, by the king's abfolute power, without the
confent of the focieties. But the bifhop of *Rochefter*
modeftly oppofed this counfel, and with great calmnefs
diffented though refolute and determined not to violate
the king's honor, and his own confcience, by forcibly
invading the liberties and properties of the mafter and
fellows of *Clare-Hall*, yet not cenfuring his fellows, but
exhorted them to act fo as is to fatisfy their own confciences, and if it fhould be fo that he could not concur,
he defired leave to fatisfy his own confcience, by abfent-
ing himfelf, or by filence to refufe his confent This
put a ftop to the proceedings at prefent The commiffioners acquainting the protector with this interruption
from the bifhop of *Rochefter*, complained, that he *by his
barking* hindered them from proceeding in the king's fervice, imputing his diffent to a partial affection for his
own countrymen, with whom at that time *Clare-Hall*
abounded This exafperated the protector, who wrote a
chiding letter to the bifhop To which the bifhop immediately returned the following anfwer.

" Right honourable,
" I Wifh your grace the holy and wholefome fear of
"   God, becaufe I am perfuaded your grace's goodnefs
" to be fuch unfeignedly, that even wherein your grace's
" letter doth fore blame me, yet in the fame the adver-
                                            " tifement

" tifement of the truth fhall not difpleafe your grace
" And alfo perceiving that the caufe of your grace's
" difcontent was wrong information, therefore I fhall
" befeech your grace to give me leave to fhew your grace
" wherein it appeareth to me that your grace is wrong
" informed

" Your grace's letters blame me, becaufe I did not
" (at the firft before the vifitation began, having know-
" ledge of the matter) fhew my mind. The truth is,
" before God, I never had, nor could get any foreknow-
" ledge of the matter, of the uniting the two colleges,
" before we had begun and had entered two days in the
" vifitation, and that your grace may plainly thus well
" perceive

" A little before *Eafter*, I being at *Rochefter*, received
" letters from Mr Secretary *Smith*, and the dean of St
" *Paul*'s, to come to the vifitation of the univerfity, and
" to make a fermon at the beginning thereof Where-
" upon I fent immediately a fervant up to *London* to the
" dean of St *Paul*'s, defiring of him to have had fome
" knowledge of things there to be done, becaufe I
" thought it meet that my fermon fhould fomewhat have
" favoured of the fame From Mr. Dean I received a
" letter inftructing me only, that the caufe of the vifi-
" tation was to abolifh ftatutes and ordinances, which
" maintained papiftry, fuperftition, blindnefs, and igno-
" rance, and to eftablifh and fet forth fuch as might
" further God's word and good learning And elfe, the
" truth is, he would fhew me nothing, but bad me be
" carelefs, and faid, there were informations how all
" things were to be done The which, I take God to
" witnefs, I did never fee, nor could get knowledge
" what they were, before we were entered in the vifita-
" tion two days, although I defired to have feen them in
" the beginning

" Now when I had feen the inftructions, the truth is,
" I thought peradventure the mafter and company would
" have furrendered up their college But when their
" confent, after labour and travail taken therein two
" days, could not be obtained, then we began fecretly
" to confult, (all the commiffioners thinking it beft,
" that every man fhould lay his mind plainly, that in
" execution there might appear but one way to be taken
" of all) There, when it was feen to fome, that with-
" out the confent of the prefent incumbents, by the
" king's abfolute power, we might proceed to the uniting

" the two colleges, I did, in my courfe, fimply and
" plainly declare my confcience, and that there only,
" fecretly among ourfelves alone, with all kind of foft-
" nefs, fo that no man could juftly be offended   Alfo,
" I perceive by your grace's letters, I have been noted of
" fome for *my barking* there   And yet *to bark*, left God
" fhould be offended, I cannot deny, but indeed it is a
" part of my profeffion, for God's word condemneth the
" dumb dogs that will not *bark*, and give warning of
" God's difpleafure

" As for that, that was fuggefted to your grace, that
" by my aforefaid barking, I fhould difhonour the king's
" majefty, and diffuade others from the execution of the
" king's commiffion, God is my judge, I intended, ac-
" cording to my duty to God and the king, the main-
" tenance and defence of his highnefs's royal honour
" and dignity. If that be true, that I believe is true,
" which the prophet faith, *Honor regis judicium diligit,*
" *(The king's power loveth judgement,)* and as the com-
" miffioners muft needs, and I am fure will all teftify,
" that I diffuaded no man, but contrariwife, exhorted
" every man (with the quiet of other) to fatisfy his own
" confcience, defiring only, that if it fhould otherwife
" be feen unto them, that I might either by my abfence
" or filence, fatisfy mine   The which my plainnefs,
" when fome, otherwife than according to my expecta-
" tion, did take, I was moved thereupon (both for the
" good opinion I had, and yet have, in your grace's
" goodnefs, and alfo efpecially becaufe your grace had
" commanded me fo to do) to open my mind, by my
" private letters freely to your grace

" And thus I truft your grace perceiveth now, both
" that anon, after knowledge had, I did utter my con-
" fcience, and alfo that the matter was not opened unto
" me before the vifitation was two days begun.

" If in this I did amifs, that before the knowledge of
" the inftructions, I was ready to grant to the execution
" of the commiffion, truly, I had rather herein acknow-
" ledge my fault, and fubmit myfelf to your grace's
" correction, than, after knowledge had, wittingly and
" willingly commit that thing whereunto my confcience
" doth not agree, for fear of God's difpleafure

" It is a godly wifh that is wifhed in your grace's
" letters, that flefh, and blood, and country, might not
" more weigh with fome men than godlinefs and reafon
" But the truth is, country in this matter (whatfoever
" fome

I

" fome men do fuggeft unto your grace) fhall not move
" me And that your grace fhall well perceive, for I
" fhall be as ready as any other, firft thence to expel
" fome of my own country, if the report which is made
" of them, can be tried true

" And as for that your grace faith of flesh and blood,
" that is, the favour or fear of mortal man Yea, marry
" fir, that is a matter of weight indeed, and the truth
" is, (alas! my own feeblenefs) of that I am afraid But
" I befeech your grace, yet once again, give me good
" leave, wherein here I fear my own frailty, to confefs
" the truth

" Before God, there is no man this day (leaving the
" king's majefty for the honour only excepted) whofe
" favour or difpleafure I do either feek or fear, as your
" grace's favour or difpleafure, for of God, both your
" grace's authority, and my bound duty for your grace's
" benefits bind me fo to do So that if the defire of any
" man's favour, or fear of difpleafure, fhould weigh more
" with me than godlinefs and reafon, truly, if I may
" be bold to fay the truth, I muft needs fay, that I am
" moft in danger to offend herein, either for defire of
" your grace's favour, or for fear of your grace's dif-
" pleafure And yet I fhall not ceafe (God willing)
" daily to pray to God fo to ftay and ftrengthen my frailty
" with holy fear, that I do not commit the thing for
" favour or fear of any mortal man, whereby my con-
" fcience may threaten me with the lofs of the favour of
" the living God But that it may pleafe him of his gra-
" cious goodnefs (howfoever the world goes) to blow
" this in the ears of my heart, *Deus diffipavit offa eorum*
" *qui hominibus placuerint* (God hath broken the bones of
" *them that pleafe men*) And this, *Horrendum eft incidere*
" *in manus Dei viventis* (It is a fearful thing to fall into
" *the hands of the living God.*) And again, *Nolite timere*
" *eos qui occidunt corpus* (Fear not thofe who kill the body)

" Wherefore I moft humbly befeech your grace for
" God's love not to be offended with me, for renewing
" of this my fuit unto your grace, which is, that wherein
" my confcience cannot well agree, if any fuch thing
" chance in this vifitation, I may, with your grace's
" favour have licence, either by mine abfence or filence,
" or other like means, to keep my confcience quiet I
" wifh your grace, in God, honour and endlefs felicity.

" Your grace's humble and daily orator,

From *Pembroke-Hall*, in   " NICHOLAS ROFFEN "
Cambridge, June 1, 1549.

The

The protector was at that time with the king at *Richmond* And on the receipt of the bishop of *Rochester's* letter, he conferred with the archbishop, who was *Ridley's* chief intimate, to difcover the fecret motives, if any he had, why the bishop difliked the proceedings at the vifitation And in a little more than a week the protector returned the following anfwer,

‘ **A**FTER our right hearty commendations to you
‘ We have received your letters of the firft of *June*,
‘ again replying to thofe which we laft fent unto you
‘ And as it appeareth, you yet remaining in your former
‘ requeft, defire, if things do occur fo, that according to
‘ your confcience, you cannot do them, that you might
‘ abfent yourfelf, or otherwife keep filence We would
‘ be loth any thing fhould be done by the king's majefty's
‘ vifitors, otherwife than right and confcience might
‘ allow, and approve And vifitation is to direct things
‘ to the better, not to the worfe, to eafe confciences,
‘ not to clog them Marry, we would wifh the execu-
‘ tors thereof fhould not be fcrupulous in confcience,
‘ otherwife than reafon would Againft your confcience
‘ it is not our will to move you, as we would not gladly
‘ do, or move any man to that which is againft right and
‘ confcience, and we truft the king's majefty hath not
‘ in this matter. And we think in this you do much
‘ wrong, and much difcredit the other vifitors, that you
‘ fhould feem to think and fuppofe, that they would do
‘ things againft confcience We take them to be men
‘ of that honour and honefty, that they will not My
‘ lord of *Canterbury* hath declared unto us, that maketh
‘ partly a confcience unto you, that divines fhould be
‘ diminifhed That can be no caufe, for firft, the fame
‘ was met before in the late king's time, to unite the two
‘ colleges together, as we are fure you have heard, and
‘ Sir *Edward North* can tell And for that caufe, all
‘ fuch as were ftudents of the law, out of the new-erected
‘ cathedral church, were difappointed of their livings,
‘ only referved to have been in that civil college The
‘ *King's-Hall* being in a manner all lawyers, canonifts
‘ were turned out and joined to *Michael-Houf*, and made
‘ a college of divines, wherewith the number of divines
‘ was much augmented, civilians diminifhed Now at
‘ this prefent alfo, if in all other colleges, where lawyers
‘ be by the ftatutes, or the king's injunctions, you do
‘ convert them, or the more part of them, to divines, ye
‘ fhall

' fhall rather have more divines upon this change than
' ye had before The *King's College* fhould have fix
' lawyers, *Jefus College*, fome, the *Queen's College*, and
' other, one or two apiece And as we are informed by
' the late king's injunctions every college in *Cambridge*,
' one at the leaft All thefe together do make a greater
' number than the fellows of *Clare-Hall* be, and they
' now made divines, and the ftatutes in that reformed,
' divinity fhall not be diminifhed in number of ftudents,
' but encreafed, as appeareth, although thefe two colleges
' be fo united And we are fure you are not ignorant,
' how neceffary a ftudy that ftudy of civil law is to all
' treaties with foreign princes and ftrangers, and how
' few there be at this prefent to do the king's majefty's
' fervice therein For we would the encreafe of divines,
' as well as you Marry, neceffity compelleth us alfo to
' maintain the fcience, and we require you, my lord, to
' have confideration how much you do hinder the king's
' majefty's proceedings in that vifitation, if now you,
' who are one of the vifitors, fhould thus draw back, and
' difcourage the other, you fhould much hinder the whole
' doings, and peradventure, that thing known, maketh
' the mafter and fellows of *Clare-Hall* to ftand the more
' obftinate Wherefore we require you to have regard
' of the king's majefty's honour, and the quiet perform-
' ings of that vifitation, moft to the glory of God, and
' benefit of that univerfity The which thing is only
' meant in your inftructions To the performing of
' that, and in that manner, we can be content you ufe
' your doings as you think beft, for the quieting of your
' confcience. Thus we bid you heartily farewel From
' *Richmond*, the tenth of *June*, 1549.

' Your loving friend,

' E SOMERSIT '

By which letter it appears how earneft the protector
was to perfuade, or intimidate, this worthy prelate to
countenance the proceedings by his concurrence The
reigning vice of the age was *fpoliation*, from which the
duke of *Somerfet* was not free, as appears not only from
his palace of *Somerfet-Houfe*, as was before taken notice
of, but one of the articles againft him was, ' That he did
' difpofe offices of the king's gift for money, and made
' fale of the king's lands ' This, perhaps, will give us
to guefs at the fecret of this vifitation, while the eftablifhing a college of civilians, by uniting two colleges
together,

together, was the pretence for demolifhing *Clare-Hall*, the fale of the lands belonging to that fociety was probably the leading motive The other vifitors, who were privy to the defign, durft not acquaint *Ridley* with it, but induftrioufly concealed the inftructions from him, till they had engaged him to preach on the occafion, and proceeded fome time in the bufinefs of the vifitation, when they hoped they fhould entangle him fo far, that for fear or fhame he could not recede But he boldly rifked the difpleafure of the protector, who was now grown very imperious and arbitrary, rather than concur in fuch unjuft meafures The affair dropt The protector had his attention immediately drawn off to fupprefs feveral infurrections raifed by the difcontented commons almoft throughout the kingdom The vifitors, efpecially the bifhop of *Rochefter*, had another commiffion to execute, which was to prefide at a public difputation appointed to be held at *Cambridge*, as there had been one a little before at *Oxford*, relating to the facrament of the Lord's Supper

Two pofitions were appointed to be the fubjects of this public difputation, and after they had been fufficiently ventilated, a determination of the matters debated was to be made by the bifhop of *Rochefter*. The two pofitions were,

1 Tranfubftantiation cannot be proved by the plain and manifeft words of fcripture, nor can thereof be neceffarily collected, nor yet confirmed by the confents of the antient fathers for thefe one thoufand years paft

2 In the Lord's Supper is none other oblation or facrifice, than one only remembrance of *Chrift*'s death, and of thankfgiving

The firft difputation was on *Thurfday* the twentieth of *June*, Dr. *Madew* of *Clare-Hall*, refpondent, maintaining the above pofitions Dr *Glyn*, Mr *Langdale*, *Sedgwick* and *Young*, opponents The fecond difputation was held on *Monday* the twenty-fourth, Dr *Glyn*, refpondent, maintaining the contrary pofitions Mr. *Perne*, *Grindal*, *Geft*, and *Pilkington*, opponents. The third was on *Thurfday* the twenty-feventh of *June*, Mr *Perne*, refpondent, maintaining the pofitions Mr *Parker*, (not *Matthew*, who was afterwards archbifhop of *Canterbury*) *Pollard*, *Vavafor*, and *Young*, opponents. There is one difference obferved between the difputations at *Oxford* and at *Cambridge* *Peter Martyr* admitted a change in the elements, and *Langdale*, one of the opponents, the firft day at *Cambridge*, afked, fuppofing a change admitted,

" Whether

' Whether that change was wrought in the substance, or
' in the accidents, or else in both, or in nothing?'
When *Ridley* interposed and answered, "There is no
" change, either of the substances or of the accidents;
" but in very deed there do come unto the bread other
" accidents, insomuch, that whereas the bread and wine
" were not sanctified before, nor holy, yet afterward they
" be sanctified, and so do receive then another sort or
" kind of virtue, which they had not before "

After the disputations were finished, the bishop determined,

I Against transubstantiation, on these five principal
grounds

  1 The authority, majesty, and verity of holy scripture.
I will not hereafter drink of the fruit of the vine St.
Paul and St *Luke* call it bread after consecration. They
speak of *breaking*, which agrees with bread, not with
Christ's body. It was to be done *in remembrance* of him
This is the bread that came down from heaven, but *Christ's*
body came not down from heaven *It is the Spirit that
quickeneth, the flesh profiteth nothing*

  2 The most certain testimonies of the antient catholic
fathers, who (after my judgement) do sufficiently declare
this matter.

Here he produced many fathers, *Dionysius, Ignatius,
Irenæus, Tertullian, Chrysostom, Cyprian, Theodoret, Ge-
lasius, Austin, Cyril, Isychius,* and *Bertram,* who call it
bread after consecration, sacramental bread, the figure of
Christ's body And expressly declare, that bread still continues after consecration, and that the elements cease not
to be the substance of bread and wine still

  3. The nature of a sacrament In which he supposes
natural symbols to represent like spiritual effects, which
in the sacrament of the Lord's Supper are unity, nutrition, and conversion They who take away the union
of the grains making one bread, of which partaking we
become one mystical body of *Christ*, or they who deny
the nutrition, or substance of those grains, by which our
bodies being nourished is represented the nourishment of
our souls by the body of *Christ*, these take away the simi-
litude between the bread and the body of *Christ*, and
destroy the nature of a sacrament As neither is there
any thing to signify our being turned into *Christ's* body,
if there be no conversion of the bread into the substance
of our bodies.

The 4th ground was, that transubstantiation destroys
one of the natures in *Christ*.

They

They, which say that *Christ* is carnally present in the eucharist, do take from him the verity of man's nature *Eutyches* granted the divine nature in *Christ*, but his human nature he denied So they, that defend transubstantiation, ascribe that to the human nature, which only belongeth to the divine nature

The 5th ground is the most sure belief of the article of our faith, *He ascended into heaven*

He quotes from St *Austin* on St *John*, ' The Lord ' is above, even to the end of the world But yet the ' verity of the Lord is here also For his body wherein ' he rose again must needs be in one place, but his verity ' is spread abroad every where.'

By verity he means an essential divine presence by his invisible and unspeakable grace, as he distinguishes on *Matth* xxviii 'As touching his majesty, his providence, ' his invisible and unspeakable grace, these words are ' fulfilled, which he spake, *I am with you unto the end of* ' *the world* But according to the flesh which he took ' upon him, *so ye shall not have me always with you* And ' why? because as concerning his flesh he went up into ' heaven, and is not here, for he sitteth at the right hand ' of the Father And yet concerning the presence of his ' divine majesty he is not departed hence.' And from *Vigilus* he quoted, ' Concerning his flesh we look for him ' from heaven, whom, as concerning the WORD (or di- ' vine nature) we believe to be with us on earth ' And again, ' the course of scripture must be searched of us, ' and many testimonies must be gathered, to shew plainly ' what a wickedness and sacrilege it is, to refer those ' things to the property of the divine nature, which do ' only belong to the nature of the flesh And contrari- ' wise, to apply those things to the nature of the flesh, ' which do properly belong to the divine nature ' Which he observes the transubstantiators do, who affirm *Christ*'s body not to be contained in any one place, and ascribe that to his humanity, which properly belongs to his divinity.

II. Against the oblation of *Christ* in the Lord's Supper he determined on these two grounds

1. Scripture, as *Paul* saith, *Hebrews* ix. Christ *being become an high priest of good things to come, by a greater and more perfect tabernacle not made with hands, that is, not of this building Neither by the blood of goats and calves, but by his own blood, entered once into the holy place, and obtained eternal redemption for us And, now in the end of the world he hath appeared* ONCE *to put away sin by the sacrifice of himself.*

himself And again, *Christ was* ONCE *offered to take away
the fins of many*. Moreover he faith, *With* ONE *offering
hath he made perfect for ever thofe that are fanctified*
Thefe fcriptures do perfuade me to believe, that there is
no other oblation of *Chrift* (albeit I am not ignorant that
there are many facrifices) but that which was ONCE made
on the crofs

2 The teftimonies of the antient fathers *Auftin ad
Bonif* epift 23 Again, in his book of forty-three queftions, queftion forty-one, *contra Tranfubftan* lib 20
cap 21, 22, where he writes, how the Chriftians keep a
memorial of the facrifice paft, with an oblation, and participation of the body and blood of *Chrift Fulgentius*,
in his book *de Fide*, calls the fame oblation a commemoration. And thefe things are fufficient at this time for
a fcholaftic determination of thefe matters.

Yet this was more than a mere fcholaftic exercife, the
occafion of appointing this difputation arofe at *Oxford*,
where Dr *Smith*, taking offence at *Peter Martyr*'s expofition of fcripture, challenged *Martyr* to a public difputation Which *Martyr* declared himfelf ready to engage
in, but not without the king's leave The privy council
gave leave, but *Smith* ran away from his challenge Then
Martyr challenged all the *Roman* catholics in that univerfity to maintain their tranfubftantiation, and the privy
council appointed delegates to hear and prefide at the difputation And like difputations were appointed at *Cambridge*, that the papifts there might likewife have an
opportunity of defending their opinions, if they could

Langdale, one of the difputants, and for his zeal made
archdeacon of *Chichefter* by queen *Mary*, compofed a pretended refutation of bifhop *Ridley*'s determination But
with this fufpicion of unfairnefs in his account of ma-
naging the difpute, that though he had the king's licence
for printing it, at *Paris, February* 1553, yet it was not
printed till three years after, when *Langdale* was fecure
that *Ridley* could make no reply However, *Pilkington*,
another of the difputants, afterward bifhop of *Durham*,
fays, that the bifhop made all things fo clear in his determination, and the auditors were fo convinced, that
fome of them would have turned archbifhop *Cranmer*'s
book on that fubject into *Latin*

Ridley affifted *Cranmer* in the firft edition of the liturgy,
or common-prayer, which was publifhed in 1548 He
was ranked with *Cranmer*, *Hooper*, and *Ferrar*, among
thofe called the *zealous proteftants*, in oppofition to *Gardiner*, *Tunftal*, and *Bonner*, who were called *zealous papifts*

Ridley printed the injunctions which he had set forth for the visitation of his diocese, and they clearly shew the progress that the Reformation had made in *England*. They particularly enjoined, that none should receive the communion, but such as should be ready with meekness to confess the articles of the creed upon request of the curate   That the homilies should be read orderly, without omission of any part thereof, and that the common-prayer be read in every church upon *Wednesdays* and *Fridays*   That none should maintain purgatory, invocation of saints, the six articles, bead-rolls, pilgrimages, relics, rubrics, primmers, justification of man by his own works, holy bread, psalms, ashes, candles, creeping to the cross, hallowing of fire, or altars, or such like abuses

The king was under a visible decay, and bishop *Ridley* preached before him about the latter end of his sickness   The bishop enlarged much in his sermon on the good effects of charity, and the king was so moved with what he said, that immediately after the sermon he sent for the bishop, whom he commanded to sit down and be covered   His majesty resumed the heads of the discourse, and said his lordship must give some directions how he might acquit himself of his duty   The bishop, astonished at so much tenderness and sensibility in so young a prince, burst into tears, but desired time to consider of the particular channel in which the royal charity should be directed, and that the king would give him leave to consult with the lord-mayor and aldermen about it   His majesty accordingly wrote them a letter by the bishop, who returned to him with a scheme of three foundations, one for the sick and wounded, another for such as were willfully idle or mad, and a third for orphans   And his majesty endowed St. *Bartholomew*'s hospital for the first, *Bridewell* for the second, and *Grey-Friars* church for the third.

The king died in 1553, and was succeeded by his sister *Mary*, whose reign was polluted with the blood of martyrs, of whom *Ridley* was one of the chief   The queen was a rigid papist, and caused lady *Jane Grey* to be beheaded, who openly professed the protestant religion, and to whom *Edward* had conveyed the crown by his will. The duke of *Northumberland* and his son, and the duke of *Norfolk* and his brother, were also beheaded for attempting to place that most excellent lady on the throne, and bishop *Ridley* was sent to the *Tower*, among others, whom *Mary* was determined to sacrifice to her vengeance

The queen released *Gardiner* and *Bonner* out of the *Tower*, and employed them to pull down the Reformation

The

The mass was restored, the protestants inhumanly persecuted, and several laws enacted for re-establishing popery. The parliament revived the statutes against heresy, and the queen commissioned *Gardiner*, as her bloody instrument, for the extirpation of what she called heresy He was particularly ordered to purge the churches of all married bishops and priests, in consequence of which, four bishops were deprived for marriage, as also three for preaching erroneous doctrines, and of 16,000 of the inferior clergy then in *England*, 12,000 were turned out for having wives.

As *Gardiner* was for forcing the protestants into the pale of the *Romish* church, he began with exerting his rage against the bishops, and the most eminent divines. The bishops *Ridley*, *Latimer*, *Hooper*, and *Ferrar*, were all imprisoned, and all suffered martyrdom, which caused an universal consternation, and the popish bishops themselves seemed ashamed of these barbarities

The convocation was adjourned, and removed to *Oxford*, that the dispute with the protestant divines might be held before the whole university, To give a colour of justice to this conference, archbishop *Cranmer*, and bishops *Ridley* and *Latimer*, were sent from the *Tower* of *London* to the prison at *Oxford*, where they were ill accommodated, denied the convenience of their books and papers, the conversation of each other, and any mutual assistance in the conference, for each was to have his day separate from the others To these three prelates, under such disadvantages, a committee from the convocation and the two universities were to be opposed The queen sent her precept to the mayor and bailiffs of *Oxford*, to bring the prisoners into the public schools, at the times appointed for the disputations, calling *Ridley* a doctor, and *Latimer* only clerk It was intended to expose these three great prelates to insolence and abuse. ' This disputation (says *Fuller*) was intended ' as a preparative or prologue to the tragedy of these bi- ' shops' deaths, as it were to dry their bodies the more ' afore-hand, that afterwards they might burn the brighter ' and clearer for the same '

The government and clergy are charged with the most infernal proceedings The queen was married to *Philip* of *Spain*, and imagined herself pregnant But she declared, she could not be delivered till the heretics, who now filled all the jails about *London*, were burnt, while the clergy and council of *England* were to be the executioners of the bloody purpose ' All the nation seemed ' to be in a blaze from persecuting flames,' and three

martyrs

martyrs were particularly fingled out—*Ridley*, *Latimer*, and *Cranmer*.

Commiffions for trying them were directed to three bifhops and feveral others But the imprifoned prelates, at their different appearances, refufed to acknowledge the papal authority. *Cranmer* was brought out firft before the committee. The next was *Ridley*, who began with a folemn declaration, that though he was once of another opinion than what he was of at prefent, yet he had not changed it upon any worldly confiderations, but merely for love of truth And fince it was the caufe of God he was now to maintain, he protefted that he would have leave to add to, or alter, any argument, as he fhould fee caufe for it; and defired he might be permitted to fpeak without interruption, All this was promifed him, but not complied with, and, though all the committee af-failed him by turns, even fometimes four or five at once, he maintained his ground, till the prolocutor put an end, by faying, ‘ You fee the obftinate, vain-glorious, crafty, ‘ and inconftant mind of this man, but you alfo fee the ‘ force of truth cannot be fhaken, therefore, cry out ‘ with me, truth has the victory.’

The three bifhops were adjudged to be obftinate here-tics, and declared to be no longer members of the church, to which they all objected *Ridley* told the commif-fioners, that although he was not of their company, yet he doubted not but his name was written in another place, whither this fentence would fend him fooner than by the courfe of nature he fhould have gone

The prifoners were then parted, and conducted to their feparate prifons, where *Ridley* wrote a letter to the pro-locutor, complaining of the noify and irregular manner with which the difpute was carried on, wherein he had not the liberty of making a full defence, nor of urging his arguments at length, being overpowered with clamor, and the indecent abufe of four or five opponents at a time He defired, however, that he might have a copy of what the notaries had fet down, which was not granted

Ridley and *Latimer* refufed to recant, or to renounce their reafon upon the unintelligible jargon of a popifh eucharift, the common watch-word for murder in thofe days, and they were to be delivered over to the fecular arm. The bifhops of *Gloucefter*, *Lincoln*, and *Briftol*, were fent to *Oxford*, to proceed againft them. When the com-miffion was read, and it appeared that the judges pro-ceeded in the name of the pope, *Ridley* put on his cap and refufed to pay any reverence to thofe who acted by fuch

a com-a commiſſion. *Latimer* alſo proteſted againſt the papal authority, and being both accuſed of the opinions, which they had maintained in the public ſchools a year and a half before, were allowed till the next morning to conſider, whether they would retract, or perſevere in them. Both adhered to the anſwers they had already made, and on the next morning they were pronounced guilty of hereſy, degraded from prieſts orders, and conſigned over to the ſecular magiſtrate to be puniſhed.

Great attempts were made on *Ridley* to perſuade him to accept of the queen's mercy, which he refuſed, and a warrant was ſent down for the execution of him and *Latimer*. They ſuffered on the ſixteenth of *October*, 1555, on the north ſide of *Oxford*, in the ditch oppoſite *Baliol-College* When they came up to the ſtake, they embraced each other with great affection, and *Ridley*, with an air of pleaſure, ſaid to *Latimer*, " Be of good heart, brother; " for God will either aſſuage the fury of the flame, or " elſe enable us to bear it" He then returned to the ſtake, and, falling upon his knees, kiſſed it and prayed very fervently After which ſetting himſelf to ſpeak to the ſpectators, ſome perſons ran to him and ſtopped his mouth Being afterwards ſtripped, he ſtood on a ſtone near the ſtake, and offered up the following prayer, " O " heavenly Father, I give thee hearty thanks for that " thou haſt called me to be a profeſſor of thee, even unto " death I beſeech thee, Lord God, have mercy on this " realm of *England*, and deliver it from all its enemies " They were not permitted to ſpeak, in anſwer to a long ſermon preached by a Dr *Smith*, unleſs they would recant. To this *Ridley* replied, That he would never deny his Lord, nor the truths of which he was perſuaded, but " God's will be done " He ſaid, he had received fines when he was biſhop of *London* for leaſes which were now voided, and deſired that the queen might give order, either that the leaſes might be made good, or the fines reſtored to the tenants out of the effects he had left behind him, which were more than ſufficient for that purpoſe. After this, they were ordered to fit themſelves for the ſtake, and as a ſmith was knocking in the ſtaple, which held the chain, he ſaid to him, " Good man, knock it in " hard, for the fleſh will have its courſe " Some gunpowder was hanged about their bodies to haſten their deaths, and the fire was put to the wood The powder took fire with the firſt flame, which inſtantly put *Latimer* out of his pain But there was ſo much wood thrown on the fire where *Ridley* was, that the flame could not break

through

through it, fo that his legs were almoft confumed before it was obferved, and then a paffage being made to the flame, it put an end to his life, in the fifty-fifth year of his age A little before he gave up the ghoft, he cried with a loud voice, " Into thy hands, O Lord, I com-" mend my fpirit. Lord, receive my foul!"

The ftation which both thefe martyrs had held, the regularity of their lives, the peaceablenefs of their tempers, their age, and their behaviour at the ftake, raifed great commiferation in the fpectators, and fent them home greatly difpleafed with thofe who had brought them to this end

Ridley's fine parts, and his great improvements in all the branches of literature neceffary to a divine, gave him the firft rank in his profeffion, and his life was anfwerable to his knowledge. He was of an eafy obliging temper, and though he wanted not a proper fpirit to fupport his character, or to do himfelf juftice againft the great and powerful, yet he was always ready to forgive any injuries, or offences His zeal for religion did not fhew itfelf in promoting feverities againft thofe who differed from it, but in diligently explaining the parts that were mifunderftood, and fhewing their foundation in fcripture and antiquity The grace of his Mafter was not only fhewn in the candor and charity of his fentiments, but he did good offices for thofe who differed from him, he was a great benefactor to the poor, he expended his revenue in a way becoming a bifhop, he maintained and treated *Heath*, the deprived bifhop of *Worcefter*, for a year and a half, in the fame fplendor as though Fulham-houfe had been his own, and *Bonner*'s mother, who merited nothing on her own account, dined always there at the table with him, whilft her fon was in the *Tower*. The Reformation was greatly promoted by his zeal and learning while he lived, as well as by his courage and conftancy at his death. For of all who ferved the altar of the church of *England*, he bore, perhaps, the moft ufeful teftimony, both in life and death, to her doctrine

To this we may add the character given of him by his learned biographer, Dr. *Gloucefter Ridley*, whofe mafterly performance we would recommend to our Readers for the hiftory, not of bifhop *Ridley* only, but of the whole time in which he lived Bifhop *Ridley* (fays he) was ' meek ' and gentle to tender confciences, patiently bearing with ' their weaknefs, but where he faw the will was in fault ' from vanity, malice, or obftinacy, he fet himfelf with ' great earneftnefs and fteadinefs to reduce it to a fub-' miffion,

' mission —With respect to himself, he was mortified,
' and given to prayer and contemplation With respect
' to his family, careful and instructive His mode of
' life was, as soon as he rose and had dressed himself, to
' continue in private prayer half an hour, then (unless
' other business interrupted him) he retired to his study,
' where he continued till ten of the clock, at which hour
' he came to common prayer with his family, and there
' daily read a lecture to them, beginning at the acts of
' the apostles, and so going regularly through St *Paul's*
' epistles, giving to every one that could read a New
' Testament, and hiring them to learn by heart some
' chosen chapters, &c '

He was a person small in stature, but great in learning,
and profoundly read in divinity Among several things
that he wrote, were these A treatise concerning images,
not to be set up, nor worshipped in churches A brief
declaration of the Lord's Supper A treatise of the blessed sacrament A piteous lamentation of the miserable
state of the church of *England*, at the time of the late
revolt from the gospel A comparison between the comfortable doctrine of the gospel, and the traditions of popish religion He had a hand in compiling the common
prayer-book, as also disputations and conferences about
matters of religion

Here follow two of his letters.

I.

" MASTER *Cheke*, I wish you grace and peace. Sir,
" in God's cause, for God's sake, and in his name,
" I beseech you of your help and furtherance towards
" God's word I did talk with you of late what case I
" was in concerning my chaplains I have gotten the
" good will and grant to be with me, of three preachers,
" men of good learning, and (as I am persuaded) of ex-
" cellent virtue, which are all able, both with life and
" learning, to set forth God's word in *London*, and in
" the whole diocese of the same, where is most need of
" all parts in *England*, for from thence goeth example
" (as you know) into all the rest of the king's majesty's
" whole realm The men's names be these, Mr *Grindal*,
" whom you know to be a man of virtue and learning
" Mr *Bradford*, a man by whom (as I am assuredly in-
" formed) God hath and doth work wonders, in setting
" forth of his word The third is a preacher, the which
" for detecting and confuting the Anabaptists and Papists

3 I " is

" is enforced now to bear *Chrift's* crofs The two firft be
" fcholars in the univerfity The third is as poor as
" either of the other twain Now there is fallen a pre-
" bend in *Paul's,* called *Cantrells,* by the death of one
" *Layton* This prebend is an honeft man's living of
" thirty-four pounds and better in the king's books I
" would with all my heart give it unto Mr *Grindal*, and
" fo I fhould have him continually with me, and in my
" diocefe to preach

" But alafs! Sir, I am letted by the means (I fear me)
" of fuch as do not fear God One Mr *William Thomas,*
" one of the clerks to the council, hath in times paft fet
" the council upon me, to have me to grant that *Layton*
" might have alienated the faid prebend unto him and
" his heirs for ever God was mine aid and defender,
" that I did not confent unto his ungodly enterprife Yet
" I was then fo handled before the council, that I granted,
" that whenfoever it fhould fall, I fhould not give it be-
" fore I fhould make the king's majefty privy unto it
" Now *Layton* is departed, and the prebend is fallen, and
" certain of the council (no doubt by this ungodly man's
" means) have written unto me, to ftay the collation.
" And whereas he defpaireth, that ever I would aflent
" that a preacher's living fhould be beftowed on him, he
" hath procured letters unto me, fubfcribed with certain
" of the council's hands, that now the king's majefty hath
" determined it unto the furniture of his highnefs's ftable
" Alafs! Sir, this is a heavy hearing When papiftry was
" taught, there was nothing too little for the teachers
" When the bifhop gave his benefices unto ideots, un-
" learned, ungodly, for kindred, for pleafure, for fervice,
" and other worldly refpects, all was then well allowed
" Now, when a poor living is to be given unto an excel-
" lent clerk, a man known and tried to have both dif-
" cretion and alfo virtue, and fuch a one as, before God,
" I do not know a man yet unplaced and unprovided for,
" more meet to fet forth God's word in all *England*
" When a poor living, I fay, which is founded for a
" preacher, is to be given unto fuch a man, that then in
" ungodly perfon fhall procure in this fort letters to ftop
" and let the fame; alafs! Mr *Cheke,* this feemeth unto
" me to be a right heavy hearing Is this the fruit of
" the gofpel? Speak, Mr *Cheke,* fpeak for God's fake,
" in God's caufe, unto whomfoever you think you may
" do any good withal And if you will not fpeak, then
" I befeech you let thefe my letters fpeak unto Mr. *Gates,*

" to

" to Mr. *Wrothe*, to Mr *Cecil*, whom all I do take for men
" that do fear God.

" It was said here constantly, my lord chamberlain to
" have been departed Sir, though the day be delayed,
" yet he hath no pardon of long life, and therefore I do
" beseech his good lordship, and so many as shall read
" these letters, if they fear God, to help that neither
" horse, nor yet dog, be suffered to devour the poor liv-
" ings appointed and founded by godly ordinance to the
" ministers of God's word. The causes of conscience,
" which do move me to speak and write thus, are not only
" those which I declared once in the cause of this prebend
" before the king's majesty's council, which now I let
" pass, but also now the man, Mr *Grindal*, unto whom
" I would give this prebend, doth move me very much,
" for he is a man known to be both of virtue, honesty,
" discretion, wisdom and learning And beside all this,
" I have a better opinion of the king's majesty's honour-
" able council, than (although some of them have sub-
" scribed, at this their clerk's crafty and ungodly suit, to
" such a letter) than, I say, they will let, and not suffer
" (after the request made to them) the living appointed
" and founded for a preacher, and be bestowed upon so
" honest and well a learned man

" Wherefore, for God's sake, I beseech you all, help,
" that with the favour of the council, I may have know-
" ledge of the king's majesty's good pleasure, to give this
" preacher's living unto Mr *Grindal*. Of late there have
" been letters, directed from the king's majesty and his
" honourable council unto all the bishops, whereby we
" be charged and commanded, both in our own persons,
" and also to cause our preachers and ministers, especially
" to cry out against the insatiable serpent of covetousness,
" whereby is said to be such a greediness amongst the
" people, that each one goeth about to devour another,
" and to threaten them with God's grievous plagues,
" both now presently thrown upon them, and that shall
" be likewise in the world to come Sir, what preachers
" shall I get to open and set forth such matters, and so
" as the king's majesty and the council do command them
" to be set forth, if either ungodly men, or unreasonable
" beasts, be suffered to pull away and devour the good and
" godly learned preachers' livings? Thus I wish you in
" God ever well to fare, and to help *Christ's* cause, as
" you would have help of him at your most need From
" *Fulham* this present, the 23d of *July*, 1551

" Your's in *Christ* "

II

" GOOD Mr *Cecil*, I muſt be a ſuitor unto you in
" your good maſter *Chriſt's* cauſe. I beſeech you be
" good to him. The matter is, Sir, alaſs! he hath lain
" too long abroad (as you do know) without lodging, in
" the ſtreets of *London*, both hungry, naked and cold.
" Now, thanks be to almighty God! the citizens are
" willing to refreſh him, and to give him both meat, drink,
" cloathing and firing. But alaſs! ſir, they lack lodging
" for him. For in ſome one houſe I dare ſay they are fain
" to lodge three families under one roof. Sir, there is a
" wide, large, empty houſe of the king's majeſty's, called
" *Bridewell*, that would wonderfully well ſerve to lodge
" *Chriſt* in, if he might find ſuch good friends in the
" court to procure in his cauſe. Surely I have ſuch a
" good opinion of the king's majeſty, that if *Chriſt* had
" ſuch faithful and hearty friends who would heartily
" ſpeak for him, he ſhould undoubtedly ſpeed at the king's
" majeſty's hands. Sir, I have promiſed my brethren the
" citizens to move you, becauſe I do take you for one
" that feareth God, and would that *Chriſt* ſhould lie no
" more abroad in the ſtreets."

J O H N   P H I L P O T.

THIS very learned divine, ſon of ſir *Peter Philpot*,
was born near *Wincheſter*, and was, in his youth,
put to *Wyckham*, or *New-College*, *Oxford*, where he ſtudied
the civil law for ſix or ſeven years, beſides the other
liberal ſciences, and eſpecially the languages* From
Oxford he ſet out upon his travels through *Italy*, where
he was in ſome danger on account of his religion, a
Franciſcan friar at *Padua*, endeavoring to trouble him for

* Mr *Strype* records an amuſing incident, relative to Mr *Philpot*,
after he went to *Oxford*,—' Where (ſays he) he profited in learn-
' ing, ſo well, that he laid a wager of TWENTY PENCE with *John*
' *Harpsfield*, that he would make two hundred verſes in one night,
' and not make above two faults in them. Mr *Thomas Tuchyner*,
' ſchoolmaſter, was judge: And adjudged the TWENTY PENCE to
' Mr *Philpot*.' *Strype's* eccl. mem. III. p. 263.

herefy

herefy But returning to *England* in the time of king *Edward*, he was collated to the preferment of archdeacon of *Winchefter* by the pious and excellent Dr *Ponet*, the first proteftant bifhop of that fee Stephen Gardiner, (*Ponet's* predeceffor) bifhop of *Winchefter*, (fays *Strype*[*]) ever bore ill-will againft this godly gentleman [Mr *Philpot*], and forbad him preaching, oftentimes in king *Henry's* reign But he [*Philpot*] could not in confcience hide his talent, under this prince, and in fo popifh a diocefe At laft, the bifhop fent for certain juftices, who came to his houfe And there calling Mr *Philpot*, ROGUE, *Philpot* faid to the bifhop, " My lord, do you keep a privy feffions in your own houfe for me, and call me ROGUE, " whofe father is a knight, and may fpend a thoufand " pounds within one mile of your nofe? And he that " can fpend TEN POUNDS by the year, as I can, I thank " God, is no vagabond "

Mr *Philpot*, when archdeacon of *Winchefter*, labored abundantly in word and doctrine, with great fuccefs, in *Hampfhire*, during the time of king *Edward* He was very well furnifhed both by grace and natural acquirements for his calling, to which he zealoufly devoted them all Bifhop *Ridley* and our martyr were efteemed the two moft learned of all our *Englifh* Reformers *Philpot* appears to have poffeffed great fervency of fpirit, which appeared in all his controverfies and troubles with the papifts, whom he boldly attacked, leaving all confequences in the hand of God He had the glowing ardor of a martyr, and defired the martyr's crown He was valiant for the truth, and feared not the faces of men, for, at the beginning of queen *Mary's* reign, in a convocation of bifhops and dignitaries, appointed for the purpofe of changing religion from proteftant to popifh, our learned archdeacon, with a few others, bore a noble teftimony againft the defign, and, for his vigorous oppofition, notwithftanding the promifed liberty of free debate, he was called before the chancellor, the faid bifhop of *Winchefter*, his ordinary, and by him committed a clofe prifoner for about a year and a half He was then fent to *Bonner*, bifhop of *London*, and other commiffioners, who confined him in the bifhop's coal-houfe, to which adjoined a little dark houfe with a great pair of ftocks, both for hand and foot. There he met with two fellow-fufferers in the fame good caufe, one of whom was a clergyman of *Effex*,

a godly

a godly minister, and a married man *, who, upon hearing that archdeacon *Philpot* was brought to the coal-house, desired much to see him, to whom he grievously lamented, that in the hour of temptation, through the frailty of the flesh, and the extremity of imprisonment, he had sinfully complied, by writing, with the bishop of *London* He added, that he was immediately set at liberty, but afterwards felt such a hell in his conscience, that he could scarce refrain from laying violent hands on himself Nor could he be at peace in his mind, till he went to the bishop's register, desiring to see the writing in which he had yielded to the bishop, which he had no sooner got into his hands, than he tore it in pieces The bishop, being informed of this, sent for him, and acted indeed more in the character of a popish bishop, than of a bishop of *Jesus Christ, who must be no* STRIKER, for he fell upon him like a lion, beat his face black and blue, and pluckt off great part of his beard. He then sent him to be confined hand and foot in the stocks in the dark hole, where Mr. *Philpot* found him, " as joyful (said he) under the cross " as any of us, and very sorry for his former infirmity "

The second day after Mr *Philpot* had been in the coalhouse, he was sent to make his appearance before *Bonner*, who, among other things, said, ' I marvel that you are so ' merry in prison, singing and rejoicing in your naugh- ' tiness, when you should rather lament and be sorry.' Mr *Philpot* answered, " We are in a dark comfortless " place, and therefore as St. *Paul* wills us, we make " *merry in the Lord, singing together, in hymns and psalms* " After some further altercation, he was remanded back to the coal-house, " where, (said he) I, with my six fellow " prisoners, do rouze together from the straw, as chear- " fully, we thank God, as others do from their beds of " down " But as though resolved, if possible, to put a stop to the rejoicing of this great and godly man, the papists were continually adding new severities, so that when bishop *Bonner*, in one of his fawning fits, asked him, ' If he could shew him any pleasure, and he would ' do it ' Mr *Philpot* answered, " My lord, the pleasure " that I will require of your lordship is, to hasten my " judgement which is committed unto you, and to dif- " patch me forth of this miserable world, unto my eternal " rest For notwithstanding this fair speech (added he

---

* This was the Revd Mr *Thomas Whittle*, a most excellent man, as appears by his writings preserved by Mr *Fox* He suffered in the flames with great joy and constancy, not long afterwards.

" in

" in his account of this matter) I cannot obtain hitherto,
" for this fortnight paſt, either fire, or candle, or good
" lodging. But it is good for a man to be brought low
" in this world, and to be counted amongſt the vileſt,
" that he may in time of reward receive exaltation and
" glory. Therefore, praiſed be God, that he hath hum-
" bled me, and given me grace with gladneſs to be con-
" tent withal."

Mr *Philpot* was examined fifteen or ſixteen ſeveral times
before biſhop *Bonner* and others, but being well ſkilled
in the civil and canon law, he pleaded his privilege of
exceptionem fori, and refuſed to be examined before the
biſhop of *London*, becauſe he was not his ordinary, being
archdeacon of *Wincheſter*. The biſhop urged his right of
being his judge, becauſe the convocation, in which Mr
Philpot was accuſed of hereſy, in zealouſly maintaining
the proteſtant doctrines of the church of *England*, as then
by law eſtabliſhed, was held in St *Paul*'s church, and
conſequently in his dioceſe. ' Therefore as you were ſent
' hither to me (ſaid the biſhop) by the queen's commiſ-
' ſioners, and are *now* in my dioceſe, I will proceed againſt
' you as your ordinary.'

" I cannot deny (ſaid Mr *Philpot*) but I am in your
" coal-houſe, which is in your dioceſe, yet am I not *of*
" your dioceſe. I was brought hither through violence,
" and by ſuch men as had no juſt authority ſo to do, and
" therefore my being at preſent in your dioceſe, is not
" enough to deprive me of my own ordinary's juriſdic-
" tion, nor does it make me willingly ſubject to your
" juriſdiction, any more than a ſanctuary man, being by
" force brought forth of his place of privilege, loſes his
" privilege, but may always claim his privilege whereſo-
" ever he is brought. Nor does my conduct in the con-
" vocation ſubject me to your juriſdiction, or make you
" my ordinary, for although St *Paul*'s be in your dio-
" ceſe, it is neverthelefs a *peculiar* of the dean and chap-
" ter, and therefore not *of* your dioceſe." The biſhop
then endeavored to enſnare him in private examinations,
but Mr *Philpot* ſaid, " My lord, *Omnia judicia debent*
" *eſſe publica*, i.e. all judicial proceedings ought to be
" public. Therefore, if your lordſhip have any thing to
" charge me lawfully withal, let me be in judgement
" lawfully and openly called, and I will anſwer accord-
" ing to my duty, otherwiſe in corners I will not."

Biſhop of London. ' No, wilt thou not knave? Thou
' art a fooliſh knave, I ſee well enough. Thou ſhalt
' anſwer whether thou wilt or not.'

I   *Philpot.*

Philpot   " I will make no further answers than I have
" said already."

Bishop of London   ' Have him away, and set him in
' the stocks What, foolish knave '"

The next morning early, an hour before day, Mr *Philpot* was sent for by the bishop, but fearing some foul play,
because it was at so unseasonable a time, he refused to
go. The bishop then ordered him to be brought by violence, and charged him to take the book and swear to
answer truly to all such articles as he should demand of
him But as the bishop was not Mr *Philpot's* ordinary,
he would not swear The consequence of which was,
the bishop ordered him to be put into the stocks, " where
" (says *Philpot*) I sat from morning till night, when the
" keeper upon favour let me out "

For a great while, they pretended to examine him every
day, and sometimes oftener, and meanly to abuse him
with the taunts of *blockhead, knave, fool,* &c. But this
good man's arguments, on account of his great superiority
in learning and knowledge of the scriptures, they could
neither answer nor refute, ' so that (says Mr *Fox*) bishop
' *Bonner* having taken his pleasure with Mr *Philpot* in his
' private talks, and seeing his zealous, learned, and immu-
' table constancy, thought it high time to rid his hands
' of him And therefore sitting in the consistory at St
' *Paul's,* he caused him to be brought before him and
' others, as it seemeth, more for order's sake, than for any
' good affection to justice and right judgement '

Bonner then began by charging Mr *Philpot* with being
fallen from the unity of *Christ's* catholic church—with
blasphemously speaking against the sacrifice of the mass,
calling it idolatry—and with speaking against, and denying, the real presence of *Christ's* body and blood to be in
the sacrament of the altar He labored, with the rest of
the bishops, both by persuasions and promises, and by
cruel threatenings, to make him abjure To all which
he answered, " You, and all your sort, are hypocrites,
" and I would all the world knew your hypocrisy, your
" tyranny, ignorance, and idolatry."

After a great deal more altercation upon a variety of
matters, which served only to shew the bishop's tyranny
and the martyr's constancy, *Bonner* asked *Philpot* if he
had any just cause to alledge why he should not condemn
him as a heretic ? " Well, (said Mr *Philpot*) your ido-
" latrous sacrament, that you have found out, you would
" fain defend, but you are not able, nor ever shall "

                                                        ' Mr

' My lords, (said *Bonner*) my predeceſſor, *Stokeſley,*
' when he proceeded to give ſentence againſt a heretic,
' made uſe of a certain prayer, whoſe example I will now
' follow, and ſo with a loud voice prayed, *Deus, qui*
' *errantibus, ut in viam poſſint redire, juſtitiæ veritatiſque*
' *tuæ lumen oſtendis, da cunctis, qui Chriſtianâ profeſſione*
' *cenſentur, & illa reſpuere quæ huic inimica ſint nomini,*
' *& ea quæ ſint apta ſectari, per Chriſtum Dominum noſ-*
' *trum, Amen*'

Philpot " I wiſh you would ſpeak in *Engliſh,* that all
" men might underſtand you, for St *Paul* commands,
" that all things, ſpoken in the congregation, ſhould be
" ſpoken in a tongue that all men may underſtand and
" be edified " The biſhop then repeated it in *Engliſh,*
and when he came to theſe words—' to refuſe thoſe things
' which are enemies to his [i e. *Chriſt*'s] name,' *Philpot*
ſaid, " Then they muſt all turn away from you, for you
" are enemies to that name May God ſave us from ſuch
" hypocrites, as would have things in a tongue that the
" people cannot underſtand." ' Whom do you mean?'
ſaid the biſhop —" You, anſwered *Philpot,* and all who
" are of your congregation and ſect And I am ſorry to
" ſee you ſit in the place you now do, pretending to ex-
" ecute juſtice, while you do nothing elſe but deceive
" all men " And turning to the people, he ſaid, " O all
" you gentlemen, beware of theſe men [the biſhops] and
" all their doings; for they are contrary to God's word
" and the primitive church "

The biſhop then pronounced ſentence of condemnation
againſt him as a heretic, upon which *Philpot* ſaid, " I
" thank God, I am an heretic out of your curſed church.
" But I am no heretic before God.—But God bleſs you,
" and give you grace to repent of your wicked doings, but
" let all men beware of your bloody church "

In *Newgate* he was treated moſt cruelly by the keeper,
though Mr *Philpot* begged of him, upon the foot of old
acquaintance, not to do it He ordered him on the block,
and as many irons to be rivetted on him as he was able
to bear, and allowed his man to extort money from him,
before he would allow him to be taken from the block.
And notwithſtanding Mr *Philpot* pleaded his being a
long time in priſon, and his conſequent poverty, and that
he would willingly ſell his gown off his back for twenty
ſhillings, (" for, ſaid he, the biſhop told me, I ſhould
" ſoon be diſpatched") the keeper demanded four pounds,
and becauſe Mr. *Philpot* had it not to give him, he or-

3 K　　　　　　　　　　　　　　　　　　dered

dered his man to take him on his back, and carry him into *limbo*

When notice was given him, the night before he suffered, that he was to be burnt the next day, he said,—"I am ready, God give me strength, and a joyful re-"surrection" He then poured out his spirit in prayer to the Lord, giving him hearty thanks for accounting him worthy to suffer for his truth. As he was going into *Smithfield*, the way being very dirty, two officers took him up, in order to bear him through the dirt, on which he merrily said—"What! will you make a pope of me?" When he was come into *Smithfield*, he kneeled down and said, "I will pay my vows in thee, O *Smithfield!*" Being come to the stake, he kissed it, and said, "Shall "I disdain to suffer at this stake, when my Lord and "Saviour refused not to suffer a most vile death upon "the cross for me." When he was bound to the stake, he repeated the hundred and sixth, seventh, and eighth *Psalms*, and prayed most fervently, till at length, in the midst of the flames, with great meekness and comfort, he gave up his spirit to God.

THOMAS CRANMER, D.D.

The first PROTESTANT ARCHBISHOP of *Canterbury*.

THIS great and good man was the son of *Thomas Cranmer*, esq, a gentleman of an antient and wealthy family, which came in with the conqueror, and was born at *Aslacton*, in *Nottinghamshire*, *July* 2, 1498. His father died, when he was very young And his mother, when he was fourteen years old, sent him to *Cambridge*. He was elected fellow of *Jesus-College*, where he was so well beloved, that when his fellowship was vacant by marriage, yet his wife dying about a year after, the master and fellows chose him again. This favor he so gratefully acknowledged, that when he was nominated to a fellowship in cardinal *Wolsey*'s new foundation at *Oxford*, though the salary was much more considerable, and the way to preferment more ready by the favor of the cardinal, he nevertheless declined it, and chose rather to continue with

       his

From an Original Painting in the British Museum

his old fellow-collegians, who had given him so singular a proof of their affection

In the year 1523, he commenced doctor of divinity, being then in the thirty-fourth year of his age, and being in great esteem for theological learning, he was chosen reader of the divinity-lecture in his own college, and appointed by the university to be one of the examiners of those, who took their degrees in divinity These candidates he examined chiefly out of the scriptures, and finding many of them grosly ignorant thereof, having thrown away their time on the dark perplexities and useless questions of the schoolmen, he rejected them as insufficient, advising them to apply themselves closely to the study of the holy scriptures, before they came for their degrees, it being shameful for a professor of divinity to be unskilled in that book, wherein the knowledge of God, and the grounds of divinity lay And though some hated him for this, yet the more ingenuous publicly returned him thanks, for having been the means of their great improvement in the sound knowledge of religion

During his residence at *Cambridge*, the question arose concerning king *Henry's* divorce, and the plague breaking out in the university about that time, he retired to *Waltham-Abbey* Where casually meeting with *Gardiner* and *Fox*, the one the king's secretary, the other his almoner, and discoursing with them about the divorce, he greatly commended the expedient suggested to the king by cardinal *Wolsey*, of consulting the divines of our own and the foreign universities, which he thought would bring the matter to a short issue, and be the safest and surest method of giving the king's troubled conscience a well-grounded satisfaction This conversation *Fox* and *Gardiner* related to the king, who was so much pleased with it, that he said, ' *Cranmer* had got the sow by the right ' ear,' and immediately sent for him to court, and admiring his gravity, modesty and learning, resolved to cherish and promote him. Accordingly he made him his chaplain, and gave him a good benefice He was also nominated by him to be archdeacon of *Taunton*. At the king's command he drew up his own judgement of the case in writing, and so solidly defended it in the public school at *Cambridge*, that he brought over many of the contrary part to his opinion, particularly five of those six doctors, who had before given in their judgement to the king, for the lawfulness of the pope's dispensation with marrying the brother's wife.

In

In a matter of so great importance, it may not be improper to give an abstract of those arguments, on which they, who, with doctor *Cranmer*, favored the divorce, grounded their judgement. These were taken partly from scripture, partly from fathers, councils, and schoolmen.

From scripture they argued, ' That the prohibited degrees in *Leviticus* were not only obligatory to the *Jewish* ' nation, but moral precepts and the primitive laws of ' marriage, as appeared from the judgements denounced ' against the *Canaanites* for the violation of them, and their ' being said to have polluted the land thereby, which ' cannot be accounted for, if these were only positive ' *Jewish* constitutions That among those prohibited degrees, the marriage with the brother's wife was one, ' *Lev.* xviii. 16. and 20, 21 And that the breach of ' these precepts was called an unclean thing, wickedness ' and an abomination That the dispensation in *Deuteronomy*, of marrying with the brother's wife, only shewed, ' that the foundation of the law was not in its own nature ' immutable, but might be dispensed with by immediate ' divine revelation, but that it did not follow, that the ' pope by his ordinary authority could dispense with it. ' And to pretend the sense of the precept to be only a ' prohibition of having the father's wife in his life time, ' was a poor low cavil, it being universally unlawful to ' have any man's wife whatever, while he was yet living

' The constant tradition of the church was clear against ' the lawfulness of the marriage. *Origen* on *Lev* xx St ' *Chrysostom* on *Matth* xxii. and St *Basil* in his epistle to ' *Diodorus*, expresly assert these precepts to be obligatory under the gospel, and in the *Latin* church, St ' *Ambrose*, *Jerom*, and *Austin*, were of the same opinion ' And *Tertullian*, who lived within an age after the apostles, in his fourth book against *Marcion*, affirms, that ' the law of not marrying the brother's wife does still ' oblige Christians Pope *Gregory* the Great had given ' the same determination, in answer to *Austin*, the first ' archbishop of *Canterbury*, and directed him to advise ' all, who had married their brother's wife, to look on ' the marriage as a most grievous sin, and to separate ' from her society Other popes had declared themselves ' of the same judgement, and particularly *Innocent* the ' Third had wrote with great vehemence against such ' marriages '

To these were added many testimonies from the writers of later ages, and the schoolmen and canonists, but the judgement of the purest antiquity being so full and express, prefs, we shall pass them over, as less material, only observing, that on the contrary side none could be produced, before *Wickliffe* and *Cajetan*, who looked on these prohibitions as only branches of the judicial law of the *Jews*.

' The second canon of the council of *Neo-cæsarea* de-
' crees, that if a woman were married to two brothers,
' she should be excommunicated till death, and that the
' man, who married his brother's wife, should be anathe-
' matized Which was confirmed in a council held by pope
' *Gregory* the Second. The fifty-first canon of the council
' at *Agde* reckons the marriage with his brother's wife
' among incestuous marriages, and decrees, that all such
' marriages are null, and the parties so contracting to be
' excommunicated till they separate from each other And
' the contrary doctrine and error of *Wickliffe* had been
' condemned, not only in convocation at *London* and
' *Oxon*, but in the general council of *Constance*.'

And because some endeavors were used to evade all this by a pretence, that the marriage with prince *Arthur* was never consummated, it was farther alledged, ' that con-
' summation was not necessary to make a marriage com-
' plete, as might be inferred from *Deut* xxii 24 where
the woman, who was only espoused to a man, if she
' admitted another to her bed, is commanded to be stoned
' as an adulteress, and the man is said to have humbled
' his neighbour's wife And though *Joseph* had never
' consummated the marriage with the blessed virgin, yet
' it appears from *Matt* i. 19, that he could not put her
' away, without a solemn bill of divorce '

But, in this case, there was not the least ground to imagine, that the marriage had not been consummated. The marriage-bed was solemnly blessed when they were put into it, they were seen publicly in bed together, for several days after. The *Spanish* ambassador had, by his master's order, taken proofs of the consummation of the marriage, and sent them into *Spain* And the young prince, who was then sixteen, had by many expressions given his servants cause to believe, that it was consummated the first night Nay it was thought, that his too early marriage hastened his death, he having been strong, vigorous, and healthy, before it, but afterwards declined apace, which was attributed to his being too uxorious After his death, his brother was not created prince of *Wales*, till ten months were elapsed, that they might be certain that the princess was not with child, before they conferred that honor upon him She herself never said any thing then to the contrary, and in the petition offered to the pope in her name, as repeated in his bull, it is said, that the marriage was perhaps consummated Nay farther, in the pope's brief, it is plainly confessed, that the marriage was fully consummated

In the year 1530, doctor *Cranmer* was sent by the king to dispute on this subject at *Paris, Rome,* and in other foreign parts At *Rome* he delivered his book to the pope, and offered to justify it in a public disputation But after sundry promises and appointments, none appeared to oppose him publicly, and in more private conferences he forced them to confess, that the marriage was contrary to the law of God The pope constituted him pœnitentiary general of *England,* and dismissed him. In *Germany,* he gave full satisfaction to many learned men, who were before of a contrary persuasion, and prevailed on the famous *Osiander,* to declare the king's marriage unlawful, in his treatise of incestuous marriages, and to draw up a form of direction, how the king's process should be managed, which was sent over to *England.* Before he left *Germany,* he was married to *Osiander's* niece, whom, when he returned from his embassy, he did not take over with him, but sent for her privately in 1534

In *August,* 1532, archbishop *Warham* departed this life, and the king, thinking Dr *Cranmer* the most proper person to succeed him in the see of *Canterbury,* wrote to him to hasten home, concealing the reason But *Cranmer* guessing at it, and desirous to decline the station, moved slowly on, in hopes that the see might be filled, before his arrival. But all this backwardness, and the excuses which his great modesty and humility prompted him to make, when after his return the king opened his resolution to him, served only to raise the king's opinion of his merit, so that at last he found himself obliged to submit, and undertake the weighty charge ' This de-' clining of preferment (says bishop *Burnet*) being a ' thing of which the clergy of that age were so little ' guilty, discovered, that he had maxims very far dif-' ferent from most church-men.'

The pope, notwithstanding *Cranmer* was a man very unacceptable to *Rome,* dispatched eleven bulls to complete his character By the first, which is directed to the king, he is, on his nomination, promoted to the see of *Canterbury,* by the second, directed to himself, notice is given him of this promotion, the third absolves him from all censures; the fourth was sent to the suffragans, the fifth to the dean and chapter, the sixth to the clergy of *Canterbury,* the seventh to all the laity, the eighth

to

to all that held lands of the fee, requiring them to acknowledge him as archbishop, by the ninth his confecration is ordered, upon taking the oath in the pontifical; by the tenth the pall was fent him, and by the eleventh, the archbishop of *York*, and bishop of *London*, were ordered to put it on These bulls, the archbishop according to cuftom received, but immediately furrendered them to the king, becaufe he would not acknowledge the pope's power of conferring ecclefiaftical dignities in *England*, which he efteemed the king's fole right.

He was confecrated on *March* 30, 1533, by *John Longland*, bishop of *Lincoln*, *John Voicy*, bishop of *Exeter*, and *Henry Standish*, bishop of St *Afaph* And becaufe in the oath of fidelity to the pope, which he was obliged to take before his confecration, there were fome things feemingly inconfiftent with his allegiance to the king, he made a public proteftation, that he intended not to take the oath in any other fenfe than that which was reconcilable to the laws of God, the king's juft prerogative, and the ftatutes of this kingdom, fo as not to bind himfelf thereby, to act contrary to any of thefe. This proteftation he renewed, when he was to take another oath to the pope, at his receiving the pall, and both times defired the protonotary to make a public inftrument of his proteftation, and the perfons prefent to fign it.

The firft fervice the archbishop did for the king, was pronouncing the fentence of his divorce from queen *Catharine*, which was done *May* 23 *Gardiner*, bishop of *Winchefter*, and the bishops of *London*, *Bath*, and *Lincoln*, being in commiffion with him The queen, after three citations, neither appearing in perfon, nor by proxy, was declared contumax, the depofitions, relating to the confummation of the marriage with prince *Arthur*, were read, together with the conclufions of the provinces of *Canterbury* and *York*, and the opinions of the moft noted canonifts and divines in favor of the divorce. And the archbishop, with the unanimous confent of the reft of the commiffioners, pronounced the marriage between the king and queen *Catharine* null, and of no force, from the beginning, and declared them feparated and divorced from each other, and at liberty to engage with whom they pleafed In this affair the archbishop proceeded, only upon what had been already concluded by the univerfities, convocations, &c. and did no more than put their decifions into a form of law. On the twenty-eighth of *May* he held another court at *Lambeth*, in which he confirmed the king's marriage with *Anne Boleyn*.

The

The pope, alarmed at thefe proceedings, by a public inftrument, declared the divorce null and void, and threatened to excommunicate the archbifhop, unlefs he would revoke all that he had done. Whereupon the archbifhop appealed from the pope to the next general council, lawfully called, and fent the appeal under his feal to *Bonner*, defiring him and *Gardiner* to acquaint the pope with it, in fuch a manner, as they thought moft expedient.

On the feventh of *September*, the new queen was delivered of a daughter, who was baptized the *Wednefday* following, and named *Elizabeth*, archbifhop *Cranmer* ftanding godfather.

When the fupremacy came under debate, and the ufurped power of the bifhop of *Rome* was called in queftion, the archbifhop anfwered all the arguments brought in defence of the papal tyranny, with fuch ftrength and perfpicuity, and fo folidly confuted its advocates from the word of God, and the univerfal confent of the primitive church, that the foreign power was, without fcruple, abolifhed by full confent in parliament and convocation. The deftruction of this ufurped jurifdiction *Cranmer* had prayed for many years, as himfelf declared in a fermon at *Canterbury*, becaufe it was the occafion of many things being done contrary to the honor of God, and the good of this realm, and he perceived no hopes of amendment while it continued. This he now faw happily effected, and foon after, he ordered an alteration to be made in the archiepifcopal titles, inftead of *Apoftolicæ fedis legatus*, ftyling himfelf *Metropolitanus*.

The king, whofe fupremacy was now almoft as univerfally acknowledged, as the pope's had been before, looked on the monaftries with a jealous eye, thefe he thought were by their privileges of exemption engaged to the fee of *Rome*, and would prove a body of referve for the pope, always ready to appear in the quarrel, and to fupport his claim. This, it is probable, was the chief motive which inclined the king to think of diffolving them. And *Cranmer*, being confulted on this head, approved of the refolution. He faw how inconfiftent thofe foundations were with the Reformation of religion, which he then had in view, and propofed, that, out of the revenues of the monaftries, the king fhould found more bifhoprics, that the diocefes being reduced into lefs compafs, the bifhops might the better difcharge their duty according to fcripture and private practice. He hoped alfo, that from thefe ruins there would be new foundations erected in

every

every cathedral, to be nurseries of learning, under the infpection of the bifhop, for the ufe and benefit of the whole diocefe. But thefe noble defigns were unhappily defeated, by the finifter arts of fome avaricious courtiers, who, without fear of the divine vengeance, or regard to the good of the public, ftudied only how facrilegioufly to raife their own fortunes out of the church's fpoils.

When queen *Anne Boleyn* was fent to the *Tower*, on a fudden jealoufy of the king, the archbifhop was greatly concerned for her misfortune, and did his utmoft endeavor to affift her in her diftrefs He wrote a confolatory letter to the king, in which, after having recommended to him an equality of temper, and refignation to Providence, he put him in mind of the great obligations he had received from the queen, and endeavored to difpofe the king to clemency and a good humor. Finally, he moft humbly implored him, that, however unfortunate the iffue of this affair might prove, he would ftill continue his love to the gofpel, left it fhould be thought, that it was for her fake only, that he had favored it. But neither this letter of the archbifhop, nor another very moving one wrote with her own hand, made the leaft impreffion upon the king For her ruin was decreed, and (after *Cranmer* had declared her marriage with the king null and void, upon her confeffion of a præ-contract with the earl of *Northumberland*) fhe was tried in the *Tower*, and executed on the nineteenth of *May*, 1536.

In 1537, the archbifhop, with the joint authority of the bifhops, fet forth the famous book, entitled, " The " Erudition of a Chriftian-man." This book was com- pofed in convocation, and drawn up for a direction to the bifhops and clergy It contains an explication of the creed, the Lord's-prayer, the ave-maria, juftification, and purgatory. This was a great ftep towards the future Reformation, for in this book the univerfal paftorfhip of the bifhop of *Rome* is declared to have no foundation in the word of God, the church of *England* is afferted to be as truly and properly a catholic and apoftolic church, as that of *Rome*, or any other church where the apoftles perfonally refided, and all churches are affirmed to be equal in power and dignity, built upon the fame foun- dation, governed by the fame Spirit, and on as good grounds expecting the fame glorious immortality ——In the article of the facrament of the altar, though the cor- poral prefence is afferted, yet it is only faid, that the facra- ment is to be ufed with " all due reverence and honor," without any mention of the adoration of the elements.

3 L The

The superstitious notions of the people concerning the ceremonies and injunctions of the church, in thinking them of stricter obligation than moral duties, are censured In the exposition of the second commandment, bowing down to, or worshipping of images, is expresly condemned The invocation of saints is restrained to begging their intercession for us, and health of body and mind, remission of sin, grace and future happiness, are said to be above the disposal of created beings, and blessings, for the obtaining which, we must apply only to God Almighty The clergy are forbid to pretend to temporal jurisdiction, independent on the civil magistrate, passive obedience is asserted without restriction, and all resistance, on what pretence soever, condemned The people are cautioned against mistaking the *ave-maria* for a prayer, which is only an hymn of praise Justification is attributed to the merits and satisfaction of *Jesus Christ* ALONE, exclusive of the merit of good works And the pope's pardon, masses at *Scala Cœli*, or before any celebrated images, are declared unprofitable to deliver souls out of the middle state of punishment, concerning the nature and degrees of which it is affirmed, that we have no certainty from revelation —All this was doing something towards a more perfect Reformation, when Providence should afford both time and opportunity

Archbishop *Cranmer*, from the day of his promotion to the see of *Canterbury*, had continually employed his thoughts on getting the scriptures translated into *English* He had often solicited his majesty about it, and, at length, obtained a grant that they might be translated and printed. For want of good paper in *England*, the copy was sent to *Paris*, and by *Bonner*'s means a licence was procured for printing it there As soon as some of the copies came to the archbishop's hands, he sent one to the lord *Cromwell*, desiring him to present it in his name to the king, importuning him to intercede with his majesty, that by his authority all his subjects might have the liberty of using it without constraint, which lord *Cromwell* accordingly did, and the king readily assented Injunctions were forthwith published, requiring an *English* bible of the largest size to be procured for the use of every parish church, at the expence of the minister and church-wardens, and prohibited all discouraging the people from reading or hearing the scriptures The book was received with inexpressible joy, every one, that was able, purchased the same, and the poor greedily flocked to hear it read. Some persons in years learned to read on purpose

that

ens they might peruse it, and even little children crouded with eagerness to hear it

The archbishop was not yet convinced of the falseness of the absurd doctrine of transubstantiation, but continued a stiff maintainer of the corporal presence, as appears from his being unhappily concerned in the prosecution of *Lambert*, who was burnt, *November* the 20th, 1538, for denying transubstantiation

In 1539, the archbishop and the other bishops, who favored a Reformation, fell under the king's displeasure, because they could not be persuaded, to give their assent in parliament, that the king should have all the revenues of the monastries which were suppressed, to his own sole use. They had been prevailed upon to consent, that he should have all the lands which his ancestors gave to any of them, but the residue they would have bestowed on hospitals, schools, and other pious and charitable foundations. In particular, *Cranmer* had projected, that a provision should be made, out of this fund, in every cathedral, for readers of divinity, and of *Greek* and *Hebrew*, and so to render them, instead of stalls of laziness, seminaries of learning. *Gardiner*, bishop of *Winchester*, and the rest of the popish faction, took this opportunity to insinuate themselves, by their hypocrisy and flattery, into the king's favor, and to incense him against the archbishop. This is thought to have been the cause of the king's zeal, in pressing the bill containing the six bloody articles, by which none were allowed to speak against transubstantiation, on pain of being burnt as heretics, and forfeiting their goods and chattels, as in case of treason. It was also thereby made felony, and forfeiture of lands and goods, to defend the communion in both kinds, or marriage of the clergy, or those who had vowed celibacy, or to speak against private masses and auricular confession

The archbishop argued boldly in the house against the six articles, three days together, and that so strenuously, that though the king was obstinate in passing the act, yet he desired a copy of his reasons against it, and shewed no resentment towards him for his opposition to it. The king would have persuaded him to withdraw out of the house, since he could not vote for the bill, but, after a decent excuse, he told his majesty, that he thought himself obliged in conscience, to stay and shew his dissent. When the bill passed, he entered his protest against it, and soon after he sent his wife away privately to her friends in *Germany*. The king, who loved him for his probity and courage, fent the dukes of *Norfolk* and *Suffolk*, and the lord *Cromwell*, to acquaint him with the efteem he had for him, and to affure him of his favor, notwithftanding the paffing of the act. Bifhop *Burnet* fays, upon this matter, ' that *Cranmer* put his reafons againft the fix ' articles together, and gave them to his fecretary to be ' written out in a fair hand for the king's ufe But the ' fecretary croffing the *Thames* with the book in his bo- ' fom, met with fuch an adventure on the water, as might ' at another time have fent the author to the fire There ' was a bear baited near the river, which breaking loofe, ' ran into it, and happened to overturn the boat in which ' *Cranmer's* fecretary was, and he, being in danger of ' his life, took no care of the book, which falling from ' him floated on the river, and was taken up by the bear- ' keeper, who put it into the hand of a prieft that ftood ' by, to fee what it might contain The prieft prefently ' found it was a confutation of the fix articles, and fo ' told the bear-keeper, that the author of it would cer- ' tainly be hanged So when the fecretary came to afk ' for it, and faid it was the archbifhop's book, the other, ' being an obftinate papift, refufed to give it, and reckoned ' that now *Cranmer* would certainly be ruined But the ' fecretary acquainted lord *Cromwell* with it, who called ' for the prieft, and feverely chid him for prefuming to ' keep a privy counfellor's book, and fo he took it out ' of his hands. Thus the archbifhop was delivered out ' of his danger '

In 1540, the king iffued out a commiffion, to the archbifhop, and a felect number of bifhops, to infpect into matters of religion, and explain fome of the chief doctrines of it. The bifhops drew up a fet of articles favoring the old popifh fuperftitions, and, meeting at *Lambeth*, vehemently urged the archbifhop, that they might be eftablifhed, it being the king's will and pleafure But, neither by fear nor flattery, could they prevail upon him to confent to it; no, though his friend the lord *Cromwell* lay then in the *Tower*, and himfelf was fuppofed to lofe ground daily more and more in the king's affections. He went himfelf to the king, and expoftulated with him, and fo wrought upon him, that he joined with the archbifhop againft the reft of the commiffioners, and the book of articles was drawn up and paffed according to *Cranmer's* judgement

In this year the largeft volume of the *Englifh* bible was publifhed, with an excellent preface of the archbifhop's prefixed to it, and the king required all parifhes to pro-

vide

tide one of them by the next *All-hallowtide*, under the penalty of forty shillings a month, till they had got one. The people were also charged not to dispute about it, nor to disturb divine service by reading it during the mass, but to read it humbly and reverently for their instruction. Six of these were set up in several parts of St *Paul's*, but *Bonner*, afraid of the effect, posted up near them an admonition, ' that none should read them with vain glory and ' corrupt affections, or draw multitudes about them when ' they read them ' But such was the eager desire of the people after this *new-old* treasure (if I might so speak) that great numbers gathered about those who read, and such as had good voices used to read them aloud, in succession, almost all day long. Many sent their children to school, and when they had learned to read, they carried them to church to read the bible. In short, the eyes of the people being opened, they began boldly to speak against those doctrines of the church of *Rome*, which either contradicted or could not be found in the bible, insomuch that *Bonner* set up a new advertisement, threatening to take away the bibles, if this use were made of them. And upon the complaints he and his brethren presented upon this subject, the free use of the scriptures was afterwards much restrained.

After the fall of the lord *Cromwell*, archbishop *Cranmer*, observing the restless spirit of his adversaries, and how they lay upon the watch for an opportunity to bring him into trouble, thought it prudent to retire for a season, and to live in as great privacy as the duties of his station would permit him. Notwithstanding which, his implacable enemy, bishop *Gardiner*, was daily contriving his ruin, and he having procured one Sir *John Gostwicke* to accuse the archbishop in parliament, of encouraging novel opinions, and making his family a nursery of heresy and sedition, divers lords of the privy council moved the king to commit the archbishop to the *Tower*, till enquiry should be made into the truth of this charge.

The king, who perceived that there was more malice than truth in these clamors against *Cranmer*, one evening, under pretence of diverting himself on the water, ordered his barge to be rowed to *Lambeth* side. The archbishop's servants acquainting their lord of his majesty's being so near, the archbishop came to the water-side, to pay his respects to the king, and to invite him into his palace. The king commanded the archbishop to come into the barge, and made him sit down close by him, having so done, the king began to complain to him, of the nation's

being

being over-run with herefy and new notions of divinity, which he had reafon to fear might be of dangerous confe-quence, and that the faction might in time break out into a civil war, and be the caufe of much blood-fhed, and the total ruin of many of his honeft and peaceable fub-jects. To prevent which, his majefty told him, he was refolved to feek after the grand incendiary, and to take him off by fome exemplary punifhment And then pro-ceeded to afk the archbifhop, what his opinion was of fuch a refolution, Though *Cranmer* foon fmelt the meaning of that queftion, yet he freely, and without the leaft ap-pearance of concern, replied, that his majefty's refolution was greatly to be commended, and that not only the prime incendiary, but alfo the reft of the factious heretics ought to be made public examples to the terror of others But then he cautioned the king, not to charge thofe with herefy, who made the divinely-infpired fcriptures the rule of their faith, and could prove their doctrines by clear teftimonies from the word of God. Upon this, the king came clofer, and plainly told him, he had been informed by many, that he was the grand herefiarch, who encou-raged all this heterodoxy, and that his authority had oc-cafioned the fix articles to be contefted fo publicly in his province. The archbifhop modeftly replied, that he could not acknowledge himfelf to be of the fame opinion, in refpect of thofe articles, as he had declared himfelf of, when the bill was paffing, but that notwithftanding he was not confcious to himfelf, of having offended againft the act Then the king, putting on an air of pleafantry, afked him, whether his bed-chamber would ftand the teft of thofe articles, the archbifhop gravely and ingenuoufly confeffed, that he was married in *Germany* during his embaffy at the emperor's court, before his promotion to the fee of *Canterbury*, but, at the fame time, affured the king, that on the paffing that act, he had parted with his wife, and fent her abroad to her friends. His anfwering thus, without evafion or referve, fo pleafed the king, that he now pulled off the mafk, and affured him of his favor; and then freely told him of the information preferred againft him, and who they were that pretended to make it good The archbifhop faid, that he was not afraid of the ftricteft fcrutiny, and therefore was willing to fubmit himfelf to a legal trial. The king affured him, he would put the caufe into his own hands, and truft him entirely with the management of it This, the archbifhop remon-ftrated, would be cenfured as partiality, and the king's juftice called in queftion But his majefty had fo ftrong

an

an opinion of *Cranmer*'s integrity, that he was resolved to leave it to his conduct, and, having further assured him of the entire confidence he reposed in him, dismissed him.

The archbishop immediately sent down his vicar-general, and principal register, to *Canterbury*, to make a thorough enquiry into the affair, and trace the progress of this plot against him. In the mean time his adversaries importunately pressed the king to send him to prison, and oblige him to answer to the charge of heresy. At length his majesty resigned so far to their solicitations, as to consent, that if the archbishop could fairly be proved guilty of any one crime against either church or state, he should be sent to prison. In this the king acted the politician, intending, by thus seemingly giving countenance to the prosecution, to discover who were *Cranmer*'s chief adversaries, and what was the length of their design against him. At midnight he sent a gentleman of his privy-chamber to *Lambeth*, to fetch the archbishop, and, when he was come, told him, how he had been daily importuned to commit him to prison, as a favorer of heresy, and how far he had complied. The archbishop thanked his majesty for this timely notice, and declared himself willing to go to prison, and stand a trial, for being conscious that he was not guilty of any offence, he thought that the best way to clear his innocence, and remove all unreasonable and groundless suspicions.

The king, admiring his simplicity, told him, he was in the wrong to rely so much on his innocence, for if he were once under a cloud, and hurried to prison, there would be villains enough to swear any thing against him, but while he was at liberty, and his character entire, it would not be so easy to suborn witnesses against him. ' And therefore, continued he, since your own unguarded ' simplicity makes you less cautious than you ought to ' be, I will suggest to you the means of your preserva- ' tion. To-morrow you will be sent for to the privy- ' council, and ordered to prison, upon this you are to ' request, that since you have the honor to be one of the ' board, you may be admitted unto the council, and the ' informers against you brought face to face, and then, ' if you cannot clear yourself, you are willing to go to ' prison. If this reasonable request is denied you, appeal ' to me, and give them this sign, that you have my ' authority for so doing.' Then the king took a ring of great value off his finger, gave it to the archbishop, and dismissed him.

The

The next morning, the archbishop was summoned to the privy-council, and, when he came there, was denied admittance into the council-chamber. When Dr *Butts*, one of the king's physicians, heard of this, he came to the archbishop, who was waiting in the lobby amongst the footmen, to shew his respect, and to protect him from insults. The king soon after sending for the doctor, he acquainted his majesty with the shameful indignity put upon the archbishop. The king, incensed, that the PRIMATE OF ALL ENGLAND should be used in so contumelious a manner, immediately sent to command them to admit the archbishop into the council-chamber. At his entrance he was saluted with an heavy accusation, of having infected the whole realm with heresy, and commanded to the *Tower*, till the whole of this charge was thoroughly examined. The archbishop desired to see the informers against him, and to have the liberty of defending himself before the council, and not to be sent to prison on bare suspicion. But when this was absolutely denied him, and finding that neither arguments nor intreaties would prevail, he appealed to the king, and producing the ring he had given him, put a stop to their proceedings. When they came before the king, he severely reprimanded them, expatiated on his obligations to *Cranmer* for his fidelity and integrity, and charged them, if they had any affection for him, to express it, by their love and kindness to the archbishop. *Cranmer*, having escaped the snare, never shewed the least resentment for the injuries done him, and, from this time forwards, had so great a share in the king's favor, that nothing farther was attempted against him.

These troubles of the good archbishop are somewhat differently related by doctor *Burnet* and Mr. *Strype*, but I rather chuse to follow archbishop *Parker*'s account, who, living in those times, must be allowed to be a much better authority in things of this nature, than any who lived at so great a distance.

The archbishop's vicar-general and register, being found negligent and dilatory, the king sent doctor *Lee* privately to *Canterbury*, to examine into this conspiracy against the archbishop, and make his report of what he could discover. On a strict enquiry, he found letters from bishop *Gardiner*'s secretary, by which it appeared, that that prelate had been the principal promoter of this prosecution against *Cranmer*. When the bishop of *Winchester* perceived, that his designs against the archbishop were detected, fearing the consequence, he wrote him a very penitent letter, in which

which he acknowledged himself to have been guilty of great folly in giving credit to those slanderous reports, which were raised against the archbishop, is if he had been a favorer of heresy and false doctrines, declaring, that he was now entirely satisfied, that these accusations were wholly false and groundless, asking pardon in most submissive and affectionate terms, for his great rashness and undutifulness, and promising all future obedience and fidelity to the archbishop, whom he stiled his good and gentle father. On the reception of this letter, the archbishop, laying aside all resentment against him, resolved to forget what was past, and said, since *Gardiner* called him father, he would prove a father to him indeed. And when the king would have laid the bishop of *Winchester's* letter before the house of lords, *Cranmer* prevailed with him, not to give the bishop any trouble about it, but to let the matter drop.

The same lenity he shewed towards doctor *Thornton*, the suffragan of *Dover*, and doctor *Barbar*, who though entertained in his family, and entrusted with his secrets, and indebted to him for many favors, had ungratefully conspired, with *Gardiner*, to take away his life. When he first discovered their treachery, he took them aside into his study, and telling them that he had been basely and falsly abused by some, in whom he had always reposed the greatest confidence, desired them to advise him, how he should behave himself towards them. They, not suspecting to be concerned in the question, replied, that such vile abandoned villains ought to be prosecuted with the utmost rigor, nay, deserved to die without mercy. At this the archbishop, lifting up his hands to heaven, cried out, " Merciful God, whom may a man trust!" and then pulling out of his bosom the letters, by which he had discovered their treachery, asked them if they knew those papers. When they saw their own letters produced against them, they were in the utmost confusion, and, falling down on their knees, humbly sued for forgiveness. The archbishop told them, that he forgave them, and would pray for them, but that they must not expect him ever to trust them for the future.

And now I am upon this subject of the archbishop's readiness to forgive and forget injuries, I cannot but take notice of a pleasant story which happened some time before this. The archbishop's first wife, whom he married at *Cambridge*, lived at the *Dolphin-inn*, and he often resorting thither on that account, the popish party had raised a story, that he was hostler of that inn, and never had the

benefit

benefit of a learned education　This idle story a *Yorkshire*
priest had with great confidence asserted, in an ale-house,
which he used to frequent, railing at the archbishop, and
saying, that he had no more learning than a goose　Some
of the parish, who had a respect for *Cranmer*'s character,
informed the lord *Cromwell* of this, who immediately sent
for the priest, and committed him to the *Fleet* prison
When he had been there nine or ten weeks, he sent a relation of his to the archbishop, to beg his pardon, and
humbly sue to him for a discharge　The archbishop instantly sent for him, and, after a gentle reproof, asked the
priest whether he knew him, to which he answered, no
The archbishop expostulated with him, why he should
then make so free with his character　The priest excused
himself by his being in drink　But this, *Cranmer* told
him was a double fault, and then let him know, that if
he had a mind to try what a scholar he was, he should have
liberty to oppose him in whatever science he pleased　The
priest humbly asked his pardon, and confessed himself to
be very ignorant, and to understand nothing but his mother tongue　" No doubt then, (said *Cranmer*) you are
" well versed in the *English* bible, and can answer any
" questions out of that　Pray tell me who was *David*'s
" father ?" The priest stood still a while to consider, but
at last told the archbishop, he could not recollect his name.
" Tell me then (says *Cranmer*) who was *Solomon*'s father ?"
The poor priest replied, that he had no skill in genealo-
gies, and could not tell　Then the archbishop advised
him to frequent alehouses less, and his study more, and
admonished him, not to accuse others for want of learning,
till he was master of some himself, discharged him out of
custody, and sent him home to his cure

　Thus much may suffice concerning the clemency and
charitable forgiving temper of the archbishop.　He was
much blamed by many for his too great lenity, which, it
was thought, encouraged the popish faction to make fresh
attempts against him.　The king, observing their implacable hatred towards him, and the perils to which he was
exposed, on account of the zeal for the Reformation of
those abuses under which the church groaned, changed
his coat of arms, from three cranes, to three pelicans,
thereby intimating to him, that he must, like the pelican,
shed his blood for his spiritual children's benefit, if it
should please God to call him thereto.

　And now the archbishop, finding the juncture somewhat
favorable, argued against the sanguinary act of the six articles, in the parliament house, and pressed for a mitigation
of

of its severity, and made such an impression on the king, and the temporal lords, by his strong and persuasive reasoning, that they agreed to moderate the rigour of the statute

Soon after, the king prepared for an expedition against France, and ordering a litany to be said for a blessing on his arms, the archbishop prevailed with him to let it be set forth in English, the service in an unknown tongue making the people negligent in coming to church This, with the prohibition of some superstitious and unwarrantable customs, touching vigils and the worship of the cross, was all the progress the Reformation made, during the reign of king Henry For the intended Reformation of the canon law, was, by the craft of bishop Gardiner, suppressed for reasons of state, and the king, towards the latter end of his life, seemed to have a strong byass towards the popish superstitions, and to frown on all attempts of a Reformation.

On the 28th of *January*, 1546, king *Henry* departed this life, and was succeeded by his son *Edward*, who was godson to the archbishop, and had been instructed by men who favoured the Reformation Archbishop *Cranmer* was one of those, whom the late king had nominated for his executors, and who were to take the administration of the government into their hands, till king *Edward* was eighteen years old And when the earl of *Hertford* was afterwards chosen protector, his power was limited, so as not to be able to do any thing, without the advice and consent of all the other executors

The bishops of the popish party (says bishop *Burnet*) took strange methods to insinuate themselves into the late king's confidence, for they took out commissions, by which they acknowledged, that ' all jurisdiction, civil and ec- ' clesiastical, flowed from the king, and that they exercised ' it only at the king's courtesy, and would resign it at his ' command ' That archbishop *Cranmer* adopted this error, is plain, not only from his answers to some questions relating to the government of the church, first published by doctor *Stillingfleet*, in his *Irenicum*, but from the commission, which he now took out from the new king, whom he petitioned for a revival of his jurisdiction, and that as he had exercised the functions of an archbishop during the former reigns, so that authority determining with the late king's life, his present majesty would trust him with the same jurisdiction On this error of the archbishop, the modern papists make tragical outcries, forgetting, that it was the common mistake of those times, and that *Bonner* not only took out the same commission now, but had before taken out that other in the reign of king *Henry*, in which

3 M 2 (as

(as we have obferved) the king was declared the fountain of all authority, civil and ecclefiaftical, and thofe, who formerly exercifed ecclefiaftical jurifdiction, are faid to have done it precarioufly, and at the courtefy of the king, and that it was lawful for him to revoke it at pleafure And therefore, fince the lord *Cromwell*, the king's vicar-general in ecclefiaftical affairs, was fo far employed in matters of ftate, as not to be at leifure to difcharge his function every where, the king gave *Bonner* authority to exercife epifcopal jurifdiction in the diocefe of *London*

This feems to have been the precedent, after which the new commiffions were now formed Mr *Strype*, indeed, confidently affirms the archbifhop to have had a hand in drawing them up, but the very words, which he quotes to prove it, are manifeftly taken from the preamble to *Bonner*'s commiffion But from thefe unprimitive and uncatholic notions, our archbifhop was happily recovered by that bright luminary of our reformed church, bifhop *Ridley.*

The late king, who died in the *Roman* communion, (though his imperfections are fo freely charged on the Reformation by the papifts) had, in his will, left fix hundred pounds per annum, for mafles for his foul, with provifion for four folemn obits every year, but, by the influence of the archbifhop, this fuperftitious part of his will, notwithftanding his ftrict and folemn charge for its execution, was neglected

On the 20th of *February*, the coronation of king *Edward* was folemnized at *Weftminfter Abbey* The ceremony was performed by archbifhop *Cranmer*, who made an excellent fpeech to the king, in which, after a cenfure of the papal encroachments on princes, and a declaration, that the folemn ceremonies of a coronation add nothing to the authority of a prince, whofe power is derived immediately from God, he goes on to inform the king of his duty, exhorts him to follow the precedent of good *Jofias*, to regulate the worfhip of God, to fupprefs idolatry, reward virtue, execute juftice, relieve the poor, reprefs violence, and punifh the evil doer It may not be improper, to tranfcribe what he fays concerning the divine original of kingly power, in his own words, to rectify fome prevailing notions amongft us " The folemn rites of corona-
" tion (fays he) have their ends and utility, yet neither
" direct force or neceffity, they be good admonitions to
" put kings in mind of their duty to God, but no increafe-
" ment of their dignity For they be God's anointed, not
" in refpect of the oil, which the bifhop ufeth, but in
" confideration of their power which is ordained, of the
" fword

" fword which is authorized, of their perfons which are
" elected of God, and indued with the gifts of his Spirit,
" for the better ruling and guiding of the people The
" oil, if added, is but a ceremony, if it be wanting, the
" king is yet a perfect monarch notwithstanding, and
" God's anointed, as well as if he was moiled." Then
follows his account of the king's duty, after which he
goes on, " Being bound by my function, to lay thefe
" things before your royal highnefs, yet I openly declare,
" before the living God, and before the nobles of the land,
" that I have no commiffion to denounce your majefty
" deprived, if your highnefs mifs in part, or in whole, of
" thefe performances "

This fpeech had fo good an effect on the young king,
that a royal vifitation was refolved on, to rectify the diforders of the church, and reform religion. The vifitors
had fix circuits affigned them, and every divifion had a
preacher, whofe bufinefs it was, to bring off the people
from fuperftition, and difpofe them for the intended alterations And to make the impreffions of their doctrine
more lafting, the archbifhop thought it highly expedient
to have fome homilies compofed, which fhould, in a plain
method, teach the grounds and foundation of true religion, and correct the prevailing errors and fuperftitions.
On this head he confulted the bifhop of *Winchefter*, and
defired his concurrence, but to no purpofe For *Gardiner*,
forgetting his large profeffions of all future obedience to
the archbifhop, was returned with the dog to his vomit,
and wrote to the protector, to put a ftop to the Reformation
in its birth When *Cranmer* perceived that *Gardiner* was
obftinate, he went on without him, and fet forth the firft
book of homilies, in which himfelf had the chief hand
Soon after, *Erafmus*'s paraphrafe on the New Teftament
was tranflated, and placed in every church, for the inftruction of the people

On *November* 5, 1547, a convocation was held at St.
Paul's, which the archbifhop opened with a fpeech, in
which he put the clergy in mind of applying themfelves
to the ftudy of the holy fcriptures, and proceeding according to that rule, in the throwing off the corrupt innovations of popery. But the terror of the fix articles being
a check on the majority, they acquainted the archbifhop
with their fears, who, reporting it to the council, prevailed
to have that act repealed In this convocation, the communion was ordered to be adminiftred in both kinds, and
the lawfulnefs of the marriage of the clergy affirmed by a
great majority,

In

In the latter end of *January*, the archbishop wrote to *Bonner*, to forbid, throughout his diocese, the ridiculous processions, which were usual in the popish times, on *Candlemas-Day*, *Ash-Wednesday* and *Palm-Sunday*, and to cause notice thereof to be given to the other neighboring bishops, that they might do the same. He was also one of the committee appointed to inspect the offices of the church, and to reform them according to scripture and the purest antiquity. And by them a new office for the holy communion was drawn up, and set forth by authority.

This year was also published the archbishop's catechism, entitled, " A short instruction in Christian religion, for " the singular profit of children and young people," and a *Latin* treatise of his, against unwritten verities. From this catechism, it is plain, that he had now recovered himself from those extravagant notions of the regal supremacy, which he had once run into; for here he strenuously asserts the divine commission of bishops and priests, inlarges on the efficacy of their absolution and spiritual censures, and earnestly wishes for the restoring the primitive penitentiary discipline.

In 1550, the archbishop published his " Defence of " the true and catholic doctrine of the sacrament of the " body and blood of our Saviour *Christ*." He had now, by the advice and assistance of bishop *Ridley*, overcome those strong prejudices he had so long labored under, in favor of the corporal presence, and in this treatise, from scripture and reason, excellently confuted it. The popish party were alarmed at the publication of it, and soon after two answers to it were published, the one written by Dr *Smith*, the other by *Gardiner*. The archbishop defended his book against them both, and was allowed, by all impartial readers; vastly to have the superiority in the argument. The archbishop's book was afterwards translated into *Latin*, by sir *John Cheke*, and was highly esteemed by all learned foreigners, for the great knowledge in scripture and ecclesiastical antiquity therein discovered.

The next material occurrence relating to the archbishop, was the publication of the forty-two articles of religion, which, with the assistance of bishop *Ridley*, he drew up for preserving and maintaining the purity and unity of the church. They were also revised by several other bishops and learned divines, and, after their corrections, farther enlarged and improved by *Cranmer*. These articles were agreed to in convocation in 1552, and in 1553 were published by royal authority, both in *Latin* and *English*.

The

The archbishop had formed a design, in the reign of the late king *Henry*, to review and purge the old canon law from its popish corruptions, and had made some progress in the work. But by the secret artifices of *Gardiner* and others, that king was prevailed upon not to countenance or encourage it. In this reign he resumed his design, and procured a commission from the king, for himself, with other learned divines and lawyers, diligently to examine into the old church-laws, and to compile such a body of laws as they thought most expedient to be practised in the ecclesiastical courts, and most conducive to order and good discipline. The archbishop prosecuted this noble undertaking with great vigor, and had the principal hand in it. But when a correct and complete draught of it was finished and prepared for the royal assent, the unhappy death of the good young king blasted this great design, and prevented its confirmation. The book was published by archbishop *Parker*, in the year 1571, entitled, *Reformatio legum ecclesiasticarum.*

King *Edward* was now far gone in a consumption, not without some strong suspicions of being brought into that condition by slow poison, and, finding himself decay apace, began to think of settling the succession. He had been persuaded by the artifices of the duke of *Northumberland*, to exclude his sisters, and to bequeath the crown to the lady *Jane Grey*, who was married to *Northumberland*'s son. This, the duke pretended, was absolutely necessary for the preservation of the reformed religion, which would be in great danger from the succession of the princess *Mary*. —But, in fact, he had nothing at heart but the aggrandizing his own family, and intailing the crown on his posterity, for he was even then a secret papist, as he afterwards confessed at his execution. The archbishop did his utmost to oppose this alteration of the succession. He argued against it with the king, telling him, that religion wanted not to be defended by such unrighteous methods, that it was one of the gross errors of the papists, to justify the excluding or deposing princes from their just rights, on account of religion, and, let the consequence be what it would, justice ought to take place, and the protection of the church committed to the care of that righteous providence, which was never known to give a blessing to those, who endeavored to preserve themselves from any imminent danger by unlawful means. But his majesty, being over-persuaded by *Northumberland*'s agents, was not to be moved from his resolution. The will was made, and subscribed by the council and the judges. The archbishop

I

bishop

bishop was sent for, last of all, and required to subscribe But he plainly told them he could not do it without perjury, having sworn to the entail of the crown on the two princesses, *Mary* and *Elizabeth* To this the king replied, that the judges, who best knew the constitution, should be most regarded in this point, and they had informed him, that, notwithstanding that entail, he might lawfully bequeath the crown to the lady *Jane* The archbishop desired to discourse with them himself about this matter, and they all agreeing, that he might lawfully subscribe the king's will, he was, after many persuasions, prevailed upon to resign his own private scruples to their authority, and at last, not without great reluctancy, he set his hand to it.

On the sixth of *July*, in the year of our Lord 1553, it pleased Almighty God to take to himself this pious and good prince, king *Edward*, and the archbishop, having subscribed to the king's will, thought himself obliged, by virtue of his oath, to join the lady *Jane* But her short-lived power soon expired, and queen *Mary*'s title was universally acknowledged, and submitted to

Not long after her accession, a false report was raised; that archbishop *Cranmer*, in order to make his court to the queen, had offered to restore the *Latin* service, and that he had already said mass in his cathedral church of *Canterbury*. To vindicate himself from this vile and base aspersion, the archbishop published a declaration, in which he not only cleared himself from that unjust imputation, but offered publicly to defend the *English* liturgy, and prove it consonant to scripture, and the purest antiquity, and challenged his enemies to a disputation This declaration soon fell into the hands of the council, who sent a copy of it to the queen's commissioner's, and they immediately sent for the archbishop, and questioned him about it *Cranmer* acknowledged it to be his, but complained that it had, contrary to his intent, stolen abroad in so imperfect a condition For his design was to review and correct it, and then, after he had put his seal to it, to fix it up at St *Paul*'s, and on all the church-doors in *London* This bold and extraordinary answer so irritated them, that they sent him, within a week, to the *Tower*, there to be confined, till the queen's pleasure concerning him was known. Some of his friends, who foresaw this storm, had advised him to consult his safety, by retiring beyond sea, but he thought it would reflect a great dishonor on the cause he had espoused, if he should desert his station at such a time as this, and chose rather to hazard his life, than give such just cause of scandal and offence. The substance of this remarkable paper was as follows. That he found the devil was, more than ordinary, busy in defaming the servants of God, and that whereas the corruptions of the mass had been cast out, and that the Lord's Supper was again set up, according to its first institution, the devil now, to promote the mass, which was his invention, set his instruments on work, who gave it out, that it was now said in *Canterbury* by the archbishop's order. Therefore he protested, that it was false, and that a dissembling monk (meaning *Thornton*, suffragan bishop of *Dover*) had done it without his knowledge. He also offered, that he and *Peter Martyr*, with four or five more whom he could name, were ready to prove the errors of the mass, and to defend the doctrine and service set forth by the late king, as most conformable to the word of God, and to the practice of the antient church for many ages.

In the middle of *November*, archbishop *Cranmer* was attainted by the parliament, (which in those times yielded to any thing, and to every thing) and adjudged guilty of high treason, at *Guildhall*. His see was hereupon declared void. And on the tenth of *December* the dean and chapter of *Canterbury* gave commissions to several persons to exercise archiepiscopal jurisdiction in their name, and by their authority. Archbishop *Cranmer* wrote a very submissive letter to the queen, in the most humble manner acknowledging his fault, in consenting to sign the king's will, acquainting her, what pressing instances he made to the king against it, and excusing his fault, by being over-ruled by the authority of the judges and lawyers, who, he thought, understood the constitution better than he did himself. The queen had pardoned so many already, who had been far more deeply engaged in the lady *Jane's* usurpation, that *Cranmer* could not for shame be denied, so he was forgiven the treason. But, to gratify *Gardiner's* malice, and her own implacable hatred against him for her mother's divorce, orders were given to proceed against him for HERESY.

The *Tower* being full of prisoners, archbishop *Cranmer*, bishop *Ridley*, *Latimer*, and *Bradford*, were all put into one chamber, for which they blessed God, and for the opportunity of conversing together, reading and comparing the scriptures, confirming themselves in the true faith, and mutually exhorting each other to constancy in professing it, and patience in suffering for it.

3 N

In

In *April*, 1544, the archbishop, with bishop *Ridley*, and bishop *Latimer*, was removed from the *Tower* to *Windsor*, and from thence to *Oxford*, to dispute with some select persons of both universities. At the first appearance of the archbishop in the public schools, three articles were given him to subscribe. In which the corporal presence, by transubstantiation, was asserted, and the mass affirmed to be a propitiatory sacrifice, for the sins of the living and dead. These, he declared freely, he esteemed gross untruths, and promised to give an answer concerning them in writing. Accordingly he drew it up, and when he was brought again to the schools to dispute, he delivered the writing to Dr *Weston*, the prolocutor. At eight in the morning the disputation began, and held till two in the afternoon, all which time the archbishop constantly maintained the truth, with great learning and courage, against a multitude of clamorous and insolent opponents. And three days after, he was again brought forth to oppose Dr *Harpsfield*, who was to respond for his degree in divinity. And here he acquitted himself so well, clearly shewing the gross absurdities, and inextricable difficulties of the doctrine of transubstantiation, that *Weston* himself, as great a bigot as he was, could not but dismiss him with commendation.

In these disputations, among other slanderous reproaches, the archbishop was accused for corrupting and falsifying a passage, which in his book of the sacrament he had quoted from St *Hilary*. In answer to which, he replied that he had transcribed it *verbatim* from the printed book, and that Dr *Smith*, one of their own divines there present, had quoted it word for word also. But *Smith* made no reply, being conscious that it was true. When the disputation was over, one Mr *Halcot*, remembering that he had *Smith*'s book, went directly to his chamber in *University-College*, and comparing it with *Cranmer*'s, found the quotations exactly to agree. He afterwards looked into a book of *Gardiner*'s, called, ‘The devil's sophistry,’ where the same passage was cited, and both the *Latin* and *English* agreed exactly with *Cranmer*'s quotation and translation. Upon this he resolved to carry the said books to the archbishop in prison, that he might produce them in his own vindication. When he came thither he was stopped, and brought before Dr *Weston* and his colleagues, who, upon information of his design, charged him with treason, and abetting *Cranmer* in his heresy, and committed him to prison. The next day he was again brought before them, and they threatened to send him to bishop

Gardiner, to be tried for treason, unless he would subscribe the three articles, concerning which the disputation
had been held This he then refused, but being sent for
again, after the condemnation of *Cranmer*, through fear
he consented to do it, yet not till they had allured him,
that, if he sinned by so doing, they would take the guilt
upon themselves, and answer for it to God And yet
even this subscription, of which he afterwards heartily
repented, could not prevail for the restoring his books,
till he should shew them to their shame, nor for his entire
discharge, the master of *University-College* being commanded
to keep a strict watch over him, till *Gardiner*'s pleasure
concerning him was known, and if he heard nothing from
him in a fortnight's time, then to expel him the college
for his offence

On the twentieth of *April*, *Cranmer* was brought to St.
Mary's, before the queen's commissioners, and refusing
to subscribe, was pronounced an heretic, and sentence of
condemnation was read against him as such Upon which
he told them that he appealed from their unjust sentence and
judgement, to the judgement of the Almighty, and that
he trusted to be received to his presence in heaven, for
maintaining the truth of whose spiritual presence at the
altar, he was there condemned. After this, his servants
were dismissed from their attendance, and himself closely
confined in prison

The latter end of this year a popish convocation met;
and did archbishop *Cranmer* the honor, to order his book
of the sacrament to be burnt, in company with the *English*
bible and common-prayer-book *Cranmer*, in the mean
time, spent his melancholy hours in writing a vindication
of his treatise concerning the eucharist, from the objections of *Gardiner*, who had published a book against it,
under the feigned name of *Marcus Antonius Constantius*.
Many learned men of the *Romish* persuasion came to visit
him in prison, and endeavored, by disputations and conferences, to draw him over to their church, but in vain

In 1555, a new commission was sent from *Rome*, for the
trial of archbishop *Cranmer* for heresy, the former sentence
against him being void in law, because the authority of
the pope was not then re-established, The commissioners
were Dr *Brooks*, bishop of *Gloucester*, the pope's delegate,
Dr. *Story*, and Dr *Martin*, doctors of the civil law, the
queen's commissioners On *September* 12, they met at St.
Mary's church, and being seated at the high altar, commanded the archbishop to be brought before them To
the queen's commissioners, as representing the supreme

authority of the nation, he paid all due respect, but absolutely refused to shew any to the pope's delegate, lest he should seem to make the least acknowledgment of his usurped supremacy. Brooks, in a long oration, exhorted him to consider from whence he was fallen, advising him, in the most earnest and pathetic manner, to return to his holy mother, the Roman catholic church, and, by the example of his repentance, to reclaim those whom his past errors had misled.

In this oration, he betrayed great ignorance both of scripture and antiquity, of scripture, by affirming, that the Arians had more texts, by two and forty, to countenance their errors, than the catholics had for the maintenance of the truth, of antiquity, by making Origen write of Berengarius who lived near eight hundred years after him, and by confounding the great St Cyprian with another Cyprian of Antioch, laying the magical studies of the latter to the charge of the former.

When he had finished his harangue, Dr Martin, in a short speech, began to open the trial, acquainting the archbishop with the articles alledged against him, and requiring his answer. The articles contained a charge of perjury, incontinence, and heresy, the first, on account of his opposition to the papal tyranny, the second, in respect to his marriage, and the last, on account of the Reformation in the late reign, in which he had the chief hand. The archbishop having liberty to speak, after he had repeated the Lord's-prayer and the creed, began with a justification of his conduct, in relation to his renouncing the pope's supremacy, the admission of which, he proved by many instances, to be contrary to the natural allegiance of the subject, the fundamental laws of the realm, and the original constitution of the Christian church. And in the close, he boldly charged Brooks with perjury, for sitting there by the pope's authority, which he had solemnly abjured. Brooks endeavored to vindicate himself, and retort the charge on the archbishop, by pretending, that he was seduced by Cranmer to take that oath. But this, the archbishop told him, was a gross untruth, the pope's supremacy having received the said blow from his predecessor, archbishop Warham, by whose advice king Henry had sent to both the universities, to examine what foundation it had in the word of God, to which they replied, and gave it under their seal, that, by the word of God, the supremacy was vested in the king, not in the pope, and that Brooks had then subscribed this determination, and therefore wronged him, in pretending that he was seduced by him,

him At this *Brooks* was in a great confusion, and cried, ' We come to examine you, and, I think, you examine us '

Then Dr *Story* began to rail at the archbishop, in an indecent manner, for excepting against the authority of his judge, and moved bishop *Brook*, to require from him a direct answer to the articles, whereof he stood accused, or, if he continued to deny the pope's authority, and to decline answering, to proceed to sentence against him

After this, doctor *Martin* had a short conference with the archbishop, about his conduct in relation to the supremacy, and the doctrine of the eucharist, and then they proceeded to demand his answer to certain interrogatories, concerning the crimes laid to his charge, to which he replied in so full and satisfactory a manner, that *Brooks* thought himself obliged to make another speech, to take off the impression his defence might have made upon the people. The speech was much unbecoming the gravity of a bishop, consisting only of scurrilous and unchristian railings, and uncouth and sophistical misapplications of scripture and the fathers After this, the archbishop was cited to appear at *Rome*, within fourscore days, and there to answer in person To which he replied, that he would very willingly content, if the queen would give him leave to go to *Rome*, and justify the Reformation to the pope's face But this was only a mock citation, for he was kept all that time close confined, and yet at the end of fourscore days was declared contumax, for wilfully absenting himself from *Rome*, whither he was legally summoned, and in consequence thereof was degraded, as we shall see hereafter

It is worth while to observe his last judgement, concerning the extent of the regal supremacy, is contained in his answer to Dr *Martin* When that doctor asked him, who was supreme head of the church of *England?* the bishop answered, " *Christ* is head of this member, as he is " of the whole body of the catholic church " When the doctor again demanded, whether he had not declared king *Henry* head of the church ? " Yes, said the archbishop, of " all the people in *England*, as well ecclesiastical as tem- " poral." ' What, says *Martin*, and not of the church?' ' No, replied the archbishop, for *Christ* only is head of " his church, and of the faith and religion of the same "

In the *February* following, 1556, a new commission was given to bishop *Bonner* and bishop *Thirlby*, for the degradation of the archbishop When they came down to *Oxford*, the archbishop was brought before them, and, after they had read their commission from the pope, *Bonner*, in

a scurril-

a scurrilous oration, insulted over him, after a most unchristian manner, for which he was often rebuked by
bishop *Thirlby*, who had been *Cranmer*'s particular friend,
and shed many tears upon the occasion   In the commission it was declared, that the cause had been impartially
heard at *Rome*, the witnesses on both sides were examined,
and the archbishop's counsel allowed to make the best defence for him that they could   At the reading this, the
archbishop could not forbear crying out, " Good God,
" what lyes are these¹ that I, being continually in pri-
" son, and not suffered to have council or advocate at
" home, should produce witnesses, and appoint my coun-
" sel at *Rome!* God must needs punish this open and
" shameless lying "   When *Bonner* had finished his invective against him, they proceeded to degrade him , and,
that they might make him as ridiculous as they could, the
episcopal habit which they put on him, was made of can-
vass and old clouts.   Then the archbishop, pulling out
of his sleeve a written appeal, delivered it to them, saying,
that he was not sorry to be cut off, even with all this
pageantry, from any relation to the church of *Rome*, that
the pope had no authority over him, and that he appealed
to the next general council   When they had degraded
him, they put on him an old threadbare beadle's gown,
and a townsman's cap , and in that garb delivered him over
to the secular power   As they were leading him to prison,
a gentleman came, and gave some money to the bailiffs,
for the archbishop   But this charitable action gave such
offence to *Bonner*, that he ordered the gentleman to be
seized , and, had he not found great friends to intercede
for him, would have sent him up to the council, to be
tried for it

While the archbishop continued in prison, no endeavors were omitted to win him over to the church of *Rome*.
Many of the most eminent divines in the university resorted to him daily, hoping, by arguments and persuasions
to work upon him , but all in vain, for he held fast the
profession of his faith, without wavering, and could not
be shaken by any of the terrors of this world, from his
constancy in the truth.   Nay, even when he saw the barbarous martyrdom of his dear companions, bishop *Ridley*
and bishop *Latimer*, he was so far from shrinking, that he
not only prayed to God to strengthen them, but also, by
their example, to animate him to a patient expectation
and endurance of the same fiery trial

At last the papists bethought themselves of a stratagem,
which proved fatal to him.   They removed him from pri-

fon, to the lodgings of the dean of *Christ-church*, they treated him with the greatest civility and respect, and made him great promises of the queen's favor, and the restitution of his former dignities, with many other honors and preferments accumulated, if he would recant. And now, behold a most astonishing instance of human frailty! The man, who had with such undaunted resolution, such unshaken constancy, and so truly primitive a spirit of martyrdom, faced the terrors of death, and defied the most exquisite tortures, sinks under this last temptation, falls a prey to flattery and hypocrisy, and consents to recant!

It is a vulgar error, even in our best historians, to suppose, that the archbishop acknowledged the whole of popery at once, and subscribed but one recantation. But this mistake is now rectified by the labor of the industrious Mr *Strype*, who has discovered how subtilly he was drawn in by the papists, to subscribe six different papers, the first being expressed in ambiguous words, capable of a favorable construction, and the five following pretended to be only explanations of the first. It is very probable, that had they acquainted *Cranmer* with the whole of their design at once, he could never have been seduced to redeem his life with such a dishonorable compliance. But when they had, by their hypocrisy and artifice, drawn him in to a first and second recantation, a shame to retreat after he had gone so far, and unwillingness to lose the benefit of his past subscriptions, prevailed with him to go on. The path of duty is the only path of comfort and safety. Yet we have instances in holy writ, that some of the greatest believers have been so left to their own wills, as to be suffered to commit the foulest crimes, that he who thinketh he standeth may take heed lest he fall, and to convince all Christians, that their perseverance is in God's faithfulness and strength, and not in their own.

The copy of the archbishop's first subscription ran thus.

"Forasmuch as the king's and queen's majesties, by
" consent of their parliament, have received the pope's
" authority in this realm, I am content to submit myself
" to their laws herein, and to take the pope for the chief
" head of this church of *England*, so far as God's laws,
" and the laws and customs of this realm will permit.

"THOMAS CRANMER."

This paper was immediately sent up to the queen and council, but being not satisfactory, another was offered him to subscribe, in fewer words, but more full, and with less reserve, and was as follows.

"I *Thomas*

" I *Thomas Cranmer*, doctor in divinity, do subscribe
" myself to the catholic church of *Christ*, and unto the
" pope, supreme head of the same church, and to the king
" and queen's majesties, and unto all their laws and or-
" dinances　　　　　　　T HOMAS CRANMER "

This also being thought too brief and ambiguous, a
third, yet fuller and more express, was required of him,
which was this

" I am content to submit myself to the king's and
" queen's majesties, and to all their laws and ordinances,
" as well concerning the pope's supremacy, as others
" And I shall, from time to time, move and stir all others
" to do the like, to the uttermost of my power, and to
" live in quietness and obedience to their majesties, most
" humbly, without murmur, or grudging against any of
" their holy proceedings　And for my book which I have
" written, I am content to submit to the judgement of
" the catholic church, and the next general council
　　　　　　　　　" T HOMAS CRANMER "

This, like the rest, not giving satisfaction, was immediately followed by a fourth, in these following words, viz.

" Be it known by these presents, that I *Thomas Cranmer*,
" doctor of divinity, and late archbishop of *Canterbury*, do
" firmly, stedfastly, and assuredly believe, in all articles and
" points of the Christian religion and catholic faith, as
" the catholic church doth believe, and hath believed from
" the beginning　Moreover, as concerning the sacraments
" of the church, I believe unfeignedly in all points, as
" the said catholic church doth, and hath believed from
" the beginning of Christian religion　In witness whereof
" I have humbly subscribed my hand unto these presents,
" the eighteenth day of *February*, in the year 1555
　　　　　　　　　" T HOMAS CRANMER."

Having gained ground upon him thus far, they grew
bold and barefaced, and in the fifth paper (which is in
Fox's martyrology, and has been commonly thought to be
his only recantation) they required him to renounce and
anathematize all *Lutheran* and *Zuinglian* heresies and errors, to acknowledge the one holy catholic church, to be
that, whereof the pope is the head, and to declare him the
supreme bishop, and *Christ*'s vicar, to whom all Christians
ought to be subject　Then followed an express acknowledgement of transubstantiation, the seven sacraments, purgatory, and of all the doctrines of the church of *Rome* in
general, with a prayer to God to forgive his past opposition to them, and an earnest entreaty to all, who had been
misled

misled by his doctrine and example, to return to the unity of the church

And yet even this, full and express as it was, did not give content, but a sixth was still required, which was drawn up in so strong and ample terms, that nothing was capable of being added to it, containing a prolix acknowledgment of all the popish errors and corruptions, and a most grievous accusation of himself as a blasphemer, an enemy of *Christ*, and a murderer of souls, on account of his being the author of king *Henry*'s divorce, and of all the calamities, schisms, and heresies, of which that was the fountain. This last paper he subscribed on the eighteenth of *March*, not in the least suspecting, that the papists designed, notwithstanding all these subscriptions, to bring him to the stake, and that the writ was already signed for his execution.

These six papers were, soon after his death, sent to the press by *Bonner*, and published, with the addition of another, which they had prepared for him to speak at St. *Mary*'s, before his execution. And though he then spake to a quite contrary effect, and revoked all his former recantations, yet *Bonner* had the confidence to publish this to the world, as if it had been approved and made use of by the archbishop.

The day appointed for his execution was the twenty-first of *March*, and Dr. *Cole* was sent to *Oxford*, to prepare a sermon for the occasion. The day before, *Cole* visited him in the prison, whither he was now removed, and asked him if he stood firm in the faith he had subscribed. To which *Cranmer* gave a satisfactory answer. The next morning *Cole* visited him again, exhorted him to constancy, and gave him money to dispose of to the poor, as he saw convenient. Soon after he was brought to St. *Mary*'s church, and placed on a low scaffold, over against the pulpit. Then Dr. *Cole* began his sermon, the chief scope whereof was, to endeavor to give some reasons why it was expedient that *Cranmer* should suffer, notwithstanding his recantation. And, in the close, he addressed himself particularly to the archbishop, exhorting him to bear up with courage against the terrors of death, and, by the example of the thief on the cross, encouraged him not to despair, since he was returned, though late, into the bosom of the catholic church, and to the profession of the true apostolical faith. The archbishop, who, till now, had not the least notice of his intended execution, was struck with horror, at the base inhumanity, and unparallelled cruelty [not to be exceeded in the infernal regions!] of these proceedings. It is ut-

terly

terly impoſſible to expreſs what inward agonies he felt, and what bitter anguiſh his ſoul was perplexed with During the whole ſermon he wept inceſſantly, ſometimes lifting up his eyes to heaven, ſometimes caſting them down to the ground, with marks of the uttermoſt dejection ! When it was ended, being moved to make a confeſſion of his faith, and give the world ſatisfaction of his dying a good catholic, he confented, and, kneeling down, began the following prayer

" O Father of heaven, O Son of God, Redeemer of
" the world, O Holy Ghoſt, proceeding from them both,
" three perſons, and one God, have mercy upon me moſt
" wretched caitiff and miſerable ſinner ! I ! who have
" offended both heaven and earth, and more grievouſly
" than tongue can expreſs ! whither then ſhould I go, or
" where ſhall I fly for ſuccour ! To heaven I am aſhamed
" to lift up mine eyes, and on earth I find no refuge !
" What ſhall I then do ? Shall I deſpair ? God forbid !
" O good God, thou art merciful, and refuſeſt none, who
" come unto Thee for ſuccour To Thee therefore do
" I run, to Thee do I humble myſelf, ſaying, O Lord
" my God, my ſins be great, but yet have mercy upon
" me for thy infinite mercy ! O God the Son, thou waſt
" not made man, this great myſtery was not wrought, for
" few or ſmall offences only, neither didſt thou give thy
" Son to die, O God the Father, for our ſmaller crimes,
" but for the greateſt ſins of the whole world, ſo that the
" ſinner return unto Thee with a penitent heart, as I do
" now in this moment · Wherefore take pity on me, O
" Lord, whoſe property is always to have mercy, for
" though my ſins be great, yet thy mercy is greater —I
" crave nothing, O Lord, for my own merits, but for thy
" name's ſake, and that it may be glorified thereby, and
" for thy dear Son *Jeſus Chriſt*'s ſake, in whoſe words I
" conclude Our Father, &c."

Having finiſhed the Lord's-prayer, he roſe from his knees, and made a confeſſion of his faith, beginning with the creed, and concluding with theſe words " And I be-
" lieve every word and ſentence taught by our Saviour
" *Jeſus Chriſt*, his apoſtles and prophets, in the Old and
" New Teſtament And now added he, I come to the
" great thing that ſo much troubleth my conſcience, more
" than any thing I ever did or ſaid in my whole life, and
" that is, the ſetting abroad a writing contrary to the
" truth, which I here now renounce as things written
" with my hand contrary to the truth which I thought in
" my heart, and written for fear of death, and to ſave

" my

" my life if it might be, that is, all such bills or papers
" which I have written and figned with my hand fince
" my degradation, wherein I have written many things
" untrue And for as much as my hand offended, writ-
" ing contrary to my heart, my hand fhall firft be pu-
" nifhed For, *may* I come to the fire, it fhall be firft
" burned As for the pope, I refufe him as *Chrift's* enemy
" and antichrift, with all his falfe doctrine And as for
" the facrament, I believe as I have taught in my book
" againft the bifhop of *Winchefter* "—Thunder-ftruck, as
it were, with this unexpected declaration, the enraged
popifh crowd admonifhed him not to diffemble " Ah,
" replied he with tears, fince I have lived hitherto, I
" have been a hater of falfhood, and a lover of fimplicity,
" and never before this time have I diffembled " Upon
which they pulled him off the ftage with the utmoft fury,
and hurried him to the place of his martyrdom over againft
Baliol-College Where he put off his cloaths with hafte,
and, ftanding in his fhirt and without his fhoes, was faftened with a chain to the ftake Some preffing him to
agree to his former recantation, he anfwered, fhewing his
hand, " This is the hand that wrote, and therefore it fhall
" firft fuffer punifhment " Fire being applied to him,
he ftretched out his right hand into the flame, and held it
there unmoved, except that once he wiped his face with
it, till it was confumed, crying with a loud voice, " This
" hand hath offended," and often repeating, " This un-
" worthy right hand " At laft, the fire getting up, he
foon expired, never ftirring or crying out all the while;
only keeping his eyes fixed to heaven, and repeating more
than once, " Lord *Jefus*, receive my fpirit " He died in
the fixty-feventh year of his age

He was an open, generous, honeft man, a lover of truth,
and an enemy of falfhood and fuperftition He was gentle
and moderate in his temper, and though heartily zealous
in the caufe of the Reformation, yet a friend to the perfons of thofe who moft ftrenuoufly oppofed it Thus in
the year 1534, he endeavored to fave the lives of bifhop
Fifher, and of *Thomas More*, and afterwards, when *Ton-
ftall* bifhop of *Durham* came into trouble, and a bill was
brought into the houfe of lords for attainting him, *Cranmer*
fpoke freely, nay proteefted, againft it He was a great
patron of learning and the univerfities, and extended his
care alfo to thofe proteftant foreigners, who fled to *England* from the troubles in *Germany*, fuch as *Martin Bucer*,
made profeffor of divinity, and *Paulus Fagius*, profeffor of
the *Hebrew* tongue at *Cambridge*, *Peter Martyr*, profeffor

of divinity at *Oxford*, *John à Lasco*, *Bernardine Ochinus*, *Emmanuel Tremellius*, &c He was a very learned man in himself, and author of several works, printed and unprinted

His printed works are, 1 An account of Mr *Pole's* book, concerning king *Henry* the VIIIth's marriage 2 Letters to divers persons, to king *Henry* VIII secretary *Cromwell*, Sir *William Cecil*, and to foreign divines 3 Three discourses upon his review of the king's book, entitled, The erudition of a Christian man 4 Other discourses of his 5 The bishops' book, in which he had a part. 6 Answers to the fifteen articles of the rebels in *Devonshire* in 1549 7 The examination of most points of religion 8. A form for the alteration of the mass into a communion. 9 Some of the homilies 10 A catechism, entitled, A short instruction to Christian religion, for the singular profit of children and young people 11 Against unwritten verities 12 A defence of the true and catholic doctrine of the sacrament of the body and blood of our Saviour *Christ*, &c 13 An answer to *Gardiner*, bishop of *Winchester*, who wrote against the defence, &c *Lond* 1551, reprinted 1580 It was translated into *Latin* by sir *John Cheke*. *Gardiner* answered, and *Cranmer* went through three parts of a reply, but did not live to finish it However it was published 14. Preface to the *English* translation of the bible 15 A speech in the house of lords, concerning a general council 16 Letter to king *Henry* VIII in justification of *Anne Boleyn*, *May* 3, 1535 17 The reasons, that led him to oppose the six articles 18 Resolution of some questions concerning the sacrament 19 Injunctions given at his visitation within the diocese of *Hereford* 20 A collection of passages out of the canon law, to shew the necessity of reforming it. 21 Some queries in order to the correcting of several abuses 22 Concerning a further Reformation, and against sacrilege. 23 Answers to some queries concerning confirmation 24 Some considerations offered to king *Edward* VI to induce him to proceed to a further Reformation 25 Answer to the privy council 26 Manifesto against the mass

Those works of *Cranmer's*, which still remain in manuscript, are, 1 Two large volumes of collections out of the holy scripture, the antient fathers, and later doctors and schoolmen These are in the king's library When they were offered to sale, they were valued at a hundred pounds But bishop *Beveridge* and doctor *Jane*, appraisers for the king, brought down the price to fifty pounds 2 The lord *Burleigh* had six or seven volumes more of his

writing.

writing. 3 Doctor *Burnet* mentions two volumes more that he had seen 4 There are also several letters of his in the *Cotton* library

---

JOHN PONET, or POYNET,

BISHOP of WINCHESTER

THOUGH the life of this excellent man was but short, and the memorials of that life are handed down to us but in fragments, he was of eminent import-ance in his time, and was a burning and a shining light in the church of God Bishop *Godwin*, in his book *de præsulibus Angliæ*, says of him, that he was born in the county of *Kent*, in or about the year 1516, and received his academical education in *King's-College, Cambridge*. He must have obtained the knowledge of the gospel pretty early in life, for he was in so much confidence with the great Reformers, that, so soon as the beginning of king *Edward's* reign [*June* 26, 1550] when *Ponet* could not have been more than three and thirty years of age, he was consecrated bishop of *Rochester*, and, upon the deprivation of *Gardiner*, was, within a year afterwards, translated to the see of *Win-chester* The reason of his preferment does as much honor to the admirable young king *Edward*, as it could reflect credit upon the bishop, for, we are told, that it was, by the king's own motion, on account of some very excellent sermons which *Ponet* had preached before him —A ladder of episcopal advancement, which is but too rarely ascended!

He was a man of very great learning, as well as grace, and possessed the knowledge, not only of the *Latin* and *Greek*, but (what is not a frequent attainment among di-vines) a thorough acquaintance with the *Dutch* and *Italian* tongues He was, in particular, a very great *Grecian*, and had engaged his mind, probably when quite a young man, very deeply in mathematical learning To such a pro-ficiency had he arrived in the mechanical branch of the mathematics, that he constructed a clock, by the effort of his own genius, which pointed both to the hours of the day, the day of the month, the sign of the Zodiac, the lunar variations, and the tides This was presented to *Henry* the VIII and was received very graciously, for (what indeed it was in those days) a wonderful piece of mecha-nism Besides all this variety, as well as extent, of know-ledge, in so young a man, *Heylyn*, who was by no means partial

partial to 'he principles of our Reformers, informs us, that he was ' well-studied with the antient fathers '

Thus fraught with human knowledge and with divine grace, we cannot wonder, that Dr *Ponet* was so soon and so much taken notice of Above all, God gave him the desire to devote his great abilities to the cause and service of the gospel He not only preached much, but is said to have written much for the truth, both in *Latin* and *English* But the piece, for which he is most remembered, is the composition called, "King *Edward*'s catechism," which was approved and passed by the synod, which passed the book of articles, under the king's warrant *Fuller* says, that this catechism ' was first compiled (as appears by the ' king's patent prefixed) by a single divine, charactered ' pious and learned, but afterwards perused and allowed ' by the bishops, and other learned men, &c and by royal ' authority commanded to all schoolmasters to teach it ' their scholars ' Some have supposed, that this pious and learned divine was Dr. *Alexander Nowel*, dean of St *Paul's*, but others, upon better warrant, have given it to Dr *Ponet*, then bishop of *Winchester* However, all the great Reformers revised it, and particularly archbishop *Cranmer*, without whom nothing was undertaken or set forth in religion, during king *Edward*'s reign.

This catechism is highly calvinistic, and perfectly correspondent with the articles, which were published about the same time. It came out in the year 1553, in two editions, the one *Latin*, and the other *English*, with the royal privilege Indeed, the pious king himself prefaced this catechism by a letter, dated at *Greenwich*, *May* the twentieth, in which he ' charges and commands all schoolmasters ' whatsoever, within his dominions, as they did reverence ' his authority, and as they would avoid his royal displea- ' sure, to teach this catechism, diligently and carefully, ' in all and every their schools, that so, the youth of the ' kingdom might be settled in the grounds of true reli- ' gion, and furthered in God's worship '—At that time, and afterwards in the reign of queen *Elizabeth*, the catechizing children and servants was thought to be of so much importance to posterity, that the neglect of it was entitled to some very severe penalties*.—But we are grown *wiser*

in

' * The care of sending their *children* and *servants* is by the rubric laid upon fathers, mothers, mistresses, and dames, who are to *cause them to come to church at the time appointed, and obediently to hear, and be ordered by the curate, until such time as they have learned all that is here* [in the catechism] *appointed for them to learn* The same is required by the 59th canon of the church, which farther orders, that if any of these

neglect

From an Original Engraving published under the Inspection of Be...

in thefe days, and above defcending to inculcate Chriftian principles upon the minds of youth, for which realon, among others, our young people are fo pious, decent, and virtuous, are fo full of good notions, and fo ready to follow them, as we find them in the prefent age. Were nine tenths of the nation examined, it would be found that they had not fo much as once read through their bibles. And as to catechifms, it feems as if they were very well for parifh-boys and charity-children, but as to the offfpring of other people, it appears to be a fettled point, that they fhall know no more of God and his gofpel than their parents before them.—Such are the times, and fuch our manners!

As we have mentioned the fubject of catechifms, we will only add upon this head, that the prefent catechifm of the church of *England* was, at the command of king *James* the firft, revifed by the bifhops, and that in addition was made to it, giving the explanation of the facraments. This was done by the pen of bifhop *Overal*, then dean of St *Paul*'s, and approved.

When queen *Mary* came to the crown, and gave a bloody earneft of what proteftants may ever expect to receive from bigotted papifts, Dr *Ponet*, with fome other great and good men, thought it prudent to quit the kingdom. He accordingly retired to *Strafburgh* in *Germany*, where he departed this life, on the eleventh of *April*, aged only forty years.

Bifhop *Godwin* mentions, that *Ponet* publifhed feveral works in *Latin* and *Englifh*, which were extant in his time, but which we have not feen. They are however fuppofed to be chiefly upon theological fubjects.

PHILIP MELANCTHON.

THIS celebrated divine, who was one of the wifeft and greateft men of his age, was born, on the fix-

neglect their duties, as the one fort in not caufing them to come, and the other in refufing to learn as aforefaid, they are to be fufpended by the ordinary (if they be not children), and if they fo perfift by the fpace of a month, they are to be excommunicated. And by the canons of 1571, every minifter was yearly, within twenty days after *Eafter*, to prefent to the bifhop, &c. the names of all thofe in his parifh, who had not fent their children or fervants at the times appointed. And to enforce this, it was one of the articles which was exhibited, in order to be admitted by authority, that he, whofe child of TEN years old or upwards, or his fervant at fourteen or upwards, could not fay the catechifm, fhould pay ten fhillings to the poor's box.' WHEATLY *upon the Common Prayer* p 396 4th edit.

teenth

teenth of *February*, 1497, at *Bretten*, in the palatinate of
the *Rhine* His father was *George Schwartferd*, which fignifies *black earth* in German, and *Melancthon* in *Greek*,
therefore, *Reuchlin* gave *Philip* the name of *Melancthon*, in
the fame manner as *Hermolaus Barbarus* changed the name
of *Reuchlin* into that of *Capnio*, from *Capnos*, which in the
Greek fignifies fmoak, as the word *Reuch* does in the *German* language. It was cuftomary among the learned men
of that time to exprefs their names in *Greek*, when they
could find any word in that language into which they
could turn them   Thence come *Oecolampadius, Erafmus,
Chytræus, Reuchlin, Melancthon*, and others But *Reuchlin*
was the only man whom *Germany* had, in his time, to put
in competition with all the learned men in *Italy*, and it
was he that advifed *Frederic* duke of *Saxony* to fend for
Melancthon to *Wittenberg*, in 1518, to be the *Greek* profeffor in that univerfity

Melancthon gave very early marks of his capacity But
his inftruction and education were chiefly committed to
the care of his grandfather *Reuterus*, becaufe his father's
time was taken up with the affairs of the elector palatine,
whom he ferved as engineer, or commiffary of the artillery.
He ftudied firft in the place of his nativity, at a public
fchool, and then under a tutor   He was afterwards fent
to *Pfortfheim*, a fmall city in the marquifate of *Baden*,
where there was a famous college, and he lodged with
one of his relations, who was fifter to *Reuchlin* Upon
this occafion, he became known to that learned man, who
loved him with great tendernefs. He went to the univerfity of *Tubingen*, in the duchy of *Wirtemberg*, and from
thence to *Heidelberg*, that of the metropolis of the palatinate, in 1509, where he was matriculated on the thirteenth
of *October*, and made fuch confiderable improvement, that
he was intrufted to teach the fons of count *Leonftein*, and
was made batchelor, though he was under fourteen years
of age   But he was refufed his degree of mafter of philofophy, on account of his youth, which, together with the
air of *Heidelberg*, which did not agree with his conftitution,
occafioned him to leave that univerfity in 1512, and return
to that of *Tubingen*, where he continued fix years.

Melancthon has been juftly reckoned among illuftrious
youths, and Mr. *Baillet* has juftly beftowed a chapter
upon him in his ' hiftorical treatife of young men, who
' became famous by their ftudies or writings.' He was
employed to make the greateft part of the harangues and
difcourfes of eloquence, that were publicly fpoke in the
univerfity of *Heidelberg*. He ftudied divinity, law, and
mathematics,

mathematics, at *Tubingen*, where he heard the lectures of all sorts of professors, and publicly explained *Virgil*, *Terence*, *Cicero*, and *Livy* He also found time to serve *Reuchlin* in his quarrel with the monks, and diligently applied himself to the reading of the word of God. *Reuchlin* made him a present of a copy of the bible which *John Frobenius* had lately printed at *Basil* in a small volume *Melancthon* always carried this bible about him, and chiefly when he went to church, where those, who saw him hold it in his hands during divine service, believed he was reading quite another thing than what the time and place required of him, because it was much larger than a prayer-book, and those, that envied him, took occasion from hence to make him odious with others.

He taught at *Tubingen*, both in public and private, with great applause and admiration, and published some works as first fruits, from which it sufficiently appeared what a crop might be afterwards expected. He was so remarkable, in 1515, that *Erasmus* then said of him, ‘ Good ‘ God, what hopes may we not conceive of *Philip Me-* ‘ lancthon, though as yet very young, and almost a boy, ‘ equally to be admired for his knowledge in both lan- ‘ guages ! What quickness of invention ! What purity of ‘ diction ! What vastness of memory ! What variety of ‘ reading ! What modesty and gracefulness of behaviour !’ *John James Grynæus* made a parallel between the prophet *Daniel* and *Melancthon*, in which he introduced this fine encomium of *Erasmus*

In 1518, he accepted the *Greek* professorship in the university of *Wittenberg*, which *Frederic* the elector of *Saxony* offered him upon the recommendation of *Reuchlin* His inauguration speech was so fine, that it removed the contempt to which his stature and mien exposed him, and raised great admiration of himself He soon contracted a friendship with *Luther*, who taught divinity in that university, and *Andrew Caroloſtadius*, archdeacon of *Wittenberg*, joined their acquaintance, and was of their opinion.

Erasmus had heard, that *Melancthon* had censured his paraphrases, for which this learned man, in 1519, wrote a very civil letter to justify himself to *Erasmus*, who accepted of these excuses, but told *Melancthon*, that men of letters ought to love each other, and be united to defend themselves against their common enemies. *Erasmus* spoke very kindly to *Melancthon*, and told him, all the world was agreed in commending the moral character of *Luther*, but there were various sentiments touching his doctrines. *Luther* had a great love and esteem for *Melancthon*, and

3 P

Luther,

Jovius, after having abused *Luther* in a most scandalous manner, pays a compliment to *Melancthon* *Melancthon* had so much scrupulous honour and disinterestedness, that he refused to receive his salary, as a reader in divinity, because he could not bestow such close attendance, as he thought that office required

Melancthon read lectures at *Wittenberg* upon *Homer*, and upon the *Greek* text of the epistle of St *Paul* to *Titus*, which drew a great croud of auditors, and excited in them an earnest desire of understanding the *Greek* tongue He reduced the sciences into a system, which was then difficult, as they had then been long taught in a very confused manner.

In the year 1520, *Jerom Alexander*, the pope's nuncio, solicited the emperor, and *Frederic* elector of *Saxony*, to punish *Luther* In consequence of which, the diet of *Worms* was held on the sixth of *January*, 1521, when *Luther* nobly vindicated his doctrine The remarks of *Melancthon* upon these transactions, and upon the conduct of *Frederic*, are judicious and important " So far, says he, was *Luther* " from being suborned and instigated by the courtiers and " princes, as the duke of *Brunswick* affirmed, that, on the " contrary, the elector of *Saxony* was much concerned at " the foresight of the contests and disorders which would " ensue, though the first attacks made by *Luther* were " upon very plausible grounds. By his own sagacity and " judiciousness, and by long experience in the art of " reigning, he knew well how dangerous all changes were " to government But, being truly religious, and one " who feared God, he consulted not the dictates of mere " worldly and political wisdom, and was determined to " prefer the glory of God, to all other considerations, and " at the hazard of any public or private detriment. Yet " he presumed not to rely entirely upon his own judge- " ment concerning an affair of so great importance, but " took the advice of other princes, and of men venerable " for age, experience, learning, and probity " Speaking of these troubles to *J Jonas*, says, ' What a deplo- ' rable thing would it be, that *Philip Melancthon*, an ' amiable youth of such extraordinary abilities, should ' be lost to the learned world upon this account !' And, in 1522, *Erasmus* was apprehensive of being attacked by *Melancthon*, with whom he was very unwilling to have any dispute But, in 1523, *Erasmus* was well pleased to find, that both *Luther* and *Melancthon* were offended at the be- havior of *Hutten*, who had wrote a furious libel against

Erasmus

Erasmus And *Melancthon* declared how sorry he was, that the contention between *Luther* and *Erasmus* was continued.

The Sorbonne at *Paris* condemned the writings of *Luther* in 1521, and *Melancthon* made an apology for *Luther* against this censure, which he called, *Furiosum Parisiensium theologastrorum decretum* i e the furious decree of the *Parisian* theologasters, or small divines. The same year *Melancthon* was appointed by the elector of *Saxony* one of the deputies to give him their opinion concerning the abolition of private masses at *Wittenberg*, which they approved, and desired the elector to abolish them throughout all his dominions The elector told the deputies, by *Christian Beyer*, that he conceived their advice was grounded on the gospel, and required them to order that affair with such moderation as to raise no troubles, divisions, or seditions, among the people The deputies answered, that they believed private masses might be abolished, without noise or trouble, but the abuse was so great, that, though it could not be effected without some disturbance, it ought to be attempted That the ordinance of the mass, prescribed by the holy scripture, was visibly so different from that of private masses, that it was needless to deliberate farther about it That the antient foundations of the monastries, colleges, and churches, were not made to say a certain number of masses, or to chant canonical hours, but to instruct youth in the holy scripture and religion That the foundations made, four or five hundred years before, to say masses, were abusive, and that those who made them, were mistaken That inconveniency ought not to be regarded in such an enterprize, nor such impediments as might be surmounted, since it was the cause of truth and religion *Stork*, *Marcus Stubnerus*, and *Martinus Cellarius*, in 1522, went from *Zwickau* to *Wittenberg*, to preach their fanatical doctrine But *Melancthon* and the other Reformers wrote to the elector of *Saxony*, and to *Luther*, about these men, whom they took to be enthusiasts, and, when they were discovered to be such, the elector drove them out of his territories.

Erasmus, in 1524, owned that the state of things disheartened him from adventuring his person in the *Low Countries*, where *Hulst* and *Egmond* were his inveterate enemies 'When these saints, says he, want to do any
' one a mischief, they first clap him in prison, and then his
' affair is decided by a few confederates, who are judges
' and parties There the most innocent man alive must
' suffer the vilest treatment, lest their authority should

suffer

' ſuffer And when they have been totally miſtaken, they
' cry out, that the ſide of religion muſt always be favor-
' ed!' ' *Melancthon*, continues *Eraſmus*, would gladly have
' a conference with me, but is loth to expoſe me to any
' hatred and obloquy, which however I ſhould have deſ-
' piſed. He is a youth of great candor' But there is
ſome room to doubt, whether he would have been glad of
a viſit from *Melancthon*, who, with all his mildneſs and
candor, was little leſs hated than *Luther* by the Romaniſts.
The ſame year, *Eraſmus* wrote a long epiſtle to *Melancthon*, which began with an invective againſt *Hutten* He
commended the *Loci Communes* of *Melancthon*, as very fit
and able to encounter and demoliſh phariſaical tyranny
But he added, that they contained alſo ſome things which
he did not underſtand, ſome concerning which he had
doubts and ſcruples, and ſome which he thought it need-
leſs to profeſs openly He then boaſted of the mild and
moderate councils which he had given to popes and princes,
but he ſpoke very ill of *Zuinglius*, *Oecolampadius*, *Farel*,
Capito, and *Hedio*.

He apologized for having written againſt *Luther*, and
ſaid, that the calumnies of eccleſiaſtics, who made him
paſs for a Lutheran, and the importunity of princes, had
conſtrained him to it ' Although, ſays he, I were a
' moſt bigotted papiſt, yet would I condemn cruelty, be-
' cauſe opinions oppoſed with cruelty ſpread the more,
' Therefore, the prudent *Julian* would not put Chriſtians
' to death. Our *Theologers* thought, that if they burned
' a man or two at *Bruſſels*, the reſt would be corrected by
' it. On the contrary, the ſufferings of theſe men made
' many embrace Lutheraniſm.'

Melancthon anſwered *Eraſmus* politely, and with a much
better temper, telling him, that the vices of particulars
ſhould not bring any prejudice againſt a good cauſe, and
that *Luther* did in no wiſe reſemble thoſe whom he had
painted in ſuch odious colors. He gently reproved him for
drawing up a catalogue of vile fellows, and inſerting ſuch
perſons as *Oecolampadius*, and other men of merit, amongſt
them. As for himſelf, he declared, that in his conſcience
he was perſuaded of the truth of *Luther*'s doctrine, and
would never forſake it. But, as to the diſſertation of
Eraſmus upon free-will, he ſays, " We are not at all
" ſhocked at it, for it would be mere tyranny to hinder
" any man from giving his opinion in the church of *Chriſt*,
" concerning any points of religion. This ought to be
" free to every one, who will deliver his ſentiments with-
" out paſſion and partiality. Your moderation in that
                                                    " treatiſe

" treatife hath been applauded; and yet fuffer me to tell
" you, that fometimes you bite too hard   But *Luther* is
" not fo eafily provoked, as to be unable to bear diffent,
" and he promifeth to obferve the fame moderation in his
" reply   It is alfo your duty to be very cautious not to
" bring an odium upon a caufe, which the holy fcrip-
" tures fo evidently favour   As you yourfelf have not as
" yet condemned it, if you attack it with vehemence, you
" will wound your own confcience   You know that we
" ought to examine, and not to defpife prophecies "

Erafmus replied, in another long epiftle to *Melancthon*,
that he had not much exhorted him to forfake the Reformers, knowing it would be labor loft, but could have
wifhed that *Melancthon* had applied himfelf entirely to good
literature   And yet, if *good literature* was not compatible
with the ftudy of divinity, it would have been *bad literature*, or *malæ litera*, as the monks then called it   He
declared, his only view was to promote the good of both
parties, and to diffuade tumults, and he wifhed, that a
Reformation might be made without ftrife and contention
This was wifhing impoffibilities, confidering the temper
of the Romanifts

All *Europe* was convinced, that *Melancthon* was not fo
averfe, as *Luther*, to an accommodation with the Romanifts, and that he would have facrificed many things for
the fake of peace   This appears chiefly by the book he
wrote concerning things indifferent, which was fo ill received by *Illyricus*. *Melancthon* advifed the Reformers not
to contend fcrupuloufly about indifferent things, provided
thofe rites and ceremonies had nothing of idolatry in them,
and to bear fome hardfhips, if it might be done without
impiety   *Illyricus*, on the contrary, cried out, that people
fhould rather defert all the churches, and threaten an in-
furrection, than to bear a furplice.   Some Romanifts have
been infpired with the fame fpirit, which calls to mind
what a Jefuit faid, ' that they would not put out one wax-
' taper, though it were to convert all the Hugonots '

The elector of *Saxony*, and fome other princes, fupported the Reformers at the diet of *Spires*   But, after
feveral debates, it was ordered, ' that the doctrine about
' the eucharift fhould not be entertained   That the mafs
' fhould be continued, and the celebration of it permitted
' even in thofe places where the reformed doctrine pre-
' vailed   That the Anabaptifts fhould be profcribed
' And, that one prince fhould not protect the fubjects of
' another.'   The reforming princes oppofed this decree,
and alledged, ' that their minifters had proved, by invin-
' cible

' cible arguments taken out of scripture, that the popish
' mass was contrary to the institution of *Jesus Christ*, and
' the practice of the apostles That they could not permit
' the Lord's Supper to be administered in a different man-
' ner in the same church That there was nothing more
' certain than the word of God, which explained itself;
' and therefore they would take care, that nothing else
' should be taught than the Old and New Testament in
' their purity. And they declared, that the decree of the
' former diet was made for the preservation of peace, but
' that this would infallibly occasion wars and troubles in
' *Germany*' This was put in writing by way of *protesta-*
tion, and published, on the nineteenth of *April*, 1529, as
a solemn instrument of appeal to the emperor, and a general or national council This gave the Reformers the
name of PROTESTANTS.   The instrument of protestation
was signed by the electors of *Saxony* and *Brandenburgh*,
Ernest, and *Francis*, dukes of *Lunenberg*, the landgrave of
Hesse, and the prince of *Anhalt*, as also by the deputies
for the fourteen cities of *Strasburgh, Nuremberg, Ulm, Con-*
stance, Reuthingen, Windesheim, Memmingen, Lindau, Kemp-
ten, Hailbron, Isne, Weissemberg, Nordlingen, and St *Gall*.

Oecolampadius wrote to *Melancthon*, desiring him to declare his opinion in favor of the *Zuinglians*, that the contest might cease between them and the *Lutherans*   *Me-*
lancthon answered, that he could not approve of the opinion of the Sacramentarians, but that, if he would act
politickly, he should speak otherwise, as he knew there
were many learned men among them, whose friendship
would be advantageous to him, so that, if he could have
concurred with them, in their opinion about the Lord's
Supper, he would have spoken freely   He observed, that
the *Zuinglians* supposed the body of *Jesus Christ* to be
absent, and only to be represented in the sacrament, as
persons are represented upon a theatre   But he considered,
that *Jesus Christ* had promised to be with us to the end of
the world   That it is not necessary to separate the divinity from the humanity, so that he was persuaded, the
sacrament was a pledge of the real presence, and that the
body of *Jesus Christ* was truly received in the Lord's Supper   That the proper import of the word was not contrary to any article of faith, but agreed with other places
of scripture where the presence of *Christ* was mentioned.
He declared, it is an opinion unbecoming a Christian, to
believe that *Jesus Christ* is, as it were, imprisoned in heaven   That *Oecolampadius* only propounded some absurdities, and the judgement of some fathers, against it, neither

of

of which ought to influence thofe who know, that the myfteries of religion are to be judged by the word of God, and not by geometrical principles, as they muft alfo know that many contradictions are to be met with in the writings of the antients But he faid, that the greateft number of the expreffions in the moft eminent authors, proves the doctrine of the real prefence to be the general fenfe of the church.

Oecolampadius replied, and the confequence was a friendly conference at *Marpurg*, in *October* following, between the heads of the Lutherans and Zuinglians The landgrave of *Heffe* was prefent at this conference, where *Zuinglius*, *Oecolampadius*, *Bucer*, and *Hedio*, appeared on one fide, and *Luther*, *Melancthon*, *Juftus Jonas*, *Ofiander*, *Brentius*, and *Agricola*, on the other fide. The Lutherans propofed fuch articles as they objected againft in the doctrine of the Zuinglians Firft, That there was no fuch thing as original fin, but it was only a natural infirmity and weaknefs, and that baptifm did not take away any fin in children. Secondly, That the Holy Ghoft is not conferred by the ufe of the word of God, and the facraments, but without that word, and thofe facraments Thirdly, That fome of them were fuppofed to have erroneous thoughts about the divinity of *Jefus Chrift*, and the holy Trinity Fourthly, That they let the value of faith as to our juftification, high enough, but feemed to attribute juftification to good works. Fifthly, That they did not think the body and blood of *Jefus Chrift* were really in the Lord's Supper Zuinglius and Oecolampadius cleared themfelves fully of the fufpicion they lay under about the Trinity, and Divinity of *Jefus Chrift* But they had long difputes about original fin, and the operation of the facraments, in which points *Melancthon* agreed with *Zuinglius*, by explaining, or altering his former opinions, fo that they differed only about the eucharift. *Luther* could not fo fully agree with *Zuinglius*, as may be feen in his life.

The diet of *Augfburg* was held in *June*, 1530 Nothing coft *Melancthon* more pains, than the tafk that was given him this year, to draw up a *confeffion of faith*, which is called the *Augfburg* confeffion, becaufe it was prefented to the emperor at the diet in that city *Melancthon* drew up this *confeffion of faith* out of the memoirs fent to the elector of *Saxony* It was divided into two parts The firft contained twenty-one articles upon the chief points of religion, as the unity of God, original fin, the incarnation, juftification, the gofpel-miniftry, the church, the civil government, the day of judgement, free-will, the caufe of fin, faith, good works, and the adoration of faints The other part was concerning the ceremonies and ufages of the church, which the proteftants faid were abufed, fuch as the communion in both kinds, the marriages of priefts, confeffion, abftinence from meats, monaftic vows, and ecclefiaftical jurifdiction

Melancthon had revifed, and corrected, this confeffion feveral times, but had much difficulty to pleafe *Luther* at laft. Indeed, it is probable, that *Luther* would not have tempered his ftyle with fo much moderation It was a difficult time, and all fweetnefs of expreffion, which affected not the merits of their caufe, was then neceflary to be added

This confeffion was figned by the proteftant princes, and read before the emperor in a fpecial affembly of the empire, who were then difmiffed, that they might confult what refolutions they fhould come to in this affair Their judgements were divided The more violent faid, that the edict of *Worms* ought to be put in execution, and fuch, as would not obey, fhould be compelled by the civil powers Others were for choofing a certain number of honeft, learned, and indifferent perfons, according to whofe judgement the emperor was to decide all matters And a third party were for giving the confeffion of faith to the popifh divines to confute, and the confutation to be read, in a full diet, before the proteftants This laft advice was taken, and *John Faber*, *John Cochlæus*, *Eckius*, *Wimpina*, *Collinus*, and fome other popifh divines, were appointed to draw up a confutation, which they finifhed, and delivered to the emperor and the popifh princes, who were of opinion that all the fevere expreffions, which the divines could not refrain from bringing in, fhould be taken out. When this was done, the emperor called the proteftants together, on the third of *Auguft*, and told them, he had communicated their confeffion to fome learned and religious perfons, to give their opinion of it, and to obferve what was found, or what was contrary to the faith of the church That they had given their judgements in writing, which he had approved, and then ordered it to be read before them by one of his fecretaries.

The *Romifh* divines examined the proteftants confeffion of faith ftep by ftep in their anfwer They fully approved of fome articles, as the firft about the holy Trinity; the third about the incarnation, the eighth about the wicked in the church, and that the facraments adminiftered by wicked perfons are good, the ninth about the neceffity of baptifm, and the baptifm of infants, the tenth about the

Lord's

Lord's Supper, the thirteenth about the operation of the
facraments, though they judged that article to be defective, because they would not acknowledge feven facraments, the fourteenth about the calling of ministers,
provided they allowed of a canonical ordination, the fixteenth about the authority of the magistrates, the feventeenth about the last judgement and the refurrection, and
the eighteenth about free-will But they rejected other
articles, as the fourth, fifth, fixth, and twentieth, that
men are not justified by the merit of good works, but by
faith alone, the feventh, that the church is a congregation
of faints, and that it is fufficient, to preferve its unity,
that men agree in the doctrine of the gospel, and about
the administration of the facraments, without following
the fame ufages and traditions The twenty-first, about
the invocation and worship of faints Thofe, which they
partly received, and partly rejected, were the fecond, about
original fin, which they approved, except the definition of
fin given in it, which feems to agree better to actual than
original fin, the eleventh alfo, about abfolution, they
allowed of, but difliked what is faid in it about confeffion,
in the twelfth, about repentance, they did not like the
affertion that faith is a part of repentance, and what concerns fatisfaction, the fifteenth was approved, as to what
is faid there, that the rites and ceremonies of the church
are to be obferved, but rejected fo far, as it fays, that the
cuftoms received by tradition, as celibacy, and vows, are
of no ufe to obtain grace, or make fatisfaction to God.

As to the fecond part of the confeffion of *Augfburg*, in
which the proteftants afferted, that the communion under
one kind, celibacy of priefts, the ceremonies of the mafs,
private maffes, the name of facrifice given to the mafs,
monaftic vows, abftinence, fafts, and auricular confeffion,
are abufes The popish divines maintained, in their anfwer, they were not abufes, but religious and holy ufages,
commanded by fcripture, and confirmed by tradition Yet
they acknowledged, there were fome abufes in them that
wanted reformation, and which the emperor promifed to
obtain

The *Romish* divines defired the proteftants to return to
the old communion of the church. The elector of *Saxony*
anfwered for the proteftants, that if the Romanifts could
prove, that the proteftants had advanced any error, they
would recant it, and if they defired any farther explication, they were ready to give it · That, fince they had approved of fome articles of their doctrine, and rejected

others

others, it was neceffary they fhould confirm and explain thofe in difpute

In confequence of this, a conference was held at *Augsburg* on the feventh of *Auguft*, between feventeen *Romifh* divines, and fome of the proteftants But this was of no effect. The Romanifts faid, if the Proteftants would not fatisfy the emperor, by uniting in matters of faith with the princes and members of the empire, they would bring great troubles upon *Germany* by the wars and tumults, which their feparation would raife. The proteftants anfwered, by *George Brucke*, their deputy, that they took it ill to be threatened, and complained, that the emperor would not fuffer them to be heard fufficiently That they could not be allowed a copy of the confutation of their confeffion, but upon hard terms, and that it was expected, they fhould approve of it, without reading or examining it, which they could not do with a fafe confcience That though it was promifed and concluded, in the laft diet of *Spires*, that a council fhould be held, nothing was done in it fince. The committee of the *Romifh* deputies replied, that the proteftants had no reafon to complain of his imperial majefty That the condition on which he offered them a copy of the confutation of their confeffion was not hard, becaufe he was fenfible how they ufed the edict of *Worms* · That they might with greater fafety confent to the doctrine of the univerfal church, than of a fmall number of heretics and apoftates, who could not agree among themfelves And that the emperor, having two wars upon his hands, could have no hopes of holding a council at that time.

The proteftants fhewed reafons for their feparation, and offered to chufe a fmall number of perfons on both fides, who might treat amicably together, and confult if they could not find out fome way of agreement This propofal was received, and feven perfons were nominated by both parties to confer about religion, two princes, two lawyers, and three divines The Romanifts were the bifhop of *Augfburg*, and the duke of *Brunfwick*, the chancellor of the archbifhop of *Cologne*, and the chancellor of the marquis of *Baden*, *Eckius*, *Wimpina*, and *Cochlæus*. For the proteftants were the elector of *Saxony*'s fon, and the marquis of *Brandenburg*, the lawyers *Brucke* and *Heller*, and the divines *Melancthon*, *Brentius*, and *Schepfius* They met, and agreed upon fifteen of the twenty-one articles of the confeffion of *Augfburg*, fo that there remained but fix, three of which were only difputed againft in part, and the other three were remitted to the fecond part of their confeffion,

feffion, about which it was more difficult to come to an agreement Melancthon, and the other Lutherans, agreed to their points of doctrine That men fhould not be faid to be juftified by faith alone, but by faith and grace That good works are neceffary That reprobates are included in the church That man hath a free-will That the bleffed faints intercede for us, and may be honored In the other feven articles, they agreed, that the body and blood of *Chrift* were contained in both elements, and that they would not condemn the laity, who would receive the eucharift only under one kind That the ufual veneration fhould be given to the holy facrament That the public mafs fhould be celebrated with the ufual ceremonies, and that they fhould obferve what is effential in the confecration That the fafts on the vigils might be ftill obferved, and fome holydays kept That the bifhops fhould hold their jurifdictions, and that parifh priefts, preachers, and other ecclefiaftical perfons, fhould fubmit to them in fpiritual matters, and that their excommunications fhould not be contemned.

The *Romifh* divines, on the twenty-fecond of *Auguft*, made their report to the diet, upon what terms they ftood with the Lutherans It was then thought, that it would be a fpeedier way to perfect the agreement by reducing the deputies to three, and that both parties fhould appoint two lawyers, and one divine *Melancthon* was chofe by the Proteftants, and *Eckius* by the Romanifts. The points upon which they debated, were principally the mafs, vows, and celibacy of priefts The Romanifts confented, that the married priefts might live with their wives, but they would not relax in the bufinefs of the mafs and vows. *Melancthon*, who was very much inclined to peace, might have come nearer, if he had been invefted with ample powers But the other Proteftants had been diffatisfied with his condefcenfion, and ordered him to advance no further This put an end to all kinds of accommodation But *Melancthon* drew up " An apology for the *Augfburg* " confeffion," which the proteftant princes offered to prefent to the emperor, who refufed to receive it, and it was publifhed the next year.

Luther was not at the diet of *Augfburg*, but he wrote to *Melancthon* about the tranfactions there. The former was of opinion, that all propofals of an accommodation would be ineffectual, but the latter tried to moderate the mind of *Luther*, and ftop his heat.

Erafmus alfo wrote to *Melancthon* in thefe words, ' Go ' alone, my dear *Philip*, can unravel the intricate plot of

       ' the

' the tragedy which is now acting. Ten councils affem-
' bled together could not do it, much lefs fuch an one as
' I If a man fays a reafonable thing, it is ftraightway
' called Lutheranifm ' *Melancthon* anfwered *Erafmus* from
Augfburg, and prayed him to continue the charitable office
of exhorting the emperor to moderation *Erafmus* replied
with fome peevifhnefs and refentment, faying, that he
would not concern himfelf in behalf of the evangelics.
However, he was better than his word, and did write to
cardinal *Campejus*, defiring him to diffuade the emperor
from making a religious war.

The fweating ficknefs, which broke out in *England* in
1485, raged this year in *Germany*, among other calamities,
and the affairs of the poor proteftants were fo bad, in all
appearance, that *Melancthon* was quite dejected, and overwhelmed with forrow. *Luther*, who had more courage,
wrote him many excellent letters of confolation

Archbifhop *Cranmer* had a very great regard for *Melancthon*, whom he invited to *England*, and expected there.
Peter Martyr, and his companion *Ochinus*, had their annual allowance from the king, but fome more extraordinary annuity was intended for *Melancthon*

Francis I king of *France*, had a great love for learning
and learned men. He eftablifhed profeffors of the *Hebrew*,
Greek, and *Latin* languages at *Paris*. The revival of letters in *France*, which had been in a manner extinguifhed
for feveral ages, was owing to this prince, who was therefore called the *Father of Letters* He married *Eleanor*, the
emperor's fifter, in 1530, at which time there was a great
controverfy about religion in *France*, and the king was
defirous of having *Melancthon* to come there, as he judged
him a proper perfon to pacify the difputes. We are told,
that the queen of *Navarre* often talked to the king her
brother of a very good man, as fhe faid, who was called
Philip Melancthon, whom fhe was continually praifing as
the moft learned man of his time, and that fhe did not
doubt, but if fo holy and able a man could confer with
the doctors of the *Sorbonne*, they would quickly find the
means of reftoring peace to the church. Whereupon this
prince, who otherwife had a great defire to bring into
France the ableft men of his time, wrote to *Melancthon*,
and invited him to come to *Paris*, to join his endeavors
with the *French* divines to reftore the antient difcipline of
the church This letter was dated at *Guife*, the twenty-
eighth of *June*, 1535, and declared the pleafure the king
had, that *Melancthon* was difpofed to come into *France*, to
endeavor to pacify the controverfies, *Melancthon* wrote

to the king, the twenty-eighth of *September* following, and assured him of his good intentions, but that he was sorry he had not surmounted the obstacles to his journey *Langey* was ordered to sound *Melancthon*, if he was inclined to change his chair of theology at *Wittenberg*, whose income was only two hundred crowns a year, for a royal professor's chair in the university of *Paris*, at twelve hundred crowns a year. *Varillas* says, ' the elector of *Saxony* per-
' mitted *Melancthon* to go into *France*, in hopes that he
' would make all the *French* turn Lutherans But *Luther*,
' who could not be without *Melancthon*, detained him a
' long time, upon pretence that he was to concert, or, to
' speak more properly, to polish with him his last book
' against the Anabaptists.' *Bayle* contradicts *Varillas*, and says, the elector of *Saxony* could not be prevailed upon to grant *Melancthon* the liberty of going to *France*, and wrote his excuses to *Francis* I *Luther* did not detain *Melancthon*, but made repeated instances to the elector for his journey In fact, *Melancthon* could never obtain leave from the elector to make it, although *Luther* had earnestly exhorted that prince to consent to this journey, by representing to him, that the hopes of seeing *Melancthon* had put a stop to the persecution of the protestants in *France*

The king of *England* also desired to see *Melancthon* · But neither of these two monarchs ever saw him However, *Melancthon* sent a small piece into *France*, which contained his advices about reconciling of the controversies

Luther, in 1536, wrote upon his table these words following *Res et verba Philippus, verba sine rebus Erasmus, res sine verbis Lutherus, nec res nec verba Carolostadius* 'Philip
' *Melancthon* is both substance and words, *Erasmus*, words
' without substance, *Luther*, substance without words,
' and *Carolostad* neither substance nor words.' *Melancthon* unawares coming to *Luther* at that time, and reading the same, smiled, and said, " Touching *Erasmus* and *Caro-*
" *lostadius*, it is well judged and censured, but too much
" is attributed unto me, also good words ought to be
" ascribed to *Luther*, for he speaketh exceeding well "

Melancthon, in 1541, assisted at the conferences of *Spires* and *Ratisbon*, where the controversies between the Romanists and Protestants were warmly disputed. At the former, the papists chose *Eckius*, and the protestants appointed *Melancthon*, to confer about the points in controversy, and agreed that they should begin to discourse about original sin. They entered upon it, and continued the conference three days, when *Nicholas Granville*, who was then prime minister to the emperor, and his commissioner

at

at the conference, received a letter from his imperial majesty, which ordered that the conference should be discon-
tinued, and all things referred to the diet of *Ratisbon*,
where the protestants were ordered to meet. This diet
was opened in *March*, in the presence of the emperor, who
appointed *Eckius, Pflugius,* and *Gropper*, to manage it for
the Romanists, and, for the Protestants, *Melancthon, Bucer,*
and *Pistorius*. He commanded them to lay aside all passion,
and to respect the glory of God only in that conference.
Frederic, brother to the elector palatine, was appointed
president, who opened the conference on the 27th of
April, when a writing was produced, which contained
twenty-two articles, wherein the whole substance of religion was comprized. It was imagined, that this writing
was drawn up by *John Gropper,* but the emperor said, it
was presented to him by persons of learning and piety, to
forward the peace. He therefore desired them to examine
it, that they might approve of what was well, correct
what was amiss, and terminate all differences. *Dupin* has
set forth all these articles, which are too long to be in-
serted here. The protestants examined, and objected to
several of them, which was resented by the legate, and
the diet was concluded by the emperor, who commanded
that the decree of the diet of *Augsburg* should still continue, but he suspended all prosecutions in the imperial
chamber concerning matters of religion, till either a general or national council was held. In the course of this
disputation, it ought to be mentioned to the honor of *Melancthon,* that when *Eckius* proposed a sophism somewhat
puzzling, *Melancthon* paused a little, and said, " that he
" would give an answer to it next day." Upon which
Eckius represented to him the disgrace of such a scholar
requiring so long a time, but *Melancthon* replied, like an
honest man, " *Mi doctor, non quæro meam gloriam in hoc*
" *negotio, sed veritatem.*" i. e. My good doctor, I am not
seeking my own glory in this affair, but the truth. However, he got a complete victory over *Eckius,* who dared no
more to shew his face in the controversy.

In 1543, *Melancthon* went to the elector of *Cologne,* to
assist him in introducing a Reformation into his diocese,
which proved ineffectual. *Bucer* and *Pistorius* assisted *Melancthon* in drawing up the articles for the elector. But
Gropper composed a treatise against those articles, and the
divines of *Cologne* stood so firm against their archbishop,
that he was unable to introduce the protestant religion in
his electorate. However, the elector of *Cologne,* and the
elector palatine, renounced popery.

Melancthon

Melancthon had two sons, and two daughters, by Catharine Crappin, the daughter of a burgomaster of Wittenberg, whom he married in the year 1520, and lived very
happily with till the year 1557, when she died His
daughter Anne was married to George Sabinus, of Wittenberg, in 1536, when she was only fourteen years old.
Sabinus was one of the best poets of his time, and Erasmus,
in 1534, had highly recommended him to Melancthon
Anne understood Latin well, and was very handsome Her
father loved her tenderly. But there had been several
quarrels between the father-in-law and the son-in-law,
because Sabinus was ambitious to obtain civil employments, and disliked the humility of Melancthon, who confined himself to literary employments, and would be at
no trouble to advance his children Sabinus, in 1543,
carried his wife into Prussia, to the great grief of Melancthon, and she died at Konigsberg in 1547. Melancthon's
other daughter was married, in 1550, to Gasper Peucer,
who was an able physician, and was very much persecuted.
Melancthon, was certainly a good father, as appears by this
story. A Frenchman found him one day holding a book
in one hand, and rocking a child with the other Melancthon, seeing him surprized at this, made such a pious
discourse to him about the duty of a father, and the state
of grace in which children are with God, that this stranger
went away much more learned than when he came in

Melancthon had much of his time taken up by the affair
of the Interim. He attended seven conferences upon this
subject in 1548, and wrote all the pieces that were presented there, as also the censure of that Interim

About this time Melancthon was expected in England,
by king Edward VI. to which he was excited by bishop
Latimer, the great court-preacher, who said before the
young monarch, in one of his sermons, ' I hear say, Mr
' Melancthon, that great clerk, should come hither. I
' would wish him, and such as he is, two hundred pounds
' a year. The king should never want it in his coffers
' at the year's end.'

Melancthon was one of the deputies, whom Maurice,
elector of Saxony, was to send to the council of Trent in
1552 He waited some time at Nuremberg for a safe-
conduct, but he returned from thence to Wittenberg, on
account of the war which was ready to break out His
last conference with the doctors of the Romish communion
was at Worms, in 1557, and of the dissentions that afflicted
him, there was none more violent than that which was
raised by Flavius Illyricus.

Melancthon

Melancthon was of a mild and peaceable difpofition He had a great deal of wit, much reading, and vaft knowledge. He lived among a fort of people who appeared to him paffionate, and too forward to mix human methods, and the authority of the fecular power, with the affairs of the church His tender confcience made him fear there was a mark of reprobation in it But he muft have well weighed all inconveniences, when he caft his eyes upon *Paleftine*, as *Ablard* had formerly done, to retire there, in cafe his enemies fhould drive him away "I am not de-"jected, fays he, at the cruel clamour of my enemies, "who have threatened they will not leave me a footftep "in *Germany*. But I commit myfelf to the Son of God. "If I fhall be driven away alone, I am determined to go "to *Paleftine*, and, in thofe lurking places of *Jerom*, by "calling upon the Son of God, to write clear teftimonies "of the divine doctrine, and in death to recommend my "foul to God."

The teftimonies of piety with which *Melancthon* ended his days were admirable And it is obfervable, that one thing which made him look upon death as a happinefs, was, that it delivered him from theological perfecutions. Some days before he died, he wrote on a piece of paper, in two columns, the reafons why he ought not to be forry for leaving this world. One of thofe columns contained the bleffings that death would procure him The other contained the evils from which death would deliver him. The firft column had fix heads. Firft, That he fhould come to the light Secondly, That he fhould fee God. Thirdly, That he fhould contemplate the Son of God. Fourthly, That he fhould underftand thofe admirable myfteries which he could not comprehend in this life. Fifthly, Why we are created fuch as we are. Sixthly, What is the union of the two natures in *Jefus Chrift*. The fecond column had only two articles Firft, That he fhould fin no more. Secondly, That he fhould be no longer expofed to the vexations and rage of the divines.

The ftate of man appeared to this great divine to be one of the moft incomprehenfible myfteries of religion; and yet there is not one among thofe who believe without examining, that imagines there is any difficulty in it.

Melancthon faid, he had held his profeffor's place forty years, without ever being fure that he fhould not lofe it before the end of the week. None liked his mildnefs, which expofed him to all forts of flander, and deprived him of the means of anfwering a fool according to his folly. The only advantage it procured him was to look

S

upon death without fear, by considering that it would secure him from theological hatred and contentions

Hoornbeeck attributed to Melancthon the Greek version of the Augsburg confession, which appeared under the name of Paul Doscius And Placcius also believed that the translation of Ecclesiasticus and the Psalms into Greek verse was the work of Melancthon It is certain, that he assisted Luther in translating the New Testament into the German language But Melchior Adam, Teissier, and Grou, were mistaken, as well as Placcius, about his Greek version of Ecclesiasticus, and the Psalms, for Lyserus has proved that it was done by Doscius. Melancthon, in 1559, wrote in Greek to the patriarch of Constantinople, and said, "I send "you the Greek version of the confession, which was pub-"lished without my advice However, I like the style, "and have sent it to Constantinople' Melchior Adam says, that this version was made by Melancthon, though it was published under the name of Doscius, who was rector of the college of Hall in Saxony But Melancthon's own words shew that he did not make this version

Peucer was heard to say, that Melancthon, his father-in-law, having read the dialogue de Coena domini, wrote by Occolampadius, forsook the opinion of the oral manducation, and that afterwards he triumphed in the argument from the doctrine of the fathers He said, "The doctrine "of consubstantiation was unknown to the fathers, and "that Augustine was a gross Zuinglian"

Melancthon explained himself freely to an Hungarian, who asked his opinion about the eucharist This was reported to Pomeranus, who afterwards addressed himself in this manner to the people in a sermon 'Most dear bre-'thren, the church is in great danger Pray to God for 'some great persons that are fallen into error' Melancthon was present, and understood that this was meant of him He could not suppress his anger, and went out of the church in sight of all the congregation. Hospinian has undertaken to prove, that Melancthon turned from Lutheranism, as to the point of the real presence, though the fear of oppression prevented him from declaring his judgement openly

Melancthon spent all his life in study, and seemed not to be capable of any other labor He subsisted upon the salary he received from John Frederic, elector of Saxony, as professor of divinity in the university of Wittenburg, which was just sufficient to maintain his family His constitution was very weak, and required great tenderness and management, which made Luther, zealous as he was,

blame

blame him for laboring too earneſtly in the vineyard   'I
' am extremely grieved, ſays he, for your very bad ſtate
' of health, and my prayers are continually offered up for
' your recovery, that there may be ſomebody, when I am
' dead, who may be a bulwark to the houſe of *Iſrael*
' againſt the ragings of *Satan*   In the mean time, why
' do you embarraſs and load yourſelf with ſo much buſi-
' neſs and labour, regardleſs of all the admonitions which
' have been given you?   The time will come, when you
' will condemn, but it will be too late, this inconſiderate
' zeal, which now poſſeſſes you, and urges you to under-
' take ſo much more than you are able to bear, as if you
' had a conſtitution of iron or ſtone.'

In the beginning of his ſickneſs, he ſaid, "I deſire to
" be diſſolved, and to be with *Chriſt*"   And when his
intimate friend *Camerarius* took his laſt leave of him, and
commended him to God, *Melancthon* ſaid, "*Jeſus Chriſt*,
" the Son of God, who ſitteth at the right hand of the
" Father, and giveth gifts to men, preſerve you and
" yours, and us all"   Feeling himſelf very ſick, he cried;
" O Lord, make an end!"

Having received letters from *Francfort*, concerning the
perſecution of ſome godly men in *France*, he ſaid, "that
" his bodily diſeaſe was not comparable to the grief of
" his mind for his godly friends, and for the miſeries of
" the church"   Raiſing himſelf up in his bed, he cried
out, "If God be for us, who can be againſt us?"   After
this he prayed to himſelf, and being at length aſked by
his ſon-in-law, if he would have any thing, he anſwered,
" Nothing but heaven, therefore, trouble me no more
" with ſpeaking to me"   Soon after this he gave up the
ghoſt, at *Wittenberg*, on the nineteenth of *April*, 1560,
which was the ſixty-third day of his ſixty-fourth year
He was honorably buried near *Luther*, in the church of
the caſtle, two days after   And his funeral oration was
ſpoken by *Winſhemius*, a doctor of phyſic, and profeſſor
of the *Greek* tongue.

When he was firſt converted, he thought it impoſſible
for his hearers to withſtand the evidence of the truth in
the miniſtry of the goſpel, but, after preaching awhile,
he complained, "That old *Adam* was too hard for young
" *Melancthon.*"

It is aſtoniſhing, that, amidſt ſo many other occupations, *Melancthon* could write ſo many books   The number of them is prodigious; and a chronological catalogue
of them was publiſhed in 1582, by *Mylius*. *Chriſtopher
Pezelius*, profeſſor of theology at *Wittenberg*, in 1578, publiſhed

lifhed fome extracts of *Melancthon's* works, in which he
put the objections and anfwers concerning theological
matters in a very good method, and interfperfed fome fhort
obfervations This work contains eight volumes in oc-
tavo, which have been printed feveral times at *Neuftat.*
Melancthon finifhed few pieces, and publifhed many imperfect He found his writings were profitable to the
youth, and he rather chofe to print many of them, than
to perfect a fmall number, as he preferred the advantage
of the public to his own glory We may believe, that
the happy genius wherewith he was naturally endowed,
gave him fome affurance that his works would be efteemed,
though unfinifhed His *Latin* verfes pleafed the hyper-
critical *Julius Cæfar Scaliger* And *Gafpar Bufchius*, poet-
laureat to *Ferdinand* king of the *Romans*, tranflated *Melancthon's* catechifm, and his poftilles, into *German*, as alfo a
letter of his to the count *de Weda*

Melancthon was fo cool in his temper, that he examined
matters the more freely on both fides, and was not peremptory in his opinions, becaufe he was convinced that
his knowledge might daily increafe, for he remembered
that he had corrected many things in his own writings,
which he had believed to be good when they were firft
publifhed. His modefty and experience rendered him a
little diftruftful He loved peace, and deplored the confufion of the times. He was even difpofed to judge favorably of feveral doctrines to facilitate a re-union Modefty, moderation, and love of peace, form in the minds
of the moft knowing men, a certain principle of equity,
which makes them lukewarm and irrefolute, and this
feems to have been the character of *Melancthon.* In fome
cafes, however, (as *Zanchius* obferved of him) his natural
timidity led him to concur with and do many things,
which his judgement difapproved, and which were afflicting to many good men, who loved him fincerely

He publifhed feveral books on rhetoric, logic, and
grammar, as well as on theology. His common-places
were publifhed in 1521, when he was only twenty-four
years of age, and there is reafon to believe that he was
an author in print before the age of twenty The parliament at *Paris*, in 1523, cenfured fome of his works, is
they did thofe of *Luther* and *Carolostadius* The court
condemned the writings of *Melancthon*, as containing
' things contrary to holy fcripture, found reafon, the
' councils, the doctrine of the univerfal church, and judge-
' ment of the catholic fathers; being full of fchifmatical
' and heretical propofitions already condemned, contain-

' ing the doctrines of *Luther*, and more dangerous than
' his books, because of the artifices and smoothness of his
' discourse And to shew that they had reason to con-
' demn them, they joined a general censure of some pro-
' positions taken out of his book of common-places, his
' commentary upon the epistle to the *Romans*, his treatise
' against the censures of the Sorbonne, his letters, and
' declarations ' The Lutheran doctrine was then encouraged in the *French* court, and it is no wonder that every
Reformer was censured by the Sorbonne and parliament,
who condemned *Mafgret* for favoring the licence which
Wickliff had introduced, and passed a general censure
upon the colloquies of *Erasmus*, while that eminent genius
paid *Melancthon* the highest compliments, and said he was
desirous of joining with him in his endeavors for the peace
of the church, but that there were some men, of reputation and authority, who treated all those as heretics that
had any correspondence with *Melancthon*

     Melancthon, *Cruciger*, *Bugenhagius*, and *Auroga'lus*, assisted
Luther in his *German* translation of the bible. *Luther* pre-
sided over the work, and collated the *Vulgate* translation,
his new one, and the original text *Melancthon* compared
these with the *Septuagint* *Cruciger* conferred the *Hebrew*
with the *Chaldee*, and the other assistants explored the
rabbinical writings Every one came to conference prepared for the particular passages under consideration, and
each delivered in his judgement upon the several texts
These were all collated and examined, before they concluded upon and determined the final expression.— This
was a great work, highly valuable in itself, and the most
effectual means, in the hand of God, both of preparing
and establishing the REFORMATION.

JOHN à LASCO:

The POLISH REFORMER.

GOD calleth his church out of every people, and
nation, and tongue It is declared that every country under heaven shall bear witness of the power of his
grace, as well as participate the blessings of his providence;
and that he is, and will be, *rich unto all that call upon* HIM.
This

This excellent man was born of a noble family, (which took its name from *Lasco*, or *Latzki*, or *Latzco*,) in *Poland*, and received a very learned and accomplished education. His brother *Jerom* was also a very able and considerable man, and was employed by the emperor *Ferdinand* to negotiate an affair of great importance with the *Turks*, as his ambassador. And he had an uncle, of his own name, who was archbishop of *Gnesna* in *Poland*, to whom *Erasmus* dedicated his edition of St. *Ambrose*'s works.

To attain the knowledge of every thing worth knowing, he set out upon his travels. His distinguished abilities procured him an easy access to several crowned heads, whose countries he visited; and his eloquence, as well as his learning, made him acceptable every where.

In the course of his learned pursuits, we find him traversing the *Alps*, and sitting himself down in the barren cold region of *Switzerland*. It seems, that divine grace, while he was visiting the world, here first visited his heart. It not only visited, but fixed its abode within him. *Zuinglius* appears to have been the instrument; for we find, that he staid some time with him at *Zurick*, and that *Zuinglius*, being fully acquainted with his eminent talents as well as gracious affections, prevailed upon him to study divinity, with a view of promoting the cause of the gospel.

After some stay at *Zurick*, he returned to his own country. But *Poland* was no favorable place for his profession of protestantism, or the increase of his spiritual knowledge, as a divine. Accordingly, though his family and connections opened his way for any sort of preferment, he left his country, his friends, and all human expectation, in order to propagate the truth with freedom, and to enjoy it with safety. He did not quit the kingdom, however, without the knowledge and consent of the king. But, having obtained the royal licence, he chose rather to suffer afflictions (like *Moses*) with the people of God, than to enjoy all the riches and honors, which the world could afford him. He had been made provost of *Gnesna* and bishop of *Vespr'm* in *Hungary*, but these dignities had no weight with him to quit or conceal the knowledge of the truth, for which he was accused of heresy, and even sentenced without hearing. He afterwards wrote to the king upon a similar occasion, and told him, " That his doctrine of " the sacrament had been condemned by a preconceived " determination, without any real or just knowledge of " the matter by those who condemned him; and that it " was the manner of the papists, not to attempt convic- " tion by scripture and reason, but to employ force and " authority,

" authority, accufing thofe of herefy, who will not fwal-
" low all they fay, or maintain whatever abfurdities they
" are pleafed to affirm."

Sic volo, fic jubeo　ftet pro ratione voluntas.

It appears by a popifh hiftorian, quoted by *Melchior
Adam*, that our noble profeffor left *Poland* in the year 1540.
We find him retired, however, to *Embden* in *Friefland*
about the latter end of the year 1542, where he took upon
him the office of a paftor, and preached conftantly at his
church in that town　In the following year, he was engaged, by *Anne* countefs dowager of *Oldenburg* in *Eaft
Friefland*, to introduce and eftablifh the reformed religion
in that territory　This he attempted with great fuccefs,
and continued in this labor, till he received an invitation
from *Albert* duke of *Pruffia* for the fame purpofe.　He fent
the prince, in a fpirit of fairnefs and candor, a declaration
of his doctrine of the facrament, which accorded with the
doctrine of *Zuinglius*, and therefore, as the duke was a
Lutheran, the affair dropped between them.

He had labored in the work of the gofpel near ten years
in *Eaft Friefland*, not daring to venture into *Germany* on
account of the threats of *Charles* V. and the conteft upon
the bufinefs of the *Interim*, when he was invited into
England, by our great and good archbifhop *Cranmer*, to
affift in the work of the Reformation.　This was about
the year 1549.　He arrived in *England*, when the publication of the *Interim* drove the proteftants into any country,
that would grant them a toleration, and fuch they found
in *England*, where they had feveral privileges granted them
by king *Edward* the VIth　Three hundred and fourfcore
were naturalized, and erected into a corporate body, which
was governed by its own laws, and allowed its own form
of religious worfhip independent of the church of *England*;
which at that time was a moft extraordinary conceffion,
and proved how highly they were held in eftimation.　A
church in *London* (the *Auftin Friars*) was alfo granted to
them, with the revenues belonging to it for the fubfiftence
of their minifters, who were either exprefsly nominated,
or at leaft approved, by the king.　His majefty alfo fixed
the precife number of them.　According to this regula-
tion, there were four minifters, and a fuperintendant;
which poft was affigned to *John à Lafco*, who had been
invited over, and who, in the letters patent, is called a
perfon of illuftrious birth, of fingular probity, and great
learning　In the midft of thefe favors, it was certainly
neither prudent nor grateful to attack the eftablifhed

church,

church, which we find he did by writing a book against
her ritual, her ecclefiaftical habits, and the gefture of
kneeling at the facrament. What a pity, when fo many
effentials were concerned, that good men fhould occupy
themfelves and differ about modes, and forms, and trifles!

About this time, ' the emigrants from *Germany* (fays
' Dr *Glocefter Ridley*) on the fcore of religion, who agreed
' in fubftance with us, but under a different difcipline,
' were to be protected, but, under their wing, crept mul-
' titudes of frantic enthufiafts, or lurking papifts perfo-
' nating new fectaries. For fifting of thefe, in *June* 1550,
' *Auftin Friars* was given to the *Germans* and other fo-
' reigners, for their church, under the fuperintendency
' of *John à Lafco*, the *Polander*, *for avoiding of all fects of*
' *Anabaptifts and fuch like*, as king *Edward* fets it down
' in his journal. Thefe were indulged to ufe their own
' rites and ceremonies, and an injunction was given to
' all bifhops, judges and officers, not to moleft them for
' their non-compliance with the order of religion efta-
' blifhed here. So that every ftranger, who was not pro-
' tected by *John à Lafco*, became amenable to the *Englifh*
' governors.'—Thus affairs ftood (for *Lafco's* book did
not operate to his prejudice), till the death of that excellent prince, our *Englifh Jofiah*, gave a new turn to public
expectation, and for a time unhinged the eftablifhment of
the reformed religion.

King *Edward* the VIth was taken from the world on
the fixth of *July*, 1553. The change of public meafures
and counfels was foon written in blood. However, *John
à Lafco* and the other foreigners of the proteftant faith,
were fuffered to depart, or rather were fent away, upon
the acceffion of queen *Mary*. They formed a great company of *Polifh, Germans, French, Scots, Italians, Spaniards*,
and others. *John à Lafco* embarked on the feventeenth of
September following, with one hundred and feventy-five
of his flock, and his colleagues, all, except two, who ftaid
in *England* concealed, together with the reft of the *German* proteftants, who were deprived of their churches, and
all their privileges taken away. Thefe diftreffed exiles
arrived on the coaft of *Denmark*, in the beginning of a
very fevere winter, but they met with a reception as cold
and as barren as the country itfelf. For, though they
were known to be proteftants, yet becaufe they profeffed
the Zuinglian doctrine concerning the facrament, to the
lafting difgrace of the *Danes*, both as men and as Chriftians, they were not fuffered to difembark, nor to anchor
longer than two days, without daring to put their wives
and

and children on fhore An inftance of brutality, which would have difgraced the *Algerines* ! They were treated in the fame inhofpitable and unchriftian manner at *Lubec*, *Wifmar*, and *Hamburgh*, becaufe, with thefe Lutherans and the papifts, they could not believe, contrary to the evidence of their fenfes, and without the leaft authority from the fcripture to look after a miracle, that the bread and wine in the facrament actually became that very body and blood of *Jefus Chrift*, which is afcended to heaven, and which, it is declared, fhall remain there, till the final reftitution of all things If the manners and difpofitions of thefe people had been ever fo much more churlifh, felfifh, and unfeeling, than they are by nature, furely, grace, if they had any, muft have melted their bofoms at the fight of fo much outward fuffering, and efpecially of fo much Chriftian woe. After fpending the winter, which is commonly very fevere in thofe countries, in this dreadful manner, toffed about from place to place, they at length refolved to fteer for *Embden*, where, after a multitude of perils and hardfhips, they did not arrive till *March*, 1554, when the worft of the winter was nearly over From *September* to *March*, they had wandered to and fro, and were driven about upon the feas. Through the wide world thefe people fought after a home, of whom the world, indeed, was not worthy

At *Embden* they were received with kindnefs and hofpitality; and moft of them fettled in the country The good countefs dowager, *Anne* of *Oldenburg*, became their immediate patronefs, and probably procured for them all the good offices, which they found in *Friefland* *John à Lafco*, however, did not remain here, for, in 1555, he went to *Frankfort* upon the *Maine*, where he obtained leave of the fenate to build a church for the reformed ftrangers, and particularly for thofe of the low countries While he was at this city, he wrote an apologetical letter to *Sigifmund* king of *Poland*, againft the afperfions of *Joachim Weftphale*, of *Timann*, and of *Pomeran*, who had all reprefented him as a vagabond, defirous of drawing away people after him This letter was written in 1556, and we have given a hint of its contents before.

In this year, 1556, with the confent of the duke of *Wirtenberg*, he maintained a difputation againft *Brentius* the Lutheran, upon the fubject of the euchariſt *Brentius* publifhed a very unfair account of this controverfy, in which he ftated many things, which *John à Lafco* had not faid, and omitted many others, which he had urged, but which bore too hard upon the Lutherans. He alfo abufed

the

the church of the ftrangers, over which *John à Lafco* prefided, calumniating them for differing from the confeffion
of *Augfburg*, refpecting the facrament   This obliged our
noble fufferer to publifh an apology for himfelf and his
church, about the beginning of the year 1557, in which
he proved, " That their doctrine did not militate with
" the *Augfburg* confeffion concerning the prefence of *Chrift*
" in the fupper," as their adverfaries had charged upon
them   " But that, if even they did differ from that con-
" feffion, it did not follow they were to be condemned,
" if they could juftify their diffent from that confeffion
" by the word of God "

Weftphale feems to have been his principal adverfary,
and carried his oppofition with a bitternefs, very unbecoming a minifter and a Chriftian.   He called thefe poor
refugees by opprobrious names, railed feverely at *John à
Lafco*, and even went fo far as to fay, ' That thofe, who
' had fuffered, upon the doctrine of the facrament, in
' *England, Holland, France*, and elfewhere, were only the
' martyrs of the devil '—A rafh expreffion indeed, which
involved in its cenfure fome of the brighteft and moft ufeful inftruments of the Reformation, whofe very books
Weftphale was not worthy to bear after them!   Such hot-
headed opinionifts only injure the caufe, which has the
misfortune of their approbation

After an abfence of twenty years, our noble *Pole* returned to his native country, where, notwithftanding the
bifhops and other ecclefiaftics did their utmoft to drive him
away, their efforts proved ineffectual, through the favor
of *Sigifmund* the king, who made ufe of his talents in his
moft important affairs   In *Poland*, the harveft truly was
plenteous, but the laborers were few   The popifh clergy
obftructed every attempt of a Reformation, and would have
deftroyed *John à Lafco*, but for fear of the confequence to
themfelves.   They once attempted to remove him from
the king's confidence, and had the boldnefs to addrefs his
majefty upon the fubject.   But the king nobly replied,
' That he had indeed heard, that the bifhops had pro-
' nounced him an heretic, but the fenate of the kingdom
' had determined no fuch matter   That *John à Lafco* was
' ready to prove himfelf untainted with heretical pravity,
' and found in the catholic faith '

When open attacks would not ferve, they attempted (in
the true fpirit of their profeffion) to deftroy him by fecret
arts   No lie, no calumny, was too grofs or bitter for circulation, if there was the leaft profpect of its gaining
belief among the multitude   They fet it about, that he

was a trumpet of fedition, and would foon 'introduce a civil war into the land But thefe artifices, likewife, had no other effect, than to fhew the malice and wickednefs of his enemies

However, it pleafed God, in a fhort time, to remove his fervant out of this turbulent world, and to bring him happily, where the wicked ceafe from troubling, and where the weary are at reft. He was taken away by a fhort ficknefs in *January*, 1560

King *Sigifmund* (as we have obferved) very highly efteemed him, and advifed with him upon his moft weighty affairs. *John à Lafco* continued in the Helvetic or Zuinglian doctrine of the facrament, without any variation, but took very great pains to conciliate the difference, which fubfifted upon that article, in the proteftant churches He was a man of peace, a minifter of the gofpel of peace, and peace he wifhed to promote And fo do all thofe, who have *the peace of God ruling in their hearts*

The hiftorians of his time fpeak very highly in his praife, *Erafmus*, who much efteemed him, declares, that he had learned fobriety, temperance, modefty, difcretion and chaftity of him, although being then old, and *John à Lafco* yet young, he ought to have been the mafter, and not the fcholar And *Zanchius*, in a letter to him, writes thus, ' *Servavit te huc ufque Deus, ut ficut* Lutherus *fuæ Ger-* ' *maniæ,* Zuinglius *fuæ Helvetiæ,* Calvinus *fuæ Galliæ,* ' *ita tu tuæ Poloniæ fis Apoftolus* ' i e. God hath hitherto preferved you, that as *Luther, Zuinglius*, and *Calvin*, were the apoftles of their own refpective countries of *Germany, Switzerland,* and *France*, fo *You*, in like manner, might be the apoftle of *Poland*, your native land,

His writings were 1 A book upon the Lord's Supper 2 An epiftle, containing a brief difcuffion of the controverfy upon the Lord's Supper 3 A confeffion of our communion with the Lord *Chrift*, and the exhibition of his body in the facrament, addreffed to the minifters of the churches in *Eaft Friefland* 4 An epiftle to the minifters of the church at *Bremen* 5 A tract againft *Mennon*, the chief of the catabaptifts. 6 Three epiftles, concerning the right method of church-government. 7 An epiftle apologetical to king *Sigifmund* and the ftates of *Poland*, 8 A defence of the church of refugees at *Frankfort*, upon the calumny about the Lord's Supper 9 An anfwer to the virulent addrefs of *Joachim Weftphale* upon the fame fubject. 10 The manner and reafon of the whole ecclefiaftical conduct of *Edward* the VIth. towards the church of refugees in *London*,

I

PETER

PETER MARTYR

From an original Engraving published under the Inspection of Be.

PETER MARTYR:

OR

PETER MARTYR VERMILIUS.

THIS excellent man was born in the city of *Florence*, the metropolis of the dukedom of *Tuscany* in *Italy*, on the eighth of *September*, 1500. His father was *Stephen Vermilius*, who gave him such a liberal education, that, at sixteen years of age, he became a canon regular of the order of St. *Augustine* in the college at *Fifcoli*, about a mile from *Florence*. It is said, that he received the first rudiments of literature from his mother, who was a very ingenious lady, and ufed to read *Terence* and the other *Latin* clafics to him in the original. He fpent three years at this college, and was then fent to *Padua*, to enlarge his learning in that univerfity, which was in a flourishing condition He fettled there in the monaftry of St. *John de Verdera* of the fame order of Augustines, where he continued eight years studying philofophy, and the other liberal arts But he more particularly applied himself to the fludy of the *Greek* tongue, and poets, which he completely maftered.

He began to preach in 1526, and the first time he performed that office was in the church of St. *Afia* in *Brefcia*, or *Brixia*, a city belonging to the republic of *Venice* He afterwards preached in the moft confiderable cities of *Italy* But all the time that he could obtain from his function was devoted to facred learning, philofophy, and in acquiring the *Hebrew* tongue. He became fuch a celebrated fcholar, that he was made abbot of *Spoletto*, in the duchy of *Umbria*, fubject to the pope, where he continued three years. From thence he was translated to the city of *Naples*, where he became abbot of the monaftry of his order called St *Peter ad Aram*, which was much more confiderable than that of *Spoletto*

At *Bononia* he applied himself to the fludy of the *Hebrew* tongue, and purfued at the fame time his ftudies in divinity

It was at *Naples* that *Martyr* first read the works of *Bucer* and *Zuinglius*, which opened his eyes to the verity

of

of the gofpel But he did not embrace the proteftant religion till the year 1542 One *Valdes*, a *Spanish* lawyer
and learned proteftant, was the means of eftablifhing him
in the knowledge and love of the truth , fo that, it is faid,
he even ventured to preach it privately at *Rome* itfelf to
fome perfons of quality, and proceeded fo far as to attack
the doctrine of purgatory openly , but was foon filenced.
He fell into a dangerous ficknefs after he had been three
years at *Naples*, but the ftrength of his conftitution over-
came it, and his phyficians advifed him to take better air
than what *Naples* afforded The fathers therefore chofe
him general vifitor of their order, that he might be abfent
from his cure with convenience And he was foon after
elected prior of St *Fridian* in the city of *Lucca* in *Tufcany*,
where he enjoyed his native air Here he lived with *Zanchius* and *Tremellius*, whom he is faid to have been the inftrument of converting to the knowledge and profeffion
of the gofpel, with many others, who were afterwards
obliged to abandon their native country upon that account.

This priory was a place of great dignity, and had epifcopal jurifdiction in the middle part of the city. He
inftituted a moft admirable method of ftudies for the young
ftudents at *Lucca* But his opinion concerning a Reformation of the church was difcovered, and fnares were laid
for him by the monks, which prevented him from declaring his fentiments. He therefore committed the beft part
of his library to the cuftody of one of his friends, gave
another part to the college, and departed from *Lucca* to
Pifa, a city eight miles diftant from the other

He wrote from *Pifa* to cardinal *Pole*, and fhewed him
the reafons of his departure Afterwards he went into
Switzerland with *Bernardinus Ochinus*, who was alfo lately
converted from the *Romifh* fuperftitions, after having been
one of the moft popular preachers in *Italy*, and continued
fome time at *Zurick*, from whence he went to *Strafburgh*,
by means of *Bucer*, where he read and taught divinity
about five years.

While he was at *Strafburgh*, he followed the example of
Luther and *Bucer*, by taking a wife, who had lately been
a nun, and whofe name was *Catharine Dampmartin* This
caufed his enemies to fay, that he left his order and monaftic vows for the fake of a woman She lived with him
eight years, went with him to *England*, and died at *Oxford*.

Bucer endeavored to perfuade *Peter Martyr* to follow his
example about the euchrift. *Martyr* conformed himfelf
for fome time to *Bucer*'s language, and afterwards left it,
when he faw the dangerous confequences of it, which
were,

were, that the Lutherans were not fully satisfied, while it gave offence to the weak and perplexed, and embarrassed them in such a manner, that they could not tell what to believe on that point. However, *Bucer* was convinced of *Martyr*'s orthodoxy, and they continued their friendship. *Bucer* and *Fagius* were invited to *England* in the reign of *Edward* VI. *Peter Martyr* was also invited there in that reign, to assist in the Reformation. Though *Naudæus* erroneously says, he fled thither for refuge.

In 1547, *Edward Seymour*, lord protector, and archbishop *Cranmer*, invited *Peter Martyr* to *England*, ' that his ' assistance might be used to carry on a Reformation in the ' church.' He arrived in *December* the same year, in this kingdom, with *Bernardinus Ochinus*, another *Italian*. They were kindly received by archbishop *Cranmer* at *Lambeth*, and entertained there for some time. The stipends, allowed them, were handsome for the time, though indeed no stipends could deserve any consideration, which might draw over and subsist men of such eminence and learning. We were but just emerged from barbarism in this country; and the introduction of learned foreigners afforded both a polish to our manners, and an improvement to our minds. True knowledge beat down the outworks of superstition, and the gospel of truth invested the capitol.

Bucer was made professor of divinity at *Cambridge*, and, in 1548, *Martyr* was admitted doctor of divinity at *Oxford*, as he had stood at *Padua*. The government, at that time, had a watchful eye over both the universities, where *Bucer*, *Martyr*, and the other learned foreigners, were hard pressed in disputes with popish *English* divines. *Oglethorpe*, the president of *Magdalen-college* in *Oxford*, was particularly obnoxious, as being backward in the work of Reformation, and there was some talk of prosecuting him before the council. But he prevented this, by sending a letter to *Cranmer*, setting forth his own conduct in the most favorable light, wherein he declared his dislike to transubstantiation, yet he thought that *Christ* was present in the sacrament in some inconceivable manner, on which account, he was of opinion, that it ought to be administred with great devotion and caution. We shall find that doctor *Oglethorpe* was afterwards made bishop of *Carlisle*, and that it was he who crowned queen *Elizabeth* in 1559, notwithstanding the other bishops refused to assist at the solemnity, because that princess had sufficiently declared herself against the church of *Rome*.

Doctor *Smith*, another eminent professor in *Oxford*, had been remarkably inconstant in matters of religion, and was

was therefore removed from his public professorship of divinity, to make way for *Peter Martyr*, notwithstanding he was more addicted to the Zuinglian than to the Lutheran doctrines in point of the sacrament.

The same year, *Martyr* was appointed by the king to read a public lecture to the academians in the divinity school, and to have an annuity of forty marks for his reward. He maintained public disputations with the Romanists, who behaved to him more like personal enemies than religious adversaries.

It is necessary to observe, that the main spring which actuated all measures, was religion. The young king, and the duke of *Somerset*, were sincerely and virtuously disposed towards a Reformation, and their measures were directed by the cool and politic head of archbishop *Cranmer*, who made an admirable use of that knowledge of mankind, which he had acquired by his long experience. He could not, indeed, prevent many, who assisted in the work of Reformation, from profiting themselves by the spoils of the church. But he took care, that what she lost in her property, she should make up in her establishment.

The spirit of Reformation seems to have been quickened by the arrival of the foreign divines from *Germany* and other places. They were in general against the imparity of church government. But, in other respects, their opinions were not much repugnant to those now received by the church of *England*. The calling in those foreigners had this happy effect, that their authority, which was great in *England* on account of their reputation abroad, proved an useful counterpoize at the universities, to the influence of the papists and the popish professors, who continued still numerous there.

The privy-council were informed of the tumult at *Oxford*, and appointed some delegates to hear and preside in the disputation which the professor had undertaken. *Martyr* accordingly maintained, against three opponents, that in the sacrament of thanksgiving there is no transubstantiation of bread and wine into the body and blood of *Christ*. That his body or blood is not carnally or corporally *in* the bread and wine, nor *under* them. But that his body and blood are united to the bread and wine sacramentally. His adversaries, finding no advantage could be gained by argument, had recourse to more forcible measures. They stirred up the multitude against him so successfully, that he was obliged to retire to *London*, till the tumult was suppressed.

In

In 1550, the king beſtowed a canonry of *Chriſt-church* upon *Martyr*, who was inſtalled the twentieth of *January* He then entered upon the lodgings belonging to him, which joined on the north-ſide of *Chriſt-church* great gate leading into *Fiſh-ſtreet* His wife *Catharine* ſettled with him there; as the wife of doctor *Cox* did about the ſame time with him in the dean's lodgings It was obſerved, that theſe were the firſt women, who reſided in any college or hall at *Oxford*, by whoſe example any other canon was permitted to marry, and introduce women and children into thoſe ſeminaries, which was looked upon as ſuch a damnable matter by the papiſts, that they uſually ſtiled them concubines, and called the lodgings that entertained them and their children ſtews and bawdy houſes

While *Martyr* continued in theſe apartments, he continually, and eſpecially in the night time, received very opprobrious language from the papiſts, as well ſcholars as laics, who frequently broke his windows This diſturbed his ſtudies and ſleep, and obliged him to change his lodgings for thoſe in the cloiſter, where he peaceably ſpent the remaining part of his abode in the univerſity. However, for the cloſer enjoyment of his ſtudies, he erected a fabric of ſtone in his garden, ſituated on the eaſt-ſide of his apartments, wherein he partly compoſed his commentaries on the firſt epiſtle to the *Corinthians*, and his epiſtles to learned men. This fabric contained two ſtories, and ſtood till 1684, when it was pulled down

Doctor *Hooper*, profeſſor of divinity, was preferred to be biſhop of *Glouceſter*, but when he came to be conſecrated he ſcrupled the wearing of ſome of the epiſcopal ornaments. Archbiſhop *Cranmer* ſuſpended *Hooper*, as is mentioned in his life The doctor conſulted *Bucer* and *Martyr* upon the affair, and the latter wrote him an anſwer to all his objections, which was fuller than *Bucer's* letter to the archbiſhop, but exactly conformable to the ſentiments expreſſed in it He commended *Hooper* for his pains in preaching, but adviſed him not to exert his zeal upon points that are indefenſible, and things of little moment, leſt the people ſhould from thence be led to call in queſtion the judgement of the reformed preachers, and give no credit to what they delivered in the moſt important articles. He reminded him, that an abſtinence from things ſtrangled, and from blood, was a part of the *Jewiſh* inſtitution, and yet that the council at *Jeruſalem* commanded the gentiles to obſerve it, to avoid giving offence, In anſwer to one objection of *Hooper's*, ‘ that

‘ we

' we ought to have an exprefs warrant from fcripture for
' every thing belonging to religion ' *Martyr* told him,
that if the general rules of order were obferved, the governors of the church had a difcretionary latitude in little
matters   Thus, for inftance, our receiving the communion in a church, in a forenoon, not in a declining pof-
ture, and in a congregation of men only, ftood upon no
other than ecclefiaftical, that is, human authority, to
which he prefumed, that *Hooper* had always fubmitted
without any fcruple   He told him further, that it would
be difficult to produce any warrant from the New Teftament for finging pfalms in public worfhip, and that the
Chriftian church from the beginning, in many particulars, had a regard to the *Jewifh* polity, efpecially in the
great feftivals of *Eafter*, and *Whitfuntide*. Suppofing,
what he could not grant, that the epifcopal habit and veftments were introduced into the church by the fee of *Rome*,
yet he did not think the contagion of popery fo very malignant as to carry infection to every thing which it
touched   That to govern by fuch narrow maxims would
lay an inconvenient reftraint upon the church of God,
and that our anceftors moved much more freely, who
made no difficulty of turning heathen temples into Chriftian churches, and of tranflating the revenues facred to
idolatry, to pious ufes, and the maintenance of the clergy.

Hooper for fome time continued his non-conformity,
but he was afterwards confecrated bifhop, and died a martyr   *Peter Martyr*, and his companion *Ochinus*, had their
annual allowances from the king, as all other learned followers had, according to bifhop *Latimer*, who faid, in one
of his court fermons, ' There is yet among us two great
' learned men, *Peter Martyr* and *Bernard Ochin.*, which
' have an hundred marks a piece.   I would the king would
' beftow a thoufand pounds on that fort '   Such were the
fentiments of this moft venerable prelate and martyr, the
pious *Latimer*

The death of *Bucer*, which happened in 1551, was
greatly lamented by king *Edward* VI and all the friends
of the Reformation in *England*.   He was no friend to the
book of Common Prayer as it ftood at the time of his death,
and his remonftrances, with thofe of *Martyr* and *Calvin*,
prevailed with archbifhop *Cranmer*, and the other prelates
of the Reformation, to fuffer it to be revifed and corrected.
Catharine, the wife of *Peter Martyr*, died about the fame
time, and fhe was buried in the cathedral church of *Oxford*,
near to the place where the reliques of St. *Fridefwide* had
been

been reposed. But, about four years after, her body was taken up, thrown out of the church with scorn, and buried in a dunghill, where it lay till queen *Elizabeth* came to the crown, when she ordered the body to be taken up and reburied. ' The wife of *Peter Martyr* had been suf-
' pected of heresy. But, as she was a foreigner, and did
' not speak *English*, it was impossible to prove the charge
' against her, yet this did not prevent her body being
' taken out of its grave, and buried in unconsecrated
' ground.' The bodies of *Bucer* and *Fagius* were taken up and burnt under the farce of law. ' The like difficult
' process was also carried on against the body of *Peter*
' *Martyr's* wife. But the visitors could not hear of any
' witnesses that had heard her utter any heresy. They
' sent up therefore to cardinal *Pole* for fresh instructions,
' who directed, that since it was notorious she had been a
' nun and had married contrary to her vow, her body
' should be taken up, and buried in a dunghill, as a per-
' son dying under excommunication, which was done
' accordingly.' *Melchior Adam* says, that the true reason of this low indecency was founded in a motive of resent-ment, which cardinal *Pole* had conceived against her hus-band. The cardinal had formerly been the most intimate friend of *Martyr*, and even continued to appear so, after he had expressed his dislike of the errors of the church of *Rome*. But when *Martyr* left *Italy*, *Pole* became his most inveterate enemy, and exercised this indignity to the wife, in order to express his hatred of the husband. When queen *Elizabeth* came to the throne, her body was removed again by an order, and solemnly interred in the most ho-norable part of the church. And, to prevent the papists from treating her in the same opprobrious manner again, if they should ever have come into power, her bones were mixed with the bones of the saintess *Fridefwide*, that it might not be possible to distinguish or separate them.

King *Edward* VI died in 1553, in the sixteenth year of his age, which gave a violent blow to the Reformation. He was succeeded by his sister *Mary*, the daughter of *Catharine* of *Arragon*, who had been educated a papist, and whose reign was polluted with the blood of martyrs. Upon her accession, all the popish bishops were restored, and the protestant bishops set aside. A letter was issued to the bishops, attended by a proclamation, forbidding all exercises of preaching and expounding the scriptures with-out the queen's licence. Thus, the supremacy, for this time, was borrowed by a popish sovereign, to be the scourge of the Reformation. In the beginning of this

3 T   reign,

reign, many proteftants forefaw the approaching perfecutions which difhonored the nation, and retired abroad ;
fome to *Switzerland*, and others to *Germany*. A refolution was taken to bring into the univerfities a teft for
purging them of all proteftants, and to prevent their re-
admiffion for the future   This was done by way of oath,
as follows

‘ You fhall fwear, by the holy contents of this book,
‘ that you fhall not keep, hold, maintain, and defend, at
‘ any time, during your life, any opinion erroneous, or
‘ error of *Wickliffe*, *Hufs*, *Luther*, or any other condemned
‘ of herefy   And that ye fhall keep, hold, maintain, and
‘ defend generally and efpecially, all fuch articles and
‘ points as the catholic church of *Rome* believeth, holdeth,
‘ or maintaineth, at this time   And that ye fhall allow
‘ and accept, maintain and defend, for their power, all
‘ traditions, inftitutions, rites, ceremonies, and laudable
‘ cuftoms, as the faid church of *Rome* taketh them, al-
‘ loweth them, and approveth them   And that you fhall
‘ namely and fpecially hold as the faid catholic church
‘ holdeth in all thefe articles, wherein lately hath been
‘ controverfy, diffention, and error, as concerning faith
‘ and works, grace, and free-will, of fin in a good work,
‘ of the facrifice of the New Teftament, of the priefthood
‘ of the new law, of communion under both kinds, of
‘ baptifm and Chriftian liberty, of monaftic vows, of faft-
‘ ing and choice of meats, of the fingle life of priefts, of
‘ the church, of the canonical books, of the firm holding
‘ of matters not expreft in the fcriptures, of the inerra-
‘ bility of general councils in faith and manners, of the
‘ power of the church to make laws, of the church’s
‘ facraments and their efficacy, of the power of excom-
‘ munication conferred upon the church, of punifhing
‘ heretics, of the facrifice of the mafs, of purgatory, of
‘ worfhipping faints and praying to them, of worfhipping
‘ the images of faints, of pilgrimages, of evangelical pre-
‘ cepts and councils   And likewife of all other articles,
‘ wherein controverfy or diffention hath been in the church
‘ before this day ’

The roman-catholics at *Oxford*, without waiting for
any directions from the court, drove *Peter Martyr* from
the divinity chair, and brought the old fervice into the
churches with all the train of ceremonies formerly ufed.
Martyr then left *Oxford*, and went to *London*, where the
queen granted him a fafe-conduct, with which he returned to *Strafburgh*, where he met doctor *Cox* and fome
other

other *English* fugitives, and renewed his lectures in philosophy and divinity Ochinus went to *Strasburgh* with his
friend *Martyr*, and it was in the year 1553, that they
repassed the sea Ochinus went to *Switzerland*, where he
continued ten years, when he was banished for his writings, in the seventy-sixth year of his age, and then went
to *Moravia*, where he died of the plague There are express and unexceptionable proofs that *Ochinus* fled from
Basil to *Poland*, and died in those parts, yet the capuchins
made no scruple to publish, that he died a roman-catholic
martyr at Geneva 'Tis very certain, that he was not
found in the faith

Martyr, upon an honorable invitation from the magistrates, travelled to *Zurick* in 1556, to which place he was
accompanied by our excellent doctor *Jewel*, and several
other exiled divines of *England* In this city he took for
his second wife one *Catharine Merenda* He lived at *Zurick* seven years in high esteem with the inhabitants of the
place, and in great friendship with *Bullinger* and other
learned men. While he continued there, *Maximilian
Celsus*, an exiled count, and the chief minister of the *Italian* church of *Geneva*, died, whereupon *Martyr* was invited to succeed him, which he refused for several reasons
When queen *Mary* died, queen *Elizabeth* invited him to
return to *England*, and accept of what preferment he
pleased, which he modestly declined He continued at
Zurick to the time of his death, which happened on the
twelfth of *November*, 1562, in the sixty-second year of his
age. He died with great comfort, meekness and tranquillity, in the presence of *Bullinger*, and some other friends,
before whom he declared, with a voice which could scarce
be heard, "That he expected life and salvation only
" through *Jesus Christ*, who alone was appointed by the
" Father for the salvation of men." To this declaration
he added several reasons for this hope, concluding with
this sentence, " This is my faith, and in this I die
" But those, who teach otherwise and lead men to expect
" salvation upon any other ground, will God destroy "
Then, stretching forth his hands, he gently said, " Fare-
" well, dear friends and brethren, farewell "

It appears that *Martyr* was in *France* in 1561, when he
paid a visit to *John Anthony Caraccioli*, a bishop, who
had openly declared himself a protestant This prelate
had not been confirmed or elected by the church and
people, which made him in doubt, whether he could
lawfully exercise the pastoral function? He convened the

elders

elders of the reformed church, who met at *Poiſſy*, and referred the affair to the church of *Geneva* ' In the mean
' time, paſſed through *Troyes*, (ſays *Beza*) that great man
' *Peter Martyr*, in his return from *Poiſſy* to his church at
' *Zurick*, by whoſe advice, the biſhop made his abjura-
' tion, ſigned the confeſſion of faith, promiſed to quit his
' biſhopric, and was received into the miniſtry '

He had two children by his ſecond wife, who both died
very young, and before him, and he left her with child
of a third, which proved a daughter

Peter Martyr is ſaid to have been a man of a large
healthy body, and of a very grave ſedate and well-compoſed
countenance. His parts and learning were very uncommon, as was alſo his ſkill in diſputation, which made him
as much admired by the proteſtants, as hated by the papiſts He was very ſincere and indefatigable in the work
of the Reformation, yet his zeal was never known to run
headſtrong before his judgement He was always moderate and prudent in his outward behavior; nor, even in
diſputation, was he ever tranſported into intemperate
warmth, or driven to unguarded expreſſions None of his
works raiſed his reputation higher in *England*, than his
defence of the orthodox doctrine of the Lord's Supper,
againſt biſhop *Gardiner*, which all the foreign divines likewiſe allowed to be a moſt able and accurate performance.
Biſhop *Jewel* ſaid of him, that he was ' an illuſtrious man,
' and ought never to be named without the higheſt reſpect
' and honor ' And *Simlerus*, who ſpoke his funeral oration before the people of *Zurick*, told them, ' That they
' might have another in *Martyr's* room, but another
' *Martyr* they would never have '

His writings were very conſiderable The *Engliſh* titles
of them are as follow 1 A catechiſm or expoſition of
the creed, publiſhed in *Italian*. 2 A prayer book compoſed out of the *Pſalms* 3 Commentaries upon *Geneſis*
4 Upon the book of *Judges*. 5 Upon the two books of
Samuel 6 Upon the firſt book of *Kings*, and eleven chapters of the ſecond 7 Upon *Paul* to the *Romans*. 8 Upon
the firſt epiſtle to the *Corinthians* 9 Diſputations at
Oxford, about the Lord's Supper. 10 Defence about the
orthodox doctrine of the Lord's Supper, againſt *Stephen
Gardiner* 11 An abridgement of the ſaid defence made
by him afterward 12 Confeſſion exhibited to the ſenate
of *Straſburgh*, concerning the Supper of the Lord. 13.
Judgement concerning the preſence of *Chriſt's* body in the
ſacrament, delivered at the conference at *Poiſſy* 14 A
diſcourſe

discourse concerning the mass   15 A dialogue concerning the place of *Christ*'s body, against the *Ubiquitaries*   16 Refutation of *Richard Smith*'s two books, concerning single life and monkish vows   17 Commentaries on the first and second books of *Aristotle*'s *Ethicks*, and part of the third   18 Common places gathered out of his commentaries by others, and digested into heads   19. Certain treatises of free-will, God's providence, predestination, and the cause of sin   20 Propositions, some necessary, some probable, out of *Genesis*, *Exodus*, *Leviticus*, and *Judges*, together with solutions of a question or two concerning some Mosaical laws and oaths   21 Divers sermons and orations of several subjects, and made upon several occasions   22 His letters to sundry persons, concerning much variety of useful discourse.

THOMAS GRYNÆUS.

GOD, in his great mercy to his church, has appointed ministring servants, of various gifts and qualifications, for the building up of his people, and forwarding them in their most holy faith. Where the soft language of a *Barnabas* would probably fail, the Lord sends the thunder of a *Boanerges* to the soul. And he rarely employs the meek and placid spirit of a *Melancthon*, when the raging passions of men are better opposed by the magnanimous heart of *Luther*. Some of his ministers are most instrumental in public speaking, and others are perhaps more permanently and extensively useful in writing for the public. Divine grace confers different talents, proportioned to the different work designed. But still it is the *same* Spirit and the *same* Lord, *who worketh all in all*. Whatever good is done upon earth, the Lord doeth it himself.

This excellent man, *Thomas Grynæus*, seems to have eminently possessed *the ornament of a meek and quiet spirit*, which, though it has but little splendor in the eyes of men, *in the sight of God is of great price*. He made but little noise in the world, but was, however, of great use in promoting the cause of Reformation.

He was born at *Veringen* in *Germany*, of a good family, about the year 1512, and received the rudiments of his
education

education at home. While he was yet very young, he was removed to the care of his good and learned uncle *Simon Grynæus* (whose life we have given) at *Heidelberg*, under whose tuition he studied very hard, and in time became a great proficient in almost every branch of science.

In the year 1529, he accompanied his uncle to *Basil*, in the seventeenth year of his age, and was so far advanced in his studies, as to be able, at a time, when others are little more than school-boys, to assist his learned relation privately in the tuition of young persons, and in some respects, by teaching others to instruct himself. He does not appear to have remained long at *Basil*, for we find him, while a mere youth, in the capacity of a public teacher of the languages and philosophy at *Bern* in *Switzerland*, where he obtained great esteem by his life and learning. In this station he continued about eleven years, till theological disputes, in which he was necessarily involved, began to run very high. Upon which account, being a man of a quiet spirit, and wearied with the contentions about him, he returned to *Basil*, where he pursued his studies for a while, with great diligence and privacy.

He had not sate down long at *Basil*, in 1547, before the rectors of that university, desirous to shew honor to so learned a man, as well as wishing for his able assistance, conferred upon him the degree of master of arts. While he was employed in this business of public and private tuition, to which he added the labors of a preacher in the neighboring villages, *Charles*, marquis of *Baden*, who was awakened by the grace of God from the idolatry and superstition of the times, was employed in purging his dominion of the *Romish* errors, and in establishing the pure doctrine of the gospel. His territory lay close up to *Basil*. Wishing, therefore, for an able and faithful minister, he applied earnestly to *Grynæus* to accept of the charge, and the more, as it was no great distance from his beloved seat of learning. Accordingly, *Grynæus* complied with the marquis's wishes, and performed his pastoral duty with so much faithfulness, solemnity, and kindness of behavior, that he was exceedingly endeared to his flock, and beloved by all those, who had any concern for truth and knowledge. In this function he continued about eight years; at the expiration of which, an epidemical disorder, which raged in *Basil* and through all the neighboring country, carried off this valuable servant of *Jesus Christ* to his Master's presence, on the second of *August*, in the year 1564,

and

and in the fifty-second year of his age His body was buried in his own church, where he had been the first preacher of the gospel, and where an honorable monument was afterwards erected to his memory

It does not appear, that he published any writings, but he left behind him a noble treasure for the church in his four excellent sons, whose names were, *Theophilus, Simon, John James,* and *Tobias,* all of them eminent for their piety and learning But *John James,* whose life we shall give hereafter, was the most distinguished of the four, and succeeded his father in his pastoral charge, as well as in faith and doctrine He was indeed a burning and a shining light, as our Readers will probably perceive in the account of him. Such a father and such sons are not often met with in the history of the world.—Blessed be God for *them* May the Lord of the vineyard send forth many more such laborers into his harvest!

PETER PAUL VERGERIO,

BISHOP of ISTRIA,

SCARCE any thing proves the almighty efficacy of the grace of God with more demonstration, than the conversion of the determined opposers of the gospel. That *such* men should build the faith, which once they attempted to destroy, not only shews that there is some extraordinary circumstance in the case, but excites the public astonishment, and leads to the strictest enquiry This enquiry, when conducted with candor and seconded by grace, has often ended in the conversion of others, and what was at first imagined to be only a private matter, has eventually turned out a public blessing. The wonderful change made in the apostle *Paul* had this happy effect, and as the sincerity of such persons, as the apostle and some others were, cannot reasonably be questioned, the surprizing alteration of their sentiments and conduct has been produced, as a strong argument of the truth and glory of the gospel And, perhaps this argument has been treated by nobody with more force and perspicuity (so far as relates to the power of words), than by the late lord *Lyttleton* in his tract, entitled, ' Obfervations upon the converfion of St. ' *Paul* '

The fubject of our prefent confideration is another very remarkable inftance of the fame kind *Vergerio*, as well as the apoftle we have juft mentioned, had too much knowledge to be deceived by mere artifice, had too great an intereft, as well as gave up too great an intereft, on the oppofite fide, to be queftioned of their uprightnefs, and had nothing to hope for, by efpoufing the caufe of truth, but reproach, and perfecution, and poverty

There were two of this name of *P P Vergerio*, and both very learned men   By way of diftinction, our *Vergerio* is called junior, probably from being the younger of the two, The other was a layman, and a pupil of *Chryfoloras*, of *Conftantinople*, who revived the knowledge of the *Greek* tongue and other learning in *Italy*, after a barbarifm of above feven hundred years. It does not appear in what part of *Italy* our *Vergerio* was born or educated, but we find him celebrated for his knowledge in the canon law and fcholaftic divinity, and, in confequence of it, employed by the pope, as his nuncio, at the ever memorable diet of *Augfburg* in the year 1530   *Vergerio* had almoft unlimited confidence placed in him, and was entrufted with a very ample commiffion. His chief inftructions were, that he fhould ufe all endeavors to prevent the holding of a national council in *Germany*, and to induce king *Ferdinand*, the emperor's brother, to oppofe any treaty of that kind   *Vergerio* very fedul-oufly acquitted himfelf according to the tenor of his commiffion, and left no ftone unturned to perplex and mortify the Lutherans, by fhewing every liberality to *Eckius*, *Faber*, *Cochlæus*, and others, who were their adverfaries, in order to induce them to make the warmer oppofition   He alfo made *Eckius* a canon of *Ratifbon*, a piece of preferment, which, as the pope's legate, he could confer, being prefent, the chapter's right of election, in that cafe, being fufpended

Vergerio had conducted his truft with fo much addrefs, that when *Rango*, the bifhop of *Rhegio*, (who had been fent by *Clement* VII in quality of Ambaffador to *Germany*, to conciliate the breaches in religion, and to negotiate the affair of a general council) was thought too old and infirm to carry on the artifices of the *Roman* fee, nobody was thought more capable, or more attached, to fucceed in that commiffion than *Vergerio*   His bufinefs was to profefs, in behalf of the pope, his holinefs's ardent defire to convene a general a general council, while, secretly, he was to throw the most insurmountable obstacles in the way of effecting of that measure, which might be in his power. It was a work of darkness, and he was enjoined to be as silent as death.

Pope *Clement* dying, cardinal *Farnese* was elected in his stead, and assumed the name of *Paul* the third. This good man, as one of his first acts, created two of his grandchildren (very much under age, and issue of his bastards) cardinals of his holy church. He recalled *Vergerio* from *Germany*, in order to be exactly informed of the state of religion (or most likely of other things) in that country, and ' consulted (says *Sleidan*) with the cardinals, by what ' means they might best prevent the calling of a national ' council, till, by private and unsuspected contrivances, ' they should have embroiled the emperor and other princes ' in a war.' The piety of this design needs no comment. However, the new pope resolved at length to send *Vergerio* back again into *Germany* to proffer a general council, but to take care at the same time, under the appearance of the greatest openness and simplicity, to learn what form the protestants would insist upon in reference to the qualifications, votings, and disputations of the council, that there might be such terms and rules imposed on them, as he might be sure they would never consent to. By this means, the odium of not holding the council would apparently fall upon them. He was also instructed, to exasperate the princes of the empire against the king of *England* [*Henry* the eighth] whose dominions the pope had in contemplation to bestow upon those, who would conquer them. And he received a secret article, to tamper with *Luther* and *Melancthon*, in order to bring them over to the cause of *Rome*. ' One great reason (says *Sleidan*) why ' *Vergerio* was sent back upon this commission to *Germany* ' was, because king *Ferdinand* had recommended him to ' the pope, as a person extremely well qualified to under- ' take that employment.'

Early in the spring of the year 1535, *Vergerio* set out to execute this hypocritical commission, in which he was exceedingly industrious, and negotiated with almost all the princes of *Germany*. At *Prague* he met with the good elector of *Saxony*, with whom he dealt with all imaginable subtilty, and according to the coloring of his commission. He proposed, among other things, that the council desired should be called at *Mantua*, pretending the convenience of its situation with respect to plenty and access, but meaning, really to get all the heads of the protestant party into *Italy* under his master's power. But the design was seen

through,

through, and fell to the ground *Vergerio* went also to *Wittenberg* upon the object of his commiſſion with *Luther*, but *Luther* knew not the value of gold, and did not eſtimate high enough all the preferments of the world, to give the pope's nuncio any proſpect of ſuccefs

In the year 1556, *Vergerio* returned to the holy father, in order to give in a ſtate of aſſairs, and to explain his management in the commiſſion. His report was, that the proteſtants demanded a free council, in a convenient place, which place muſt be within the territories of the empire, as the emperor had promiſed them   With reſpect to *Luther* and his party, there was no hope of prevailing upon them by any other means, than abſolute force and entire ſuppreſſion.   As to the motion about the king of *England*, the proteſtants would on no account hear of it, and the reſt of the princes received it but coldly   Indeed, *George* duke of *Saxony* [*Luther*'s bitter enemy] did ſay, that the greateſt danger was from the proteſtants, which was only to be avoided by the pope and emperor declaring war againſt them, as ſoon as poſſible

Upon the force of this laſt hint, the pope ſent off *Vergerio* to *Naples*, where the emperor then was, in order to propoſe a war upon the Lutherans, as the beſt and quickeſt method of ſettling the controverſy   The emperor came to *Rome* to debate this matter, and propoſed earneſtly the calling a general council   The pope inſiſted that it ſhould be held in ſome city or town of *Italy*, to which the emperor, not knowing the pope's holy motives, conſented, and accordingly a bull was drawn up by the nine cardinals out of the conſiſtory, by the archbiſhop of *Brundiſi*, by the biſhop of *Rhegio*, and by our *Vergerio* juſt made biſhop of *Modruſch* and ſoon after of *Capo d' Iſtria*   *Mantua* was the place fixed by the bull, and the twenty-third of *May* enſuing was the time

It was foreſeen, that the proteſtants, from every reaſon of ſafety and propriety, which could be dear to them as men and as Chriſtians, would never conſent to put themſelves into the pope's clutches   Accordingly, they told the emperor, that they could not truſt themſelves out of their own country, and eſpecially, as in the caſe of Dr *Huſs*, it might not be eaſy to procure ſuch a ſort of *ſafe-conduct*, as would bring them back again   They laid open at large the fallacy and deceit of the pope's conduct, and gave very broad hints to the emperor, that they could neither truſt him nor any of the papiſts. *Sleidan* enters, at full length, all the debates upon this occaſion, to whoſe commentaries we muſt refer the inquiſitive Reader

Vergerio

Vergerio was called from his embassy in *Germany* by the pope in the year 1537, as a man, who well understood and could well be trusted with his holiness's affairs, and therefore could give him the most precise account and advice upon them From this time to the year 1541, he seems to have remained in *Italy* But, in this last year, he was commissioned to go to the diet at *Worms*, under an assumed character for the *French* king, as it was thought he might do his holiness more service under a borrowed form, than he could do in a real appearance *Vergerio*, with his usual industry and address, made a speech here, upon the unity and peace of the church, which he printed and circulated In this speech, he insisted chiefly upon arguments against holding a national council, for the pope, of all things, could not endure that step, and *Vergerio* knew very fully his secret thoughts. By *Vergerio*'s means, in co-operation with other instruments, the conference at *Worms* was impeded, and at length dissolved Every thing, that artifice and evasion could do, was attempted, and unhappily succeeded

We have mentioned, that *Vergerio* was in great favor with king *Ferdinand*, of *Hungary*, to which may be added, that he was in such terms of esteem with him, as to be godfather to one of his children, with the marquis of *Brandenburgh*, and the archbishop of *Lunden*

When *Vergerio* returned from *Worms* to *Rome*, the pope, in reward for his services, designed to have made him a cardinal, among some other persons, whom he intended to promote, but, upon some insinuations, that he was leaning towards Lutheranism, through his long residence in *Germany*, the pope changed his purpose Upon the information of this circumstance (which seems to have had no other foundation than malice or envy) from cardinal *Grinucio*, to whom the pope had told it, *Vergerio* was quite astonished, and, in order to put an end to all suspicions of that sort, he retired into the country, and began to compose a book, to which he prefixed this title, " *Adver-* " *sus apostatas Germaniæ*," against the apostates of *Germany* This work naturally led him into strict investigations of the doctrines of the protestants, which he had never duly examined before, in order to give them the most exact and forcible confutation. Divine grace took this occasion, which he meant for opposition, to bring about what he least expected—his conversion. The apostle *Paul* was called to the truth, when he meditated its ruin, and so was *Vergerio*, and the great *Francis Junius*, whom we shall mention hereafter. He found himself overcome and vanquished by a careful perufal of the writings, which he wished to explode, and he faw the rottennefs and impiety of that church, whofe interefts it had been the main bufinefs of his life to uphold In the utmost perturbation of mind, and relinquishing his views of a cardinal's hat, he went to confer with his own brother, *John Baptift Vergerio*, bishop of *Pola*, in *Iftria*, which territory is part of the *Venetian* ftate. His brother, in the laft degree of aftonishment, began to bewail the ftate and condition of *Vergerio's* underftanding, and feemed rather at a lofs what to do with himfelf than how to give advice to another At length, by *Vergerio's* repeated entreaties, they applied themfelves together in fearching the fcriptures, and particularly in examining by the fcriptures that important article—the juftification of a finner before God The refult was, the Spirit of God fet home his word on both their hearts, and they became brethren in grace, as well as in blood They faw, in this pure glafs of the word, the error of the church of *Rome* upon this doctrine, as well as the abfurdity, fallacy, and impiety of many other tenets, which it maintains. Convinced of the truth in their own minds, they faw it was too precious a light to be confined *under a bufhel*, or in their bofoms They, therefore, preached to the people of *Iftria* the true doctrine of the gofpel, according to the meafure of grace given them. This foon alarmed the inquifition, as well as raifed the indignation of the monks The officers of the inquifition came quickly to *Pola*, and *Capo d' Iftria*, where the brothers had preached, and committed their ufual outrages upon the people, and one of them, *Grifonio*, went into the pulpit, and, amongft other terrors, excommunicated all, who would not *inform* againft perfons *fufpected* of *Lutheranifm* What would he fay to Lutherans themfelves? He and his colleagues fearched after thofe, who had been guilty of reading the New Teftament in the vulgar tongue, which it feems *Vergerio* and his brother had procured to be diftributed among the people This occafioned much perplexity and diftrefs The inquifitors preached alfo frequent fermons againft the perfon and doctrine of *Vergerio*, who was obliged to fly, for fafety, from the approaching ftorm. If he had been in the ecclefiaftical ftate, under the immediate dominion of the pope, probably he had not fo efcaped He firft retired to *Mantua*, and fought the protection of cardinal *Hercules Gonzaga*, who had been his intimate friend. But he foon found, that no man of the world will protect from perfecution on account of the gofpel, for *Gonzaga*, urged by letters from *Rome*, and by *John Cafa* the pope's legate at

Venice,

Venice, foon thought it expedient to let *Vergerio* know, that his company could be difpenfed with. In this fituation, he thought it was proper to go to *Trent*, where the general council was convened, in order to explain his cafe to the fathers, among whom he had a right to fit. But the pope, though he wifhed to have had him prifoner, yet finding it neceffary to remove all fufpicion (efpecially in *Germany*) concerning the freedom of the council, wrote to his legates, who prefided there, to get him profcribed from appearing among them. Being in confequence expelled, he went to *Venice*, where *Cafa* the pope's legate, advifed him to go by all means to *Rome*, and reconcile himfelf. Whether *Cafa* was fincere or not, *Vergerio* knew better than to truft himfelf in the lion's den, and therefore went to *Padua*, where he remained for fome time.

During *Vergerio*'s abode at *Padua*, there occurred in *Citadella*, near that city, a circumftance, which has been much talked of all over the Chriftian world, and which it may not be thought tedious or impertinent to relate — In *Citadella* lived *Francis Spira*, a lawyer of great abilities and practice at the bar. This man had embraced the reformed religion with remarkable zeal and earneftnefs, and, as he made proficiency in it, freely expreffed his opinion of the feveral points of the controverted doctrine, both to his friends and to every body. A conduct of this fort could not long be concealed in *Italy*, but was at length noticed to *John Cafa**, archbifhop of *Benevento*, and the pope's legate at *Venice*. When *Spira* was informed of this, he was very fenfible of his danger, and therefore, after revolving the matter in his thoughts, he followed eafy counfels, and went to the legate, who had fent for him. Before the legate, he recanted his errors (as he termed them), begged his abfolution, and promifed obedience for the future. Though the legate was glad of his voluntary confeffion, yet, for the fake of example, he enjoined him, by way of penance, to return home, and make a public recantation of the proteftant doctrines. All this he promifed to do, againft the impreffions of his mind, and the clear conviction of his confcience, which reproached, and reproached him again, for his fhameful defertion and denial. When he came home, the folicitations of his friends, (who urged, that the welfare of himfelf,

* This being (for one would fcarce honor him with the name of *man*) wrote an execrable book in celebration of an unnatural vice, which he had the impudence to call a *divine work*; and fo protefs that he followed it. This book was written in verfe, to render his abominable lafcivioufnefs the more pleafing.

I of

of his wife, children, estate, and all, depended upon it) prevailed, and he made his formal recantation Soon afterwards his foul was struck with horror at what he had done, and he fell into the most dreadful despair of God's mercy Growing worse and worse, and expressing himself in language almost too dreadful to repeat, concerning his crime, and his assured damnation from God, he was removed by his friends from *Citadella* to *Padua*, that he might both have better advice of physicians, and the constant conference of learned men His physicians soon confessed his malady beyond their art, and prescribed for him, as the best and only remedy, good advice and spiritual consolation. Accordingly, many of the clergy and others constantly attended him, and labored to heal his mind by such portions of scripture, as exhibit the riches and extent of the mercy of God to repenting sinners He allowed the truth of those passages, and of all they could say respecting the love of God in *Christ*, but still insisted, that *he* was particularly excluded to be an instance of the divine vengeance, and that the promises did not belong to him, who must justly be damned to everlasting torments, because he had abjured the truths of God, knowing them to be so, and against the repeated admonitions of his conscience He said, in language as dreadful as ever was heard, that he felt the pains of damnation, even then, in his foul, that he wanted to be at the worst, which hell could inflict upon him, as the expectation of more torments increased those he already sustained, and that, though he saw all glory and excellency in God, yet he was so far from loving him on that account, that he most horribly hated him the more. In this condition he continued for some time, refusing all sustenance, and spitting it out again, when forced upon him. *Vergerio* frequently visited him, and set before him the freedom and fullness of the divine grace, urging the instances of *Peter* and others, who had fallen from God, but were received into mercy again, but all his exhortations were in vain Whatever could be said, was thrown away upon poor *Spira*, and his malady increased more and more In short, he languished, and sunk, and died, in all the agonizing tortures of the most miserable despair*

Vergerio, as an eye-witness of God's wrath for the denial of his truth, was deeply struck with this dreadful example, and in consequence was the more confirmed by it in his

* The account of *Spira* is delivered by several creditable authors, who were eye-witnesses of his melancholy end, viz *Matthew Gribaldo*, a lawyer of *Padua*, by *Sigismund Gelou*, *Henry Scot*, and *Vergerio*

attachment

attachment to the proteftant doctrine Till this period, he had evidently hefitated, and wifhed to keep himfelf as fafe as he could, without entirely making fhipwreck of confcience But this awful inftance determined him He, therefore, fully refolved to abandon his native country and all he had, and to become, in a double fenfe, a *ftranger and pilgrim upon earth* Every true Chriftian muft be this in his fpirit, but every one is not called to be fo both in body and mind, as *Vergerio* undoubtedly was He underwent this voluntary banifhment, that he might live where he might freely profefs the doctrine of *Chrift* He quitted the fine country of *Bergamo* for the bleak barren hills of the *Grifons* The *Grifons* became a fpiritual *Eden*, far more delightful than the *Italian* plains, through the fweet manifeftation of the gofpel If *Chrift* and a dungeon have been preferred by many martyrs to a palace without him , furely *Chrift* and the *Grifons* muft be far more welcome than all the bufy fcenes of life, where inward peace is a ftranger, and where outward felicity flies off in a dream *Vergerio* counted the coft, and had made a wife eftimate of the honors, the riches, and the pleafures, of a giddy world. He was certainly able to do fo, in the ftrength of grace, for he had feen and known them all in their higheft fplendor and magnificence And, with *Solomon*, he could write upon them all , —*vanity and vexation of fpirit*

Vergerio preached the gofpel partly amongft the *Grifons*, and partly in the *Valteline*, for feveral years At length, he was invited to *Tubingen*, in *Swabia*, by the duke of *Wurtemburg*, where he paffed the remainder of his days

Vergerio's brother, *John Baptift Vergerio*, bifhop of *Pola*, who was converted to the truth at the fame time (as we we have mentioned) died before he left *Italy*, and it is fufpected, that he was poifoned by thofe defperate and implacable papifts, who hunted likewife for *Vergerio's* blood.

While *Vergerio* was among the *Grifons*, the emperor and pope had endeavored to draw the *Swifs* to the council of *Trent* But the *French* king, having oppofite views, inftructed *La Morliere*, his ambaffador or envoy to the Cantons, to diffuade them from it *La Morliere*, finding it a work of difficulty, prevailed upon *Vergerio*, who was expert in negotiation and bufinefs, to come to him from among the *Grifons* *Vergerio* fupplied him with arguments, and, foon afterwards, publifhed a book againft repairing to the council By thefe means, *Switzerland* and the *Grifons* were preferved from that corrupt leaven, and from being enfnared by the policy of *Rome*.

In

In this book *Vergerio* exhibited the pride, pomp, luxury, ambition, bribery, and diffolute manners of the court of *Rome*, which he declared he well knew, and from his heart detefted That the council of *Trent* was not called by the pope, to eftablifh the doctrine of *Chrift*, but thofe human inventions which they had brought in contrary to the word of God, not to purge God's fold, but to diffeminate their inveterate errors, not to reftore Chriftian liberty, but to introduce a miferable bondage and oppreffion on the fouls of men. That this appeared, from there being none but bifhops and abbots, who had taken an oath prefcribed by the *Roman* ceremonial, allowed to fit there That the inferior clergy and fecular princes had only a right to come, without the leaft power of deliberating or voting, fo that every conclufion muft be *ex parte*, as all, who differed from *Rome*, were without influence And that, in fhort, no good thing would be done, nor any corruption complained of remedied, though to remedy corruptions was the exprefs end for which the council was pretended to be called.

The event proved the truth of *Vergerio*'s affertion, as we may more fully learn from the celebrated hiftory of that council, written by the excellent *F Paulo* of *Venice*

This good man *Vergerio* finifhed his labors and his life at *Tubingen* on the fourth of *October*, in the year 1566 His funeral fermon was preached by Dr. *James Andreas*, on 1 *Tim* 1 12,13 *I thank* Chrift Jefus *our Lord, who hath enabled me, for that he counted me faithful, putting me into the miniftry, who was before a blafphemer, and a perfecutor, and injurious But I obtained mercy, becaufe I did it ignorantly in unbelief.* Upon this text he drew, and might draw, no very diftant parallel between thofe two perfecuting converts, the apoftle *Paul* and bifhop *Vergerio*

Pezelius fays, that ' of a wolf God made *Vergerio* one of ' his fold, and a paftor of his flock,' and *Trithemius* fpeaks of him, that ' he was a man, diligent in fearching the ' holy fcriptures, and very learned in human fcience, ' celebrated as a philofopher and a rhetorician, and per- ' fectly fkilled in the *Greek* and *Latin* tongues ' *Thuanus* mentions him likewife in very handfome terms, and perhaps as handfome as he dared But *Vergerio* has a much better commendation than all thefe,—the applaufe of his Mafter—*Well done, good and faithful fervant, enter thou into the joy of thy Lord*

End of the

CPSIA information can be obtained at www.ICGtesting.com
Printed in the USA
BVOW082007150312

285159BV00004B/61/P